ANTIOCH

This is a complete history of Antioch, one of the most significant major cities of the eastern Mediterranean and a crossroads for the Silk Road, from its foundation by the Seleucids, through Roman rule, the rise of Christianity, Islamic and Byzantine conquests, to the Crusades and beyond.

Antioch has typically been treated as a city whose classical glory faded permanently amid a series of natural disasters and foreign invasions in the sixth and seventh centuries CE. Such studies have obstructed the view of Antioch's fascinating urban transformations from classical to medieval to modern city and the processes behind these transformations. Through its comprehensive blend of textual sources and new archaeological data reanalyzed from Princeton's 1930s excavations and recent discoveries, this book offers unprecedented insights into the complete history of Antioch, recreating the lives of the people who lived in it and focusing on the factors that affected them during the evolution of its remarkable cityscape. While Antioch's built environment is central, the book also utilizes landscape archaeological work to consider the city in relation to its hinterland, and numismatic evidence to explore its economics. The outmoded portrait of Antioch as a sadly perished classical city par excellence gives way to one in which it shines as brightly in its medieval Islamic, Byzantine, and Crusader incarnations.

Antioch: A History offers a new portal to researching this long-lasting city and is also suitable for a wide variety of teaching needs, both undergraduate and graduate, in the fields of classics, history, urban studies, archaeology, Silk Road studies, and Near Eastern/Middle Eastern studies. Just as importantly, its clarity makes it attractive for, and accessible to, a general readership outside the framework of formal instruction.

Andrea U. De Giorgi is Associate Professor of Classical Studies at the Florida State University, USA. He specializes in Roman urbanism and visual culture from the origins to Late Antiquity, with emphasis on the Greek East. He is the author of *Ancient Antioch: from the Seleucid Era to the Islamic Conquest* (2016, paperback 2018), editor of *Cosa and the Colonial Landscape of Republican Italy* (2019), and co-editor of *Cosa/Orbetello. Archaeological Itineraries* (2016). Dr. De Giorgi has directed excavations and surveys in Turkey, Syria, Georgia, Jordan, and the UAE. Since 2013, he has codirected the Cosa Excavations in Italy, and currently studies the 1930s Antioch collections at the Princeton University Art Museum, USA. He has also collaborated with the Museo di Antichità di Torino, the Museo di Cosa in Ansedonia, and the Museum of Fine Arts in St. Petersburg, Florida.

A. Asa Eger is Associate Professor of the Islamic World in the Department of History at the University of North Carolina at Greensboro, USA. His research centers on Islamic and Byzantine history and archaeology of the eastern Mediterranean, with a focus on frontiers and the relationship between cities and hinterlands. He is the author of *The Islamic-Byzantine Frontier: Interaction and Exchange Among Muslim and Christian Communities* (2015), winner of ASOR's G. Ernest Wright Book award for 2015; *The Spaces Between the Teeth: A Gazetteer of Towns on the Islamic-Byzantine Frontier* (2012, 2nd edition 2016); and editor of *The Archaeology of Medieval Islamic Frontiers* (2019). Dr. Eger has directed excavations and surveyed all around Antioch (Antakya) in Turkey since 2001, as well as in Israel, Cyprus, and Greece. He currently studies the 1930s Antioch collections at the Princeton University Art Museum, USA, and 1970s survey material from the Tell Rifa'at Survey, the hinterland of Aleppo, at the Louvre Museum, France.

Cities of the Ancient World

Cities of the Ancient World examines the history, archaeology and cultural significance of key cities from across the ancient world, spanning northern Europe, the Mediterranean, Africa, Asia and the Near East. Each volume explores the life of a significant place, charting its developments from its earliest history, through the transformations it experienced under different cultures and rulers, through to its later periods. These texts offer academics, students and the interested reader comprehensive and scholarly accounts of the life of each city.

Damascus
A History, 2nd edition
Ross Burns

A History of Siena
From its Origins to the Present Day
Mario Ascheri and Bradley Franco

Ebla
Archaeology and History
Paolo Matthiae

Carthage
A Biography
Dexter Hoyos

Antioch
A History
Andrea U. De Giorgi and A. Asa Eger

www.routledge.com/classicalstudies/series/CITYBIOS

ANTIOCH

A History

Andrea U. De Giorgi and A. Asa Eger

Routledge
Taylor & Francis Group
LONDON AND NEW YORK

First published 2021
by Routledge
2 Park Square, Milton Park, Abingdon, Oxon OX14 4RN

and by Routledge
52 Vanderbilt Avenue, New York, NY 10017

Routledge is an imprint of the Taylor & Francis Group, an informa business

British Library Cataloguing-in-Publication Data
A catalogue record for this book is available from the British Library

Library of Congress Cataloging-in-Publication Data
Names: De Giorgi, Andrea U., author. | Eger, A. Asa, author.
Title: Antioch : a history / Andrea U. De Giorgi and Asa Eger.
Other titles: Cities of the ancient world.
Description: Abingdon, Oxon ; New York, NY : Routledge, 2021. | Series: Cities of the ancient world | Includes bibliographical references and index.
Identifiers: LCCN 2020048152 (print) | LCCN 2020048153 (ebook) | ISBN 9781138845244 (hardback) | ISBN 9780367633042 (paperback) | ISBN 9781315727608 (ebook)
Subjects: LCSH: Excavations (Archaeology)—Turkey—Antioch. | Antioch (Turkey)—History. | Antioch (Turkey)—Antiquities.
Classification: LCC DS99.A6 D43 2021 (print) | LCC DS99.A6 (ebook) | DDC 956.4/8—dc23
LC record available at https://lccn.loc.gov/2020048152
LC ebook record available at https://lccn.loc.gov/2020048153

ISBN: 978-1-138-84524-4 (hbk)
ISBN: 978-0-367-63304-2 (pbk)
ISBN: 978-1-315-72760-8 (ebk)

Typeset in Bembo
by Apex CoVantage, LLC

This book is dedicated to the people of Antioch, who carry within them this history, distinctive identity, and power of resilience, even in the face of recent conflict.

CONTENTS

FIGURES

TABLES

ABBREVIATIONS

AAES	*Publications of an American Archaeological Expedition to Syria in 1899–1900*; New York, 1903–1930 I. R. Garret, *Topography and Itinerary*, 1914 II. H. C. Butler, *Architecture and Other Arts*, 1903 III. W. K. Prentice, *Greek and Latin Inscriptions*, 1908
IV.	E. Littmann, *Semitic Inscriptions*, 1904
ANS	*American Numismatic Society*; New York
Antioch Archives	Excavations Diaries, Field Reports, Correspondence and Objects Catalogue, 1932–1940. Antioch Expedition Archives, Department of Art and Archaeology, Princeton University; Princeton
Antioch I	G. Elderkin (ed.), *Antioch on the Orontes I. The Excavations of 1932*; Princeton, 1934
Antioch II	R. Stillwell (ed.), *Antioch on the Orontes II. The Excavations. 1933–1936*; Princeton, 1938
Antioch III	R. Stillwell (ed.), *Antioch on the Orontes III. The Excavations. 1937–1939*; Princeton, 1941
Antioch IV.i	F.O.Waagé (ed.), *Antioch on the Orontes IV. Part One. Ceramics and Islamic Coins;* Princeton, 1948
Antioch IV.ii	D. Waagé (ed.), *Antioch on the Orontes IV. Part Two. Greek, Roman, Byzantine, and Crusader Coins*; Princeton, 1952
Antioch V	J. Lassus, *Les Portiques d'Antioche*; Princeton, 1972
Antioche de Syrie	B. Cabouret, P.L. Gatier, C. Saliou (eds), *Antioche de Syrie. Histoire, images et traces de la ville antique.* Topoi Supplément 5; Lyon, 2004
Braidwood, Mounds	R. Braidwood, *Mounds in the Plain of Antioch. OIP* 48; Chicago, 1937

BE	*Bulletin Épigraphique*, annually in *Revue des Études Grecques*
BMC	*A Catalogue of the Greek Coins in the British Museum;* London, 1873-
Chronicon Paschale	M. Whitby and M. Whitby, *Chronicon Paschale 284–628.* Liverpool, 1989
Chron. 1234	A. Hilkens, *The Anonymous Syriac Chronicle of 1234 and its Sources*. Leiden, 2018.
City of Mosaics	Scott Redford (ed.), *Antioch on the Orontes. Early Explorations in the City of Mosaics* *Asi'deki Antakya. Mozaikler Şehrinde İlk Araştirmalar*; Istanbul, 2014
CRAI	*Comptes-rendus des séances de l'Académie des Inscriptions et Belles-Lettres*
CJ	P. Krueger, *Codex Justinianus. Corpus Iuris Civilis, II*; Berlin, 1914
CTh	P. Krueger, P. M. Meyer, T. Momsen, *Codex Theodosianus*; Hildesheim, 2000
Downey, History	G. Downey, *A History of Antioch in Syria from Seleucus I to the Arab Conquest*; Princeton, 1961
Dussaud	R. Dussaud, *Topographie historique de la Syrie antique et médiévale*; Paris, 1927
East & West	K. Ciggaar and M. Metcalf. *East and West in the Medieval Mediterranean I: Antioch from the Byzantine Reconquest until the end of the Crusader Principality:* Acta of the Congress held at Hernen Castle in May 2006. OLA 147. Leuven, 2006
Euseb.HE	I. Boyle and C. F. Crusé, *The Ecclesiastical History of Eusebius Pamphilus, Bishop of Caesarea, Palestine*: New York, 1856
Evagrius	M. Whitby, The Ecclesiastical History of Evagrius Scholasticus; Liverpool, 2000
Expositio	G. Lumbroso, *Expositio Totius Mundi et Gentium*; Roma, 1903
Gourob, Papyrus	Holleaux, M. (1906) 'Remarques sur le papyrus de Gourob (1). Flinders Petrie Papyri, II; XLV; III; CXLIV'; *BCH* 30: 330–348
IG	*Inscriptiones Graecae*
IGLS	*Inscriptions grecques et latines de la Syrie*
ILS	H. Dessau, *Inscriptiones Latinae Selectae*; Berlin, 1892–1916
Isaac of Antioch	G. Bickell (ed.) *S. Isaaci Antiocheni, Doctoris Syrorum, Opera Omnia*; Giessen, 1873
John of Nikiu	R. H. Charles (ed.), The Chronicle of John, Bishop of Nikiu; London, 1913
Levi, Pavements	D. Levi, *Antioch Mosaic Pavements*; Princeton, 1947
Life of St. Symeon	P. Van den Ven, *La Vie ancienne de St. Syméon Stylite le Jeune. Vie grecque de Sainte Marthe, mère de St. Syméon*; Bruxelles, 1962–1970

Lost Ancient City	C. Kondoleon, *Antioch. The Lost Ancient City*; Princeton, 2000
P. Macarius	*Voyage du Patriarche Macaire d'Antioche*. Texte Arabe et traduction française par B. Radu. Patrologia Orientalis, 22, 30, fasc. 1
Malalas	E. Jeffreys, M. Jeffreys, and R. Scott. *The Chronicle of John Malalas. A Translation*; Melbourne, 1986
McAlee, Coins	R. McAlee, *The Coins of Roman Antioch*; London, 2007
Michael the Syrian	R. Bedrosian, *Chronicle of Michale the Great Patriarch of the Syrians;* Long Branch, 1871
Petit	P. Petit, *Libanius et la vie municipale à Antioche au IVe siècle après J.-C.*; Paris, 1955
Proc. *Wars*	Procopius, *History of the Wars*, Volume I: Books 1–2 *(Persian War)*. Translated by H. B. Dewing. Loeb Classical Library 48; Cambridge, MA, 1914
PUAES	*The Princeton University Archaeological Expeditions to Syria in 1904 and 1909*; Leiden, 1907–1949 I. H. C. Butler, F. E. Norris, E. R. Stoever, *Geography and Itinerary*, 1930 II.B H. C. Butler, *Architecture. Northern Syria*, 1920 III.B W. K. Prentice, *Greek and Latin Inscriptions. Northern Syria*, 1922 IV.B E. Littmann. *Semitic Inscriptons. Arabic Inscriptions*, 1949
Pietro Della Valle	Pietro Della Valle, *Viaggi di Pietro della Valle il Pellegrino descritti da lui medesimo in lettere familiari all'erudito suo amico Mario Schipano, divisi in tre parti, cioè la Turchia, la Persia e l'India colla vita e ritratto dell'autore*, II; Torino, 1843
PLRE	A.H.M. Jones et al., *The Prosopography of the Later Roman Empire*; Oxford, 1971–1972
RE	*Paulys Real-Encyclopädie der classischen Altertumwissenschaft.*
Res Gestae Divi Saporis	Ernest Honigmann e André Maricq, *Recherches sur les Res Gestae Divi Saporis, in* Mémoires de l'Académie royale de Belgique, Classe des lettres et des sciences morales et politiques, XLVII.4; Bruxelles, 1953
SEG	*Supplementum Epigraphicum Graecum*
SGLIBulg	*Spätgriechische und spätlateinische Inschriften aus Bulgarien*
Socr.HE	E. Walford and H. de Valois, *The Ecclesiastical History of Socrates, named Scholasticus, or the Advocate*. London, 1853.
Stephanus of Byzantium	Augustus Meineke, *Stephani Byzantii Ethnicorum Quae Supersunt*. Reimer, 1849
Synkellos, Chron.	*The Chronography of George Synkellos*. A Byzantine Chronicle of Universal History from the Creation. Translated with Introduction and Notes by W. Adler and P. Tuffin; Oxford, 2002

Tchalenko, Villages	G. Tchalenko. *Villages Antiques de la Syrie du Nord. Le massif du Bélus à l'époque romaine*, III vols; Paris, 1953
Theod.HE	L. Parmentier and G. C. Hansen, *Théodoret de Cyr. Histoire ecclésiastique*; Paris, 2006
Theod.HR	P. Canivet and A. Leroy-Moninghen, *Théodoret de Cyr. Histoire des Moines de Syrie*; Paris, 1977–1979
Theophanes	C. Mango and R. Scott, *The Chronicle of Theophanes Confessor*. Oxford, 1997
TIB	K. P. Todt and B. A. Vest, *Tabula Imperii Byzantini 15. Syria Prōtē, Syria Deutera, Syria Euphratēsia*; Vienna, 2014
WSM	E.T. Newell, *The Coinage of the Western Seleucid Mints from Seleucus I to Antiochus III*; New York, 1977

INTRODUCTION

> Antioch is among the cities in which the stranger finds comfort away from his homeland.
>
> – 'Alī b. Abī Bakr al-Harawī[1]

It is an exciting time to be writing a history of Antioch, the most significant and continuously occupied major city of the eastern Mediterranean. An ongoing flurry of research initiatives attests to the vitality of the field of Antiochene studies. Whether bringing into focus the materiality of the city or its pivotal role in the religious discourse of Late Antiquity, which reverberated throughout the medieval period, these analyses teem with the energy, contradictions, and dilemmas of a city that eludes firm characterizations. We thus align ourselves to the group of scholars who are magnetically attracted to and, at least in our case, more often than not baffled by the city on the Orontes.

It seems that the more one engages with Antioch (modern Antakya in the Republic of Turkey), the more it deceives its beholder. Topography, foundation, political orientation, religion, demographics, downfall: these are but some of the topics with unanswered questions the city still poses. Antioch's vast literary repertoire, primarily Late Antique and Crusader, indeed affords glimpses into the here and now of life in the city, but it is hardly a coherent narrative of the community. More to the point, the voices of the actors that *made* Antioch are missing. The meager numbers of inscriptions – fewer than 100 – further inhibit the braiding together of stories of the families, notables, and folks at large who inhabited the city. And if the epigraphic record for the classical and post-classical periods is lamentable, that for the Islamic epoch is equally regrettable.

Another challenge is the fact that the number of textual sources regarding Antioch far outweighs the archaeological work done on the city, particularly in certain periods. Merging and aligning these two is frequently not possible. On the one hand, we have a mountain of allusions to toponyms, places in the city where a myriad of events took place, from the largest conquests and sieges of its gates to the smallest sales of garden plots. Yet aside from the city wall, citadel, and hippodrome, we know virtually nothing about where any of these places were actually located in the city.

Of course, we are not the first authors to foreground Antioch's paradoxes while stressing the city's centrality. Glanville Downey wrote his masterly *A History of Antioch in Syria from Seleucus to the Arab Conquest* (1961), which remains a seminal work for any Antioch research. We have drawn greatly on his work and benefited from its unparalleled marshaling of the sources. But much has happened since 1961. For all his enthusiasm and stamina, Downey wrote in the aftermath of the Princeton excavations (1932–1939), a project that ultimately fell short at meeting the expectations of the scholars and stakeholders involved. Downey's lukewarm treatment of the excavations reveals the shared sense of modest returns that he and others – especially one of the team's primary (and non-Princetonian) field excavators, Jean Lassus[2] – stressed in their work. In the end, the excavations failed to expose the materiality of the city they had so adamantly sought to achieve, even as Downey's personal involvement (on the 1932 Daphne Road dig) yielded no trace of the florid past of Antioch's suburbs. Overall, his limited recourse to the archaeological record shows how Downey sidelined information that generally seemed impractical and convoluted. Corollary to this, publications and exhibitions on Antioch have focused much as the original excavators eventually did – on its mosaics. The significant volumes since Downey – including the Worcester Art Museum's *The Arts of Antioch* and *Antioch: The Lost Ancient City* and Doro Levi's study of mosaics[3] – all elevate the Antiochene mosaics above all else, as does the city's brand new Hatay Archeological Museum. The dispersal of this collection, with hundreds of pavements scattered among key North American museums from Honolulu to Richmond, to name but two, further reinforces Antioch's reputation as "the city of mosaics."[4]

Conversely, our book seizes the opportunity to take up the 1930s excavations with a view toward enriching and finessing existing narratives. To that end, this book offers three contributions to the study of Antioch, from which emerge four dominant themes to connect each period of the city's long history.

Contributions

New research

First, this study harnesses unpublished Antioch collections at the Princeton University Art Museum and the Visual Resources Collection of its Department of Art and Archaeology, as well as the latest published field research, to imbue the historical data with new topographic and material perspectives. For instance, the discovery between 2010 and 2012 of an extensive sixth-century bath complex and fifth-century villa and shops at the site of construction for a new high-end hotel raises new questions about the buildings that articulated life in Antioch, whether in its public areas or along its axes of movement. We also still have much to learn about the city's topography and how it was experienced in antiquity. A German-Turkish archaeological survey of the city studied its walls and water systems and conducted geophysical work, particularly on the plateau on top of Mt. Staurin, from 2004 to 2008, and produced a new topographic work with 355 archaeological features on both the plain and the mountains. It also discerned building phases for the Iron Gate via photogrammetry as well as for the citadel.[5] Current Turkish excavations in the area of the former Island by the local Mustafa Kemal University have also begun to pour new information into our understanding of the city's physicality. Further, our study also gathers important new work that has appeared recently, such as the large, wonderfully well-researched, meticulous description of the city in the *Tabula Imperii Byzantini* volume on Syria and the almost completed French *Lexicon Topographicum Antiochenum*, based largely on written sources.[6] A US-based international team, the New Committee on the Excavations of Antioch and Its Vicinity, has also begun piecing together the material culture derived from the Princeton excavations of 90 years past, infusing the archival data with new studies on ceramics, glass, metal, coins, and small finds, and new interpretations on stratigraphy.[7] One of these areas that we incorporate into almost every period is an overview of the coin evidence and how that informs wider questions of economy and links to the city's political history. Certain key periods also continue to be the foci of new research, such as the Late Antique and Crusader eras, together with ongoing studies on Christianity, churches, and so forth, as well as the Crusader Principality of Antioch. Lastly, with the tremendous help of Steve Batiuk, we have pieced together a plan of the city for each of its main ten periods of occupation. These plans show the changing fortification walls, water supply and river channels, and gates of the city and all the features discussed therein (see Appendix 1). To be sure, these plans are not the final word on how Antioch appeared; however, they incorporate historical maps, excavations, topography, hydrology, geology, remote sensing, and textual accounts to show a city, not frozen in one specific time period (as numerous plans of Antioch show, not least Downey's), but as constantly transforming, evolving to reflect the constraints of its time and meet the needs of its citizens.

Longer life and afterlife

Second, the book builds a narrative that, starting with the city's foundation under the Seleucids, continues well into the twentieth century; this is a biography of a city. The version of Antioch typically remembered is invariably the classical one culminating in the fourth and fifth centuries, when it was an imperial capital city at its largest and most populated. Arguing that 900 years was its lifespan, Downey devoted but a single page to Antioch following the Islamic conquest of 638.[8] The *Arts of Antioch* volume, meanwhile, completely ignores the medieval period, including not a single object and only two coins dating to the Crusades, while *Antioch: The Lost Ancient City* was similarly published in this vein, with hardly any mention of medieval Antioch. The historical overview of the recent exhibition hosted by Koç University's Research Center for Anatolian Civilizations, *Antioch on the Orontes: Early Explorations in the City of Mosaics*, likewise winds down with the fourth century and draws a line after the Islamic conquests.[9] A book entitled *Antiochia sull'Oronte*, published in Italy by Capuchin Christians of Antioch, mentions the Islamic periods in two sentences.[10] This limited version of the city indeed comes from the Byzantine authors themselves, like Libanius, whose biased descriptions concealed any notion of urban decline, neglect, or change in favor of a literature praising the city and its political prominence. We feel, however, that this presentation of the city does not adequately serve the discourse of a community that in the postclassical epochs reinvented itself time and again as it negotiated new realities of power and religion. We therefore offer a novel, holistic treatment of Antioch that intends to illustrate the history of the city in full.

Downey's own omissions fit into a much larger pattern of how postclassical cities in the Mediterranean have been regarded. Despite a growing body of scholarship on the nature of early medieval cross-cultural interactions[11] and a recent trend in trans-Mediterranean history, most Western civilization, art history, philosophy, and literature surveys still follow a common and entrenched assumption: that "Western" culture was manifested in the great classical cities of the Greek and Roman periods in the Mediterranean, and when they declined, all achievements in learning, art, economics, and social organization transferred to medieval Europe. What is left out of this model and continues to remain uncritically engaged with is the crucial role played by post-Roman cities, mostly under Islamic rule, in shaping Mediterranean and European cultures, east and west. With few exceptions, archaeologists have excavated classical cities and discarded their later (Islamic and medieval) levels, granting institutions continue to give money to classical excavations and not Islamic or medieval ones, and tourist and antiquities departments of various countries present these cities to the public with their Islamic and medieval incarnations eviscerated. Inaccurate and incomplete knowledge about the development of Mediterranean society after the Roman period is thus a form of history-making that substantiates a fictional West-versus-East division, thereby disconnecting the West from an interconnected history with its Islamic forebears.

In contrast, we operate here within a theoretical framework of urban transformation as opposed to postclassical decline. This book thus significantly expands and revives Downey's seminal volume, with its second half comprising entirely these "forgotten" chronologies: Early Islamic (638–969), Middle Byzantine (969–1084), Saljūq (1084–1098), Crusader (1098–1268), Mamlūk (1268–1516), and Ottoman (1516–1920). In doing so, the narrative of Antioch we present negates that of the seventh- or even sixth-century decline of the city, arguing instead for transformation from the classical city into a medieval one. Scholars have demonstrated that Antioch underwent substantial changes already in the sixth century, just *before* the Islamic conquests; however, the city was not abandoned and did not become useless, and it did not decline, an evaluation that serves only to discourage continuing inquiry after this period.[12] In fact, archaeological reanalysis shows that the city continued to thrive and transform well into the Islamic/medieval periods as a religious, intellectual, and economic center.[13] With the available data, this volume thus seeks to shed light on the specific changes manifested in the city's physical topography, economic life, and civic administration over the entire course of its occupation, to illuminate *how* urban space can show a society's changing priorities, and to better trace the complicated systems of networks and cross-cultural exchange that took place across the Mediterranean between the seventh and early twentieth centuries.

Focusing on the built environment and its evolution will address why transformations occurred during the medieval period when, for example, the city contracted and was more densely populated, public areas filled in and became private, villas were abandoned, and entertainment and public institutions were transformed into industrial zones. It also serves to demonumentalize the city somewhat by bringing together equally processes of ruralization, encroachment, industrialization, and spoliation. Meanwhile, the material culture provides valuable data on the city's economic health, the provenance of goods coming into or leaving the city gives evidence for trade, and excavated workshops show local production. Indeed, this study shows that the roots of privatization of commerce, globalization, and capitalism in far-reaching market economies, commonly seen in medieval European cities,[14] in fact have their origins in early medieval Islamic cities such as Antioch.[15] Antioch is also a perfect case study of a border town inhabited by diverse populations. In addressing these matters, this book thus significantly fills in the rather large omission of Antioch's influence at this time, apparent in all the scholarship on Late Antique and medieval Mediterranean archaeology, economy, settlement, urbanism, and social life over the last 80 years.

Wider vistas

The book's third contribution is to bring together a discussion of the city within its landscape, both its immediate hinterland and its broader region bridging Anatolia and Syria. Antioch was a classical city, founded as one of several Seleucid imprints on a new landscape. Its location, in geographic and historic Syria, was along the Orontes River in a narrow valley sandwiched between two substantial mountain ranges – the more gradually rising foothills of the Amanus Mountains to the west and the steep, sharply rising Mt. Silpius (1,660 feet) and Mt. Staurin, part of the Jibāl al-Aqra' range to the east. Its location made it particularly susceptible to intense winds, mentioned in several sources, which, coming through the Amuq Plain along the Orontes and funneling between the narrow river plain, are to this day a hallmark of the city's location.

Antioch's position was not merely strategic in a micro-topographical sense. It was situated within the southwest corner of the Amuq Plain, a large, triangular, fertile lowland watered by four rivers, three of which, the northern Kara

Su, the northeastern Yaghrā, the eastern Afrin, and the Orontes – emptied into the marshy Lake of Antioch (Amik Gölü) and surrounding wetlands. Exiting the lake, they joined the Orontes River, which watered the plain from the south. The lake drained just 15.5 kilometers north of Antioch via the Küçük Asi River.

The Amuq Plain has been one of the most important nodes of habitation since the earliest history of human settlement (Figure 0.1).

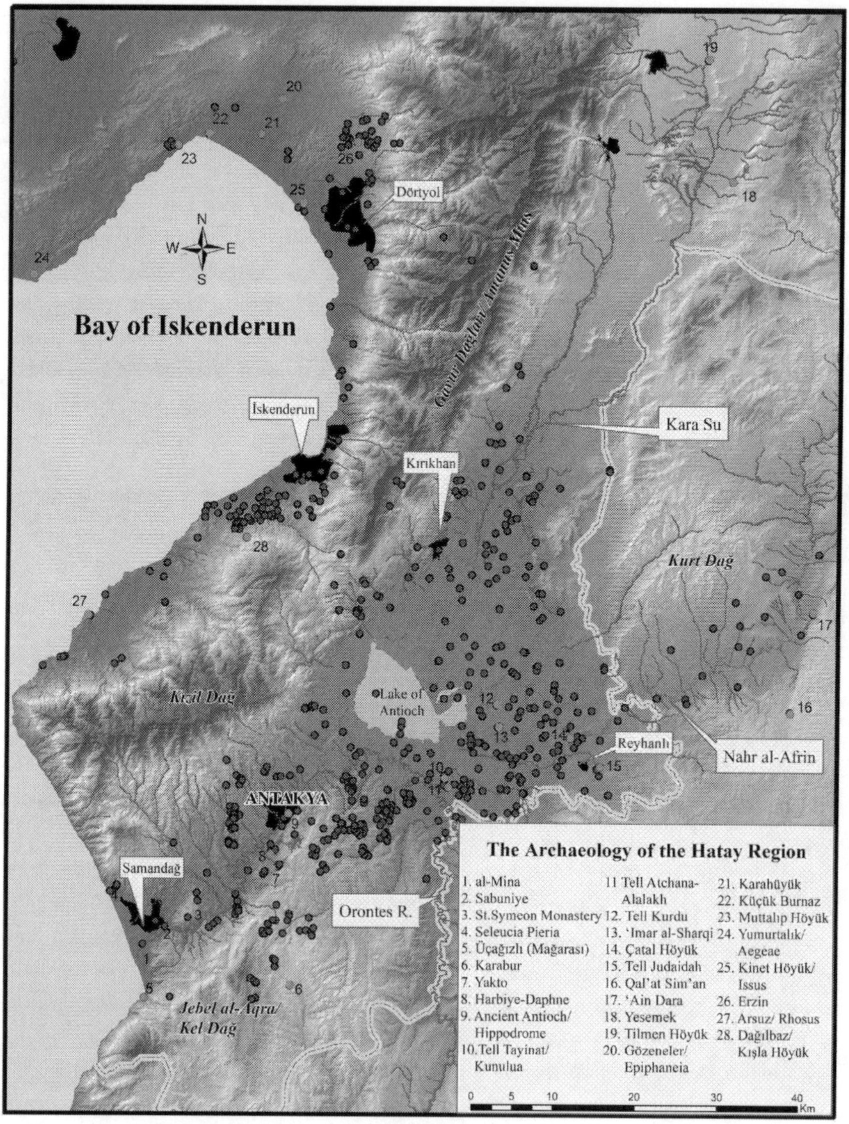

FIGURE 0.1 Archaeological sites in the Hatay region of Turkey

Source: Courtesy of Stephen Batiuk

Virtually every traveler in every period for which written sources remain has waxed eloquently on its productivity and abundance. Today, the Amuq unassumingly continues its role as the predominant agricultural provider in the area, while beneath its irrigated soils and on its many tells are literally hundreds of potential archaeological sites.

The Amuq Plain's importance throughout human history also owes to its regional location as a zone of transition, travel, communication, and trade, one of the few links connecting Anatolia with Syria and the western coastal mountainous zones with the eastern deserts of the Middle East. The Orontes River also gave it direct access to the Mediterranean Sea. Until the Late Roman/Early Islamic periods, the Orontes was navigable from the Mediterranean Sea to the city, facilitating its importance in the Mediterranean world. When the river was no longer usable, caravans began taking merchandise along the local road from the Orontes delta to Antioch, a distance of about 24 km.

The route into the Amuq Plain also acted as a funnel for routes from the Belen Pass westward over the Amanus to Cilicia, the Kara Su Valley north to Mar'ash, the Afrin River Valley northeast to the Upper Euphrates Valley and the eastern frontier, and the Orontes Valley south from Apamea. For the wider region, Antioch was a major stop for east-west routes to Aleppo and the Euphrates (and then to Baghdad) and north-south routes across the Taurus Mountains to the *thughūr* frontier and to Anatolia via the Cilician Plain.

This work builds on research conducted by many teams of archaeologists, including the authors', on surveys and excavations in the vicinity of Antioch. At present, the Amuq Survey, launched in 1932 by Robert Braidwood in the same year that Princeton began its excavations and restarted in 1995 as the Amuq Valley Regional Project, sponsored by the Oriental Institute of the University of Chicago, has covered some 1,875 km^2 and recorded nearly 400 sites.[16] Meanwhile, the Orontes delta Archaeological Project, recording 55 sites and covering 150 km^2, was part of the Amuq Valley Regional Project from 1999 to 2001 and in 2002 became independent.

These projects have revealed the importance of considering the pre-Hellenistic landscape of the Amuq Plain as a palimpsest of *longue durée* dominant capital cities in most every period. Excavations at the major Chalcolithic (4500–3300 BCE) site of Tell Kurdu, the Middle and Late Bronze Age (2100–1200 BCE) regional capital city of Tell Atçana (Alalakh), the Early Bronze (3300–2100 BCE) and Iron Age (1200–539 BCE) capital city of Tell Tayinat, the Iron Age settlement of Çatal Höyük, and the multi-period site of Tell Judaidah reveal that the Amuq Plain was a focal point of human settlement, economy, and power.[17] By the Hellenistic period, however, these cities and most of the Bronze and Iron Age tell sites on the plain had been abandoned. A new settlement system began to appear – that of a dense network of small, dispersed rural farms and cultivated lands connected to a large city. By the time of the Seleucid founding of Antioch, the plain had come to be dominated by a large standing lake, noted by authors such as the fourth-century CE rhetor Libanius as key to the fertility and transportation of agricultural products and a natural resource itself. As Libanius boasted in his Oration *in Praise of Antioch* (*Antiochikos*):

> The river and the lake are a source of profit to the city not merely in that they provide fare for our tables, but also because all the produce of the soil comes into the city's possession through the ease by which it is transported, for the import of corn is not reduced to the meager amount brought in by pack animals. The countryside is divided up between them; the river flows through the areas which derive no assistance from the lake; similarly, the lake extends over those areas where there is no aid from the river. By lake and river craft they empty the countryside of its produce and transport it to town. The first stages of transportation are separate, but then, instead of both being used, the river acts as host for the convoy of lake-borne goods as well as of its own, and brings them into the center of the city.[18]

As we will see, throughout much of its history, Antioch benefited from this breadbasket outside its gates.

Seleucid Antioch (303 BCE–64 BCE), therefore, on the one hand represents a continuity as the successor capital of the Amuq Plain yet also demarcates a significant change in the relationship between urban and rural sites and, accordingly, the city's dependence on the productivity of the plain. This arrangement remained a key infrastructure for the city in the Roman (64 BCE–193 CE) and the successive Late Antique (193–458 CE) and Early Byzantine epochs (458–638 CE). While Antioch remained the dominant city of the plain from this period onwards, its dependency on its rural hinterland broke down beginning in the sixth century and continuing throughout the Islamic period. From that point until the early twentieth century, the city became more self-sufficient and ruralized as parts of it were given over to cultivation within its own walls, while farms in the plain aggregated together into small towns of importance. This transformation in the way the city related to the plain has traditionally been regarded by scholars as one of the major signposts of Antioch's decline. Yet in the larger scheme, Antioch's role in the larger region remained as an important frontier town between the Islamic and Byzantine lands, as a local center and production node for the surrounding frontier villages and towns, and as an entrepôt between the Islamic and Byzantine empires.[19]

Themes

A resilient city

There is no possible conclusion to the biography of a city still densely inhabited, vibrant, and dynamic. We offer, however, four themes that repeat themselves from period to period as hallmarks of Antioch, something quintessentially Antiochene, perhaps. The first, that of the city's resiliency, presents a contradiction to the important role played by the landscape in creating a fertile and prosperous hinterland. By all rights, like its conquest, a near-biblical series of natural disasters that afflicted Antioch and are known from descriptions in textual sources – earthquakes, famine, plague, and river flooding (Figure 0.2) – ought to have broken the city a dozen times over and decimated its population. Antioch, straddling the northernmost fault line of the Dead Sea/Great Rift Valley, has been especially earthquake prone. Nearly 60 earthquakes are recorded in the city's history, about ten of which caused extreme damage and loss of life and would have scaled more than 7 in today's magnitude measurements. For comparison, the 2010 earthquake that devastated Haiti had a magnitude of 7. Further, many of these major ones have often clustered together, for example in the sixth, twelfth, and nineteenth centuries, making recovery challenging. Yet the city has survived period after period, down to the present day. To be sure, these disasters had some effect: the double earthquakes in the sixth century appear to have altered the composition of the classical city permanently and ushered in its medieval transformation. Similarly, the wave of strong earthquakes in the twelfth century stretched the city's resources thin, allowing only the most important features – walls and key churches – to be rebuilt, leaving the rest of the city heavily damaged. This in turn may have facilitated the ease of the 1268 siege by the Mamlūks, who had no interest in restoring Antioch to its former size and glory but rebuilt the city as a town on a much smaller scale that was built up internally but remained physically contracted for another 500 years. Other disasters, like fires, plagues, and famine, were sometimes tied to earthquakes and sometimes to changes in climate. River flooding was a near annual occurrence that was managed in many periods but not always. Indeed, the Princeton excavators had to deal with flooding of the mountain streams and Orontes as a feature of seasonal occurrence that frustrated their excavations occasionally. But disasters, like conquests, become tropes and part of the city's lore. The real effects of these were likely not as extreme as depicted, as the city and its residents endured, though with hardship and loss, every time. In many ways, this is an encouraging historical example of resilience, particularly as the world, at the time of publishing this book, is going through a global pandemic of the coronavirus COVID-19, alongside a host of other worldwide natural disasters such as wildfires in California and Australia, an uptick in

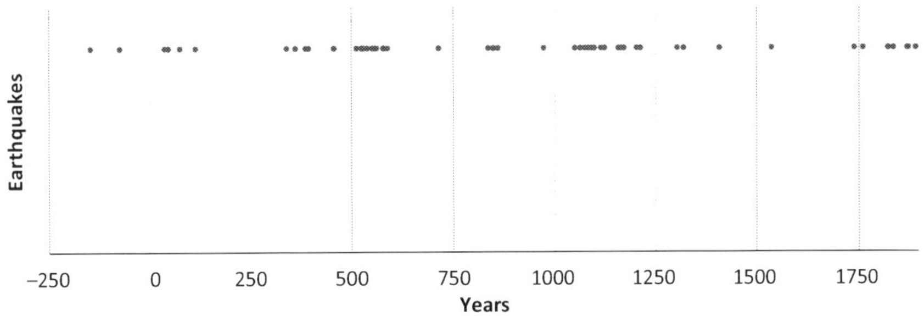

FIGURE 0.2 Antioch earthquakes by year, 250 BC to 1900 CE

powerful hurricanes and monsoons, and earthquakes, as well as humanitarian crises in Yemen and Syria, huge refugee movements in Central America, Burma, and the Mediterranean, social justice protests in Hong Kong, racial justice and police reform protests in cities throughout the United States and other world cities, the storming of the U. S. Congress building by right-winged insurrectionists, and, of course, a comet and a great conjunction of Jupiter and Saturn. Indeed, it seems, as many Muslim and Christian writers in the Near East wrote in the seventh century, that the apocalypse is nigh. Studying Antioch through all of its ages, replete with crises and transformations, teaches us a valuable lesson on the capacity of a city and its citizens to rebuild and to be resilient.

One interesting outcome is how the city and its inhabitants reacted to these disasters. The current global pandemic is showing us how nearly all aspects daily life and economy have been overturned and have necessitated dramatic social changes. In premodern (and pre-internet) Antioch, where hygiene and sanitation were far less than what they are now, we can be sure that these disasters had profound physical and psychological effects on the population. Yet while population fluctuated, the city was never abandoned. This is a significant point, in that many cities of the classical world were eventually abandoned by the medieval period, if not earlier. Antioch has been continuously inhabited. Further, calamities such as earthquakes and fires can be seen as allowing for new growth. The ancient and medieval city is often envisioned as clean, museified, and antiseptic, when in fact cities were the reverse; we have to imagine porticoes, streets, and alleys as cluttered, stinky, noisy, and teeming with crowds of people and animals. Thus, a disaster and clean-up in its aftermath could also expose and remove clutter such as old, abandoned, or disused structures and spaces, and allow for reshaping. Archaeological evidence for Antioch indeed reflects this continuity, showing much rebuilding and restructuring yet very few instances of destruction.

A conquered city

The second theme, accordingly, is that of conquest. Nearly every period in Antioch's history begins with a conquest, many of which are elaborately described in the sources, such as the almost legendary Crusader and Mamlūk sieges and those of the Persians, Arabs, Byzantines (their reconquest), and Saljūqs. These conquests in many ways bear striking similarities, as the enemy was nearly always kept at bay by the sheer impenetrability of Antioch's walls, and so the city had to be taken by treachery. That the city's taking had to be an inside job – a Trojan horse if you will – attests to its strength and invincibility. Often the access point was from the summit of the mountain (as in the sixth-century Persian and Middle Byzantine conquests), farthest from the city itself. This points to a general weakness of Antioch – that the mountains are steepest within the city, but the slopes eastward are more gradual. After the Middle Byzantine period, the citadel on Mt. Silpius featured prominently during sieges, often creating in effect two cities, with either the conquerors holding down the citadel and attacking the lower city or vice versa, with the remaining town taking refuge in the citadel. The conquests also frequently involved bloody massacres, and a good number of the town's citizens were killed and buildings destroyed. But however graphic these descriptions are, the overarching narrative of continuity compels us to question how transformative or devastating these sieges initially were, as the city's history following each conquest was quite active and rich. The archaeological evidence also supports the argument for continuity, failing as yet to show any evidence of conquest. The Mamlūk conquest, of all of these, might have come closest to greatly diminishing Antioch. If at any point the city witnessed a substantial "decline" in the sense that it was dramatically reduced in physical size and depopulated, it was following the Mamlūk conquest of the city in 1268. Yet even this perceived nadir cannot be considered a decline; just months after the siege, the city was the subject of significant royal patronage with the establishment of six to eight mosques and four bathhouses, it was a home to intellectual communities, and it continued as a center for trade. Antioch's importance was unwavering.

A cosmopolitan city

Seemingly at odds with the theme of conquest is the continued heterogeneity of Antioch's population in language, ethnicity, and religion. Indeed, this has been a matter of pride for the city to this day. This third theme, the city's cosmopolitan nature and diverse communities, appears in every period. We see strong representations of Persians, Greeks, Roman colonists, orthodox Chaldean communities and Melkites who spoke Arabic, West Syrian Orthodox/Jacobites and Armenians, Arabs and Zuṭṭ, and Jewish communities earliest of all. Indeed, today the pluralism and tolerance of Antioch's many religious and ethnic communities are cited as a model for Turkish cities. Present throughout nearly all periods of Antioch's history was also an intellectual community of scholars, some of whom lived there, others who passed through and temporarily resided. To this we can add that Antioch, despite its many foreign or outsider rulers, was largely run by the nobles of the city from at least the sixth century onwards through the Islamic period. Such diversity makes talking about the Antiochenes, if we can use this term, rather problematic in any period. Although we will mention whenever possible which specific group was involved in any aspect of the city's history, the ancient and medieval sources themselves did not always distinguish among the peoples of Antioch, frequently lumping them together, and in such cases we will follow suit. But though social tensions were ever present in the city and we highlight them frequently, they remain beyond the focus of this volume.

Yet despite the city's diversity and tensions, its citizens repeatedly came together and acted in unison to protest against officials and rulers they did not approve of or even shake off foreign conquerors and governors. Whether it was the Emperor Julian, the Saljūqs, the Crusaders, the Hamdānid Sayf al-Dawla, or various local officials, the Antiochenes' exertion of their own power over whom they supported to govern them is notable, particularly given the number of foreign attempts to conquer the city. In doing so, they reinforced the Antiochene local identity and their efforts to act as an autonomous community. This theme also challenges the narrative of a city in decline and ruin, besieged and conquered, its population massacred. Rather, it shows how the city was able to survive each conquest and produce narratives of local resistance steeped in its own rich socio-cultural, economic, religious, and built environment.

A celebrated city

The final theme is that of foundation and legacy. Antioch's foundation is shrouded in myth and legend, from its Seleucid beginnings through the Ottoman period. Even in the Middle Byzantine, Crusader, and Ottoman periods, the story of Seleucus I Nicator was remembered and woven together with talismans and images around the city, such as the iconic Tyche (divine fortune) of Antioch, as well as important figures in Antioch's own spiritual landscape. These were not necessarily proper gods – like Apollo, whose oracle resided in the suburb of Daphne – but patron saints who became divine. They include St. Peter and St. Paul, who brought Christianity to the city; St. Ignatius, St. Babylas, whose burial in pagan Daphne, one of the earliest instances of a cult of relics, later defied an emperor and started a revolt; St. Barbara, St. Luke, St. Symeon Stylites the Younger, the influential Church Father John Chrysostom; and the Patriarch Christopher, whose murder ignited the Byzantine reconquest of the city. Habīb al-Najjār, a carpenter, was its most famous Islamic resident, identified often as a hero of the Qur'ān, and likely one of its first citizens to accept monotheism. The continuity of the recollection of persons throughout its entire history lent Antioch and its diverse population an elevated status *sui generis*, making it a city worth visiting and conquering. The walls of Antioch, depicted so carefully in the fifth-century Byzantine Peutinger Table map (Figure 3.10), are their own legendary site, a wonder of the world, and the city's star attraction. Indeed, as the city's biography shows, they were as much centers of action, or *omphaloi* of the city, as they were its edges. The city remained powerful and tantalizing in the eyes of rulers and ruling dynasties and numerous travelers: pilgrims, merchants, academics, and explorers, all of whom wished to reengage with its profound past. In fact, in every period after the Islamic conquests, the city was regarded as legendary – the place where true monotheism took root, where prophets and apostles were buried, and where relics were enshrined. It was the invincible city with impenetrable walls, a town steeped in history and antiquity that continuously beckoned visitors and conquerors alike. In many instances, the city's classical past is evident in its medieval and early modern incarnations, consciously expressed, remembered, and etched into the buildings and walls themselves. This constant awareness of Antioch's history was for some periods a longing for the past, for others a legitimizing of its importance in the present. Thus, not only is the city of Antioch like a palimpsest, where the past is visible, but throughout its history it has also consciously connected with its past, including rather than rejecting it while at the same time rewriting it.

A few more words

Presenting the full history of Antioch has been no easy task. Condensing information culled from many primary and secondary sources written over the city's 2,324-year history into a book of this size is not for the faint of heart. Therefore, this book presents an enormous wealth of information on the city, some of it for the first time, including new and reinterpreted archaeological results along with material culture and numismatic studies and new translations. Moreover, much of the material is combined together for the first time and done so in a contextualized way set against a proper and full chronology. We have done this also by deliberately sidelining the main capitals of our periods such as Rome, Constantinople/Istanbul, Baghdad, and Jerusalem. These have received sufficient scholarly attention, and Antioch has always appeared as peripheral to their stories. Therefore, this narrative seeks to invert that hierarchy and foreground the life of Antioch as main actor and the imperial/caliphal cities as support. Our presentation of Antioch is intended for a broad readership; we have tried to write a compelling and rich narrative that effectively weaves together our own arguments and descriptions in book form. To that end, we have limited the citations of primary sources while directing the reader toward essential scholarship. So, too, we have often chosen to cite a translation of a source in a modern language, where possible, so as to encourage more accessibility to general readers. We have also trimmed the use of excessively technical terms while also providing Greek, Latin, Arabic, and Ottoman Turkish translations, some of which may seem obvious to more expert readers.

No doubt this book will need revising as publications on the Princeton excavations are systematically reanalyzed, textual sources reveal more clues as to the city's topography, and new excavations and surveys – conducted mainly by Mustafa Kemal University and the Hatay Archeological Museum – are published. At present, it is our hope that this volume will be helpful both to researchers familiar with the city and to newcomers visiting it for the first time. It is also certain that the scholarly landscape of the city will transform and evolve much as the city itself has, from period to period.

With this book we also continue our own long history of affiliation with Antioch and its community, and we take this opportunity to express gratitude to all of our friends in Hatay. This book has depended on the kindness and generosity of many colleagues and friends to come to fruition, indeed a pantheon in their own right. We would like first to thank Alan Stahl and Charles Gates for reading the manuscript and providing invaluable feedback, and also Darby Scott, Charlie Bloom, Scott Redford, Tasha Vorderstrasse, Malike Dekkiche, Alyssa Gabbay, Derek Krueger, Scott Kennedy, Fahri Dikkaya, Rick Barton, Robyn LeBlanc,

Cybelle McFadden, and Andrew Wasserman for reading and commenting on individual chapters. We are grateful to Gunnar Brands, Ulrich Weferling, the late Andrea Zerbini, Dimitri Gondicas, Michael Padgett, Michael Koortbojian, Nathan Arrington, Julia Gearhart, Britt Bowen, Hakan Boyacı, Aaron Miller, Peter van Alfen, Michael Bennett, Elif Denel, and Marina Milella for their support, images, and suggestions. Also, thanks to Choukri Heddouchi, Hussein Algudaihi, Kate Sheeler, Peter Klempner, Yusuf Enis Sezgin, Esmanur Şamiloğlu, Kyle Brunner, and Raymond Farrin for help with translations. Special praise must go to Steven Batiuk for his long hours in producing the plans of Antioch and Claire Ebert for her work on the maps. We also owe immense thanks to the American Council of Learned Societies for a grant to A. Asa Eger and to the FSU students of Andrea U. De Giorgi's seminar on Antioch in 2017. Last, but certainly not least, we are indebted to Jan Ryder, our editor, who worked tirelessly on polishing and refining this manuscript.

Note on style and transliterations: We use Antioch throughout, even when the city was referred to in the Islamic periods as Anṭakīya and in Turkish as Antakya; similarly, we use Orontes River (rather than 'Asī, Maqlūb, etc.). Names, terms, and toponyms, with the exception of major cities, are transliterated in Arabic and Ottoman Turkish following IJMES style except Appendix 2; however, the majority of well-known cities also retain a standard non-transliterated name in every period. We also use Julian-Gregorian dating throughout, not the Islamic calendar or any other.

Notes

1 Harawī 2004.
2 *Antioch V*, 3–12. Particularly for sector 17-O, as we shall see in this volume.
3 Becker and Kondoleon 2005; Kondoleon 2000; *Levi, Pavements*.
4 See the recent catalog of the 2014 exhibition of photographs from the Princeton excavation, Redford 2014.
5 Brands 2016a.
6 *TIB*; also Bergjan and Elm 2018.
7 These have been presented at a three-year panel at the Annual Meeting of the American Schools of Oriental Research (2016–2018) and will be published in a volume, still in progress.
8 *Downey, History* De Giorgi 2015, 11.
9 De Giorgi 2017; Najbjerg and Moss 2014, 34. There is no other chapter on Antioch's history after this time range.
10 Zambon et al. 2000.
11 Horden and Purcell 2000; McCormick 2002; Wickham 2005.
12 Kennedy 1985a; Guidetti 2010.
13 Eger 2014b, 95–134.
14 Lopez 1976; Thomas 1997.
15 Abu Lughod 1989.
16 Yener et al. 2005; *Braidwood, Mounds*; Casana 2004, 2007.
17 Haines 1971; Gerritsen et al. 2008; Pucci 2019; Osborne et al. 2019.
18 Lib. *Or.* 11.260–262.
19 Eger 2012, 2015.

1

THE EAGLE OF ZEUS ARRIVES (303 BCE–64 BCE)

> Even without seeing it, one can have full knowledge of it from hearsay, for there is no corner of land or sea to which the fame of the city has not spread.
>
> – Libanius, *Oration 1*

Introduction

Why Antioch was founded on a rather unpromising site, how its community developed an urban infrastructure, and how it grew to become a capital under the Seleucid kings are the main themes of this chapter. The political instability in the aftermath of Alexander the Great's unexpected death in 323 BCE and the establishment of the Seleucid dynasty are, however, the fundamental antecedents to the city's foundation. In this vein, we cannot separate the analysis of Antioch's genesis and growth from presenting the agency behind it or the motives that prompted the formation of an enclave of Greeks along the riverbanks of the Orontes.

Upon Alexander's death, the vast empire he had conquered was carved up by his leading generals, who established their own kingdoms and dynasties; among these was Seleucus I Nicator (305–281 BCE), whose far-flung Seleucid Empire stretched from the furthest reaches of Alexander's conquests in modern-day Pakistan back through what is today Afghanistan, Iran (Persia), Iraq, Syria, and into central Turkey. The recent burgeoning interest in the Seleucid monarchy has brought into sharper focus the political and cultural outlooks of this dynasty.[1] The nature of its rule, suspended between Greek and Persian paradigms, has drawn interest from scholars of various learned traditions (Figure 1.1).

More to the point, a wealth of studies have debunked the myth that the Seleucid world was peripheral to Greece and Persia, bringing more and more into focus the centrality of the kingdom's mechanisms, above and beyond the questions of what

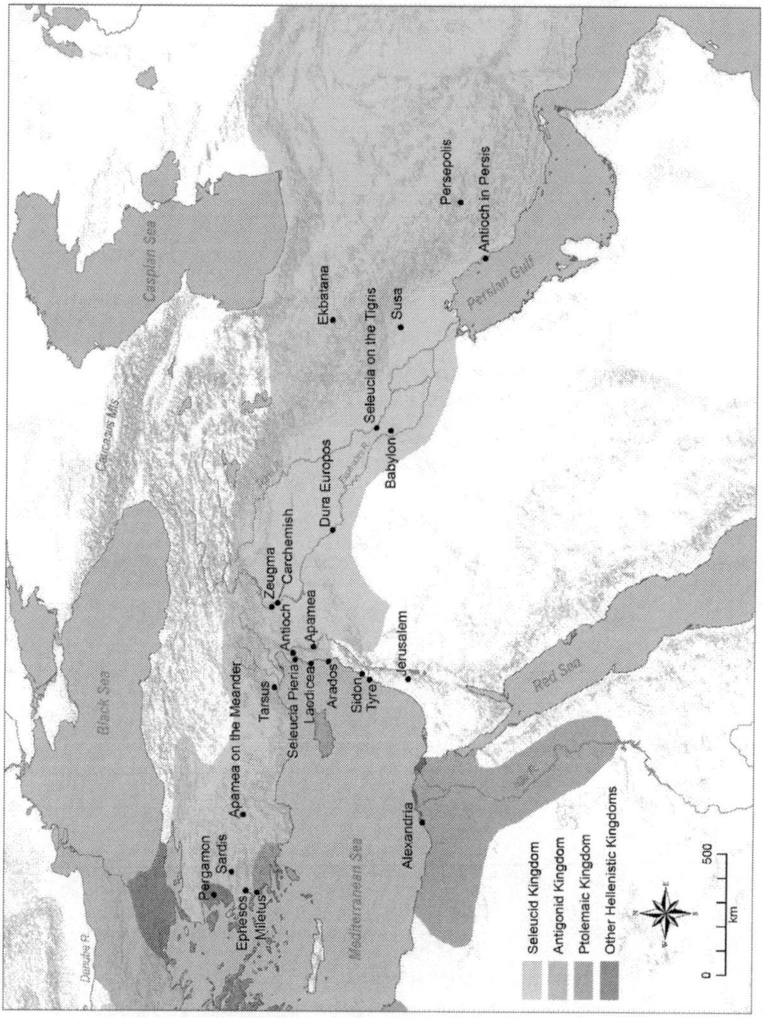

FIGURE 1.1 The Hellenistic kingdoms

Source: Created by Claire Ebert

is Western and what is Eastern.[2] How the Seleucids effectively negotiated realities of power and forged a novel monarchic discourse through local allegiances and universalistic aspirations is a question that continues to be vigorously debated.[3] Indeed, the patchy and skewed textual records of the Seleucids have failed to hamper a growing scholarly veering toward the Hellenistic kingdoms. The biased, pro-Roman voices of Polybius, Livy, and Appian, to name but a few, remain nevertheless key to reconstructing the historical discussion of the Seleucids. In particular, emphasis on the lives and deeds of Seleucus I Nicator, Antiochus III the Great, and Antiochus IV Epiphanes illustrates the role of the kingdom as it forged its own concept of "state" and made its mark on the political realities of the time. Antioch is typically foregrounded in much of this scholarship, for the city was central in Seleucid politics and indeed transformed the Hellenistic East in fundamental ways.[4] Yet much as the ancient accounts contribute to the discourse of the city coalescing and rising to unexpected heights under these monarchs, the dearth of textual and epigraphic sources has hindered analysis of the city's socio-political configuration. One can only lament the epigraphic habit of the city, the condition by which the local culture minimized the dissemination of its public records, constituting a hurdle that ultimately frustrates insights into the lives of Antioch's inhabitants. But disquieting though the picture might seem, new archaeological and numismatic data offers ways to further our understanding of the city's history and materiality.

Topography

Antioch on the Orontes lies at the junction between the southernmost extension of the Amuq Plain (Amik Ovası) and the slopes of Mt. Staurin and Mt. Silpius (Kusseyr Dağı, Habib Neccar Dağı, part of the Jibāl al-Aqra); here the Orontes River (Asi River, also known in antiquity as Drakon or Typhon)[5] bends its course southward as it points decisively toward the Mediterranean coast. Crucial though it was for providing the region with plenty of water, the Orontes also dictated the shape and conditions of the ancient settlement (Figure 1.2). In particular, its unpredictable regime, affected as it was by climatic, hydrological, and, indeed, anthropogenic factors as well as propensity to flood, greatly affected the topography of Antioch. Any facile determinism aside, the river commanded Antioch's nucleation as well as urban development for centuries.

Indeed, Antioch's location was completely ill suited for urban expansion; hemmed in between the Amanus Mountains (Nur Dağı), the river, and the slopes of Mt. Silpius and Mt. Staurin, the city from its outset had to reckon with conspicuous runoff from the mountain massifs and the capricious regime of the Orontes, such as when fall and winter rainstorms gusted through the region, causing rivers and streams to swell beyond measure. The rushing waters would spill over their banks, inundate homes, and sweep away livestock, mills, and bridges, flooding freshly tilled fields. In the city, people would often resort to jars, buckets, and sponges to bail out their shops and houses.[6] All the same, a complex system of conduits, dams, and aqueducts attests to the tenacity with which the Antiochenes

FIGURE 1.2 The Orontes River and Antioch

Source: Declassified Corona imagery, 1967

coped with this frail ecology and sought to control the impetus of seasonal streams from the adjacent mountains. In particular, the Antioch excavations in 1937 recovered what the archaeologists referred to as a Hellenistic system of tunnels designed to impound inflows and channel them under the main thoroughfare.[7] The reign of Justinian in the sixth century saw the consolidation of the so-called Iron Gate, incorporating centuries of waterworks and man-made modifications planted deep in the gorge between Mt. Silpius and Mt. Staurin. Serving as both gate and dam, it was the city's most spectacular effort to curb the erratic waters of the Parmenios, a torrential stream flowing into the Orontes and also known as the Onopniktes or "donkey drowner" (and today, Haci Kürüş Deresi).[8] Yet even the Iron Gate and its infrastructure of canals and tunnels could only partially contain the seasonal impact of the streams: thick gravel and cobble alluvial fans accumulated for centuries at the foot of the two mountains and now bury large tracts of the ancient city under meters of sediment.

The role of the Orontes, inasmuch as it shaped the local topography, has not been sufficiently brought into focus by previous scholarship.[9] Erratic in the extreme, 30 to 35 meters wide, with an average discharge of 11 cubic meters per second, the river rises in the Lebanon mountains near Hermel and enters the plain of Homs in Syria via the Wadi al-Rablah, then driving north past Homs and Hama and turning decisively west.[10] From Syria, the Hatay corridor drives the Orontes into Turkey, eventually bending west at the modern village of Demirköprü, ancient Gephyra. Some 15 kilometers southwest the Orontes waters the site that, poised on the slopes of Mt. Staurin and Mt. Silpios, accommodated the foundation of Antioch. Because of its endemic propensity to change course, today the Orontes skirts the northwestern sector of Antioch, no longer forming the Island, that is, the "city within the city," which retained its centrality for centuries. Further south, the river skirts the Daphne plateau on its left and then continues its course all the way to the Mediterranean coast, emptying its waters some 22 km from Antioch. The Tyche (deity of fortune) of Eutychides of Sykion (Figure 1.3), showing the divine fortune of Antioch with turrite crown, holding a sheaf of grain and sitting on the

FIGURE 1.3 The Tyche of Antioch by Eutychides, Roman copy

Source: Photo Copyright Governorato SCV-Direzione dei Musei Vaticani

rock of Mt. Silpius with the personified Orontes swimming at her feet, lulls us into believing the harmonious unity between the city and the river. The sculptural group was commissioned by Seleucus Nicator and executed by Eutychides, a pupil of the great artist Lysippus.[11] A mid-third-century CE coin depicts on the reverse the Tyche under the baldachin of a four-column shrine (*tetrakionion*), which is the building that accommodated Eutychides's statue at least until the sixth century CE,[12] though where this shrine was located cannot be established. But the truth is that the Orontes compromised the fortunes of the city time and again; its tendency to swell in the winter season – when sheets of rain pummel the region – led conspicuous alluvial debris and sediment to accumulate along its course, as attested by the disappearance of the ancient Island in the late medieval era.[13]

An urban port presumably existed in the vicinity of the Philonauta Gate, where the Orontes bends slightly eastward (near sector 21-H), and riverine transport once connected Antioch to the Mediterranean; a day of navigation, it seems, led from the city to sea outlets in the vicinity of Seleucia Pieria, one of Antioch's twin cities. To that end, the good health and taming of the river were crucial, and for centuries emperors and city administrators saw to the upkeep of the Orontes' drainage and navigability in ways reminiscent of waterworks on the Tiber in Rome.[14] Whether for the hauling of goods or the convenient drowning of political enemies,[15] the life of Antioch was thus braided together with that of the river.

A similarly relentless negotiation with the forces of nature occurred, albeit on a larger scale, in the greater territory surrounding Antioch, a topographically diverse basin loosely corresponding to the Amuq Valley. Central in it is the plain of Antioch, known today as the Amik Ovası; in antiquity as today, it functioned as a hinge between the Mediterranean and northern Mesopotamia. The plain was long dominated by the conspicuous Lake of Antioch (Amik Gölü), which seemingly began to form during the late Bronze Age as a result of the aggradation of the Orontes floodplain;[16] presumably the basin reached its maximum capacity during Late Antiquity, as rates of sediment aggradation reached their peak.[17]

Framed by the metalliferous Amanus Mountains to the west[18] and hill systems jutting from the Syrian Jibāl to the east, this region was the locus of an impressive mesh of sites dating from the Chalcolithic era (roughly 4500–3300 BCE) down to the Ottoman age (Figure 1.4).

But this is not all, for Antioch and its territory lay on the northernmost extension of the Dead Sea Rift Valley, the zone of faults between the convergence of the African and Arabian Plates that gave rise to the long streak of earthquakes that wreaked havoc in the city, especially during the sixth century CE, and almost led to its wholesale demise at least twice, in 113 and 519 CE. "Wretched Antioch" reads one of the Sibylline Oracles.[19] Whether spurious or not, this text nevertheless introduces a characterization of the city that oozes time and again in the textual sources of the Late Roman Empire and medieval periods. Yet the misfortunes and calamities punctuating the city's history hardly outweigh the trajectory of a community that with a good deal of pride, and indeed legitimate claim, styled itself as the center of the Greek world and rose to the highest plateau of prominence.

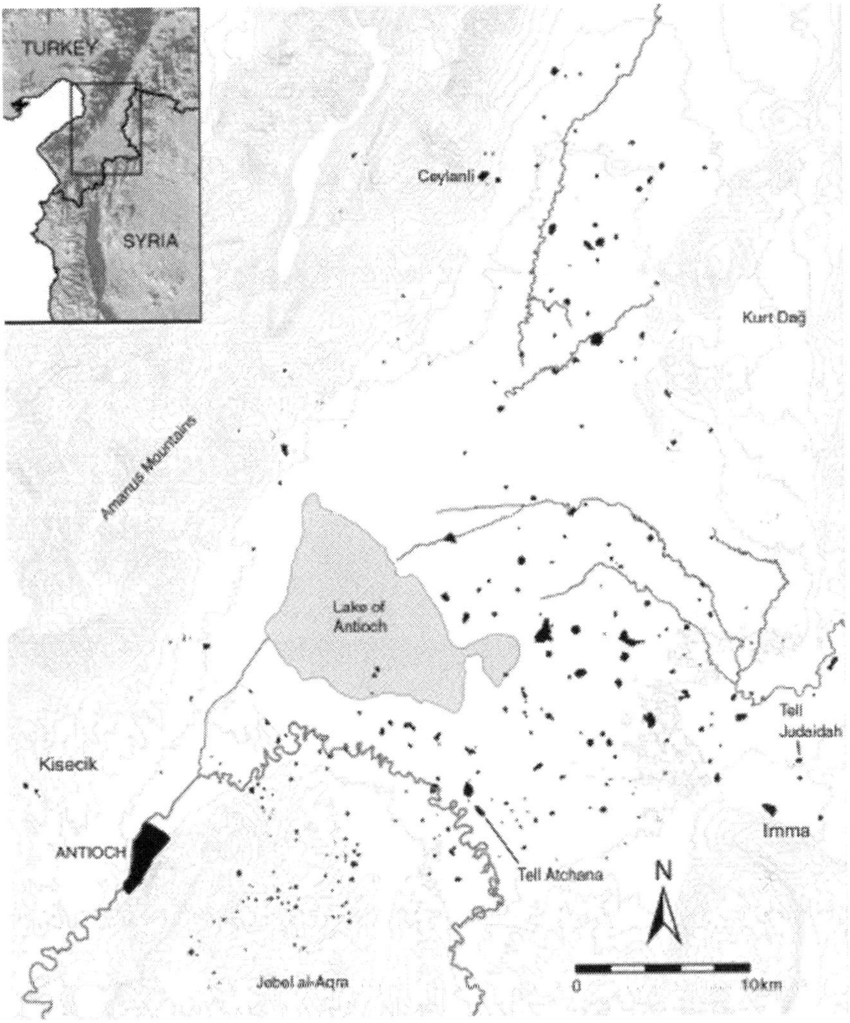

FIGURE 1.4 The Amuq Valley Regional Project survey 1999–2004

Source: Courtesy of the Amuq Valley Regional Project, Oriental Institute, University of Chicago

The early landscape

The Seleucid foundation of Antioch was grounded in a landscape that had been in use from time immemorial, as revealed by decades of archaeological research conducted in the Antioch plain.[20]

The settlement systems of the Late Bronze Age–Early Iron Age, as well as their web of interconnected foci, trade routes, and canals, were instrumental in building the armature underpinning the urbanism of later epochs. The formation of the kingdom of Alalakh in the late Bronze Age is a good case in point.

Seminal excavations conducted by Sir Leonard Woolley in the 1930s at the site of Tell Atchana, some 20 miles northeast of Antioch following the road to Aleppo, revealed parts of Alalakh's sacred architecture as well as sectors of a palace.[21] Woolley's excavations also yielded caches of cuneiform texts, most of which date to circa 1600 BCE and attest to a dominant Hurrian culture, albeit tinted with Canaanite accents. Of course such cultural commingling has significant bearing on the study of the Hebrew Bible, and studies on Alalakh's personal names and social practices also resonate in Genesis and Exodus.[22] The cultural diversity of this landscape in the middle-to-late second millennium BCE, however, needs to be highlighted, traversed, and experienced as it was by western Semitic, Anatolian, and Syrian communities. In tandem with that, in following centuries the expanses of territory from the Mediterranean coast to the Syrian rolling hills were transformed into engineered landscapes demarcated by boundaries, axes of traffic, and canals seeking to prevent the flooding of fields and settlements. The kingdom of Alalakh, overlooking the Amuq Plain from its conspicuous mound and fortifications, typifies these trends and is the manifesto of a culturally defined basin as early as the second millennium BCE.[23] The region's crossroads character, permeability to other cultures, and firm control of the land and its resources continued well into the Iron Age: recent textual and archaeological and epigraphic evidence from the nearby site of Tell Tayinat (Kingdom of Kunulua) resonates with the political tensions of the early seventh century, amid the rise of the Anatolian powers, the divided kingdom of Israel, and the consolidation of Assyria.[24] Here the discovery of palaces, a large temple, and beautifully carved stone reliefs document the rise to prominence of the capital of the kingdom of Patina/Unqi.

While the material and historical records for the Persian period and the Archaic era remain poorly known, it is nonetheless accepted that the Amuq Plain and the upper Orontes Valley heightened increasingly their role as a link between the Levantine peoples of the eastern Mediterranean and the Aegean world, as attested by the finds at Tell al-Mina on the Mediterranean coast, six miles south of the Orontes delta. The agency behind the establishing of this trading post has long been a matter of dispute, amid hypotheses of founders hailing from the Greek mainland or of mixed Levantine and Hellenic constituencies.[25] Telling though Tell al-Mina's material culture may be, with its rich repertoire of Greek imports of the eighth and seventh centuries, it more fundamentally signals the rise and fall of a hub that propelled far-flung, large-scale trade and commercial exchanges between the delta of the Orontes and regions such as Attica in Greece. Whether the presence of Greek ethnic elements can legitimately be read through the lenses of some ethnic brewing that preceded the establishment of Seleucid colonies is a possibility entertained in the past.[26] By this view, Antioch's founding myths and the role of the Greeks were not mere exercises of etiology but episodes grounded in concrete evidence. It is perhaps safer, however, to consider the extraordinary degree of connectivity and crosspollination that pervaded the eastern Mediterranean in the Iron Age, stimulated as they were by flows of goods and information radiating from Greece, the islands, and the coast of the Levant.

From the Seleucids to Antioch

It stands to reason that by the time the Seleucid surveyors reached the region during the last decade of the fourth century BCE, a thriving constellation of communities was apparently in place. In the closing years of that century, Seleucus Nicator secured his northern Syrian holdings through a cluster of new urban foundations.[27] These sites varied greatly in size and topography, at times consisting of *ex novo* foundations or, conversely, exploiting previously occupied tells (mounds). All the same, the landscape that Seleucus so thoroughly intended to urbanize was hardly a blank canvas. As mentioned, small kingdoms, cities, and their infrastructure had created a vast network of roads and sites for the exploitation of resources and the simple channeling of traffic into the heart of Mesopotamia or toward the Mediterranean. Indeed, the existing infrastructure facilitated Seleucus's work; in his mind, northern Syria, a district loosely defined as the Seleucis, was to become the heart of the kingdom.[28] Put simply, the establishment of the dynastic resting place and, more subtly, a reconfiguration of Seleucus's territorial holdings around this new regional pivot let the king's intentions be known. Capillary control of the territory was the main impetus of this operation; to that end, old arteries of traffic, the Mediterranean seaboard, and riverine basins witnessed an almost synchronic flurry of new establishments and urban effervescence.[29] Many of the sites and toponyms carried either dynastic names or replicated the nomenclature of places in Greece and Macedonia in an effort to both draw upon a glorious past and assert the new world order. A mesh of sites carrying the names of members of the royal family or reminiscent of a Greek/Macedonian ancestry thus spanned Asia and Persia, signaling the new realities of power. Rural districts adjacent to these foci, by turns, underwent dense occupation by a peasantry that remained amenable to serving in the royal army as the situation arose.[30] The case of Europos (Carchemish), for instance, illustrates well the functioning of these settlements, equipped with a halo of small sites, presumably small villages and farmsteads gravitating toward the urban center.[31] Other foci like Dura Europos and Jebel Khalid, conversely, declared the essentially military nature of their settlement, poised as they were on the Euphrates.[32]

More ambitious still, however, was the establishment of the so-called Tetrapolis:[33] a system of four sibling cities, two on the Mediterranean coast (Laodicea and Seleucia Pieria) paired with two inland (Antioch on the Orontes and Apamea) that was intended as the centerpiece of Seleucid rule over northern Syria. Much has been written on these putative twin cities;[34] although the textual sources offer a narrative of synchronic settlement, the archaeological record seems to suggest a great degree of diversity in setting, size, and outcomes. Hardly matching the scale, prestige, and accolades of Antioch, these other sibling cities nevertheless remained tied to the city on the Orontes for the rest of their history by indissoluble links, their relationship characterized by episodes of brotherhood, fierce competition, open conflict, and submission. All the same, these four cities were equally implicated in the extraordinary narrative of settlement, growth, and evolution that occurred on the shores of the Orontes and that led to realizing one of the greatest cities of the ancient world. Earthquakes, too, inflicted equal shares of destruction to the four cities of the Tetrapolis.

Antioch's establishment in the textual record

Antioch was not, however, meant to retain any primacy in Seleucus's project, for it became the fully fledged capital of the Seleucid kingdom only in the second century BCE.[35] Instead, Seleucia Pieria had apparently been designated as a royal mainstay, accommodating as it did the mortal spoils of the king and his successors. Antiochus III (223–187 BCE), also known as the Great, brought to completion the gradual transformation that was to change Antioch's course of history. The gradual increase of production in silver tetradrachms in Antioch (of the Apollo sitting on the Omphalos type, with the prominent cone representing the navel or the mythical center of the world) at the expense of Seleucia in the aftermath of Seleucus's death may bear witness to this phenomenon of gradual political reorientation (Figure 1.5).[36] But let us now return to the city's foundation, conventionally dated to 300 BCE, and its implications.

The Greek geographer and historian Strabo informs us that the growth of the city consisted of four major stages, each carried out under a Seleucid king, namely Seleucus I Nicator, Seleucus II, Antiochus III the Great, and Antiochus IV Epiphanes.[37] The ill-promising site did not curb the zest of the kings in concentrating their efforts and energies here. In particular, John Malalas, a

FIGURE 1.5 Tetradrachm of Antiochus III. Obverse: diameded head of Antiochus facing right. Reverse: Apollo seated on Omphalos, testing arrow and resting left hand on grounded bow; ΒΑΣΙΛΕΩΣ ΑΝΤΙΟΧΟΥ

Source: Courtesy of the American Numismatic Society, ANS 1944.100.75135, Edward T. Newell bequest

sixth-century CE historian and native of Antioch, implied that Seleucus's surveyors were aware of the environmental challenges, and not least the torrential runoff, brought by situating a foundation at the foot of Mt. Silpius and Mt. Staurin.[38] Whether any prudence was exercised is a matter of dispute; the will of the gods prevailed, and Seleucus Nicator made no attempt to shrink from the divine plan. Accordingly, he placed the new community on the valley floor, where the Orontes River bent forming the Island, in the vicinity of a village known as Bottia.

The existence of a predecessor to Antioch remains a thorny issue, for the archaeological record hampers any safe reconstruction. Nor is the textual record less murky. For all its wealth of information, the chronicle of John Malalas offers a perspective on historical events, recent and old, redolent with anachronisms and historical inaccuracies. As for the circumstances of the foundation, Malalas claims that after defeating his enemy Antigonos I Monophthalmus, another of Alexander's successor generals, at Ipsos in 301 BCE, Seleucus established a first foundation at Seleucia Pieria, which would become Antioch's port.[39] The modality of the foundation followed a three-part template that applied to the other cities of the Tetrapolis as well: (1) sacrifices to Zeus Kasios/Keraunios, (2) an eagle appearing and snatching the sacrificial meats, and (3) dropping of the same meats at the site that was to become the new city. The implications of the eagle's presence, symbolizing Zeus and echoing the myth of the foundation of the Serapeion in Alexandria by Alexander the Great, informed the royal propaganda that imbued these foundations.[40] As Daniel Ogden has noted, the lamination between Seleucus and Alexander the Great could not be more apparent, as the former exploited the well-known iconographies of thunderbolts, eagles, and heads of Zeus into the coinage of Antioch and Seleucia from the early days.[41] Not surprisingly, the city of Antioch was not slow in developing monumental programs celebrating the same visual symbols of the foundation and the royal family. Eagles, the gods who attended to the foundation, and Tychai (images of the city's divine fortune), among other symbols, punctuated the sculptural townscape of Antioch from its establishment and identified urban landmarks like towers and street junctions for the successive centuries.[42]

According to Malalas, Antioch's site of choice was that of the village of Bottia, opposite the site of Iopolis, situated somewhere on the slopes of Mt. Silpius near an altar dedicated to Zeus. The two enclaves may thus have been separated by the course of the Orontes. Pleased with their plan, Seleucus and his loyal priest Amphion laid the grounds for the new foundation. The vagaries of Malalas's text frustrate any attempt to establish a firm sense of topography, let alone any historical coherence. Nevertheless, it is likely that Antioch's foundation aimed at defining a new urban base at a site built upon previous settlements. This was, however, a somewhat crowded landscape, and careful choices had to be made as far as incorporating old establishments went. In particular, the plan for the new city had to avoid encroaching on the one urban community that powerfully signaled Seleucus's enemy, namely, Antigonos. In fact, a city boasting a 70 stade (about 13 km) perimeter named Antigonia had been previously founded by Antigonos himself somewhere between the slopes of the Amanus Mountains and the Lake of Antioch, presumably near the outlet to the lake of the Kücük Asi River, known as the ancient Arkeuthas or Iaphta.[43] It stands to reason that in the immediate aftermath of Antigonos's defeat at Ipsos, Antigonia was fully dismantled; its materiality and memory could neither survive nor compromise Seleucus's new project. Ironically, though, in the thirteenth century the account of Ibn al-'Adīm still stressed the fact that Antigonia was the material predecessor of Antioch, while also attesting to the durable legacy of the Seleucid foundation.[44]

The defeated city's Tyche, however, survived the pillaging. In a unique transfer of religious prerogatives, she was handed over to the new community, thus signaling the appropriation of Antigonia's most intimate religious essence. More concretely, the story of Antigonia's Tyche is reminiscent of the trope of spoliation that defeated cities typically had to undergo during the third century BCE. The description of the 212 BCE capture and plunder of Syracuse by the Romans, as penned by Plutarch, Livy, and, partially, Polybius, balanced between moralistic overtones and the extolling of the winner's magnanimity, may have served as a viable textual template for the Late Antique presentation of the theme.[45] Indeed, it appears that the spoils of the entire disgraced city of Antigonia were relocated – whether forcibly or not we cannot tell – to the new city on the Orontes. All in all, the staged destruction of Antigonia, the human sacrifice of a young girl (Aimathe, designated as the new Tyche of the city), the establishment of a temple dedicated to Zeus Bottios, and, lastly, the definition of the city's perimeter all characterized the beginning of Antioch's urban narrative. That the name Antioch was that of Seleucus's father (Antiochus) rather than of his son is now accepted; all the same, the nomenclature of the city reflected once again the dynasty's attention to toponyms in this region.[46]

But John Malalas is not the only voice that informs us of Antioch's early days. The narrative of Libanius – the fourth-century sophist who was a major intellectual figure of his time and, not least, a native of Antioch – in his oration *Antiochikos* affords insights into the unfolding of the events and the founding myths of the city.[47] Originally penned for the 356 CE Olympic Games in Antioch, this text has been heavily treated by modern historians in an effort to glean its validity as a topographic and historical excursus of the city.[48] The text is complicated; suspended between aspirations of a victory ode and the partisanship expected of a true son – and indeed broker – of Antioch, it offers important insights into the life and topography of the city, to be treated here in subsequent chapters. Suffice to say for now that Libanius narrates at length the vicissitudes leading to Antioch's foundation, substantially underpinning the story as presented later by Malalas, although the latter's account varies in several instances.[49]

More to the point, Libanius's text is paramount for any reconstruction of Antioch's foundation and urban growth, for he surveys both town and country and altogether draws on a vast body of poorly known scholarly traditions on the city. His allusion to a "mass of past history" is especially telling.[50] In particular, the oration's different sections individually shed light on the city, its surroundings, and local society. The second section is particularly relevant, since Libanius describes within it the panoply of settlements preceding Antioch's foundation as well as their mythical framework. In particular, it explores the migrations of the Argives from Greece who, under the leadership of the demi-god Triptolemos, wandered in the quest of Io, a hapless Argive princess loved by Zeus but transformed into a white heifer to protect her from Hera's jealous wrath, who in turn sent a tormenting gadfly that compelled her to roam the earth. Attracted by the beauty of the land, the Argives went on to settle at Iopolis, establishing a temple dedicated to Nemean Zeus. Then entered King Casos from Crete who, under the whims of Zeus, joined the Argives, founded one Kasiotis (a refoundation of Iopolis?), and invited a contingent of Cypriots led by Amyke, the daughter of King Salaminus of Cyprus and immortalized in the name of the Amuq Plain. The Heraklidae, descendants of the demigod, and a group of Eleans from Greece seemingly established their own enclave of Herakleia, a new appendix to the city that cannot be safely located. The Persian king Cambyses and Alexander the Great, too, are not spared by this narrative, for the latter, according to Libanius, initiated the settlement that foreshadowed the official foundation by Seleucus. In particular, the great king established the temple of Zeus Bottios and the citadel of Emathia. This whirlwind of heroes/heroines, demigods, and, indeed, deities, follows the convention of Greek mythography. Put simply, Libanius not only writes of scores of people involved in city's making but also braids a teleological structure into stories of dispossession and migration. Fundamentally, the narrative reaches its apex with the grand moment of Antioch's foundation, with elephants at each corner of the delineated space sanctioning the layout of the future city.[51] It should not be ruled out that the so-called Tetrapylon of the Elephants, the monumental four-arched passageway of unknown layout and décor that spanned the main street intersection on the Island with its bays,[52] may have commemorated this particular event.

Much emphasis in Libanius's text, however, is also accorded to the foundation of Apollo's sanctuary at Daphne, Antioch's picturesque southern suburb (modern Harbiye).[53] Today, this heavily built development, crammed with tall concrete buildings and densely populated by restaurants and hotels, hardly reflects Daphne's ancient splendor. In antiquity, this plateau overlooking the Orontes Valley owed its renown to the springs and the sanctuary of Apollo and its sacred grove of laurels and cypresses.[54] The beauty of the place in antiquity, it seems, had no match. Its description by Edward Gibbon, eighteenth-century author of the monumental *History of the Decline and Fall of the Roman Empire*, is particularly poignant:

> The temple and the village were deeply bosomed in a thick grove of laurels and cypresses, which reached as far as a circumference of ten miles, and formed in the most sultry summers a cool and impenetrable shade. A thousand streams of the purest water, issuing from every hill, preserved the verdure of the earth, and the temperature of the air; the senses were gratified with harmonious sounds and aromatic odors; and the peaceful grove was consecrated to health and joy, to luxury and love.[55]

Notably, Antioch during the Hellenistic era was often referred to as "Antioch near Daphne," and her characterization "on the Orontes" appeared only at a further point in the Roman era.[56] The ties between the two communities remained indissoluble until Daphne's abandonment in the late Middle Ages. Allegedly, it all began with Seleucus's serendipitous discovery of one of Apollo's sacred arrows the god had shot after the loss of the beloved nymph Daphne as she transformed into a beautiful laurel tree. Seleucus then dedicated the site to Apollo and built a sanctuary that rose to unparalleled centrality. John Malalas substantiates the Daphne foundation myth, inferring that the king planted cypress trees right where Heracles had established the enclave of Heraklea.[57] Be that as it may, the original laurel tree remained as testament to this miracle for centuries to come.[58] Divination, politics, and the tenets of Greek religion thus coalesced into a cult that played a paramount role in the fortunes of the Greco-Roman world, with kings and emperors going to the lengths of traveling to Daphne to consult the god. The great, oracular milieu of Apollo in Delphi, Greece, now had its doppelgänger in the Greek East. Castalia, the name of one of the springs, powerfully conveyed this wholesale replica of Delphi's religious prerogatives in this suburb of Antioch.

In more mundane terms, however, the myths of Daphne, Apollo, and tangentially King Seleucus resonated in the visual culture of the city, appearing as it did in numerous media, from mosaic pavements to portable commodities.[59] These myths, as with the founding myths of Io, Triptolemos, and Heracles, are ones that with their emphasis on migration, quests, and divine implication shaped the cultural outlook of the city and reverberated in its festivals and religious parades, as, for instance, attested by an annual celebration of the search for Io.[60] Whether serving religious purposes or as a simple attestation of belonging, these images inform the durability of these foundation myths.

Yet Daphne was also a milieu that had long accommodated a sizable Jewish community and, plausibly, the Matrona, one of the main synagogues, a temple that was "as profane as the sanctuary of Apollo and populated by demons," according to John Chrysostom, the bishop of Antioch between 386–397 CE and, ultimately, a key figure among Church Fathers.[61] As with any other sacred building in Antioch, this synagogue remains elusive both in location and layout; its shape, décor, and fruition are matters of guesswork. But it was not built in a vacuum. In particular, Talmudic traditions contend that the settlements of Hamath and Ribla preceded that of Antioch and Daphne, while also serving as stations of the Babylonian exile.[62] Nor may it be too far-fetched to think that *Ex praeda Iudea* (From the booty of Judea), the celebratory inscription on the theater built by Titus in Daphne, above and beyond its rhetoric, was a manifestation of rulers fundamentally pitted against a community that had a firm foothold on that plateau. Overall, the piecemeal archaeological investigation of Daphne inhibits the clear definition of these problems, as the following chapters will show.

Traces of substantial quarrying operations that plausibly preceded the installation of the elegant houses and amenities of the Roman period suggest that the Daphne plateau may also have supplied the stone for the monumental programs of the early Seleucid kings.[63] Regrettably, though, the quest for Daphne's most famous site – the temple of Apollo and its surrounding cluster of other pagan sanctuaries – remains illusory. The Caesarea Cup (Figure 1.6), a fourth-century CE bronze vessel now at the Louvre, may offer a rendition, albeit on a small scale, of the prostyle building with two columns on the front, four slender fluted columns on the side, exquisitely carved Corinthian capitals, pediment, and a cella with a frieze of garlands and a sequence of three niches.[64] As for the temple's archaeological evidence, examining the systems of terracotta pipelines that tapped into five springs, the 1930s archaeologists noted trajectories that seemingly skirted a mound-like prominent area. Strewn with broken column drums and other fragments of monumental architecture, the site appeared as a promising area for the location of the great temple of Apollo. Its archaeological inspection, however, was not added to the excavation agenda, with the Daphne exploration soon veering toward safer targets, and not least the mosaics.[65] As a consequence, the temple's architectural configuration, both in its original Seleucid plan and Roman imperial overhauls with gardens, porticoes, and baths cannot be determined. Nor does the picture of Seleucid religious monuments in the region offer any support to a speculative plan;[66] the two known Seleucid temples of Seleucia Pieria and Jebel Khalid (Syria) are rare examples of a religious architecture that, in the early Hellenistic period, sought to reconcile Greek architectural idioms with oriental accents. Yet these buildings differ greatly in size, aesthetics, and cultic practice, so that the eclecticism of their Doric style defies the notion of a fixed architectural module applying to Seleucid sanctuaries.[67] Though patchy, the textual sources are a redress for the loss of the temple of Apollo. They extol the magnificent décor, with the statue of the god as centerpiece. It was made of marble and wood by the hand of the great Athenian artist Bryaxis, who owed his renown to previous work at the island of Rhodes. The rhetorician Libanius offers a gripping description of the statue, seemingly portraying the god in the act of singing while holding a lyre.[68]

Ultimately, how the oracle of Apollo operated and how space around it framed its consultation are the crux of the problem. The Caesarea Cup, is by all accounts the only visual rendition of the religious mysteries that unfolded at Daphne, with the god Apollo sitting in the front of the sacred laurel and the temple in Daphne,

FIGURE 1.6 The Caesarea Cup

Source: Musées du Louvre, Courtesy of ART RESOURCE

as the divine fortune of Caesarea (the Tyche of Caesarea) with turrite (in the shape of walls and towers) crown and in the garb of an amazon receives the oracle (Figure 1.6).[69]

The establishment of the oracle of Apollo during the early days of the city also spearheaded the appearance of other cults: the successive addition of the temple of Zeus is a good case in point. That one priest presided over the functioning of all the sanctuaries at Daphne is also a concrete possibility. An inscription dating to the days of Antiochus III makes plain that an unknown priest supervised all the cults and was presumably chosen by the king.[70]

The foundation of Antioch was thus predicated on episodes of migration and wanderings, with the uncanny horizon of quasi-divine beings, heroes, and supernatural events. The project, however, more fundamentally mobilized a presumably considerable number of settlers, most of whom were enlisted in the Seleucid army. Athenians, Thracians, Macedonians, Cretans, Cypriots and Jews were but some of the constituencies that apparently landed on the shores of the Orontes and built a conglomerate of ethnicities.[71] As already mentioned, many of these groups migrated from Antigonia; it is plausible that the setting up of a large bronze statue to Athena in Antioch was an act of piety by the very Athenians who were relocated from the city of Antigonos. Whether fiction or a *captatio benevolentiae* seeking to capture the audience's goodwill, almost eight centuries later the empress Eudocia, wife of Theodosius II (408–450) recognized and boasted of Antioch's Athenian legacy in a public speech that, if anything, attests to the durability of these founding myths as well as the cultural positioning of the city.[72] Athenians aside, mercenaries and soldiers represented the bulk of the new settlers at Antioch. But their identity can hardly be established, nor do we have any names of individuals who can be assigned to this enterprise. Nevertheless, two stelae found in the vicinity of the city and now in the Hatay Archaeological Museum in Antakya offer a glimpse of these early settlers (Figure 1.7).

These sculptures, bearing the names of Aristophanes and Polemos, are considered as the earliest in a collection of mostly unprovenanced funerary reliefs now on exhibit at the Turkish museum.[73] Their iconography is quite remarkable: a small shrine with gable and slender columns frames the visual presentation of the deceased. The stele of Aristophanes, in particular, offers a plastic rendering of the human silhouette, with emphasis on posture and treatment of the garments. This type of imagery can be safely assigned to the early Hellenistic period, and it fits the cultural horizon of early Antioch. Further, the stele of Polemos, of presumably similar chronology, showcases a warrior in full military paraphernalia

FIGURE 1.7 The gravestones of Aristophanes and Polemos

Source: From De Giorgi 2019

sporting an assault posture. This iconography is well known throughout Asia Minor and the Greek East. One painted stele from Sidon (Lebanon), that of Dioskurides, a soldier – from Balboura, Pisidia (a mount-region of southwestern Anatolia) – illustrates perhaps the best rendition of this visual template.[74] Overall, it can be surmised that similar images, redolent as they were with allusions to the military sphere, found a fertile territory in the area of Antioch, where throngs of veterans had just settled with their families. Funerary stones of this kind would have no doubt found the appreciation of those who fought for the establishment of the city and hoped and aspired to the memorialization of their services.

To sum up, Antioch was not built in a day: it rose from the ashes of Antigonia and occupied the small swath of land left as the river Orontes encroached upon Mt. Silpius, the massif overlooking the city. A spate of settlements with evocative names – Bottia, Kasiotis, Iopolis – seemingly preceded the royal foundation or coalesced within it. They can be reasonably linked to constellations of sites archaeologically known in the environs of Antioch. In concrete terms, however, Antioch was planned in a way that would exploit the potential of the Orontes to the fullest, adjusting its layout to the river and setting the urban fulcrum on the plain near the highway running southwest-northeast and connecting the Mediterranean to the heart of Syria.

The foundation's physical appearance

Geopolitical and religious concerns thus coalesced in the plan developed under the guidance of Seleucus; from the very outset Antioch occupied the northern sector of what became "classical" Antioch and was presumably equipped with a system of defenses. The nucleation and successive growth of the city in the following centuries and its inhabitants' ability to adapt to a complex environment illustrate the character of this foundation. Seleucus himself, though warned by his entourage, adamantly moved forward with the foundation, its importance demanding the utmost attention.[75] Its legacy remained ingrained in the visual culture of the city, as attested by numerous mosaics in which the personified foundation, the *Ktisis*, appears in all her splendor.[76] But amid environmental pressures, historical conundrums, and religious preoccupations, the question remains: what did the city of Seleucus look like? Above and beyond the textual accounts, what can we infer about the city's materiality in the aftermath of its foundation? Wolfram Hoepfner has suggested that Antioch's establishment must be seen in the context of a response to Alexandria;[77] by this rationale, he observes it to be no coincidence that the two cities equally occupied a surface of approximately 600 hectares. But two problems arise: first, the topographies of the two cities are in no way comparable, and second, at least in the initial plan, Antioch's foundation was not pitted against the great city of Alexander the Great, nor meant to be vying with it. Antioch grew organically in the following centuries, with the fortifications of Tiberius,

Theodosius, and Justinian eventually girding an expanse that neared Alexandria's measurement.

It is now apparent that the city's first settlement occupied the northern, level space between the Orontes River and the slopes of Mt. Silpius and Mt. Staurin (Figure 1.8). While this is conjectural, the material evidence seems to corroborate this possibility. In particular, the presence of third-to-second-century BCE coins is suggestive of patterns and accumulations that may not be haphazard.[78] As for the urban amenities and administrative buildings that were part of the original plan, we can infer that the main thoroughfare served to order space. It also created a grid that, oriented northeast to southwest, was demarcated by city blocks following the axis of the Parmenios and Phyrminos (Hamşen Deresi) mountain torrents. As for the size of these city blocks, they measured on average 120 by 60 meters, figures generally in line with the evidence from two other cities of the Tetrapolis, namely Apamea and Laodicea.[79] Whether there was one or more than one agora remains difficult to answer.[80] Glanville Downey modeled the layout of Antioch as that of Dura Europos and proposed the existence of an agora replicating the size of that in the city on the Euphrates. As recent studies have shown, however, the urban fabric of Dura needs to be situated in the second century BCE.[81] A more fitting template may be found at Seleucia on the Tigris, the early capital of the kingdom, established around 306 BCE and consisting of two, possibly three large plazas connected to the main canal. In a similar vein, it may be suggested that Antioch's early agora lay near the gate that in the days of the emperor Jovian was referred to as the Philonauta Gate, which may have demarcated the zone of a riverine harbor near where the Orontes shifted its course from south to southwest. While this is speculative, the topography makes plain this was an ideal site where the main thoroughfare, the river, and the highways radiating from Antioch met. Further, in the late fourth century CE, the incident of the bishop Meletius rushing to leave the city from a gate adjacent to the agora, amidst an angry mob, corroborates this possibility.[82] All the same, it is possible that within a few generations this agora turned out to no longer meet the needs of the locals, and so new public spaces were added by Seleucus and his successors. Downey also inferred that the city had to be equipped with a theater,[83] but while plausible, and indeed the topography was suited for one, no material evidence has supported this hypothesis.

Another piece of infrastructure that cannot be firmly established is an alleged early wall of Seleucus. Walls better than any other architectural feature capture the might and the whims of the ruling power that commissioned them. That Antioch was girded by a monumental enceinte from its early days is thus likely.[84] Downey proposed a system of linear defenses following the long artery of traffic around which Antioch grew, thus marking the eastern extent of the settlement (Figure 1.8). He was not too off the mark, it seems.

The city wall, comprising at least eight different building phases and numerous repairs and dating from the early days of the city to the Crusader phase, remains an object of debate.[85] While the 1930s excavations identified no trace of Seleucus's

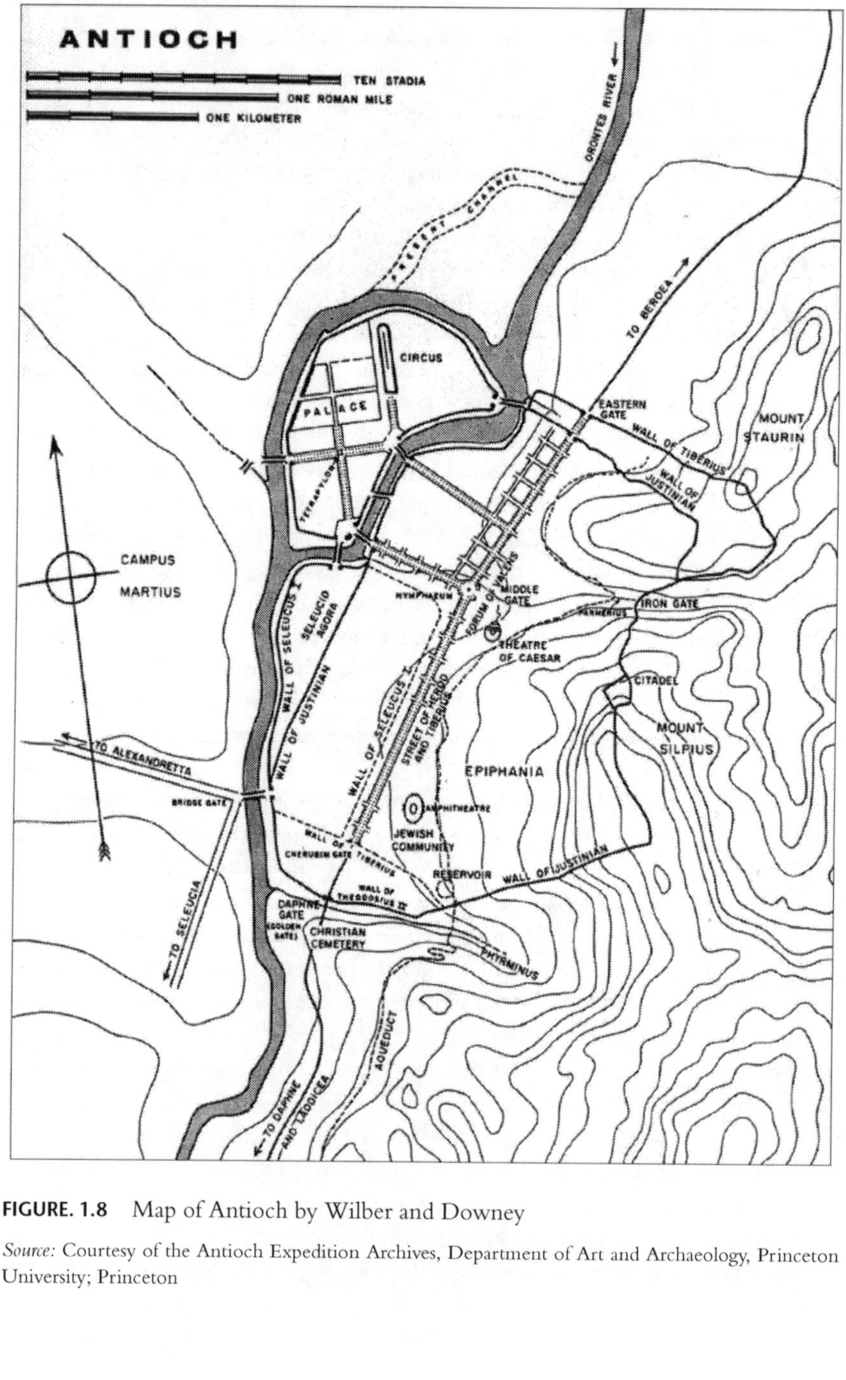

FIGURE. 1.8 Map of Antioch by Wilber and Downey

Source: Courtesy of the Antioch Expedition Archives, Department of Art and Archaeology, Princeton University; Princeton

wall lining up with the main thoroughfare, it is plausible that some of the fortifications on Mt. Staurin, especially a few stretches of polygonal masonry on its eastern flank, effectively date to the city's early Hellenistic phase, if not from the days of its foundation.

Christiane Brasse's study in particular shows two key trends. First, some of these early works appear to have been later incorporated into the Roman and Byzantine defenses (Figure 1.9). Second, stand-alone wall segments run southeast-northwest on the slopes of Mt. Staurin, following an axis parallel to the main thoroughfare, while others punctuate the saddle between that mount and Mt. Silpius. These may identify walls designed to enclose discrete settlements, as will be discussed in greater detail. Worth noting is that Seleucid fortifications at Seleucia Pieria, Ibn Hani, Cyrrhus, Apamea on the Orontes, Apamea on the Euphrates, and Jebel Khalid, to name but the best known, utilized seemingly heavy polygonal masonry and negotiated the local rugged topography in similar fashion. What is more, the inclusion of a fortified citadel, as in the case of Cyrrhus, should not be ruled out, though the archaeological evidence has not shown any evidence for it.[86]

In sum, putting together the textual sources and the archaeological datum, it can be surmised that the polygonal walls on Mt. Staurin may actually have been part of the original defenses of the city, aligned as they were with the main thoroughfare. This defensive circuit apparently had to negotiate the asperities of the rocky terrain and the presence of deeply cut gullies, as attested by the southeastern sharp turn of the section, plausibly to allow the presence of a gate. On these grounds, it is now possible to visualize the armature of the early city plan, as in Figure 1.9. The existence of gates, however, is still a matter of guesswork. All the same, Malalas remarks that Seleucus placed a statue of the seer Amphion at the site later to be occupied by the Romanesia gate, which in the fourth century connected the Island to the vast Amuq plain.[87] While the account cannot prove the existence of a Hellenistic predecessor of the Romanesia gate, it nevertheless enriches the picture of a city skyline punctuated by dozen of images stemming from the glorious days of Antioch's foundation. That of Amphion, however, may have triggered in the beholder a sense of localized historical memories as well as leaving testimony of the great unique story that spawned from the vision of the seer who accompanied the king.

Seleucus also saw to the completion of all stringent practicalities entailed by a large-scale urban project; his architects completed the first network of aqueducts that, tapping water from the Daphne springs, fed the city and may have contributed to realizing a sewage system.[88] Indeed, the siphoning off of water from Daphne initiated a pattern of exploitation that continued in the course of antiquity. Daphne was not only the seat of Apollo, and later a resort where affluent Antiochenes would escape the scorching heat of the summer months, but also the key strategic partner that contributed fundamentally to Antioch's growth, thanks to its abundant water supply.

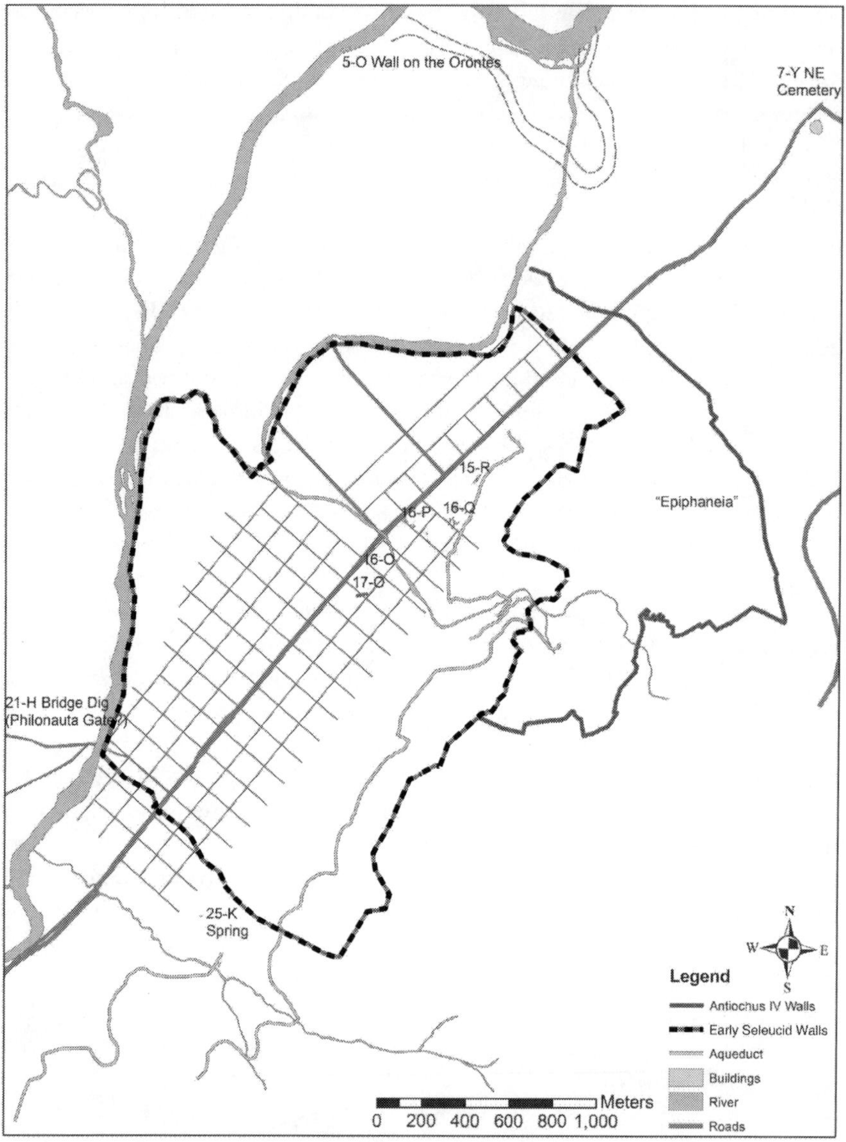

FIGURE 1.9 Antioch and its fortifications. Highlighted are the early perimeter and a possible location for Epiphaneia

Source: Adapted from Brasse 2010; courtesy of Stephen Batiuk

Elusive though early Antioch may seem for the disquieting absence of concrete information, the city was essentially a space shaped by the royal institution, with prominent institutional buildings and statues of kings, eagles, and horses signaling the extent of the urban expanse.[89] The lack of archaeological data does not hamper the possibility of visualizing early Antioch based on the social relations it engendered, the sharing of space, or the commemoration of the local collective memory. The main thoroughfare, the city grid, and the celebration of Seleucid military achievements all held this ambitious project together.

New expansions

Under successive kings, Antioch raised its profile, for the city plan was plausibly enlarged to accommodate new settlers,[90] a phenomenon that could be filed under the city's second expansion. At that time, however, the city became entangled in a long struggle for hegemony between the Seleucids and another of the rival dynasties of Alexander the Great's successors – the Ptolemies of Egypt. In particular, the mandate of Antiochus II Theos (261–247 BCE) inaugurated a season of insecurity. Libanius's ambiguous reference to Antioch's "difficulties" at that time[91] may indicate mounting political tension in the region, as the following developments suggest. In particular, the Egyptians and their occupation of large tracts of Syria, and not least the city of Seleucia Pieria, exerted pressure on the kingdom of Seleucus II Callinicus (246–226 BCE). The so-called Gourob papyrus offers documentary evidence, albeit complicated, of the days of Seleucid faltering in front of the Egyptian royal house, with a Ptolemaic delegation and army making it all the way to Antioch after having presumably followed the course of the Orontes sometime in the year 246 BCE, that is, during the Third Syrian War.[92] Patchy and poorly preserved, the text also contains a reference to a lofty reception that the Antiochene officers offered to Ptolemy III and a bewildered Egyptian delegation outside the city walls. Impressed by the monumentality of the city, the Egyptians were met in front of an unknown monumental gate: a curtain of walls, it seems, girded the city at that time. What gate the text specifically alludes to is impossible to determine. All the same, Seleucus II, in 244 BCE, succeeded at driving the Egyptians out of Antioch and parts of Syria. Seleucia, however, remained in foreign hands until 219 BCE.[93]

The loss of what soon became the Attalid kingdom in Asia Minor and attempts to regain a firm foothold in Parthia further led to a significant channeling of resources into Antioch and the reconfiguration of the monarchic role in the city, as manifested by an ambitious new urban expansion on the Island, formed by the Orontes northwest of the original settlement.

This third great expansion, which significantly enlarged the original nucleus of the city, as suggested by Strabo, took place under Seleucus II (and his successor Antiochus III). Further, this project brought about a wholesale reorientation of the city's topography, both in the new itineraries it imposed and in leadership. Put simply, while the project led to the city's enlargement and responded to necessities that were most likely demographic, the establishment of a new constellation of buildings on the Island – not least a royal palace (Basileion) under Antiochus III[94] – informs both the heightening of Antioch's role and a new idea of monarchy, one defined by the perimeter of the royal residence and its infrastructure of streets, bridges, and annexes. A system of defenses strengthened the fabric of the royal enclave; in their flurry of activities, the Princeton excavations of 1932 identified in sector 5-O, an area that now lies right under the modern course of the Orontes, a short stretch of dry-laid ashlar block wall of rather impressive proportions (Figure 1.10).

Although hastily excavated, this flimsy evidence illustrates the presence of ramparts that defined the northernmost perimeter of the Island and its monumentalization. As often happened with the Princeton excavations, however, this dig was rapidly jettisoned. What matters here is to underscore how this building project signaled a new phase for Antioch: the arrival of new settlers, all of Greek origin, Libanius implies;[95] the increase of rural settlement across the plain of Antioch; and overall economic prosperity, as possibly indicated by the unflagging pace at which the local mint apparently issued coins of the king. At that time, the city struck coins at a sustained pace, thus confirming its role as capital of the western Seleucid world. Gold octadrachms of the Apollo of omphalos type and silver tetradrachms of the same iconography stand out in this production. Further, the king may have reformed the mint upon his return to the city on the Orontes in

FIGURE 1.10 The 1932 excavation on the Island of Antioch: sector 5-O

Source: Courtesy of the Antioch Expedition Archives, Department of Art and Archaeology, Princeton University; Princeton

204 BCE, introducing a new portrait with mature features and less godlike appearance. That these octadrachm issues were meant to celebrate specific events is a grounded possibility.[96] It is likely that the losses in Asia Minor, turmoil in Greece, and overall reconfiguration of the Seleucid universe that occurred under Antiochus III spawned episodes of migration toward the rapidly growing capital.[97]

The intellectual stature of the city, it seems, was also a preoccupation of the king. To heighten Antioch's profile, Antiochus III established a great library, directed by Euphorion of Chalcis,[98] who seemingly wrote a now-lost history of the city on which Posidonius of Apamea greatly drew for his narrative. The competition for primacy with Alexandria (and its own renowned library), at that time one of the greatest cities of the ancient world, cannot be more obvious. The state treasury lavishly funded building programs and urban décor, while games and festivals contributed to enhancing the city's centrality; evidence for games in 197 BCE is attested by the epigraphic record.[99]

Political structure and economy

By the second century BCE, Antioch, seat of the Seleucis satrapy and the royal court,[100] had outgrown every other city in the area, becoming one of the most prominent cities of the kingdom.[101] As we shall see, during the civil wars and strife of the late second century BCE, when the kingdom was essentially reduced to Syria and Phoenicia, the possession of Antioch was key for a ruler to lay his claim and be recognized as the legitimate Seleucid king.[102]

Worth noting is that the Seleucid state had a somewhat peculiar configuration, consisting of a highly centralized government of a loosely Persian matrix and a network of local governors who enacted the king's policies. At times the king himself would personally deal with the cities, especially when granting special rights, civic charters, and tax exemptions. This dense administrative web was superimposed on the individual poleis, which in turn were governed through the political apparatus of Greek tradition and referred to themselves as independent. Based on their independence, they would negotiate agreements with the king on a broad range of matters, from fiscal regulations to military expectations. They also negotiated with other communities and poleis for religious and political purposes;[103] many inscriptions pertaining to these transactions and treaties illuminate the relationships among the polities of Seleucid Asia Minor.[104]

Antioch's political conduct plausibly followed these lines, and both king and city were legitimized by a common set of values played out through a shared language of honors and *euergetism*, a well-known practice in the Greek East whereby grandees and notables would distribute part of their wealth to local communities in the form of public buildings, doles, and moneys.[105] That said, coercion and exorbitant extraction of surplus through taxes were key to the kingdom's survival, and the most prominent cities and communities were obliged to feed the state coffers and sustain military expenditures. The contemporary, rival Ptolemaic kingdom had a system of revenues that, in all likelihood, was predicated on similar mechanisms.

Incidentally, the letter sent by a Ptolemaic officer to the community of Arsinoë in Cilicia captures the tax problem of the second century BCE, when the official remarks that "the city has to prosper so as to pay more taxes."[106] How this system of revenues was occasionally tapped for the support of individual communities we cannot determine; it is interesting, however, that following the earthquake that struck Rhodes and the East in 227 BCE, Seleucus II was not slow in offering his aid. In particular, Polybius tells us that the king, "besides exempting Rhodian trading to his dominions from custom duties, presented them with ten quinqueremes [warships] fully equipped, two hundred thousand medimni of grain, ten thousand cubits of timber and a thousand talents of hair and resin."[107] The recourse to rescue measures of this nature may have also been in place when Antioch was, by turn, hit by an earthquake in 148 BCE, for the city was apparently rebuilt from scratch.[108] It is hard to assess the impact, duration, and aftermath of this event. We shall see that Antioch's history will be punctuated by similar institutional rescue efforts combined with remarkable local tenacity.

Since the days of Seleucus Nicator, however, Antioch benefited from its centrality, and the road network linking the city to other foci like Cyrrhus, Seleucia Pieria, and Apamea was reasonably effective as early as the third century BCE. As for its administrative side, two inscriptions illustrate the presence of a board of magistrates, priests, and city council, as well as authorities appointed for religious festivals and games.[109] Antioch had a democratic constitution, as appears from a document of *isopoliteia* (the grant of citizenship) agreements made with the city of Teos in Asia Minor under Antiochus III and that were signed by the *demos* of Antioch.[110] According to John Malalas, the initial population of the city tallied 5,300 units, cited as "men," a sum to which one may add a reasonable number of women, children, foreigners, and slaves. This assessment must, however, be taken with all due caution, as Malalas' appraisals often appear vague.[111] The parallel with the 6,000 adult males residing in Seleucia Pieria in 220 BCE is, however, indicative[112] and suggests that these early cities were inhabited by the thousands at this stage. As for the demographic composition of the *khora* (territory) surrounding Antioch, guesswork is our only option. The settlement of veteran soldiers was crucial to the Seleucid colonization of the countryside and the rest of northern Syria. Military obligations were essential to an empire in a state of constant war. Posidonius states that during the Parthian wars under Antiochus VII, in the late second century BCE, "no home in Syrian Antioch escaped the loss of sons."[113] Citizenship and military service in particular went hand in hand. In Seleucus Nicator's plan, all colonies in Syria granted a *kleros* (plot of land) of unknown acreage to each individual who enjoyed political rights.[114] The examples of entire garrisons in Syria obtaining citizenship privileges and land allotments might thus account for the spreading of rural settlement in the Antiochene countryside from the beginning of the foundation.[115] Overall, the distribution of these *kleroi* was essential to meeting the goals of extracting a surplus and recruiting new troops. This rationale also underpinned the configuration of the rural landscape of Seleucid cities. Farms, villages, and small estates were the entities the Romans would thus have to reckon with upon annexing

Syria. Antioch was no exception, and a dispersed pattern of sites straddling the plain and the highlands began to vividly emerge in tandem with the foundation, as shown by the archaeological survey of the Amuq Plain.[116]

As befitted a royal foundation, Antioch also had its own mint.[117] Its silver tetradrachms, however, appeared in the markets of northern Syria slightly later than those of Seleucia Pieria, thus reinforcing the possibility that Seleucia was intended as the main hub.[118] Moreover, it appears that the tetradrachms of Antigonia were appropriated by Seleucia rather than Antioch. The question is convoluted, but, as Georges Le Rider suggests, by the end of Seleucus's life Antioch had probably become the main mint of the Seleucis (i.e., the satrapy of northern Syria) as manifested by types, weights, and iconography, as well as a pervasive sense of royal control over production.[119] The head of Heracles on the obverse, Zeus in a throne holding a miniature Nike in his outstretched hand signifying victory on the reverse, with the legend ΒΑΣΙΛΕΩΣ ΣΕΛΕΥΚΟΥ, are the first official tetradrachms of the Antioch mint, as well as a copy of Alexander the Great's tetradrachm minted in Macedonia, Babylon, and other eastern mints. Only under Antiochus I did a variation set in, with the king's portrait on the obverse and Apollo sitting on the omphalos on the reverse. From the days of Seleucus Nicator, Antioch produced bronze municipal coins and silver royal issues without break; the Ptolemaic intermission between 246 and 244 BCE, when the city was briefly occupied by Ptolemy III, may be the sole exception.[120] The city issued substantial royal and occasional municipal coinage to permit payments by the administration and generate circulation of currency for tax obligations, while military campaigns occasionally demanded additional series. Contingencies, too, drove the output of the royal mint of Antioch: the example of the heightening of production and weight standards of tetradrachms under Seleucus IV Philopator (187–175 BCE) to pay the indemnity imposed by Rome after the 188 BCE treaty of Apamea is a good case in point.[121] It has been argued that in the early days, Seleucus Nicator had deliberately founded cities to stimulate cash circulation and spur local economies, with raw materials from the rural districts converted into currency that in turn the treasury would cash in as forms of tribute.[122] But the monetized economies that long preceded the Seleucid foundations[123] and the role of cities like Antioch as hubs, markets, and centers of craft production rather invite considering urbanism as the ultimate force driving the royal economy.

Although we cannot easily calculate the overall output of Antioch's royal mint, it has been suggested that approximately 1,300 dies were used over the 235-year time span covering the dynasty, which is a modest sum compared to later Roman mints.[124] These measures should also be put in their context. As for the third century BCE, evidence from hoards indicates that Seleucid royal coinage represented still a minor percentage, albeit increasing, of coins in relation to issues with the iconography of Alexander the Great.[125] The 1930 excavation datasets are also particularly revealing. Alan Stahl has shown that in the area of the greatest concentration of early digs – that is, the Island (sectors L-10–11, M-10, and N-7–10) – coin finds of the Hellenistic period were almost abysmal, with a few issues dating no earlier than 162 BCE. Only the so-called "street digs" – trenches aimed at intercepting the main thoroughfare – reversed this trend, yielding as they did evidence from the early days of Seleucus,[126] thus reinforcing the already-mentioned possibility that the early city was first settled on that flat expanse between Mt. Staurin and the Orontes.

Epiphaneia

The fourth and last fundamental enlargement of the city's layout, after those of Antiochus II and Seleucus II/Antiochus III, occurred under the tenure of Antiochus IV Epiphanes (175–164 BCE). He spared no efforts in continuing, and indeed outshining, the work of his predecessors, making sure he would come across as Antioch's second founder. In less than a century, the city had grown to become a full-fledged metropolis and capital, and so its layout and urban décor had to meet the momentous growth of the community and its political prominence. Textual sources describe Antiochus IV as a visionary, adept in letters, with a bent for megalomania. Fittingly, the reverse of his 173 BCE bronze tetradrachms in Antioch bore the epithet Theos Epiphanes (God Manifest), while successive 168 BCE issues on precious metal issues celebrated the man as Nicephorus (Bearer of Victory) after the Egyptian campaigns.[127] It should be borne in mind, however, that Antioch was the king's principal mint, for the volume of the coinage it produced, and new iconographies as well as titles were devised in the city of the Orontes.[128] Not trivial is the detail that the king was an avid bath-goer in Antioch, as reported by Polybius, thus suggesting that at that time public bathhouses were already established in the city.[129] Overall, these are the main traits of the king, as gleaned from the textual sources. One of his military parades, as reported by Polybius, on the occasion of the 167 BCE games in honor of Apollo, epitomizes his grandiose vision.[130] Featuring an infantry of 50,000 men from all regions of the kingdom, the procession probably proceeded from Antioch to Daphne along the city's main thoroughfare. The visual effect it produced can easily be conjured, for it must have dazzled bystanders through its sequences of elephants, chariots, treasures, and gladiators proceeding toward Daphne's sanctuary. As a buffoon, the king rode on a donkey. The festival, banquets, and gladiatorial games lasted for days. More subtly, the event was designed to let the Greeks and Romans know that the Seleucid kingdom was alive and well despite its defeat of 189 BCE against the Romans at Magnesia. Polybius makes plain, however, that the sources of such a lavish display were the looting of Egypt, moneys from friends, and ultimately the pillaging of unspecified sanctuaries. That Antiochus also followed a well-rehearsed Mesopotamian template, however, should also be considered. As Lauren Ristvet noted,[131] the parade of Daphne, with its marshaling of military formations, cosmologic symbolism, divine images, and humiliation of the king, followed the template of the *akkitu*, a festival that took place every spring in Seleucid Babylon yet predicated on ancestral practices. Central in the *akkitu* was indeed the public degrading of the royal figure in front of the city priests.

However, Antiochus IV's greatest achievement in Antioch remains the establishment of Epiphaneia, an eponymous highland development physically divorced from Antioch (Figure 1.9).[132] It was intended as a measure to accommodate the city's swollen population and a means to decentralize the political and administrative apparatus of the capital city, ultimately shedding new prestige on the king. More subtly, though, the addition of this new quarter completed the urban layout of Antioch, which would remain virtually unvaried for centuries. Thus, Epiphaneia's constellation of public and religious buildings, essential for the unfolding of the city's political and spiritual routines, reoriented the habits and routines of the Antiochenes. In short, the pendulum of the city swung away from the Island and the agoras between the thoroughfare and the Orontes as Antiochus relocated the city's core components on higher ground, presumably on the flat, nondescript highland saddle between Mt. Silpius and Mt. Staurin, roughly 1.5 km east of the city.[133]

It is hard to determine how this transition affected Antioch's population and whether this enclave, like Bottia and Iopolis, had preceded the city's foundation. Wherever we locate this development, it is apparent that from the mid-second century BCE, Epiphaneia stimulated mobility from the city thanks to the services it provided. In particular, it functioned as a political and religious hub, as the textual sources inform us. Among its public buildings were a *bouleuterion* (council chamber), a temple to Zeus Olympius, and a shrine dedicated to the Muses.[134] Moreover, a new commercial agora – presumably the so-called tetragonal agora – and a building accommodating the royal archives, both of which were seemingly destroyed by fire in 69/70 CE, further added a sense of centrality to Epiphaneia.[135] Whether a fortification wall symbolically encircled the quarter, giving it the configuration of a discrete, almost separate entity within the city, remains to be established.[136] All the same, based on the textual sources, it is safe to contend that Epiphaneia tied its fortunes to those of Antioch and went on to be inhabited during the classical and late antique periods. It cannot be excluded that a prominent sanctuary dedicated to the Roman Jupiter Capitolinus was also situated in the new settlement;[137] through this shrewd expedient Antiochus offered his token of recognition to Rome.

The Epiphaneia building program, however, was focused not simply on establishing a single borough; rather, it reasonably entailed creating a network of aqueducts aimed at impounding the waters of the Parmenios and channeling them into cisterns. Some of the waterworks were noted by the 1930s archaeologists in sector 16-O North (Digs IV and VIII). In particular, two vaulted channels may be assigned to this epoch, when the impounding of the Parmenios catchment was essential to safeguard the rest of the water infrastructure.[138] Behind this ingenious project was probably Cossutius, a well-known architect whose credentials included the temple of Zeus in Athens, according to Vitruvius. The possibility that he worked for Antiochus IV in Antioch is corroborated by graffiti on the lining of a tunnel, discovered upon the inspection in 1934, seemingly mentioning the architect.[139]

Lastly, in addition to Epiphaneia, Antiochus and his successors are said to have added new buildings in the city – to wit, temples of Minos, Demeter, and Heracles, and a theater.[140] That Antiochus monumentalized the main thoroughfare, or cardo, is also a possibility taken up by Karl Otfried Müller in his 1839 seminal work and reinforced by the 1930s archaeologists as they came across signs of an evident reconfiguration averaging 16 meters in width and dating to the second century BCE.[141] It cannot be determined whether at this early stage the 2,275 m of the cardo's length were lined by colonnades. Moreover, traditional hypotheses hold Herod the Great (37 BCE–c. 4 BCE) responsible for monumentalizing Antioch's main axis of traffic.[142] At any event, other projects of urban décor unfolded at this time. Of interest is the dedication of a sculptural group to the king by the Cilicians. Antiochus had apparently freed Antioch of the Isaurian threat, that is, gangs of bandits and renegades that seemingly populated the woods of the Amanus Mountains.[143] As befitted a Seleucid king, he appeared in all his glory as he wrestled a bull. Whether the sculptural group was associated with the Tauriane Gate, a prominent landmark within the city walls possibly near the river, has been disputed.[144] The sculptural group nonetheless continued the tradition of kings leaving their powerful, permanent imprint on the built environment.

Environmental concerns, massive building programs, geopolitics, and excessive antics thus were factors that played out in the making of Antiochus IV's Antioch. It is fair to say that he also sought to transfer the "model" of Antioch that he contributed to build. Enmeshed in Jewish affairs, he went as far as commissioning the construction of a stadium and a gymnasium at the foot of Temple Mount in Jerusalem, ostensibly promoting a new appendix of Antioch in the heart of Israel, thanks to the support of local Hellenized Jews.[145] The rift and riots that ensued were brought to a halt in 167 BCE with the looting of Jerusalem and the defiling of the Temple. He is also believed to have unleashed his wrath on Antiochene Jews, for tradition has it that during his reign the synagogue of the Seven Maccabean Martyrs was established as a memorial to a family of Jews tortured and murdered for their refusal of eating swine. The building was presumably located in the southern expanses of the city, on the slopes of Mt. Silpius, but its exact position, let alone its convoluted transformation into the Christian church of Ashmunit, remain a matter of dispute.[146] An episode of pestilence, further, also afflicted the city during his tenure. When exactly this happened cannot be determined, plausibly around 180 BCE, but the measures adopted to curb the epidemic are of interest. A monumental talisman was carved into the rock of Mt. Staurin, under the suggestion of one Leios, a wonder worker;[147] this was the *Charonion*, an image of a female divine figure, veiled and presumably donning a mask (Figure 1.11).

On her right shoulder is a small, draped figure wearing a calathus, a lily-shaped basket presumably for rituals honoring the goddess Demeter. It was perhaps the first example of a recursive, local tradition where such media were accorded agency and thus harnessed in moments of anxiety. In Near Eastern fashion, these devices were expected to mediate between supernatural powers and earthly communities, warding off the latter from all types of perils. The heterogeneous character of the local population with its commingling of Greeks and easterners may explain these practices.

The last days of the Seleucids

After the life of Antiochus IV Epiphanes was cut short in the aftermath of the 164 BCE Parthian campaign,[148] Antioch in subsequent decades was affected by the volatility of Seleucid politics and its inability to challenge the rise of Rome. Antiochus's death opened a century during which Antioch was locus to dynastic strife, usurpation, Ptolemaic entanglements, and Roman interference. In his *Syriaca*, the Greek historian Appian chronicled the slow demise of the dynasty amid regents, heirs, and infant rulers. The reigns of Antiochus V Eupator (164–162 BCE) and Demetrius I Soter (162–150 BCE) in particular demarcate a watershed in Seleucid history, not least the beginning of the struggle for the throne as well as the crescendo of Roman and Attalid interference in Syrian affairs. Geopolitics aside, no tangible work of Demetrius went down in history, with the exception of an elusive fortress outside Antioch in which he secluded himself.[149] Of interest, however, are some issues of the Antioch mint at this time, which seemingly heightened its output on account of the hostilities in Judea and the internal tension with Demetrius

FIGURE 1.11 The Charonion

Source: Courtesy of the Antioch Expedition Archives, Department of Art and Archaeology, Princeton University; Princeton

I Soter.[150] A silver tetradrachm in particular departs from the almost canonical iconography of Apollo on the omphalos on the reverse to propose a Tyche holding a cornucopia and seated on a low pillar adorned with a fish-tailed winged monster (Figure 1.12). Equally compelling are two smaller denominations, namely a drachma with a cornucopia on the reverse and a drachma with a horse protome (head and upper torso) on the obverse and an elephant head on the reverse.[151]

For a monarch whose claim was the rule of a kingdom spanning Antioch and Ekbatana,[152] the subtle allusions to the horse of Alexander and the iconic pachyderms of the Seleucid army were fitting. Alexander Balas (152–145 BCE), however, subverted this state of affairs and, with the support of the Maccabees, defeated Demetrius and seized the throne.[153] He seemingly approved a new league between Antioch and Seleucia Pieria; bronze coin issues celebrated a new season of partnership and concord "of the brother peoples," so the legend reads.[154] This was also a rather short-lived manifesto of political harmony, as tension in the region was mounting.

The ambivalence of Ptolemy VI Philometor (186–145 BCE) and claims to the Seleucid house advanced the position of Demetrius II (146–138 BCE; 129–125 BCE). With the governors Diodotus and Hierax handing the city over to Ptolemy VI and the Seleucid crown passing from the latter to Demetrius, the final showdown against Alexander Balas occurred in 145 BCE on the plain of Antioch, near the Oinoparas River (the modern Afrin).[155] The victorious Demetrius then inaugurated a season of military reforms aimed at shrinking the size of the army, dismissing mercenaries and forces previously stationed in Antioch. He also took revenge on Antioch for having originally sided with Balas and presumably punished the alleged supporters of his former rival. Perhaps not coincidentally, after two years of bronze coinage production of mainly tetradrachms and drachms, the mint ceased to strike for Demetrius in 145–144 BCE.[156] What measures triggered the local dissent cannot be surmised, but unrest and widespread dissatisfaction loomed large in the city at that point. The ensuing revolt soon got out of hand, with the king hiding in the palace on the Island. With Antioch close to falling, Judaean troops hired by Demetrius resorted to fire. The outcome was the incineration of large tracts of the city as well as the subsequent slaying of apparently 100,000 individuals.[157] Numbers in the ancient textual sources, of course, are often speculations or transcend reason. The Jewish historian Josephus, however, makes plain that the calamity and destruction of the city were indeed extraordinary.[158]

At this juncture Diodotus Tryphon (142–138 BCE) enters the picture. Possibly the same associate of Balas who had allowed Ptolemy VI to enter Antioch, he teamed up this time with the son of Balas, Antiochus VI (144–142 BCE). More fundamentally, he built his enclave in the satrapy of Apamea, probably using Chalcis as his base, and garnering troops, resources, and indeed elephants, he launched his offensive against Demetrius.[159] In 144, Antioch thus passed under the control of Tryphon and Antiochus VI, with the royal mint advertising the new era and Demetrius confining himself to Seleucia Pieria, only a few kilometers away.[160] The idyll

FIGURE 1.12 Tetradrachm of Demetrios I Soter. Obverse: Diademed head of Demetrios facing right. Wreath border. Reverse: Tyche seated facing left, holding a scepter in her right hand and a cornucopia in her left; winged Tritoness supporting throne; ΒΑΣΙΛΕΩΣ ΔΗΜΗΤΡΙΟΥ ΣΩΤΗΡΟΣ

Source: Courtesy of Gift of the Estate of Nathan Whitman, Mount Holyoke College Art Museum, South Hadley, Massachusetts. Photograph by Laura Shea 2004.13.9

between Tryphon and Antiochus VI was, however, short lived, the latter dying soon after military activities in Judaea, presumably in 141 BCE.[161] With Rome's validation,[162] Tryphon thus began his mandate as king, the mint of Apamea issuing at full swing images of the king together with military iconography. But boasting though he may have been of his successes, Tryphon failed to foster unity in a kingdom still under the influence of Demetrius II and that recognized the line of Antiochus VI, while also being embroiled in a long quarrel with Judaea.

At this very time Antiochus VII Sidetes (138–129 BCE), Demetrius's brother, appeared in Antioch. Following the clash of his armies with Tryphon's, Antioch began to strike coins in his name, now raised to monarchic dignity; a well-documented issue showcases the portrait of the king on the obverse and the eagle of Zeus on the reverse.[163]

With Tryphon's eclipse in 138 BCE,[164] Antioch and the Seleucid Empire entered a phase of new confidence and, arguably, unity. *Reconquista* whims and the utopia of regaining the energies of old characterized the mandate of Antiochus VII. In particular, he succeeded in assembling an impressive army to unleash a campaign against the Parthians, thus seeking the restoration of Seleucid control in Persia; the Antioch mint stuck coins at a furious pace, it seems.[165] The tragic outcome of the enterprise in 129 BCE, however, leading to the loss of Mesopotamia all the way to the Euphrates, is said to have brought grief to virtually every household in Antioch.[166] Demetrius II now seized the throne a second time for five years, to the dismay of the Antiochene community.[167] No wonder then that the materialization of Antiochus VII's alleged son, one Alexander adopted by the Ptolemaic house, triggered local hopes for a better settlement. This Alexander II Zebinas (128–122 BCE) ushered in a phase in which brothers fought against brothers and the line of kings became susceptible to fabrication. He soon had to vie with Antiochus VIII Grypus (121–96 BCE), son of Demetrius II, who defeated him in 122/121 BCE. Despite Antioch's initial support, Alexander Zebinas also compromised his chances of popular consensus by perpetrating the greatest sacrilege against the gods of the city, as he sought to seize illegally the golden statue of Zeus.[168] Ironically, he had previously issued tetradrachms with the iconography of the enthroned Zeus Nikephoros.[169] What, however, stands out is the condition of cities like Antioch and also Apamea, which in these conflicts invariably paid a hefty price as well as being forced to fill the royal armies with citizen troops.[170]

On a more positive note, Antiochus VIII fostered a sense of royal dignity that Antioch had not seen in decades; the celebration of games and festivals in Daphne[171] must be interpreted as a deliberate effort to continue the legacy of the great Seleucid kings. The magnificent tetradrachm of the king and his wife Cleopatra Thea, wearing a veil and crown,[172] vividly attests to the effort of heightening the image of the royal family and the dynasty altogether. As turned out in successive years, however, this was an ephemeral attempt to regain a prestige and sense of royal authority now on the wane. Amid internal attempts to seize the throne and family intrigues, Seleucid rule was fiercely contested by Antiochus VIII and Antiochus IX Philopator Cyzicenus (114–95 BCE) in a whirlwind of at least three different reigns for each king.[173] The reports are redolent with the familiar trope of the decadent king, yet they bring into focus the conflict between the two half-brothers and the duality between Antioch and Selucia Pieria, now raised to the status of a royal seat after many decades.[174] The squabble, however, led to further depletion of the kingdom's resources, with both cities ceasing to mint silver coins and forced to tap into sacred treasuries. Antiochus XI Philadelphus (94–93 BCE) in 93 BCE seemingly had to pay for the damage caused by previous conflicts. His resolve to bring Antioch back to its former glory was quite firm: Malalas informs us that he commissioned extensive repairs of the temples of Apollo and Artemis in Daphne, presumably restoring the treasury and gold objects looted by his predecessors.[175]

The following decades were marred by further intra-dynastic conflicts to the detriment of a now comatose state and a city, Antioch, having to grapple with the continuous royal turnover. Moreover, the textual sources consist of reports that can hardly be collated in a coherent sequence, with corrupt kings and usurpers taking center stage.[176] Earthquakes, too, may have compounded the situation with damage to the infrastructure and a heightened sense of social distress. The historian Justin reports on a catastrophic seism that struck Syria during the first quarter of the first century BCE and allegedly killed 170,000 people. Several unknown cities were greatly damaged.[177] Further, the frail premises that had underpinned the Seleucid state appeared in their true colors: external domination and seceding dynasts. In this sorry state of affairs, the phase of Armenian domination in Antioch would go almost unnoticed were it not for the appearance of the Tyche type on bronze tetradachms for the first time in the city's history (Figure 1.13). The Tyche appears first on local coinage under Tigranes II of Armenia (83–69 BCE). The reverse type was used for bronze coins and tetradrachms during the first and second centuries CE.[178] This same iconography was also appropriated for other purposes around the same time by other types of media.

The white marble stele of Tryphe was acquired by the Princeton team in 1937 in Seleucia Pieria as they were beginning the limited archaeological exploration of the site (Figure 1.14). This noble image of a woman ensconced in a high, thronelike chair brings to mind the well-known template of Tyche of Eutychides. In that same vein, the stele showcases Tryphe in the guise of the divine fortune of Antioch, with a footstool occupying the space typically held by the personified, swimming Orontes. Some hammering defaced Tryphe's head and right hand, while a succinct inscription offers a laconic, unpersonal farewell to the viewer: "to Tryphe, wife (or daughter) of Egias. Farewell, you who are now without pain. (ΑΛΥΠΕ ΧΑΙΡΕ)" However, the stele is redolent with an Antiochene artistic sensibility and, not least, sense of belonging. More importantly, this arresting image of a fierce local spirit at a time of political uncertainty, foreign domination, and violence may be no coincidence. That images of this kind circulated far and wide at this time may not be a mere coincidence.

At last Armenian rule came to an end. In 69 BCE a powerful earthquake struck Syria and its cities[179] – that Antioch was shaken and suffered damage is quite likely, for the sources imply that the event was a sign of the coming end of Armenian domination. According to literary traditions, many cities and communities were greatly affected by the quake across the Syrian region and plausibly Armenia, though there is a possibility that the shocks also caused serious damage in Palestine.[180] But a new political scenario was appearing at the horizon. Rome's erosion of Antioch's freedom and independence in the early 60s BCE foreshadowed what lay ahead: the establishment by Quintus Marcius Rex, proconsul of Cilicia, of a

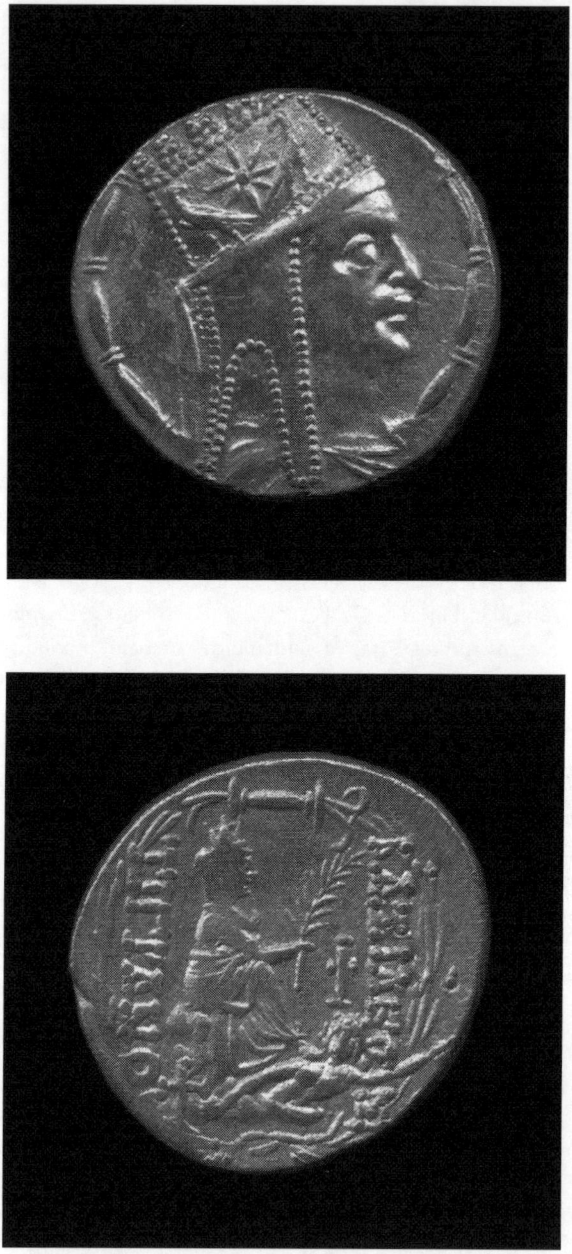

FIGURE. 1.13 Tetradrachm of Tigranes II. Obverse: Head of Tigranes the Great facing right, wearing beaded headdress (called Armenian tiara) with side flaps and bird and star motifs. Fillet border. Reverse: Tyche of Antioch, draped and wearing turreted crown, holding a palm branch. At her feet, the river god Orontes swims past; ΒΑΣΙΑΕΩΣ ΤΙΓΡΑΝΟΥ

Source: Courtesy of Gift of the Estate of Nathan Whitman, Mount Holyoke College Art Museum, South Hadley, Massachusetts

FIGURE 1.14 The funerary stele of Tryphe

Source: Courtesy of the Antioch Expedition Archives, Department of Art and Archaeology, Princeton University; Princeton

Roman base consisting of palace and hippodrome on the Island of the Orontes bespeaks Rome's aims.[181]

Constricted between Parthia, Armenia, and the rising hegemony of the Romans in the East, the Seleucid kingdom saw its rule abolished in 64 BCE by the Roman general Pompey. A once-powerful and wide-embracing empire, one that at the time of Seleucus I had been the largest of the Hellenistic period, came to an end. We shall see in the next chapter, in the history of Roman Antioch, how the role of the city was reconfigured as it transitioned under new realities of power.

The materiality of Hellenistic Antioch

What did Hellenistic Antioch actually look like? What monuments can be safely assigned to the pre-Roman phase of the city? How much did the 1930s excavations contribute to gleaning the city's configuration?

From the slopes of Mt. Staurin the austere bust of the Charonion, the monumental talisman commissioned by Antiochus IV Epiphanes, continued to affect local superstitions and religious beliefs in the sixth century CE, as attested by the words of Malalas.[182] It is fair to say that the Charonion is the sole survivor of Antioch's Seleucid heyday. Depicting a female with veiled head, as noted earlier, the Charonion worked in synchrony with the sculptural cityscape of Antioch, punctuated as it was by dozens of statues, large and small, alluding to the city's momentous foundation – Malalas alone tallies 11 of these:[183] heads of horses, bulls, gods attending the establishment of the city like Zeus Keraunios, the eagle of Zeus, the Tyche, and Seleucus's main priest Amphion. All strategically placed on the most conspicuous monuments and seemingly overcoming the ephemeral, ever-changing panorama of Roman images, they succeeded at carrying on the cult of these ancestral figures. In any event, it is apparent that Antioch's constituents recognized the city's mythical past and proclaimed its legacy as successor to the Macedonian and Seleucid empires, thus rising to the role of its most strenuous upholders. Consequently, the city's built environment shaped and was in turn shaped by people who styled themselves as descendants of Seleucus Nicator and Antiochus IV.

The city of the early kings, however, was not a target when the seminal Antioch excavations of 1932 began. The aims, achievements, and shortcomings of a remarkable constellation of scholars and institutions – namely Princeton University, the Musées de France, the Worcester Art Museum, the Baltimore Museum of Art, and the Fogg Art Museum – as they grappled with one of the most complex and indeed elusive cities of antiquity are well known.[184] Filed under "fiasco" by some and extolled by others, these seminal excavations, however, invite reconsideration, for they inadvertently afford insights into the Hellenistic past of the city and offer important underpinnings for ongoing research. We shall reprise this story separately in Chapter 11, yet a few points of relevance should be highlighted here.

It was Charles Rufus Morey of Princeton University who initially mapped out a plan to resurrect the Antioch of the fourth century CE and its Daphne suburbs. The navigation of the city's ancient space, however, was predicated on the text and vision of Karl Otfried Müller, who, for all his remarkable erudition, never set foot in Antioch.[185] In 1839, the German scholar had produced an authoritative map including the "Seleuci Nicatoris Urbs" and sites like Bottia, Epiphaneia, and Iopolis (Figure 1.15). It followed that the 1932 excavations' signature map, as drawn by Donald Wilber and Glanville Downey, situated monuments and urban features based on Late Antique textual records and on Müller's projections rather than concrete archaeological data. More fundamentally, it illustrated the sites that the 1932–1939 excavations of Antioch had unsuccessfully sought to locate (Figure 1.8). Put simply, this map was their wish list. But it is also a map that has had great implications for our understanding of Hellenistic Antioch and its topography, for it located Seleucus's fortifications and a tentative space occupied by the Seleucid agora (though no material evidence has supported this hypothesis). A manageable *Altstadt*, the ancient core of the city, was thus firmly placed in space, creating a small enclave and its future pendant, Epiphaneia, on the slopes of Mt. Silpius.

Overall, the results of the 1932 campaign epitomized the trajectory the expedition was to pursue in the next seven years. With a frenzy of investigations taking

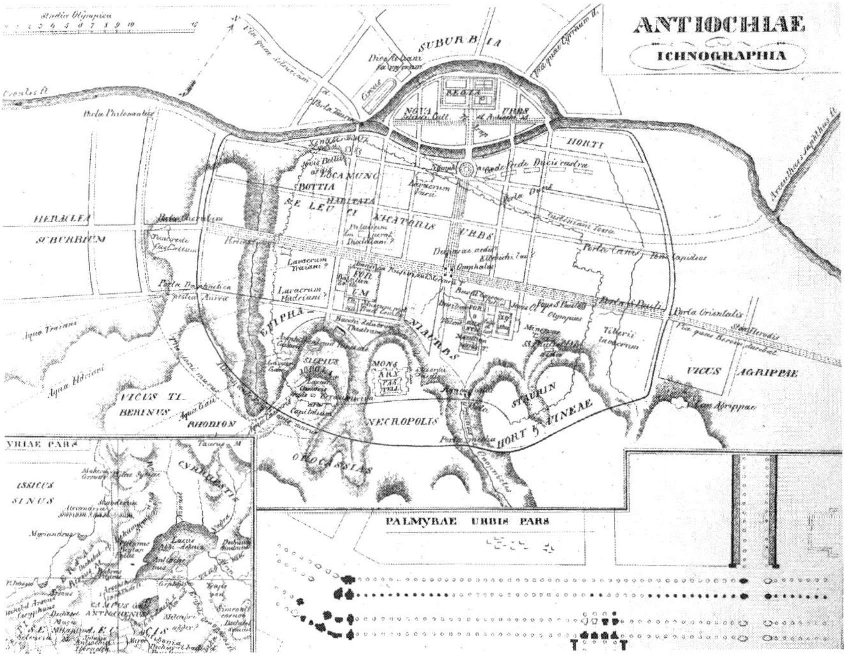

FIGURE 1.15 Antioch's map by Müller

Source: From Müller 1839

place on the Island, Downey began investigating, to no avail, a building outside Daphne. Its many column shafts sticking out of the ground had suggested a tentative location for the great sanctuary of Apollo, or perhaps one of the sanctuaries that were corollary to the oracular temple. The evidence that turned up, however, yielded no trace of Daphne's ancestral cults. Rather, all that came to light was a small medieval church with a modest decorative apparatus and no identifier. The seemingly unpromising excavation of the church was terminated at the end of the campaign, and other apparently unfruitful sites were similarly jettisoned in successive seasons.

An unsystematic strategy of sound investigations of select sectors and occasional exploration of orchards and fields to rapidly lift mosaics ensued. Occasional glimpses of the Hellenistic city got in the way of the excavators, whether the already discussed stretches of the ashlar defensive walls on the Island (sector 5-O) or fortifications in polygonal masonry near the Charonion and along on the slopes of Mt. Staurin (sector 16-Q and environs). The "Street Digs," not least sector 16-P, identified elusive traces of the Hellenistic epoch. But this evidence, no matter how telling, was rapidly dismissed. The goals of the expedition and its sponsoring institutions lay rather in the lofty buildings of Late Antique Antioch celebrated by the literary tradition.

For all their shortcomings, the Antioch excavations did produce a wealth of archaeological data from the city and its environs. The excavations in the city, as well as in Daphne and Seleucia Pieria, though limited, raised questions of space use and integration of the hinterlands into the greater Antioch urban system. The cursory inspection of Seleucia Pieria, other than yielding beautiful pavements, shed light on the city's topography while bringing to light two extraordinary buildings, namely a Doric temple of the early Hellenistic period and a church of the end of the fifth century CE.[186] Prominently placed on a spur, the Hellenistic temple was of a Doric peripteral plan with 18.60 × 36.90 m foundations and six by 12 columns (Figure 1.16). It had a bipartite cella and a deep distyle pronaos in antis, that is, its sidewalls extended to the front of the temple's porch and ended in a pillar or post on either side of the entrance.

Its weathered foundations are its only remains, with column drums still scattered across the site. Most of its superstructure has been scavenged for centuries, and it is no exaggeration that the monument has served as quarry for the villages nearby. Use, access, and experiencing of the temple are beyond our grasp. Further, the deity to which this temple was dedicated remains to be established, and whether Zeus Keraunios, the Dioscuri, or Isis were worshiped here cannot be determined.[187]

And we should not dismiss the archaeological collections now stored at the Princeton University Museum of Art as they also help shed light onto Antioch's

FIGURE 1.16 Seleucia Pieria, Doric temple. Central portion of the temple showing crypt (center) and fallen column drums (right)

Source: Courtesy of the Antioch Expedition Archives, Department of Art and Archaeology, Princeton University; Princeton

Seleucid days. Ongoing analysis of the ceramics from sector 17-O is producing rich evidence about wares of the third and second centuries BCE, from black glaze to brown and red slipped wares, that identify use and deposition along the main thoroughfare, thus reinforcing the hypothesis that this axis of traffic was central in the nucleation and growth of the city. Of the same chronological horizon are also a pair of terracotta heads, parts of figurines, from sector 16-P that seem to adhere to the conventions of productions in places like Seleucia on the Tigris, thus bringing to the fore the blend between oriental and Greek visual traditions (Figure 1.17).[188]

And what to make of Antioch's collection of pavements that now line up the halls of museums worldwide? They are arguably the most arresting illustration of Hellenism in the service of the Antiochenes. While their chronology spans the second century BCE to early sixth century CE, it is a matter of record that many of them utilized images, models, and visual idioms of the Hellenistic period. It is plain that the iconography of these pavements more likely derives from Hellenistic models than from any theme or subject elicited by contact with the Roman world: Orpheus, Narcissus, Dionysus. Equally prominent are river gods, the myth of Daphne, and the topography of Syria and Cilicia, in an effort to reconcile a mythical currency common to the whole Mediterranean with the specificities of Antioch's landscape. The well-established genre of the narrative mythological mosaic with accompanying text, attested throughout large parts of the Oriens,

FIGURE 1.17 Early Hellenistic terracotta figurines from sector 16-P

Source: Courtesy of the Antioch Expedition Archives, Department of Art and Archaeology, Princeton University; Princeton

also figures prominently at Antioch. Overall, these are but some of the themes that the mosaicists selected from a vast repertoire that was readily available. We should remember that Antioch was seat of one of the ancient world's richest libraries, which had been founded by Antiochus III; it plausibly included, among its holdings, a vast collection of *paradeigmata*, that is, models that an artist could draw upon for his compositions.

All in all, the early Princeton archaeologists identified a few buildings on the Island and exposed a complex stratigraphy, ultimately showing how multilayered Antioch and its entire district were. A recent urban survey by Gunnar Brands, however, has shown a way forward for our understanding of Hellenistic Antioch, thereby opening new avenues of research:[189] rectifying the approximate topography of the 1930s excavations, it has thereby built a new plateau from where the archaeological collections at the Princeton Museum of Art can be recontextualized within their original setting. Moreover, this data has been plugged into a real, concrete city plan defined by the perimeter of fortifications.[190] These new and promising underpinnings now make it possible to take up again settlement narratives that the Antioch excavations left suspended and to build a more concrete urban image of Antioch from its nucleation. In particular, the city's first settlement can be reasonably situated on the tract of land between the Orontes River and the slopes of Mt. Silpius and Mt. Staurin, as attested by the numismatic and ceramics evidence.[191] It is likely that, less than a century after its foundation, Antioch expanded its original core to the Island – as attested by the small stretch of a fortification found in 1932 – and then eastwards, to incorporate the rugged slopes of the two mounts. Central in this new research, however, is determining the location of the highland quarter of Epiphaneia under *Antioch*, IV, Epiphanes (Figure 1.9 and Figure 1.18).

Better dividends can be clinched with the archaeology of the highlands of Antioch. In particular, the whereabouts of Epiphaneia have long been a matter of dispute. The textual sources of classical and Late Antiquity offer limited insights into its topographic setting, loosely situating it on the slope of Mt. Silpius. In addition, the 1930s archaeological investigations failed to offer any concrete material evidence, despite some reconnaissance on the slopes between Mt. Silpius and Mt. Staurin, a saddle that is rich with traces of architecture, aqueducts, and ceramics on the surface. After a long impasse, however, Wolfram Hoepfner, in the framework of renewed interest in Antioch's topography in the 1990s, took up the issue of Epiphaneia's location, assigning to it the stretches of polygonal walls visible on the slopes of Mt. Staurin.[192] His analysis was furthered by Brands's fieldwork in 2004–2005, a component of his multi-dimensional survey of the Mt. Silpius and Mt. Staurin districts of Antioch, which took place between 2004 and 2009. Consisting of archaeological, architectural, and geophysical surveys of the areas that Antioch straddled, the project illustrated previously unknown features and rectified the old datasets of the 1930s excavations. During the 2006–2007 seasons, Brands conducted both archaeological and geophysical surveys on the saddle separating Mt. Silpius from Mt. Staurin, a discrete area measuring approximately 200 by 500 meters and demarcated by a weathered perimeter of polygonal walls and traces of

FIGURE 1.18 The tentative location of Epiphaneia between Mt. Silpius (in the background) and Mt. Staurin

Source: Photograph by Andrea U. De Giorgi

conspicuous water systems (Figure 1.19). Ground-penetrating radar (GPR) and systematic collection of artifacts have also contributed to a picture of settlement spanning the Hellenistic and Late Antique phases of the city, thus corroborating the possibility that a small urban entity grew in this area. Whether this site corresponds to Epiphancia remains to be established.

Conclusions

Overall, this piecemeal, jarring evidence frustrates the physical description of the Seleucid capital. However that may be, Antioch's layout and armature, as planned by the early kings, dictated its successive development during the Roman era. All in all, Antioch maintained a continuous dialogue with its founding agents and relevant events throughout the course of classical and late antiquity. Many of the monuments celebrating the achievements of Seleucus were apparently still visible during the days of John Malalas in the sixth century and even later.[193] A repertoire of these ancestral figures – whether the king, his horse, or the Tyche, to name but a few – engaged local viewers, effectively communicating meanings and memories in dialogue with an ever-evolving built environment. This dialectic between old and new and, more to the point, between the Seleucid imprint of the city and its

FIGURE 1.19 Early polygonal fortifications on Mt. Silpius

Source: Photograph by Andrea U. De Giorgi

development during the Roman epoch, would become particularly evident as the city sought to enlarge its fabric from the early imperial period onwards.

Notes

1 Boehm 2018; Ogden 2017; Chrubasik 2016; Kosmin 2014.
2 See especially Sherwin-White and Kuhrt 1993; Strootman 2011.
3 Ma 2011; Strootman 2011.
4 Bowersock 1994b.
5 Paus. 8.29.3–4 and Jones 2000. See also Polyb. 5.59 on the Orontes watering the city of Antioch. The landmark study on the Orontes and its basin is Weulersse 1940; for a recent survey of the river's characteristics and geological context, see Bridgland et al. 2012.
6 Chrysostom, Hom. 13.3 in 1 Tim. [PG 62, 568C].
7 *Antioch III*, 13–14.
8 Brands 2009.
9 See Gatier 2016, 250–251, on the symbiosis between the river and the city, underscored as it was by the textual sources.
10 Bridgland et al. 2012.
11 Paus. 6.2.7 (transl. by W.H.S. Jones: "This Eutychides made for the Syrians on the Orontes an image of Fortune, which is highly valued by the natives." For the stylistic discussion of the statue, see Ridgway 2000, 243–244. The best known Roman replica, found in 1780 in the Barberini villa near Quadraro, is at the Musei Vaticani; see Meyer 2006, pl. 5.2. Three bronze miniature versions are now at the Worcester, Louvre, and

Firenze museums, respectively. Gnoli 2013 adds further depth to the issue, divorcing the tutelary deity from the concept of the Tyche. For a comprehensive discussion of the Tyche's iconography, see Christof 2001.

12 McAlee, *Coins* 1181. *Tetrakionia* are landmark monuments that typically signaled an intersection of two avenues of traffic. See Balty 2000 for the study of a sixth-century CE *tetrakionion* in Apamea, Syria. Antioch could also boast a Tychaion, mentioned by Lib. *Ep.* 88.2 and *Theod.HE.* 3.26.2; under Theodosius II the building was apparently transformed into a place of cult dedicated to St. Ignatius, with substantial activity in the late sixth century CE, as recorded in *Evagrius* 1.16. How the building looked remains uncertain. That it replicated that of Alexandria, established presumably during the early days of the foundation, is a suggestive possibility. See McKenzie and Keyes 2013, 37–52.

13 De Giorgi 2016, 42.

14 Trajan deserves particular credit for the shoring up of the Tiber banks, as part of his greater project for Ostia and Portus. Noteworthy are also the efforts of Valens during the famine of 370 CE in Lenski 2002, 388.

15 The drowning of enemies in the Orontes is a literary trope. However, the Emperor Valens imposed this punishment on many affiliates of the Orthodox bishop Meletius in 370 CE; see Soc. 4.2. and the Life of Athanasius of Alexandria, in Photius, Bibliothèque, cod. 258, 485a.

16 Wilkinson 1997; Wilkinson et al. 2001; Yener et al. 2000; Yener et al. 2005.

17 Lib. *Or.* 11.26; on the geomorphological configuration of the basin, see Batiuk 2007; Gerritsen et al. 2008; Casana 2007. The lake came to an abrupt end in the 1960s after the Turkish government spearheaded an ambitious reclamation plan to secure new land, primarily for the cultivation of cotton. Silt and sand dunes in the central and northern sweeps of the plain are the visual relics of the ancient lake, while seasonal floods in the central sector – where today the modern Hatay Airport (Hatay Havalimanı) operates – punctually remind the community of the ills of poor drainage.

18 On the "Amanus" etymology, see the twelfth-century grammarian John Tzetzes reporting on the myth of Orestes and the relieving of his madness (a-mania) after his matricide somewhere in those mountains: Tzetzes, *Schol. On Lycophron* 1374. A survey of the archaeology in the Amanus district can be found in Alkım 1969.

19 *Oracula Sybillina* 13, 125 (transl. by Dodgeon and Lieu 1991, 50–51). Other than the repeated destruction of Antioch through the centuries, tangible signs of telluric action may be identified in two uplifts of the coastline in the vicinity of Seleucia Pieria that may have impacted the dynamics of settlement between the first millennium BCE and Late Antiquity; see Erol and Pirazzoli 1992.

20 Gerritsen et al. 2008.

21 Woolley 1955.

22 Hess 2002, 209–221.

23 Casana 2007.

24 Harrison and Denel 2017; Harrison et al. 2018.

25 On al-Mina and its cultual implications, see Descœudres 2002.

26 See *Downey, History* 53 and the discussion in Ogden 2017, 157. For the religious perspectives on Greek settlers in Antioch and Seleucia Pieria, see Strootman 2016.

27 See Cohen 2006.

28 Cohen 2006; Kosmin 2014, 103.

29 Appian reports 56 cities founded by Seleucus Nicator: see App. *Syr.* 57.295–298. Cohen 2006 offers an in-depth catalog of dynastic foundations.

30 Grainger 1990, 82.

31 Newson 2016. For an early archaeological survey of the region, see Archi et al. 1971.

32 On Dura Europos the literature is vast; see, however, the comprehensive survey of Baird 2018 and especially Kosmin 2011 for a detailed account of the foundation. On the Dura

excavations and archaeological record, see Brody 2011. For the Jebel Khalid excavation, see tentatively identified as Amphipolis, see Clarke et al. 2002.

33 Strab. 16.2.4. (Transl. by H. L. Jones):

> Seleucis is not only the best of the above-mentioned portions of Syria, but also is called, and is, a Tetrapolis, owing to the outstanding cities in it, for it has several. But the largest are four: Antiocheia near Daphnê, Seleucia Pieria, and also Apameia and Laodiceia; and these cities, all founded by Seleucus Nicator, used to be called sisters, because of their concord with one another. Now the largest of these cities [Antioch] was named after his father and the one most strongly fortified by nature after himself, and one of the other two, Apameia, after his wife Apama, and the other, Laodiceia, after his mother. Appropriately to the Tetrapolis, Seleucis was also divided into four satrapies, as Poseidonius says, the same number into which Coelê-Syria was divided, though Mesopotamia formed only one satrapy. Antiocheia is likewise a Tetrapolis, since it consists of four parts; and each of the four settlements is fortified both by a common wall and by a wall of its own. Now Nicator founded the first of the settlements, transferring thither the settlers from Antigonia, which had been built near it a short time before by Antigonus; the second was founded by the multitude of settlers; the third by Seleucus Callinicus; and the fourth by Antiochus Epiphanes.

The satrapy thus featured Antioch, Seleucia, Apamaea, and Laodikeia (and presumably Cyrrhestice and Commagene). Strabo's statement is rather problematic, as it presupposes that the institutions of the Tetrapolis and those of the satrapy were interlocked in some way. How the two worked both independently and in conjunction remains unclear.

34 Cohen 2006 offers a comprehensive historical survey of these sites. Archaeologically, Apamea is the best known of the four, thanks to decades of extensive fieldwork at the site. See in particular Balty and Balty 1977 and 1981; Balty 1981, 1988, 1994. Seleucia Pieria was modestly investigated by the Antioch excavations of the 1930s; the investigation led to the identification of a Doric temple, a church (previously referred to as a martyrion), some spectacular houses, the so-called Market Gate, and tracts of the city wall and gates; see *Antioch III*, 31–34. The city walls are of interest: while stretches of polygonal masonry survive on the eastern flank of the acropolis, the rest of the perimeter uses an isodomic technique that seemingly harkens back to the early days of the Seleucid foundation; see McNicoll 1997, 85–89. The site's topography, however, remained that of Chapot 1907, with Boselli's general plan; see Uggeri 2006; Van Berchem 1985, though the latter is primarily interested with the Roman imperial phase. Of relevance, too, is Seyrig 1938. See also Pamir 2014b for some recent additions. As for Laodicea, well known is its numismatic repertoire, for the city served as a royal mint from the early days of Seleucus, exporting a great deal of its silver coinage with iconic dolphin design; see Houghton and Lorber 2002, xx–xxi. With regard to Laodicea's archaeological record, limited information can be found in Sauvaget 1934. It should be noted that Sauvaget's reconstruction of classical Laodicea was long upheld to illustrate the transition from the classical colonnaded street to the enclosed and covered market, the suq of the Islamic period. As it stands, this model is based on a notion of cultural decline and degeneration from an age of order to one of political chaos.

35 Chrubasik 2016, 184. It is now accepted that Antioch became capital not earlier than the second half of the second century BCE. See Houghton and Lorber 2002, 9.

36 *Downey, History* 66. It should be borne in mind that under Seleucus Nicator the Antioch mint struck predominantly bronze issues, with the exceptions of gold staters of the Alexandrine type, silver tetradrachms, and silver hemiobols. See Houghton and Lorber 2002, 18.

37 Strab. 16.2.4, see n. 33.

38 *Malalas* 8.13.

39 *Malalas* 8.12.

40 Saliou 2009–2010, 360–366.

41 Ogden 2017, 110.

42 As we will see later, in Oration 11, Libanius also reinforces the point of the visual rhetoric enforced by the Seleucid kings: see in particular *Or.* 11.91–92.

43 Diod. Sic. 20.47.5; Dio Cass. 40.29.1–3; *Strab.* 16.2.4. The remains of this elusive and apparently large city (it boasted a perimeter of 70 stades, approximately 13 km) have yet to be identified, though Cohen 2006, 47 tentatively situates the site northeast of Antioch. To date, no archaeological survey in the region has identified traces of Antigoneia. Lastly, for Antigonia's coinage, see Le Rider 1999, 11–13.

44 Fictitious and murky though it may be, Ibn al-'Adīm 1988, 8 (transl. by K. Brunner) reiterates some of the foundation's topical points. In particular:

> Seleucus built certain cities and he completed the building of Antioch, decorated it and he named it after his son Antiochus and it is Antioch, previously Antigonus initiated the building of it. In the 6th year of the death of Alexander. It was mentioned he built it on the River Orontes and named it Antūghīnā and he said the first king of Syria and Babel, Slūqūs Nīqṭūr who was Syrian, and he ruled in the 13th year of Baṭlamiyūs b. Lāghūs [presumably Ptolemy].
>
> *(1996, vol. 1, pp. 8–9)*

45 Plut. *Marc.*19.1–3; Livy 25.31; Polyb. 8.37.

46 See the report by John Tzetzes, *Chiliades* 7.167 (transl. by V. Dogani):

> As Pausanias writes on the foundation of Antioch, Antioch was founded by Seleucus Nicator, according to some, as the namesake of his own father Antiochus, according to Lucian, as the namesake of his son Antiochus, the one, whom they called *Soter*, whose wife was Stratonice, the one, who was diagnosed by Erasistratus, just from his pulse, to be in love with his own stepmother. Seleucus founds this city of Antioch, as well as seventy-four other cities. But as for those, who foolishly claim that Antiochus founded this one, Attaeus and Perittas, as well as Anaxicrates shall refute them most wisely and will expose them to be absurd, along with them Asklepiodoros, who happened to be a fellow-slave. Those men, whom at that time Seleucus made the supervisors of the constructions.

Of interest are the names of the three supervisors who may have assisted Seleucus with the practicalities of the foundation, at variance with that provided by Malalas and nowhere else attested.

47 Ogden 2011, 149–160.

48 The literature on Libanius' Oration 11 is vast: see the masterly Festugière 1959, 23–61; Downey 1959; Fatouros and Krischer 1992; Norman 2000; Wiemer 2003; Saliou 2006; Cribiore 2007, 24–30.

49 Ogden 2017, 105.

50 Lib. *Or.* 11.43. Pausanias of Antioch is in all likelihood one of Libanius's sources. See *Downey, History* 36.

51 The reference to Alexander the Great's foundation of Alexandria with the ritual demarcation of the future city on the ground could not be more obvious. See *AR* 1.32. Malalas corroborates this account, adding that one Xenaios was the architect in charge; see *Malalas* 8.13.

52 *Malalas* 3.19; Balty 2000, 231.

53 The fourth century CE historian Ammianus Marcellinus described Daphne as "the charming and magnificent suburb of Antioch," Amm. Marc. 19.12.19.

54 Stenger 2018, 193–196; Kalleres 2015.

55 Gibbon 1776, I.23, in which Daphne is also treated as the epicenter of Antioch's luscious rituals and festivals. Also, on the ineffable beauty of Daphne: Jul. *Ep.*58 (transl. by W.C. Wright):

> I should not have hesitated to compare Daphne with Ossa and Pelion or the peaks of Olympus, or Thessalian Tempe, or even to have preferred it to all of them put together. But you have composed an oration on Daphne such as no other man 'of

> such sort as mortals now are' could achieve, even though he used his utmost energies on the task, yes, and I think not very many of the ancient writers either. Why then should I try to write about it now, when so brilliant a monody has been composed in its honour? Would that none had been needed!

Orientals, too, were in awe when seeing the place, as in the case of Antioch's 540 CE siege by the Persians. Thus wrote Procop. *B. Pers*. 2.14 (transl. by H. B. Dewing):

> Accordingly he (the king Khosrow) first went up to Daphne, the suburb of Antioch, where he expressed great wonder at the grove and at the fountains of water; for both of these are very well worth seeing. And after sacrificing to the nymphs he departed, doing no further damage than burning the sanctuary of the archangel Michael together with certain other buildings.

56 Habicht 1992. Also, Ogden 2017, 106 and n. 29; Strootman 2016, 16–19. It is worth noting, however, that the characterization of Daphne as "that near Antioch" is used by Josephus in Joseph. *BJ*. 1.12.5.

57 *Malalas* 8.20.

58 Aus.*Clar. Urb*. i.i. Of interest Lib. *Or*. 1.255 and especially 262. In the fourth century CE, the establishment of the local Christian community eroded more and more the religious significance of Daphne, to the detriment of the sanctuary and the sacred grove. See in particular Libanius' tirade against the governor Cynegius and his plan to fell the cypresses in Daphne (transl. by A. F. Norman):

> He had decided to lay the axes on the cypresses in Daphne and I, realizing that such a course would bring no good to any who chopped them down, advised one of his boon companions that he should not incur the anger of Apollo because of the trees, especially since his temple had already been afflicted by similar misdeeds.

Current legislation saw to the protection of the grove; see *CTh* 10.1.12 of 379 CE and then the later *CJ* 11.78.1–2.

59 The presence of statues is particularly meaningful; see Saliou 2006 on the role of urban sculpture that allegedly added to the city's urban décor, as filtered through the lenses of Malalas's *Chronographia*. See also Balty 2004.

60 *Malalas* 2.8: "From the time when the Argives came to the search of Io to the present the Syrians of Antioch have performed this memorial rite, knocking at the houses of the Hellenes at this time each year."

61 Chrysostom, *Adv. Jud*. 1, 6.

62 *Jerusalem Talmud* 10.61.

63 *Antioch Archives*, Field Report of 1932.

64 Will 1983, 8.

65 In a few years Daphne was to become the arena where the so-called "mosaic crew" operated. Following the lead of local villagers, and often actually salvaging ancient domestic buildings under threat, these archaeologists were tasked with the recovery and lifting of mosaics. Their pace quickened between 1933 and 1936, with hundreds of pavements excavated, packed, and shipped to the United States and France. Because of these finds, the opulent houses of Daphne of the Roman and Late Roman period are now central in the archaeological discourse of this suburb.

66 For a broader discussion of the issue, see in particular the survey of Syrian sacred architecture in Gawlikowski 1992, 323–346.

67 *Antioch III*, 34; Clarke 2015, 143–155.

68 Lib. *Monod.de Daphnaeo Templo* 3.334.

69 Will 1983, 1–25.

70 Waddington 1870, n. 2713.

71 This issue of the Athenian and diverse legacy is recursive in Libanius, see *Or.* 15.79 (transl. by A. F. Norman):

> Our city claims descent from the race of Inachus that wandered far in search of Io; she has an Athenian element; she is a city of Macedonians, of Alexander who trod the same path as yourself; he admired its spring and gladly drank of its water.

72 *Evagrius* I. 20. The speech dates to 438 CE, as she was en route to Jerusalem to fulfill a vow.

73 Laflı and Meischner 2008, ns 1–2 in their catalogue. On funerary stelae from Antioch, see also Laflı and Christof 2014; Meischner 2003; Parlasca 1982; De Giorgi 2019.

74 Pisidia is a region that loosely corresponds to western Anatolia, near modern Isparta and Burdur. For the technical description of the reliefs, see Parlasca 1982, taf. 2 and 3.

75 Tzetzes, *Chiliades* 7.118, 176–180.

76 The image of the *Ktisis*, the foundation, popular on Antioch pavements of the fifth century has been interpreted as the visual upholding of a distant past and bolstering of a Greek genealogy. I would add that this image better than any other encapsulates the Antiochene unremitting allegiance to the city and determination to look at the future. On the significance of the personified foundation, see Becker and Kondoleon 2005, 210–215.

77 Hoepfner 2004, 7.

78 Stahl 2017.

79 Leblanc and Poccardi 1999.

80 Libanius mentions one agora; see *Or.* 1.102.

81 Leriche 2007, 86.

82 Chrysostom, *De s. Meletio* 1.3.

83 *Downey, History* 72.

84 On the construction of the city walls, see also Guidi 1897, 153, a translation of the late medieval Codex Vaticanus 286. Although believed to be anachronistic and arguably inaccurate, it nevertheless offers a narrative on the king seeking to incorporate the plain and the slopes of the mountains within the city walls. Also of interest is the thirteenth-century biography of the Mamlūk sultan Baybars, in which many of the tropes of Antioch foundation coalesce, albeit in fabricated form:

> They presented to their king these details. Thus, [the king] ordered for its construction, and procured the expenses. They requested excellent stone (*ḥajaran jayyidan*) for its construction. They found [the stone] within a two day's [journey] from [the city]. He hired for [the project] men, security, and the rest – 80,800 men, 600 carts (*ʿajala*), 1,900 donkeys, and 100 skiffs (*zawraq*) to transport the stone blocks apart from the carts, men, and skiffs in Port al-Suwaydiyya, carrying the marble, the columns (*ʿumud*), and [their] bases (*qawāʿid*). It was demanded that [the project] should be completed within three and a half years. Its walls and towers were built, as there are 153 towers, 153 *badana*(?), and seven gates – five of which are large but two of them are small. He made there seven drains/diverts(?) that cast out to the river, near the *wādī* named al-Kashkarūt. A gate was placed in the mountain by [the king] from which [water] could go down to the city, and over which there are bridges for the people to cross. When [the channel] becomes full, it exits from underneath the wall. [The people] led the water to [the city] in two qanāts al-Būlīṭ and al-ʿĀwiya. When [the project] was finished, the king came to see it.

See Ibn ʻAbd al-Zāhir 1976, 314. Adaptation of the text courtesy of Kyle Brunner.

85 Brasse 2010.

86 See Abdul Massih 2009.

87 *Malalas* 8.17.

88 Disentangling the evidence of at least three different surviving water systems is particularly complicated; see Benjelloun et al. 2015, 4. The archaeological surveys of Gunnar

Brands on the southern slopes of Mt. Staurin show water collection systems and channels impounding water that may date to the early days of the city; see Brands et al. 2009; Pamir and Yamaç 2012. In his survey of the topography of Selucia and Antioch, however, Polybius makes plain that the latter discharged its sewage into the Orontes; Polyb. 5.59. A system reminiscent of Rome's Cloaca Maxima may have reasonably been in place, funneling "bad" waters and mountain runoff along the Parmenios channel into the river.

89 *Malalas* 8.16–17.

90 Strabo's "phase two" of the city's growth may be situated between the mandates of Seleucus Nicator and Seleucus Callinus, with the latter apparently spearheading a development on the Island. See n. 33.

91 Lib. *Or.* 11.112.

92 See *Gouroub, Papyrus*. Text and commentary of this text can be found in Mahaffy 1893; Mahaffy and Gilbart Smyly 1905; Holleaux 1906 and, more recently, in Piejko 1990. The issue of the Orontes' navigability and the modality of the Egyptian expedition reaching Antioch has generated little consensus among scholars: see for instance *Downey, History* 18–19; Van Berchem 1985, 68.

93 Just. *Epit.* 27, 1–2; *Downey, History* 90. During the days of the Egyptian occupation, the Antioch mint may have ceased its operations, replaced, as it was, by an unknown establishment nearby that used Antioch dies and continued to strike coins at least until 204 BCE. See Houghton and Lorber 2002, xxiii.

94 Strab. 16.2.5. Demetrios II apparently hid in the palace during the riots of 147 BCE.

95 Lib. *Or.* 11.119.

96 Houghton and Lorber 2002, 394–404.

97 The AVRP archaeological survey attests to an uptick of rural settlement and site increase during the second century BCE; see Gerritsen et al. 2008, 248–252.

98 Euphorion, *Testimonia* 1.

99 Cohen 2006, 82.

100 *TIB* 15, 541.

101 Grainger 1990, 125.

102 Sherwin-White and Kurht 1993, 7–38.

103 On the treaty between the obscure Antioch in Persis and Magnesia on the Meander, which also included Antioch on the Orontes, see Austin 1981, n. 190.

104 Grainger 1990, 152.

105 Ma 1999, 181.

106 *SEG* 39.1426.

107 Polyb. 5.89.9.

108 *Malalas* 8.25, reporting on the earthquake using the information of the historian Domninos: "It was rebuilt better, 152 years after the laying out of the city walls" the text reads. See also *Downey, History* 120.

109 Austin 1981, n. 220, on the papyrus describing Ptolemy III's visit to Antioch and the greeting of the population. In addition, particularly telling is the obscure document published by Kraeling 1968, 178–179, referring to religious festivals and a probable list of individuals offering their liturgies.

110 Herrmann 1965, 29–160. Section 2, block D, lines 100–104.

111 *Malalas* 8.15. It is likely he referred to the population of the Platonic ideal city; see Pl. *Lg.* 737e. On the use of Malalas as a primary source, see Liebeschuetz 2006 and *Downey, History* 38–40.

112 Polyb. 5.61.1.

113 Diod. Sic. 34.17.

114 Cumont 1934, 187–190.

115 Joseph. *Ap.* 2. 4. 39; Gerritsen et al. 2008.

116 Gerritsen et al. 2008, 249–252.

117 Newell 1918.

118 Le Rider 1999, 28.
119 Ibid., 27–30.
120 Cohen 2006, 82.
121 Houghton et al. 2008, 13.
122 Aperghis 2001.
123 Boehm 2018, 104.
124 Metcalf 2000, 105.
125 Aperghis 2001, 93.
126 Stahl 2017, 233–234.
127 Houghton et al. 2008, 44. The victory was intended as the outcome of the second Egyptian campaign of that same year. The minting in Antioch of the so-called "Egyptianizing" series, with iconographies of Serapis, Isis, and the Ptolemaic eagle, let it be known who the new force to reckon with was.
128 Houghton et al. 2008, 44.
129 Polyb. 26.12–13. The portrait of the king and interactions with the Antiochene folks as reported through Athenaeus 5.193d (transl. by W. R. Paton) is not the most flattering, amid claims of erratic behavior and Roman dignity aspirations:

> Antiochus surnamed Epiphanes gained the name of Epimanes by his conduct. Polybius tells us of him that, escaping from his attendants at court, he would often be seen wandering about in all parts of the city with one or two companions. He was chiefly found at the silversmiths' and goldsmiths' workshops, holding forth at length and discussing technical matters with the molders and other craftsmen. He also used to condescend to converse with any common people he met, and used to drink in the company of the meanest foreign visitors to Antioch. Whenever he heard that any of the young men were at an entertainment, he would come in quite unceremoniously with a fife and a procession of musicians, so that most of the guests got up and left in astonishment… . Upon being elected, he would sit upon the ivory curule chair, as is the Roman custom, listening to the lawsuits tried there, and pronouncing judgment with great pains and display of interest. In consequence all respectable men were entirely puzzled about him, some looking upon him as a plain simple man and others as a madman… . He also used to bathe in the public baths, when they were full of common people, having jars of the most precious ointments brought in for him.

Athenaeus himself in *The Learned Banqueteres*, 2, 45, reports on Heliodorus (FGrH 373 F 8) inferring that Antiochus Epiphanes, whom Polybius refers to as Epimanēs ("the Madman") because of how he acted, mixed wine into the spring in Antioch, presumably for a heightened bath experience.

130 Polyb. 30.25–27. The games were announced to far away cities so that "people in Greece were eager to visit Antioch then" (transl. by S. Douglas Olson).
131 Ristvet 2014.
132 Strab. 16.2.4; *Malalas* 8.205.
133 Hoepfner 1999; 2004, 6–8; Brands et al. 2007 and 2008.
134 As for the *bouleuterion*, the building is mentioned by Libanius in several occasions, for there he offered some of his teaching (*Or.* 1.104; 11.125; 20.42; 22.30; 46.16). He provides occasional vistas onto the built surroundings, namely porticoes and a covered theater (*Or.* 20.42). Of interest is also the report in the *Chronicon Pascale* 585, 1.5, with reference to the statue of the empress Eudocia, commemorating her visit of 438 CE. As for the temple dedicated to Zeus Olympius (likely to be identified with the temple of Jupiter Capitolinus), the textual record is also compounded by the establishment in the second century CE, under Commodus, of another sanctuary dedicated to the same god. It was situated within the premises of the *plethron*, that is the Theater of Zeus Olympius; see Lib. *Or.* 10.23 and *Malalas* 12.2. The sanctuary of the Muses may also be identified with a "Mouseion" reported by Malalas to be destroyed by a wildfire under Tiberius in 23/24 CE but assigned to one Antiochus Philopator (*Malalas* 10.10); the

title "Philopator" however, was assigned to three different Antiochi, to wit, Antiochus IX, X, and XII; see Downey 1961, 132. Malalas also infers that the Mouseion was built (presumably repaired) during the days of Marcus Aurelius (*Malalas* 11.30), decorated by Probus, and later transformed into a *praetorium* in 335 CE; see *Malalas* 13.4. See also Lib. *Or.* 1.102 on the use and popularity of the temple in the fourth century CE.

135 Joseph. *Bell. Iud.* 7.55:60–61. The text alludes to the archives and other public buildings nearby. It was seemingly affected by 70 CE wildfire that struck the quarter of Epiphaneia.

136 *Malalas* 8.22 excludes the presence of fortifications.

137 1 Macc. 23–24 suggests that the spoils of Jerusalem's destruction were instrumental in building the sanctuary dedicated by Antiochus IV to Jupiter in Antioch. Livy reports on the building in 41.20.9 (transl. by E. T. Sage and A. C. Schlesinger): "at Antioch he built a magnificent temple to Jupiter Capitolinus, which had not merely its ceiling panelled with gold, but also its walls wholly covered with gilded plates." Also, Livy *Per.* 41, in which the building is paired with the great sanctuary of Zeus Olympios in Athens, one of the other great accomplishments of Antiochus IV Epiphanes: "Apart from his piety, because of which he built many grand temples in many places – at Athens, the temple of Jupiter Olympius, and at Antioch, that of Jupiter Capitolinus – he played a very tawdry role as king." On Malalas assigning the construction of a temple dedicated to Jupiter Capitolinus at a further point in time under the mandate of Tiberius see Saliou 2012, 30.

138 For the description of the two vaulted tunnels, see *Antioch V*, 101–118.

139 Vitr. *De arch* 7.15. For the graffiti, see *Antioch II*, 90. The excavation in object is that of sector 17-Q, where presumably the aqueduct changed its direction.

140 On the sanctuary of Minos: Lib. *Or.* 11.125. The sanctuary of Demeter: Lib. *Or.* 11.124–127; Lib. *Or.* 15.79; Julian *Mis.*15, 346. An elusive *Eleusinion*, mentioned in Lib. *Ep.* 1221F.2, should also brought into focus; whether it was related, and in what way, to the sanctuary of Demeter is a matter of guesswork. The sources are vague when it comes to the sanctuary of Heracles: while Libanius assigns it to the Hellenistic period, see *Or.* 11.125, Malalas mentions the site only inasmuch as it was razed by the earthquake of 39 CE that struck many cities of Asia, see *Malalas* 10.23.

141 Müller 1839, 56. See, however, the traces of the road's pre-Roman pavement in sector 16-P, *Antioch V*, 62; 143. Other sectors of the 1930s so-called Street digs yielded traces of the Hellenistic layers: among these are 16-O, 17-N, and 19-M. The limited extent of these operations and their complicated stratigraphy hinders the collating of this data, as Jean Lassus recognized.

142 *Downey, History* 107.

143 Lib. *Or.* 11.143. On the Isaurians and their history, see Shaw 1990.

144 Saliou 2000.

145 1 Macc. 1.11–15 where it is mentioned the construction of a stadium. 2 Macc. 4.9 on the enrolling of people of Jerusalem as citizens of Antioch and the establishment of a gymnasium.

146 The literature on the theme is vast. Among the ancient sources are: 2 Macc. 6–7; 4 Macc. 5–18; St. Jerome *De situ et nomin. Hebraic.*, *PL* 23.958; St. Aug. *Sermo* 300.6=*PL* 23.958; *John of Nikiu* 62; Anonymous "Descrizione Araba"160. Veneration of the Maccabees at Antioch is alluded by John Chrysostom in *De ss. Martyrbus* (PG 50–645–47). The account of Augustine, in particular, has led to the belief of Antioch as the place of martyrdom and altogether seat of the cult. For a recent discussion of the sources, their traditions, and the downright dismissal of a synagogue that accommodated the relics of the Maccabees in Antioch, as well as its Christian reincarnation, see Triebel 2005.

147 *Malalas* 8.22. See *Antioch I*, 83–84. His inspection of the monument yielded no trace of a shrine and led to inferring that the "colossal bust was never finished." Pamir 2017

offers a new reading of the sculpture's significance, suggesting that it may showcase a symbolic synthesis between the mother goddess and Charon, the mythical ferryman.
148 2 Macc. 9.5–9 on the death of the king. On the king and his intrusion in Jewish affairs, see *Malalas* 8.23.
149 Joseph. *AJ.* 13.35–36.
150 Houghton et al. 2008, 133.
151 Windham 2005, 278.
152 Chrubasik 2016, 129.
153 1 Macc. 10.48–50. Joseph. *AJ.* 13.59–61.
154 Cohen 2006, 82.
155 Joseph. *AJ.* 13.116; Diod. Sic. 32.9d, 10.1.
156 Houghton et al. 2008, 280.
157 1 Macc. 11.43–51.
158 Joseph. *AJ.* 13.137.
159 Chrubasik 2016, 136.
160 *Downey, History* 124.
161 Joseph. *AJ.* 13.218; Livy *Per.* 55.137.
162 Diod. Sic. 33.28a.
163 Windham 2005, 280.
164 Strab. 16.2.10.
165 App. *Syr.* 68. Houghton et al. 2008, 350, 363.
166 Diod. Sic. 34.17.
167 The impasse of the Antioch mint at this time is particularly telling, for no bronze emissions are recorded for Demetrius's second stint in Antioch; see Houghton et al. 2008, 418.
168 Diod. Sic. 34.28; Just. *Epit.* 39.2.5–6; Joseph. *AJ.* 13.269.
169 Windham 2005, 280.
170 Hoover 2007, 280.
171 Just. *Epit.* 39.2.7–9; App. *Syr.* 69.
172 The Antioch issue may date to 122–121 BCE: Houghton et al. 2008, 474; see also Metcalf 2000, 106.
173 Hoover 2007, 284–288.
174 *Downey, History* 130.
175 *Malalas* 10.9. The entity of Antiochus's repairs or intervention cannot be inferred from Malalas's text. See Downey 1961, 84. The king allegedly drowned in the Orontes; see Joseph. *AJ.* 13.369.
176 Hoover 2007, 280.
177 Just. *Epit.* 40.2.1.
178 *McAlee, Coins* 7.
179 Just. *Epit.* 40.2.1: "But although Syria was safe from its enemies, it was laid waste by an earthquake, in which 170 000 men died and many cities were destroyed. The soothsayers read this portent as auguring a change in affairs."
180 Ambraseys 2009, 96.
181 *Downey, History* 140.
182 *Antioch I*, 83–84.
183 Saliou 2009–2010.
184 De Giorgi 2015.
185 Müller 1839.
186 *Antioch III*, 33–54. Of relevance are also the houses that were discovered at the end of the campaign, namely the House of Cilicia and the House of the Drinking Contest, *Antioch III*, 32. See also the 3D reconstruction of the church in Kondoleon 2000.
187 Uggeri 2006, 155.
188 Menegazzi 2012.
189 Brands and Pamir 2007; 2008; 2009.

190 Brands 2016a, Figure 2.
191 Stahl 2017. The ongoing analysis of sector 17-O of the excavations, along with samples of ceramics from other soundings, corroborate the picture of the city's nucleation on the northern swath of what became Antioch in the Roman and successive periods.
192 Hoepfner 1999–2004.
193 Saliou 2006. See the many references to the survival of the classical city in Chapters 6, 8, and 10.

2

ORIENTIS APEX PULCHER

The Roman "Beautiful Crown of the East" in the making (64 BCE–192 CE)

> While the emperor was tarrying in Antioch a terrible earthquake occurred; many cities suffered injury, but Antioch was the most unfortunate of all. Since Trajan was passing the winter there and many soldiers and many civilians had flocked thither from all sides in connexion with law-suits, embassies, business or sightseeing, there was no nation or people that went unscathed; and thus in Antioch the whole world under Roman sway suffered disaster.
>
> – Cassius Dio, *Roman History*, 68.24

Introduction

Here we will examine the Roman period of Antioch between the city's establishment as capital of the province of Syria in BCE 64 to the end of the second century CE, a yardstick traditionally demarcating the phase of the Early Roman Empire (Figure 2.1). More to the point, we aim to highlight the city's transition from liminal provincial capital to the main military and commercial hub of the Eastern empire. Cassius Dio's account of the 115 CE earthquake is meaningful at two levels: one, it shows the city's endemic susceptibility to earthquakes and their cascade of consequences (geological, structural, and humanitarian),[1] and two, it makes known the cosmopolitan character of Antioch's population and, to a further degree, the city's integration within the realities of the Roman Empire. How these catastrophic events reverberated both in the city and in centers of power will be a recurring theme in this and the following chapters on Late Antique and Byzantine Antioch.

We also bring into sharper focus here the relentless construction of Antioch and the city's complicated catalog of buildings. The pounding of hammers, rasping of saws, and hauling of stones identified a typical day in imperial Antioch. How the built environment changed and new buildings contributed a new presentation of the old remains the focus of inquiry. The truth is that few of these monuments have

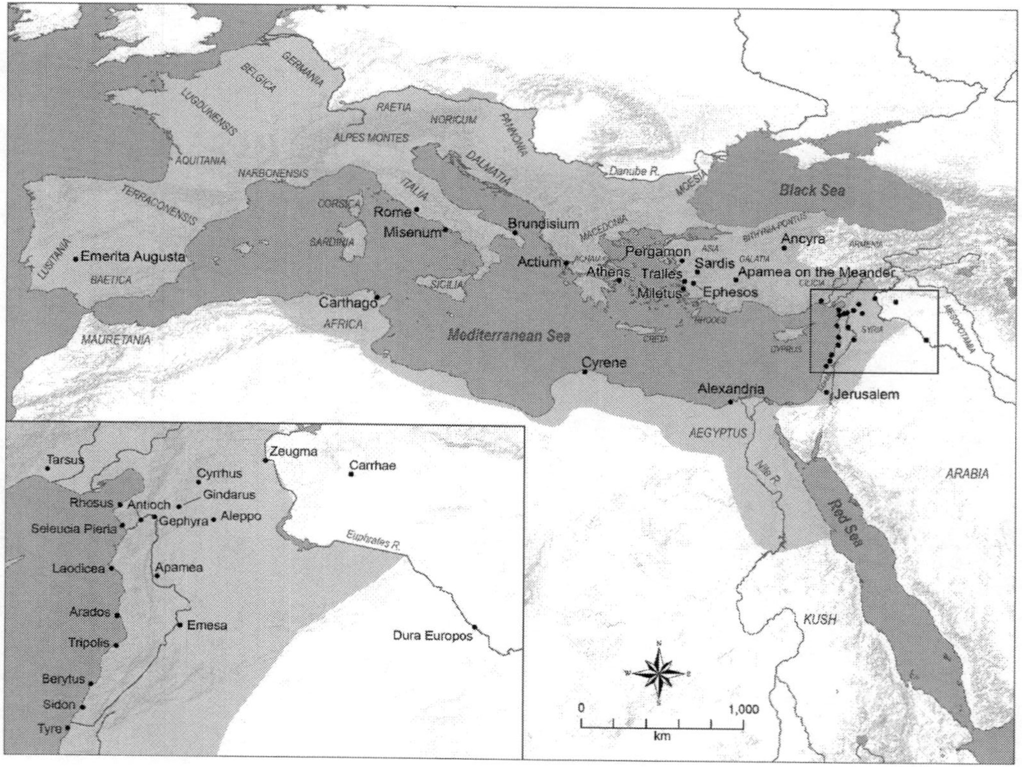

FIGURE 2.1 Antioch and the Early Roman Empire

Source: Created by Claire Ebert

been excavated or identified on the ground. The gulf between the city's materiality as excavated and its ancient descriptions could not be wider. Only do occasional glimpses afford insights into a topography that, still grounded in its Seleucid layout, had to negotiate the ambition and physical expansion of the provincial capital.

The days of Pompey and Roman administration in Antioch

Roman Antioch and its materiality are difficult to pin down; although as early as the Late Roman Republic in 64 BCE it gained back its political centrality as capital of the province of Syria, nonetheless, the city remains poorly documented by both literary sources and the archaeological record.[2] By and large, the historians of Rome decried the evils originating on the banks of the Orontes and spreading throughout the Roman universe; at best, Antioch, in tandem with Daphne, was perceived as the place where entertainment and festivals were paramount; hence the depiction of a city with a bent for luxury and debauchery.[3] As for the city's material record, of the many trappings aligning Antioch with most Greco-Roman cities, only a few heavily weathered remains illustrate the extensive building programs that shaped the urban fabric. Among these are stretches of the Hadrianic waterworks, short segments of walls in the lower city, and a good deal of the original perimeter of defenses, albeit greatly repaired and reconfigured during the course of Antioch's life. At the same time, however, new research on Roman Antioch has harnessed the scanty evidence available to put forth new interpretative frameworks.

The Roman general Pompey (106–48 BCE) arrived in Antioch in the spring of 64 BCE, following his military activities against the pirates of Cilicia. Officially about to embark on an expedition against the Nabatean king Aretas III (87–62 BCE), he seized the opportunity to easily overthrow the last of the Seleucid kings, Antiochus XIII Asiaticus (69–64 BCE), who still ruled despite the destabilization of his comatose kingdom. Pompey thereby annexed Syria to Rome.[4] The Roman historian Justin believed that Pompey's intervention was aimed at eliminating the depredations of the Jews and Arabs.[5] While this may well have been part of his agenda, it was not the only goal; the occasion at hand, personal ambition, economic opportunities, and Syria's prestige are but some of the many factors accounting for the climax of military operations in the region.[6] The turn of events was also not random; Pompey had carefully mapped out a strategy from the beginning of hostilities against Mithridates VI, king of Pontus and one of Rome's most formidable enemies. Syria was the natural extension of Cilicia, and indeed, Pompey's intervention was foreshadowed by the presence of Roman *negotiatores*, businessmen and entrepreneurs alike, in the region since the early first century BCE. This was in tandem with the 67 BCE visit to Antioch of Quintus Marcius Rex, proconsul of Cilicia, who may have disbursed funds for construction of the palace and an adjacent circus, also referred to as "Hippodrome A" (Figure 2.2).[7]

The 1930s archaeological investigations on the Island explored the layout and foundations of the 510 × 75 m circus in sectors 7/8/9-N.[8] Presumably, the emperor

FIGURE 2.2 The Roman circus: concrete core of stairway 4

Source: Photograph by Andrea U. De Giorgi

Justinian had already stripped down the building in the sixth century in completing new fortifications, so little testimony remained of the 80,000 seating arena that had identified centuries of spectacles in Antioch. Nevertheless, it appeared to the excavators that a substantial first-century CE layer predated the later monumental fourth-century CE phase. That the former potentially replicated the building commissioned by Q. Marcius Rex in the late first century BCE is a likely possibility.[9] The excavators cleared debris and dug trenches so as to expose the wall between the arena and seats, three main access gates (*carceres*), and parts of the eastern seating area (*cavea*), as well as the system of two rows of rectangular bays, ambulatories, and piers supporting the tiers of seats. The excavations showed that the hippodrome had a continuous *spina* (the concrete median at the arena's center around which the chariots raced) of rubble concrete with a drain on each side, while the goal posts (*metae*) had large, semicircular foundations.[10] West of the circus was presumably the imperial palace and its Hellenistic predecessor, although no structure could be safely assigned to it.[11] East of the arena were found the austere, rubble-core foundations of a temple showcasing a unique T-shaped articulation in the cella that had already been stripped of its superstructure and revetment in antiquity. It boasted an impressive 78 × 45 m podium; a third-century CE chronology is predicated on structural similarities with the imposing Donuktaş Temple in Tarsus. Similarly, it may have been dedicated to the cult of the emperor, a trend that greatly pervaded the cities of Asia and the Greek East in the second and third centuries CE.[12] In

FIGURE 2.3 Aerial view of the circus and temple complex on the Island

Source: Courtesy of the Antioch Expedition Archives, Department of Art and Archaeology, Princeton University; Princeton

its fourth-century configuration (Figure 2.3), the temple was likely connected by walls and water conduits to the hippodrome, thus adhering to a template well-documented elsewhere in the empire. Suffice to say here that the 1930s excavations failed to bring these monuments together and firmly establish the earliest phase of the Island's monumentalization.

But let us return to the momentous days of the province's establishment. The Roman Senate knew well what Syria could offer, and Pompey acted accordingly.[13] His settlement, though, did not significantly alter the status quo. Making no attempt to revive the centralized administration of the Seleucids, neither did Pompey divide Syria into city-states, as he had done previously in Pontus. The province was too vast and was safer to control through local dynasts rather than expecting free cities to administer the various ethnic groups present in the region.[14] The first political measures enacted by Pompey and recorded in Antioch prescribed a change of calendar from Seleucid to Pompeian, a system that reckoned retrospectively from its starting unit in the autumn of 66 BCE, namely, the defeat of Tigranes the Great, king of Armenia. Administratively, Pompey entrusted the province's command to *praetors* who held the appointment for two years[15] and whose main duty was to defend the newly acquired territory from the continuous threat of large groups of nomadic Arabs. L. Marcius Philippus was the first *de facto* governor of the province. As for its status, Antioch itself remained a *civitas libera*: independent and self-governed, though still liable to pay taxes.

After 55 BCE, the province's command was theoretically bestowed on officials of consular rank because of the heavy military implications the appointment carried.[16] No sooner had the provincial infrastructure adjusted to this new arena than the fiscal machinery in Antioch was in full swing.[17] The proconsul Aulus Gabinius's decision to divest the *publicani* (revenue agents) of their right to collect taxes,[18] both for his own gain and for the relief of the local population, suggests that revenues were levied shortly after Syria's establishment as a province. Far from being driven by altruism, however, Gabinius operated under the assumption that the *publicani* contributed to the dispersion of the already-vexed finances of the Syrian communities. Therefore, not only did he severely curtail their sphere of influence in both legal and civic matters,[19] but he also canceled contracts between Roman farmers and local administrations. This is a procedure Pompey had enacted in Pontus, where territories were ultimately assigned to cities instead of being handed over to *publicani*.[20]

How taxes were extracted, however, and how the folks in Antioch, and Syria at large, responded to Roman law and order is hard to tell. Ultimately, the crux of the problem is how the Roman administrative apparatus worked in Antioch and in the hinterlands of the city, where a dense rural settlement grew in tandem with the capital city. We can, though, safely infer that Pompey employed the Seleucid system and its channels to make Syria a stipendiary province, following the example of Asia.[21] By this rationale, Antioch and the Syrian cities in all likelihood resorted to civic *pactiones*, that is, special agreements to collect revenues from their territories, thus reporting solely to the proconsul and legally preventing the *publicani* and their companies from performing their usual, coercive collecting activities. We can also assume that Antioch retained the ability to administer its territory and possibly to allot *ager publicus*, that is, public land, in the way the community saw fit, thus bypassing Roman interests. On these enactments, however, ancient historians offer divergent perspectives. Cicero minced no words when he rebuked both Gabinius and Pompey for the measures they adopted, allegedly detrimental to the Roman people.[22] Josephus, conversely, praised the governor and his populist actions, that is, the overall fair treatment of the Syrian and Jewish communities, though he tangentially referred to the illegality of Gabinius's personal fortunes.[23] A silver tetradrachm in the name of Gabinius, albeit essentially replicating types of Philip II Philadelphus (a client king under Pompey in 88–83 BCE) on the obverse and Zeus enthroned on the reverse, with the monogram of the Roman governor, was minted in Antioch at this time.[24]

As prescribed by Pompey's *libertas* grant, in the second half of the first century BCE Antioch enjoyed the status of a free city,[25] which, at the very least, enabled the community to retain its own political constitution, eschew Roman garrisoning, be exempt from paying certain taxes, and, more subtly, create a base of local officials who would assume accountability for collecting taxes and fees, thus acting as brokers for the Roman state. It is difficult to tell whether the Antiochenes bribed Pompey to attain that status, as some sources contend.[26] Be this as it may, "freedom" carried benefits like the rebuilding of the *bouleterion* (council chamber, presumably that in Epiphaneia), some economic exemptions, as well as prestige;[27] also, tax liability could not be challenged. But the changes in Antioch occurred not only at the strictly administrative level. The increasing presence of *negotiatores* in the city[28] and a new series of bronze coin issues continuing the iconography of Seleucid rulers signaled a community slowly recuperating its economic strength and tapping into new streams of commerce and trade.[29] The so-called "municipal coinage" of Antioch spanning the first century BCE and the first three centuries CE and bearing the ethnic – that is, the Metropolis of the Antiochenes – in tandem with the names of kings, emperors, and the Roman senate,[30] gained momentum at this very time.

Two factors may account for the likely economic growth the region witnessed at the end of the first century BCE and present in the archaeological record especially through evidence of active minting and the undertaking of building programs. First, it is likely the city offered incentives and encouraged settlement and cultivation of the *ager publicus* in the hinterlands. In doing so, the city operated under a sensible strategy: if a fixed tax quota had to be met and handed over to the Romans, it had to enlarge the taxpayer base. Markets and new allocations of land in Antioch's territory were thus appropriate means of increasing the city's internal revenues and of meeting the hefty cost of Roman taxes. Second, this period also witnessed the introduction of the Roman army, which shaped the community in fundamental ways. The magnitude of military operations, which brought at least seven legions to Syria by the end of the century, had strong economic and social impacts on the Antiochene district, as well as complex ramifications for the relationship between locals and the Romans.[31] Here suffice it to say that the presence of the legions fostered economic benefits because it was accompanied by considerable purchasing power and so fueled the monetization of Antioch's economy. Starting in 63 BCE, Antioch was the locus of the continuous deployment of legions, which increased in 53 BCE prior to the Parthian expedition of the Roman general and politician Marcus Crassus, as well as between 51 and 43, when troops were likely stationed in the metropolis.[32] But deploying military contingents on such a scale also required a reliable and efficient communication network. In particular, operations in the province's southern sector and the transfer of troops to the Euphrates district demanded ease of movement from Antioch, where some cohorts as well as headquarters were seemingly situated. The existence of a military camp in the environs of the city, however, is still a major question. The swath of land north of the island, across the river, may have accommodated the infrastructure of the Roman military, as allusions in the textual record suggest.[33]

In all likelihood, by the end of the first century BCE, Antioch was effectively connected with the rest of Syria and into Lebanon through an efficient network of roads. At this time, the Seleucid routes were probably paved, and new arteries, like the road to Aleppo-Beroea, were likely built (Figure 2.4).

FIGURE 2.4 The Roman Road that connected Antioch to Aleppo, near Tell Abiqrin, Syria

Source: Photograph by Andrea U. De Giorgi

Through these endeavors, not only did the Romans create a system that facilitated movement of troops, supplies, and commerce, but they also stimulated settlement in areas lying athwart these arteries. The plain of Antioch in the Amuq Valley was no exception. The town of Gephyra (modern Demir Köprü) (Figure 2.5), for instance, probably developed around the bridge over the Orontes at that very time, becoming a nodal point from which various routes east and south branched off.

Much of the military mobilization, predicated on this network of roads (Figure 2.6), was motivated by the region's political volatility. Vast regions of Antioch's surrounding plateaus were inhabited by groups of nomadic Arabs, referred to as "nomads" and "bandits" by the sources.[34] Although the precise extent of the territories they settled is not exactly known, some groups reached and inhabited the Orontes Valley beginning in the early Hellenistic period and were involved in the struggle for control of the Seleucid kingdom in the early 60s BCE.[35] The example of Gindaros, located in the Afrin Valley between Antioch and Cyrrhus[36] and governed by an Arab confederation, suggests that these *ethne* were a significant component of the Syrian landscape.

Nor were these communities sedentary, according to the sources; Strabo reinforces this notion when he calls them a people of *skenitai*, that is, tent-dwellers.[37] It is also evident from his text that these tribal entities had their own political structure; *phylarcs* and *tetrarchs* retained supreme authority, which they extended to conquered cities and territories.[38] Of course, the term "tribe" is misleading, as we

FIGURE 2.5 Ancient Gephyra (modern Demir Köprü): the Roman/Ottoman bridge

Source: Photograph by Andrea U. De Giorgi

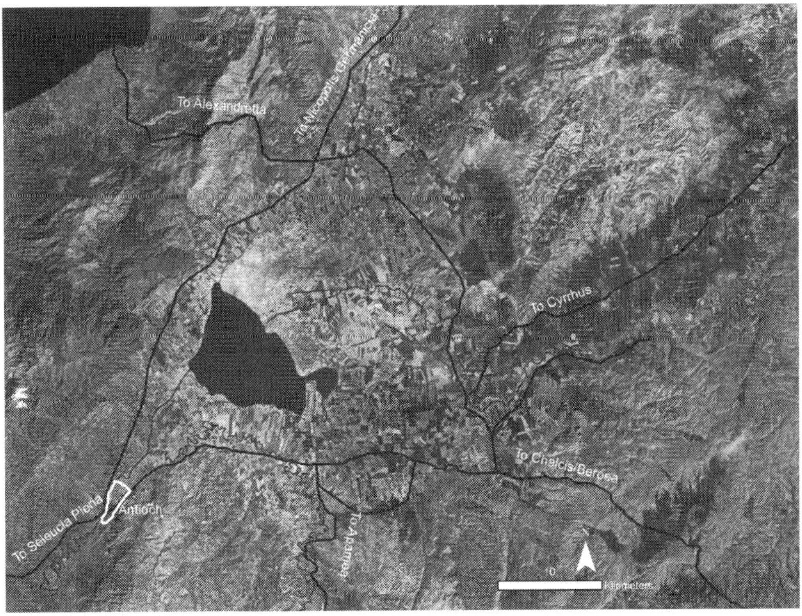

FIGURE 2.6 Roman roads in the territory of Antioch

Source: Created by Andrea U. De Giorgi

are dealing with ethnically defined groups administered by magistracies and owning land. The impact of the Roman institutional machinery on these communities remains to be determined. That they were involved in the political reconfiguration of the region is a matter of record. Strabo makes plain that the kingdom of Emesa supplied troops to Quintus Caecilius Bassus, a Pompeian officer who sought to arm the resistance against Julius Caesar.[39] All the same, the unsung military operations waged against these polities are the first tangible sign of a Roman hand on the Orontes Valley and the whole of Syria during the last decades of the first century BCE.[40] The outcome of these activities was positive for the Romans in that the pressure pushed some of these tribes to the south. The Romans thus plausibly succeeded in pacifying the northern Orontes district and the region of Antioch.[41] By the time of Augustus (27 BCE–14 CE), the entire northern district of Syria had been presumably subjugated, while the southern sectors still had to reckon with groups like the Ituraeans and Nabateans, who represented a continuous threat to the region's stability.[42] In any event, after 12 BCE, the year of the last revolt in the Trachonitis region, we hear no more of rebellions or guerilla activities waged by the Arabs in southern Syria (Figure 2.7).

After Rome's catastrophe under Crassus at Carrhae (modern Harran) in 53 BCE, the Parthian siege of Antioch in 51 BCE,[43] and the brief Persian occupation of the city in 40–39 BCE, no single invasion or threat destabilized Syria or the district of Antioch until the attack of the Sasanian ruler Shāpūr I in 256 CE.[44] Peace indeed offered grounds for a new era; it is not only rhetoric to infer that the *Pax Romana* carried benefits.[45] Cities like those of the Tetrapolis – that is, Antioch, Seleucia Pieria, Apamea, and Laodicea – were given the opportunity to govern themselves and administer their own territory[46] and were seemingly spared the deprivations experienced by many other communities under the civil war between Pompey and Caesar.[47] Moreover, the territory of Antioch was apparently exempt from settlement by veteran soldiers or the redistribution of land.

Libertas: Antioch under Julius Caesar

The ills of the civil war, however, reverberated greatly in Antioch, with the city allegedly siding with Caesar against Pompey; according to Caesar's own account:

> There [in Cyprus] he learned that the people of Antioch and all of the Roman citizens in business there had by common consent seized the citadel in order to keep him out, and had sent word to the Pompeians who, people said, had gone to nearby communities after their escape: "Do not come to Antioch. If you do, your lives will be in great danger."[48]

Nonetheless, Caesar made no delay in declaring Antioch's status as capital and a "free city" when he visited the city the year following his defeat of Pompey in 48 BCE.[49] According to Malalas, Caesar confirmed Antioch's autonomy in an edict in which he referred to the city as a "metropolis, sacred, inviolable, autonomous,

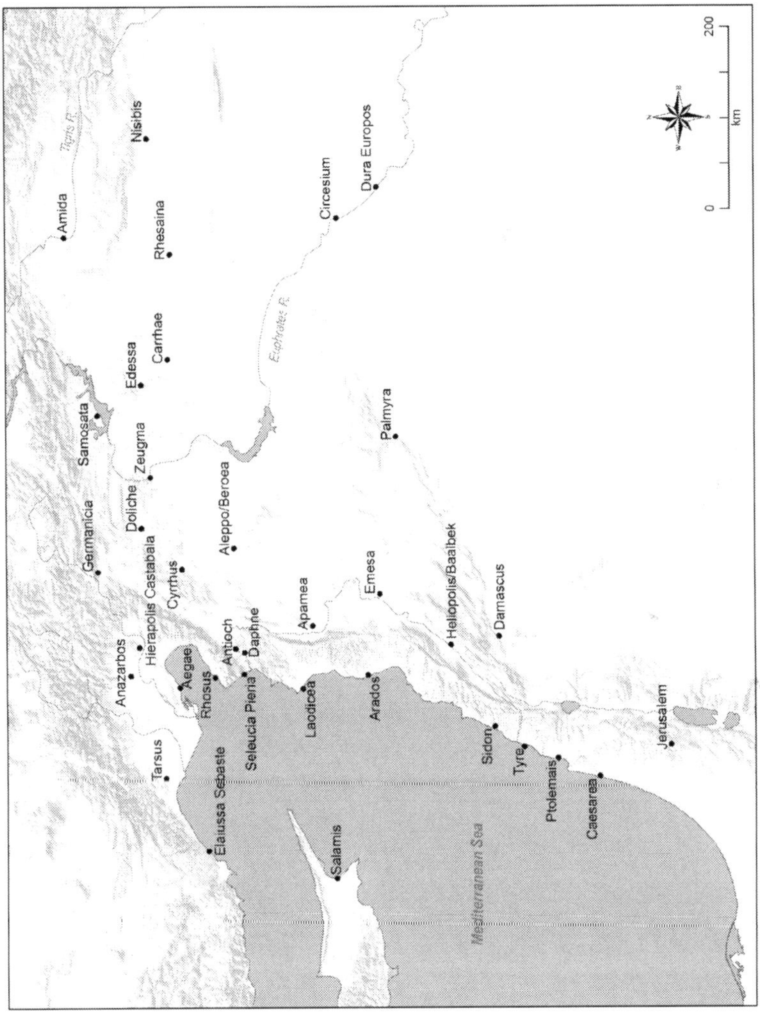

FIGURE 2.7 The cities of Roman Syria

Source: Created by Claire Ebert

sovereign and capital of the East."[50] At this time the city, in addition to adopting the Caesarian system of reckoning time,[51] received the first organic building program of a Roman general in consequence of its political stature, and, presumably, demographic growth.[52] Isolated acts of munificence such as those of Quintus Marcius Rex and Pompey were surpassed by a wide-embracing construction plan reminiscent of Caesar's building projects in Rome, grounded as it was in utilitarian and institutional ends, as well as with much attention to entertainment. John Malalas offers the catalog of works under the auspices of Caesar. While it is difficult to infer whether some of these projects consisted of repairs of previous buildings, he mentions a bath on the acropolis supplied by an aqueduct that presumably tapped into a source near the Laodicea road, independent of the Daphne line of water supply. In particular, the construction of the *Kaisarion* (a basilica) in front of the Temple of Ares, with the statue of the Tyche of Rome, a theater, a *Monomacheion* (an amphitheater for gladiatorial combats later transformed by Valens into the *Kynegion*), aqueducts, and repairs of an altar dedicated to the ancestral gods were the main feats of the Caesarian plan for Antioch. Although none of these survives (excepting the possible identification of the theater in 1934), either dismantled by successive projects like the Forum of Valens or simply decayed with time, they arguably added a new Roman veneer to the fabric of the former Seleucid capital.[53]

Under Caesar, Antioch retained both the ability to administer its territory and to collect dues from the communities settled in the hinterlands. Improved living conditions, demographic growth, a slowly recovering economy, the introduction of public amenities, and, most of all, a fertile territory made Antioch and its territory a pole of attraction. The gradual increase of settlement in the districts surrounding the city during the last decades of the first century BCE can indeed be understood in these terms.[54] But there is more to the situation. It may be that Roman legislation played a decisive role by stimulating, in various forms, the farming of new land. The enactment of the *Lex Agraria* in 58 BCE relied heavily on revenues coming from Pontus and Syria.[55] Considering that the entire southern sector of the latter province was still hostile, only a few communities within the Euphrates and Orontes basins could meet tax demands and feed the state coffers. Cities like Apamea and Antioch were conceivably at the forefront of this program, and to offset the fiscal burden, it is possible they offered incentives to settlers and parcels of *ager publicus* for tax-farming.

Caesar's death in 44 BCE of course shook the Roman world, and Antioch was not spared from being drawn into the frenzy of events following his murder. The arrival of Gaius Cassius, one of the chief assassins, in that same year led to a state of anxiety, for he confiscated properties belonging to the local Jews, won the favor of the military, and kept at a distance Cornelius Dolabella, the appointed governor, who sought in vain to enter Antioch with his modest forces.[56] Only after the battle of Philippi and defeat of Cassius and fellow-conspirator Brutus in 42 BCE did Marc Antony restore order and return Jewish assets to their rightful owners.[57] During his short tenure, Antony may have stripped the city of some of its prerogatives of independence and inviolability. Moreover, his departure from Antioch led to the

FIGURE 2.8 The tetradrachm of Cleopatra and Mark Antony, c. 36 BCE. Obverse: Diademed, draped bust of Cleopatra: ΒΑΣΙΛΙΣΣΑ ΚΛΕΟΠΑΤΡΑ ΘΕΑ ΝΕΩΤΕΡΑ. Reverse: bust of Antony facing right, border of dots: ΑΝΤΩΝΙΟΣ ΑΥΤΟΚΡΑΤΩΡ ΤΡΙΤΟΝ ΤΡΙΩΝ ΑΝΔΡΩΝ

Source: Courtesy of Coin Archives

Parthian invasion and short-lived occupation of the city by the Persian Pacorus, who apparently received the favor of the poulation.[58] Antony's return in 39 BCE led to freeing Antioch and the settling of local crises in Commagene (a small kingdom in eastern Syria) and Judea, with a view toward preparing a campaign against the Parthians. In addition, his marriage with Cleopatra VII led to a new arrangement of the East, along with a reconfiguration of client kingdoms and web of alliances. The dynastic coinage issued by the Roman governors and virtually replicating the iconography of the Seleucid Philip II Philoromaeus was interrupted between 37 and 31 BCE, when the Antioch mint presumably issued the silver tetradrachms of Antony and Cleopatra (Figure 2.8).[59]

In the following year Antioch became the headquarters of Antony's ill-conceived military campaign against the Parthians. As the tension in Rome between Octavian (the future Augustus) and Antony soared, however, Antioch presumably aligned itself with the latter, as indicated by the arrival of a party of gladiators willing to serve against Octavian.[60] The Battle of Actium of 31 BCE, however, determined who the sole leader of the Roman world would be, and Antony's death in the following year sanctioned the beginning of the Augustan phase for the Greek East and Antioch.

Imperial Antioch

Halfway through the process of pacification, Syria became an imperial province and was thus to be governed by a *legatus* instead of a proconsul.[61] The territory still consisted of a patchwork of kingdoms, cities, and *ethne* that Rome strove to coalesce into a single unit, and where internal strife still loomed large. It was clear to Augustus that a geographically undefined province comprising the whole of the Roman Levant and extending all the way to Egypt's borders was both politically and administratively unwieldy.[62] But under him, the political configuration of the Antiochene district remained unchanged, and the privileged status of the metropolis was once again recognized. Antioch thus retained its administrative apparatus consisting of the *boule*, or council, and *demos*, or people. This political orientation appears in a public letter sent by Augustus from Ephesus around 36/34 BCE to the small, loyal community of Rhosus, a few miles west of Antioch on the Syrian coast, which granted citizenship to the *navarkos* (fleet admiral) Seleucus and extended benefits to the community.[63] From the Capitol in Rome the document was copied in Tarsus, Seleucia, and Antioch, thus making known the networks and mechanisms with which Augustus was to build alliances in the East.

Nor did the military connotation of Syria change – hence the province's attribution to "Caesar" rather than to the "People of Rome."[64] According to the historian Tacitus, four legions were stationed in the region under the Julio-Claudians.[65] The region's heavy militarization, however, had important effects on the economic outlook of the Antiochene district and Syria as a whole.[66] The supply system was notably affected in that much of the tax revenue presumably stayed in the province and was recycled as army pay. Local economies like that of Antioch drew enormous advantages by supplying the legions. Evidence that military officials in both Western and Eastern legions were assigned to this type of commercial transactions with the local communities reinforces our hypothesis.[67] It follows that the economy's monetization found ideal ground and, as a result, the mint of Antioch started producing coins of various denominations at an industrial rate; the silver tetradrachm with the portrait of Augustus on the obverse and the Tyche on the reverse offers an exquisite fusion of both imperial authority and local identity.[68] More fundamentally, though, as Roman rule was gaining more momentum in the region, imperial bronze issues with the *SC* iconography (*senatus consulto*), radiating from Antioch, began to circulate widely, thus supplementing traditional silver tetradrachm currency. The new type foregrounded the iconography of the emperor and effectively communicated the new realities of power, while subtly seeking to enforce a sense of loyalty.[69] As Kevin Butcher has shown, however, Syrian cities on the coast seem to have been recalcitrant in minting this new currency, at least until the later years of Augustus' reign. The adherence to Roman values was clearly a nonhomogeneous phenomenon, at least in the province of Syria.

Religious implications were not foreign to this new monetary state of affairs. *SC* coins issued under the governorship of Varus in 5 BCE also celebrated Augustus as *archiereus*, high priest, thus advertising the cult of the emperor and the pervasiveness of his divine persona.[70] But more mundane matters fueled the functioning of the Antioch mint. We can infer that the substantial striking of Augustan bronze and silver tetradrachms in the year 5 BCE must be linked to the movements of the legions in response to potential threats from Armenia and Parthia.[71] Some of the issues revived the iconography of the Tyche, last adopted by the Armenian occupants under Tigranes II in 83 BCE. More fundamentally, Augustan silver coinage circulated far and wide within Syria, and countermarks featuring the names of the legions *Legio III Gallica*, *VI Ferrata*, *X Fretensis*, *XII Fulminata*, and *XV Apollinaris* reinforce the military motivation behind this series. This synchrony between minting activity and the presence of legions in Antioch had important effects on the district's economic configuration. Although the legions' purchasing power clearly improved monetization of the local economy, we must also assume that the army's presence often demanded irregular exactions in kind, essentially the provision of free supplies or at a fixed cost.[72] Nevertheless, it also had some positive effects: for instance, large-scale acquisitions of grain to supply the Roman troops benefited local economies.[73]

The census in 6 CE was a turning point for life in Antioch and for the province of Syria as a whole.[74] It consisted of a property survey intended to provide a basis for setting the taxes levied on the provincial populations.[75] Some cities and territories in Syria were exempt from Roman taxes, but although it enjoyed privileged status, Antioch was not one of them. In Syria, it was carried out under the supervision of the legate Sulpicius Quirinus.[76] Owing its fame to a mention in the Gospel of St. Luke,[77] the census is also referenced by the famous Berytus (Beirut) inscription at the Archaeological Museum in Venice, which provides information on the population of Apamea, Antioch's former twin-city, as reckoned in the year 7 CE.[78] Importantly, this epitaph provides the only census figures for the Roman world outside of Egypt;[79] the inscription specifically reports the presence of 117,000 inhabitants in Apamea alone. These numbers, however, fail to clarify who the *homines cives* (citizens) were, whether they included women and children, as the juridical definition of *homo* entailed, or if the number pertained to taxpayers only. If so, excluding slaves and foreigners, one reaches figures well beyond 117,000, at least doubling this sum. But this estimate also seems exaggerated for the whole of Apamea's town and countryside. Moreover, what can one make of the numerous Arab confederations settled in the territory of Apamea?[80] The problem is riddled with difficulties, nor do legal sources help much. The Roman jurist Ulpian makes clear that in a Roman census, all Roman subjects in Syria were expected to pay the poll tax, both men and women, provided that males were at least 14 years old, that females were at least 12, and that neither were older than 65. That children were counted in the census was a given.[81] By the same token, the Egyptian census of 47/48 CE listed a number of slaves who were seemingly working for Roman citizens and filing their returns relative to property but not the persons living on it.[82]

Although the subject is a thorny one, what matters here is to underscore the intimate connection between the provincial census and the poll tax. Antioch, based on its urban layout, could at the time boast a population in no way inferior to that of Apamea, at least some 150,000 citizens, excluding slaves and foreigners.[83] Based on the 10 km long perimeter of walls and an overall 1,750–2,100 ha suitable for living, Liebeschuetz estimates a population for fourth-century CE Antioch approximately in the order of 200,000, assuming people did not live in high tenements, unlike elsewhere in the Mediterranean.[84] Things may have not been much different for the early imperial period. Further, if the administration adhered to the ancestral laws, however, only those who owned land could be considered members of the citizen body and thus enjoy all privileges. Ownership of a *kleros* (plot of land) had been the decisive factor in all citizenship disputes under the Seleucids. Because of the land allocation strategies adopted by Antioch following the creation of the province of Syria, we can safely infer that it was in the city's best interest to incorporate the greatest number of citizens possible. This was especially true under Pompey, when a lump sum was due at the end of the year as the provincial tax payment. Whatever the case, both the town and countryside of Antioch shared a common set of obligations by the end of the first century BCE, and the reckoning of a poll tax followed the same procedure. Once implemented, the new tax system fully integrated the province of Syria within the economic system of the empire, thereby creating new financial options for Rome and, apparently, great distress for the populations of Syria and Judea: Tacitus alleges they were vexed by the heaviness of the tribute.[85] How Antioch coped with plausibly increasing demands from the Roman imperial treasury and the provincial administration remains to be established.

But the Augustan age coincided not only with the administrative overhaul of the region: Antioch's materiality in both town and countryside also underwent major transformations, presumably in tandem with Augustus's visits in 31 and 20 BCE.[86] The monumentalization of the Antioch–Alexandretta route undertaken under Augustus attests to the imperial administration's involvement in building a new road infrastructure and channeling traffic with it. Paving a key axis of traffic leading to the Mediterranean, however, was only part of the equation. A triumphal arch in all likelihood spanned the road in the vicinity of the modern village of Beylan,[87] while the subsequent addition of a *ianus* (arcade), a monument of similar configuration, plausibly in those same environs, reminded viewers and passersby of the life and achievements of the great general Germanicus, whose life was cut short in Daphne in 19 CE.[88] Aside from the visual conventions of Julio-Claudian propaganda subtly played out at nodal points of traffic, the urban fabric of Antioch underwent heavy-handed modifications, for Augustus spared no effort in stamping his own mark on it. Mediated by the vision of Marcus Vipsanius Agrippa, the man behind numerous conspicuous building projects in Rome and Athens, the upgrade of the city on the Orontes entailed first of all establishing an enclave, the *Agrippitai*, which in true Seleucid fashion identified its main agent.[89] How the *Agrippitai* development looked and where exactly it was located cannot be established. Nor is its date of foundation firm, though Agrippa is known for having been bestowed with *imperium* (command) in the East between 23 and 21 BCE. The new neighborhood plausibly included the *Agrippeion*, a bath located "near the mountain" that tapped into a local spring for its supply. No physical attestation remains, yet the eclectic bath of Agrippa in the Campus Martius in Rome, with its dedicated water supply system and unique design of ponds and canals, is a gripping example of the level of creativity and engineering dexterity that may have also been employed in Antioch.[90] Second, during the first decade of the first century CE, Herod the Great may have sponsored the paving of Antioch's colonnaded street, an overt act of loyalty and friendship. The project was seemingly brought to completion under Tiberius.[91] Although the 1930s archaeologists successfully intersected the long avenue only in small segments of the main street digs (16-P and 19-M, among others),[92] they nevertheless proposed a tentative history of the evolution of this axis of traffic, from a modest road in the days of Seleucus to its 16-meter wide monumentalization under Antiochus IV Epiphanes.[93] Herod would then have paved it, while Tiberius flanked it with porticoes. The enlargement of the sidewalks from 1.30 to 4.30 m may bear witness to this transformation (Figure 2.9).[94] Thus relentlessly modified, buried, and repaved, Antioch's colonnaded street and porticoes had a life of their own and bear witness to the vicissitudes suffered by the city's built environment during the course of the ages. Again, they are a palimpsest of Antioch's long history, and as such are an essentially textual reality; Libanius's written text, as we will see in the next chapter, helps to conjure their configuration and social ramifications.[95]

As a third fundamental project, Agrippa embarked on clearing of its debris the great stadium on the Island, originally established by Quintus Marcius Rex.[96] The earthquake that struck Syria in the first quarter of the first century BCE and neglect had apparently made the venue unserviceable. That this occurred in synchrony with the establishment of games at this time is a possibility, hence the necessity of better, larger venues. As with the Circus Maximus in Rome, Agrippa was thus

FIGURE 2.9 Sector 16-P, Dig 5: remains of the early Roman street and Hellenistic sidewalk under it

Source: Courtesy of the Antioch Expedition Archives, Department of Art and Archaeology, Princeton University; Princeton

involved in the embellishment of a building that better than anyone would broadcast the new realities of power and, altogether, the high profile of the city on the Orontes.[97] Further, John Malalas reported that an endowment for theatrical and sport games was instituted at this time by Sosibius, an Antiochene senator and personal friend of Augustus.[98] All the same, we are in no position to confirm whether these projects were brought to completion during Augustus's reign. For all his lukewarm propensity at building, Augustus's successor Tiberius (14–37 CE) is nevertheless credited with the city's most outstanding feature, that is, a new perimeter of fortifications that enlarged the original Seleucid perimeter (Figure 2.10).[99]

The autopsy of these famous fortifications, however, has brought to light at least eight different styles of masonry, the chronology of which is fraught with difficulties.[100] Evident modifications in antiquity and significant medieval repairs confound the viewer and compress several centuries of building activities. Moreover, the expansion of a modern quarry now threatens the survival of entire stretches of fortifications. Nevertheless, Christiane Brasse succeeded at mapping almost 3 km of fortifications, in the main of the sixth century CE and Crusader periods, identifying two main systems of walls, "internal" and "external," along with a mesh of lesser walls, especially along the slopes of Mt. Staurin, that seemingly date to the Hellenistic period (Figure 1.9).[101] The internal perimeter is characterized by rather precipitous heights and mighty towers of predominantly late antique construction, as well as the inclusion of the medieval citadel; for these reasons, the treatment of

FIGURE 2.10 A section of the external fortifications of Antioch, possibly dating to the early Roman period

Source: Photograph by Andrea U. De Giorgi

the enceinte will be taken up again by successive chapters. More relevant here is the second enceinte, tentatively assigned to the Early Roman period, with stretches of small mortared limestone blocks superimposed on previous Hellenistic polygonal masonry (Figure 2.11). It is approximately 2.3 Km long and lies some 400m east of

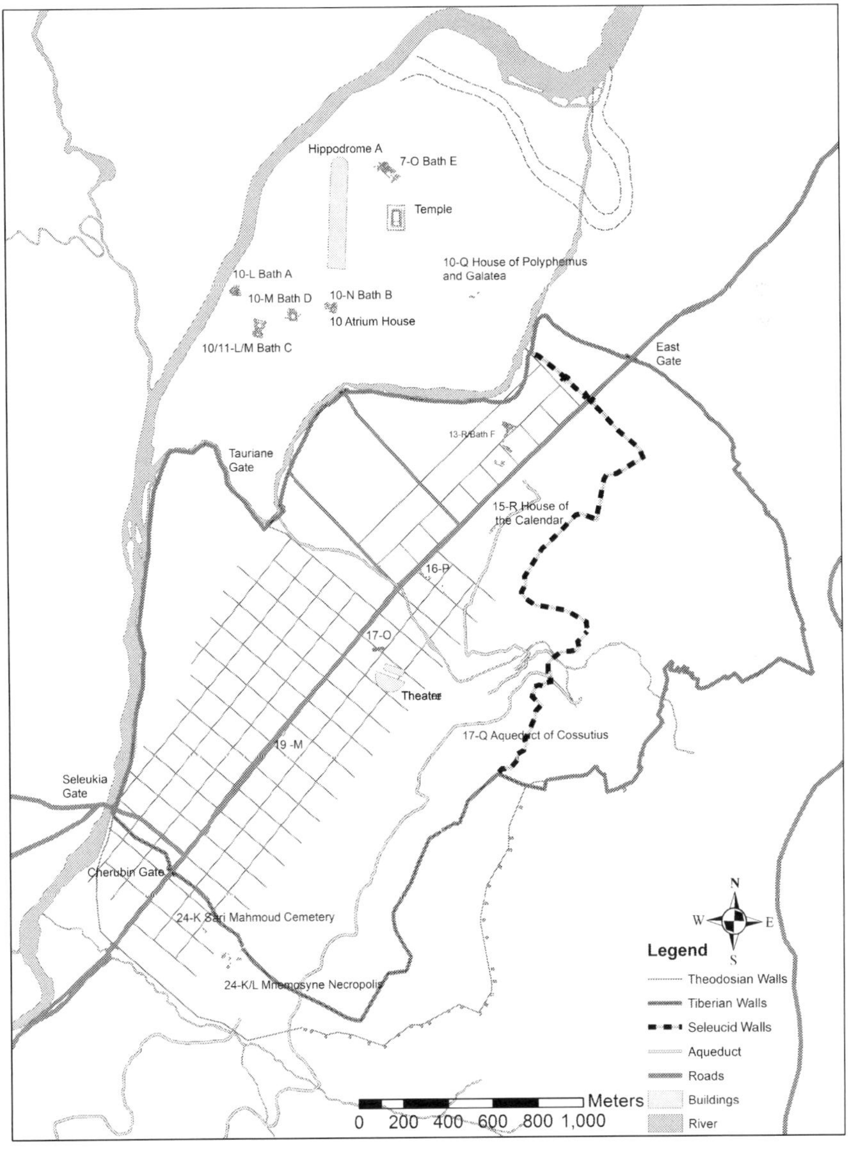

FIGURE 2.11 Roman Antioch

Source: Created by Stephen Batiuk

the internal perimeter, straddling the southern sector of Mt. Staurin, with long sections, especially along the southeastern ridge of the mountain, not well preserved. It should be stressed that this extraordinary enlargement of the enceinte required an enormous output of resources and labor, for the asperities of Mt. Silpius posed paramount challenges to the builders and the hauling of stone. But it also signaled a city raising its confidence, molding its surroundings, while also bolstering its political and military agendas.

As for the general contour of the enceinte, the two main circuits can best be described as starting their course at the southern slope of Mt. Silpius at a point marked by the conspicuous Justinianic hexagonal tower (Tower 1). The wall then heads east against the rugged and steep terrain, then jerks decisively north, where it converges, or splits, between an "internal" and "exterior" wall, with critical chronological implications to be determined. The former continues along the crest of Mt. Silpius for approximately 500 m and then precipitously drops to encroach upon the Iron Gate, which in its earliest phase served as a bridge for one of the aqueducts from Daphne, either of the Julio-Claudian period or of Trajan's.[102] The perimeter then continues north so as to encircle the slopes of Mt. Staurin, then turns west and descends into the city, with a few stretches of extremely weathered sixth-century CE masonry still observable in Antakya. Conversely, the "external" wall, 2.3 km long and encircling the plateau on which Epiphaneia has been tentatively situated, is less well preserved and presents a staggering blend of construction techniques, not least segments of polygonal masonry seemingly harkening back to the heyday of Seleucid Antioch, as seen in the previous chapter. How the Tiberian program of defenses can be extracted from the complexity of the evidence is the question at issue. Further, the southwestern section of the wall as it descended from Mt. Silpius and reached the Orontes is also a matter of guesswork.[103] Nonetheless, it is apparent that the enceinte had to leave the gorge of the Phyrminos stream outside its ramparts, for the torrential regime of the waters may have significantly endangered the stability of the building program (Figure 2.11). To corroborate this point, two partially investigated clusters of tombs at Sarı Mahmud (24-K) and Mnemosyne (24-K and -L), which have yielded traces of first- and second-century CE depositions,[104] make it very likely that the defensive wall ran northwest of them, thus leaving the burial grounds outside the city. At any event, based on the textual record, we can situate an ambitious enlargement of the city walls during the Julio-Claudian dynasty for a community that had hitherto grown considerably.[105] Lastly, it is a truism that these curtains, towers, and their itineraries reflected the priorities, outlooks, and, indeed, routines, of the folks who lived in Antioch. Thanks to a web of trails that traversed Mts. Silpius and Staurin, these highland districts were integrated within the city and created a host of new foci that expanded the community. Fallen vaulting, sections of aqueducts, and ubiquitous traces of architecture on the eastern slopes of Mt. Staurin inform the enlargement of the civic infrastructure that presumably took place around that time. Community like that of Epiphaneia may have attracted new settlement. The city was growing, and the monumental architecture of the walls met the demands of a community that may have witnessed a demographic uptick. Contemporary rural settlement data in the hinterlands and Amuq Valley supports this picture of growth.[106]

Antioch under the Julio-Claudian Dynasty

By the end of Augustus's reign, the city of Antioch had thus added a substantial imperial veneer that did not, however, modify the Hellenistic armature. Rather, the addition of the Augustan building programs coalesced into the Hellenistic fabric. The funeral of the great general Germanicus in 19 CE,[107] who died in Antioch, was perhaps the first staged event that foregrounded the forum (presumably one of the Hellenistic agoras) and plausibly the new colonnaded street, replicating the long tradition of parades that had unfolded on that same avenue. If Malalas is to be believed, Tiberius also added a panoply of temples, old and new, to the city and Daphne: to wit, a new restoration of the temple of Jupiter Capitolinus previously established by Antiochus III; a shrine to Pan on the slopes of Mt. Silpius, presumably in the environs of the theater of Caesar; and, lastly, a temple to Dionysus "near the mountain." In Daphne, the temples of Apollo and Artemis were also repaired.[108] New foci like colonnades, a bath that tapped into the waters of the Olympias spring – where allegedly Alexander the Great had quenched his thirst – and monumental talismans to curb the torrential fury of the Parmenius further contributed to the city's new image.[109]

Whether the project of adding these new landmarks was spurred by the fire of 23 CE is a possibility. Assessing the magnitude of this catastrophe is difficult, and one surmises that Epiphaneia suffered a heavy toll, with the destruction of the *bouleuterion* and the Temple of the Muses, both previously built under Antiochus IV Epiphanes.[110] Navigating the catastrophism of the ancient sources is a complicated task, but the fact is that powerful natural disasters played a major role in shaping the city from this juncture onward. The responses of the community and its stakeholders were central; how sectors of the city were rebuilt by institutional agencies and the population returned to daily activities is a key theme in analyzing this and successive epochs.

Tiberius also renamed the river from "Drakon" to "Orontes" and set up a statue of the she-wolf of Rome's founding myth on one of the eastern gates. How this symbol coalesced or competed with the sculptural landscape previously established by the Seleucid kings needs more investigation. The Antiochenes, too, contributed to an already cluttered urban fabric;[111] lavished as they were with all these building programs, they returned the favor to Tiberius by setting up a statue in his honor.[112]

Tiberius's successor Caligula (37–41 CE) also took up the legacy of commissioning public buildings and baths under the aegis of the imperial family; the scale of the earthquake that befell the city in 37 CE may have encouraged repairs in the city and in Daphne, as well as to the water infrastructure.[113] More importantly, this event, whatever its magnitude, signaled the disaster-relief strategy of the Roman state, with allegedly the dispatching of the senators Pontus and Varius, as well as the governor Salvianus, to assist the city and mobilize funds for reconstruction. From the days of Tiberius, the Roman state had already sought to implement a viable relief-effort strategy, whether through tax remission or concrete resources. Ultimately, the case of Antioch in 37 CE sheds light on the nature of the relationship between the city and Rome, the well-being of the former foregrounded by the apparent rapid intervention of the imperial administrators. The infusion of silver coinage, typically commemorating Germanicus and his wife, Agrippina the Elder, parents of the new emperor, may signal the government's financial efforts.[114]

Whether a byproduct of the cataclysm or because of public demand, under Caligula the city witnessed the construction of an aqueduct tapping waters from Daphne. The archaeological record of Mt. Silpius and Mt. Staurin, however, shows an intricate mesh of tunnels, reservoirs, and channels that cannot be safely assigned either to Caligula's plan or to that of the second-century emperors.[115] In particular, two different distribution systems have been identified on the slopes of Mt. Staurin, consisting mainly of tunnels and small cisterns for decantation.[116] The presence of a nexus of open conduits that presumably impounded water from a source on Mt. Silpius and distributed it across Mt. Staurin is also a possibility. As with the city walls and their complex history of repairs, these features attest to a host of different projects and overhauls spanning the city's life during the entire course of antiquity. That they sought to provide water to the boroughs and baths on the left side of the Orontes is an attractive possibility (Figure 2.11).

Brimming though the city was with prestige and imperial décor, it also began to suffer civil strife and street violence, especially pitted at the local Jewry; in particular, during the third year of Caligula's reign, the emperor ordered that his statue be set up in the Temple in Jerusalem. This enactment, likely promulgated in Antioch by the governor Petronius, spiraled into violent protests by the Jews, and presumably military repression.[117] Furthermore, Malalas reported in the sixth century that confrontations between the two rival factions of the Blues and the Greens at the circus became part of the civic political discourse, although his account seems to conflate the realities of his time with the days of Caligula.[118] Importantly, Glanville Downey points out the role of a small yet very active Christian community[119] – the first in fact to refer to itself as such at this time – as possibly instrumental in the growing religious tensions and widespread political anxieties. Not surprisingly, Caligula's accession marked a number of changes in the region as well as in the nature of the Roman administration. In particular, the period that the new emperor inaugurated was the last for the kingdoms, tetrarchies, and dynasts in the southern sector of the province. Independent territories like those of Commagene and Emesa survived another quarter of century, to be, however, terminated under Vespasian.[120]

The reign of Caligula's successor Claudius (41–54 CE) also reckoned with the consequences of yet another earthquake. In Antioch, the imperial house stipulated tax exemptions for professional guilds in return for repairs to the damaged porticoes of the colonnaded street.[121] Apparently the temples of Artemis, Ares, and Hercules, mentioned earlier, were also damaged, although their location is unknown.[122] Equally taxing on the city were the effects of the famine that spread throughout the Near East between 44 and 47 CE. The nature and duration of the event, as well as its effects on population trends, are, however, hard to fathom. At this juncture, the Christian community of Antioch is reported as having come to the aid of their brothers in Jerusalem.[123] Such an early momentum should not surprise: Antioch was where St. Paul's more inclusive approach to the practice and teaching of Christianity took the upper hand over St. Peter's more restrictive stance, thereby fundamentally severing ties with Judaism and mapping out a universal mission.[124]

Such an early momentum should not surprise, for from the beginning Antioch was a vital center for the new faith, as described in the Acts of the Apostles; indeed, Antioch was the city where Christians first styled themselves as such and where the apostle Paul began his ministry.[125] Here the importance of the Jewish community settling in Antioch becomes manifest, for the spread of Christianity was initially connected to those locations where Jews had already established themselves in earlier centuries. The dialectic between Judaism and Christianity, and not least the crosspollination between the two, offers a fundamental lens for understanding Antioch's early church. By tradition it was the apostle Peter himself who founded the church of Antioch and served as its first bishop. These early events are reported by the New Testament:

> So then those who were scattered because of the persecution that occurred in connection with Stephen made their way to Phoenicia and Cyprus and Antioch, speaking the word to no one except to Jews alone. But there were some of them, men of Cyprus and Cyrene, who came to Antioch and began speaking to the Greeks also, preaching the Lord Jesus. And the hand of the Lord was with them, and a large number who believed turned to the Lord. The news about them reached the ears of the church at Jerusalem, and they sent Barnabas off to Antioch. Then when he arrived and witnessed the grace of God, he rejoiced and began to encourage them all with resolute heart to remain true to the Lord; for he was a good man, and full of the Holy Spirit and of faith. And considerable numbers were brought to the Lord. And he left for Tarsus to look for Saul (Paul); and when he had found him, he brought him to Antioch.[126]

One Nicolas and Stephen also helped established the initial core of the group. Barnabas, a prominent early Christian, and Paul also made converts and taught at length, though the number of members cannot be established.[127] Nor can their activities be firmly situated in space; as Downey notes, houses would have served as places for congregation and celebration of the Eucharist;[128] the example of the church in a domestic context at Dura Europos attests to these practices. Aside from references in the Acts of the Apostles and the Epistles to the preaching of Paul, Barnabas, and possibly Peter, it appears that a variety of groups articulated different forms of doctrine drawing on the Jewish faith as well as pagan beliefs. The ensuing blend of approaches may account for many of the theological controversies and heresies that from the early days permeated the life of the Christian

Church and threatened its unity in the succeeding centuries. In particular, Antioch was the locus of the famous clash between Peter and Paul over whether Gentile converts should have to undergo circumcision and follow Jewish dietary laws.[129] The eventual victory of Paul's more inclusive approach over Peter's more restrictive stance fundamentally severed ties with Judaism and mapped out a universal mission, thereby facilitating the spread of the new religion beyond Palestine and throughout the Roman Empire. Antioch's importance to the new faith is further reflected in the fact that many of the early Christian missionary efforts were dispatched from there, including the various missions of Paul. Additionally, the line of bishops, stemming from St. Peter and continuing with St. Evodius (c. 53–c. 69) and St. Ignatius (c. 70–c. 107), gave stamina to a community that, thanks to almsgiving and a strong sense of brotherhood, was now connected to other groups across the Eastern Empire.[130] As Susan Ashbrook Harvey poignantly noted, thanks to its blend of Pauline leadership and Petrine gravitas, in the early days of Christianity Antioch was the beacon from which Christian authority radiated in the east and beyond.[131]

Meanwhile, civic life in Antioch was further enriched by new Olympic festivals,[132] thus fully inserting the city into the network of pan-Mediterranean Greco-Roman cities. Rights and privileges of the local Jews were reinstated, thus substantially rectifying the policies of Caligula.[133] Claudius thereby hoped to establish concord in a much-troubled orient. Yet political events in the regions adjacent to the Antiochene district reverberated greatly at this time. The history of the Judean and Syrian provinces between 44 CE and 66 CE is exceptionally well documented, as the period is accurately covered by Josephus's account; however, scanty information is available for the capital of the region, except for a few allusions to secondary events related to the First Jewish War (66–73 CE). Antioch maintained its prominent role of capital and continued to mint its independent issues, essentially silver tetradachms as well as dynastic types with the iconographies of Agrippina the Younger and her son, the young Nero, designated heir of Claudius.[134] Furthermore, the Antiochene district continued to deal with arrivals of new military contingents because of the worsening situation in Judea. A substantial number of new detachments landed in Antioch, most notably under the governorship of Quadratus in 51/52 CE, and were soon deployed in southern Syria and stationed in Ptolemais, closer to Judea.[135]

The military situation in the region escalated in the wake of Nero's accession to the imperial throne in 54 CE. By 62, the Syrian legions were fully equipped and reorganized both for the Jewish rebellion and for a grand-scale invasion of Parthia. Antioch presumably served as the logistical center as well as headquarters for the expedition, thus accommodating the military apparatus as well as organizing the supply system. High profile commanders like Q. Cornelius Aquinus were in the city at that time; he was the legate of the Legion VI Ferrata in Antioch shortly before moving to Pannonia in 68 CE. An epitaph commemorates the burial of his slave Antiochus.[136] The mint also operated at a sustained pace, emitting silver tetradrachms with the laureate head of the emperor on the obverse and a spread-winged eagle, thunderbolt, and palm branch on the reverse. With the new

FIGURE 2.12 Silver tetradrachm of Antioch (59–65 CE) under Nero. Obverse: Laureate bust of Nero wearing aegis: ΝΕΡΩΝΣΣ ΚΑΙΣΑΡΟΣ ΣΕΒΑΣΤΟΥ. Reverse: Eagle standing left on thunderbolt; to left, palm branch. Date to right. Border of dots: Ζ ΘΡ

Source: Courtesy of the Harvard Art Museums

iconography, the Antioch mint also introduced a new standardization of the tetradrachm, deemed to be excessively overvalued against the denarius. A shift of four denarii (previously three) at the rate of one tetradrachm corrected the apparent unbalance (Figure 2.12).[137]

Jewish affairs, however, took the upper hand, with a full-fledged revolt starting in 66 CE that the Syrian governor, Cestius Gallus, was unable to curb. Tacitus makes plain that only the intervention of Vespasian, as governor of Judea, brought an end to the incendiary situation.[138] Regardless, anti-Jewish sentiment radiated in the East; Antioch was not exempt, as one Antiochus, a local Jewish renegade, ignited a most tragic pogrom and then was tasked with surveilling the Jews and their religious observances.[139] The paucity of information on Antioch at this time is, however, jarring. Even Malalas, typically garrulous in his penning of Antioch-related anecdotes and stories, had to limit his account to the only notable event occurring at this time: the death of the bishop Evodius in 66 CE and appearance on the horizon of his successor Ignatius (50–117 CE), the next leader of the Christian community, believed to have been an auditor of St. John, to have been bestowed the seat of Antioch from the Apostles themselves, and finally to have been martyred in Rome under Trajan.[140]

Antioch and the Flavians

Following the death of Nero, Antioch played an important role in the ensuing civil wars. The Year of the Four Emperors, 69 CE, proved once again the city's centrality and its key profile in military terms, with Mucianus, governor of Syria, securing the support of the Syrian legions to Vespasian and the favor of the Antiochenes in the assembly.[141]

During this time the socioeconomic configuration of the province of Syria and the district of Antioch were modified by the Flavian emperors of Vespasian and his two sons, Titus and Domitian, when a series of political measures mapped out better communications and industrial productivity and created the conditions for a period of economic vitality.[142] As for the city, a devastating fire in 70 CE presumably destroyed the tetragonal agora, the offices of the public records, and basilicas in Epiphaneia;[143] arguably, it may have been an incentive for building projects. More to the point, the incident drove a further wedge between the Jewish community and the rest of Antioch's population in the aftermath of Titus's destruction of Jerusalem and the Temple that same year. The renegade Antiochus again let it be known that Antioch's Jews had deliberately set the city on fire, with consequent stir in the city and ensuing atrocities.[144] The events of 70 CE thus had fundamental repercussions on the life of the local Jewry, stripped of its visibility and prestige.[145]

The East as a whole was also transforming its administrative and political configurations at that time: Judea became a detached entity, while the kingdoms of Commagene, Emesa, and Palmyra were fully integrated within the province. Governors acquired particular centrality as well. For instance, the long governorship of Ulpius Traianus (begun in 73/74 CE) coincided with some important innovations in the territory of Antioch.[146] The father of the future emperor Trajan was the successor of A. Marius Celsus. Upon beginning his tenure, he enhanced the road network in the Euphrates district and the Antioch-Seleucia Pieria corridor, and this, together with his service in the Jewish war and a probable Parthian campaign, earned him the *ornamenta triumphalia*, an event amply celebrated by Pliny.[147] The sustained production of SC coinage by the Antioch mint around 74 CE may support the hypothesis of the military operations against the Persians.[148]

It is legitimate, in view of these structural changes, to ask what impact Vespasian's Eastern policy as well as the elder Traianus's activities had on Antioch and its hinterlands. Unlike in other districts, where substantial overhauls of the fiscal system took place,[149] the Antiochene administrative scheme appears to have remained unchanged, while the role of the metropolis as economic propeller of the province was further increased with the adoption of a series of measures.[150] First, at the military level, the dense garrisoning of the province underwent structural changes;[151] legions were more rationally relocated on Syrian and Antiochene territory so as to maintain them at fighting pitch[152] and diminish the negative effects of the presence of troops in urban areas.[153] As mentioned, the road network in the region was apparently enhanced, and the legions and their engineers were clearly those who executed the plans. The rationale behind these intense activities was rather simple: Vespasian was interested in having a rapid and efficient network of roads connecting Antioch to the Euphrates in response to the Parthians' increasingly hostile activities.[154] The many honors bestowed on Traianus for his activities in Syria, including the minting of an ad hoc bronze "name and wreath" coin, do not rule out the possibility of a campaign in the years 73–74 CE.[155]

Ulpius Traianus deserves particular mention, since several major building projects in the territory of Antioch were carried out under his governorship.[156] These activities strongly suggest increased attention from the Roman state toward northern Syria and, more specifically, on the Antioch-Seleucia Pieria corridor (Figure 2.13), which functioned as the terminal of Roman communications by sea

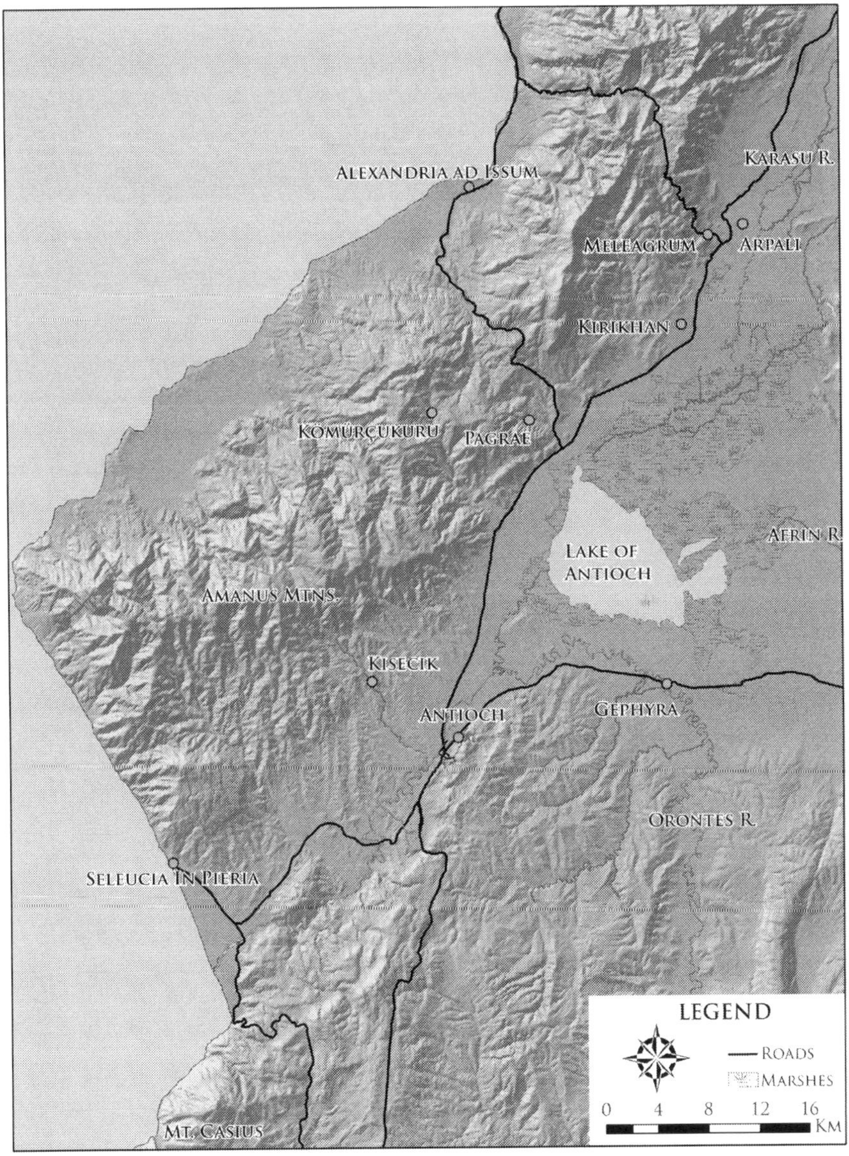

FIGURE 2.13 Map of the southern Orontes district

Source: Created by Stephen Batiuk

and the nexus of various land routes.[157] In particular, three important inscriptions recovered in the northern hinterlands of Antioch refer to a series of canalizations of the Orontes carried out around the city in the 122nd year of the Caesarian era, that is, the years around 73–74 CE, under the auspices of Vespasian and the city of Antioch respectively. The first text is a milestone of cylindrical shape found at the site of Küçük Dalyan Köyü (today a borough in the northern Antakya districts), commemorating the excavation of a canal of three Roman miles, with bridges, under Traianus in 73–74 CE with the blessings of the imperial family, and presented to the city of Antioch.[158] The text's interpretation, however, presents two major difficulties. The first is to spatially locate the undertaking, for it indicates that the canal tapped the waters from the "*Dipotamia(e) Flumen*," possibly the point where the Orontes and the Little Orontes rivers met in the "between two rivers" basin north of Antioch and Küçük Dalyan Köyü.

The second interpretative problem is the rationale behind the work. According to the text, all four Syrian legions, that is, III Gallica, IV Scythica, VI Ferrata, and XVI Flavia Firma, contributed to the project.[159] Given the scale of the Roman army's involvement, we can thus assume this canalization primarily served a military purpose and must have been quite large. The design essentially facilitated the river's navigability and thus eased the transport of troops from Seleucia to Antioch. It is likely the Orontes's sinuous course north of the city hampered navigation and the maneuvers of large cargoes and barges; hence the decision to cut a canal. In addition, the geographer Pausanias mentions the undertaking of major canalization work in the territory of Antioch under an unnamed emperor, whom at this point we can safely identify with Vespasian. His text is actually fairly precise in pinpointing the purpose of the canal, which diverted waters so as to avoid ledges of rock and make the river perfectly navigable.[160] This ambitious project was part of the construction of a new harbor at Seleucia Pieria, carried out by the same legions and cohorts used in the Antiochene district. It consisted of a fortified external harbor connected via a gateway to an inner harbor, now entirely silted. Traces of breakwaters, piers, and a light house have been noted by early travelers and archaeologists alike. The same agency also excavated a tunnel that diverted the torrential waters of the Değirmendere stream and thus avoided the inundation and silting of the military harbor; the site today is known as Titus Tüneli (Figure 2.14).[161] Several inscriptions around the harbor, referring to the deified Vespasian and Titus, leave no doubt about who undertook these works, while a cluster of gravestones document the presence of a detachment of the Misenum fleet, the *classis misenensis*, that is the senior fleet of the Roman imperial navy, based in Misenum, Italy.[162] Triremes by the lofty names of Providentia and Tigris, among others, were moored in the imperial harbor as late as the second century CE. All in all, this grand design of waterworks had one precise goal: to use the Orontes for transporting military cargoes, supplies, and troops all the way to Gephyra, whence the routes to Beroea and Zeugma leading to the Euphrates frontier could be easily accessed (Figure 2.5).

Additionally, in his history of Late Antique Antioch,[163] J.H.W.G. Liebeschuetz argued, on the basis of Libanius's statement, that ships unloaded their cargoes in

FIGURE 2.14 Titus Tüneli: one of the great waterworks of the Flavian era

Source: Photograph by Andrea U. De Giorgi

front of people's houses and that water-borne commerce was important in providing the city with alternative sources of sustenance. While the shape of such riverine transports can hardly be assessed, we can infer their potential was more systematically exploited in the late first century CE. The drastic fluctuations in the Orontes riverbed may have severely impaired navigation of medium-to-large vessels both upstream and down to the harbor of Seleucia Pieria. As shown, Vespasian's important construction of the 4.5 km-long canal in 75 CE was a corrective that eased the transport of supplies and opened a new artery of communication into the city, channeling the waters of the Kara Su and Orontes Rivers.[164]

But this is not all. In 73–74 CE, a year earlier, a similar undertaking, albeit with different ends, had been commissioned and excavated by Antioch's population to benefit the local fullers and their workshops. Twin inscriptions record the project's completion under Traianus's governorship.[165] The project consisted of a 2.5 km water channel for use by the fullers and was intended for civilian and industrial use only; according to the inscriptions, it tapped water from the Orontes and then led to a reservoir on the slopes of Mt. Amanus.[166] To accomplish such a massive undertaking, the canal had to be excavated by means of a corvée labor force from different quarters of the city and supervised by the imperial legate, but having no military involvement. The name of the emperor himself is inscribed in the heading somewhat dismissively, almost to underscore this was an affair of the Antiochene community alone.[167] In this case, we can see that the administrative scheme at work in the city depended on individual contributions for mobilizing the labor force, a procedure followed for similar public works at Arsinoë in Egypt. It follows that discrepancies in allocating funds for the project by Antioch's various quarters can be understood through the financial disparities among their respective constituents.[168] The importance of these extraordinary inscriptions is indeed threefold. First, they inform us of the means through which a polity had to pursue its own economic agenda. Second, they underscore the magnitude of the waterworks along the Orontes, and not least the investment of the imperial house; the text makes plain this was a fairly complex infrastructure, equipped with dams, barriers, and a terminal reservoir, and paid for by the community. Lastly, the names of the boroughs convey the ethnic diversity of the community, for some are imbued with Semitic and Persian accents. The names of the city blocks, referred to in the inscriptions as *plintheia*, vary from very Greek-sounding names like Theophrastos to those of various Eastern origin, like Bagadates, Pharanakes, and Damasaphernes.[169] Ultimately, they are instrumental in shedding some light onto the materiality of the city and making known the whereabouts and toponyms of neighborhoods possibly located on the right shore of the Orontes, from which stemmed the canal.

In summary, Vespasian conspicuously entrusted the territory of Syria and the Antioch district to Traianus,[170] whose building and planning programs across the Syrian province, from Commagene to Bostra and from Palmyra to Gerasa (modern Jarash), bespeak both his military and civil accomplishments.[171] In particular, worsening relations with the Parthians stimulated the development of an unprecedented communications network in the region, with Antioch prominently positioned as portal to the East. These developments were further likely to bring tangential benefits to the communities in the Antiochene district, especially in the form of economic opportunities, technologies, and highways. The archaeological record of the territory of Antioch moreover shows a trend of increasing settlement and connectivity in the first and second centuries CE.[172]

Visual mementos of the Flavian achievements in Judea by the hand of Titus (79–81 CE) also began to populate Antioch's cityscape: through its sign "*Ex praeda Iudaea*," a new theater at Daphne apparently was an example of the didactic powers of imperial architecture, built as it was on the ruins of a former synagogue. The theater was excavated in 1934 and 1935. It is one of the largest operations carried out by the Princeton team (sector 2-N) and brought to light a heavily robbed building that had been originally lavishly decorated by exotic marbles and provided with a sophisticated water system that enabled the flooding of the orchestra for entertainment purposes.[173] In addition, the Cherubim of Jerusalem's Temple were allegedly hung on a gate and paired with a sculptural group of the moon goddess Selene and four bulls (a subtle commemoration of the Jerusalem attack at night); this visual program added an eclectic feature to Antioch's crowded skyline and sent a clear and intimidating message to the local Jewry.[174]

The last of the Flavian dynasty, Domitian (81–96 CE), also added a host of the typical trappings of a Roman city: a temple dedicated to Asclepius and a monumental bath "of Medea near the slopes of the mountains."[175] Of interest also is the evidence of administrators or imperial grandees sponsoring building projects. Indeed, the presence of the Roman bureaucratic apparatus must have also increased at this time, as evidenced by the inscription of Lucius Maecius Postumus, possibly on the architrave of a building near the hippodrome, which informs us of the presence in Antioch of the former promagister of the Arval Brothers collegium as well as his likely act of munificence.[176]

In this political context, the overhaul of the provincial coinage as orchestrated by Antioch and the Flavian administrators should be brought into sharper focus. In particular, from the days of Vespasian, the volume and types of silver tetradrachms reached hitherto unprecedented heights.[177] Roman imperial aurei and denarii were also issued by the Syrian mints; as Richard McAlee suggests, at this time Antioch was supported by at least four other mints, namely at Tripolis, Aradus, Tyre, and, not least, Rome.[178]

Earthquakes, Trajan, and Antioch in the second century CE

It is no overstatement that Antioch became virtually the second imperial capital under the reign of Trajan (98–117 CE). Cassius Dio's vivid description of the city at the time of the 115 CE earthquake, which opens this chapter, gives us a glimpse of the city's size and degree of urbanization.[179] The event must have reached a high magnitude, killing thousands of people; again, the words of the historian capture the gravity of the drama:

> There had been many thunderstorms and portentous winds, but no one would ever have expected so many evils to result from them. First there came, on a sudden, a great bellowing roar, and this was followed by a tremendous quaking. The whole earth was upheaved, and buildings leaped into the air; some were carried aloft only to collapse and be broken in pieces, while others were tossed this way and that as if by the surge of the sea, and overturned, and the wreckage spread out over a great extent even of the open country. The crash of grinding and breaking timbers together with tiles and stones was most frightful and an inconceivable amount of dust arose, so that it was impossible for one to see anything or to speak or hear a word.

Trajan himself miraculously escaped the fury of the event; in all likelihood he resided on the Island and then sought shelter in the hippodrome. To appease the gods, he offered a generous thanksgiving in Daphne. Yet the numbers of Antiochenes killed by the earthquake must have been staggering. Klaudia may have been one of the casualties, or, if she chanced to survive, may have been an eyewitness of the calamity (Figure 2.15). The laconic, succinct text of her epitaph "Farewell, you are now without pain (ALUPE XAIRE)" leaves a lot of room for the imagination. Further, the formulaic early second-century CE iconography

FIGURE 2.15 The funerary stele of Klaudia, early second century CE

Source: Courtesy of the Antioch Expedition Archives, Department of Art and Archaeology, Princeton University; Princeton

hardly reveals anything meaningful about Klaudia's life. Yet one could imagine that it was people like her who experienced those momentous days and contributed to rebuilding Antioch, once the rattles had subsided. Indeed, the surviving Antiochenes wasted no time in recovering from the earthquake and quickly tapped into provincial funds for the reconstruction of the city. After hastily offering their thanksgiving in a new shrine to Zeus Soter in Daphne, they went on to deploy efforts and labor in the areas where assistance was most needed. How the relief effort was coordinated we are not in position to tell, nor is the financial output from the imperial authorities known.

But the earthquake of 115 CE did not only elicit large-scale, state-sponsored responses and top-down optimism. Countless citizens of Antioch had lost their homes, goods, and bonds across generations. They were living now in that sort of estrangement, having lost the perception of belonging to a recognized and recognizable place, while entering the realm of the displaced. Facing a traumatizing field of ruins in lieu of a densely inhabited space, some decided to part company with the place that had framed their lives for many decades.

The so-called House of Trajan's Aqueduct (26-L) may be a good representative of buildings that were abandoned after the earthquake (Figure 2.16).[180] Heavily damaged around that time and subsequently buried by a landslide, this house, unlike other units in the district, was never reoccupied. Its foundations rested on the vaulting of the Trajanic aqueduct that from Daphne flows all the way to the lower slopes of Mt. Silpius, serving a reservoir and a host of baths. Two weathered pavements with decoration of shaded cubes and a winged female figure are the only remaining décor of a house that may have been in use for a few decades only. While the aqueduct was restored after the earthquake, the house was abandoned to its fate of ruins.

But In the context of widespread destruction, some people conversely resorted to reconstructing their emotional and material dimension, both public and private. The House of the Calendar (15-R), on the slope of Mt. Staurin, brings testimony to new expressions of resistance; through its reconstruction and aggrandizing, the

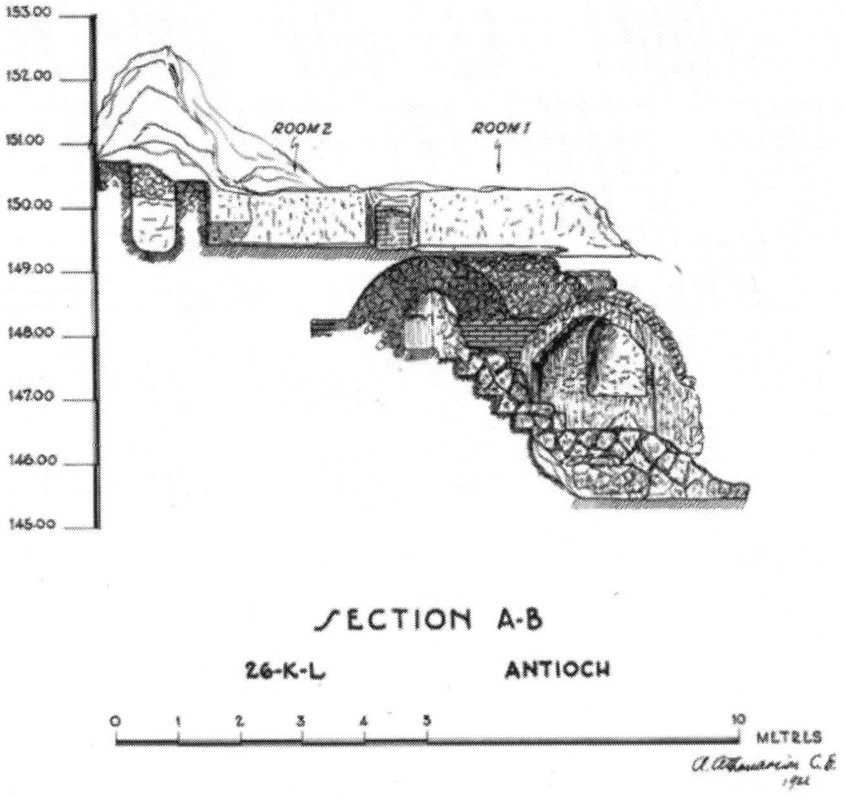

FIGURE 2.16 The House of Trajan's aqueduct

Source: Courtesy of the Antioch Expedition Archives, Department of Art and Archaeology, Princeton University; Princeton

domestic unit becomes the locus where nature and natural disasters are questioned while new modes of understanding human frailty are enabled. This house of Hellenistic origin was presumably razed by the 115 CE earthquake. Its debris, ashes, and broken mosaic pavements formed the bedding for the construction of a new, larger unit provided with a triclinium, colonnaded portico, and pool. The eccentric visual program of the triclinium is of interest, for it accommodated, among panels with apotropaic symbols and marine deities, the representation of a calendar. Though weathered, only the winter and spring quadrants survive; the composition includes names of the months in Greek (*Dustros*, *Xanthikos*, *Artemeisios*, *Daisios*) and personified seasons (Spring-*Trope Earine*) (Figure 2.17).

FIGURE 2.17 House of the Calendar: the panel with the personified Spring

Source: Courtesy of the Antioch Expedition Archives, Department of Art and Archaeology, Princeton University; Princeton

In his analysis of the iconography of this pavement, Doro Levi stressed the allusions to divinities and rituals suggested by the personified months, carrying paterae (vessels), torches, and pouring libations.[181] While this angle should not be discounted, it is apparent that what mattered the most to the patrons and the artists of the House of the Calendar was illustrating the cyclical alternation of the seasons and months at a critical moment in the history of the city. More poignantly, they aimed at celebrating the overall restoration of the course of nature against the catastrophe.

The main artery of traffic, that is the colonnaded street, formerly paved by Herod the Great and embellished architecturally by Tiberius, in the aftermath of the earthquake was in all likelihood no longer serviceable. Of course, in a context of widespread destruction, ease of movement along the main axis of traffic is vital, whether for hauling away heaps of rubble or simple movement of goods and people. How Antioch quickly reacquired mobility and used reconstruction to mint a new version of the main thoroughfare can be gleaned thanks to the 1930s excavation data sets.

Amid sparse investigations in the territory of Antioch, the Princeton Excavations in 1934 devised a thoughtful, albeit complicated, plan of "street digs" with large and deep soundings loosely following Antakya's Kurtuluş Caddesi, the modern reincarnation of the cardo.[182] Soundings 19-M and 16-P documented the stratigraphy of the main road, and altogether its "biography." Narrow and redolent with cultural phases, these sounding had to be peeled off from twelfth-century houses all the way down to the Hellenistic levels. However, these excavations illustrated one fundamental aspect of the issue at stake; the dismantling of the street of Herod and Tiberius and the wholesale replacement of it with a new, monumental axis of traffic in the aftermath of the earthquake. This enterprise entailed clearing heaps of debris for at least a 40 m width.[183]

The new road of Trajan was grounded in deep foundations, essentially a 1 m layer – thick with debris and rubble. The road alone was 9.25 m wide and flanked by porticoes and *tabernae* (shops) each 16 m wide, as apparent in sector 19-M (Figure 2.18).

Put simply, after the 115 earthquake, to planners and architects it seemed more expeditious and cost-effective building a new colonnaded street from scratch rather than seeking to repair the old one. In so doing, the overall width of the operations must have exceeded 40 m of width in clearing of structures for the entire length of the cardo, approximately 7 km.

Ultimately, the project almost doubled the size of the previous road and porticoes, and presumably went on until the mandate of Antoninus Pious (138–161 CE),[184] when the decoration of the colonnade was officially completed. Through this project, however, Antioch was presented with a new logic of space for vehicles, pedestrians, and retail. The monumental aesthetics and functionality of the time brought to bear an architectural configuration that was going to change life in Antioch. More to the point, the imposing size of this undertaking resonated with the solutions that Trajanic planners and builders had adopted around the same time in Rome at the Markets of Trajan. In particular, the realization of the great hemicycle

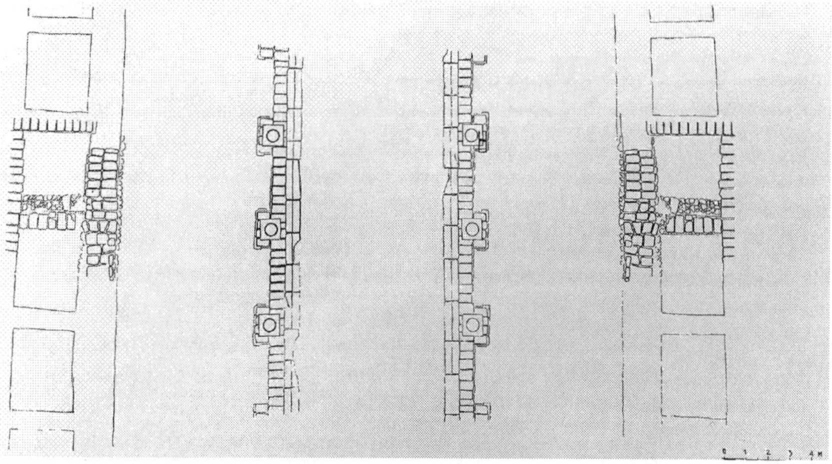

FIGURE 2.18 Lassus's hypothesis for the colonnaded street of Trajan, as suggested by the 19-M excavation

Source: Adapted from *Antioch V*

and its lining of small barrel vaulted *tabernae*, curvilinear configuration aside, reverberates with the same bent for stimulating movement along and behind these retail spaces, fueling commerce and fostering a new sense of community. It should be stressed, though, that with the exception of a few fragments of entablature and columns, not a scrap of the ancient boulevard survives, thus making its volumetric and monumental appearance impossible to determine. Tenuous traces of basalt slabs and red and gray granite columns are all that is left of this magnificent axis of traffic.

In Trajan's view, Antioch's new thoroughfare was the centerpiece of an organic plan that included the *Mese Pule*, the middle gate near the Temple of Ares and spanning the Parmenius. Presumably, this served a celebratory purpose only, for it was located on the slope of Mt. Silpius near the space that in the late fourth century became forum of Valens. It may have been conspicuous and visible from a distance, though. Moreover, its decorative apparatus could not be more telling: on it was a relief of the she-wolf of Rome's founding legend.[185]

Overall, Trajan's tenure also had positive effects, inasmuch as the emperor commissioned the construction of a number of other monumental projects, some of which may have started before the 115 CE cataclysm. In that vein, the frenzy of repairs and new building programs also included the construction of new baths as well as completion of the theater.[186] The latter's sculptural program deserves attention: on the proscenium was apparently a nymphaeum with the sculptural Kalliope group. Malalas's detailed description makes plain that this statue replicated that of the Tyche, with the addition of kings Seleucus and Antiochus bestowing a crown upon her. More to the point, the legendary powers of the city were still being referenced in the sixth century and beyond.[187]

The suburb of Daphne, too, received post-earthquake assistance, and the reconstruction of the temple of Artemis must be seen in this context.[188] Major repairs and, presumably, new feeders and ramifications of the aqueduct of Daphne were also undertaken at this time. The 8 km-long and 1 km-wide valley separating Antioch from Daphne was then traversed by another major system of tunnels, bridges, and conduits. Again, extrapolating the exact agency amid a mesh of waterworks spanning the Seleucid to Crusader periods is complicated. The 1930s archaeologists identified at least three systems on the ground when conditions and visibility were optimal,[189] but whether these belong to Seleucus, Caligula, or Trajan, respectively, remains to be established. Nevertheless, it appears that the series of bridges overcoming the roughness of the valley between Antioch and Daphne may be assigned to Trajan's project. To reduce the velocity of water (100 m of fall over 8 km) and thus enable a steady and regular flow downstream into, presumably, a terminal *castellum*, the builders resorted to a winding pattern of curves at right angles. A first, heavily battered segment of this aqueduct survives in Antioch between Yayla Sokak and Dere Sokak over the Phyrminus gorge in the Bağrıyanık quarter. Possibly connected to it are the remains of a large reservoir, very similar to one in the Havuzlar quarter. A second surviving stretch of the aqueduct survives in the Sümerler area, near Dere Sokak (Figure 2.19).

FIGURE 2.19 The remains of Trajan's aqueduct in Antakya

Source: Photograph by Andrea U. De Giorgi

New beginnings and a city rising from its ashes: it is no overstatement that Trajan acted as new founder of Antioch.

Central though the earthquake may have been, it nevertheless represents but one episode in the complicated mesh of events occurring in the city during Trajan's reign. Malalas, for instance, informs us of a Persian coup in the days preceding the military campaign against the Persians in 113 CE.[190] The city at that time probably harbored a not-so-latent pro-Persian sentiment, with the presumably vast constituency of local Easterners keen on handing the city over to Persia's Arsacid rulers. But as soon as Trajan entered the city, it became a "base" for the emperor and accommodated the logistics of a massive expedition. Ultimately, the war against the Parthians produced two new appendices to the Roman Empire: the provinces of Mesopotamia and Armenia. Though abortive in a few years, these novel entities required a conspicuous investment in the military and in the logistics of the supply system, especially considering the numbers of troops entering the province and the equally high number of captives.[191] As Denis van Berchem points out, the naval base at Seleucia and the military headquarters of the expedition in Antioch were working at full swing between 113 and 116 CE.[192] The output of the Antioch mint, too, was critical in sustaining the demands of the military; fittingly, the volume and diversity of types replicated those of Vespasian. Recourse to other mints, namely Tyre and Caesarea in Cappadocia, proved effective in meeting the challenges of the provincial government. There were also important ties with the mint of Alexandria, as shown by the resemblance of several tetradrachms and at least one die link.[193]

Altogether, Trajan resided in Antioch between 114 and 117 CE; at that juncture, the city became a de facto military headquarters for the Roman army, a tradition that continued under emperors Lucius Verus, Pescennius Niger, and Caracalla.[194] Violence against Christians is reported during Trajan's sojourn. Their community was no doubt enjoying momentous growth; incidentally, the gospel of Matthew, presumably written in the city during the 80/90s BCE, attests to the local reception of Christ's message and stresses the role of the *ekklesia*, that is the assembly.[195] Under Trajan, the pastoral guide of Ignatius set the example for the role that the ecclesiastical authority was to have in the following centuries, with regard to the enforcement of theological doctrines and the configuration of the local church. From the martyrdom of Ignatius, later to be elevated as saint, to five virtuous Antiochene women who were burned alive in front of Trajan, it is nevertheless apparent that the imperial administration flexed its muscles in front of a fast-growing Christian community.[196] The violence pitted against Antioch's church also spawned new legends and examples to follow: the myth of Saint Thecla and her extraordinary virtues in making proselytes once again placed Antioch prominently on the map of early Christianity.[197]

Antioch under Hadrian

New changes occurred under Trajan's successor Hadrian (117–138 CE),[198] a former governor of Syria who had experienced firsthand the catastrophe of the earthquake and who proclaimed himself emperor in Antioch.[199] In political terms, one of the first measures he adopted upon taking power was to introduce an ad hoc official for the province of Syria alone; this official functioned as the financial overseer of the senatorial state.[200] Though the exact competence the appointment carried is difficult to pinpoint, one fact is clear: the enormous investment for military activities in Syria was taking its toll on the precarious provincial treasury, and corrective measures were needed. It is likely, however, that the introduction of these officials was successful, for the appointment continued under the following emperors.[201] We can better understand Hadrian's decision to abandon promptly all the newly acquired Trans-Euphrates territories as well as the immediate cutbacks on military expenditures as an effort to curtail expenditures and protect the provincial treasury. Adjustments to the Antioch mint were in order, too. The sustained pace of striking operations under Trajan was downgraded to the *status quo* that had preceded the Parthian campaigns. As Kevin Butcher poignantly noted, the minting activity of northern Syria can be best described as "depressed."[202]

Hadrian came to Antioch repeatedly, at least three times between 123 and 130 CE. As befitted a legitimate imperial transition, a temple dedicated to the divine Trajan was added to Antioch's cityscape, though under Julian (361–363) this was transformed into a library.[203] The city amply benefited from Hadrian's presence through a series of new games and building programs that offered new amenities to urbanites. In particular, major investments brought to completion the aqueduct of Trajan and led to establishing new baths carrying his name, cited in one third-century CE papyrus from the Dura Europos region.[204] Bath establishments also went hand in hand with healing cults; the stunning second-century CE marble statue of Hygieia from "Bath F" (sector 13-R),[205] discovered next to that of Asclepius and now on display at the Worcester Art Museum, attests to the most common commingling of cultural and religious practices at Antioch (Figure 4.10). Moreover, central in the Hadrianic building program for Antioch was the construction of a spectacular *castellum* regulating the flow of water from Daphne's main spring of Castalia, site of the Apollonian oracle near the temple of Apollo. Much has been made of the appearance of this building (also referred to as the *theatron*), its visual configuration, and rationale.[206] What matters to us, however, is that Hadrian clearly reinvigorated the centrality of the sanctuary's oracular faculties, while also claiming ownership, as his deliberate effort to exclude everyone from the divinatory powers of the Castalia spring shows.[207]

The new presentation of Daphne and its religious mission was further corroborated by the addition or architectural embellishment of the theater (Figure 2.20). While lifting mosaics in Daphne in 1934, the American archaeologists explored a terraced orchard that had been plundered by villagers seeking large limestone blocks. The two-year excavation led to the recovery of the building's north *parodos* (a vaulted passageway connecting the outside to the orchestra), a portion of the *cavea* and orchestra, as well as fragments of the superstructure, not least the marble décor of the stage, from statues to capitals. Altogether, the archeological record

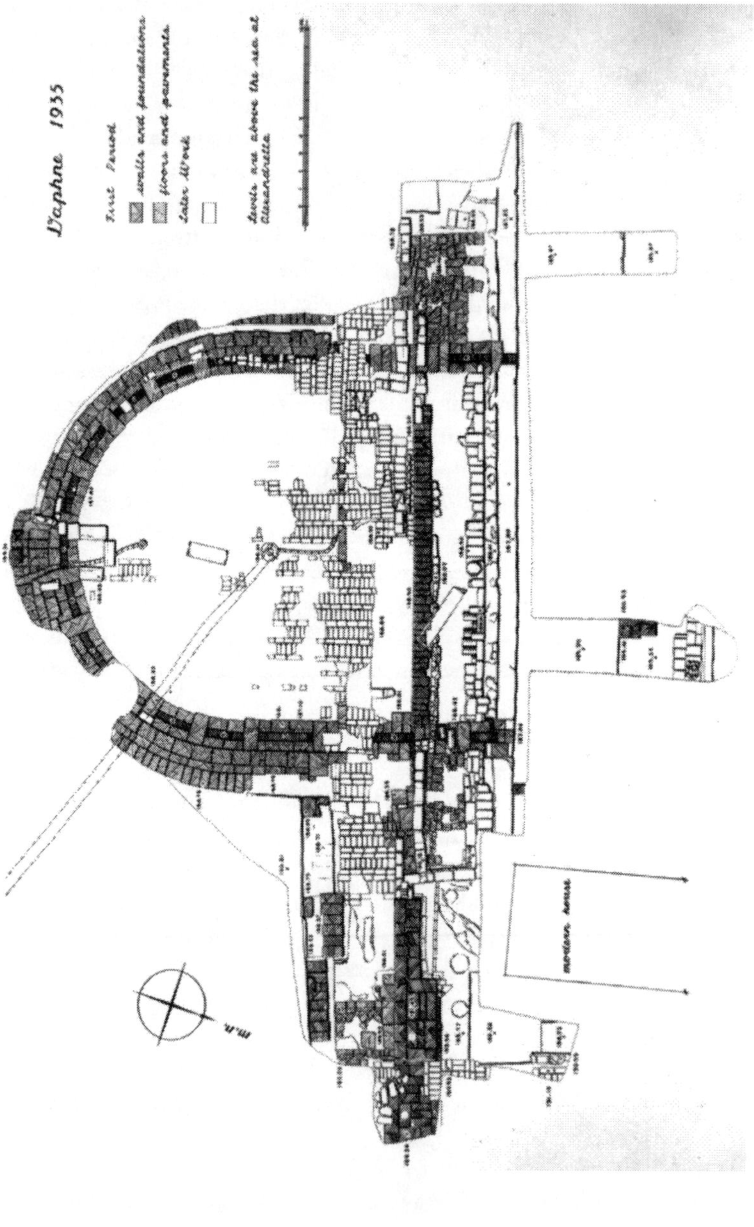

FIGURE 2.20 The theater in Daphne

Source: Courtesy of the Antioch Expedition Archives, Department of Art and Archaeology, Princeton University; Princeton

offers a fairly coherent second-century CE horizon, though the patchy architectural decoration opens the possibility of third-century CE repairs or additions.[208]

While Hadrian's building programs had a fundamental impact on the city and its community, less-tangible phenomena were occurring in the countryside during this same period. As demonstrated by the mid-1930s' reconnaissance survey of Russian archaeologist Georges Tchalenko, the region of the highlands east of Antioch, the so-called *Massif Calcaire*, also referred to as the "Dead Cities," began to thrive economically thanks to the wine and olive oil industry at the beginning of the second century CE.[209] In all likelihood, improvements in tenancy systems accounted for the increase of settlement on the highlands as well as the expansion of oil and wine production. Laws like the *Lex Manciana* and *Lex Hadriana* enabled tenants to have a guaranteed return and gave them an incentive to work more land for better profit within the sharecropping framework.[210] These schemes were ideal for farmers who had no money or land to cultivate, or who simply would not risk investing in an olive orchard, since it carried only long-term profits. The archaeological finds from the highlands around Antioch, as well as the evidence recorded by Tchalenko, strengthen this hypothesis. Olive oil and wine production in Antioch during the second century CE were profitable activities, and, not surprisingly, the price of land began to rise.[211] Overall, the increase in Antioch's rural settlement suggests that the city economically produced networks of villages and farms essential for its sustenance. One may speculate that the city's large population, the constant presence of the legions, the economic opportunities that came with developing a large-scale administrative and legal apparatus, and the availability of work to support the civic infrastructure each generated demands for goods and services that could be met from the villages.[212] Libanius's orations incidentally afford insights into the city's supply system. In his *De Angariis*,[213] for instance, the Antiochene rhetorician offers a captivating snapshot of the city's rural landscapes and of the daily routine of local farmers happily trundling into the city to supply local markets with their loads of grain. While this bucolic picture fails to represent the complexity of the situation, let alone pre-fourth-century CE realities, it nevertheless suggests the reliance of the city on the rural hinterlands for supplies.[214]

In summary, the archaeological data confirm a plausible trend of substantial economic and demographic growth in the territory of Antioch during the early second century CE. By 117, the provincial tetradrachm mint had been transferred from Tyre to Antioch, with consequent appearance of issues celebrating the event and carrying the very symbols encapsulating the myth of Antioch's foundation: the eagle and Seleucus Nicator's sacrificial meat.[215] Once again, a bridge to the Seleucid legend connected the city to modern politics and ancestral rituals and strengthened its sense of centrality.

Antioch and the Antonines

The Antonine era under Antoninus Pius (138–161 CE) and his successors, Lucius Verus, Marcus Aurelius, and Commodus, furthered Antioch's prominence even more, underwriting substantial building programs throughout the city. Campaigns against the Parthians once again projected Antioch at the center of the Roman world. A fire, however, raged out of control under Antoninus Pius,[216] forcing evacuations and destroying homes and public buildings, once again testing the Antiochenes' resilience. The damage caused by the blaze may have led to yet another scheme of urban repairs funded by the state coffers; allegedly, the emperor completed the paving of the colonnaded street, thus bringing to conclusion the project started by Trajan.[217] Fragments of a monumental frieze with garlands that can be stylistically ascribable to the Antonine period were recovered in a hasty 1936 excavation; in all likelihood they were part of a building or a portico not reported by the sources.

As for key events, in 162 CE Marcus Aurelius (161–180) and Lucius Verus (161–169) came to Antioch to prepare for a campaign against Vologeses III, the Parthian king. The escalation of the Parthian crisis ushered in new opportunities for Antioch, though not everything was rosy. Lucius Verus's long sojourns in Antioch and his local lukewarm reception began the literary trope of the emperor and his failure to win the hearts of the city on the Orontes. Lucius's apparent bent for spectacles, shows, and hunting apparently alienated the Antiochenes' sympathies.[218] For the first time in imperial history we hear of Antioch's disconnect with the authorities in Rome as well as a sense of agency by the local community. Much was brewing in Antioch; on one hand, the victorious campaign of 166 against Vologeses III met the expectations of the Roman state in securing its position in the East and the usual uptick in *SC* bronze coinage, with at least five different issues accompanied the military operations.[219] On the other hand, this war bolstered the claims of the *deus ex machina* of the expedition, the commander Avidius Cassius, a Syrian of Cyrrhus. How this episode led to Avidius Cassius's attempt to usurp the empire in 175 and to Antioch's punishment for siding with him is widely known;[220] the Olympic games were banned, and fiscal sanctions in all likelihood had a negative impact on civic life.

Such an impasse, however, did not hinder the undertaking of imperial building programs: a bath called the *Centenarium* and a temple dedicated to the Muses are assigned to Marcus Aurelius's reign.[221] More ambitious projects, however, may have occurred under Commodus (180–192), with the construction of a bath known as the *Commodium*, restoration of the adjacent temple of Athena, and the addition of the *Xystos* (a possible monumental entrance to the Olympic complex), and a temple to Zeus.[222] Suffice to say, this cluster of buildings was the key locus to the revival of civic life brought about when the Olympic games were restored.

Indeed, festivals and Olympic games received the blessings of the imperial house, for the whole system was revised with a view toward merging the emperor's contribution with that of the city. The old endowment of Sosibius was also brought to fruition, thus ending the endemic misuse of those funds[223] and greatly enlarging the scale of the games. *Venationes* (hunts), gladiatorial spectacles, chariot races, and theatrical plays were but some of the events, which occurred every five years and were regulated by a host of magistrates.[224] An inscription from Tralles dating around 180 CE makes plain there were at least three types of games at this time: the Hadrianea, the Commodeia (the Olympic games), and those sponsored by one Eucrates.[225] Much civic brio, however, was at variance with Antioch's halting of minting activities at this very time. Both bronze and silver issues were discontinued, and only Caracalla, some decades later, restored the Antioch production of SC issues to normal standards. Abundance of previous coinage may have led to this phase of stagnation.[226]

The archaeology of Early Imperial Antioch

All this energy and centrality of Antioch under the Early Roman Empire, however, stands once again in contrast with the meager material record of the city. The archaeology of the middle/late second century CE is still largely unknown; fine tuning the dating for any structures to match the more precisely dated textual history remains difficult. Nevertheless, the 1930s excavations brought to light tenuous traces of domestic units, thus offering a glimpse into the lives of the Antiochenes: the so-called Atrium House on the Island (10-N) is a well-documented example (Figure 2.21). Excavated in 1932, this unit south of the hippodrome brought to the fore a complex established during the Augustan Age that underwent drastic modifications in the following epochs.[227]

In a way, this house stands out as a manifesto of the protean qualities of Antioch's houses, as they shifted their orientation and itineraries through time yet remained true to their original core – that is, the emphasis on a courtyard. More fundamentally, the Atrium House was decorated by the exquisite craftsmanship of Antioch's mosaicists. The floor of its triclinium (dining room) accommodated five panels and what is arguably deemed of one Antioch's finest mosaics, the well-known *Judgement of Paris* (Figure 2.22). The pavement was laid on an earlier floor of plaster between 115 and 119 CE following damage to the house in the 115 earthquake.

This is a stunning example of an Antiochene sensibility that by the late second century CE had already established its canon and was to inspire countless artists across the Greek East. Other domestic units that suffered massive damage and, eventually, termination by the hand of the 115 CE earthquake also afford insights into house design and decoration practices in Antioch. A gripping example is provided by the House of Polyphemus and Galatea, sector 10-Q. Despite the lamentable archaeological record of the context, what appears vividly is the degree of destruction that led to the curving and breaking of the pavements. What is more, the central panel of one of the mosaics makes it now possible for us to understand some of practices that regulated the creation of what we may characterize as an "Antiochene interior." In particular, it shows the recursive use of *emblemata*, that is, pieces of mosaics that were presumably prepared by workshops to be later mounted and fitted to the domestic context and the rest of the decorative apparatus.[228]

But the Atrium House was not alone in presenting its excavators with a heady decorative apparatus and a unique plan. To clinch similar rapid rewards, a number of houses were hastily dug up. Among these, the House of the Calendar and

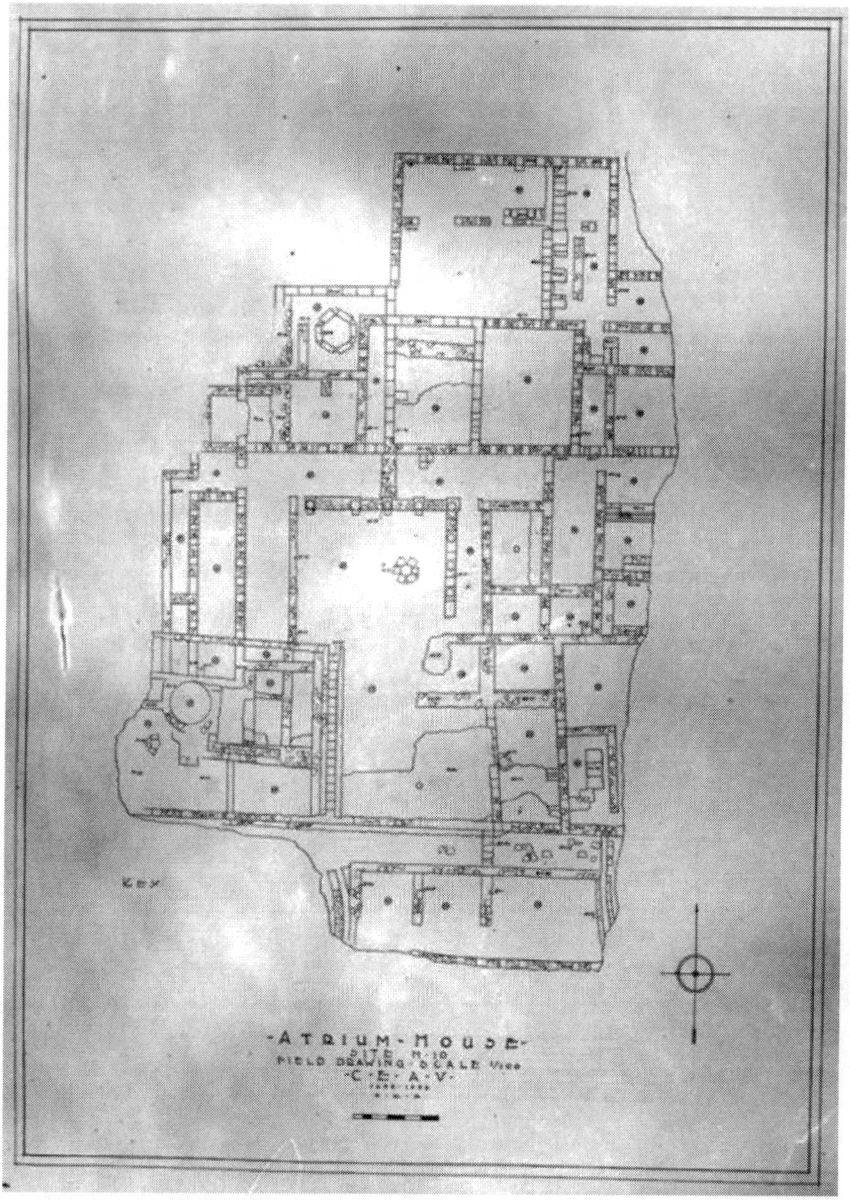

FIGURE 2.21 The Atrium House on the Island

Source: Courtesy of the Antioch Expedition Archives, Department of Art and Archaeology, Princeton University; Princeton

FIGURE 2.22 The *Judgment of Paris* mosaic

Source: Courtesy of the Antioch Expedition Archives, Department of Art and Archaeology, Princeton University; Princeton

the House of the Drunken Dionysus are but a couple of examples of domestic architecture containing other splendid mosaics. The context in which these pavements were found, however, was never fully documented.[229] Equal treatment was accorded to the domestic contexts situated in the nearby district of Daphne,[230] where the theater of the second century CE and several houses dating between the third and early sixth centuries were excavated.[231] Many villa sites were thus discovered on this plateau, among which the House of the Boat of Psyches and the House of Menander stand out for their magnificent mosaics.

Craftsmanship, workshops, and the provenience of the stones used in assembling the mosaics are questions several scholars are currently exploring in this field.[232] Less well known is, of course, Daphne's narrative of settlement (Figure 2.23); how the site, above and beyond its obvious religious implications, went from being treated as a quarry in the Hellenistic period to prime real estate in the imperial period remains to be established.

Also of interest is a cluster of domestic units investigated in 1938–1939 near Seleucia Pieria. Among these is the House of the Drinking Contest, typically dated around 200–230 CE and owing its renown to a large mosaic reiterating the recurring theme of a divine symposium (Figure 2.24).[233] The layout is remarkable insofar as it stresses again the centrality of the triclinium through opening a series of itineraries

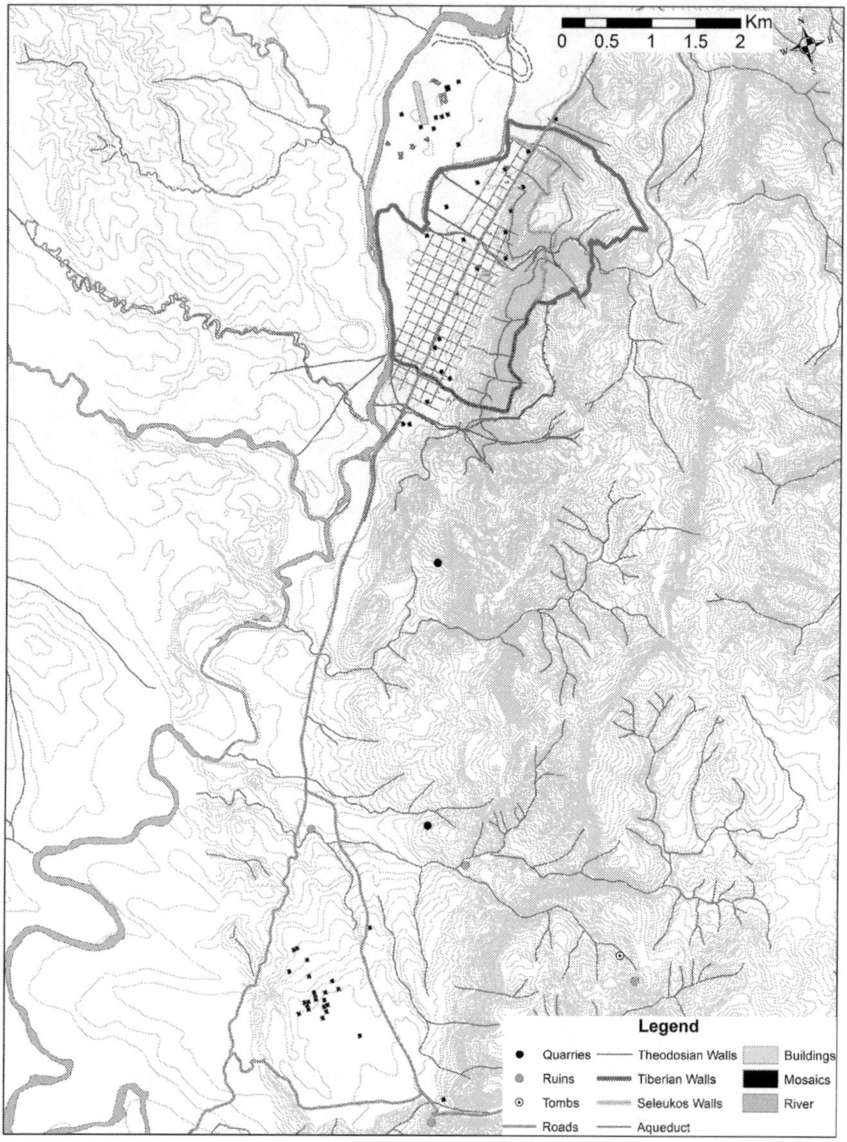

FIGURE 2.23 Antioch, Daphne, and the 1932–1939 excavations: the small squares correspond to the individual digs

Source: Created by Stephen Batiuk

and lines of sight across the nymphaeum (fountain and basin), the porticoes, and the corridors. Patchy though the record of this house may be, it nevertheless reveals the presence of the triclinium/nymphaeum formula that became the hallmark of many houses in the Antiochene district.

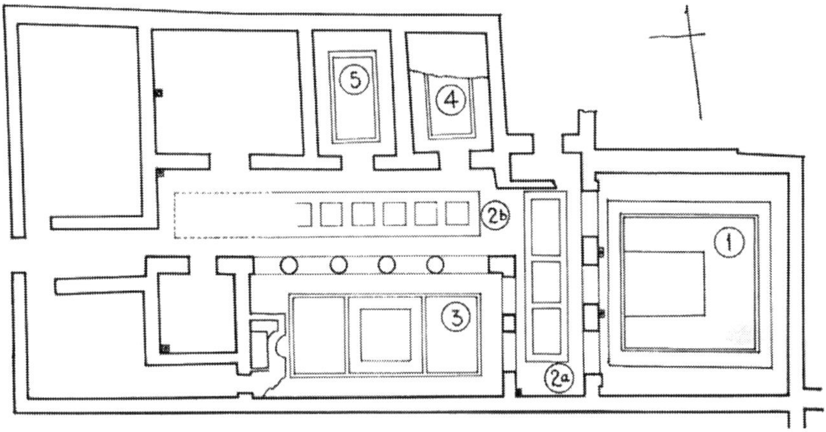

FIGURE 2.24 The House of the Drinking Contest, plan

Source: Courtesy of the Antioch Expedition Archives, Department of Art and Archaeology, Princeton University; Princeton

Further, the identity of the patrons of these remarkable houses remains a key issue.[234] The scant evidence available points in the direction of the Antiochene elites who, through recursively adopting Greek myths and their visual metaphors, shaped their living space in a way that celebrated a shared corporate identity. Ironically, this Hellenic spirit and its visual repertoire were at odds with the expectations of Charles Rufus Morey, director of the Princeton excavations, to find the traces of the "barbarization of classical art."

Overall, the question of where most of Antioch's population concentrated and whether these units represent the only housing solution available to them remains paramount. No tenements like those known, for instance, in Rome or Ostia were identified by the early Antioch excavations or recent salvage digs in Antakya. What kind of structures were available to the bulk of the population and, not least, to the less affluent strata remains to be established. It is nevertheless apparent that all the known houses, for all their opulence and attention to décor, had one aspect in common. Their layout and presentation were constantly revamped and transformed during the course of time, thus adhering to a practice that was the signature of public architecture in the city.[235] Ultimately, the action of earthquakes was a key factor in the reorientation and restructuring of these houses. Whether they also reflect an idiosyncratic perspective toward housing and domestic space is also a cogent possibility.

There should, however, be no doubt that the Romans found here, in this corner of the Levant, both groups and individuals keen to mediate between them and the local communities and equally eager to obtain privileges and visibility within their own polities. The epigraphic record for Antioch is very limited, and one can hardly construct a prosopography on the few names available, let alone patterns of social mobility. The narratives available for families in Ephesus, Antioch in Pisidia, and Aphrodisias are simply not conceivable in Antioch. Nevertheless, documents like the letter of Augustus to the town of Rhosus, noted earlier, bestowing citizenship and privileges to the *navarkos* Seleucus, are proof of the amalgamation under way.[236] The pinnacle of this trend was reached during the Flavian period, when Rome welcomed the first Antiochene senators, thus inaugurating a trend that continued in the following decades. The process was formulaic: members of local elites became prominent, first within the city and then in the *koinon* (assembly) of the province,[237] and eventually gained access to the Roman Senate. Eight families from Antioch between the end of the first and second centuries CE achieved the highest excellence following this trajectory.[238] It is likely that the key to their prominence resided in land assets and the economy of the rural district. In this perspective, the villas excavated in the 1930s likely served strictly residential purposes and, especially those located in the vicinity of Daphne, as an ideal retreat from the city during the hottest summer months. Even the physical characteristics of this district suggest this hypothesis. Densely forested in antiquity, the area was unsuitable for extensive agriculture, let alone the villa economy of Italian tradition or the farmstead module observed on the plain of Antioch or the rolling hills of the southeastern Jibal.[239]

Conclusions

In conclusion, we have observed Antioch's gradual positioning at the center of the Roman world. As provincial capital, the city was not slow in developing a dense network of rural settlements that were held together by new administrative frameworks. A panoply of causes, from Daphne's heightening as pivotal religious center in the eastern Mediterranean to the escalation of hostilities with the Parthians, led to forging a new image of the city while also imbuing the community with a new sense of confidence and civic pride. The built environment, so greatly enriched by empire-sponsored projects, whether for water infrastructure or entertainment, demonstrably distanced Antioch from the countless Greco-Roman cities of the Greek East. No community could boast comparable investments by the imperial administrators. The grand waterworks of the Flavians along the lower Orontes Valley let it be known that Antioch was to become the bulwark of Rome in the years to follow.

As Roman provincial capital, Antioch retained its Hellenistic urban layout and ancestral customs. Both Pompey and then Caesar felt the allure of the city on the Orontes and were not slow in bestowing *libertas* on its prestigious community. The occasional makeover of buildings and addition of imperial veneer, however, signaled the new law and order. Julius Caesar, Agrippa, Tiberius, and virtually every emperor that had an interest in stamping their pride onto this city left a permanent mark on Antioch's built environment. But unlike the other cities of the Roman East, it was no mere embellishment of a prestigious and loyal community.

Rather, the gradual eastward tilting of the empire and the growth of a formidable foe east of the Euphrates increasingly added political and administrative gravitas to Antioch, while also making the city the vital center of a confrontation against the Persians that spanned the first and the seventh centuries CE. Fittingly, long imperial sojourns like those of Trajan and Lucius Verus inaugurated a season of extended stays and ambitious monumental expansion.

Notes

1 Mordechai and Pickett 2018.
2 Will 1997.
3 The literary trope of the city as a locus of excesses reverberates greatly in the sources. See, for instance, Plut. *Cat. Min.* 13, *Hist. Aug.* Marcus Aurelius 8.12. On Roman soldiers distracted by Antioch, see Fronto *Ep.* 19. For a general discussion of the military and the dangers of Antioch, see Wheeler 1996.
4 Millar 1993, 27; Burns 2005, 46; Ball 2000, 11–12.
5 Just. *Epit.* 40.2.
6 Rey-Coquais 1978, 45.
7 Downey 1937. See also Leblanc and Poccardi 1999, 115–122, for a thorough discussion of the topography on the Island.
8 W.A. Campbell was at the helm of the circus excavation; see his report in *Antioch I*, 34–41. His identification of the building with that of Q. Marcius Rex is grounded in the late Hellenistic pottery and a coin of Antiochus VI Dionysus (144–142 BCE) in the strata below the level of the top of the foundations.
9 Humphrey 1986, 455. He stresses the lack of any decisive evidence pointing to the late first century BCE and suggests an early second-century CE date based on select pottery deposits. This hypothesis, however, does not rule out the existence of the early predecessor of Q. Marcius Rex known through the textual sources. For the ongoing excavation of the circus, see Pamir 2019.
10 For the concise report, see *Antioch I*. On curse tablets found at the circus, see Hollmann 2003. An ongoing Turkish excavation has taken up the area again, exposing a portion of the *spina* and the seats in the western sector. The recovery of a grave, potentially of the Hellenistic period, opens suggestive possibilities in how the area was used prior to Antiochus III's development. See Pamir 2016, 77.
11 *Antioch Archives*, Diary Summer of 1934–1937.
12 The discussion of Antioch as center of the imperial cult from the days of Augustus until its fall from grace in the Severan period can be found in Butcher 2004, 13. For the general phenomenon of imperial temple wardens, that is, the *neokoria*, see Burrell 2004.
13 App. *B Civ.* 1.68.309.
14 Jones 1998, 258.
15 Brennan 2000, 411.
16 Sherwin-White 1983, 271.
17 Dio Cass. 39.56.6. infers that Gabinius first organized the taxation system for both Judea and Syria, thereby changing the procedure introduced by Pompey, which essentially consisted of a lump sum. Though intriguing, no other sources substantiate this information.
18 Sherwin-White 1983, 271–279; Eilers 2003, 91. For Cicero's criticism on Gabinius's administration, see Cic. *Prov.cons.* I-20. Whether it was real maladministration or just personal enmity is difficult to tell. See *Downey, History* 149.
19 On measures affecting the *publicani* and their activities, and particularly on the loss of proconsular favor in legal matters, see Sherwin-White 1983, 276.
20 Strab. 12.3.34.
21 Vell.Pat. 2. 37.
22 Cic. *Prov.cons.* 10.
23 Joseph. *AJ.* 14.6.4.

24 Butcher 2004, 51.
25 *TIB* 15, 144.
26 *Downey, History* 144.
27 Malalas reports that Pompey "laid claim to the Antiochenes and, entering the city of Antioch, he made it subject to the Romans, giving generously to them and rebuilding the *bouleuterion*, for it had fallen down." Pompey also allegedly praised the Antiochenes for their Athenian origin, a trope in the Antioch sources. See *Malalas* 8.30. On the possibility that an earthquake may have led the bouleuterion to its sorry state, see Downey 1937, 150.
28 Caes. *BCiv*. 3.102.
29 On the bronze issue using Seleucid types, see *McAlee, Coins* 1–2. On the continuity of minting coins that continued the Seleucid traditions, see Metcalf 2000, 107. With regard to coinage in the Pompeian era, and especially the discrepancies among the former cities of the Tetrapolis, see Butcher 2004, 26.
30 *Antioch IV*, ix, 24–69.
31 For a thorough study of the Roman legions and their impact on the societies of Syria, see Pollard 2000. With regard to the military operations in Syria and beyond the Euphrates during the days of the Julio-Claudian dynasty, see Dabrowa 2020, 17. As the Polish scholar remarks, a precise timeline of the military operations in Syria as well as the names of the legions involved remains a difficult task. The loss of Zeugma and, especially, Samosata by the construction of massive dams on the Euphrates hampers the understanding of the military infrastructure in the early days of the Roman Empire.
32 Cic. *Att*. 5.18.1.
33 On the size of the Syrian army during the first century CE, see Wintjes 2018, 79. On Antioch as a base, see Isaac 1990, 436–438. The textual sources refer in passing to the existence of a military camp near Antioch: Lib. *Or*. 15.76; *Theod.HR* 2.15; 2.19; 4.25.6; 4.26.3; 8.8; Passio Bonosi et Maximiliani (BHL 1427) AAS 21, 431F; Ps. Athanas, *Petitiones Arianorum*, PG 26, 820.
34 Tate 1997, 55. Tribes and nomads are often confused. Thoughtful in this sense is Whittaker 1978, 331–362, based on a thorough analysis of the archaeological evidence from Roman Africa.
35 Dio Cass. 36.17.3; Jones 1998, 264.
36 Jones 1998, 264. For the archaeology of Gindaros, see Kramer 2004.
37 Strab. 16.5.
38 Butcher 2003.
39 Strab. 16.2.
40 *Downey, History* 143–151.
41 Rey-Coquais 1978, 44.
42 Tate 1997, 57.
43 Dio Cass. 40.29.1 states that after failing to take Antioch, the Parthians sought to regroup around Antigonia. This information is of course controversial, for it would attest to the survival of the city after Seleucus Nicator's dismantling.
44 Millar 1993, 159.
45 Cumont 1934, 188.
46 Butcher 2003, 36.
47 Eilers 2003, 95.
48 Caes. *BCiv*. 3.102.
49 On the battle of Pharsalus see the hyperbolic account of Julius Obsequens, 65a (transl. by A. C. Schlesinger), perhaps reporting a local legend:

> On that very day, it is well known that in many places statues turned about of their own accord, battle-cries and the clash of arms were heard at Antioch, so that twice the walls were manned; the same sounds were heard at Ptolemaïs, and the noise of timbrels at Pergamum.

As for Antioch's titles, they occur in some of the Julio-Claudian issues, see Downey 1951. For a synthetic report on Antioch's mint and the coins recovered by the Antioch expeditions, see Metcalf 2000, 105–111.

50 *Malalas* 9.5. spells out the provisions of Antioch's freedom grant. The titles of "metropolis, sacred, inviolate, and autonomous" also figure prominently on the early Caesarian bronze coinage in Antioch; see Butcher 2004, 26.

51 *Downey, History* 157.

52 Rey-Coquais 1978, 45.

53 *Malalas* 9.5. A German-Turkish archaeological survey identified an aqueduct tapping water from a spring above the village of Kuruyer and presumably entering the city from the valley of the Phyrminus stream; see Pamir and Yamaç 2012. Early 1930s surveys of Antioch's aqueducts were conducted by the Princeton team: see *Antioch I*, 49–56. For the textual reference, see also Lib. *Or.* 11. 219 and 10.33. The theater of Caesar was presumably a repair of the Seleucid theatre of Dionysus; an early theater is mentioned by Lib. *Or.* 11. 125. Antakya's topography of the city in the area of Sofular Mahallesi (sector 18-O–P) may have accommodated a venue of that nature, as suggested by a large, semicircular plaza still visible in 1934 despite "30 ft. of silt." A sounding using robber's trenches and a shaft identified at least two rows of seats: *Antioch Archives*, Diary Summer 1934. It played a central role in the politics and entertainment of Antioch: see Lib. *Or.* 11.125; Amm. Marc. 33.5.3; Severus of Antioch *HC* 18, *PO* 37, p. 18; *Evagrius* 6.7. The latter, in particular, attests to the longevity of the building as locus for political debates.

54 Gerritsen et al. 2008; De Giorgi 2007.

55 App. *B Civ.* 2.20.

56 Cic. *Ad Fam.* 12.15.

57 Joseph. *AJ.* 14.5.

58 *Downey, History* 161–160.

59 Olivier and Parisot-Sillon 2013, 258–259. The Antony and Cleopatra silver tetradrachm allegedly produced at Antioch is controversial; see Butcher 2004, 55–58.

60 Dio Cass. 51.8.

61 Millar 1993, 27.

62 Though acknowledged by several emperors, the problem was finally resolved by Septimius Severus at the end of the second century CE by creating the twin provinces of Syria Coele and Syria Phoenice.

63 *IGLS* 3. 1. 718. See also Sherk 1969, 58. Another case in point is that *of C. Julius Menoes Antiochensis Syriae ad Daphnem* (*CIL* IX, 41=*ILS*, 2819), an Antiochene presumably stationed in the navy base of Misenum under Vipsianus Agrippa (Dio Cass. 58.5; Suet. *Aug.* 16), whose daughter married Malchius, a trierarch of Augustus. On Greeks and Orientals getting citizenship rewards during the civil wars, see Mancinetti Santamaria 1983, 125–136.

64 See Millar 2002, 271–291, for a comprehensive analysis of senatorial versus imperial provinces and their ramifications.

65 Tac. *Ann.* 4. 5; Millar 1993, 32.

66 Dabrowa 2020.

67 Erdkamp 2002, 47–69.

68 As Carlos F. Noreña writes: "The record of the Antiochene civic coinage under Augustus is twofold, then, characterized by a consistent interplay of imperial and local in its themes, images, and texts." See Noreña 2016, 296–297. Also, Stahl 2017, 235 on the clustering of first-century-CE coins in sectors 15-M (House of Aion) and 10-N (Bath B and the Atrium House); Jones 1998, 263. The go-to reference for the catalog of denominations of Antioch's coinage during the Augustan Age is *McAlee, Coins* 110–121. See also some general indications in Metcalf 2000, 105–111.

69 Horster 2013.

70 Butcher 2004, 29.

71 Howgego 1982, 12.
72 Pollard 2000, 176. Also, more generally, Erdkamp 2002, 47–69.
73 See the Dura Final Report 5.1 in Welles et al. 1959, 270–278.
74 Plin. *HN* 5.19. features a list of Syrian cities. Odds are good that in compiling the report, Pliny amply drew from the census data of 6 CE, yet inconsistencies and discrepancies make his list controversial. The main problem is the division between Syria Coele and the "rest of Syria," which causes a "muddle," as Jones puts it. For a detailed discussion on Pliny's Syrian Cities list, see Jones 1998, 262–263.
75 Dabrowa 1998, 28.
76 Joseph. *AJ*. 18.26. Dabrowa 1998, 27–30.
77 Luke 2. 1–2. The correlation between the census and the birth of Jesus Christ presents a series of problems, chiefly the fact that Galilea at the time was under the independent tetrarchy of Herodes Antipas, and thus no Roman census took place there during Jesus's lifetime.
78 *ILS*, 2683.
79 See Bagnall and Frier 1994 for a thorough discussion of the census in Roman Egypt.
80 Plin. *HN* 6.145.
81 Ulp. *dig*. 50. 15. 3.: "Aetatem in censendo significare necesse est, quia quibusdam aetas tribuit, ne tributo onerentur; veluti in Syriis a quattuordecim annis masculi, a duodecim feminae usque ad sexagensimum annum tributo capitis obligantur."
82 Bagnall and Frier 1994, 12–14.
83 The population of Antioch is a debated issue, with figures ranging from 150,000 to 500,000; see Callu 1997.
84 Liebeschuetz 1972, 92–93. His focus is Libanius's Antioch, that is, the city of the fourth century CE. Nevertheless, this tally can also be applied to the Roman city, given the spatial implications. Of relevance here also Lib. *Ep*.119, loosely referring to 150,000 men in Antioch, and Chrysostom, Hom. in Matth. 85.4, inferring that the city could boast 150,000 Christians.
85 See Tac. *Ann*. 2. 42. 7, where Tacitus alludes to a petition that aimed to protect the population of Syria and Judea. It is likely that Tacitus's elusive argument was simply intended to the detriment of the Tiberius. The rub is whether taxation remained quantitatively low. A later reference to the hefty tributes levied in Syria can be found in the *Historia Augusta*, life of Pescennius Niger, where the complaints of the Palestinian population are completely disregarded by the emperor, as seen in SHA. *Pesc. Nig*.7. 9.
86 *Downey, History* 169.
87 *IGLS* 3. 744: – *mque/–rumque/–li arcu donatus/–noster/-us Augustus-/–mum Caesarem/–Illyricum/-secutus sit.*
88 Tac. *Ann*. 184–191 (II 69–73); Suet. Cal. 2; *Tabula Siarensis* I, 35–37: *Alter ianus fieret in montis Amani iugo quod est in* [---]. See J. Gonzales 1984. A cenotaph located in Antioch's forum also commemorated the place of Germanicus's funeral pyre. On Germanicus in Antioch, see also *IGLS* 3. 836.
89 *Malalas* 9.14.
90 Kontokosta 2018.
91 Joseph. *AJ*. 16, 148; Joseph. *BJ*. 1.21.11; Dio Chrys. *Or*. 47.16; Lib. *Or*. 11.196; *Malalas* 9.17; *John of Nikiu* 66.2.
92 *Antioch V*, 41–81.
93 See previous chapter, p. 44.
94 *Antioch V*, 143.
95 Although mainly concerned with Antioch during the time of Libanius, Cabouret 1999 provides a comprehensive commentary on the porticoes and their social discourse.
96 See p. 71. See also Humphrey 1986, 456 on the genesis of the building and its textual references.
97 Dio Cass. 49.43.2.
98 *Malalas* 9.20 reports on the endowment and its handling by some administrators, who evidently profiteered from it. See also Liebeschuetz 2006; Saliou 2016 on Malalas's anachronisms and complicated flashbacks in his text.

99 Lib. *Or.* 1.14.

100 Brasse 2010. Early travelers to Antioch, too, sought to identify the different agencies behind the construction of Antioch's walls. See, for instance, the report of James Buckingham (1826, 561), who upon seeing the citadel and crosses etched on walls, remarked as follows:

> An examination of the masonry itself, and the general style of their construction, is sufficient, however, to convince any one the least conversant in antiquities, that the whole is either a work of the romans, or of Seleucus Nicator, the founder of the city, at the death of Alexander, and that the cross is, therefore, a more recent addition.

101 Brasse 2010.

102 Brands 2009, 12.

103 The map by Downey and Wilber situates the southern section of the wall of Tiberius in this same fashion, though the Theodosian addition ends up in the gorge of the Phyrminus, which is not a tenable solution. Brasse 2010; Brands 2016a, by turn, safely avoid tracing any walls, limiting their analysis to visible or recorded remains.

104 The Sari Mahmud excavation was a rapid foray of the Princeton team into the demolition of an old *khān* during the summer of 1934. The inspection of the site, though cursory, yielded a host of funerary slabs of the first two centuries CE as well as fragments of marble architecture. While the Mnemosyne necropolis is mostly known for the beautiful and enigmatic fourth-century CE mosaic of a funerary symposium, evidence that attests to previous phases is well documented, in the main small marble slabs with images and dedicatory inscriptions. See in particular De Giorgi 2019, 30–31.

105 On the demography of Antioch, see Callu 1997.

106 Gerritsen et al. 2008, 252–260.

107 Tac. *Ann.* 73 (transl. by C.H. Moore and J. Jackson): "The body, before cremation, was exposed in the forum of Antioch, the place destined for the final rites." Also, Dio Cass. 57.18 (transl. by E. Cary and H. Foster):

> His death occurred at Antioch as the result of a plot formed by Piso and Plancina. For bones of men that had been buried in the house where he dwelt and sheets of lead containing curses together with his name were found while he was yet alive; and that poison was the means of his carrying off was revealed by the condition of his body, which was brought into the Forum and exhibited to all who were present.

108 *Malalas* 10.8–10. As for the temple of Dionysus, Malalas reports that two statues of Amphion and Zethos lay in the courtyard of the building. The temple of Pan is also mentioned by Libanius among other civic cults in *Or.* 15.79.

109 On the Olympias spring and the myth of Alexander the Great in Antioch see Lib. *Or.* 11.72–74; 88; 250; 15.79. On the recurring use of monumental talismans and their cultural implications, see pp. 44–45; *Downey, History* 181, refers to these talismans as "products of local folklore." Rather, these traditions were rooted in the eastern matrix of the city and its ancestral traditions.

110 See previous chapter, p. 43.

111 Saliou 2006, 69–73.

112 *Malalas* 10.8.

113 *Malalas* 10.18–19. A Slavonic version of Malalas's manuscript also refers to a landslide that may have occurred in tandem with the event. See Ambraseys 2009, 111.

114 Metcalf 2000, 108.

115 Lib. *Or.* 11.243; Antioch on the Orontes II, 53–54. See also Leblanc and Poccardi 2004, 241–242.

116 Leblanc and Poccardi 2004, 241–243.

117 Kraeling 1932, 148–149.

118 *Downey, History* 192–195. Malalas's text may be corrupted by anachronism in this particular context: see Liebeschuetz 2006, 147.

119 Acts 11.26; *Downey, History* 192.
120 Millar 1993, 56.
121 *Malalas* 10.23. Ephesus and Smyrna apparently were hit, along with other cities of Asia. The year of the episode is unknown. Of interest is also a report by Philostratus, *VA*. 6.38 (transl. by C. Jones), presumably referring to this very event, whereby

> The governor of Syria was throwing Antioch into turmoil by sowing suspicion that had divided the citizens. The city was holding an assembly, when a major earthquake occurred that caused them to cower and, as usually happens in divine visitations, to pray for one another.

122 *Downey, History* 196.
123 Uggeri 2009, 95.
124 Gal. 2. 11.
125 Acts 11.26: "And for an entire year they met with the church and taught considerable numbers; and the disciples were first called Christians in Antioch."
126 Acts 11.19–26.
127 For the discussion of the early Antiochene community, see in particular Dauer 1996, 12–22.
128 *Downey, History* 277.
129 Gal. 2. 11.
130 *Downey, History* 285–286.
131 Harvey 2000, 39.
132 On Sosibius' donation for the games, see n. 98. The administrative framework of these games, however, merits attention. As Johannes Hahn recently notes, this is the first-and-only instance of a city acquiring the rights to organize games from Elis in Greece, which had authority over Olympia and the Olympic games. Permission was allegedly granted for a period of 90 penteric cycles. On this issue and the wider discussion about this controversial transfer of authority, see Hahn 2018, 55.
133 Joseph. *AJ*. 19.279.
134 Rey-Coquais 1978, 50.
135 Millar 1993, 64.
136 31 *Antioch I*, 158.
137 *McAlee, Coins*; Metcalf 2000, 108; Windham 2005, 287. For the full discussion of new standards and iconography under Nero at the Antioch mint, see Butcher and Ponting 2009, 60. Relevant is also the discourse of the metrology; the Antiochene talent weighed the same as an Attic one but apparently valued at three quarters of it; see Butcher 2004, 199.
138 Tac. *Hist.* 5.10 (transl. by C.H. Moore):

> When Cestius Gallus, governor of Syria, tried to stop it, he suffered varied fortunes and met defeat more often than he gained victory. On his death, whether in the course of nature or from vexation, Nero sent out Vespasian, who, aided by his good fortune and reputation as well as by his excellent subordinates, within two summers occupied with his victorious army the whole of the level country and all the cities except Jerusalem.

139 At stake, of course, was their refusal to sacrifice to the gods. Joseph. *BJ*. 7.46–53.
140 *Malalas* 10.32; Chrysostom, Hom. in St. Ig., 4. 587. See also the spurious account of the *Martyrium Ignatii*; though problematic in terms of nature and sources, it nevertheless documents the rise to prominence of the church of Antioch.
141 Tac. *Hist.* 2.80 (transl. by C.H. Moore):

> Then he entered the theatre at Antioch, where the people regularly hold their public assemblies, and addressed the crowd which hurried there, and expressed itself in extravagant adulation. His speech was graceful although he spoke in Greek, for he knew how to give a certain air to all he said and did.

142 Rey-Coquais 1978, 53.
143 Joseph. *BJ*. 7.54–60.
144 Joseph. *BJ*. 7.46–52.
145 Kraeling 1932, 153.
146 On Traianus's career, see Dabrowa 2020, 69–76. On his governorship between 73 and 78 CE, see Dabrowa 1998, 64–67; Bowersock 1973, 133, is of a different opinion, suggesting a 73–77 CE tenure, which would precede the appointment of Commodus by a year.
147 Plin. *Pan*. 16. 1. On the senate's bestowing of the *ornamenta triumphalia*, the highest honor for a military commander, to Ulpius Traianus, see also Drabowa 2020, 74.
148 Butcher 2004, 34.
149 On Flavian policy in Asia Minor, see Dabrowa 1980; for Judea, see Millar 1993, 70–79.
150 On Flavian building activities within the city, see *Downey, History* 206–207.
151 Dabrowa 1986, 93.
152 See Wheeler 1996, 229–276, on the alleged laxity of the Syrian legions and the birth of the literary *topos* of their lack of discipline. See also Tac. *Ann*. 13. 35. 1 for the ironic characterization of the troops under Corbulo, incapacitated by their unprofessional behavior in Syrian cities.
153 The changes applied initially to the Cappadocian legions and then subsequently to the Syrian. Moreover, a new unit, Flavia Firma, was introduced in 72 and stationed in Samosata, modern Samsat, now under the waters of the Atatürk Dam. For the logistics and the movements of the Syrian legions, however, see Millar 1993, 8; Dabrowa 1986.
154 Van Berchem 1985, 61.
155 On the coinage at issue, see *McAlee, Coins* 159. For Traianus's accolades, see Millar 1993, 80. On the possibility of a campaign against the Parthians in 73–74 CE carried out under Vespasian by Traianus, see Van Berchem 1983, 189.
156 Bowersock 1973, 133–135.
157 Millar 1993, 86.
158 For an extensive analysis of the document, see Van Berchem 1983, 186–196. Also, Dabrowa 2020, 74.
159 For long it has been held that a detachment of Antiochenes from Pisidia had contributed to the undertaking, as suggested by the controversial reading of the last lines of the inscription. Van Berchem inferred that the Antiochene detachment was a unit recruited among the Syrian Antiochenes; though suggestive, the interpretation is not substantiated by any evidence, and no textual or epigraphic source supports the existence of such a unit. A *cohors* of Pisidian Antiochenes had instead been active in Asia Minor since the inception of that Augustan colony in western Asia Minor, but its deployment in Syria in that moment of fairly stationary legions and detachments is somewhat problematic. However, the recent discovery of a Greek copy of the same text has brought the matter to an end, excluding any involvement of folks from Pisidia. In particular, Catherine Saliou has conclusively demonstrated that this great undertaking had been presented to the city of the Antiochians, i.e., those on the Orontes (Ἀντιοχέων πόλει). See her compelling discussion of the text in Aydın and Saliou 2020.
160 Paus. 8.29.3 (transl. by W.H. S. Jones):

> The Syrian river Orontes does not flow its whole course to the sea on a level, but meets a precipitous ridge with a slope away from it. The Roman emperor wished ships to sail up the river from the sea to Antioch. So with much labour and expense he dug a channel suitable for ships to sail up, and turned the course of the river into this.

Augustus and Tiberius have been typically identified as the unnamed emperor, though there is no evidence of any major work on the Orontes under their mandate. It is safer, then, to assign Vespasian to this allusion. Also, we shall see how a similar project was carried out under Justinian in the sixth century CE.

161 On the Roman navy and the Seleucia harbor under the Flavians, see Van Berchem 1985, 47–87 and *Antioch III*, 2–5. For an up-to-date illustration of Seleucia's harbors and infrastructure, see Pamir 2014a, Figure 5. Also, noteworthy is Buckingham 1825, 547–548: at the time of this early report, the harbor and a good portion of its internal configuration were still visible.

162 *IGLS* 1131 is an especially controversial inscription in that it refers to both Vespasian and Titus as *divi* and bears no trace of the name of Domitian, and thus hints at being an Antonine tribute to the great work at Seleucia. See Van Berchem 1985, 58–59. On the gravestones of the Misenum sailors, see Seyrig 1938.

163 Liebeschuetz 1972, 128.

164 For the problematic expression *Dipotamia(e) flumen* see Millar 1993, 86.

165 For a through discussion of the two inscriptions, see Feissel 1985, 77–103. Also, L. Robert in *CRAI*, 1951, 255–256 and *Downey, History* 232, n. 151.

166 Feissel 1985, 89.

167 The text bears no mentions of the emperor's *Cursus Honorum*, and Vespasian is hastily dismissed as *Titus Flavius* in lieu of the conventional formula *Imp. Caesar Vespasianus Aug.*

168 Feissel 1985, 94–95.

169 Ibid., 95–100.

170 Dabrowa 1980, 39–41.

171 Millar 1993, 80–90; Rey-Coquais 1978, 53.

172 Gerritsen et al. 2008, 252–260; De Giorgi 2008.

173 *Malalas* 10.45. It is quite likely that the theater in Daphne was built under Hadrian, though one cannot rule out the possibility that the project began in the Flavian period. The excavators called into question Malalas's interpretation and suggested a first building phase in the late first century CE and a second after the 341 CE earthquake. Based on coins, the abandonment of the building may date to the mandate of the Emperor Tiberius II (578–582); see Wilber 1938, 57–62. Overall, however, the evidence of a Flavian phase is tenuous at best, and the building's fragmentary architectural decoration rather points toward the second century CE and the Hadrianic horizon.

174 On the display of the spoils and its topographical implications, see Saliou 2013.

175 *Malalas* 10.50.

176 *Antioch I*, 53; *AE* 1968; Scheid 1990 on the prosopography of the Arval Brothers.

177 Metcalf 2000, 108.

178 *McAlee, Coins* 152–172.

179 Dio Cass. 68. 24. 1–2 (transl. by E. Cary and H. B. Foster):

> For as Trajan was wintering there, and many soldiers had gathered there as well as many civilians, whether for judicial hearings or on embassies or as traders or out of curiosity, there was not a province or a community which remained unharmed, and thus in Antioch the whole world under the Romans suffered disaster.

180 *Levi, Pavements*, 34–36.

181 *Levi, Pavements*, 36.

182 *Antioch V*, 146.

183 See especially ibid., 41–81.

184 *Malalas* 11.24.

185 *Malalas* 11.9.

186 Dio Cass. 8.404–409; on the water infrastructure, see Leblanc and Poccardi 2004, 239–256; *Levi, Pavements*, 1.34. Stretches of the aqueduct survive between Harbiye and Antakya; see Pamir 2014a.

187 *Malalas* 11.9. See also Lib. 1. 102–103.

188 *Malalas* 11.11.

189 *Antioch Archives*, Diary 1934–1937.
190 *Malalas* 11.3.4.
191 Millar 1993, 103.
192 Van Berchem 1985, 47–87.
193 *McAlee, Coins* 2003, 187. Silver issues of Trajan radiating from Antioch, following the so-called "Antioch style," began in 108/109 CE. Of interest is the interplay with the Rome mint, with the latter striking coins for the East in the early part of Trajan's reign. See Butcher 2004, 88–91.
194 Dio Cass. 69.18; *SHA*, life of Marcus Aurelius 8.12; Dio Cass. 71.2.2; 75.8–9; 78.20; 79.4–7. Antioch's continuous role as military base continued, albeit in an intermittent way, until the campaigns of Heraclius in 634 CE.
195 Harvey 2000, 39.
196 *John of Nikiu* 72, 1–12. In this context of persecution the earthquake of 113 CE reads like a sign of the "wrath of God."
197 Acts of Thecla, Hennecke and Schneemelcher 1965, 2: 353–364.
198 See Bowersock 1994c, 372, on the alleged reduction of Antioch's importance after the title of metropolis was conferred to Tyre and Damascus.
199 On Hadrian as governor of Syria, see Dabrowa 1998, 89–90.
200 *CIL*, 8, 7059.
201 Rey-Coquais 1978, 53.
202 Butcher 2004, 38.
203 John of Antioch, frag. 273.
204 *Malalas* 11.11. See also Feissel-Gascou 1989, 535, n. 1.
205 *Antioch Archives*, 1934. According to the field notes, the earliest phase of the building should be situated in the first century CE, when the apse of the building was realized. It is plausible that a portico and a mosaic pavement were added in the second century.
206 See Brands 2016b and *Downey, History* 221.
207 Amm. Marc. 22.12.8.; see also Cabouret 1994, 99–100.
208 See fragments of entablature and cornices in *Antioch II*, 89.
209 *Tchalenko, Villages* includes the results of the seminal surveys that brought into focus the district and its development between the second and eighth centuries CE. Tate 1992 finessed and reoriented the discussion, emphasizing the economic agendas that drove settlement in the region. For new interpretative frameworks and sociopolitical perspectives, see Callot 2013.
210 Mattingly 1988, 51.
211 Philostr. *VA*. 6. 39.
212 On Antioch's courts drawing visitors and litigants from all over Syria, see especially the papyrus *Euphrates I*, Chapter 3, 93.
213 Lib. *Or.* 1.26.
214 This is also demonstrated by the Amuq Valley Regional Project survey data; see Gerritsen et al. 2008.
215 *McAlee, Coins* 216; Rey-Coquais 1978, 55.
216 SHA Ant. Pius 43, 1–2.
217 *Malalas* 11.24. Dio Chrys. *Or.* 47.16 also mentions Antioch's colonnades; whether he is referring to the Trajanic repairs is difficult to ascertain.

> Yet perhaps I should not fail to add this much at least on the subject of the tombs and shrines, namely, that it is not likely that the people of Antioch did not lay hands upon anything of this kind; the reason is that they were providing much more space than we are, for their city is thirty-six stades in length and they have constructed colonnades on both sides.

218 SHA *Verus*, 6–9.
219 Butcher 2004, 39.
220 *Downey, History* 228; *TIB* 15, 547.

221 *Malalas* 11.30; on the issue of the size and supply system of this bath, see *Downey, History* 229. As for the sanctuary of the Muses or Mouseion, see Chapter 1, p. 65, n. 134. It is likely that Marcus Aurelius commissioned the restoration of the building, though it is an argument from silence.
222 Lib. *Or.* 11.219; *Malalas* 12.2; Constantinus VII Porphyrogenitus, *De Insidiis*, 167, 1.2.
223 See n. 98.
224 Lib. *Ep.* 1399–1400. See also Bru 2011, 252.
225 *ITralles* 117. See also Remijsen 2010.
226 Butcher 2004, 41.
227 *Antioch I*, 1934, 8–19, in which the site is described in its interface with Bath "B" and House "A." According to the archaeologists, the building was established in the Augustan period, possibly ruined in the 94 CE earthquake, and then devastated by that of the year 115 CE. See also Ellis 2007; Stillwell 1961, 47–48. For a recent analysis, see also Stahl 2017, 235.
228 *Levi, Pavements*, 25–28.
229 Exemplary in this sense is the so-called House of the Menander, which presumably consisted of five different suites adjacent to one another and of at least two building phases: one of the mid-second-century CE and one of the early fourth century. See Dobbins 2000.
230 *Downey, History* 647–650.
231 Wilber 1938.
232 Becker-Kondoleon 2005.
233 Dobbins 2000.
234 Ibid., 51.
235 Morvillez 2007, 54–55.
236 *IGLS* 3, 1.718. Jalabert and Mouterde 1950, 395–411. See n. 63.
237 Rey-Coquais 1978.
238 Bowersock 1994a, 141–159.
239 Gerritsen et al. 2008.

3

FROM CAPITAL TO CRISIS

Antioch in the Late Roman Empire (193–458)

> Wretched Antioch, the exacting Ares will not leave you
> while the Assyrian War is waging around you.
> For a leading man will dwell under your roofs
> who will battle against all the arrow-shooting Persians,
> he himself coming from the royal house of the Romans.
>
> – *Sibylline Oracles* 13.59–63

Introduction

The end of the Antonine period and rise of the Severan dynasty in 193 CE demarcate the beginning of the Late Roman Empire (third to fifth centuries CE), an epoch that traditionally overlaps with Late Antiquity (third to sixth centuries CE), a term used to describe the transition from the classical period to the Middle Ages. As with any major historical compartments, these labels serve the viewpoint and analysis of the individual scholar rather than offering widely accepted canonical timelines. With this chapter, however, we bring into focus Antioch at the time when it became the virtual capital of the Roman Empire and was referred to as "the city without a rival."[1] Ausonius, a fifth-century poet in Gaul who catalogued and ranked cities, made plain that Antioch equaled Alexandria and trailed not far behind Rome, Constantinople, and Carthage.[2] As for the demography, it is accepted that the population of the city at that time ranged between the 150,000 and 300,000 inhabitants.[3] The voices of Antiochene chroniclers, historians, and rhetoricians create an extraordinary unison of excellence, monumentality, and political gravitas. Indeed, for the whole of the third century and much of the fourth, Antioch was arguably the empire's capital in all but name, and no city could compete with its centrality. Intellectual currents, religious debates, the transformation of civic governance, the rise of a new extraordinary foe in the East, the logistics of wars on an unprecedented scale, and the city's status as residence of several emperors made Antioch the new pivot of the *oikoumene*, that is, the whole inhabited earth (Figure 3.1). But this was also an *oikoumene* that was redolent with the political insecurities and religious dilemmas of the times, anxieties that played out prominently in Antioch.

Here we highlight these sociopolitical realities overall as they also brought to bear on new architectural landscapes. Whether through imperial patronage, the initiative of local notables, or an extraordinary output of resources, Antioch's built environment continued to be transformed amid the establishment of new monuments and upkeep of the old. Another key line of inquiry is the foundation of Constantinople in 330, which gradually began to eclipse Antioch's fortunes and eroded its preeminence. Finally, the havoc wreaked by the earthquake of 458 – the consequences of which made evident the city's vulnerability and ultimately ushered in a new phase in the life of Antioch – bookends the chapter.

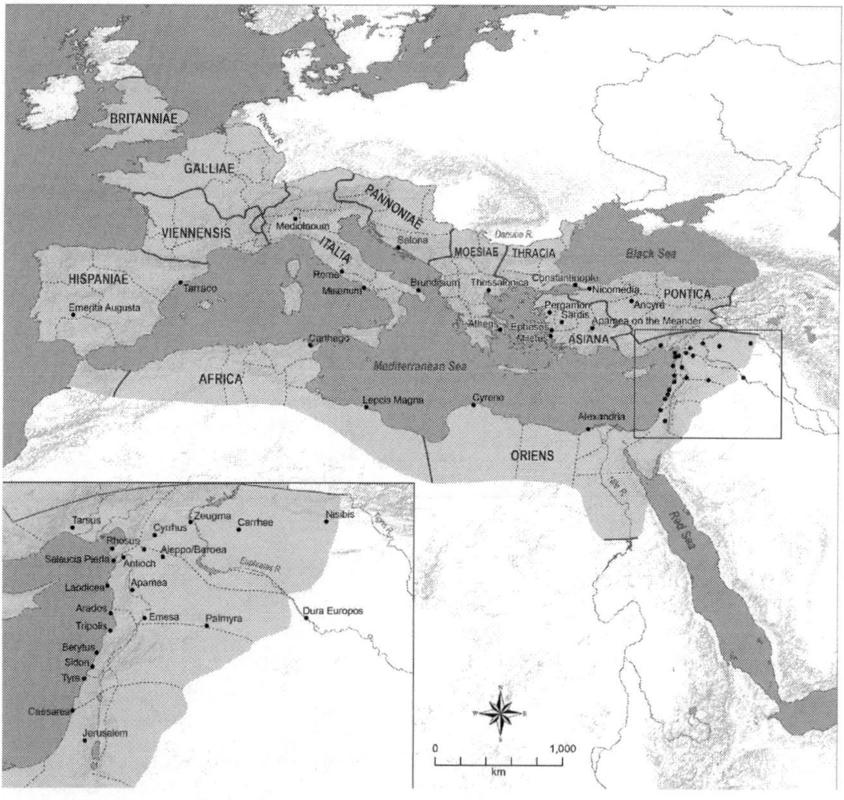

FIGURE 3.1 The Roman Empire during the fourth century CE

Source: Created by Claire Ebert

A universal empire: the Severans and the third century

The Severan dynasty rose to the highest rank at a key juncture in Roman history. The 193 failed coup by the Syrian legate Pescennius Niger showed the limitations and inner contradictions of the Roman state, as control over the Syrian legions went hand in hand with securing the highest seat in Rome.[4] In practical terms, Pescennius's brief intermezzo and Antioch's unconditional support to the usurper's cause led to extreme measures once Septimius Severus (193–211) restored normality. More to the point, the new emperor separated Syria into two units – Coele (North) and Phoenice (South)– to facilitate his political control over the region. Antioch was downgraded to the status of a village (*kome*) under Laodicea, its Seleucid twin-sister city, and also forced to renounce the Olympic games, nor was any spectacle to be held in the hippodrome thereafter.[5] Antioch was not alone in its institutional downfall. The prestigious colony of Berytus (modern Beirut), founded by Augustus, suffered equal fall from grace. In Antioch, though, the imperial enactment severely dented the confidence of a city that for centuries had boasted of its freedom, independence, and prestige. This long, unfortunate hiatus was, however, brought to a close by the mediation of Julia Domna, Severus's Syrian wife, followed by their son Geta's (209–211) veiled intention of making Antioch the capital of the East and the subsequent reinstatement of the provincial capital's prerogatives under the latter's brother, Caracalla (212–217).[6] Moreover, the imperial house once again spared none of the usual efforts to add their signature to the civic built environment. In particular, baths once again encapsulated the ruler's munificence, in the form of the *Severianum* and the *Livianum*.[7]

Nonetheless, along with the elusive *Plethron*, a venue for wrestlers previously built by Didius Julianus in 193, the Severan baths were the only buildings added to Antioch's fabric before the century's turn.[8] In general, Caracalla went to great lengths to rectify the picture of Antioch's sudden state of marginality; amid the pressures of the *Constitutio Antoniniana* social reform in 212, which granted Roman citizenship to all free men in the empire, and a new war to be waged against the Persians, he mapped out a plan to fully reinstate Antioch's provincial dignity. The title of *colonia iuris italici*, albeit essentially honorific, was but one additional accolade to be added to the city's unmatched pedigree. Antioch thus rose to the prestigious status of colony and its territory was legally treated as if it were in Italy. No longer a *kome* of Laodicea, the city's institutional impasse of nearly two decades had come to an end.[9] Whether a spate of new building programs ensued under the gaze of Caracalla himself, for he enjoyed long sojourns in the city between 215 and 216, cannot be established. His life, however, was cut short in 217 near Carrhae by the treason of Macrinus (217–218),[10] during whose short-lived regime Antioch functioned effectively as capital of the empire, with the local mint issuing billon tetradrachms at full swing.[11] From there Macrinus also responded to the Parthian invasion of Mesopotamia, reached a settlement, then became successively implicated in the dynastic struggle for control of the imperial house. The revolt radiating from Emesa, shrewdly orchestrated by Julia Maesa, sister of Julia Domna, led to Macrinus's overthrow by Caracalla's cousin Elagabalus (218–222). This restoration of the Severan line in turn brought to the fore emperors attested to have spent significant time in Antioch, namely, Elagabalus himself in 218 and Severus Alexander (222–235) in 231. Although ephemeral, Elagabalus's reign in Antioch was signaled by an extraordinary output of civic coinage, with two issues dominating the collection of the 1934 excavation of Daphne's theatre.[12] As Kevin Butcher noted, Antioch at this time not only heightened its production of bronze civic coinage, silver tetradrachm coinage, and Roman imperial radiates but also oversaw the production of local civic coinage across Syria and Arabia.[13] Severus Alexander's reign, meanwhile, confirmed Antioch's position at the center of the Roman East, with the appointment of Gaius Julius Priscus as *rector Orientis*, or governor of the East.[14] The emperor's assassination by his own troops in 235, however, also ushered in a half-century of political turmoil, as the empire cycled through no fewer than 26 claimants to the imperial throne, most of whom met a violent end. Pressure from invading barbarians, crop failures, peasant rebellions, plague, currency debasement, and breakdown of trade networks added to the turbulence.

Importantly, Severus Alexander's reign also interfaced with the rise of a new, powerful dynasty in the district of Fars in Persia, namely the Sasanians.[15] According to al-Ṭabarī, a ninth-century Persian scholar, King Ardashīr I (224–242) led a revolt that finally brought down the Arsacid kingdom.[16] The new realities of power brought forth the energy and bent for conquest of the new house, and relations between Rome and Persia reached their nadir over the following four centuries. The two powers wasted no time opening hostilities. While the initial campaigns waged by Severus Alexander from 231 to 233 led to a stalemate between the two empires, successive attacks by Shāpūr I the Great (240–270) against Roman Syria in 251, 256, and 260 made clear the Sasanians' true intentions. Antioch itself suffered greatly at the hand of the Sasanian king in 253 and 260, in the aftermath of the military catastrophes at Carrhae and Edessa (modern Urfa). Persian agents provocateur operated in Antioch, as well. Whether with the help of the Roman rebel Mariades or else by effectively exploiting the weaknesses of the city's topography, the Persians captured Antioch, enslaved a sizable portion of the population, and led them into the heart of Persia.[17] It is possible the captives wound up offering their labor and know-how to establish gridded cities reminiscent of Roman urban planning, such as Jund-i Shapūr in Khuzistan, or became involved in establishing bridges and dams in Susiana.[18] All the same, other than the vehemence of the attack and its effects on the city, we need to consider the presence not only of traitors in Antioch but also of full-fledged factions that favored Persian domination. Underlying this pattern was a vast landscape of lobbies and political factions that Septimius Severus had not silenced and that seized every opportunity of strife to ignite their own conflicts.[19]

Altogether, Antioch suffered two sacks within seven years; the inability of emperors Trebonianus Gallus (251–253) and Valerian (253–260) to keep the Sasanian threat in check led to destruction within the city. Many of the building programs that followed in successive decades, not least those of the Tetrarchic and Constantinian epochs, may have been aimed at repairing the damage caused by the

Persian attacks.[20] It is almost ironic that a bust of Trebonianus Gallus was recovered amid a cache of other sculptures, mostly dating to the fourth and fifth centuries during the 1934 excavations.[21] As for Valerian, the rock reliefs at Naqsh-i Rustam and Bishāpur (Figure 3.2) offer arresting portraits of the Roman emperor humiliated by Shāpūr; in two different combinations, he appears with Gordian III (238–244) and Philip the Arab (244–249) in a spectacular celebration of Roman subjugation to Persian rule.

Meanwhile, the Antioch mint was nearing the point when the tetradrachm system was abandoned in favor of the production of radiate coinage. That this switch was a result of the Sasanian invasion remains to be determined.[22]

Religious anxieties during the first half of the third century also came to the fore at this time. The ecclesiastical authorities in Antioch, as cited by the fourth-century historian and bishop Eusebius, had to reckon with imperial efforts to eradicate Christianity while also seeking to define an orthodoxy of belief, suspended as they were between Jewish exegesis and early Christological debates. In this context, the Severan dynasty sought to bring Christianization to a halt altogether while remaining ambivalent about the movement's intellectual aspects, as attested by the presence of the great theologian Origen (184–253) in Antioch under the invitation of Julia Mamea, mother of the emperor Alexander Severus.[23] Episodes of persecution followed especially under Maximinus Thrax (235–238), leading to an apparent clash between the great bishop of Antioch St. Babylas (237–251) and Philip the Arab (244–249). The voice of St. Babylas no doubt played a role in raising the Christian community's profile and apparently spearheading a dialogue with

FIGURE 3.2 Naqsh-i-Rustam: the rock relief of Shāpūr, Valerian, and Gordian III

Source: Photograph by Andrea U. De Giorgi

the imperial house, though whether the bishop actually forced Philip the Arab to repent of his crimes and actions remains uncertain. In any event, his life and mission were cut short by the massive anti-Christian campaign waged by Decius (249–251).[24] His martyrdom, moreover, became one of the fundamental stories of early Christianity in Antioch, and not least generated much veneration at his burial site in Daphne and, later, in Kaoussié.[25] Meanwhile, the violence against the Christians did not subside in the following decade, despite the Persian threat. All in all, the observance of ancestral religious customs and, in short, the pagan spirit still loomed large in the city. Magnificent mosaic pavements and artifacts like the mid third century so-called Antakya Sarcophagus (Figure 3.3), with its dazzling visual allusions to heroism, lion hunting, and ritual offerings, advertised the cultural and religious outlook of patrons who upheld the Greek spirit of old.

The city's bureaucratic configuration may also have changed at this time, with a heightened number of high-tier administrators coming directly from Rome. The inscription of Quintus Virius Egnatius Sulpicius Priscus, found during the 1935 excavations near Antioch's hippodrome, mentions he was appointed *praefecto frumenti dandi* (prefect in charge of grain doles) and was father of a future consul under Severus Alexander, though it is hard to infer his specific charge (Figure 3.4).

Several inscriptions in Rome and in the provinces also mention Quintus Virius Larcius Sulpicius, brother of Quintus Virius Egnatius Sulpicius Priscus, who possibly belonged to Septimius Severus's *consilium* (advisors) and as such was involved in the provincial government.[26] Along these same lines of high-echelon imperial personnel in Antioch, one can also read the 216 petition from a group of

FIGURE 3.3 The Antakya Sarcophagus

Source: Courtesy of Hakan Boyacı

FIGURE 3.4 The inscription of Virius Egnatius Sulpicius Priscus

Source: Courtesy of the Antioch Expedition Archives, Department of Art and Archaeology, Princeton University; Princeton

Syrian villagers from the vicinity of Damascus, who denounced the fiscal abuses of an individual who had apparently seized the priesthood at the sanctuary of Zeus Hypsistos, enjoyed immunity from taxes and liens on the property, and benefited from leasing out the land.[27] In this case, the villagers bypassed the governor and presented the petition directly to Caracalla in Antioch, thus illustrating the attempt to punish a man whose actions were at variance with both traditional and Roman fiscal and land customs.[28] The hearing before Caracalla was recorded by a bilingual inscription set up at the sanctuary of Zeus Hypsistos in Dumeir (Syria) and was centered upon two senatorial figures, Egnatius Lollianus and Iulianus Aristaenetus, thereby demonstrating the involvement of senators in provincial matters. It follows then that as *comites Augusti*, prominent individuals of senatorial rank, these men would fulfill legal and administrative duties in provincial contexts.[29]

Indeed, since the days of the early empire, governors had typically settled civil disputes in a capital city or in one that presided over a *conventus* or district court,[30] and so Antioch was often the arena for trials, litigations, and requests for arbitration and judgment from the inhabitants of the Antiochene district and beyond. As another example, in August 245, four farmers from Beth Phouraia, a village on the Euphrates near Dura Europos,[31] came to Antioch to petition the governor Julius Priscus at Antioch's baths of Hadrian to resolve a dispute with some fellow villagers who were threatening to take away their land and assets in open infringement of the laws enforced by the Romans.[32] The text documenting this event illustrates, first, how a thermal establishment functioned also as venue for the resolution of legal matters and, second, the reliance of the Syrian population on the Roman judicial system for land management emanating from Antioch. Instead of settling the debate among themselves, this group of farmers traveled many miles and waited eight months to consult the provincial governor in Antioch in order to prevent any actions or deprivations against them.[33] It is thus apparent that not only communities but also individuals entertained dialogue with the empire and civic administration in various ways. These included both legal and cultic purposes, a common example being the denunciation of illegal appropriations by Roman officials.[34] Whether for business or leisure, Antioch was thus a city that attracted visitors and migration from all over Syria, the Greek East, and even Persia.

Although the Persian occupation of Antioch did not last, the Sasanian threat still loomed over Mesopotamia and Syria; only intervention by the Palmyrenes under the leadership of Queen Zenobia curbed their expansion and prevented the collapse of the eastern frontier at this time (Figure 3.5).

Suspended between myth and scanty historical evidence, the kingdom of Palmyra took advantage of the political and military impasse between the powers of East and West, and not least the sorry state of affairs in the Roman world in the 260s. The kingdom spanned Anatolia and Egypt, an immense expanse of land commanded by the caravan city of Palmyra in the Syrian desert, which had grown to become one of the greatest, and indeed most beautiful, cities of the Greek East. At the helm of the Palmyrene state was Queen Zenobia with her son Vaballathus, whose hegemonic views coincided with the fundamental stalemate of the Roman

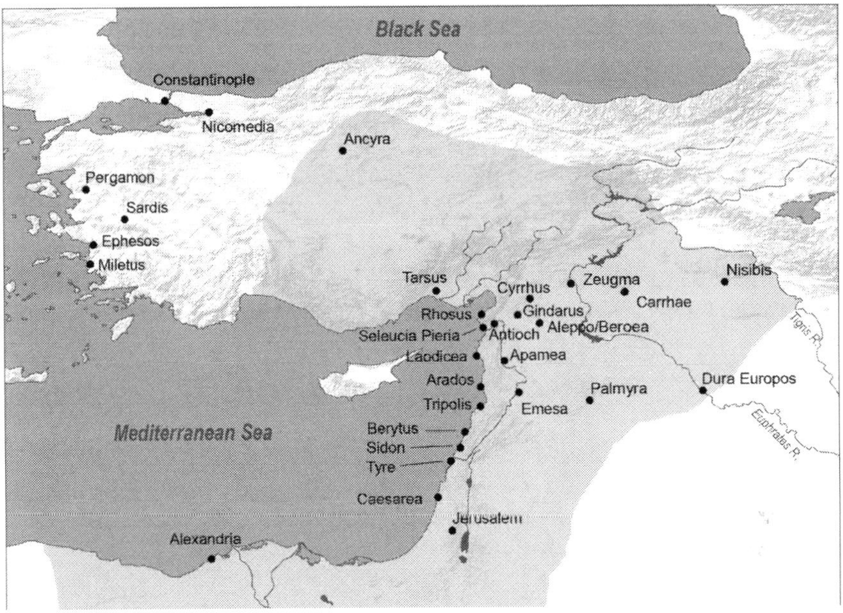

FIGURE 3.5 The kingdom of Palmyra at its greatest extent

Source: Created by Claire Ebert

state. Coins minted in Alexandria with the legend Septimia Zenobia Augusta powerfully advertised the queen's lofty plans. Other coins showing Vaballathus and the emperor Aurelian (270–275), minted in Antioch, attest to the political volatility of those days as well as an effort to reconcile Roman rule with the ambitions of the Palmyrene state.[35] Nor was Antioch exempt from the turmoil of the period, and it may have been under the grip of the Palmyrene house in 270. The defeat of the Palmyrene forces at Immae (modern Yenişehir, 40 km east of Antioch) by Aurelian in 272, however, restored Roman authority over Antioch and Syria and ended the brief Palmyrene hegemony.[36] According to Malalas, after her capture, Queen Zenobia was paraded on a dromedary camel through the streets of Antioch.[37]

This phase of unrest also coincided with religious divisions when in 260 Paul of Samosata rose to become the new bishop and new civic authority in Antioch *tout court*. Fundamentally a Syrian who apparently minced no words about welcoming Palmyrene hegemony, he steered the Christian community toward a doctrine that stressed the human nature of Christ, thereby planting the seeds for the development of Arianism in Antioch. At stake was the core understanding of the Christian message: was Christ created by God and so subordinate to him, as Arianism held, or was he one together with God and the Holy Spirit in the Trinity, as orthodoxy maintained? The liturgy, too, fell under the scrutiny of Paul, with rigorous observance of the old hymns and the introduction of a women's choir.[38] Divisive and controversial to the degree that councils were held against him in Antioch in 264 and 269, his trajectory followed that of the Palmyrene state, with his final ejection from Antioch in 272.[39] Nonetheless, his dogmas were now deeply rooted in the religious landscape of Antioch.

Shortly after Aurelian's reign, the emperor Probus (276–282) apparently enacted a series of measures to revamp civic life in the city. Grain doles, education, and restoration of public buildings conveyed a sense of imperial investment and recognized Antioch's role within Eastern politics.[40] As for Antioch's monuments, Probus is credited with having restored the original veneer to many buildings; in particular, he embellished the temple of the Muses, presumably to be identified with the shrine erected by Marcus Aurelius. Within it, Probus apparently commissioned the construction of a new nymphaeum, one that exhibited a remarkable pool and mosaic with the scene of the marine *thiasus*, or ecstatic retinue, of Oceanus and Thetys, a staple iconography among Antioch's pavements and visual décor writ large (Figure 3.6).[41] From the exquisite pavements of the House of the Calendar to the pool decoration of Bath F, the theme spanned at least two centuries of mosaic making in Antioch and epitomized the recurring use of marine imagery. Detached from complicated intellectual allusions, these pavements may have relied on such

FIGURE 3.6 Mosaic of Oceanus and Thetys, House of Menander, Daphne

Source: Courtesy of the Antioch Expedition Archives, Department of Art and Archaeology, Princeton University; Princeton

literary genres as the Greco-Roman poet Oppian's *On Fishing*, a survey on marine species apparently written at the time of Marcus Aurelius and Commodus and that may have been popular in Syria and Cilicia. In all likelihood, these themes lacked any narrative underpinning, existing only as image and fitting perfectly in locales used as monumental fountains.

The early fourth century and the Tetrarchic capital

The reign of Diocletian (284–305) marked a watershed in the history of the Roman Empire, as the new emperor brought to an end the political turmoil of the previous half-century. Among his many reforms was the addition of a co-emperor to rule in the West as he himself ruled in the East in order to better manage the sprawling empire. Known as Augusti, they were joined in rule by two junior colleagues known as Caesars, a system referred to as the Tetrarchy, or "rule by four." This political arrangement demarcated a new era in Antioch as well. In the new world order, Antioch became one of the capitals of the Diocese of the East, home of the *comes Orientis* (count of the East) and of the *magister militum per Orientem* (military commander for the East). Following at least two visits, Diocletian established his headquarters in the city with a view toward launching a military campaign against the Sasanian king Narseh (293–302). After alternating fortunes, in 298 his junior colleague Galerius (293–311) finally defeated the Persians.

A porphyry head found during the excavation of military barracks outside Antakya in 1934, buried along with a cache of other sculpture presumably discarded or hidden, may document the appearance of Diocletian's official portraiture, with its typical geometric and austere overtones, on the shores of the Orontes (Figure 3.7).[42]

Seeking to leave a durable imprint on the city, Diocletian also made his mark as a builder. In 297, he established a new imperial enclave on the Island on the site that had previously served as the residence of the Seleucid kings under Antiochus III and that may have been monumentalized by Quintus Marcius Rex in the late first century BCE (Figure 3.8). The new imperial palace had presumably already been started by the emperor Gallienus (253–268), who eventually went on to choose Milan as his headquarters.[43] As Slobodan Čurcic has noted, Diocletian's residence in Antioch has to be seen in the context of the great imperial palaces of the Tetrarchy at Thessalonica (Palace of Galerius), Milan (Palace of Maximian), Split (Palace of Diocletian), and later Constantinople.[44] Presumably drawing on the same conceptual plan, these buildings braided together the concept of the imperial, grandiose *domus* in dynamic connection with a hippodrome or other monumental amenities. More fundamentally, these palaces had great impact on their respective urban settings and overall topography, all the while broadcasting a new idea of the emperor as a ruthless and strenuous defender of the state and its ancestral values.

How the Antioch complex negotiated this template, however, is difficult to deduce, as the 1930s excavations failed to tease out its layout in relation to the

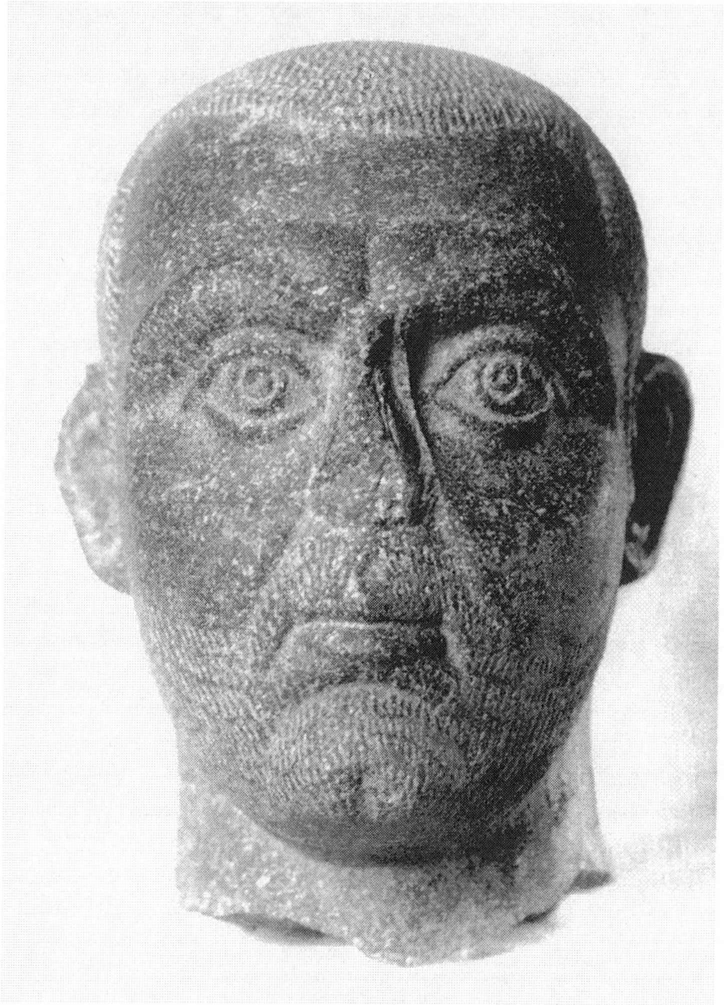

FIGURE 3.7 Head of Tetrarchic ruler (Diocletian?), also interpreted as Constantius I Chlorus

Source: Courtesy of the Antioch Expedition Archives, Department of Art and Archaeology, Princeton University; Princeton

temple, hippodrome, and tract of land west of the latter (Figure 3.9). Descriptions of the palace, albeit vague, can be found in textual sources, chiefly in the texts of Libanius and Theodoret, bishop of Cyrrhus (423–457).[45] Altogether, these texts convey the scale of Diocletian's achievement and the Island's wholesale reconfiguration, at that point effectively becoming a city within the city.

This imperial enclave was walled and equipped with its own gridded system of four porticoed streets connected to the bridges and presumably regimented by the

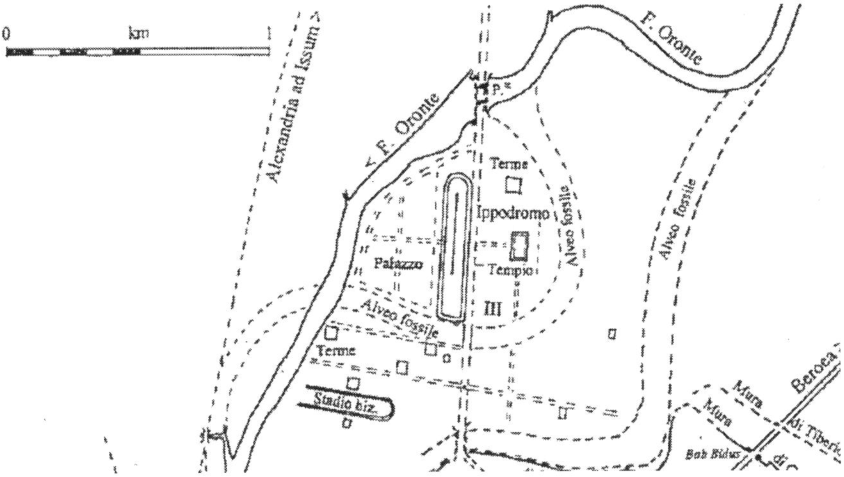

FIGURE 3.8 The conjectural plan of the Palace and the Island by Patitucci and Uggeri

Source: Adapted from Patitucci and Uggeri 2008

FIGURE 3.9 The Island: rubble core walls of the temple looking east

Source: Photograph by Andrea U. De Giorgi

Tetrapylon of the Elephants, a cubic monument of four interlocked arches that functioned as an *omphalos*, or urban nexus, and was decorated with pachyderms, a symbol that had long identified the Seleucid monarchy. From there, colonnaded streets stretched out along the compass points, with three segments all the way to the Island's fortification wall, the fourth, heading south, being presumably shorter. According to the theologian Evagrius Scholasticus (536–594), the eastern colonnade met the main *cardo* near the Parmenius stream (the future Forum of Valens, Figure 3.13).[46] As a complement to the project, the *Campus Martius* was likely situated north of the palace across the river, one of the few places we know lay on the river's west side. Subsequently, the palace and hippodrome unit also accommodated a second hippodrome south of the first, perhaps a training facility, oriented such that it led to the Island's main bridge and thence to *Tauriane* gate, one of the gates overlooking the Orontes.[47] Whether this addition can be assign to this general development or has to be assign to a later phase in the sixth century CE remains to be determined. The 1930s excavators did not provide any circumstantial evidence for the dating of the building.[48]

Overall, this transformation of the Island ushered in a new image of this district, emphasizing its centrality and more subtly bringing to bear the city's wholesale reorientation.

In tandem with the imperial palace, Diocletian also sponsored an ambitious building program spanning both Antioch and Daphne; the new edifices included a bath near the palace and four more scattered throughout the city, including the so-called *Senatorium*, all of unknown location. Granaries and a hippodrome in Daphne were added, the latter also embellished by the *Olympieion*, or temple of Zeus Olympius, and a temple to Nemesis. As Johannes Hahn remarked, these projects coalesced into the revamping of the Olympic games, which were to continue, albeit intermittently, until 520 CE. But this is not all: for these games Diocletian himself assumed the lofty title of *alytarch*, that is supreme authority of the festival.[49] In this context, Diocletian also restored the temple of Apollo, presumably the seat of the oracle, established a place for the cult of Hecate, and commissioned the construction of a residence for emperors and dignitaries visiting the Daphne sanctuary.[50] Daphne's new veneer could not have been more reminiscent of the Seleucid heyday. Malalas's mockery of the emperor in Antioch, inebriated by his role of *alytarch* and oblivious of his leadership role, hardly does justice to a shrewd emperor who sought to imbue the city and its administrators with a new sense of responsibility toward the highly centralized administration of the tetrarchy.[51] Fittingly, the emperor also promoted waterworks in Seleucia Pieria, presumably aimed at curbing the perennial silting of the military harbor built by the Flavians. But in 303 its 500 workers revolted against him and sought to burn down the imperial palace in Antioch, a sign of widespread dissatisfaction with work conditions. Once again a sense of Antiochene agency pitted against the imperial authorities seems to emanate from the event, with members of the council involved in the strife. A heavy-handed imperial response was, however, not long in coming.[52]

Equally rigorous was Diocletian's zeal in rooting out Christians from the Roman world. The year 303 and beginning of the Great Persecution of Diocletian and his Caesar Galerius marked the darkest hour of the local community, as attested by many stories of martyrdom and atrocities; apparently, this persecution represented the pinnacle of all purges orchestrated by emperors against Christians. More often than not, episodes sparked the energetic response of the Roman army, as in the cases of the emperor Decius, whose purge of Christians was allegedly caused by his resentment for the predecessor Philip, or that of Valerian, who blamed the minister of finances Macrinus. What, however, triggered Diocletian's vehement response to Christianity may have been a banal divination incident, or the trope of the abandonment of the ancestral customs, as successively explained by Galerius in his 311 edict of toleration, one that substantially curbed religious violence.[53] As befitted a city that was first to claim its Christian spirit, Antioch paid a hefty toll, and many lives of martyrs were cut short, among them that of its bishop, Cyril.[54] But no matter how widespread the violence, it failed to curb the energies of Lucian of Antioch, an Arian theologian, exegete, and priest who had a profound impact on Antioch's Christian community.[55] Through relentless teaching, he further enhanced the city's stronghold of Arianism. Martyrdom, however, cut his life short in 312, with the Arian question far from resolved.

After Diocletian's abdication and the shifting of political gravitas to other imperial capitals, Antioch found itself somewhat sidelined from the convoluted succession struggles that followed, involving several competing claimants to the throne and leading ultimately to the rise of Licinius (308–324) as emperor in the East and Constantine (306–337) as emperor in the West. But the city also became overall an intellectual milieu of the highest order. Along with Alexandria, Antioch was the locus of one of the two leading schools of theology and biblical exegesis in the empire. It was also not least a pole for Neoplatonist education. Fusing traditional Platonism with the religious eclecticism of the third century, this school investigated the relationship between the materiality of things and the "One." The Neoplatonists understood that everything that existed, physical and metaphysical, derived from the One, which was itself beyond existence. Iamblichus (c. 245–c. 325), the best known Neoplatonic authority of the time, may have established his base in Daphne in the 320s. But such a strong Neoplatonic foothold also developed its intolerant and militant aspects: the case of the imperial curator of Antioch and ardent Neoplatonist Theoctenus, a staunch opponent of Christianity and persecutor of Christians in the city, illustrates the lengths to which imperial administrators would go to expel and physically eliminate entire communities while also appropriating their properties and assets. It seems that such effective measures taken in Antioch were swiftly adopted by other communities in the East as well.[56] But violence in the city on the Orontes was targeted not only at Christians, for in 313 Licinius's troops also murdered 2,000 Antiochenes inside the hippodrome, their only crime being dissent and protest against the emperor, who had neglected to donate or offer a dole to the city and its community.[57]

The days of Constantine

The shared rule by Licinius in the East and Constantine in the West was, however, hardly amicable, as the co-emperors frequently quarreled and eventually came to military blows, ending with Licinius's defeat in 324 and execution the following year. The empire was thus once again reunited under the rule of one man. Of inestimable consequence to the empire was also Constantine's earlier conversion to Christianity in 312 in the aftermath of the battle that won him the Western throne. This conversion brought about a new era of hope and widespread sense of triumph among Christians as Constantine and Licinius met in Milan in 313, with the latter issuing the so-called Edict of Milan (rather an official correspondence with the Eastern provinces) that reiterated the recommendations of the 311 edict of Galerius, granting tolerance to all religions, including Christianity, thereby bringing to an end three centuries of persecutions. It also brought the novelty of the imperial house's direct participation in religious affairs.[58]

At this juncture we need to examine the role of Antioch and its position within the new emerging realities of a much fragmented Roman Empire. In particular, Antioch's centrality and imperial prerogatives now began to erode, as Constantine's project of founding the new city of Constantinople on the site of the ancient Greek colony of Byzantium to serve as the empire's Eastern capital gained momentum in 324. This shift in power and the resentment it inspired among many Antiochenes as they watched their city be eclipsed and their prerogatives decreased resonates in the accounts of the fourth century, not least in the later correspondence between Libanius and the philosopher Themistius.[59] But as with many cities of the Greek East, Antioch too had to pay its token to the foundation of Constantinople. Accordingly, the city was forced to give up portions of its sculptural repertoire in order to contribute to establishing the new capital's collection of ancient statuary and, more subtly, the forging of its worldly civic identity.[60] As we will see in the next chapter, in the aftermath of the 526 earthquake and 527 fire Antioch was rebuilt by Justinian with materials from elsewhere. The basilica of Anatolius, in particular, was greatly damaged and subsequently rebuilt with columns from Constantinople, almost a redress for the Antiochene monuments that 200 years earlier had been taken away to contribute to the making of the new capital on the Bosphorus.

Yet under Constantine's aegis, Antioch also received assistance and largesse from the imperial house in many ways. First and foremost, the Palaia, or Old Church, was rebuilt by the bishop Vitalis in 314, signaling the beginning of a new era for local Christians. Presumably established by the apostles themselves, this church was apparently the main locus of Christian worship.[61] This major project was later paired with the establishment of the "octagonal church" or Great Church (*Dominicum Aureum* or *domus aurea*), built on the Island near the palace between 327 and 341, when it was completed by Constantine's son Constantius II (337–361) and consecrated, though its exact location, design, and chronology are much debated issues.[62] Colonnades, ambulatories, niches, and recesses over a two-story building, negotiated an octagonal plan, or more likely a circular one, and coalesced into a building that in the fifth century was typically referred to as the "Harmony." Its superstructure, however, remains a matter of dispute. As for the location, the chronicle of the bishop Theodoret suggests the church was situated near the statue of Antiochus IV slaying the bull on the Tauriane Gate.[63] If so, this information illustrates the longevity of Seleucid landmarks in a constantly evolving built environment. The Octagonal Church was also high on the list of most coveted monuments sought by the 1930s excavation, but to no avail. Nevertheless, once again the textual sources give some redress for the disquieting dearth of archaeological evidence. They inform us of the work the construction of this imposing church and its hospice entailed.[64] The alleged transfer of a fragment of the cross in 574 CE may have greatly enhanced the sense of the sacred that radiated so potently from the building.[65] More to the point, Christianity was emerging in all of its vigor from decades of unspeakable violence and heroism. The staggering scale of the building, its innovative architecture, and lavish décor gestured at the triumph of Christ and overall the opening of a new epoch of confidence and unconditioned faith. In this light, Antioch also became an essential site of pilgrimage to the Holy Land; the *Itinerarium Burdigalense*, the oldest known Christian itinerary of sacred sites by an anonymous pilgrim from Burdigala (modern Bordeaux), makes plain that the journey to spiritual enlightenment required stops in Antioch and Daphne.[66] This concept of space and religious centrality was, however, at variance with Antioch's representation in its most traditional Tyche iconography on the Tabula Peutingeriana, a medieval map replicating one from the early-to-middle fourth century CE (Figure 3.10).[67]

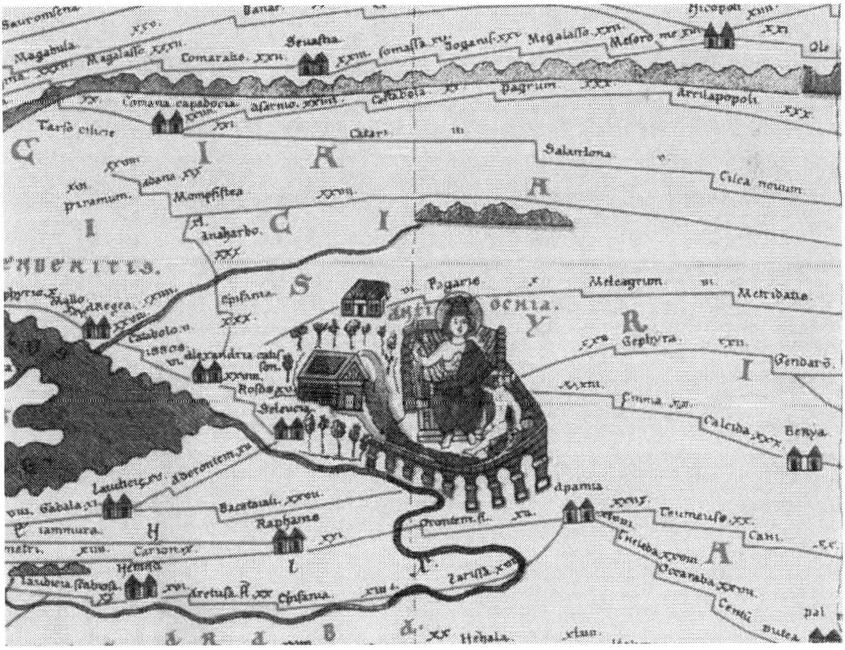

FIGURE 3.10 The Peutinger Table. Antioch and surroundings

Source: Courtesy of Mappe di Mappe

In it, the personification of Antioch appears in all of her prominence, equal in stature and décor to Rome and Constantinople. Under the goddess ensconced in her throne is the personified Orontes, while water flowing from a springhouse in Daphne is channeled into an aqueduct, thus framing the whole scene. Overall, this representation adumbrates the later references, as in the *Codex Vaticanus*, to Daphne as Bayt al-Ma, "house of water."

Yet Antioch also remained in a religious frenzy. Paul of Samosata's work had caused a chasm in the community. As a consequence, a council of bishops in Antioch held in the city firmly condemned Arianism and elected Eustathius as new bishop. Further, the same year's Council of Nicaea in 325, which ranked Antioch as an episcopal see at the same level as Rome and Alexandria, upheld the orthodox position but failed to bring concord, let alone a shared orthodoxy. Eustathius's appointment, however, was short-lived. Whether he actually drew the disdain of Helena, Constantine's mother or the ires of Eusebius of Caesarea, the emperor's confidant, is a matter of guesswork; exile of the disgraced bishop and tumults in the city were the outcome of the crisis, a pattern in the years to come. Nor did the successive appointment of a Nicene bishop, Euphronius, in 327 succeed in taming Arian voices and restoring peace in the agitated waters of Christian Antioch. Even as Constantine's great Octagonal Church was still held together by scaffolding, a schism was clearly in the works. Amid scandals of members of the orthodox clergy and Constantius II's overt imperial siding with the Arian cause, the latter doctrine gained momentum, reaching in the 350s its most radical manifestation under the bishop Eudoxius.[68]

As for more mundane matters, we have suggestive vignettes of life in the city during these days thanks to the writings of Theophanes, an imperial official who traveled from Hermopolis in Egypt to Antioch on an unspecified mission in the early fourth century. Whatever the reason of his business, he left us with vivid glimpses of the city, from traffic conditions to receipts of purchased goods, typically food. Meals mattered greatly to Theophanes, for it appears that he and his party traveled with a chef.[69] Among the goods he purchased were bread, gourds, cucumbers, lettuce, herbs, leeks, onions, carrots, eggs, olives, olive oil, fish, cheese, wine, absinthe, figs, nuts, apricots, plums, melons, apples, peaches, grapes, mulberries, nettles, *garum* (fish sauce), salt, syrup, coriander, cumin, honey, garlic, sausages, and meats. Altogether, he spent two-and-a-half months in Antioch, with at least a weekly visit to a local bath, where he would purchase slippers, oil, foam of niter/aphonitron, and soap for reasonable amounts (between 100 and 300 drachmas or one to three loaves of bread).

Tangentially, this account opens new vistas into the political realities of the day, when Antioch served as the seat of the *comes Orientis*, the count of the East. The first to be appointed by Constantine was the Christian Felicianus.[70] Residing in the Temple of the Muses (with the building presumably stripped of its religious prerogatives), Felicianus saw to the city's administration, upkeep of the water infrastructure, and conditions of the food supply, inasmuch as these were relevant to military logistics. In a civic environment prone to revolts like that of Antioch, the latter duty was essential. Indeed, a food crisis did erupt in 324, leading to widespread looting and violence, but was apparently ended by a distribution of bread sponsored by the imperial house through the ecclesiastical communities.[71] The *comes Orientis* worked in tandem with the *consularis Syriae*, that is, the governor of the Province of Syria Coele, whose headquarters were apparently located in the *Commodium* baths. Lastly, the military authority resided in the hands of the *Magister Militum per Orientem*. In short, this is the high-ranked administrative infrastructure that would interface with the imperial entourage upon visits of the emperor. Beyond Antioch, however, the political and religious affairs of the East were in the hands of the *Praefectus Praetorio Orientis*, the office that de facto enacted the plans of the imperial house.

Constantius II and the advent of Libanius

As hostilities with the Sasanians resumed,[72] Constantius II used Antioch as his imperial headquarters. He resided here for two long periods in 335–350 and 360–361 CE. As noted by Nick Henck, the city that had ridiculed emperors of the likes of Hadrian, Lucius Verus, and Septimius Severus ended up embracing this emperor in unprecedented ways, the councilors even apparently proposing to rename the city Antiochia Constantia.[73] Once again, Antiochene agency, and not least its corporate vision as it wholeheartedly upheld a representative of Rome, percolates to the surface. In any event, the local authorities had to reckon with the emperor's long sojourns in the city, when Antioch was not part of a visiting tour but rather the place from where imperial policies and military strategies were devised and enacted. Equally invested in the military and in Christological debates, Constantius diverted imperial resources for the city's embellishment, so much so that in a later encomium the emperor Julian greatly extolled the efforts of the former: "I need not stop to mention the porticoes, fountains, and other things of the kind that you caused to be bestowed on Antioch by her governors."[74] Indeed, the late fourth century represents a key juncture in the empire, for city councilors were no longer investing their own fortunes in sponsoring public projects. Rather, it was now in the hands of the emperors and their administrators to take up construction based on the availability of funds,[75] and the modifications Antioch underwent from this point forward, namely in the construction of basilicas and administrative buildings, must be read through these lenses. It is apt to situate this process as early as the tenure of Constantius, when, for instance, repairs to the Great Church were commissioned by Gorgonius, *comes* and *cubicularius* (eunuch chamberlain) in 341. Whether the restoration project was caused by the trembling of the earth that shook Antioch that same year is a possibility. The sources report extensive damage, and anywhere between three days and an entire year of aftershocks.[76] But it is also worth noting how a system of imperially funded projects and maintenance of the old fabric generally supplanted initiatives that had a more public and infrastructural purpose. The difference between Antioch in the second and fourth centuries could not be more obvious.

In 344, there commenced another long, strenuous war against the Sasanians; in the usual ebb and flow of fighting, the key cities of Singara and Nisibis were taken by the Persians and the Romans by turns. The exhausting stalemate seemingly led Constantius II to seek more energetic responses to the Sasanian threat; the completion of the harbor works at Seleucia Pieria, presumably begun under Diocletian and abruptly interrupted by the uprising in 303, attests to a strategy shift.[77] A bigger and more serviceable harbor was in order, with a view toward a more substantial and rapid disembarking of troops and adequate supply logistics. Additionally, the execution of this project illustrates the chronic condition of the harbor of Seleucia Pieria, then as today (Figure 3.11). Wedged between the coastline and the massif of Mt. Coripheus, the narrow strip of land used by the harbor was constantly under threat of silting, and lack of proper maintenance would have probably buried the harbor within a few years. Meanwhile, Antioch city councilors had to take up the burden of transporting grain at their expense so as to supply the military operations against Persia. This type of provisions may have contributed to the increasing alienation of the local *curiales*, that is the members of the council, in the governance of the city. To be sure, it effectively sustained the fiscal and military machineries of the Empire.[78]

But more stringent needs in the West, namely the revolt of the usurper Magnentius, now took precedence, and Constantius shortly thereafter left Antioch,

FIGURE 3.11 The harbor of Seleucia Pieria today

Source: Photograph by Andrea U. De Giorgi

leaving his Caesar Gallus (351–354) in charge. Despite the omen of crosses allegedly appearing in the sky upon Gallus' entrance in Antioch,[79] no junior emperor was more unfit for the job. His presence in the city inaugurated a season of terror. His wife Constantina, it seems, also greatly fueled his savagery. References to violence and slander make plain that an aura of fear loomed over the city.[80] Through incognito tours at night, Gallus would gauge the general opinion on his rule,[81] and many paid a hefty price. His excess of religious zeal had no less impact on the city, with upholders of a radical form of Arianism led by the deacon Aetius gaining a foothold in the community and influence over Gallus. Moreover, waging his own war against paganism, Gallus went as far as transposing the relics of St. Babylas, the most greatly revered local saint, to Daphne in the vicinity of the temple of Apollo.[82] In so doing, a new martyrion dedicated to the saint was intended to silence the oracle of Apollo forever.

The turning point in Gallus's short-lived and tragic stint in Antioch, however, was the food crisis of 354. Grappling with an inflammatory situation and widespread anxiety, he chose the worst course of action, resorting to force and cunning. His manipulation of the hungry masses only exacerbated the situation; singled out as the culprit, the governor of Syria Theophilus was lynched, properties of wealthy citizens were looted, and chaos reigned in Antioch.[83] In this picture of general turmoil, however, two phenomena emerged. First, having just returned to his native Antioch in 354, the figure of Libanius appeared for the first time in the political arena[84] to perform his role as broker for Antioch, conveying the voice of reason in face of the irrational forces shattering the city. As we will see, he would play that role time and again. And second, this crisis led to the downward spiral that finally alienated Gallus in the eyes of Constantius and, ultimately, to his demise. As a first measure, Constantius wiped out the network of friends and allies Gallus had created in the city, thus beginning a new round of violence.[85] Ultimately, Gallus's eclipse also demarcated the end of Antioch's role as imperial seat; from that point onward, Constantius, Julian (for a limited time), and Valens (for a longer season) sought to counter the now oppressing presence of Constantinople.[86] Political prominence was not the only asset at issue. The most revered saints of Antioch had to be surrendered to Constantinople: the 360 CE transfer of the holy spoils of the Palestinian martyrs Pamphilus and Theophilus, to be interred at the new capital in the Church of the Apostles, is a good case in point.[87]

But not even the invasion of Mesopotamia by Shāpūr II (309–379) in 358 drew Constantius back to Antioch itself. As greater border safety and military concerns increased in the West, and with Sirmium and Constantinople alternating in accommodating the imperial court for prolonged stays, Antioch remained somewhat detached from the main political discourse. But not so in religious matters, it appears. Constantius's edict against consulting pagan oracles by members of the court exacted its toll in Antioch and Syria in general.[88] A stronghold of Arianism, Antioch at this time was the locus of an even more vigorous push against orthodoxy, which culminated in 361 with the declaration of the Arian creed under the bishop Euzoius.[89] It is fair to say that the Christological crux combined with a deliberate effort to outlaw paganism made Antioch one of the most explosive urban realities of the Eastern Empire. The idyllic picture Libanius paints for the city and its territory in his well-known *Antiochikos*, penned in 356 on the occasion of the Olympic games, deliberately shunned any echoes of the rampant tension in the city and so must be treated with prudence.[90] Nor were the following years less fraught with religious predicaments, military campaigns, and conundrums of imperial succession, and Antioch once again became the venue where all of these variables played out.

Pagan capital?

Although short-lived, the reign of Constantine's nephew Julian II (361–363), known as the Apostate for his rejection of Christianity, represents a fundamental moment in the city's life (Figure 3.12). Described as "the Dragon, the Apostate, the Great Mind, the Assyrian, the public and private enemy of all in common, him that has madly raged and threatened much upon the earth, and that has spoken and meditated much unrighteousness against heaven" by the theologian Gregory of Nazianzus (329–390),[91] Julian had ambitious plans for Antioch: to make the city the epicenter of his pagan revolution and headquarters for his Persian engagements.[92]

Though born and raised a Christian, Julian had experienced firsthand the zeal, determination, and proselytism that had propelled the faith to the detriment of the traditional pantheon. His attempt to restore the latter required the wholesale

FIGURE 3.12 Gold solidus of Emperor Julian, 362–363. Obverse: AD. FL CL IVLIANVS PF AVG, pearl-diademed, draped and cuirassed bust. Reverse: VIRTVS EXERCITVS ROMANORVM, Bearded, diademed emperor in consular robes holding scepter and mappa, standing left. Mintmark: ANT B

Source: Courtesy of Harvard Museums of Art

transposal of those same qualities among pagans, and he seized the opportunity offered by a profoundly divided Christian church, at this juncture consisting of an Arian majority and two orthodox groups quarreling once again over the nature of Christ.[93] As befell Antioch time and again, a clear and present danger failed to overcome the theological debates and local feuds.[94] Moreover, Julian's plan required a religious capital, and no place, in his view, may have been more apt than Antioch.

Julian made all preparations in earnest to ensure the city met his expectations. From nominating a friendly *comes Orientis* – his own uncle Julian – to reviving municipal life, he took measures to ingrain a positive attitude toward the emperor and spared no efforts in reaching out to all constituencies. The local Jewish community in particular was a key interlocutor, eager as Julian was to rebuild the Temple in Jerusalem and gain the support of Jews all over the empire. Moreover, in Antioch, Julian could rely on the most authoritative of all voices, that of Libanius, who by that point had become one of the city's most prominent intellectuals. His welcoming speech of 362 offers a portrait of the emperor in the round: general, philosopher, and priest, to cite but a few of his talents.[95] From that point on, the relationship between the two men became one of trust and mutual respect, despite Antioch's political volatility.[96]

More fundamentally, though, the conditions under which the city fared were not as promising as expected and greatly determined the unsuccessful outcome of Julian's imperial sojourn. Vexed by the presence of legions, hit by a sequence of food crises, and lacking the means to sustain a "traditional" civic life, Antioch was not the safe harbor Julian had envisioned. Instead, the bad omens upon his entrance into the city in July 362 ushered in a phase of great conflict between the emperor and a city still loyal to the memory of Constantius and reluctant to partake in the excess of sacrifices that Julian so adamantly upheld. To his credit, Julian spared no effort in fixing the ills of the food crisis and seeking the goodwill of all parties involved. The project evidently failed, however, for within a year he also commissioned the import of vast quantities of grain from Chalcis and Hierapolis in Syria as well as from Egypt.[97] But while this measure may have palliated the immediate effects of the crisis, it failed to rectify the endemic ills of stockpiling and price jack-ups in local markets. Nor was Julian's program aimed at fully harnessing the city's land assets any more successful; the 10,000 *kleroi* or land plots that seemingly punctuated the Amuq Plain hardly reflected the actual mosaic of properties – many of which were left deliberately uncultivated – that constituted the city's main source of income.[98] Julian's forcible alienation of some of those plots and penalties, namely the imposition of civic duties on the local *curiales* surely did not gain him more support from Antioch's well-to-do.[99] The failure to enforce a new draft of qualified senators to the local senate also bespeaks the upper strata's lukewarm enthusiasm for an emperor who, among other things, had no interest in promoting games and spectacles, let alone participating.[100]

As for Julian's religious agenda, things looked no brighter. He fulfilled his obligations by offering sacrifices at most temples and shrines in the Antiochene district, from Mt. Cassius to the sanctuary of Pan on the slopes of Antioch.[101] It is a matter of record that most of these sites may not have been in good state, both in terms of lack of upkeep and downright vandalism. To counter this sorry state of affairs, Julian entrusted one Hesychios, a local priest, with the seizing of the décor, presumably columns and architectural decoration, that had been illegally apprehended by local citizens in various temples and shrines of the city for the embellishment of their houses.[102]

Evidently no shrine was exempt from rigorous observance of the ancestral rites and generous blood sacrifices. Yet the favorable local reception prophesized was nowhere in sight. Julian's attempt to reinvigorate the comatose cult of Apollo and his reinstating of the Castalia oracular spring, as well as the removal of the bones of St. Babylas (which interfered with the oracle's sight), with the ensuing parade of the coffin among hordes of chanting Christians, drove a wedge within the local population. During this turmoil, the temple of Apollo in Daphne was destroyed by fire; it had already witnessed the stripping of its marble architectural apparatus by Constantius.[103] This event further aggravated the situation, with an investigation that yielded no perpetrators but led to the closing of the Great Church and increased resistance against Julian. A round of persecutions would have probably ensued, had the *prefectus praetorio orientis* Saturninius Secundundus Salutius not coaxed the emperor to milder measures.[104]

At this juncture, all strata of the population, whether councilors or simple citizens, openly resented both the man and the emperor.[105] Overall, the blaze that incinerated the temple of Apollo marked the lowest point in the relationship between the emperor and the local population. Persecutions of Christians, even among the military, further alienated Julian from the community, for the emperor's agenda threatened their very existence. By 363, his approval in Antioch had reached its lowest level. The *Misopogon*, or "the beard hater," a vitriolic and seemingly self-deprecating satire composed by the emperor – an upholder of the long beard and attire of the traditional old days – and directed toward the people of Antioch, is the testament of his disillusion and scorn. Supposedly hung on the *Tetrapylon* of the Elephants, tentatively located near the imperial palace on the Island, this hyperbolic text may also convey the disquiet of a failed dialog and Julian's inability to fully realize his plan for the city, sidetracked as he was by the gravity of the food crisis.[106] He wrote:

> I have decided to leave this city and to retire from it; not indeed because I am convinced that I shall be in all respects pleasing to those to whom I am going, but because I judge it more desirable, in case I should fail at least to seem to them an honourable and good man, to give all men in turn a share of my unpleasantness, and not to annoy this happy city with the evil odour, as it were, of my moderation and the sobriety of my friends.[107]

Antioch never became the splendid "city of marble" Julian had intended to build,[108] and the ensuing campaign against the Sasanians in 363 cut short both his life and altogether his religious utopia.[109] Libanius, still a staunch supporter of the emperor, could not spare himself from mourning Julian though a funeral oration in his honor. He wrote:

> Why then, you gods and immortal powers, did you not bring it to pass? Why did you not make mankind happy in its knowledge of you, and him the author of their happiness? What fault had you to find in his character? Which of his actions did not meet with your approval? He erected altars, built temples, worshipped in magnificence gods and heroes, air and heaven, land and sea, fountains and rivers. He took up the fight against those who had fought against you. He was more continent than Hippolytus, as just as Rhadamanthys, more intelligent than Themistocles, braver than Brasidas. He restored to health a world that lay sick unto death. He was a hater of wrong, kindly to the just, foe to the wicked, friend to all good men.[110]

The grief of the earth, too, could not have been more acute. The strong earthquakes of 365 and 368 CE, in Libanius's words, were the expression of an infinite, cosmic sadness.[111] The former episode has gone down in history as one of the most catastrophic events to ever shake the ancient world, for it demolished cities in the eastern Mediterranean and generated a tsunami, too.[112] Whether it extended all the way into Syria cannot be determined. Surely, though, the latter temblor hit violently Nicea and the Black Sea region of Bithynia as a whole, leaving crumbled buildings and fallen facades behind, as the historian Socrates Scholasticus remarked.[113]

After Julian

In the aftermath of Julian's death, his general Jovian was elevated to the status of emperor (363–364). Arriving in Antioch, he reaffirmed the tolerance of Christianity and sought the consensus of the city's population. The loss of Nisibis to the Persians, however, led to vehement protest and turmoil. In particular, the presence of the emperor in the hippodrome ignited violence and episodes of downright anti-pagan iconoclasm, with the destruction of the temple of Trajan and the statue of Maximian.[114] The signs of a community growing exponentially uncomfortable with the imperial authorities were growing more apparent, with anger pitted at the symbols of imperial rule reaching its apex in the following decades, as we will see.

Meanwhile, the escalation of social tensions led Libanius to advocate once again on the city's behalf under the new emperor, Valentinian (364–375).[115] More mediation lay ahead for the rhetorician, as the emperor's brother, Valens (364–378), assumed the imperial seat in the East as co-emperor. Under Valens, Antioch became once again an imperial residence, from 371 to 378.[116] The effects of his rule, however, were twofold. First, fearing conspiracies, the emperor enforced policies aimed at eliminating sorcery and magic, which in turn led to trials, torture, and confiscation on a great scale; among the victims were administrators close to the emperor himself.[117] Orthodox Christians, in face of the emperor's staunch Arianism, suffered heavy-handed persecution, too, though the rifts and theological quarrels never ceased.

Second, perhaps as consequence of earthquake damage in the 360s, Valens sponsored an ambitious project that centered on creating a new forum (Figure 3.13). Gunnar Brands has suggested that this building plan drew its inspiration from the great tetrarchic capitals and resonated with a new spirit of confidence in the military strength of the Roman Empire.[118] The site presumably occupied the space of an old Hellenistic square that had been substantially modified during the Early Roman Empire and was vaulted over the Parmenius stream. Demolition of old buildings wedded a new rhetoric of power to a new, visually powerful ensemble. Charged with political and didactic gravitas, the forum blended a host of old religious and public buildings (the temple of Ares, *Mese Pule*, *Xystos*, *Commodion*, *Horologion*, *Plethron*, and *Kynegion*) with four new lavishly decorated basilicas and statues, not least that of Valens' brother Valentinian in the center of the forum.[119]

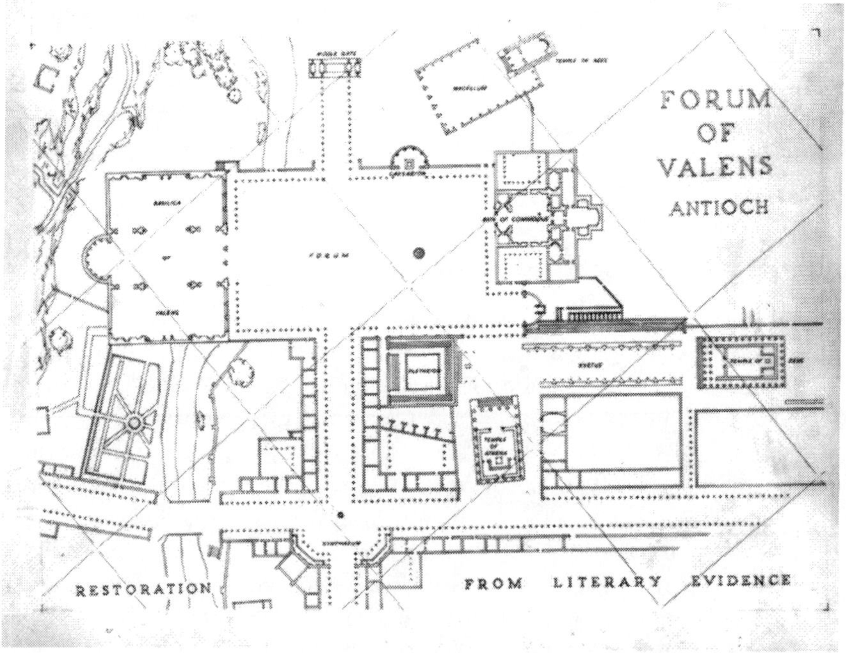

FIGURE 3.13 The Forum of Valens as envisioned by the 1930s archaeologists. None of buildings, however, were identified by the 17-O excavation

Source: Courtesy of the Antioch Expedition Archives, Department of Art and Archaeology, Princeton University; Princeton

The dynasty's presentation added a further layer to the already crowded sculptural landscape of the city, with a host of new images in the conch of the former *Kaisarion* built under Julius Caesar extolling Valens and Valentinian.[120]

Overall, as Noel Lensky stressed, this building plan cohered with the agenda of Valens, as with that of Valentinian and Gratian, which mandated that no building activity was to take place unless justified by the ruinous state of existing buildings. This institutional corollary thus led to the conservation and reconstruction of several monuments throughout the empire and, not least, in Africa: baths, amphitheaters, aqueducts, and porticoes celebrated an age of renewal and efficient public infrastructure.[121] More subtly, though, the reconfiguration of Antioch's city center was aimed at repositioning Antioch at the center of the Roman world. While stressing the key role of the Olympic games and a not-so-subtle pagan framework of reference, it also alluded to the redesign early in the fourth century of the eastern end of Rome's forum, where the temple of Venus and Roma, the great Basilica, and the so-called Temple of Romulus had forged a unique celebration of the emperor and his political outlook. Previously, under Jovian and Valentinian I, the mint of Antioch had struck gold *solidus* issues with the personifications of Rome and Constantinople on their reverse. It was significant that it was Antioch that minted a coin, and an image, that conveyed without ambiguity what the realities of power were. That through his ambitious building program in the forum of Antioch, Valens sought to reverse this trend and situate Antioch once again at the center of the *oikoumene* is a cogent possibility.[122] The exact position of the forum, however, has long been a vexatious question. Recently, a substantial bath establishment emerged during excavation of a new hotel in the Haraparası Quarter, 750 m southwest of the cave known today as St. Peter's Church, west of the main *cardo* and south of the Parmenius (an area roughly corresponding to sector 16-O of the early excavations), in an area believed to be adjacent to the forum of Valens. Indeed, the forum was one of the 1930s excavations' main targets. During the 1937 excavation of sector 17-O, the team did succeed in Level IV at intersecting with one structure that hinted at the monuments that supposedly embellished the forum, namely, the corner of a fourth-century nymphaeum (Figure 3.14). Torrential rains and security precautions, however, and what appeared to be lack of structures below the nymphaeum brought the operation to a halt, and so these efforts failed at placing the Forum of Valens in space.

What then of Antioch's fourth century grandeur? What of the city's built environment at this key juncture? These questions were central in the 1932–1939 excavation agenda. As noted in the previous chapter, exploration of the Island yielded no evidence of the imperial palace; the circus and the so-called Byzantine stadium, as well as the adjacent temple, were the only surviving features of the Island's urban development.[123] Seating about 80,000 spectators, the circus was excavated enough to expose parts of its *carceres*, or starting gates, and long sides and reveal its rubble core foundations, barrel vaulting, and piers of limestone, as well as red granite columns. What the excavators mostly found, however, were domestic units and a host of bath establishments that illustrate the nature of settlement on the Island.

FIGURE 3.14 The nymphaeum in sector 17-O. Northern corner of the building propped up

Source: Courtesy of the Antioch Expedition Archives, Department of Art and Archaeology, Princeton University; Princeton

Bath A, for instance, measuring 1,025 m^2, dates to 350–400 and rests on earlier foundations of the second century CE. This pattern is replicated by Bath B; presumably also built in the second century, it was greatly overhauled in the fourth. Baths D and E, also on the Island, in general reiterated these same cultural and chronological trends. Bath C, however, presents evident traces of looting and destruction that may harken to the moment when the complex was no longer serviceable, presumably in the sixth century after the great earthquake of 526. Other baths were also located in various districts of the town (Figure 3.15).

This remarkable concentration of thermal establishments on the Island illustrates the grounding of bathing culture in Antiochene society, all the more as the textual sources document the existence, more or less synchronic, of a panoply of baths in the city center and on the slopes of Mts. Staurin and Silpius. By the same token, this picture also begs the question of how these amenities would secure and husband water supply. While the 1930s excavations uncovered extensive systems of terracotta pipelines and storm drains, it is unclear whether these establishments impounded water from the river, via some kind of mechanical lifting devices, or simply tapped into the aquifer by means of wells. Energy, labor, water supply, and experience: these are paramount questions that invite further scrutiny of these baths.

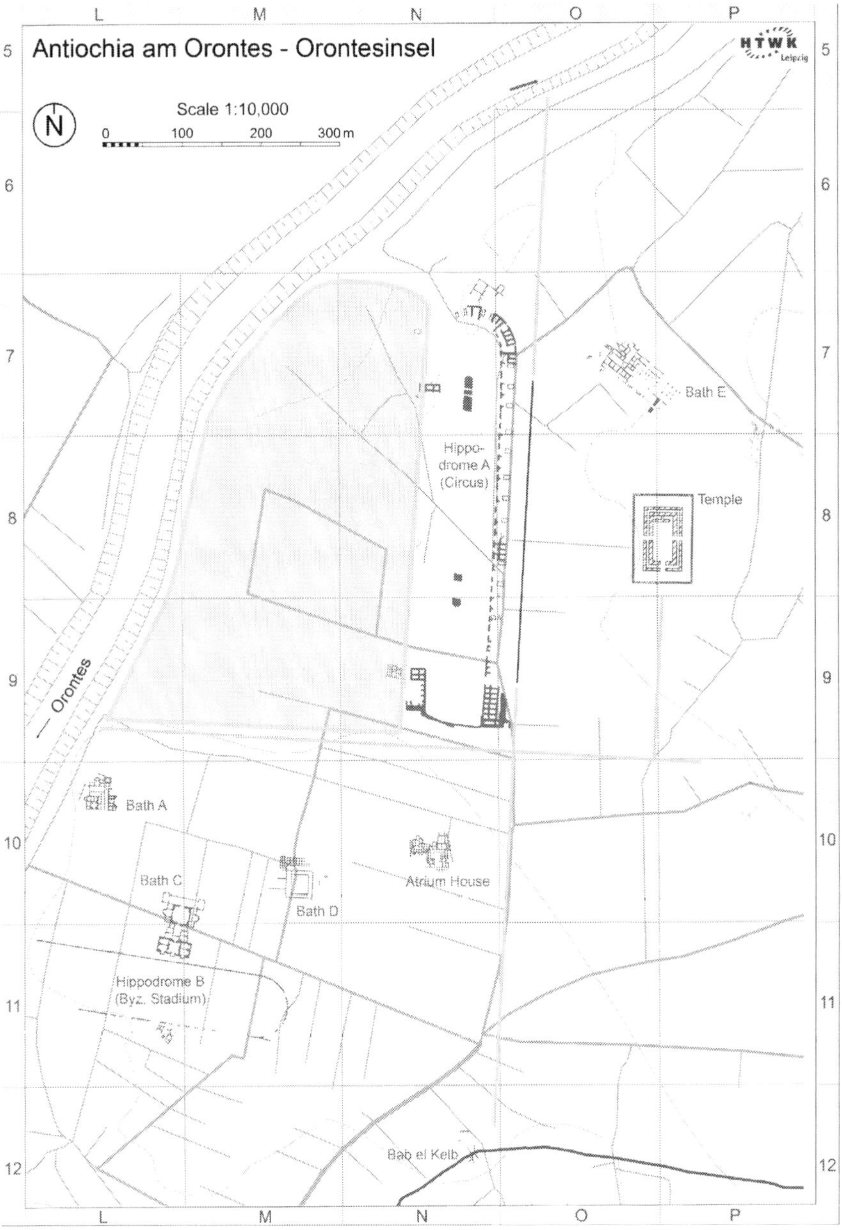

FIGURE 3.15 The Island: Baths A, C, D, E, Hippodromes A (circus) and B, and the temple. In dark gray, the area plausibly occupied by the imperial palace

Source: Courtesy of Gunnar Brands and Ulrich Weferling

Bath-going, however, remained a staple aspect of living in Antioch, even in spite of Christian doctrines that increasingly sought to cut any ties with a behavior that inevitably connected to a pagan past, and more to the point, with an environment that was laden with images of gods, nymphs, and the whole repertoire of Greek myths.

In these same years of Valens's mandate, despite much dissent and open conflict, the church of Antioch was the epicenter of Christological debates that, predicated on the nature of the son of God, garnered the most authoritative voices of the time, such as the theologian and archbishop of Constantinople, Gregory of Nazianzus, and the historians Sozomen and Socrates Scholasticus, to name but a few. It could also boast of visitors like St. Jerome. The death of Valens, however, led to a new phase of dialogue between the bishops Meletius and Paulinus and the orthodox factions they represented, after a decade that had witnessed the coexistence of essentially three different Christian congregations and ultimately a tripartite schism.[124] Through a savvy program of church building, such as the cruciform church of St.

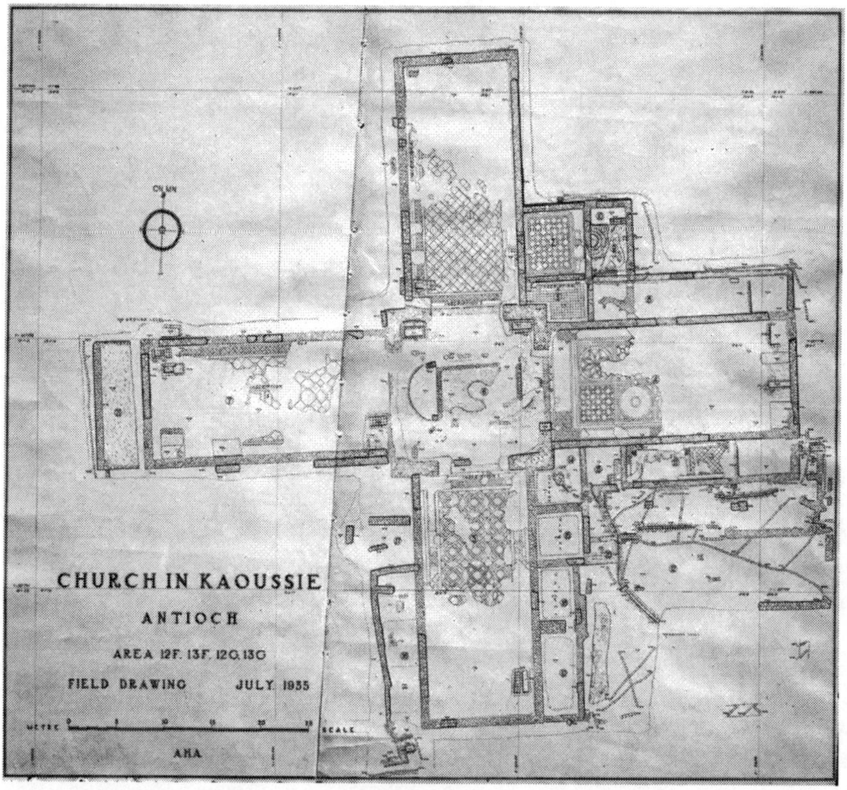

FIGURE 3.16 The Church of Kaoussié

Source: Courtesy of the Antioch Expedition Archives, Department of Art and Archaeology, Princeton University; Princeton

Babylas, built by Meletius in 379–380 in Kaoussié, a village east of Antioch on the other side of the river (Figure 3.16), and synods, the former reaffirmed the role of orthodoxy as well as its primacy.[125]

The city's economy

Of all the things that Libanius boasts about in his Praise of Antioch, perhaps none is closer to his heart than his contention that the city in the fourth century CE had unlimited access to resources: "everything is at once available," remarks the rhetorician.[126] That the city relied on its vast and fertile hinterland is a truism. Throughout these centuries of the Late Roman Empire, farmers continued to make up the economic backbone of Antioch and the surrounding area. The texts of Libanius in particular inform us of the variety of land-leasing schemes underpinning the rural districts, illustrating a variegated universe of settlement modules, from family-size farmsteads to villages. Their conflicts, anxieties, and issues of patronage resonate greatly in the text, cementing all the more the linkage of the rural hinterlands with the city.[127] One of his orations documents, for instance, a group of Jewish tenants who had rented land in his estate for four generations; he writes they had apparently failed to meet their fiscal obligations.[128] This illustrates the presence of constellations of Jewish *coloni* who had gravitated to Antioch and had the ability to plausibly run estates in ways they saw fit.

Settlement continuity and those structures of power that shaped the region during the Early Empire in fact remained substantially unaltered during the following centuries. Of course, modern historians include Roman Syria among the list of provinces that allegedly suffered during the general crisis of the third century CE.[129] The Sasanian invasions, Zenobia's revolt, crop failures, and weakening of the central power are described as accounting for a century-long catastrophic intermezzo, which ultimately preceded a new, thriving phase of apparent prosperity in the fourth and fifth centuries.[130] But references to numerous famines and food crises occurring in the fourth century and haphazardly striking the Antiochene community and economy should be considered with caution.[131] Crop failures were certainly not unheard of in the territory of Antioch; indeed, famines that had previously struck the city under Claudius and Nero indicate that the community had to cope with that problem from time to time. But the magnitude of these ecological downturns is a matter of dispute: Downey suggested that the concept of "food crisis" rather than "famine" captures the problem at issue.[132] Devastating though they may seem, these episodes were rather grounded in the issue of stockpiling and profiteering by those same Antiochenes who controlled the urban markets. Moreover, in his seminal work, Peter Garnsey underscores the vehement, yet short-term, character of these episodes.[133] As he demonstrates, crop failures were only occasionally global and catastrophic, while poor storage logistics and profiteering by the local rich were very much constant in the economy of ancient cities and could lead to traumatic results.[134]

Historical and archaeological sources further suggest that the fourth century marked the pinnacle of settlement in the Antiochene territory because of the economic opportunities the region offered. Approximately 820 rural sites punctuated the rugged 5,500 km^2 terrain of the Syrian Jibāl, east of Antioch, with an average of one settlement every 2 km^2. Also referred to as the "Dead Cities," these villages are the stunning testimony of the spreading of rural settlement from Antioch in a region that was only apparently not conducive to prospering. Lack of perennial waters, eroded landscapes, and rare cultivable plots of land did not hinder the fourth century booming of these districts. Instead, some 200,000 people may have indeed lived there at the peak of settlement, perhaps moving away from a city that was growing increasingly swollen. In spatial terms, such density was grounded in the exploitation of every pocket of land available, and accordingly the forms of human occupation vary greatly, from small farmsteads with stables and barns to fully fledged gridded villages, like in the case of Me'ez. The hallmark of these communities, however, is their agricultural character, as attested by the ubiquitous presence of pressing apparatus in virtually each farm. But their religious character also stands out, with ecclesiastical buildings reaching the staggering number of 1,200, with one church every 4.5 km^2.[135] The case of the village of Banqusa, with three churches serving a community of 30 houses, clearly shows the local degree of devotion. But this was also a landscape traversed and used by hermits, as the

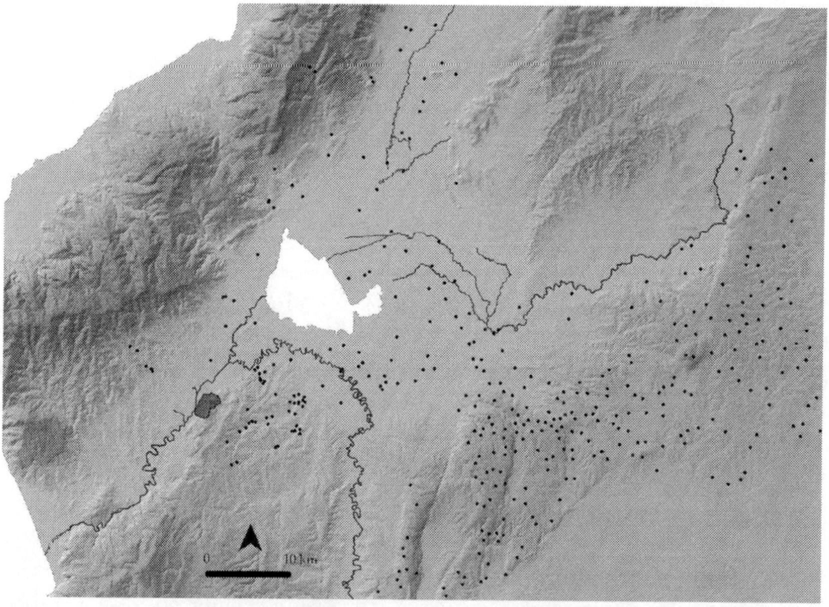

FIGURE 3.17 The late antique settlement in the territory of Antioch, straddling the plain and the Syrian highlands. This image collates survey data by Tchalenko in the 1930s and the Amuq Valley Regional Project 1999–2005

Source: Created by Andrea U. De Giorgi

late-fourth-century narrative of Theodoret of Cyrrhus illustrates. Their words, life, and experiences no doubt heightened the local sense of religious affiliation.

Overall, the evidence from the territory of Antioch, and not least from the limestone massif east of the city, can be best represented with this illustration of settlement stemming from the city (Figure 3.17).

In short, these regions witnessed intense settlement and general economic prosperity between the second and seventh centuries, essentially by means of the wide-ranging commerce of olive oil and wine, which has been long believed to be the regions' economic mainstay.[136] Fundamentally grounded in a monoculture that perpetrated itself for five centuries, the communities on the massifs produced olive oil and wine on an industrial scale for exports reaching as far as Constantinople.[137] Other economic options at their disposal were animal husbandry, mixed agricultural regimes, and various cash crops.[138] Although more economic diversification needs to enter the picture, most scholars are generally comfortable with Georges Tchalenko and Tate's settlement patterning on the limestone uplands; their assessment of these communities' ability to exploit successfully the region's scanty resources and thereby thrive (see Chapter 2), especially despite the alleged third-century crisis, has, however, been finessed by recent scholarship.[139] J.H.W.G. Liebeschuetz, in his study of fourth-century Antioch, moreover, amply relied on the evidence offered by Tchalenko's survey to argue for the region's economic and demographic growth starting in the second century.[140] In particular, he underscored that the successive diffusion of small-scale farms, each with its own olive press, indicated the growth of an independent peasantry whose wealth rested in the olive industry and the acquisition of land hitherto left abandoned or exploited solely for grazing. One important ramification of Tchalenko's work is that he recorded a landscape whose features are strikingly at odds with Libanius's more hierarchical account of Antioch's territory, which was chronically affected by heavy exactions, abuses of all kinds, and deserted lands.[141] But far from being entirely wrong or deceptive, Libanius simply tells one side of the story – the urban one; indeed, his treatment of facts was often simply aimed at creating an artificial corollary for his orations.[142]

Overall, farmers and landowners were but a facet of a multifarious universe that constituted Antioch and its markets: shopkeepers, artisans, and traders were no doubt as conspicuous in the city fabric, populating with their activities the long porticoes lining the main axes of traffic. Shops and space for retail further articulated the urban experience; *fullonicae* (fullers) and leather shops, alongside the textile industry, are mentioned for the city in the fifth century CE.[143] More fundamentally, most professions adhered to a system of guilds, which, in turn, had to reckon with imperial demands and occasional services, presumably in the context of food distribution. Whether in corporate form or individually run, these activities contributed to the circulation of cash, and it is understood that most transactions entailed recourse to currency, from salaries to the purchase of foodstuff, or fees for the admittance to baths.[144] This cash economy, of course, was predicated on monetary circulation and fueled a vast landscape of banking operations, from lending to overseas payments. While the corpus of the coins excavated in Antioch during the

1930s still awaits full publication, the early reports show trends of relevance.[145] In particular, the 1932 excavations investigated vast exposures of land on the Island, a few soundings on the colonnaded street, and Daphne. Their provisional estimate of a total of 2,990 coins offers an interesting breakdown for the Roman imperial era, with two coins of the first century CE, six of the second, 67 of the third, and 464 in the fourth, with peaks during the house of Constantine.[146] The successive study of 14,486 coins by Waagé generally corroborated these general projections.[147] Of course, bias in a very imperfect archaeological record, such as that of the early Antioch excavations, may skew the analysis of the data. Nevertheless, this information shows a trend that can hardly be disputed, one that highlights both the production pace of the local mint and, altogether, a sustained flow of cash propelled by the powers that were. Further, in a recent study Alan Stahl shows that location of the finds mattered, with higher density of Early Imperial coins along the main thoroughfare and, conversely, sparser patterns in the following centuries, with indeed an uptick of coins during the days of Constantine and followers. For instance, the finds in sector 17-O, presumably located near the Forum of Valens, very much strengthen this trend.[148] As Stahl points out, however, in terms of monetary circulation the best was yet to come in Antioch, for the greater assemblages point now in the direction of the period between 491 and 522 with even distribution of finds throughout the excavated sectors of the city, and a sequence of almost 250 coins per decade.[149] Again, prudence is in order, all the more when coinage produced elsewhere also enters the equation.

Alternatively, however, salaries and transactions could be paid in kind, with possible rolling over of funds in solid currency strictly on personal initiative. The system, as one can imagine, was amenable to all kinds of abuses, and imperial laws sought to curb the phenomenon. But levies in kind still drove the economy of the province, thereby enabling the functioning of the military: Constantius's campaigns against the Persians were sustained by grain presumably sown in Syria and dispatched by the Antioch councilors at their expenses.[150]

Inns and restaurants were part of Antioch's urban landscape, too. On the Island, we encounter Megas, Ioannes, and Anthousa, three inn-keepers of the early fourth century CE who spared no resources when it came down to give their visitors a heart warming welcome:

> Peace (be) your coming in, (you) who gaze (on this); joy and blessing (be) to those who stay here. The mosaic floor of the triclinium was made in the time of Megas and Ioannes and Anthousa, inn-keepers, in (the) month of Gorpiaios, (in the) fifth indiction.[151]

This Greek inscription, colored by Syriac borrowings in its welcoming formula, occupies the square central panel of a large mosaic with intricate geometric patterns. The 1937 excavation in sector 10-Q, on the eastern side of the Island, was hastily conducted, and the building's size and design cannot be conjured up.

Nevertheless, it is apparent that Megas, Ioannes, and Anthousa had built a partnership that administered a presumably conspicuous establishment equipped with a fancy dining room (*triclinium*). To be sure, the three entrepreneurs were not alone in the inn-keeping business.[152]

Overall, Libanius's idyllic picture of a city as a thriving market, populated by well-educated workers and catering to all of its constituencies, should not deceive us. Late Antique Antioch, though economically buoyant, thanks to a great inflow of revenues, state subsidies, and circulation of cash, was no different than any other ancient metropolis, with its landed aristocracy greatly invested in the city governance and a staggering stratum of destitute individuals, more often than not of "infinite poverty," as John Chrysostom would style them.[153] Simply put, the economy of Antioch was predicated on very frail premises. Occasional riots and widespread dissatisfaction with the administration had been the harbingers of recession since the days of the Severans.[154] No doubt that sieges, earthquakes, and food crises did not bode well for the city financial status and overall resilience, widening the schism between the well-to-do and poor, ultimately leading to episodes of economic morass that only imperial intervention could seek to rectify. Julian's attempts to curb the negative effects of the food crises in Antioch, though only temporarily palliating the emergency, captures well the nature of the phenomenon, with the situation worsening further during the last decades of the fourth century. From his Antioch viewpoint, Libanius makes it plain that "poverty is the common lot of mankind nowadays."[155]

Antioch eclipsed

As noted, during the fourth century, the city's governance was transformed from a body of well-to-do Antiochene administrators serving their fellow citizens through all kinds of curial duties to a new class of imperial officials who were central in reconfiguring the empire operated by the Tetrarchy. It has been argued that this period marks the end of "classical" Antioch, expressed by the gradual disfranchising of city councilors from civic appointments, duties, and acts of munificence.[156]

In the decades following Diocletian's political reforms, Antioch had to increasingly negotiate the local political and administrative apparatus with a growing body of imperial administrators of non-Antiochene descent.[157] Overseeing military logistics and fiscal matters were the key tasks that occupied them; meanwhile, the diversion of levies from the civic treasury to the imperial coffers naturally had a negative impact on the local economy. The city councilors of old were thus watching their prerogatives fading away. With the sense of downgrading came also the imposition of fiscal burdens and civic obligations – especially food distributions – that had the twofold result of alienating social groups that could no longer sustain these vexations while conversely strengthening the position of the few headmen (*protoi*) who could serve as providers of services.[158] The preeminence of these grandees in the civic discourse was thereby greatly strengthened, and with it their ability to tap into the imperial circles. The technicalities and nuances of the process are described through the lenses of Libanius; the picture that emerges from the fourth century onward is one of recession from the golden age of civic life. Even the *bouleuterion*, the venue that accommodated the meetings of the councilors in the aftermath of Constantine's reign, had at this point lost its vibrancy and overall raison-d'être. The physical modifications of Antioch at this time, laden with monumental basilicae and houses that look more like *palazzi*, may be grounded in the transformation of the administrative apparatus during the fourth and fifth centuries.

The reign of Valens's successor Theodosius I (379–395) represented a turning point in the religious and social landscape of Antioch as well, as his Edict of Thessalonica in 380 making Nicene Christianity the state religion of the empire sanctioned the ban on Arianism and other heresies and ended the new season of optimism that had begun with the Edict of Milan in 313. It is true that the transformation of the religious landscape between the Milan edict and the reign of Theodosius in particular led to the forging of a new image of the city, one in which churches became the main urban foci and bishops, through the heady blend of politics and sacred matters, were *de facto* political leaders. But although Antioch's scanty archaeological evidence does not preclude the evidence of a cityscape that, starting with Constantine, gestured at the new era through monumental churches and their extraordinary engineering achievements, this much confidence, zeal, and dedication failed to achieve internal cohesion and a shared sense of what true Christian orthodoxy was. Theological conflicts and disputes over dogmas drove time and again a wedge within Antioch's Christians, leading to conflicts, ejections, and social riots that reached their apex in the fourth century. In particular, far from leading to consensus, Theodosius's edict had repercussions in Antioch as competing bishops sought to gain official recognition. More importantly, empire-wide religious policies had particular resonance in Antioch; in 381, Theodosius officially outlawed paganism altogether, and the consequent destruction of temples across the Roman Empire had consequences for ancient buildings in Antioch, with monks on the frontline ready to demolish the symbols of paganism.[159] While a sense of cultural preservation may have spared urban landmarks like gates and squares, temples were endangered by the vandalism of Christian zealots. In the late 380s, Libanius decried the ongoing destruction of shrines in the countryside by the hand of hooligans, primarily monks.[160] A similar destiny may have felled urban foci, had they not already been turned into governmental buildings and protected by the imperial statute.[161] Antioch, by all accounts, was no different than other cities of Asia like Ephesus, Aphrodisias, and Sagalassos, where the display of imperial imagery with religious overtones continued into the sixth century.[162] The apparent destruction of pagan sanctuaries, however, needs to be called into question. More often than not, buildings at the end of the fourth century were repurposed for new functions, as for instance with the temple of Tyche, converted into a classroom in the 360s and the temple of Dionysus used as tribunal by the governor Tisamenus in 386.[163]

It was also during the reign of Theodosius that the voice of John Chrysostom (347–407) echoed with all his vigor in the vaults of the *Palaia*, the old church of Antioch. Born in Antioch, John Chrysostom was arguably the most prominent and tenacious of a line of religious "shepherds" who wielded the staff of authority over the city during the late fourth century. Raised to the status of religious and civic authority, he sought to steer the religious climate of Antioch in ways that would reverberate in the city's fabric. His homilies are arresting evidence of the interaction between the clergy and the community as well as of the struggles and perils of pastoral duty. Within a church redolent with dilemmas and divisions, John represented the voice of reason, but he also had to cope with its increasing "profane vigor" and intolerance of authority.[164] Further, his homilies, resonating as they did with the theological debates of the day, also brought into sharper focus the city, its poor, and the household, with much emphasis on the role of the family.[165] Deeply invested in the responsibility of guiding a community much inclined toward disobedience of religious orthodoxy as well as pagan lures, John sought to map out and enforce his own Antioch, one that shunned baths, pagan shrines, and synagogues. The saint wanted the city to part company with amenities that contaminated its spirit: theaters, hippodromes, baths, and agoras were unnecessary trappings that got in the way of holiness.[166] The opulence of houses was not exempt either, be it statues or golden roofs. The wealthy folks of Antioch, investing their assets embellishing their houses with an excess of décor, were also targets of his tirades.[167] His congregation did not have to venture far to find concrete examples of what he was speaking of: the suburb of Daphne at that time had reached its apex in the construction of rich villas and fanciful landscaping.

John Chrysostom was not, however, simply seeking to steer his community unflaggingly away from heresies. Underneath it all, he realized too well that the pagan city was far from dead and that demons of polytheism still lurked in every alley.[168] He thus had to reckon with the momentum that paganism had gained under Julian, whose plan of a pagan church based in Antioch, albeit utopian, had nevertheless given new energy to polytheism. Not even the monks and ascetics who lived near Antioch, the "athletes of Christ" described by Theodoret of Cyrrhus in his *Historia Religiosa*, could subvert this state of affairs, he believed; not even the supernatural virtues of St. Symeon the Younger, contemplating and rejecting mundane matters from his pillar 60 km east of Antioch, could lead this community to salvation.[169]

But John's homilies were directed not only against heretics and pagans but also against the Jews. Although the Seleucid king Antiochos III had granted Jews both citizenship as well as privileges, which were ratified by the Roman authorities in successive eras,[170] these were called into question in the following centuries, and while Josephus suggests that Antioch had a generally positive disposition toward the Jewish community, this did not hamper occasional escalations and overt anti-Jewish agendas endorsed by bishops, be it forcible baptism or outright violence. Indeed, John's homily of 386 against the local Jewry was a vitriolic attack that, though imbued with the rhetoric of Christian propaganda, was aimed particularly at those demi-Christians, or Judaizing Christians, of the day.[171] These were individuals of Greek descent, and apparently Christian, who nonetheless populated the synagogues of Antioch. More subtly, though, through his homilies John Chrysostom addressed the dangers the Jews posited to the integrity of Christians. Their thriving community, the apparent visual allure of their services, their ability to make proselytes, and, lastly, the rabbis' ability to treat sickness and diseases represented formidable threats to the young and shaky Christian church, in John's view. Christine Sheperdson writes:

> In fourth-century Antioch, like in third-century Carthage, synagogue-attendees bought and sold in the agora alongside their neighbors most days of the week, sat with them at the theater, bathed together in the public baths, exercised at the gymnasium, slept beside them at the cave of Matrona, and greeted them as they walked alongside Antioch's famous colonnaded and lamp-lit streets. John Chrysostom's texts employ multiple rhetorical tactics to construct *Jews*, with the result that some of his descriptions more plausibly reflect local people and practices than others.[172]

John drew upon a tradition first established by St. Ignatius, bishop of Antioch, whose letters written between 110 and 117 attested to the frailty of the local church and advocated for a Christianity free from the contamination of Judaism and Gnosticism. But perhaps John's picture of religious cross-pollination, other than unwittingly reinforcing the prominence of the Jewish community, is also arresting evidence of Antioch's multilayered character as it fused cultures, languages, and beliefs in a unique manner.

More fundamentally, Antioch's fourth-century Christianity was a universe suspended between ancestral customs and adherence to the message of bishops. The discussion over the nature of Jesus Christ, however, was far from fostering consensus. Ammianus Marcellinus makes it plain that "no wild beasts are such enemies to mankind as are most of the Christians in their deadly hatred of one another."[173] The continuous risk of religious fires flaring up in Antioch was indeed a staple condition of Late Antique Antioch.

Meanwhile, Theodosius also fueled urban modifications by mapping out a new perimeter of fortifications designed to encompass the southern districts.[174] Yet the actual works remained confined to a program of repairs presumably carried out in 397 CE. The difficulties, however, in identifying the Theodosian stretches or any other agency in the heavily manipulated masonry of the Mt. Silpius and Mt. Staurin fortifications are going to be discussed (see Appendix 1).[175]

Building programs aside, this was a community crippled by economic crisis and vexed by imperial demands. Theodosius had to reckon with the frailty and usual ills of Antioch's unstable economy. Two food crises erupted in all their force at brief intervals between 381 and 384, putting administrative personnel to a severe test. The blame game involved everyone, from the *comes Orientis* to the *consularis Syriae* to the local bakers;[176] meanwhile, the city and peasants from rural districts starved. On both these occasions Libanius rose to the challenge, negotiating solutions to the advantage of the local constituency. He, however, never feigned sympathy for the governors who, in his opinion, abused the name of the emperor, as 14 speeches addressed to Theodosius show.[177] Among the common charges of illegal practices, malevolence, and greed, some more peculiar allegations can be singled out. Noteworthy in this sense is the 392 CE speech *Against Florentius*, the *Consularis Syriae*.[178] Amid various grievances, Libanius laments Florentius's intended construction of porticoes (*stoai*) for a larger street – of unknown location – at the expense of areas hitherto used as *necropoleis*. It appears that not even the dead could stop the whims of the imperial administrators.

Meanwhile, the civic government and all strata of the population were suffering increasing requests to perform civic services; farmers, too, were expected to contribute.[179] The citizenry even had to collect and transport debris from the demolition of old buildings. In general, the gulf between the city administration and the imperial governors could not have been wider. Libanius wrote:

> I am no councilor: I have immunity because of my concern with rhetoric, but I can still be upset at the poverty of the councillors and the wealth amassed by the lackeys of the governors. Some of these, only recently hawkers of meat, bread or vegetables, have grown great on the property of the councilors and enjoy just as much respect as they, so great is the wealth they possess.[180]

Adding to all these stresses came the implementation of heavier taxes, which ignited the rage of the local population. At this point everything came to a head: in 387, Antioch finally erupted in revolt. The crowd in front of the tribunal of the provincial governor surged to unforeseen heights; their iconoclastic fury spared no image of the Theodosian house,[181] as statues of the emperor and his wife were toppled over and smashed and most of the imperial iconography in the city was razed to the ground. Libanius's report documents the irrational behavior of the mob, the crescendo of violence, and the ultimate insult against the imperial house:

> When things reached the stage of meddling with the statues, there were some offenders, but the spectators far outnumbered the performers of this outrage. Then how was it that they did not try to stop them? I repeat what I have said before – that a stronger power prevailed to stop them. There was some superhuman agency here and within them, which forced each man to look upon this and prevented him from uttering a word.[182]

Underneath it all, a shared awareness that Antioch's primacy had been fatally eroded by Constantinople loomed large, with the city on the Orontes now degraded to the same status of the thousands of communities that populated the Greek East. Executions, beheadings, and retaliation were the obvious imperial response, along with the same institutional downgrading that Antioch suffered under Septimius Severus in 193 CE.[183] This led to heady diplomatic efforts from the local *curiales* to curb the Emperor's wrath. Once again, Libanius attempted to mediate and curb the violence of the Syrian governor, Celsus, and the imperial army, while the bishop, Flavian, and John Chrysostom, whose appeals resonated in at least 21 homilies, also sought to steer the emperor's resolution to a more moderate response.[184] As trials unfolded under an ad hoc commission, even the ascetics populating the caves of Mt. Silpius and Mt. Staurin,[185] the most revered "holy men," descended into the city and partook in the discussion, urging officials toward clemency and mild punishment. The scene of these "athletes of Christ" moving down upon the city must have been theatrically stunning. It is further evident that most of these hermits would have spoken Syriac instead of Greek, and their interaction with the local population is a gripping example of linguistic diversity negotiated in unique ways.[186] As shown previously, even Greek inscriptions at inns were heavily influenced by Syriac.

Back in Constantinople, Theodosius was finally persuaded and officially granted pardon to the city; new statues of the same imperial officials were cast, and speeches of praise and religious celebrations followed in the climate of restored concord.[187] Nonetheless, by all accounts Antioch's survival had been seriously at stake. Shortly afterward, Theodosius carried out a savage repression of Thessalonica in 390, massacring 7,000 inhabitants as they revolted against the Gothic troops stationed there. At the same time, this incident illustrated the growing influence of the Church, when Ambrose, the powerful bishop of Milan, excommunicated the emperor over this massacre. This, as well as the incident in Callinicum (modern Raqqa), when in 388 an angry mob of Christians destroyed the local synagogue for which Theodosius ordered them to make compensation but was blocked by Ambrose, made plain that Christianity writ large was gaining new confidence at the expense of the secular powers.[188]

Developments in Daphne

The words of Libanius's oration addressed to Theodosius after the conciliation following the 387 riots afford important insights into the narrative of Antioch's urban evolution at this time:[189]

> Indeed, in all our many errors, we were right in this much at least, in conceiving an address to you upon the renaming of the city in the terms you have heard. You, who by your conduct have shown yourself to be our founder, must regard our storm-tossed city as your creation, and besides not destroying it, you must make additions to it worthy of your station, such as those with which you have beautified Daphne, by the eclipse of the old palace with a new one. So let the city also obtain some similar edifice, whether you

wish it to be in the island beyond the river or in the built-up district facing it. I invite you to this task, Sire, not just for the sake of its size and beauty, but also that we may learn whether we still have our erstwhile admirer, or whether he has ceased to be such.

Here Libanius alludes to the disparity in imperial patronizing that was crippling Antioch. Two more subtle points are worth sharper focus. First, as noted, Antioch was gradually losing its prestige as it was being politically eclipsed by Constantinople, and second, the emperor was directing his liberality toward other foci, and not least to Daphne, where a new imperial estate had been established and a palace built.[190] Of course imperial fortifications and churches were still to be built and bridges were still to be upgraded by the house of Theodosius in Antioch, a plan that included reconfiguring the *Keiratai* southern quarter, hitherto a Jewish enclave. Cumulatively, however, the season of the great monumental programs sponsored by emperors and aimed at creating a capital city had decidedly terminated with Valens in the late fourth century. To make matters worse, earthquakes, food crises, and military vicissitudes had contributed to Antioch's becoming a swollen, overly crowded community, to the extent that Theodoret of Cyrrhus a few decades later referred to it as a suffocating entity.[191] We can conjure thousands of Antiochenes milling about each day, populating every corner of the city and crowding its roads and plazas as they went about their business. The constant traffic of oxcarts and flow of incoming commodities added a further layer to a community that, with approximately half a million inhabitants, may have reached its maximum capacity. Sprawl had a damaging impact on the environment and also meant a poorer economy as well as poorer health and safety. We can thus safely situate a movement of sizable contingents of Antiochenes away from the city around this time. More to the point, the transformation of Antioch's social and urban fabric reverberated throughout its territory, contributing to the growth of the rural districts in the Amuq Valley and on the Syrian limestone massif, as attested by the aggregate archaeological evidence. Put simply, it appears that between the fourth and fifth centuries, the Amuq, limestone massif, and Daphne developed as an alternative to Antioch, functioning as a response to the constraints of the city, held as it was by its obsolete Seleucid armature and incapable of coming to terms with its now congested, complicated space.

With the town councilors, at that point reduced to passive spectators of their city's fortunes, Antioch's nouveaux riches now came to the fore. These were the *honorati*, rampant imperial officials who sat next to governors during trials, had a predilection for seizing the economic opportunities offered by Antioch's territory, concealing their humble origins behind false genealogies, and surrounding themselves with domestic amenities and rich basilicas.[192] Acts of munificence, too were part of the equation: the *magister militum* of 383, Ellebichus, a man of German origins, greatly invested in providing Antioch with new baths both in the city and its hinterlands. What is more, in Libanius's words Ellebichus's largesse and good taste also extended to his own domestic unit. Apparently, his new house was a true gift to the citizenry, for it enhanced the beauty of the community.[193] In that vein, the patrician Datianus is a good case in point: not only did he take up the construction – or repairs – of baths and porticoes, but he also seemingly built a host of exquisite and opulent houses that heightened his profile as *euergethes* (donor).[194] That this new crop of administrators also contributed to transforming Antioch's domestic architecture is thus a cogent possibility. Houses at Daphne, and

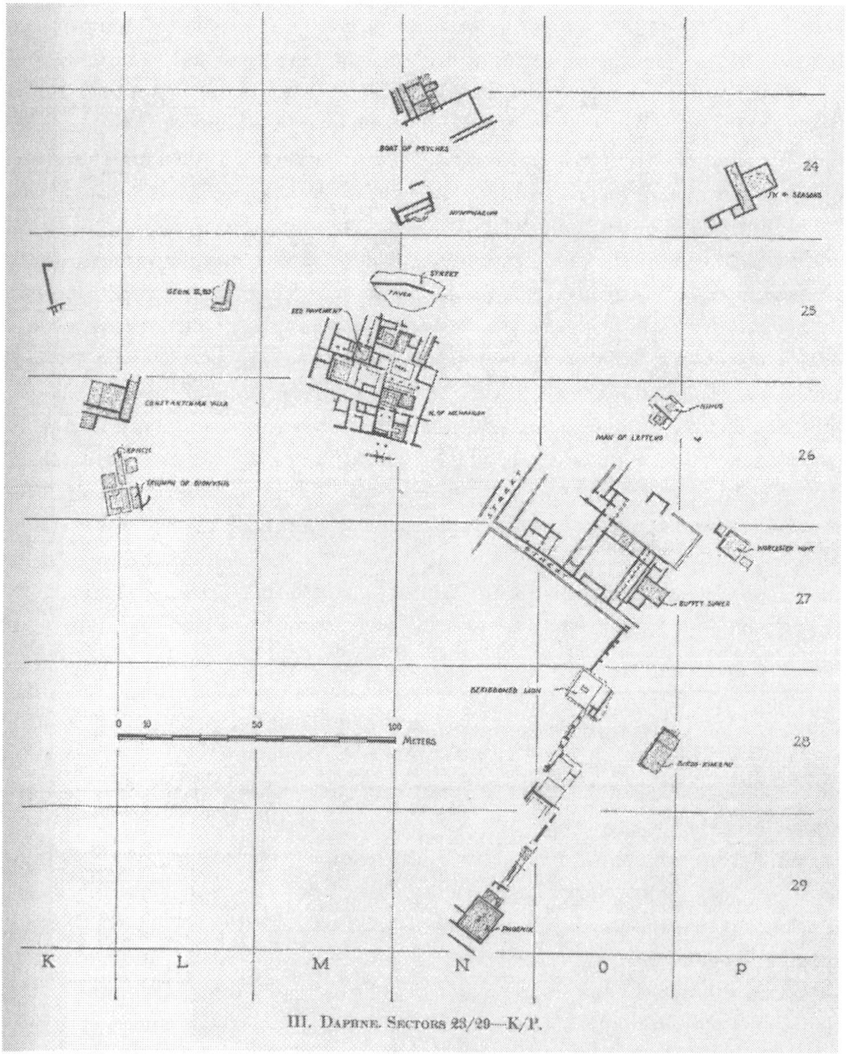

FIGURE 3.18 A cluster of houses excavated in Daphne

Source: Courtesy of the Antioch Expedition Archives, Department of Art and Archaeology, Princeton University; Princeton

primarily at the complex at Yakto, a small village outside Daphne, may reflect this phenomenon through a built environment laden with gardens and halls and lavishly decorated by the finest marbles, frescoes, and, of course, mosaics.[195] These units are indeed the only concrete evidence of the settlement straddling the plateau between the Seleucid and the Islamic ages,[196] for the excavators identified no traces of the temples, especially that of Apollo.[197] Although the excavation data is particularly complex to unravel, it is apparent that most units investigated by the Princeton team were situated away from the springs and oriented toward the northern fringes of the plateau (Figure 3.18).

Two major underground pipelines delivered water from the springs to each of the units investigated following a south–north linear trajectory. One of these conduits, however, upon encountering what was described as a conspicuous, elevated mound, apparently split in two, with its two branches skirting the feature. Centrally located in the plateau, this divided conduit may have signaled the area that accommodated the great sanctuary of Apollo and the adjacent *Olympieion*, according to the excavators.[198] Aside from scattered column drums, however, no further evidence reinforces this claim, though it may be accepted that most of the central plateau was in fact occupied by the main religious foci.

Overall, the team thoroughly investigated a number of houses on the northern fringes of the plateau via almost side-by-side trenches. If the hypothesis of the temple location is accepted, we may be able to locate the urban development of Daphne on the "periphery" of the plateau, thus in areas that would benefit from the views of the Orontes Valley. In the main, the evidence brought to light could be dated between the third and late sixth centuries CE, though it is apparent that several of the investigated suites rested on Hellenistic footings. Yet the hastiness of the 1930s excavations hampered the understanding of the distinction among several suites, and the excavators had to grapple with what they called "a complete lack of uniformity of orientation, and lack of space between individual units."[199] Modern research has focused on the structural and decorative designs of these units and put forth a "type" of house that showcases a local sensibility in its articulation of *triclinium, nymphaeum*, and peristyle.[200] The opulence of visual décor, moreover, corroborated the interpretation of Daphne as a sophisticated community flaunting its Greek culture, taste, and exuberance. The cliché of Daphne living the high life further resonates in the letters of Marcus Aurelius and the work of Libanius, to name but two ancient sources; indeed, Daphne went down in history as a place detrimental to good moral conduct.[201] Daphne's visual culture, as manifested in the aesthetics of hundreds of pavements with their dazzling mix of Greek myths, Persian accents, and personifications, further reflected the cultural eclecticism of their patrons.[202] It also contributed to realizing unique visual and structural linkages within domestic spaces, guiding movement and gaze. Yet what is particularly relevant here is the transformative character of these units and its bearing on the evolution of Daphne as Antioch's suburb.

FIGURE 3.19 The House of the Buffet Supper: the *nymphaeum*, corridor, and "buffet supper" mosaic in the foreground

Source: Courtesy of the Antioch Expedition Archives, Department of Art and Archaeology, Princeton University; Princeton

It has been shown in particular that in the fourth and fifth centuries many of these houses underwent a wholesale reconfiguration, though not as a result of the earthquakes that wreaked havoc repeatedly during that time. The frequent overlap of mosaics, as recorded by the excavators, makes this phenomenon all the more apparent. The autopsy of some units reveals the modality of this transformation. For instance, the House of the Buffet Supper provides an example of radical metamorphosis and a whole new perspective on the suburb living experience (Figure 3.19).

The third century CE building, characterized by a peculiar sequence of a garden and two *triclinia* flanking one large *triclinium* with the apse opening onto a portico and *nymphaeum*, was literally superseded by a new habitation scheme that, presumably dating to the early fifth century, reoriented the unit in fundamental ways. The longevity and transformative qualities of Antioch's domestic space need to be brought into sharper focus. The coin evidence makes it also plain that this house continued to be in use after the 526 CE earthquake, with floors that were superimposed onto the mosaics of one of the rooms.[203] In particular, the "upper level" phase of the house had its pivotal point in a new, marble-paved rectangular court framed by porticoes, with rooms and a long hall with an apse opening onto it. Also, a new façade and gardens articulated new itineraries and visual axes among the components and bear witness to a general process of revamping that perhaps we can extend to most of Daphne's built environment.[204]

FIGURE 3.20 Seleucia, House of the Drinking Contest. Raised mosaic panel B from Room 1, detail of *emblema* showing the recursive theme of the drinking contest between Hercules and Dionysus

Source: Courtesy of the Antioch Expedition Archives, Department of Art and Archaeology, Princeton University; Princeton

The House of the Drinking Contest in Seleucia is another case in point (Figure 3.20).[205] Showcasing one of the best legible architectural plans and having been excavated in relatively extensive terms, at least when compared to most houses investigated during the 1930s in the territory of Antioch, this domestic unit offers a stunning location overlooking the Orontes estuary, not to mention a vibrant decorative apparatus spanning the third and fourth centuries. As for the architecture, the unit's design gestures at traditions established in both the western and eastern Mediterranean. In particular, the emphasis on a porticoed courtyard and what appears to be an "atrium," albeit off-centered, suggest the synthesis of architectural formulas by the Antiochene builders, as well as creation of a space redolent with symbols of Greek myths.[206]

Its visual mainstay is, of course, the *triclinium*'s panel of the drinking contest, in which Dionysus and Hercules, comfortably reclining on a *kline* (the couch of the Greek symposium) hoist their cups as the drinking contest reaches its climax (Figure 3.20). A dancing maenad playing a tambourine contributes a musical layer to this stunning composition, thus blending sounds and vision in one magnificent ensemble, framed as it is by a heady pattern of lozenges, diamonds, and rhombs and small designs, like rosettes, quatrefoils, and crosses, among others. Oher panels from corridors and courtyard corroborate the visual brio of the *triclinium* through images of Eros and Psyche, fishing cupids, personified seasons, and geometric motifs. But it is the house's transformative quality, its ability to extend its locales beyond the size of the panels and offer new routines and itineraries after it underwent repairs in the fourth century that needs to be brought into sharper focus. This logic of reinventing the domestic space, whether as a response of natural wear and tear or as a more pressing remedy to telluric shocks, is their staple character, one that also brought about some decisive changes in the ways domestic space was construed and perceived.

Altogether, this architectural metamorphosis was not a mere parting with architectural models of the past;[207] rather, this scant evidence hints at the percolating of an innovative type of "house," one that within a few generations was to produce the so-called Constantinian villa and then the grandiose mid-fifth-century villa at Yakto.[208] The former owes its date of a coin under one of the mosaics that places the context safely in the early fourth century. The unit, however, consists of a partially excavated suite of three rooms, dominated by a central court that was embellished by an octagonal pool and flanked by an elegant portico with pilasters on its southern side (Figure 3.21). The decorative apparatus of the central hall is quite remarkable. The mosaic's border encompasses a geometric pattern and figured panels with scenes of rural life, cupids, birds, and flowers. The centerpiece of the composition, however, is the square section of the room. Here the artist succeeded

FIGURE 3.21 The Constantinian Villa, general view

Source: Courtesy of the Antioch Expedition Archives, Department of Art and Archaeology, Princeton University; Princeton

at visually mimicking a ceiling, perhaps to be reflected by the water pouring from the fountain, with personified seasons diagonally occupying the groins of the vaults and thus creating a system of trapezoidal panels each depicting hunting scenes of various kind, amid a menagerie of wild game, sacrifices to Artemis, and ultimately, displays of dexterity in chasing and killing prey.

Better known, of course, is the complex discovered at Yakto in 1932. This suburban *domus*, with its galleries divorcing private space from public, as well as pleasure garden, bath, and the presence of grand halls such as a great cruciform hall, makes manifest the ideology of its patrons, either imperial administrators or *curiales* who envisioned their domestic space as a locus of private matters, public events, and ultimately their work-space. The house at Yakto also obliterated a unit of the third century CE[209] and grew as a combination of four different units, connected, however, by the two prominent porticoed galleries, one of which faced on a pool and a small bath in a *viridarium*, a garden.[210] In these terms, the concept of Antiochene domestic space as defined by its modules of the third century (chiefly the *triclinium* and fountain unit) was thus supplanted by a new elaboration of space that reconciled the obligations of public life and the advantages of the suburban setting. But ultimately, the stimuli that prompted these modifications and, more subtly, the adoption of a new logic of domestic working environment imbued with the energy of public and private activities and projecting the culture of the city in the suburban

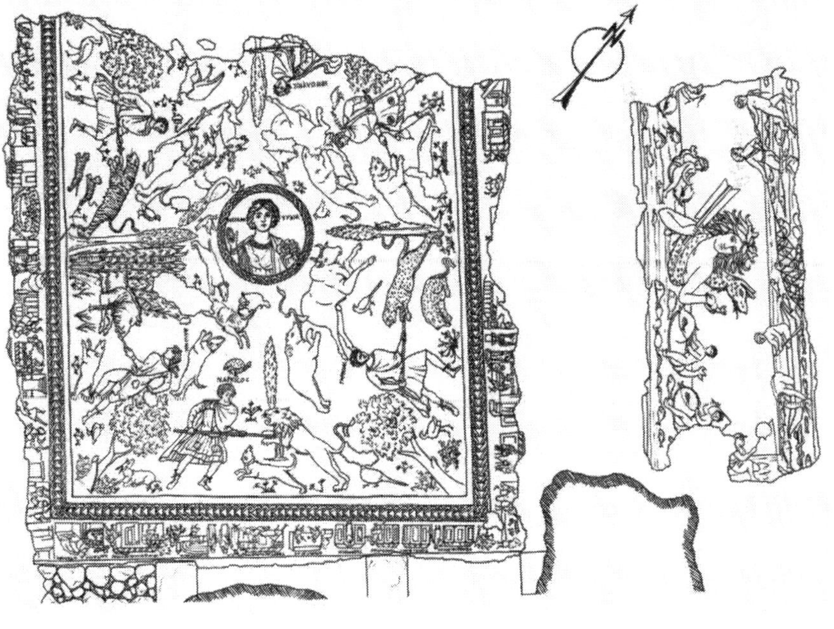

FIGURE 3.22 Yakto (Daphne). The Megalopsychia mosaic

Source: Courtesy of the Antioch Expedition Archives, Department of Art and Archaeology, Princeton University; Princeton

setting likely lay outside Daphne in the narrative of Antioch's urban evolution, and especially in the events that shook the city during the reign of Theodosius I. We may thereby be starting to comprehend Daphne's urban overhaul and archaeology a little better, when tested against the background of the social configuration of the city and, more to the point, the appearance of a new wealth, grounded as it was in the administrative and military spheres and slowly eroding the traditional realities of the Antiochene world.

Finally, worthy of discussion is the famous border of the Megalopsychia mosaic found in the Yakto villa, which may date to shortly before 458 (Figure 3.22).[211] While the pavement's central panel concerns a hunting scene typical of late antique Syrian and North African mosaics, the border, greatly damaged by the superimposition of modern buildings, presents a schematic representation of the city and select monuments. Stylistically, the composition adheres to a visual convention that figures prominently on pavements at Gerasa, Church of St. John the Baptist, with a cityscape of Alexandria or the well-known, albeit later, Madaba Map mosaic (560 CE) in Madaba.[212] It consists of a sequence of vignettes, each populated by passersby and travelers who stroll around the city, occasionally stopping in front of workshops and the facades of houses. Conspicuous monuments in the background convey a sense of depth to the panorama and suggest an itinerary comprising both city and countryside. How to view the mosaic is the question; its emphasis on physical movement and overall cinematic qualities betray a visual itinerary that is imagined, a perspective of how locals may have viewed their experience of Antioch. The discussion as to whether the implied itinerary originated in Antioch or Daphne inevitably leads to a cul-de-sac, for the mosaic offers no hints as to how to view the scenes, nor their cultural meaning. Nor does the interplay between frontal and bird's eye views help discern the rationale behind the composition. The hippodrome, the Tauriane Gate, the *Peripatos* (a portico), the Castalia spring, and private houses, to name but a few, are but some of the recognizable buildings and landmarks appearing on the pavement's frame as the journey in and outside the city unfolds in front of the viewer. Allusions to prominent citizens and their properties figure prominently in the sequence, as in the case of the bath of Ardaburius, *Magister Militum per Orientem* under the emperor Marcian and Antioch resident until 459 CE. The rhythmical sequence of porticoes and shaded walkways along the main thoroughfare surely enhanced one's experience of the city, while also hinting at their ability to foster social clustering. What is more, the houses of Antioch appear in all of their scale, one or two stories high and with gabled roofs and porticoes, thus conjuring up a domestic space that the mute foundations and robbed walls excavated by the Princeton team can only partially inform. Overall, these Yakto snippets of life and buildings in Antioch/Daphne documented key sites and served the purpose of "postcards." These images capture a fraction of a second in the ancient city's millenarian history, imbuing with life and pulsing energy its textual and material records.

Beautiful mosaics, large halls, exquisite wall decorations, and waterworks: these are but some of the traits that were common to the late antique houses of Daphne.

The modesty that John Chrysostom so vehemently had advocated for the houses of the true believers was nowhere to be found there, amid the cypress trees and the old abodes of the gods. "Make your house a church" was the unambiguous message that echoed from the *Palaia* in the city and lingered on for decades, as attested by the bishop Severus' rehashing of the same concept in 513 CE.[213] By that rationale, houses were expected to broadcast the only truth, and, as such, had to carry the sign of the cross in all of their visible parts. Not surprisingly, the Princeton excavations in the urban sector of 16-O yielded small columns and capitals with inscribed crosses that powerfully attest to this practice. But this is a rare exception amidst a material culture that still upheld the ancient Greek myths, iconography, and message.

End of an era

In the wake of the reign of Theodosius I, more troubles were to follow. The tenure of his son and successor in the East, Arcadius (395–408), witnessed another earthquake in 396, an invasion of Isaurians (tribes settled in the Amanus Mountains region and eastern Cilicia) in 399, and debates over the legitimacy of games and ancestral festivals.[214] Devastating food crises also continued; in 431 under Theodosius II (408–450) food supplies were at a premium, and a much welcome grain distribution by the empress Eudocia (408–450) in 438 suggests the city may have still been recovering from these downturns.[215] Meanwhile, largesse from the imperial house was key to restoring the bath of Valens and completing the southern extension of the city wall, with the inclusion of a new Gate of Daphne, a project presumably contemplated as early as Theodosius I.

Apparently, urban sprawl, notably in the quarter known as *Keiratai*, had greatly extended southward. Though this new development, a new curtain from the Philonauta Gate on the Orontes – presumably Antioch's fluvial port – ran to the highland Phyrminus gorge where it joined the old wall of Tiberius at a site called the Rhodion, and thus encompassed the southern boroughs along the road to Daphne. A new system of towers and defenses thus straddled Mt. Silpius south and southeast of the walls of Tiberius all the way to the citadel.[216] That the new defenses tied up nicely with the walls of Tiberius can hardly be disputed. So Evagrius Scholasticus, a sixth-century Christian intellectual native of Syria, wrote:

> At Eudocia's suggestion, Theodosius considerably enlarges the bounds of the city, by extending the circuit of the wall as far as the gate which leads to the suburb of Daphne: of which those who are disposed, may assure themselves by visible proof; for the whole wall may still be traced, since the remains afford a sufficient guidance to the eye.[217]

What is more, in the southern sectors of the city, the new enceinte wound up incorporating areas used hitherto as burial grounds and gardens, as shown by the incorporation of the *necropoleis* of Mnemosyne and Sari Mahmoud. Perhaps the *coemetarium* where the remains of St. Ignatius had been buried was one of such

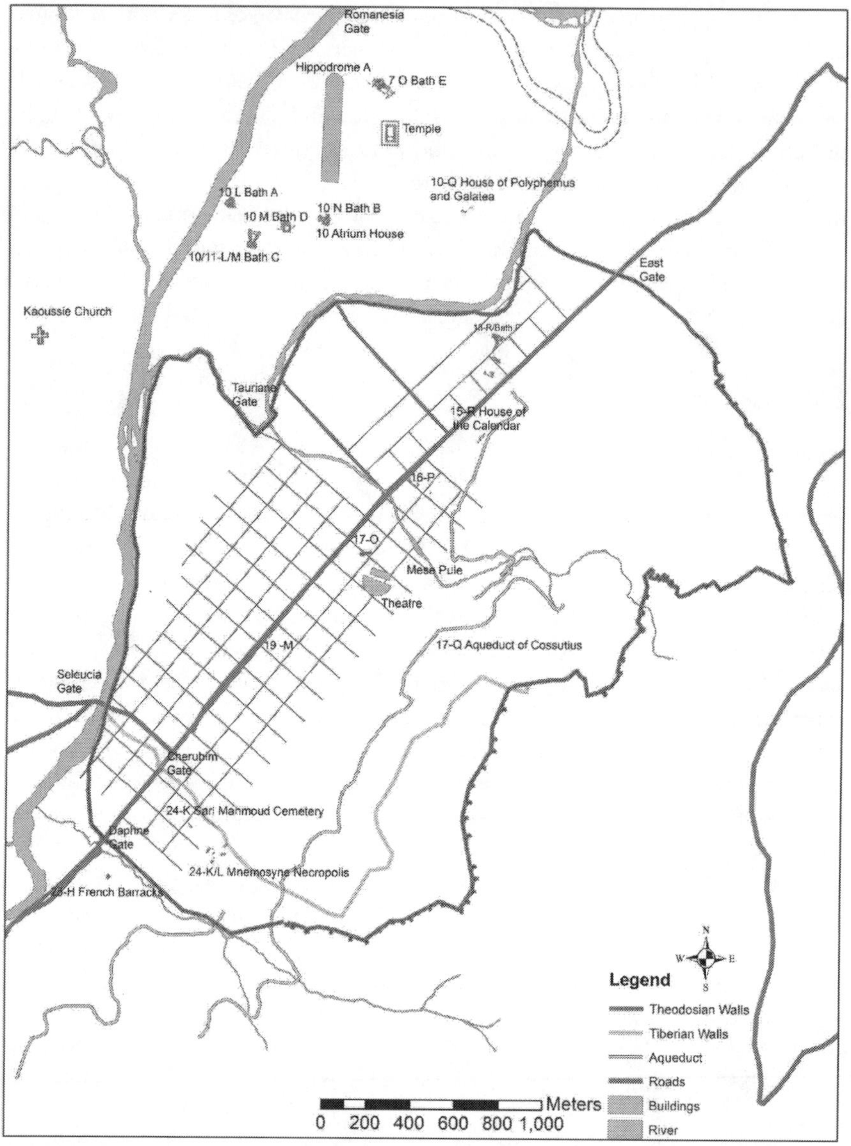

FIGURE 3.23 Plan of Late Roman Antioch

grounds now integrated in the city fabric. While stringent defensive needs drove the operation, we must also consider the desirability of building a community *ad sanctos*, to the saints, in the vicinity of Antioch's most revered saints.[218] However, the textually contested nature of the project, with the accounts of Malalas and Evagrius at variance over the agency implicated in the works, has long kept the analysis of the walls in a state of impasse (Appendix 1).[219]

The project was germane to systems of defense sponsored by the imperial house at Constantinople and Anazarbus in Cilicia, among other sites. The walls of Antioch's occasional recourse to layers of red brick with a core of mortared rubble betrays the same agency.[220] Theodosius II also had the relics of St. Ignatius moved from the cemetery in Daphne to a new church dedicated to the saint.[221] Other stand-alone buildings, designed largely for political purposes, were established by the governors with the blessings of the imperial house, the basilica of the prefect Anatolios being probably the most conspicuous example of this type of establishment. But minor projects, such as the reconstruction of the *Psephium* (a public building) by Memnonius, the basilica of Zoilus, and that of Callistus added a new sense of décor to the city, while also signaling the patronage of imperial administrators.[222] Overall, by the Theodosian age, the emphasis on the southern expanses of the city was a reflection of the gradual abandonment of the city's northern quarters, and especially the Island, which by the early fifth century had already lost its administrative purposes. But other forces were also conspiring against what had been hitherto a key sector in the life of Antioch. The seismic energy that had accumulated during the course of a century, in fact, was about to complete the divorce between the city and the island.

At this juncture the history of the city becomes fundamentally entangled with the havoc wreaked by the earthquake of September 13–14, 458. More than ever, Antioch's history during Late Antiquity is punctuated by the sequence of earthquakes, amidst other disasters, that shook its community and caused great devastation, as for instance in 215, 341, 365, and 396. Though a far greater earthquake lay in wait to strike the following century, none of these previous episodes matched the vehemence of the earthquake of September 13–14, 458, under the reign of Leo I (457–474), with an estimated loss of 80,000 lives. Authoritative voices like that of Evagrius, however, had no doubts as to the causes of the cataclysm:

> In the second year of Leo's reign there was a dreadful trembling and shaking of the earth in the city of Antiochos. Various episodes had previously occurred involving the people of the city, who showed the complete madness of those beside themselves with frenzy and a savagery beyond that of any wild animal, and these served, as it were, as a prelude to these great disasters.[223]

The seventh-century chronicle of John, bishop of Nikiu, reports that in the days of the emperor Leo the Elder "the city of Antioch was polluted owing to the earthquake that befell it."[224] Evagrius and Malalas illustrate, presumably referencing a common source, the almost wholesale destruction of buildings, especially houses, on the Island, and less extensive damage in the rest of Antioch.[225] The account of the former is particularly vivid, for it illustrates the magnitude of the catastrophe on the city's individual districts, and not least how it ravaged the Island, where apparently the palace, the *tetrapylon*, and the porticoes nearby suffered great damage. The circus, too, was not exempt from the shocks, with the reported collapse of the towers at the entrance of the building. The colonnaded street and public buildings in the rest of the city were also left apparently unscathed, while a host of baths were still functioning, though probably compromised in their stability. The *nymphaeum*, a monumental fountain in the Ostracine neighborhood, presumably in the vicinity of the Forum of Valens and possibly found in sector 17-O, was destroyed, along with houses nearby. Whether feeling to nearby highland districts or resisting the force of the event, the Antiochenes eventually had to come to terms with the destruction that had pulverized entire sectors of their city. And the memories of the event lingered for decades. Severus of Antioch's commemoration bolstered the local sense of belonging through the vicarious memory of their forebears' vicarious experience:

> But when the earthquake stopped, everyone who had fled regained confidence, putting their feet down on the ground with assurance, in order to reach the town. But all were struck with fear and were full of terror; and when they walked, they were terrified, like those who, having just crossed vast seas, disembark from a ship and are still trembling and timid. But, running between the houses, they wept inconsolably, unable to bear this sight.[226]

Overall, this event led to a definitive divorce between the city and the Island, at that point reduced to a field of ruins. More to the point, it ushered in a fundamental reorientation of the city and its axes toward the new southern extension that had been inaugurated by Theodosius II, with the imperial authority actively involved in repairs and restoration. Through tax exemptions for those who had lost their properties and the allocation of 1,000 talents of gold – which may not have been an exorbitant sum – Leo showed his positive disposition toward the city and its grieving community. But the aftershocks had not even subsided when news arrived in 459 of the death of the famed stylite St. Symeon the Elder, who had lived 37 years atop his pillar east of the city; this was followed by a new earthquake that struck the city in June 460, causing additional damage, injuries, and a widespread sense that Antioch had been abandoned by the one true God.[227] Altogether, the earthquake of 458 demarcated a major juncture in the history of Antioch.

Conclusions

Overall, we have highlighted in this chapter a key epoch in Antioch's history, when the city served as the virtual capital of the Roman Empire. A plethora of extensive building programs sponsored by the imperial house both identified Roman investment in the city and conveyed a sense of authority. The inert, generally vague description of these monuments, however, inhibits the discussion of their physical insertion into the urban plan and experience in social terms. None of them, be they the Great Church of Constantine or the Forum of Valens, have been identified on the grounds. The congregation of masses in these public spaces, whether worshippers or political cliques, cannot thus be conjured up, nor can a sense of use be gleaned. Equally jarring is the absence of the crowded tenements that accommodated the lives of the Antiochenes. The exquisitely decorated houses of Antioch and Daphne hardly informed the lives of the majority of the population. Nevertheless, the literary sources are the redress that bring into sharper focus the main actors in this city: bishops, clerics, peasants, administrators, curiales, and, indeed, the Antiochene mob, as they shaped their surroundings, drove political change and bred a modest tolerance of others. In short, the agency of the local community comes to the fore. The literary repertoire also enables a discussion of Antioch as a community, with its pulsing energy, dilemmas, conflicts, and corporate identity. How it sought, and ultimately failed, to negotiate the realities of imperial politics, going from the highest plateau of prominence to play but a marginal role, has been a key theme. More fundamentally, though, Antioch during Late Antiquity was the place where Christian debates were fiercely played out. Theological divisions nearly shattered the city time and again; only the hand of nature, through the devastating effects of earthquakes, fostered a tenuous sense of concord.

Notes

1 Amm. Marc. 16.8.8.
2 Ausonius, *The Order of Famous Cities*, 4–5.
3 Brands 2018b, 17.
4 Herodian I, 186–197 (II, 7–8); *Downey, History* 236–239.
5 *TIB* 15, 547. In so doing, Septimius Severus replicated the punishment imposed on the city by Marcus Aurelius in the aftermath of Avidius Cassius's failed coup of 175 CE. The banning of the games and prohibition of public gatherings (SHA Marcus Antoninus 25.9–10; Avidius Cassius 9.1) set the precedent taken up by Septimius Severus. See also Dio Cass. 75.14.3; Herod 3.6.9. *Malalas* also weighs in on the issue; see 12.22. Laodicea, by turn, acquired the status of colony and received all kinds of economic benefits; see Dabrowa 2020, 164.
6 *TIB* 15, 547–548.
7 *Malalas* 12.22. The former would be yet another bath on the slopes of Mts. Staurin/ Silpius, presumably tapping into the Julio-Claudian and second-century CE water feeders. The latter's position is not known, except that it was on the "level part of the city." Its name betrays that of Livia, the Antiochene citizen who apparently sold the property to the city. As for the placement of Antioch's bath, see Yegül 2000, 147. The map does not take into account the realities of aqueducts, feeders, and reservoirs: see Leblanc and Poccardi 2004, 242.
8 *Malalas* 12.16; Lib. *Or*. 11.219.
9 *TIB* 15, 548. On Caracalla's good disposition toward Antioch, see *Downey, History* 244.44.
10 Dio Cass. 9.390–395.
11 *McAlee, Coins* 278.
12 *Antioch Archives*, Field Report 1934.
13 Butcher 1988, 72.
14 Zos. 1.23.
15 Dodgeon and Lieu 1991, 9–19.
16 Potter 2004, 220.
17 On Mariades, the apparent rift he may have caused between the *curiales* and the people of Antioch, as well as his role in the siege, see *AnpD* F1 Müller, attributed to Petrus Patricius and taken up by Mecella 2018. The episode of the Persian soldiers appearing on Mt. Silpius as many Antiochenes were enjoying a play in the theater is a well-known

trope; see Amm. Marc. 23.5.3 and the reprise of the anecdote in Pseudo Hegesyppus, *De Excidio* 3.5.2 (text, translation, and commentary in Bay 2018):

> Eventually, they hold that, when theatrical plays were being frequented in that city, one of the farcical actors, raising his eyes to the mountain, saw the Persians arriving and immediately said: I am either beholding a dream or a great danger. Behold: Persians! This was possible because the mountain leaned over the city, so that not even the height of the theatre provided an impediment to seeing the mountain.

For a recent discussion of this text, its Antiochene implications, and a translation, see Bay 2018.

18 *Res Gestae Divi Saporis* 310–311. Potter 2004, 225.
19 Dio Cass. 39.59.
20 Brands 2018b, 15.
21 The Princeton team found a cache of imperial and pagan statuary in a fourth/fifth century CE villa south of Antioch. It also included imperial portraits of Pertinax and Gordian III, as well as one in porphyry of Constantius I Chlorus. It has been widely seen as a sixth-century abandonment of non-Christian iconography rather than destruction caused by the earthquakes. A further possibility is that it may have been buried in the seventh century under Islamic rule. See Brinkerhoff 1970.
22 Butcher 2004, 49.
23 Euseb.*HE*. 6.21.3.
24 Euseb.*HE*. 6.38.
25 Chrysostom, *De s. Babyla* (PG 50, 532 21–51); Soz. *HE* 5.19.
26 See *Antioch II*, 156–157. For a comprehensive discussion of the text in object and its prosopographic implications, see Chausson 1997, 244–249.
27 *SEG* 17.759. For the main edition, see Roussel and De Visschler 1942, 173–200. See also W. Kunkel's commentary in Kunkel 1953, 81–91. On the legal implications of this document, see Williams 1974, 663–667; Crook 1995, 91–95.
28 Burton 2002, 119.
29 Crook 1995, 94–95.
30 Burton 2002, 115–128.
31 Feissel and Gascou 1989, 540–545. Beth Phouraia was a village recognized by the emperor, a *kome kyriake* lying in the *conventus* of Appadana, a town located some 20 km north of Dura Europos.
32 Also known as *Euphrates* 1. The papyrus has been thoroughly translated and commented by Feissel and Gascou 1989, 535–561.
33 *Euphrates* 1, 5.
34 On the problem of illegal acts perpetrated by Roman officials against Syrian communities, see Pollard 2000.
35 Stoneman 1994, 159; Downey 1961, 265.
36 On the location of Imma, see Gerritsen et al. 2008, 253.
37 *Malalas* 12.31.
38 Harvey 2000, 42; Millar 1971.
39 Patitucci-Uggeri 2008, 13.
40 *Malalas* 12.33.
41 For a discussion of Antioch's nympheum and its visual ties with Rome's Thermae Alexandrianae, see Dunbabin 1989, 26.
42 *Antioch II*, plate 6, n. 136. For the identification of the portrait as Constantius I Chlorus, see Brinkerhoff 1970, 19–28. Considering the degree of Diocletian's engagement with Antioch, it seems more likely that the portrait in question is his, rather than that of Constantius I Chlorus.
43 Elsner 1993.
44 Ćurčić 1993.
45 Lib. *Or* 11.203: The Palace would have occupied a quarter of the Island, from the center to the river bank. The outer wall had pillars instead of battlements, and

was integrated into the urban grid by means of roads. It was beautiful and large in relation to other palaces. See also *Theod.HE*.4.26.1–2 and especially *Evagrius* 2.12, p. 64:

> The palace of the city of Antioch is washed on the north by the river Orontes: on the south there is a large portico with two stories which touch the walls of the city, and which have two high towers. Between the palace and the river is a public road leading from the city to the suburbs.

See also *Theod.HE*. 4. 26.1–2.

46 Lib. *Or*. 11.204; *Malalas* 13.19 on Julian's hanging of the *Misopogon* on the *tetrapylon*; lastly, *Evagrius* 2.12.

47 Poccardi 2001; Saliou 2000.

48 See Chapter 4, p. 218.

49 Hahn 2018, 57–58.

50 *Malalas* 12.38. As for the sanctuary of Hecate, see Lib. *Or*. 18.171 on the reference to a cult, along with those of Pan, Hermes, and Isis. An allusion to the *Olympieion* may be in Lib. *Or*. 1.122, though the question is whether he may refer to the temple of Jupiter Capitolinus, from the second century BC. The issue of the new hippodrome is a thorny one. Did Diocletian repair the building mentioned in Pol. *Hist*. 30.25–27 and Livy 33.49? Did he build a new one? Be that as it may, this stadium was the third in the Antioch district, and may be identified on the topography border of the Yakto mosaic; see Brands 2018. As for the whereabouts of the building, Leblanc and Poccardi convincingly situate it near the Lattakia (Laodicea) road. Remote sensing and a cursory inspection on the ground, moreover, seem to validate the existence of a 320 × 80 m structure; see Leblanc and Poccardi 1999–2000, 389–397.

51 *Malalas* 12.44.

52 Lib. *Or*. 20.18–19 on the unfolding of the events and *Or*. 19.45 on the measures adopted by the emperor. See also the discussion in Liebeschuetz 1972, 104, where it is conversely suggested that the capital punishment for some of the city councilors lay in their failure to maintain order in the city and environs.

53 Marcone 2012, 43.

54 *Downey, History* 329.

55 *TIB* 15, 597.

56 *Downey, History* 335.

57 *Malalas* 12.49. See also Filipczak 2017, 327.

58 Marcone 2012, 47, on the nature of the "Edict of Milan."

59 Casella 2016.

60 Bassett 2005, 50–78.

61 Mayer and Allen 2012, 100–102.

62 *Malalas* 13.3. reports on Plutarch being the "governor of Antioch in Syria" entrusted with the two undertakings. For the *Palaia*, see Eusebius *HE* 7.32.4. On the topography and architecture, see Goilav 2014. As for the Octagon Church, see Eusebius, *De Laudibus Constantini* 9.8–14 and *Vita Constantini* 3.50. The issue of the doles associated with the church is also of interest: Michael the Syrian reports in his chronicle for 259 that Constantine gave the church 36,000 measures of wheat. Ibn Shiḥna via al-Janābī reports that, every year, 36,000 mudd (1 mudd equals 1.33 lbs) of wheat were given. Also, Constantine built the statue of Maryam (Virgin Mary), octagonal on a stone similar to one in Baʿalabakk and Biʿah.

63 *Theod.HE*. 5.35.4 and Saliou 2000. For the tentative description of the monument, see in particular Kleinbauer 2006, 125–128.

64 *Malalas* 13.3. The hospice may have replicated that of Ircanus in Jerusalem. See Uggeri 2008, 29.

65 *Michael the Syrian*, 106.

66 IB 581, 4–7.

67 Talbert 2010, in which the author argues for an early date, sanctioning the solidity of the empire, rather than assisting travel; see also Uggeri 2008, 16.

68 *Downey, History* 370. How Eudoxius was able to however embrace more moderate positions and gain the coveted seat in Constantinople in the 360s has been foregrounded by Rinaldi 2015.

69 Matthews 2006.

70 *TIB* 15, 550.

71 *Theophanes*, year 5824 (transl. by C. Mango and R. Scott):

> In this year, when the 7th indiction was about to follow, a famine occurred in the East which was so extremely severe that villagers gathered together in great throngs in the territory of the Antiochenes and of Kyros (Cyrrhus, Syria) and assailed one another and stole food in attacks by night and, finally, even in daylight they would break into the granaries, looting and stealing everything in the storehouses before they went away. A modius of grain cost 400 pieces of silver. Constantine the Great graciously gave an allowance of corn to the churches in each city to provide continuous sustenance for widows, the poor in hostels, and for clerics. The Church in Antioch received 36,000 modii of corn.

72 *Theod.HR* 1.11–12.

73 Henck 2007, 148.

74 Julian *Or.* 1. 41.

75 Bassett 2004, 132. In Antioch, though, in the 390s, the governor Florentius offers a good case in point, for he commissioned the construction of a portico as well as the enlargement of the adjacent road. See Lib. *Or.* 46.4.

76 *Socr.HE* 2.10: "Antioch continued to suffer concussions through the whole year" (transl. by E. Walford and H. De Valois). Also, *Theophanes*, year 5833: "And in that year Antioch was exposed to danger for three days by great earthquakes. And it took six years to build the circular church which was completed and consecrated by Constantine, which he had also founded." See the discussion of the event in Guidoboni 1989, 674 and in Ambraseys 2009, 142–143.

77 See n. 52.

78 Liebeschuetz 1972, 91.

79 *Socr.HE* 2.28.

80 *TIB* 15, 550; *Downey, History* 196, 362.

81 Amm. Marc. 14.1.2.

82 See n. 25.

83 See Filipczak 2017, 328, where it is convincingly argued that the accounts of Ammianus Marcellinus and Libanius merge on the killing of the governor in the hippodrome. Once again, then, the venue played a fundamental role in exacerbating turmoil and instigating violence.

84 Lib. *Or.* 1. See also Libanius's concise biography in Liebeschuetz 1972, 3.

85 Julian *Mis.* 363 C, 370.

86 Liebeschuetz 1972, 4. The year 378 CE bookends the epoch of imperial sojourns in Antioch; see Kelly 2018, 137. He writes:

> if we focus on the 41-year period between Constantine's death and Valens's, Antioch was an imperial residence for well over half of that time. In the same period, Constantinople – supposedly the city with the special relationship with emperors – had only seen an emperor winter in the city on six occasions, or seven including the usurper Procopius.

87 Klein 2006, 82.

88 Amm. Marc. 19.12.

89 *Michael the Syrian* 67: the Arians of Antioch apparently built a round church at this time, and it was dedicated by Arian bishops. An earthquake, it seems, destroyed it.

90 Further, the oration's wholesale avoidance of allusions to churches, ecclesiastical authorities and people of Christian faith poignantly informs Libanius's perspective, a man who pined over an idealized Antioch that transcended its current realities; see Shepardson 2014, 172–176. His presentation of the city was anything but firm: in *Or.* 2.26, he is accused of always harping on the city's misery. In 384, he writes *Or.* 50.31, in which he laments that famine is accompanied by "locusts, flies, and snakes." In 387, *Or.* 19.6, he considers Antioch "unfortunate." See Cribiore 2007, 25.

91 Gregory, *First Invective against Julian*, 1. Also, "son of the devil" in the *passio of Cyriacus* BHG 465b; see Trovato 2014, 1–6. At least nine biographies of Julian were published between 1976 and 2009, see Bouffartigue 2009.

92 Tiersch 2018, 129, on Julian's plan to make Antioch a *hiera polis*, that is a holy city. Although fundamentally Christian, Antioch could still rely on a substantial contingent of pagans, especially among the *curiales*; see Liebeschuetz 1972, 224. The volatility of their religious affiliation, however, is the rub; Lib. *Or.* 19.26–27 suggests that the city council was quick to turn to the Christian God in the moment of the Theodosian crisis.

93 Persecutions against Antioch's Christians were seemingly part of Julian's agenda, too. Revealing in this sense is an excerpt from Augustine's *City of God*, 18.52 (transl. by W. C. Greene):

> And I will say nothing of what he essayed and would have done at Antioch, had not one most faithful and steadfast young man, who, when many were arrested for torture, was taken first and put to torture for a whole day, still singing though torn and racked, so that the emperor, astonished by his unsubdued good spirits, was awed and alarmed lest he might suffer still more ignominious disgrace if he went on with the rest.

94 *Downey, History* 380–381.

95 See Cabouret 2004. Also, Lib. *Or.* 13.51 (transl. by A.F. Norman):

> Whatever is noble in other men is present in you in greater measure. You alone have gathered to yourself all the several attributes that give renown to others. Neither orator, nor soldier, nor judge, nor teacher, nor initiate, nor philosopher, nor seer could have more admiration for himself than for you. Indeed their activities you have overshadowed by your actions, their oratory by your orations.

96 Pellizzari 2015, 78.

97 Julian *Mis.* 369A. Michael the Syrian contends that he lowered the prices of all the goods on the market, see *Michael the Syrian*, 1.279.

98 Laniado 2002, 4–5.

99 Gascou 1977.

100 *Malalas* 13.23; see Tiersch 2018, 114, highlighting Julian's effort to heighten the collaboration with local curiales at the expense of the central administration, failing, however, to provide new levels of compensation.

101 Amm. Marc. 22.14.4; Julian *Mis.* 346 B-D.

102 Alpi 2007, 41.

103 Amm. Marc. 22.13.1–5; *Socr.HE* 3.18, on Babylas silencing the demon of the oracle. For a thorough discussion of the episode, see Tiersch 2018, 121.

104 Rinaldi 2015, 35.

105 Tiersch 2018, 134.

106 Van Hoof and Van Nuffelen 2011.

107 Julian *Mis.* 364 D, transl. by W.C. Wright.

108 Lib. *Or.* 15.52. Later Crusader sources, however, stress the adage of the city sheathed in marble; see, for instance, the *Gesta Francorum*, Chapter 8, p. 354, this volume.

109 Julian began preparing his campaign against the Persians early in his tenure, probably as soon as he reached Constantinople; see Zos. 3.11.3. On March 5, 363, Julian presumably left Antioch, as in Lib. *Ep.* 98. The expedition relied on a strategy of naval support on the Euphrates that made it possible for the army to march swiftly through the heart

of Mesopotamia. As Dabrowa noted, "it should be remembered that a mere three months had elapsed from the launch of the campaign to the burning of the flotilla and the emperor's death." See Dabrowa 2020, 85. On the campaign, see Dodgeon and Lieu 1991, 231–237. On the death of Julian, see *Socr.HE* 3.21: "Some say a certain Persian hurled the javelin and then fled; others assert that one of his own men was the author of the deed, which is indeed the best corroborated and most current report" (transl. by E. Walford and H. De Valois). "Whether by treason or the hand of the enemy is a matter of dispute," See Bowersock 1978, 116. Other sources on Julian's death: Amm. Marc. 25.3.6–23; Zos. 3.28.4–29, and *Malalas* 13.21. The military repercussions and Jovian's handling of the Persian crisis and ensuing treaty with Shāpūr II are detailed in Lenski 2002, 160–167.

110 Lib. *Or.* 18.281 (transl. by A. F. Norman)

111 Lib. *Or.* 18.292. See in particular Van Nuffelen 2006 on the discussion of the earthquake's date and the composition of the funerary oration in honor of Julian.

112 For the vivid description of the tsunami, see Amm. Marc. 26.10.15–19; the discussion of the earthquake's geophysical characteristics can be found in Guidoboni 1989, 678–679. It apparently affected the coast of Egypt, Sicily, Crete, and Greece. Of interest is the perspective of contemporary church historians, who also saw in these events a reflection of the stir that agitated most Christian communities in the East.

113 Socr.*HE* 4.10–11.6. Se also Guidoboni 1989, 680.

114 Amm. Marc. 3.192–193; *Downey, History* 396.

115 *TIB* 15, 553. Lib. *Ep.* 1184–1186.

116 Zos. *NH* 4, 13.2; 4.20.2–4.21.1 for the years between 375 and 378.

117 Lib. *Or.* I. 1.163–165 and Amm. Marc. 27.7.4–8. For the discussion of the trails and their agenda, see Kelly 2018, 155–159, and especially Lenski 2002, 218–234.

118 Brands 2016a, 19–30.

119 *Malalas* 13.30; *Downey, History* 403–410. The temple of Ares was located near a *macellum* (meat and fish market) and the channel of the Parmenius; adjacent to it was the *Mese Pule*, see *Malalas* 11.9. The Xystos may have been built by Commodus and integrated into the plan of the new forum between the temple of Athena and the bath of Commodus (the *Commodium*); it consisted of porticoes, possibly functioning as gateway to a venue for gladiatorial fights: Lib. *Or.* 10.33; 11.219. In the days of Libanius, it presumably became the base of the *consularis* of Syria; how this transition came about is hard to determine. Also, the *Commodium* was adjacent to the Plethron, a venue established by Didius Julianus that accommodated wrestling. Under Valens it became a unit like a gymnasium, with two rows of seats on its four sides. It was enlarged by Argyrius in 332, then Phasganius, Libanius's uncle, in 336. Proculus, the *comes Orientis* of 383–384, proposed a further expansion of seating; see Lib. *Or.* 10.1–13. Lastly, the *Kynegion*, a nearby building that had presumably been established by Julius Caesar and then used for hunts and combats under Valens, was destroyed under Theodosius; it may have been a structure with curved sides intended for spectacles. See Lib. *Or.* 10.33; 11.219. How this cluster of buildings intersected with sectors 17-O and 18-O of the Antioch excavations still needs to be verified.

120 *Malalas* 13.30.

121 Lenski 2002, 394.

122 Michael the Syrian says that Valens gave gardens to pagans for sacrifices and let Jews perform their rites there as well. He reports that Valens built a *demosion* (a prison to hold orthodox Christians) and restored the circus; see *Michael the Syrian* 364. He also allegedly perpetrated massacres of orthodox Christians, and many of them were drowned in the Orontes; see *Socr.HE* 4.2.

123 Pamir's recent surveys and excavations in this area have substantially confirmed the topography as delineated by the 1930s excavations; see Pamir 2016.

124 By the time Meletius came back to Antioch after his exile mandated by Constantius II (360–361), two other key religious figures had materialized in Antioch. The bishop

Euzoeus, an Arian, had seized the great church, while still representing a large constituency in the city. If the gulf was not wide enough, another anti-Arian movement had meanwhile found its leader in the newly ordained Paulinus, a presbyter who had received the authoritative blessings of Lucifer bishop of Cagliari, not to mention the support of those who upheld a pro-Alexandria orthodoxy. The schism in the city could not have been more tangible; services, churches, and holy sites generated a new topography of worship that very much hinged on the vicissitudes of the day. For a thorough discussion of this momentous phase, see Shepardson 2014, 16–17.

125 See the discussion of the church's architectural features in Chapter 4, p. 224.

126 Lib. *Or.* 11.258.

127 Liebeschuetz 1972, 61–73.

128 Lib. *Or.* 47.13

129 Tate 1997, 70.

130 Decker 2001, 71.

131 Van Hoof and Van Nuffelen 2011.

132 *Downey, History* 420–421.

133 Garnsey 1988, 6.

134 The case of Pisidian Antioch petitioning the governor of Asia encapsulates the essence of a problem that affected other cities as well. See Garnsey 1988, 19. Also compelling is the case of Cibyra, see Kokkinia 2008.

135 Hull 2008.

136 *Tchalenko, Villages* and Tate 1992 are the landmark surveys of the antiquities of this region, as well as treatises on economy and religion (the former). For an excellent, concise survey of the archaeological evidence of the Syrian *Massif Calcaire*, see Ball 2000, 247–279.

137 See Callot 2013 on the new emphasis on wine production on the limestone massif and, overall, a perspective that revises the long held tenet of an industry essentially grounded in olive oil making.

138 *Tchalenko, Villages*; Tate 1992.

139 For views that substantially diverge from Tchalenko's, see Callot 1984 and 2013; Decker 2001, 71. For a thoughtful discussion of the notion of "crises," specifically the alleged large-scale crisis of the third century CE, see Garnsey 1988 and nn 133 and 134.

140 Liebeschuetz 1972, 71–73.

141 Lib. *Or.* 2.33.

142 For Libanius's modeling of himself as a *nouveau* Isocrates and performing in this capacity on numerous occasions as festival orator, see the panegyrics of the Emperors Constantius, Constans, and Julian and, obviously, the *Antiochikos*. For more on these problems and on the historical value of Libanius's orations and letters, see Downey 1959; Liebeschuetz 1972, 23–39; Norman 2000, in particular, is essentially a discussion of the *Antiochikos* and, as such, offers some valuable insights on many of the problems at issue in this study.

143 Guidetti 2010, 93.

144 Liebeschuetz 1972, 83–84.

145 While Weber 1934 and *Antioch IV.ii* illustrate a sizable portion of the collection, the cataloguing of the finds is still ongoing thanks to a new initiative at Princeton University spearheaded by Alan Stahl; see in particular www.princeton.edu/~rbsc/department/numismatics/browse20%search.html

146 Weber 1934, 80.

147 *Antioch IV.ii.*

148 Stahl 2018, 232. He infers that the sustained pace of building projects in Antioch during the Constantinian era justify this evidence.

149 Stahl 2018, 235–236.

150 Liebeschuetz 1972, 91.

151 *Antioch III*, 83–84.
152 Lib. *Or.* 11.257–258.
153 Chrysostom, Hom. 11.2. Beggars, their behavior, and their visibility are foregrounded in many a homily by John Chrysostom: see Leyerle 2018, 269.
154 *Downey, History* 241.
155 Lib. *Ep.* 60.4.
156 The exception may be the Syriarchy, perhaps the most prestigious of all the civic duties and still coveted during the days of Libanius. It involved the procurement of wild beasts for public entertainment and spectacles write large. See Lib. *Ep.* 108.3.
157 With regard to westerners in Antioch during the fourth century, see Mayer 2003, 15.
158 Lib. *Or.* 49.2, on the decline of council's membership (transl. by A. F. Norman):

> You see us standing here? You can almost count us on the fingers of your hands – twelve instead of twelve hundred. This forms the council. These are the only persons to deal with such important duties. By means of us, and us alone, is conducted the administration in the city and in the countryside, and the management of matters great and small, and the performance of duties light and heavy. That is the reason why you always hear the same names.

159 On monks interacting with the urban community, see Caner 2020.
160 Lib. *Or.* 30.8 (transl. by A.F. Norman):

> You then have neither ordered the closure of temples nor banned entrance to them. From the temples and altars you have banished neither fire nor incense nor the offerings of other perfumes. But this black-robed tribe, who eat more than elephants and, by the quantities of drink they consume, weary those that accompany their drinking. With the singing of hymns, who hide these excesses under an artificially contrived pallor – these people, Sire, while the law yet remains in force, hasten to attack the temples with sticks and stones and bars of iron, and in some cases, disdaining these, with hands and feet. Then utter desolation follows, with the stripping of roofs, demolition of walls, the tearing down of statues and the overthrow of altars, and the priests must either keep quiet or die. After demolishing one, they scurry to another, and to a third, and trophy is piled on trophy, in contravention of the law.

161 Brands 2018b, 26. See also Saliou 2018, 50, for the list of temples presumably still operating in the days of Libanius.
162 Sitz 2019, 660.
163 Lib. *Or.* 30. For the discussion of these matters, see Kalleres 2015, 31–33.
164 Brown 1988, 313. See also Mayer 2001 for a thorough presentation of John's pastoral mission in Antioch.
165 See in particular, Chrysostom, Hom. 66 *on Matthew*, where he claims that the Antioch church at that time supported 3,000 down-and-out individuals, from women with no income to the sick.
166 Chrysostom, Hom. 15 *De Statuis* 1: 153–354.
167 Chrysostom, Hom. PG 54.440.
168 Brown 1988, 313–322.
169 *Evagrius* 1.13 (transl. by E. Walford):

> This man, endeavouring to realise in the flesh the existence of the heavenly hosts, lifts himself above the concerns of earth, and, overpowering the downward tendency of man's nature, is intent upon things above: placed between earth and heaven, he holds communion with God, and unites with the angels in praising him; from earth, offering his intercessions on behalf of men, and from heaven, drawing down upon them the divine favour.

The sanctuary and settlement at Dayr Siman were built thanks to the emperor Zeno's patronage between 476 and 491. See the report in *Tchalenko, Villages* 223–276.

170 Kasher 1982.

171 Chrysostom, Hom. *Adv. Jud.* 1, 4.

172 Shepardson 2015b, 182.

173 Amm. Marc. 22.5.4. Transl. by J.C. Rolfe.

174 In actuality, the construction of new fortifications apparently unfolded under the auspices of Antiochus Kuzon, pretorian prefect in 430 and 431 and apparently consultant of Theodosius I. See Patituci and Uggeri 2008, 67–68, and the original text in *Malalas* 13.40.

175 See p. 86.

176 *TIB* 15, 554.

177 Casella 2010, 47.

178 Lib. *Or.* 46.

179 *Downey, History* 423.

180 Lib. *Or.* 2.54.

181 Lib. *Or.* 22.7.; Chrysostom *De Statuis*; *Michael the Syrian* I.306. See also *John of Nikiu* 2. 88.44.

182 Lib. *Or.* 19.31.

183 Lib. *Or.* 20.6–7; Chrysostom, Hom. De Statuis 2.2.

184 Patitucci-Uggeri 2008, 16.

185 It should be mentioned that the slopes of Mt. Silpius and Mt. Staurin are riddled with these caves, many of which are still used today by peasants for storage and shelter.

186 Shepardson 2015a. It is accepted that Syriac was widely spoken in Antioch's rural districts; see Liebeschuetz 1972, 62.

187 Lib. 22. 39–40. For the full treatment of the episode and the sources, see *TIB* 15, 554.

188 Drake 2011.

189 Lib. *Or.* 20.44 The translation is by A. F. Norman. For building projects in Antioch at the time, cf. Downey 1961, 434.

190 Lib. *Or.* 20.44. A consequence of this plan was that the cypress trees sacred to Apollo were no longer indiscriminately cut; see also Lib. *Or.*1.255; *CJ* 11.78.1.

191 *Theod.HR* 6.6. The telluric activity, in particular, never seems to have fully subsided during the last four decades of the fourth century. Ambraseys 2009, 157 situates another, modestly felt, event in 388, based on two readings of the homilies of Chrysostom.

192 As Liebeschuetz noted, imperial authorities could boast of hundreds administrators and staff members. He wrote: "It must have been possible to make money at Antioch" (Liebeschuetz 1972, 59).

193 Lib. *Ep.* 898.3. See also the discussion in Pellizzari 2012, 71–72.

194 Lib. *Ep.* 114. As for the discussion of these building initiatives seen through the lenses of Libanius's work, see Alpi 2007, 41.

195 That Daphne served as residence for wealthy Antiochenes is also proved by Lib. *Ep.* 1189.419.

196 Stillwell 1961.

197 See Leblanc and Poccardi 1999–2000 on a tentative reading of Daphne's ancient topography.

198 *Excavations Notes, Antioch Archives: Daphne*. It is worth stressing that no topographic documentation complements this hypothesis. As for the position of the Olympic stadium, see Leblanc and Poccardi 1999–2000, 391.

199 *Antioch Archives*, Field Notes of 1936.

200 For the summary of studies on Antioch's domestic context, see Kondoleon 2000.

201 Marcus Aurelius, *Letter to his praefectus* V. 5: "I have put Avidius Cassius in command of the Syrian army which is dissolved in luxury and living in the moral atmosphere of Daphne." See also Lib.*Or.* 45.7, 45.23 and 50.11.

202 Kondoleon 2000, 76.

203 *Levi, Pavements*, 311.
204 "Un habitant du quartier du IIIe siècle n'aurait certainement pas reconnu le lieu métamorphosé deux cent sans plus tard." Morvillez 2004, 280.
205 *Levi, Pavements*, 156–166. See also Dobbins 2000, 53–56 for a new interpretation of the complex.
206 Stillwell 1961, 48.
207 See, for instance, the House of Ge and Seasons, *Levi, Pavements*, 346–347.
208 For the Constantinian Villa, see *Levi, Pavements*, 226–257. As for the Yakto complex, while a number of reports dealt with the archaeology of Yakto, notably Lassus 1934, 1938, the most comprehensive treatment of the villa and its decorative apparatus is that of Levi 1947, 279–283, 323–346.
209 *Antioch II*, 98.
210 Verzone 2011, 219–225.
211 Brands 2017.
212 It is worth noting that the iconography of these "city mosaics" continued well into the Umayyad period. See Brody and Snow 2015, 22–23.
213 Alpi 2007, 46.
214 The Maïumas was in particular the rub. The Syriac name of the festival identifies the orgiastic religious rituals typically held in May and extremely popular in Antioch; see Julian *Mis*. 362 D; Lib. *Or*. 41.16; Chrysostom, Hom. in Matth. 7; Sev. Homily 95. Of interest is also Libanius's tirade against this festival in *Or*. 50.11 (transl. by A. F. Norman):

> A disgusting festival was introduced by certain persons to Daphne: its ceremonial was that of utter and absolute licence. This came to the eye of a good and prudent emperor, and he, ashamed at the behaviour and distressed for the sanctuary, put a stop to a gathering of this character, and won approval for doing so. And nobody told him how many years the festival had lasted, or that what had been the fashion should forever be the fashion, but this plague was banished from Daphne for a long time until men whose manner of life was in keeping with such kind of festivals once again introduced it.

The emperor in object was presumably Julian.
215 *Evagrius* 1.20, on Eudocia referring to the people of Antioch as fellow Athenians. See also the *Chronicon Paschale* 74.444:

> Augusta Eudocia asked Theodosius permission to go to holy places. Stopped at Antioch, spoke in council chamber a speech of encomium for Antioch, seated in the imperial throne which was of solid gold set with gems. People of city changed for her. Golden effigy of her raised up in council chamber and at the so called Museum they set up to her a bronze monument and these are standing in present day.

216 Brasse 2010, 278–279.
217 *Evagrius* 1.20.
218 Chrysostom, *Pn. in martyres* 2, in which he advocates for the worship of the local martyrs.
219 *Malalas* 13.39 *vis-à-vis Evagrius* 1.20. The latter situates the development later during the reign of Theodosius II, see also Saliou 2018, 43–44. An ongoing and soon-to-appear study of the walls by Gunnar Brands and Christiane Brasse is going to be the landmark work on the subject.
220 For the Land Walls of Constantinople, see Asutay-Effenberger 2007. On Anazarbus, Posamentir 2008.

221 De la Roque noted the large and vast though heavily damaged ruins of the Church of St. Ignatius, which he says was originally a temple first dedicated to Fortune (Tyche), built by Theodosius. Ignatius's body, however, was in a cemetery outside the Daphne Gate with other martyrs. Visiting in the mid-eighteenth century, Drummond also could not see the Temple of Fortune dedicated by Theodosius to St. Ignatius that de la Roque saw, unless it was a vestige of a church at the east end of the city dug out of the rock, measuring 102 × 59 feet. Its pillars from the nave to the choir were built of "bad stone" with brick arches. See de la Roque 1722, 246.

222 *Evagrius* 1.18; *Malalas* 14.13. The basilica was built under Theodosius II by the *magister utriusque militia per Orientem* Anatolius, in office around 438. John Malalas writes:

> He (Theodosius) also built in Antioch the Great a large illuminated basilike (…) very seemly, opposite the so-called *Athla*, which the people of Antioch call that of Anatolius, because Anatolius the *stratelates* [or/also magister militum] supervised the construction, receiving the money from the emperor when he was appointed by him stratelates of the East. And for this reason, when he finished this construction of the *basilike* he inscribed on it in gold mosaic the following "The work of the emperor Theodosius," as was fitting. Above were [representations of] the two emperors, Theodosius and his kinsman Valentinian, who ruled in Rome.

Also Nymphidianos, a consul, refurbished the gate doors, though not necessarily at the Daphne gate.

223 Guidoboni 1994, 296–300; Sbeinati et al. 2005. *Evagrius* 2.12.

224 *John of Nikiu* 88.1.

225 *Downey, History* 477, n. 6. *Evagrius* 2.12 states that the 458 earthquake was the sixth that shook the city after that of Trajan in 115 CE. This account, however, is imbued with Christian overtones, with the seismic event intended as God's punishment against the people of Antioch and their evil ways. See also *Malalas* 14.36. for an equally charged, albeit shorter, account.

226 Sev. Ant. Hom. 31. 652–660.

227 *Chronicon Paschale* 464 reports the death of St. Symeon Stylite when Ardabur, son of Aspar *magister militum*, was *comes Orientis*. Apparently, Ardabur's Gothic guard delivered the body of the saint to the Antiochenes.

4

THEOUPOLIS, THE CITY OF GOD (458–638)

> In that year [528] Antioch was renamed Theoupolis by order of the emperor. Also, a written oracle was discovered at Antioch, which read as follows: "And you, unhappy city, shall not be called the city of Antiochos."
>
> – John Malalas, *Chronographia*, 18, 29.

Introduction

Byzantine Antioch is usually mentioned in conjunction with the litany of disasters that contributed to the decline of the classical city. A rich repertoire of non-Greek sources, in particular Syriac, documents the extraordinary series of events that affected the city and its community during the sixth and seventh centuries. No surprise then that this epoch has been traditionally held to be the city's swan song, irremediably skidding to a slow demise. Downey wrote that in 540, "the Greatness of the city came to an end."[1] Indeed, he adhered to the idea of a "fall" of the city following a trajectory that borrowed much from Gibbon, except that Downey situated Antioch's zenith in the fourth century. Modern scholarship, however, has argued against this posture, proposing more nuanced narratives.[2] How a new city sprang out of Antioch's ruins, showing its transformative and resilient qualities, is thus the focus of this and the following chapters. Of course, the damage caused by the 540 Persian conquest, when Khosrow I Anūsharwān besieged and destroyed the city, the fire of 525, and earthquakes in 526 (probably the most devastating of all), 528, and 588 took a hefty toll on Antioch. Emperor Justinian (527–565), as part of his expansive building programs throughout the empire, undertook to rebuild and fortify the city, though in a contracted form, in 526 and 540 (Figure 4.1).

That Antioch looked at that point like post-World War II Dresden, as Gunnar Brands reminds us, is a real possibility.[3] But not even renaming the city

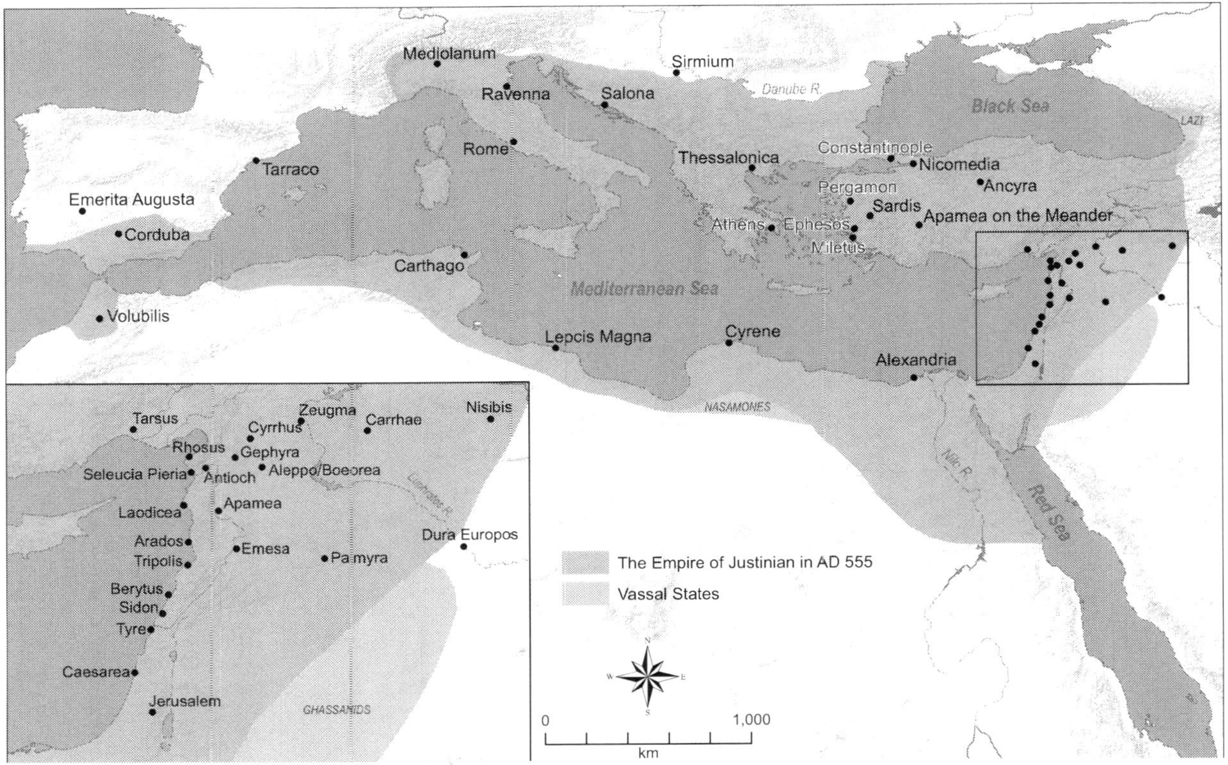

FIGURE 4.1 Antioch and the empire at the time of Justinian

Source: Created by Claire Ebert

"Theoupolis," the "City of God," spared this community from more trouble ahead, for the Persians again invaded the city in 611 under Khosrow Parviz. How these catastrophic events articulated the life of Antioch and how the city's topography adapted until the days of the Islamic conquest is the subject of what follows.

In particular, we highlight here a different image of Antioch, one that counters the notion of a city ambling toward its demise. Instead, what emerges is the picture of a community that resisted the blows by the hand of nature and man, constantly adapting and reshaping its fabric. Arguably, the earthquake disaster of 458 bookended a long phase of urban development and optimism, demarcated by the reigns of Constantius II, Valens, and Theodosius II. Overall, between 500 and 638, no fewer than 12 disasters afflicted Antioch and its surroundings. These fires, plagues, and earthquakes, combined with internal conflicts, civil war, and the Persian conquest of 540, inflicted substantial permanent damage on the city, despite the repairs undertaken after 526 and 540.[4] Moreover, Christological debates continued to widen the chasm within a fairly divided community, all the while adding widespread social unrest. And yet worse lay ahead.

But notwithstanding the repairs made to the city in the sixth century, Hugh Kennedy, in his seminal article "From *Polis* to *Madina*," argued for a city that was already being transformed before the Islamic conquest, and he seriously questioned the panegyric account by Procopius, the principal Byzantine historian of this period.[5] In short, limited urban repairs, reconstruction of the city walls, and the scanty evidence of reconstruction from Bath "F" (sector 13-R) after the 519 CE earthquake, as attested by an inscription, should not lull us into believing that Antioch could reclaim its centrality.[6]

Although Libanius and Malalas described Antioch as a city that constantly outgrew its borders, evidence for the shrinking of its urban sprawl is found as early as the reign of Justinian, who reduced the "uselessly large wall."[7] What needs to be highlighted is, however, the pivotal role of Antioch amid the geopolitical shifts. No matter how destitute Antioch may have seemed in the course of the fifth and sixth centuries, it still represented a vital focus of the Byzantine East, and as such it continued to draw imperial resources for repairs and upkeep.

The end of the fifth century

The death of St. Simeon the Elder in 459 ushered in a phase of insecurity for Antioch while driving a further wedge between the city and Constantinople, the latter being adamant about receiving the body of the saint. Qal'at Siman, the village and sanctuary from which the divine virtues of St. Symeon radiated, was under the administrative and religious jurisdiction of Antioch. It lay in the heart of the *Massif Calcaire*, that is the limestone massif east of Antioch. Here, as shown by the seminal surveys of Tchalenko and Tate and described in previous chapters, a growing rural settlement had populated the wadis, plateaus, and few pockets of land available since the second century CE (Figure 4.2). The increased density of settlement during the fifth and sixth centuries transformed these bare hills into a vast construction

FIGURE. 4.2 Rural settlement in the district of the Jabal Sam'ān during Late Antiquity

Source: From Ball 2000

zone, with churches and monasteries taking primacy in the building projects. That the sixth century vicissitudes of the city accelerated the consolidation of these communities and heightened their Christian faith is a cogent possibility.[8]

With Christianity gaining a foothold in Antioch and environs, this mountainous district manifested a remarkable bent for establishing new churches and accommodating monastic communities, while also attesting to the appearance and preaching of hundreds of ascetics. Well-to-do patrons, too, contributed to the forging of a sacred landscape, one that, however, was also grounded in a thriving oil and wine industry. Their authority over these villages covered all aspects of social life as well as the economic outlook of each small farmstead. In short, patronage was a system that enabled communities to function and thrive in a complicated landscape like that of the Jibāl. It offered financial support, legal representation in the city's courts, and accorded gravitas in the case of squabbles with nearby communities. Water, for instance, extremely scarce in nature, was more often than not a contested commodity. It was up to the village patron to smother any potential dispute and conflict, thereby ensuring the welfare of individual communities.[9] Of course, the tenuous institutional grounds on which patronage was predicated and the coercive means that framed its exercise gave way to widespread dissatisfaction and resentment.

Libanius does not mince words when denouncing the bad practices and downright exploitation of the poor that pervaded this seemingly thriving universe.[10] In this unique context of faith, profit, and competition for resources, there was ultimately a great want of spiritual guidance and leadership. Ascetics and their religious ardor provided exactly that. Furthermore, they mapped a new topography of holy sites, monasteries, and ecclesiastical communities that blended into the extant system of rural communities. The performative aspect of this form of ascetism of Syria has been already foregrounded by much scholarship, and so the arena, straddling the bare limestone hills of the Jibāl and Antioch.[11] Qal'at Siman, however, was arguably the place where these dynamics were most spectacularly played out: a village, a spectacular sanctuary, and, indeed, an imposing column (today reduced to a heavily weathered base) bear testimony to the impact of ascetism on these lands. Qal'at Siman was the beacon of religious rigor and, above all, the place that was inhabited by a saint whose religious ardor and ascetic virtues had surpassed all the other "Athletes of Christ." No hermit, really, could match the authority and vision of St. Symeon the Elder, though: he would round up masses of pilgrims and travelers, regardless of their credo and ethnicity, from anywhere in the Greek world and the eastern lands, Yemen and Persia included.[12] Textual exaggerations aside, it should be underscored how this was a landscape that brought together diverse constituencies and was traversed by folks coming from faraway lands.

Of course, miracles and exorcisms were the Saint's main assets. Less obvious, but of enormous social impact, was his involvement in litigations and general administration of the communities. As Peter Brown poignantly pointed out, in so doing the Saint thus supplanted the patronage system of old with a new, potent mix of religious and political authority.[13] A village, Telanissos (Dayr Siman) also grew in the vicinity of the sanctuary and the pillar on top of which the Saint was perched. It consisted of a cluster of generally two-story high dwellings, with gabled roofs, stables, barns, and courtyards. Hospices, inns, and small churches added to the built environment of the village. A few decades after the death of the Saint, around 480 a major building project unfolded to create a monumental corollary to the pillar (Figure 4.3). That may have curbed the emperor Leo's petition for the transfer of the body to Constantinople.

The state of affairs in Antioch, a city desperately yearning for some divine protection, ultimately prevented the departure of the divine relics of St. Symeon, for which the Antiochenes built a church in the city as well as a monastery and a monumental complex that framed the original pillar.[14] Just like in any other Greco-Roman town of the east, the latter boasted a monumental entrance: it demarcated the border between the settlement and the space where St. Symeon lived, preached, and accommodated his vast audiences, as well as conveying traffic from the processional way into the heart of the sanctuary. Throngs of pilgrims of any origin daily walked their way up to the site that had witnessed the performance of countless miracles from atop a pillar.[15] Overall, this Christianity so imbued with mysticism and hope was light years away from the urban turmoil and religious fissures that were unfolding only 90 km away.

FIGURE 4.3 Qalat Simān, the sanctuary and the pillar of St. Symeon

Source: Photograph by Andrea U. De Giorgi

Religiously zealous though it might have been, however, Antioch was also a city still imbued with pagan beliefs, as the trial against Isocasius, *quaestor* and prominent philosopher, attests. Accused of being a "Hellene," that is, a pagan, his trial caused a great stir in the days of Emperor Leo, and it is no surprise that attempts to terminate the Olympic games and other pagan festivals coincided with this historical phase. By 465, the prerogatives of the *alytarch*, or chief magistrate, had been transferred to the office of the *comes Orientis*, whereas the figure of the Syriarch, chief priest of the province of Syria, was absorbed into the cabinet of the *consularis Syriae*.[16] The reconfiguration, and indeed disappearance, of posts that had hitherto marked traditional civic appointments further signified the reorientation of public and private expenses and the wholesale distancing from the realm of games and festivals.

The successive reigns of Zeno (474–475, 476–491) marked a moment of heavy militarization in Antioch, with the *magister militum* Trokundes occupying the city with his army of Isaurians (mountain folks from Cilicia and the Amanus region), while struggles within the imperial house led to Zeno's temporary overthrow in 475 by his mother-in-law Verina. Meanwhile, the Miaphysite constituency, with its insistence that Christ had only one divine nature instead of two, divine and human, as asserted by the Council of Chalcedon in 451, heightened religious tensions. The short-lived reign of Basiliscus (475–476), who in turn upheld the Miaphysite position that Christ was both human and divine but in a single nature, contributed to the weakening of the Chalcedonian party in Antioch, which later culminated in the assassination of the patriarch Stephen in 479 by the Miaphysites and the disposal of his corpse in the Orontes.[17] The Isaurian contingent gained even more visibility when Flavius Illus, the general who had helped Zeno's restoration, was entrusted with the title of *magister militum per Orientem*. Aspiring to loftier heights, Illus maneuvered the still powerful Verina against Zeno and put forward the Syrian Leontius, one of his key collaborators, as a contender. In 484, Leontius was crowned emperor in Tarsus by Verina and recognized as such in Antioch. By turns, Antioch again became the headquarters of a usurper, with the city once again showing its inclination to side with an illegitimate ruler.[18] Zeno's response, however, was quick in coming, and the army led by Johannes the Scythian brought an end to the revolt. Four years later Illus, Leontius, and Verina were apprehended and killed;[19] fittingly, their heads were sent to Constantinople.

But peace was far from restored. The religious polarization that pervaded Antioch society reverberated far outside the naves of its churches. Riots at the hippodrome became increasingly frequent, all the more so as the two factions of the Greens and the Blues wound up identifying with the Miaphysite and Chalcedonian claims, respectively. Previously confined to the theater, rioting now became a staple feature of Antioch's political landscape in the final decade of the fifth century.[20] Three episodes of violence during the last years of Zeno's reign involving the *consularis Syriae* Thalassius and the *comes Orientis* Theodore led to partial destruction of the Forum of Valens (particularly the *Xystus*, part of the Olympic complex built by Commodus) as well as of two synagogues. Michael the Syrian, a late source, even reports on Jews being burnt alive.[21] The death of Zeno in 491 partly halted the escalation of violence; however, the quiescence of Persia also came to an end at this time, with the Sasanian Shah Kavād I (488–531) sending envoys to Antioch as the emperor lay on his deathbed. Apparently expecting his dues, the Persian king let it be known that the next ruler would have to meet his financial obligations toward Persia or otherwise could expect war.[22]

The new emperor, Anastasius I (491–518), rose to the throne at a complicated time; foreign politics, unpopular fiscal measures, and overall siding with the Miaphysite cause epitomized his reign. In Antioch, civic disturbances accompanied the city's salute of the new emperor; riots in the hippodrome led to casualties and "serious fires."[23] In 494, the Green party attacked the new *comes Orientis* Kalliopos in his *praetorium*, forcing him to flee; his successor, Constantius, restored order thanks to his special prerogatives of administering life and death;[24] it takes little imagination to envision how he did it.

Religious rifts, however, were not the only cause of distress in Antioch. Another major food crisis erupted in the early 500s and may have crippled the region all the way to Edessa and Nisibis, leading to the usual jacking up of wheat prices. So the chronicle of Joshua the Stylite reported the calamity:

> In the month of Nîsân (April) the pestilence began among the people of the city, and many biers were carried out in one day, but no one could tell their number. And not only in Edessa was this sword of the pestilence, but also

> from Antioch as far as Nisibis the people were destroyed and tortured in the same way by famine and pestilence. Many of the rich died, who were not starved; and many of the grandees too died in this year.[25]

How Antioch coped with these events is a matter of guesswork; theological and sociological debates, however, resumed shortly afterward.

The arrival in 507 of the charioteer Porphyrius Calliopas, the star of his day, known for countless victories in the arena, and his joining the ranks of the Greens further aggravated an already compromised situation. The great hippodrome of Antioch, with its more than 80,000 spectators, was a fitting venue for such an established athlete.[26] Typically, stakes were high in each competition; spells were even cast against opponents. Indeed, the Princeton team recovered 12 curse tablets as they excavated the hippodrome, the House of the Calendar, and the House of Ge and the Seasons. Magic and superstitions found a fertile turf in Antioch, where talismans, omens, and soothsayers for centuries played a major factor in the local cultural outlook. However, the tablet found in the hippodrome is of special interest for being placed on a limestone block of the drain of the *meta* (turning post) as it negotiated the curve of the arena – that is, the spot where the chances of chariot crashes were greatest. "Utterly subdue the horses of the Blue faction" reads the text, as it invokes the intervention of a panoply of lethal deities ("the dark one... conductor of the dead... destroyer of mortals, etc.").[27] How Porphyrius was involved in the politics of Antioch remains to be established, but he was on the forefront of the tragic events following the inauguration of the Olympic games in 507 and the chariot races presumably held in Daphne's hippodrome.

Anastasius had just faced the vehemence of the Greens' protest in Constantinople;[28] in Antioch their revolt was on a par with that of the city on the Bosphorus. Instigated by Porphyrius, the Greens targeted the Jews, who typically sided with the Blues, and destroyed their synagogue (plausibly the Matrona) in Daphne, looting and burning it down while killing many and desecrating the dead in their tombs. They also burned down the Temple of the Muses, previously converted by Constantine for the seat of the *comes Orientis*, while Procopius, the current *comes Orientis*, fled. The imperial forces under the *praefectus vigilium* Menas briefly overcame the rioters, but in a quick turn of events, amid atrocities and the burning of the basilicas, the Greens regained the upper hand in 508. Only the heavy-handed intervention of the new *comes Orientis*, Irenaeus Pentadiastes, stopped the mayhem. The account of Malalas, interestingly, is fraught with topographic allusions to the sequencing of facts: the Church of St. John, the basilicas of Rufinus and Zenodotus, the Prasinoi, and the baths of Olbia.[29] Of interest is the reference to an "antiforum," plausibly the forum of Valens. That the heart of the city was the locus where these riots unfolded is quite likely. Heads flung into the Orontes and atrocities of every kind, however, did not curb the recursive pattern of violence on the streets of Antioch. Events of this nature continued to plague the city and its community, as attested by the riots of 512, when, probably following the earthquake of the same year,[30] a gang of Miaphysite monks stormed the city, instigating once again the spiral of rioting. Their anti-Chalcedonian agenda was met with the uttermost dissent by the folks of Antioch, and hundreds of bodies of monks unceremoniously ended up in the waters of the Orontes.

A divided community

As noted previously, the age of Theodosius I marked the moment when powerful bishops such as Ambrose were able to challenge even the emperor. In Antioch, the tradition of powerful patriarchs continued in the following decades and appeared in all its force during the sixth century. But this was also an era that brought to the fore the balkanization of the Christian world, with Antioch as one of the main loci where vital theological debates played out. Pagans, Chalcedonians, Miaphysites, Nestorians – these are but some factions of the religious microcosm in the city loosely held together solely by a sense of belonging. Any minimal dent to the system could ignite unspeakable violence. Not even the many downturns that punctuated the history of the city in the sixth century hindered the vehemence of the conflicts.

Paganism in particular was far from dead. We have already noted how slander and accusations of following false gods still pervaded the city during the reign of Leo I. But the spread of Miaphysitism, thanks especially to proselytizing monks, was the chief thorn in the church's side. Peter the Fuller, the doctrine's mouthpiece in Antioch, seized the opportunity offered by a much-divided community and assumed the office of patriarch in 469, with the assent of Emperor Zeno.[31] The alteration of the *Trisagion* ("Thrice Holy") prayer, the hallmark of the liturgy, lay at the heart of the controversy when Peter attempted to add words suggesting that God himself had suffered crucifixion and anathematized anyone refusing to accept it; even parrots, it seems, were trained to repeat the subversive formula.[32] Needless to say, this controversy did not encourage tolerance of others in the city; rather, the murder of the Chalcedonian patriarch Stephen in 479 and the throwing of his body into the Orontes signified the wide gulf between the Chalcedonians and Miaphysites in Antioch, as elsewhere. Unlike his predecessor Zeno, Emperor Anastasius initially sought to stay neutral in the controversy, but over time came to openly support the anti-Chalcedonian movement. Not surprisingly, religious polarization still loomed in Antioch despite the presence of two somewhat moderate figures, namely, the patriarchs Palladius (488–498) and Flavian II (498–512). Nor did the elevation to the patriarchate of Severus (512–518), a former monk who established Antioch as a prominent center of Miaphysite theology, foster any sense of concord. Rather, a divisive agenda was predicated on sidelining the Chalcedonian movement, and the change in the liturgy led to a wider gulf between the two constituencies and new disputes. The hymns of the non-Chalcedonian Severus are testament to the seminal role he played in Antioch.[33] His tirades against the hippodrome and other sites like baths and brothels and polemic about all the distractions that swayed Christians in Antioch were essentially pitted against ancestral routines that were ingrained in the fabric of the city.[34] Further, his ecclesiastical message – later condemned as heretical by imperial edict in 536 – offered a firm blend of Christ's humanity and divinity and resorted, more often than not, to street violence for its enforcement.[35] By preaching relentlessly against "Christ in two natures," Severus wished to establish firm ground for the anti-Chalcedonian sentiment that was spreading east of Antioch. His proselytism, however, had to reckon with the death of Anastasius and the rise of Emperor Justin I (518–527), champion of the Chalcedonians. More fundamentally, though, this was a society that was polarized to the greatest degree, with tension resonating within the households themselves. Parents pitted against children and vice versa over Christological debates and downright religious adherence were a most common scenario in Late Antique Antioch and Syria, it seems.[36] As Jack Tannous however pointed out, the question that needs to be addressed is how was the Christian community at large in a place like Antioch individually affected by the theological discourse and its nuances?[37] With the exception of the *curiales* and the imperial administrators, presumably well cognizant of the religious issues of the day, the rest of the community was grounded in their daily economic routines and anxieties, seeking to make their ends meet in various ways. Convenience, benefits, and a more promising afterlife may have swayed the masses, perhaps. All the same, the voices of most Antiochenes are silent, and the few epitaphs that can be assigned to this momentous epoch hardly betray any sense of religious affiliation.

Justin inaugurated his reign with a generous offer to repair those cities that had suffered the blows of sectarian violence. Antioch, on the forefront in the East, received a donation of 1,000 *litrae*. Whether coincidence or not, it is a matter of record that the coin finds in Antioch during the 1930s produced the staggering number of 900 coins issued by Justin and struck by the mints of Antioch and Constantinople.[38] As Alan Stahl suggests, the Early Byzantine coin collections (491–522 CE) surpass by far previous eras and individual imperial houses, while also presenting a greater degree of dissemination, with individual finds situated in districts north of the city and west of the Orontes. Of course, patterns of circulation between the days of Justin and previous epochs were different, and there were hardly fewer coins circulating during the Roman and Late Roman periods. Nevertheless, for their relative value, the numbers of coins of the late fifth century demonstrably points in the direction of a trend of cash flow, probably fueled by the local mint functioning again at full swing.[39]

Monetary assistance was only part of Justin's vision for Antioch. The termination of the office of the *alytarch* and above all the end of the Olympic games demarcated a new watershed in the history of Antioch, one by which the city was expected to part company with its ancestral customs once and for all.[40]

Religious matters again took the upper hand, though. More subtly, a new pro-Chalcedonian agenda trickled down from Constantinople. The main target in Antioch was the patriarch Severus, who, perceiving the imminent threat, sailed off to a welcoming Alexandria. But his legacy would loom over Antioch and the East in general for many years to come. Not even the vigorous agendas of Ephraim and Gregory could eradicate the non-Chalcedonians, let alone the persecutions that were promoted in the last years of Justinian's life, as we shall see.[41] Ultimately, in

518 the seat of Antioch's patriarchate was filled by the Chalcedonian Paul (518–521), a fervent believer in violence as a good deterrent against heretics. Styled "the Jew," it appears he saw to the physical elimination of Miaphysites.[42] Many left the city and conceivably relocated on the heights of the limestone massif southeast of Antioch. The sustained growth of the rural settlement in that region may have also been predicated on the religious turmoil that was affecting Antioch at that time.[43] Of interest, too, is the report that that by the time Paul seized his seat, the city could boast of 12 monasteries.[44]

Not to be outdone by his predecessor, in 521, Euphrasius of Jerusalem (521–526) took the highest seat in the church of Antioch and furthered the anti-Miaphysite agenda, with the usual spiral of violence and coercion. Only the 523 raid of Arab forces under the leadership of al-Mundhir, a vassal of the Sasanian king, temporarily reoriented Antioch's anxieties.

But trouble in Antioch was far from over, and the looming climate of violence led the imperial authorities to suspend the Olympic games as well as other types of social gatherings at the theaters. Adding to the typical fractiousness of the exchanges among the attendants were longstanding political, social, and religious issues. In that context, the politically charged atmosphere magnified the tension and demanded radical measures; new incidents in Constantinople's hippodrome invited a similar course of action in Antioch as well.[45] But it seems the suspension hardly functioned as deterrent; episodes of turbulence in 524 made clear that military intervention alone could mend the endemic ills of cities like Antioch, and indeed Constantinople. In Antioch, accordingly, the *comes Orientis* (successively patriarch) Ephraim of Amida flexed his muscles and restored order.[46] The fraught climate of a divided city, however, continued to pervade every street and alley in Antioch.

Dark days in Antioch

At this time, Antioch's darkest season began, one punctuated by natural catastrophes on unprecedented scale. Between 525 and 542, fires and earthquakes devastated the city; only tenacity, resilience, faith, and a little help from the imperial authorities kept this community alive. From this point forward, Antioch's political profile changed in fundamental ways. The sequence of events has been amply treated by scholarship, but it is worthwhile to summarize the main episodes.[47]

In the fall of 525, a blaze incinerated the expanse of the city lying between the *martyrion* of St. Stephen and the *praetorium* of the *magister militum per Orientem*. Houses and human lives were lost as the fire raged on for days, for no source could be identified. The damage was immense, and only the swift mobilization of resources – two *centenaria* of gold – enabled reconstruction, thanks to the mediation of the patriarch Euphrasius (521–528) and imperial largesse. According to Malalas, this was just a symptom of God's displeasure with the city.[48] The trope of divine anger against a city that had repeatedly wronged the one God is one that resonates in the historical accounts of the sixth century. The Miaphysite constituency, in particular, was particularly vocal in stressing the faults of the local community; that they may have actually conspired and contributed to the catastrophe is a possibility that Uggeri takes up.[49]

But even worse was to come. No sooner had repair work begun than another massive calamity ravaged the city with all of its vehemence. On May 29, 526, one of the most devastating earthquakes of Antioch's history struck, wreaking utter havoc in the city. With an estimated magnitude of 7.0 on the surface wave scale and estimated intensity of IX (violent) on the Modified Mercalli Intensity scale,[50] the destruction was total. Although this earthquake is documented in nearly every source, the description of Malalas is particularly gripping, for he may have witnessed the tragedy first-hand. As he wrote:

> Great was the fear of God that occurred then, in that those caught in the earth beneath the buildings were incinerated and sparks of fire appeared out of the air and burned anyone they struck like lightning. The surface of the earth boiled and foundations of buildings were struck by thunderbolts thrown up by the earthquakes and were burned to ashes by fire, so that even those who fled were met by flames. It was a tremendous and incredible marvel with fire belching out rain, rain falling from tremendous furnaces, flame dissolving into showers, and showers kindling like flames consumed even those in the earth who were crying out. As a result Antioch became desolate, for nothing remained apart from some buildings beside the mountain. No holy chapel nor monastery nor any other holy place remained which had not been torn apart. Everything had been utterly destroyed. The great church of Antioch, which had been built by the emperor Constantine the Great, stood for seven days after this tremendous threat from God, when everything else had collapsed to the ground during the wrath of God. Then it too was overcome by fire and razed to the ground. Likewise other houses which had not collapsed through the divine calamity were destroyed to their foundations by fire. In this terror up to 250,000 people perished.[51]

Buildings in the city and nearby districts of Daphne and Seleucia were also destroyed, raining stone and bricks onto streets, gardens, and squares. Most landmarks of Antioch were also lost: the palace, among others, was flattened, while others, in whatever shape or form they may have survived, probably did not fare well with the 18 months of aftershocks. Michael the Syrian also reports that the church of Constantine shook for days after finally giving way amid fire and dust.[52] The number of the casualties, of course, is a speculation, and one can hardly assess the impact of the quake in terms of human lives.[53] Malalas makes it plain, however, that at that very time many outsiders had come to Antioch to partake in the celebration of the Ascension of Christ, thus making the population of the city even more swollen than it already was. One can almost conjure up those dramatic moments, with folks that had just left the great church of Constantine or the old apostolic church (*Palaia*) in peace, hoping that the huge blaze that had damaged large parts of the city in the previous year had finally appeased the wrath of God, displeased as he was with the city and its endemic religious rifts. Shortly after plazas and thoroughfares had begun to empty, the earth groaned. In the blink of an eye, a violent earthquake fissured the streets, leveled homes, caused landslides, incinerated trees and pulverized public buildings. With its vehemence, the quake stunned the city in all of its parts, from north to south. Thousands of people lost their lives.

No sooner had the rescuers started to move gingerly among crumbled buildings than new tremors began. And the dread that the worst of the shaking was far from over loomed large. As it turned out, aftershocks rattled the community for days, and more destruction was ahead.

Overall, terror, looting, bravery, and miracles all coalesced in the dramatic narrative of those days.[54] One can only imagine how survivors may have used everything at their disposal, from shovels to bare hands, rummaging through the rubble and seeking to pull people out of mounds of debris. Others resorted to inflict further punishment on the quake's victims, either by pillaging their properties or attacking them as they were leaving the city with whatever goods they could rescue. God, by turn, took vengeance on these robbers and killed them in violent ways, so Malalas reports.[55] The interplay between the community and the divine in those days, however, went beyond the mere punishment of robbers. On the third day after the quake, Malalas wrote that a cross appeared hovering above Antioch's northern districts. A communal prayer that lasted for an hour brought together all the believers and instilled a sense of hope in a community that at that point could only cling to its God. More immediate and concrete forms of assistance were garnered in Constantinople, though.

The imperial house took action, replicating, albeit on a larger scale, a similar rescue effort to that in Anazarbus, Cilicia, only a year earlier.[56] Comparable efforts were also directed at many Eastern cities during the following years; Justinianopolis (formerly Martyriopolis) and Palmyra are but two examples. In Antioch, Justin allocated the resources through the *comes Orientis* Carinus and the functionaries Phocas and Asterius. Five *centenaria* disbursed to Carinus and at least 30 allocated to the two imperial patricians apparently helped with reconstructing baths, aqueducts, and bridges, while repairing other structural damage to the civic infrastructure. How effective the disbursement was is difficult to gauge, but to some, the beauty of Antioch was no more. In Malalas's words, "everything had been utterly destroyed."[57]

It is apparent that the havoc wreaked by this and the following earthquakes invariably ushered in a new version of Antioch, as if an old world would be undone and a new one entered the scene. More to the point, seismic events in Antioch not only demolished buildings, but they also time and again reoriented the city's governance, paving the way for new social forces as well as new agencies tasked with reconstruction while relentlessly reinventing the city's skyline. Simply put, in the overturning of order that the Greek expression *kata strophe* decribes, Antioch once more succeeded in finding a new course of action.

In that vein, repairs were underway when in November 527 another fire allegedly affected the city.[58] Whether this event spurred further involvement of the imperial authorities is a strong possibility; under the patriarch Ephraim (527–545) and the *comes Orientis* Zacharias, and thanks to the munificence the new emperor, Justinian (527–565), and his wife, Theodora (527–548), more funding was secured to restore Antioch's functionality and overall dignity. It appears that the imperial couple had just commissioned churches and buildings at that time.[59] The church of the Theotokos (the holy Mother of God), that of St. Michael Archangel, that of the Saints Cosmas and Damian, along with a *xenodichion* (a hospital) and new baths, added a Justinianic stamp to the fabric of the city. In particular, the basilica built under Theodosius II by Anatolius, the *magister utriusque militiae per Orientem*, was greatly damaged and subsequently rebuilt by Justinian with columns from Constantinople, almost a redress for the Antiochene monuments that 200 years earlier had been taken away to contribute to the making of the new capital on the Bosphorus.[60]

Yet some of these projects came to naught, for on November 29, 528, still another temblor, plausibly an aftershock of the 526 quake, struck; lasting one hour, it killed an additional 4,770 civilians, as Theophanes duly noted.[61] His account is just as impressionistic as that of Malalas, with much emphasis on the horrific sounds that pervaded Antioch: the roaring noise of the earthquake, panic in the city, and collapse of the few buildings that had survived the previous tremor. Surrounding villages were also destroyed. All kinds of hardships ensued for the few remaining inhabitants, not least a frigid winter. The days of Justinian, it seems, were witnessing the lowest degree of divine support for the city on the Orontes.[62] What is more, the discovery of a written oracles and bad omens added further distress. This was the juncture where changing the name of the city to Theoupolis seemed the only viable course of action, and this was reflected on coinage (Figure 4.4).[63]

Imperial assistance, meanwhile, again reached the city. It is probable that the emperor asked that an external wall be demolished and a new defense following the river be added, promoting the excavation of a new channel of the Orontes along these new defenses, though most of these building projects may have unfolded at a further point in the 540s (Appendix I).[64] A new version of Antioch was in the making.

In financial terms, remission from taxes for three years, a measure typically implemented by emperors since the days of the Julio-Claudian emperors, was authorized for Antioch as well as for Seleucia Pieria and Laodicea.[65] Once again, the sister-cities of the Seleucid Tetrapolis formed a consortium, albeit as the target of a rescue effort. That this event coincided with military mobilization also needs to be considered, for the Sasanians were again undertaking operations in Mesopotamia. That earthquakes functioned as a stimulus for rebuilding and investing assets may be too far-fetched of a hypothesis, at least in Antioch at that juncture,[66] but it cannot be denied that the imperial administration went to great lengths in reviving the community so as to ensure continuity of settlement.[67] As Mordechai noted, one does not turn "a flourishing city into a failed one almost overnight."[68] Though struggling, the city and its customs clung to their civic institutions to keep the community alive.

FIGURE 4.4 Bronze follis, Justinian I, Antioch mint (as Theoupolis), year 13. Obverse: DN IVSTINIANVS PP AVG, helmeted, cuirassed bust facing, holding scepter and cross on globe, cross in right field. Reverse: Large M, ANNO to left, cross above, Γ below, XIII to right, Mintmark: THUPO

Source: Courtesy of Princeton University, Firestone Library Numismatic Collection, ex. Peter J. Donald Collection

Old vices die hard, however. The religious rifts in the city were far from resolved; the two earthquakes had induced a quiescence that could be disrupted at any time. The apparent ambiguity of the imperial couple, with Justinian upholding orthodoxy and Theodora leaning toward the Miaphysite cause, did not foster pacification, either. In 529, new Arab raids threatened the city, while riots still erupted in Antioch's theater, despite the imperial suspension of any sort of public spectacle.[69] As one can imagine, the local authorities promptly responded. Firmly at the helm of the patriarchate was the former *comes Orientis* Ephraim of Amida (527–545), a champion of orthodoxy with a bent for enforcing it by any means. The Miaphysite assault to the *Patriarcheion* (the seat of the Patriarch) is a good case in point.[70] Fearing exile, they sought to occupy the building but were met with the physical response of the *comes Orientis* himself. Many died, and more punishments mandated by the emperor ensued. But Ephraim was also a man who would go to any length to protect his flock, as attested by the hefty sum of gold he collected from the community to free a group of Antiochene Christians held captive by the Lakhmid Arabs, working for the Sasanians.

Amid religious collisions, a pending military threat, and new fires and tremors (still another earthquake in 532, this time inconsequential), the future of Antioch may have looked bleak to most.[71] But Justinian's commitment to the city on the Orontes was firm. Whether through the donation of his toga and jewels, displayed in the Church of Cassianus, or through donations to the city's hospices, the welfare of Antioch very much mattered to the imperial court in Constantinople.[72] Justinian also made clear that the city would serve as the base for his upcoming military response to Sasanian attacks, all while a further sense of religious gravitas was accorded by the arrival of the mortal remains of St. Marinus from Gindarus in Syria, to be interred in the Church of St. Julian.[73] As the veneration of saints thus gained new currency, Ephraim saw to the rebuilding of Constantine's Octagonal Church in 537 even as he condemned once and for all the Miaphysite heresy of Severus.

These plans, however, were disrupted by an event that further traumatized not only the Greek communities in the East but the rest of the Roman Empire as well: in 540 the Sasanians captured Antioch for the first time since the third century.[74] If the failure of a landmark 532 peace treaty with Persia had not put Constantinople under much strain, the fall of many a city – and most of all, Antioch – showed the vulnerability of the Byzantine state to the fullest degree. The implications of this event were beyond measure, for Antioch's loss was a deep blow to the imperial prestige, with the question of Justinian's fitness for the job at stake.[75] As a source for the unfolding of Antioch's fall, Procopius's account deserves primacy.[76]

The protagonist in the attack was Khosrow I Anūsharwān (531–579); not only was he equipped with a formidable army, but he also knew that Antioch was a profoundly divided city, traversed by currents of separatism and dissent. The Miaphysites, as Downey remarks, overall favored overthrowing the Greeks of Constantinople and leaned toward integration into the Persian sphere. This would free them to use Syriac in any aspects of their lives;[77] whereas in the days of John

Chrysostom the language one used in Antioch had been considered a key social marker,[78] almost a century-and-a-half later it meant spiritual and political affiliation. The visual culture of the day also attests to the influence of the Persian world in Antioch. Mosaic pavements from Daphne, in particular, document visual motifs such as parrots with ribbons or rams' heads that seem almost extrapolated from Sasanian iconography (Figure 4.5).

The sack of Antioch was the apex of Khosrow's 540 campaign, which encountered no hurdles as the Persians crossed the Euphrates, presumably at the Roman fortress of Zenobia, and marched into Syria unchecked. The account of Procopius documents the arrival of the Persian army, the pitching of their camp in front of the Orontes, the fleeing of many Antiochenes, and the overall unfolding of the siege, with consequent pillaging and destruction of the city.[79]

Weak points in the highland defenses and a lack of troops did not augur well for the withstanding against a powerful enemy. What is worst, they demoralized the resistance in Antioch, at that point under the supreme command of Germanus, one of Justinian's leading generals. Diplomacy went into motion through a whirlwind of conflicting initiatives managed singlehandedly by the city and the imperial envoys. But Germanus's efforts in seeking a peaceful settlement for the whole of Syria, not just Antioch, led to an impasse that aggravated the situation. Shortly thereafter, Germanus and Ephraim both abandoned the city, while known weak points in the

FIGURE 4.5 Daphne. The House of the Beribboned Parrots

Source: Courtesy of the Antioch Expedition Archives, Department of Art and Archaeology, Princeton University; Princeton

fortifications were left unrepaired. A contingent of 6,000 troops from southern Syria did, however, bring a sense of hope to the city at a point when many inhabitants were packing their belongings. Upon reaching the city, the Sasanians pitched their camp on the left bank of the Orontes, north of the city, and concentrated their efforts on the highland fortifications of Mt. Staurin, while also laying siege to the walls along the northern sector. Procopius's narrative at this point uses the very typical trope of a renegade who makes a final offer to the besieged. One Paulus, a man greatly disdained by most in Antioch, twice made a request on behalf of the Persians for ten *centenaria* of gold. His second attempt was met with a hurl of arrows and javelins directed at him. Taunting the enemy from the walls made matters worse, if possible. Incidentally, Procopius stresses that the Persian response came as no surprise, "for they are not seriously disposed, but are always engaged in jesting and disorderly performance.[80]" Determined to unleash his fury upon the Antiochenes, Khosrow ordered the commencement of the operations. So the siege began, directed at the weakest sectors of the defenses, presumably on the slope of Mt. Staurin. Roman soldiers supported by "the most courageous youths of the populace" fought with honor and bravery, succeeding at keeping the enemy away from the walls. The city's fierce resistance was compromised only by the lack of military supervision and defensive tactics; the collapse of a wooden walkway that had been added to the ramparts caused panic, and the forces confronting the enemy along the northern walls dispersed. The subsequent abandonment of the highland ramparts as well as the rush of soldiers and citizens toward the southern gates finally led to the city's fall, with mounted soldiers trampling over women and children seeking refuge at the gates in the lower city. The Persian army, meanwhile, found no resistance on the walls and could set its ladders and artillery for the final assault. No one tried to stop them, except a small formation of the "young men" of Antioch, some of whom were equipped with heavy armor, while others resorted to hurl stones at the enemy. In bewilderment, the Persians hesitated long enough to allow the Roman army to leave the city through the southern Daphne gate, the only gate that was spared by the attackers. From his headquarters on Mt. Silpius, Khosrow mobilized his best troops and pushed through the last, desperate defense, ruling the killing of the remaining fighters. He then ordered the survivors to be corralled, seized the treasure of the still-standing Octagonal Church, stripped buildings of their marble revetments, and ordered the city to be burned, as well as the Church of St. Michael the Archangel in Daphne. Only the southern district of *Kerateion*, where the Jewish community resided, and the Church of St. Julian were spared, as well as houses outside the city walls. Overall, he seized an enormous wealth. Lastly, Khosrow stipulated to the imperial envoys a 50-*centenaria* ransom of gold to stop the pillaging and established a perpetual tribute of five *centenaria*. Despite these huge rewards, the Persian king did not spare the city one final offense: a blaze that incinerated the whole city, save the Octagonal Church, which, of course, he had previously stripped of all of its décor.[81]

Thus Khosrow captured the city that "was both ancient and of great importance and the first of all the cities which the Romans had throughout the East both in wealth and in size and in population and in beauty and in prosperity of every kind."[82]

The surviving Antiochenes were marched into Persia, where they allegedly built Veh Antiok Khosrow ("Better-than-Antioch Khosrow [built this]"), following a practice previously established by Shāpūr I, and said to be an exact copy of the fallen city.[83] The tenth-century Persian historian Ibn al-Faqīh, in his *Kitāb al-buldān*, reinforces the story of Antioch's replica city. He writes:

> And when Anushiruwān [Khosrow] conquered Qinnasrīn and Mambij and Aleppo and Antioch and Ḥimṣ and Damascus and Jerusalem, he was pleased with Antioch and its construction, so when he proceeded to Iraq he built a city on the likeness of Antioch with its markets and streets and buildings, and he named it Zandkhusruh, and it is what the Arabs name Rūmiyya. And he ordered the captives of Antioch to enter it, so when they entered it, they found nothing strange about their homes, so every man of them was set free to go to his home except one shoemaker on whose gate in Antioch there was a mulberry tree, but he did not see it on his gate in Rūmiyya. So he was confused for a time, then he burst into his house and found it like his house.[84]

The transfer of populations and culture aside, Michael the Syrian reported that upon learning about the disgrace that had befallen Antioch, Ephraim fled in terror and hid, while Justinian wept.[85]

A new Antioch?

It is against this background of destruction and somber cityscapes that Justinian literally redesigned Antioch, though construction had to reckon with the explosion of the bubonic plague in 542, which killed many, thus severely impacting tax revenues and military enrollment empire-wide. The words of the scholar Evagrius (536–594), personally involved in this tragedy, are a powerful reminder of how pandemics stunned societies in the past as they do today. He wrote:

> In turn it overran the whole universe, leaving none among men without some experience of the disease. And whereas some cities were stricken to such an extent that they were completely emptied of inhabitants, there were parts where the misfortune touched more lightly and moved on. And neither did it strike according to a fixed interval, nor having struck did it depart in the same manner: but it took hold of some places at the beginning of winter, others while spring was in full swing, others in the summer time, and in some places even when autumn was advancing. And there were places where it affected one part of the city but kept clear of the other parts, and often one could see in a city that was not diseased certain households that were comprehensively destroyed. And there are places where, although one or two households were destroyed, the rest of the city has remained unaffected;

> but as we have recognized from precise investigation, the households which remained unaffected have been the only ones to suffer in the following year. Thus as I write this, while in the 58th year of my life, not more than two years previously while for the fourth time now the misfortune struck Antioch, when the fourth cycle from its outset had elapsed, I lost a daughter and the son she had produced, quite apart from the earlier losses.[86]

Evagrius also contends that the origin of the phenomenon was not known, but some held Ethiopia as the center of a calamity that wiped out entire cities and left no one unscathed. Against this view, new scholarship posits that the impact of the pandemic may have not been as pervasive as the sources (Procopius, John of Ephesus, and Gregory of Tours in the main) lead us to believe.[87] The demographics of the plague, couched as they are in the ideology of their reporters, are generally inflated by conjectural estimates and framed by environmental vagaries. Further, it has been shown that Mediterranean-wide land-use, coinage, and papyri from Egypt, among other indicators, betray a pattern of continuity that bears no apparent signs of disruption caused by the pandemic. Such "minimalistic" angle also finds the comfort of survey data from the Amuq Valley, where the archaeological record offers a tangible pattern of lingering on of rural settlement and apparent preservation of the land systems of old.[88] Of course, Antioch's hinterlands and territory appear almost like a Shangri-La, with its plain and mountain districts almost divorced from the dramatic events that punctuated the history of the city, be it earthquakes or food crises. In Antioch, as elsewhere, the pestilence did not strike at fixed intervals, but rather in haphazard fashion, and spreading over the urban space in ways that no one could predict. A tally of the casualties in Antioch is impossible to attain; even if one were to consider Evagrius's account laden with sensationalism, there is still a good chance that the plague caused casualties in Antioch, just like Evagrius's daughter and her baby. But no matter how dire the situation may have looked for Antioch, reconstruction plans under the auspices of the imperial house were underway.

But for whom was Justinian building? A few surviving *curiales* or the local elite writ large? The people presumably living in tenements? Provincial administrators? We may assume the city could have been entirely deserted, considering the death toll between 526 and 542, unless we question the numbers, typically swollen, offered by the textual sources. The conundrum of Antioch's population cannot be resolved here; the oscillation between 250,000 and 500,000 inhabitants at its height remains problematic.[89] What we can infer is that a segment of the population was able either to return to Antioch or to survive the various downturns. And so their resilience, in tandem with imperial assistance, resuscitated the community.

Although the scale and décor could in no way be replicated, the city aimed at retrieving its functionality and institutional prerogatives. Essentially, Justinian's reconstruction plan, which figures prominently in Procopius's *The Buildings*, was a panegyric on the public works of Justinian over all the empire: "above all he made

Antioch, which is now called Theoupolis, both fairer and stronger by far than it had been formerly."[90] The image of Antioch that emerged was one of a city that had not completely severed its ties with the Island and clustered around the southern boroughs, contained as it was by these new defenses.

Much has been written on this work; suffice it here to say that the text is often hyperbolic, as befits the encomiastic genre. Nevertheless, it contains kernels of truth to which we should give attention. Specifically, Procopius reports that Justinian rebuilt stretches of the highland fortifications that had been damaged by the attack. He writes:

> In ancient times its circuit-wall was both too long and absolutely full of many turnings, in some places uselessly enclosing the level ground and in others the summits of the mountain, and for this reason it was exposed to attack in a number of places.[91]

Justinian's builders accomplished a defensive system that was more rational, better suited to the roughness of the terrain (especially the steep section between Mt. Staurin and Mt. Silpius), and, overall, more tenable (Figure 4.6).[92]

In short, entire stretches of walls, both on the mountains and on the lower city, that had proven their vulnerability, were demolished, thus favoring a smaller, more

FIGURE 4.6 Antakya. Tower 1 of Antioch's Justinianic fortifications

Source: Photograph by Andrea U. De Giorgi

compact, and better defendable new version of the city. Cisterns were also built into the towers of the Mts. Silpius and Staurin. As noted previously, the archaeological inspection of the enceinte has proven difficult on account of the blend of repairs, masonry styles, additions, and destruction that has affected the structure during the course of the centuries (Figure 4.7); for instance, the section between Tower 5 all the way to Tower 24, along the middle section of Mt. Silpius's fortifications, exhibits substantial traces of reconfiguration, in keeping with the rectangular shape of the towers themselves.[93] Tower 20, one of the best preserved features, still standing at 9 m of height and covering an area of 12 × 14 m, in particular, is a good case in point. Connecting to the adjacent curtain at wall-walk level, it offers an extraordinary palimpsest of at least three construction phases and further repairs, from large isodomic limestone blocks to alternate courses of large and small stones. Situating each of these building techniques in their specific time and recognizing the agency that commissioned them are two paramount issues. More importantly, how the new system of defenses negotiated the lower city and its preexisting gates remains to be established. One possible postern near Tower 9 has been brought to light by the archaeological survey; at the very least it informs the existence of an alternate axis of traffic that entered Antioch from Mt. Silpius's southern sector. Overall, the crux of the problem is singling out the Justinianic phase from the blend of previous and successive building programs. In particular, discerning the interface between the allegedly extensive building program of Justinian from that of Theodosius II remains to be determined on the ground. Contrary to Downey's belief, the presence of occasional brick bands as decorative patterns, well known through a set of engravings of the walls on the southern section of Mt. Silpius by the traveler Luis Cassas, rather illustrate a type of masonry similar to Costantinople's and thus ascribable to Theodosius II. In short, as Christiane Brasse noted, better dividends can be clinched when using the insertion of cisterns in each tower as the variable that may best represent the works of Justinian.[94] Although grounded on some tenuous grounds, the argument nevertheless shows how the northern sector of the Mt. Silpius defenses showcase a sense of coherent construction and, ultimately, unity of vision.

Moreover, the emperor commissioned the repair of the water infrastructure, and not least the impounding system in the Parmenius gorge, completing the so-called Iron Gate, so as to relieve the city of the perennial problem of seasonal runoff (Figure 4.8). The Iron Gate still stands today, 20 m high, in all of its magnitude amid caves and dwellings hewn in the rock that are now being used by farmers and shepherds. It is one of the remaining testimonies of Antioch's past, deeply planted in a gully that has not been touched by Antakya's expansion.

Procopius remarks:

> he built an immense wall or dam, which reached roughly from the hollow bed of the ravine to each of the two mountains, so that the stream should no longer be able to sweep on when it was at full flood, but should collect for a considerable distance back and form a lake there. And by constructing

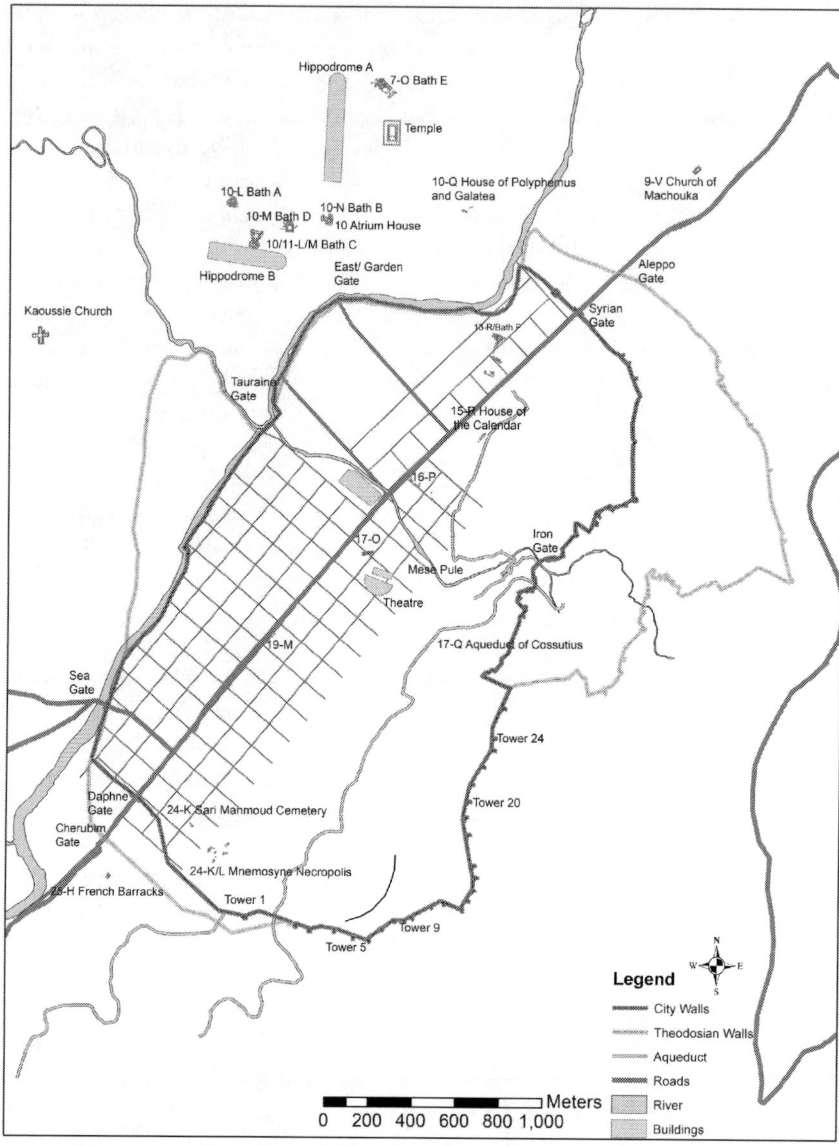

FIGURE 4.7 Antioch after Justinian's building programs

Source: Created by Stephen Batiuk

sluice-gates in this wall he contrived that the torrent, flowing through these, should lose its force gradually, checked by this artificial barrier, and no longer violently assault the circuit-wall with its full stream, and so overflow it and damage the city, but should gently and evenly glide on in the manner I have described and, with this means of outflow, should proceed through

FIGURE 4.8 The Iron Gate

Source: Photograph by Andrea U. De Giorgi

> the channel wherever the inhabitants of former times would have wished to conduct it if it had been so manageable.[95]

Little did it matter to Procopius that the Iron Gate had been long in existence, and its earlier phase, that of the early second century CE, consisted of a bridge and conduit for an offshoot of Daphne's aqueduct.[96] It was also going to be restored and strengthened in subsequent eras, as attested by the incorporation of gravestones with Arabic inscriptions in its upper masonry. All the same, this project was part of an organic plan for making Antioch a more rational and overall safer place to live, as well as an imperial bulwark against the ever present Persian threat. In that vein, Justinian also undertook a diversion of the Orontes along Antioch's land walls, in line with similar previous projects carried out under the Flavian emperors. In Justinian's intentions, the Orontes was transformed into a moat, securing the entire western flank of the city. The thoroughfare was also revamped with basalt repaving and sidewalks with drains, as attested by the excavations of sector 19-M, level III.[97] This investigation shows that a sediment of debris ranging between 90 cm and a meter covered the street of Trajan, which may have been demolished by the earthquake and its aftermath. Tenuous traces of its slabs and decorative apparatus were recovered by the excavators. A new, reduced version of the thoroughfare was thus set in place sometime between 528 and 540. More to the point, the axis appears in a new configuration: 5.45 m wide, plus sidewalks.

New porticoes and mosaic floors for shops, albeit on a scale smaller than that of Trajan's overhaul, added a sense of prestige, while also conveying that sense of return to a normal life: shops and spaces for retail articulated again the routines of the Antiochenes. Churches, too, received their fair share of attention, with restoration of the Church of the Theotokos, or Mother of God, and that of the Archangel Michael in Daphne.[98] It appears, however, that the Octagonal Church was the only structure rebuilt on the Island, and rededicated by Patriarch Ephraim.

But the city that emerged from the ashes was significantly smaller, as the archaeological evidence shows, by at least 20 percent of the former expanse,[99] with the new northern wall reducing much of the built environment, and the Island presumably reduced to a quarry. No longer was Justinian guarding the same districts as before (especially on the plain, which was too vulnerable), but only the city itself. The emperor moreover ordered the hippodrome to be dismantled in order to supplement stone for the new walls along the left bank of the Orontes; these were designed to change the course of the river so that it ran along a circuit wall via an artificial channel. The Island, however, was used not only as a quarry but also presumably for the leather industry and more of the fullers' quarters as well, thus continuing a tradition that the great water works of the Flavian period had initiated.[100] According to Doro Levi, the Princeton excavations

> not only confirm the impression that there was no longer any fervor of building activity, responsible for additional important public and private edifices, but also the suspicion that the extent and thoroughness of Justinian's restoration, which should have brought back the city to unsurpassed splendor, and added new churches to the old ones, was greatly exaggerated in Procopius' flattering account.

All in all, this was a city that in theory was expected to function again as a hub to the East and headquarters for the Eastern campaigns. But although artisans and craftsmen returned to Antioch, making it look like a vast construction zone while also conveying a sense of the place that once was, Antioch remained a city that continued to be crippled by the vicissitudes of old.

As with the previous epoch, governance of the city rested on the intersection between imperial and civic authorities. The emperor was represented by the *comes Orientis* and the *consularis Syriae*, while, as we have seen, a number of lesser officials, such as the *magister militum*, played key roles in administering the city's affairs. Overall, the great concentration of imperial bureaucrats and officials remained the staple character of the city. As for civic affairs, the patriarchs' centrality during the sixth century could not be disputed; with the almost wholesale disappearance of the city council from civic life, they became the main authority. They alone could curb the demands of the state, advocate for the city in fundamental ways, and boast the authority to discuss treaties with the enemy. But they could also be extremely divisive figures, causing rifts and widening the gap between factions.[101] The patriarchs Severus, Ephraim, and Gregory are eloquent examples of figures of this sort. Into this context of lay people and clergy we should add the few remaining town councilors and an extensive web of factions, two of which – the Blues and the Greens – were implicated in socioreligious affairs and had a propensity to create trouble. Even in the murky state of affairs of the 540s, the Christological doctrine caused grave fissures in the social fabric of the city: the synod of 542, pitted against a new spreading of the theories of Origen of Alexandria (184–253), officially condemned his works as heretic, while gesturing to the powers in Constantinople for a more drastic resolution, which came a year later with yet another synod on the Bosphorus. All the while, the chasm between the Miaphysite and the Orthodox communities in Antioch could not be mended, with a de facto partition and a deeply rooted anti-Greek sentiment after the spiral of violence. Moreover, the influence of Jacob Baradeus, bishop of Edessa and main engine behind the establishment of a Miaphysite church, further alienated the Antioch faithful from the authorities in Constantinople, while also imbuing them with a sense of belonging and resistance that only the Syriac language could capture.[102]

The ebb and flow of civic coinage reflects the events that punctuated the life of Antioch in the Early Byzantine period. The fifth century's trend of copper coins – with only two issues of gold, namely under Zeno and Leontius – continued in the following decades.[103] The gulf between the copper nummi and the gold solidus could not have been wider, with a staggering ratio of 16,800 to 1.[104] All the same, Anastasius I is recognized as the initiator of Byzantine coinage, for he enforced a series of measures that considerably changed the coinage in Syria. In short, he introduced his bronze follis, a coin valued at 40 nummi, which enabled a more reasonable conversion of 360 folles to 1 solidus. With a subsequent diameter and weight increase of the follis, he then reached a 7,200 to 1 ratio or 180 folles. With the end of Anastasius's reign and the beginning of Justinian's orbit, Antioch began to issue its own copper denominations; the post-528 series bears the legend of "Theoupolis." There were also fewer seals (lead circles that secured important documents) in the seventh century (19, compared to 36 in the sixth century and

26 in the fifth century), suggesting the rupture of Byzantine administrative life with the Persian and, later, Islamic occupations of the city.

The troubles continue

If the pandemic that swept across Antioch – and the whole Mediterranean – had not apparently decimated the population and disrupted the functioning of societies enough, a cattle plague in 553 also compounded the economic situation. A major earthquake also hit the Levant in 551, with its epicenter presumably in Lebanon; the shaking was felt in Antioch, as the *vita* of St. Symeon Stylites the Younger reports, though damage must have been minimal in the city.[105] Another followed in 557/558, with again presumably no serious consequences for the community, though the Octagonal Church and the city walls were damaged from these shocks.[106] The climate of those days, with a community balancing its existence between anxieties and hopes, resonates greatly in the *vitas* of the younger St. Symeon and his mother, St. Martha. Amid topographic allusions to Antioch, its walls, and territory, as well as references to the plague,[107] the *vitas* bring to the fore the role played by the sanctuary to St. Symeon established outside Antioch on the *Thaumaston Oron*, or "Hill of Wonders," in adding a new pivotal site in the religious landscape of the city, as well as the interfacing with the religious realities of the time. How this site began to attract throngs of visitors in the lower Orontes Valley, elaborated its own architectural idiom, and altogether strengthened the Chalcedonian cause should not be overlooked.[108] Stylitism and the highest practice of ascetic virtues were the key points of the project that unfolded on a prominent hill that had witnessed sparse settlement in the first two centuries CE. The monastery consisted of two main building phases, around 540 and in the 560s, respectively. An octagon, just like at Qal'at Siman, defined the holiest space of the monastery, while a panoply of churches, a monastery, annexes, and spaces for the pilgrims were gradually added to the main fabric of the building.[109] The sudden rise to prominence of the monastery, however, cannot be divorced from the vicissitudes of the day. In all likelihood, the genesis of the sanctuary was predicated on the events and trauma of the Persian sack of 540; by that rationale, from its inception it upheld its role of safe haven for pilgrims and believers alike. As one would expect, though, churches and martyria in sixth-century Antioch would not just simply cater to Christians at large. At that time, the balkanization of Christianity in the Antiochene region was at its apex, with Qal'at Siman having turned into Miaphysite enclave and having been the epicenter of a long season of sectarian violence since 517.[110] In this context, that the sanctuary of St. Symeon the Younger may have grown as an alternative, and, more to the point, as the Chalcedonian response to the loss of the much-revered sanctuary of Qal'at Siman, is a possibility.[111]

In the aftermath of Justinian's death in 565, Antioch became further involved in the persecutions directed against pagans and heretics. Many pagans in Antioch were arrested and imprisoned, their books burned in the hippodrome, and their idols hanged to show their insignificance.[112] The patriarch Anastasius I (561–571,

594–599), a staunch opponent of Justinian's theory of the incorruptibility of Christ, nonetheless retained his post when Justin II (565–578) succeeded to the throne in Constantinople.[113] Meanwhile, hostilities with the Persians resumed, and an army under the command of the general Adarmāhān wreaked havoc in Syria and reached Antioch, which was at that point (573) swiftly abandoned by most, including the new patriarch Gregory (571–593), a Chalcedonian.[114] But although left to fend for itself, the city was not taken. The suburbs, along with the Church of St. Julian, however, were burnt. Moreover, new earthquakes undermined the remaining confidence of the city; while the tremors of 570 are said to have caused no damage, the one of 577 apparently razed Daphne to the ground.[115] The accounts for the period are confusing, but the chronicles converge on the idea that Antioch's suburb at this time ceased to exist and would not recover.[116] The archaeology, too, corroborates this picture. No house in Daphne seems to have been built or remodeled after the middle of the sixth century, at a time when the use of mosaics also seems to have ceased in the Antiochene district. Only Bath F (sector 13-R at the Aleppo Gate) offers the most recent manifestation of a visual phenomenon that had expressed the cultural outlook of the community for more than four centuries.[117]

Slander and accusations of worshiping the old pagan gods added in the meantime a surreal layer to the already vexed community; in 577, the patriarch Gregory and Anatolius, the *vicarius* of the *praefectus praetorio* in Edessa, became heavily implicated in a plot that also involved the imperial authorities in Constantinople. Allegations of paganism and performance of forbidden rituals to Zeus caused stir both in Constantinople and Antioch. Eventually, Anatolius and his associates were executed in the capital city, thus pleasing the masses that were asking for exemplary punishment. Gregory's acquittal, however, did not dispel the shadow over the patriarch's pastoral qualities. That focus shortly thereafter shifted again to attacking Miaphysitism, however, bespeaks once again the irreparably divided condition of this community, with more riots exploding in 578. Further, as Glanville Downey poignantly noted, these episodes show that paganism was still rampant in the Greek East.[118]

With Justin II's death, Tiberius II rose to power for a brief reign (578–582). Meanwhile, the earthquake of 580 once again reminded the Antiochenes of their vulnerability. Entanglements with the Ghassanid king al-Mundhir III also document the Byzantine alliance with Arab confederations with a view toward new strategies against the Persians. This was the first time that Arabs had been directly involved in political affairs since the days of Pompey the Great, when the kingdom of Emesa supplied troops to Quintus Caecilius Bassus.[119] Further, the alliance shows that religious affinity could fill wide cultural gulfs. Miaphysitism in particular brought these entities together and overall inspired a new confidence in non-Chalcedonians in the Greek East, whose visibility had been greatly reduced by Justinian's measures. In Antioch, however, Gregory did his best to hinder any act of reconciliation with non-orthodox Christians.[120] Indeed, the patriarch remained a central figure in the years to come, yet for controversial reasons, as he was summoned to Constantinople this time on counts of sedition and incest, among other allegations. Moreover, the 588 rift with the *comes Orientis* Asterius shows the fissure between him and the imperial authorities. The people in Antioch sided with the latter, and allegedly Gregory "was openly reviled by the mob, and turned into ridicule on the stage."[121]

Gregory's acquittal in 589 in Constantinople did nothing to change the state of affairs. His histrionic skills, however, did gain him permission to build Antioch's so-called Hippodrome B – also referred to by the 1930s archaeologists as the Palaestra – on the Island as a replacement for the then decrepit ancient stadium (Figures 3.15 and 4.9), located some 300 m northeast of it.[122]

At 350 m in length, the building is elusive on more than one count: though visible via remote sensing, it appears to have never been equipped with seating and presents some eccentric solutions, such as an off-axis entrance through the semicircular east end. Its walls of stone and brick were buttressed at intervals of 3.6 m, while on some of these buttresses rested arches (Figure 4.9). Whether it was one unit with the palatial complex, intended to complement the nearby Bath "C," or rather a stand-alone unit, the excavators were not able to clarify. Nor is the role of Gregory known in making this building a viable alternative to the main hippodrome, at that point no longer serviceable and stripped of its masonry. Nevertheless, it can't be ruled out that some construction or restoration work may have occurred under the auspices of the patriarch. As Peter Brown noted, Gregory installed what John Chrysostom had previously styled "the Church of Satan."[123] That Antioch still greatly upheld its profane traditions in the sixth century should not surprise us.

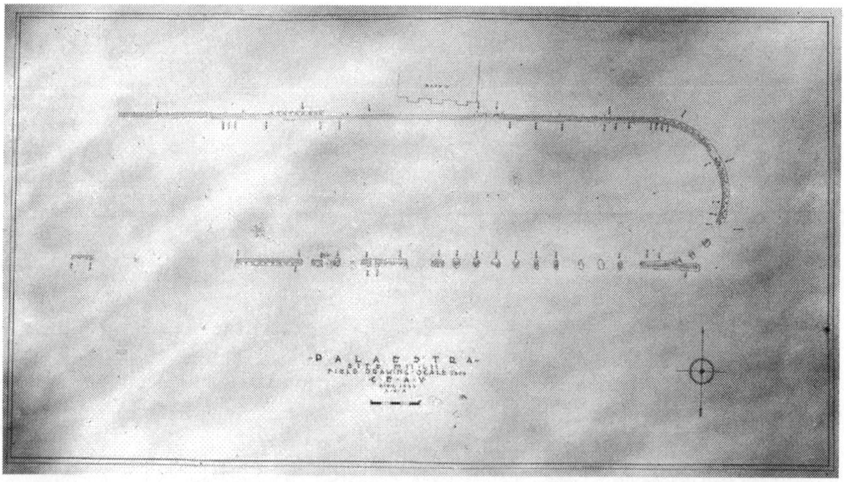

FIGURE 4.9 Hippodrome B, also referred to as the Palaestra

Source: Courtesy of the Antioch Expedition Archives, Department of Art and Archaeology, Princeton University; Princeton

Under pressure from the Avars and Slavs in the Balkans, Emperor Maurice (582–602) was able to restore confidence in the Eastern Empire despite a major military mutiny in 588 in the vicinity of Antioch against the *magister militum per Orientem* Priscus. There was also no rest for telluric activity in the region, it seems: in late October 587/588, another earthquake wrought havoc in Antioch, leveling buildings including foundations across the city and killing 60,000 inhabitants.[124] Furthermore, the scholar Evagrius, who served as an aide to Patriarch Gregory, also reported that the Octagonal Church's porticoes collapsed, with the exception of the dome, which thanks to Ephraim's 526 repairs (using wood from the sacred grove of Daphne) resisted falling until the aftershocks brought it down. That the church was not rebuilt in the succeeding years betrays both a lack of resources and a general sense of defeat. In addition, the districts of Ostracine (possibly identified in sector 17-O) and Psephium and Byrsia (of unknown location) were also affected, and not least the Church of the Theotokos. Its central nave, however, survived. Some towers on the city wall in the plain were also damaged, and stones were shifted. Other buildings, private and public, and baths, were seemingly also affected.[125] Archaeological traces of the event were seemingly discovered by Downey as he excavated a Middle Byzantine church in Daphne, "left of the modern road to Latakiya," built over a fourth-to-sixth-century rectangular building of undetermined function, possibly destroyed by fire after 583.[126] He suggests this could be attributed to the earthquake of 587/8 and was possibly the martyrion of St. Leontius (originally a synagogue) or else the Church of Michael the Archangel. Tentative evidence aside, only the will of God mitigated the effects of the event. Thus Evagrius wrote:

> Another preservation was also granted to the city, our compassionate God having mitigated the keenness of His threatened vengeance, and corrected our sin with the branch of pity and mercy: for no conflagration followed, though so many fires were spread about the place, in hearths, public and private lamps, kitchens, furnaces, baths, and innumerable other forms. Very many persons of distinction, and among them Asterius himself, became the victims of the calamity. The emperor endeavoured to alleviate this visitation by grants of money.[127]

As in a cyclical pattern, the plague struck again in 591/592, though casualties may not have been as substantial as the sources would have us believe, for the city remained politically active. Not even the damage caused by drought to olive trees (599) and weevils (600), which plausibly caused substantial long-term economic losses, interrupted the natural flow of life in the city and surrounding districts.[128] But social disruptions continued. In 608/609 under Emperor Phocas (602–610), a Byzantine army unprecedentedly marched on Antioch to prevent a revolt by Miaphysites, many of whom were killed or banished, while the patriarch Isaac was removed. Meanwhile, Jews staged an uprising over the threat of forced conversion, in the course of which the Chalcedonian patriarch Anastasius II (599–609) was murdered, though whether by Jews or Miaphysites is unclear. Troops were sent to Antioch to put down the revolt under Bonosus, the count of the East. In the immediate aftermath, many Jews were killed, maimed, or banished. Antioch thus was showing its most typical social layering and unresolved conflicts in the face of any hardship.[129]

The heavy-handed intervention of the Persians, however, owing to the breakup of the Ghassānids and eastern frontier, made clear that the city was no longer defensible, and in 611 the Sasanian king Khosrow II, also known as Parviz (590–628), once again took Antioch, along with Apamea and Edessa, after the rout of Byzantium's eastern military infrastructure.[130] But this is not all, for Caesarea Maritima in Palestine endured a two-year siege, and Jerusalem fell in 614. Syria and Palestine fell thus entirely under the Persian yoke, while a Sasanian army made it as far as Chalcedon, opposite the shores of Constantinople, in 615. North Africa shortly ensued, and Alexandria suffered Antioch's same fate. It was long, though, before Constantinople was able to muster its forces and map out a fully-fledged *Reconquista* plan.

The near 20 years of Antioch under Sasanian rule are not well documented, though echoes of the stripping of resources and enforcement of the Nestorian confession may suggest some of the events that went on. Altogether, the city remained in Persian possession until 628 (or 630), when the emperor Heraclius (610–641) was able to gain it back. But it was a small victory at a complicated time, one in which the emperor also had to come to terms with a Christianity more divided than ever. To his credit, he sought to mediate between the orthodox and Miaphysite factions: whether attempting to foster a genuine sense of concord or acting upon a shrewd calculation, Heraclius demonstrably designed an unprecedented reconciliation plan. Sergius, the patriarch of Constantinople, served as the architect and mediator of this operation, which entailed an unprecedented overture in the discussion of the nature of Christ.[131] It followed that in 630 Heraclius met with Athanasius I Gamolo, Miaphysite patriarch of Antioch, along with other Miaphysite bishops, in Mabbug (modern Mambij) Syria, previously known as Hierapolis. At the meeting, the emperor asked them to underwrite a new statement whereby Christ was declared an entity of two natures, one will, and one energy. The negative outcome of the undertaking led to another wave of prosecutions, directly mandated by the emperor, against the Miaphysites and their properties, perpetrated both by monks and civilians.[132]

Meanwhile, a threat no one had seen coming materialized at this very time in the Levant. In 636 Heraclius went down to defeat in one of the most decisive battles in history, the Battle of Yarmūk, by a new power on the scene, the rising forces of Islam.[133] The result was the loss of the Eastern provinces of the Byzantine Empire to the Islamic caliphate, effectively bringing an end to Byzantine rule in Syria. Antioch was lost; its passage in 638 CE under the Arabs went almost unnoticed.

Buildings

The destruction caused to Antioch by the hand of nature and man has been detailed previously. That Antioch also became a construction zone needs to be stressed as well, especially between 527 and 540. Presumably, most projects were imperially financed through the allocation of sums of money that may have at least helped to defray the costs of reconstruction. In all likelihood, the people of Antioch were greatly enmeshed in the repair of the city, which went from being heaps of debris (as in the aftermath of the 526 earthquake) to a condensed yet functioning urban center. As in the days of the Flavian emperors, when each borough of Antioch contributed to the excavation of a canal for the fullers, so presumably did the city take it upon itself to restore its roads, houses, and basic infrastructure. Earlier Anastasius and Justinian had created an assembly that, drawing on all the city's constituencies, would take care of public works and civic finance.[134] That this same assembly was involved in many rescue projects during the sixth century is a likely possibility.

Personal initiatives of high-tier officials, at least until the days of the great earthquake of 526, had continued to make small, albeit significant modifications to the ever-evolving fabric of the city. Illus is said to have been an active builder in Antioch, though no record of his projects survives. The damage caused by the riots in the last decade of the fifth century, with the partial destruction of the forum of Valens, was partly offset by new buildings sponsored by one Mammianus. Whether a senator in Constantinople or in Antioch, he commissioned new colonnades, a *tetrapylon*, and an antiforum in Daphne. This much munificence, rare at that point, was met with great enthusiasm in the community, which in turn dedicated a bronze statue to him.[135] The survival of this practice is noteworthy, since recent scholarship tends to consider the phenomenon of dedicating statues virtually exhausted at that point. The patriarch Ephraim also contributed a great deal to the city and its infrastructure. Public works, as for instance the Orontes bridge south of Antioch, are known to have been built under his auspices, whereas the repairs to the Octagonal Church provided the city with the functioning of one of its pivotal foci.

Imperially sponsored projects of course stemmed from the intervention of Justinian as well, as noted earlier. The fortifications on Mt. Silpius were presumably repaired in the aftermath of the Sasanian attack, as the inspection of the northern wall and its cisterns demonstrates.[136] Of the grand waterworks on the Orontes and the Parmenius, however, only the Iron Gate survives.[137] While its fabric encases the bridge of an aqueduct, the uppermost courses and its overall transformation into a dam date to the days of Justinian, when a sluice gate plausibly regulated the release of excess water. Works on the colonnaded street and its porticoes were documented by the 1930s excavations. The interspace between the Roman paved road and that of Justinian in particular makes clear that a wholesale reconfiguration of the road took place under the emperor. More tangible evidence of post-526 construction is offered by Bath F, located in Antioch's northern sector. Located in sector 13-R, this building was first inspected on the grounds of sculpture discoveries in the area and because of its location near the northern expanses of the city and the main artery of traffic. Its excavation yielded the weathered remains of a bath that in the Islamic era may have been converted into a kiln; most notably, it led to the discovery of the magnificent, albeit headless statue of Hygieia now at the Worcester Museum of Art (Figure 4.10). That it was ultimately destroyed by fire, presumably during the 540 sack, is a real possibility.[138]

The sequence of fifth and sixth century catastrophes had seemingly a minor impact on the communities living in Antioch's territory, and not least those settled in the Syrian Jibāl. The construction of ecclesiastical buildings, in particular, continued at a remarkable pace. The church of Qalblozeh is a stunning example of the architecture that developed on these barren landscapes, a blend of heavy austere volumes and delicate external decoration as made manifest by the hallmark flowing string course around windows and doors on the exterior of the building (Figure 4.11). Heavy piers, solid towers, and elegant arches constitute the armature

FIGURE 4.10 Bath F. Statue of Hygeia

Source: Courtesy of the Antioch Expedition Archives, Department of Art and Archaeology, Princeton University; Princeton

FIGURE 4.11 Qalblozeh, the church of Saints Gabriel and Michael: the interior

Source: Photograph by Andrea U. De Giorgi

of a three-nave building that, in all likelihood, was dedicated at the end of the fifth century to the Saints Gabriel and Michael.

This architectural discourse, however, was taken to new, remarkable heights by the construction of the sanctuary dedicated to St. Symeon the Elder sometime around 480–490. The vicissitudes that framed the days of his death have been already brought into focus. The monumental décor that framed the pillar, however, was one of extraordinary sophistication (Figure 4.3): an octagon surrounds the stump of the pillar and is then squared by four halls on each side that paved way to a large complex that included a monastery, baptistry, and a large court for a surface close 5,000 m^2.[139] As for churches in the city, those of St. Romanus in Antioch and St. Euphemia in Daphne are said to have been built between the late-fifth and early-sixth centuries. Justinian added the Church of the Holy Mother of God (the Theotokos), opposite the basilica of Rufinus.[140] He also built nearby the church of Sts. Cosmas and Damian. Empress Theodora by turns sponsored the Church of Michael the Archangel and the basilica of Anatolius, with columns shipped from Constantinople. A church of Job in connection with Patriarch Domninus in 545 was seemingly part of Justinian's building project and may have been located outside the city. The church in Seleucia Pieria also underwent major repairs, as attested by the 1930s excavations, while the sanctuary of St. Symeon the Younger outside Antioch became a new pole of mysticism and pilgrimage, equipped as it was with amenities for travelers and a powerful octagon around the column of the Stylite.[141]

Yet the archaeological record of Antioch's churches and ecclesiastical buildings remains somewhat patchy, if not downright absent. Nor is the location and materiality of the *coemeterium*, the burial grounds of the great saints of Antioch, known. That it was located in Daphne and accommodated the remains of the martyrs St. Ignatius, St. Babylas, St. Maximinus, St. Iuventinus, St. Julianus, and St. Drosis, as well as the ascetics St. Theodosius, St. Macedonius, and St. Thomas of Emesa, is a matter of record.[142] The1930s excavations brought to light at least four religious buildings, all outside the city walls. The first is the modest medieval Daphne church, plausibly also of the Crusader period, that was cursorily explored in 1932 at the beginning of operations.[143] Better dividends were clinched in 1935 at the site of Kaoussié (Qausīyeh), northwest of Antioch along the road to Alexandria ad Issum, where the archaeologists identified the cruciform church of Meletius, plausibly built in honor of St. Babylas around 381 and embellished with mosaic floors in 387 under the auspices of the patriarch Flavianus, the successor of the bishop Meletius (Figure 3.16). Successively, a baptistery and sacristy were added between 420 and 429 on the initiative of the patriarch Theodotus, while other annexes were added in the early sixth century, thus making this complex the quintessential template of the cruciform churches of Late Antiquity. The recovery of the sarcophagus of two men under the central bema, or bay, was one of the Antioch excavations' greatest achievements, all the more as they identified the marble flagstones that interfaced with the original mosaic floor of the building. That the occupants of the grave were the mortal spoils of St. Babylas and Meletius is a cogent possibility. How the building was referred to by the Antiochene community is the rub; the term *ekklesia* appears in one of the inscriptions. Incidentally, the decorative apparatus enables a precise chronology, and in all, the identification of a key site of worship. Three inscriptions featured in the tessellated surfaces of floors date to the episcopate of Flavianus, with one in the northern nave pinpointed to March 387, when the *presbiteros* Dorys, under the priesthood and administration of one Eusebius, laid in the exedra (the northern nave of the cross) a mosaic for the fulfillment of a vow. The same inscription is replicated, albeit with some slightly different wording, in the context of the western and southern naves of the complex, though the former may be the earliest. Also of interest is one inscription that commemorates the deacon and *paramonarius* Akkiba, who during the episcopate of Theodotus (424–428) and under Athanasius, presbyter and *oikonomos*, donated the mosaic of the *pistikon*, an ancillary room adjacent to the baptistery.[144] In the main, the decoration consists of marble opus sectile floors in the central chamber and mosaics with geometric motifs throughout the rest of the building. Of interest are the mosaic patterns of the east arm, redolent with wheels and grids set in squares and distancing themselves from the generally uniform decoration of the complex. That the décor so indicated the focus of the liturgy is a possibility that has been taken up by Wendy Mayer and Pauline Allen.[145] The first half of the sixth-century church of Machouka, in the northern districts of Antioch, was another short-lived exploration of a three-nave basilica; heavily robbed, it nonetheless showcases a well-preserved narthex and geometric/floral motifs in the mosaics of the north aisle, one of which features, amid a fleurette design, a dedicatory inscription *in tabula ansata*: "Lord, receive the offering of those whose names you know" (Figure 4.12).

No trace of the superstructure survived the destruction of the building and its consequent heavy pillaging; three graves, however, were identified by the archaeologists in the narthex. Further, the establishment of the building may have spawned settlement in its environs, as attested by much density of small sites straddling the stretch between the excavation site and the modern suburb of Narlica.[146] Lastly, the church in the lower city of Seleucia Pieria (also referred to as a martyrium), outside the immediate environs of Antioch, was hastily brought to light in 1938 (Figure 4.13).[147] Three phases of construction can be assumed: an initial phase, plausibly to be dated to the late fifth century CE, consisting of a central-plan building shaped as a double-shelled tetraconch (that is, a building with four apses) with a possible apsed chancel jutting out along the eastern axis. A wooden roof supported by the flimsy columns of the inner tetraconch would have covered the building, though its shape cannot be determined. Cross-shaped and equipped with an annular ambulatory, the church presents a choir with a rectangular base and apse, while a baptistery abutting the complex along its northern side was added by the second phase of construction. The visual décor of the church is quite remarkable, thanks to its intricate marble revetments, opus sectile floors, and

FIGURE 4.12 Machouka, church. Raised mosaic inscription from the north aisle

Source: Courtesy of the Antioch Expedition Archives, Department of Art and Archaeology, Princeton University; Princeton

FIGURE 4.13 Seleucia Pieria, church

Source: Courtesy of the Antioch Expedition Archives, Department of Art and Archaeology, Princeton University; Princeton

overall decoration of friezes and capitals. The program of mosaic flooring on three sides of the ambulatory, however, and not least its extraordinary menagerie, make the building stand out.[148]

We owe to Wendy Mayer and Pauline Allen a consideration of whether churches that have existed in the textual domain only can now be inserted into their historical framework and, in some cases, situated spatially.[149] Table 4.1, which draws from their seminal work, lists buildings in and around Antioch that can be loosely situated between the fourth and the seventh centuries. The textual sources are anything but solid, with buildings disappearing from the textual record after natural events and references to others existing only in given *itineraria*, hagiographies, or episcopal notices. The chronicle of the destruction caused by the 526 earthquake, in particular, is useful in learning about many of these buildings.[150] Nevertheless, the picture is one of sustained investment and relentless construction of sacred buildings.

Conclusions

We have considered in this chapter the sequence of disasters that affected Antioch in the late fifth and sixth centuries. Rhetorical exaggerations aside, the Antioch

TABLE 4.1 Known Church Sites in Antioch and Vicinity

Church	*Location*
Church of St. Ignatius	Within the city walls
Octagonal Church of Constantine	On the Island?
Palaia (Old Church)	Within the city walls
Church of Cassianus	Within the city walls
Church in the New City	On the Island?
Church of the Maccabees	Within the city walls, southern districts, in the Jewish quarter
Church of the Theotokos	Within the city walls
Martyrion of St. Romanus	Within the city walls
Church of Sts. Cosmas and Damian	Within the city walls
Church of Machouka	Northern districts, along the Aleppo road
Cruciform Church of St. Babylas (Kaouissié?)	West of Antioch, along the Alexandretta road
Martyrion of the Romanesia Gate	By the western city walls?
Coemeterium	Southern district along the Daphne road
Martyrion of St. Thomas	Unknown
Martyrion of St. Julian	Unknown
Martyrion of St. Barlaam	Unknown
Martyrion of St. Symeon the Elder	Unknown
Martyrion of St. Stephen	Unknown
Martyrion of St. Dometius	Unknown
Church of St. John	Unknown
Church of the Holy Prophets	? Destroyed in 526
Church of St. Zacharias	? Destroyed in 526
Church of St. John the Baptist	Unknown
Martyrion of the Maccabees	Daphne
Church of St. Michael the Archangel	Daphne
Martyrion at the temple of Apollo	Daphne
Martyrion of St. Leontius	Daphne

that Justinian rebuilt was but a pale reflection of its former self. Nevertheless, as Procopius contended, the emperor rebuilt the city from the ground up and spared no efforts in securing resources.[151] In that vein, a new cardo, porticoes, churches, fortifications, as a new course of the Orontes among other features, were laid out, thus imbuing the city on the Orontes with a new sense of relevance. Indeed, Antioch still held its place on the map of imperial politics. Although smaller and reduced, its urban core continued to signal a community still deemed crucial in articulating a military strategy against the East. Further, this was a community that did not waver even in face of the most vehement of earthquakes and other disasters.

Notes

1 *Downey, History* 559.
2 Eger 2014b.
3 Brands 2016a, 39: the degree of destruction and institutional responses are foregrounded.
4 Fires occurred in 522 and 573; earthquakes in 526, 528, 551, 557, 577, and 588; plagues affecting both humans (bubonic) and cattle in 542, 553, and 560; and drought in 599. See Foss 1997, 190–191. For a list of these events, Mordechai 2018, 25–26.
5 Kennedy 1985a, 6. This assertion partially corroborates Liebeschuetz 1972, 264, who suggests that Antioch had already begun to develop local rule and trade-based organizations, characteristic of the medieval city. On the subject of an organic and irregular street layout, however, he concedes that while it may have begun in the Byzantine period, excavations show that the grid layout persisted until the end of the Byzantine period – evidence of the enduring influence revealed by the Princeton excavations.
6 Kennedy, 1985a. Also, *IGLS* 3. 1. 786. The inscription refers to the bath as *demosion* and places the restoration in 538. The text of the inscription reads:

> In the time of Flavius…? the very grandiose and most glorious count of the East and count of the Sacred Largesses, the public bath Sigma (?) was rebuilt from the foundations, with the disposition of a four-sided, colonnaded court (tetrastoon). In the time of Indiction 1, of the 586th year (= 537/8).

See *Antioch IIII*, 89, 115; 151, pl.33.5 for the archaeological context of the find as well as Foss 1997.
7 Lib. *Or.* 11.234; *Malalas* 13.40; Proc. *De Aed.* 7.47.
8 Dagron 1979–1984.
9 Lib. *Or.* 47.19.
10 Ibid., 6–7.
11 Brown 1971, 82.
12 *Sym Styl.* 60–70.
13 Brown 1971, 91.
14 *Downey, History* 482.
15 Harvey 2000, 46.
16 Liebeschuetz 1972, 144, where it is emphasized how these measures further eroded the involvement of local notables in civic activities, whether for the channeling of their resources toward other duties or deterrent against any form of individual popularity. Reduced though they may have been, the games nevertheless survived as institution until the first two decades of the sixth century CE; see Hahn 2018, 70.
17 As for the the murder of the patriarch Stephen in 479, the Chronicle of John of Nikiu in Egypt makes it plain that the folks in Antioch hated Stephen on account of his adherence to Nestorianism, see *John of Nikiu* 88.44.
18 *TIB* 15, 556.
19 *Malalas* 15.14; *Downey, History* 496.
20 Liebeschuetz 1972, 159–160; Filipczak 2017, 329.
21 *Michael the Syrian* 149. Well known is Zeno's alleged remark that the Greens should have burned not only the corpses of the Jews but also live Jews. See *Malalas* 15.15.
22 Chronicle of Joshua the Stylite 19 (transl. by W. Wright).
23 Constantinus VII Porphyrogenitus, *De Insidiis* 36.
24 *Malalas* 16.2.
25 Chronicle of Joshua the Stylite 44 (transl. by W. Wright).
26 John of Ephesus *Hist. Eccl.* 5.17.
27 Hollmann 2003, PUAM inv. 3603-I57.
28 *Malalas* 16.3.
29 Filipczak 2017, 335–338. The Prasinoi and the Baths of Olbia are unknown locations.
30 *Evagrius* 3.32. See also the Chronicle of Zuqnin, in Pseudo-Dionysius. 512 and 518 in Chronicon ad Annum 819.

31 Bishop intermittently: 469–470, 470–471, 475–476, 484–494.
32 Severus, *Homily on the Trisagion* (125) (transl. by M. Brière).
33 Allen and Hayward 2004.
34 Alpi 2012, 154. See for instance Severus, *Homilia* 95 (PO 25, 93–94) (transl. by M. Brière): "Isn't it true that you marched in the procession and fully celebrated the rituals of Zeus Olympios?"
35 *Evagrius* 3.33.
36 *CJ* 1.15.12.18. See also *Evagrius* 4.10.
37 Tannous 2014, 32.
38 *Antioch IV.i*, 182.
39 Stahl 2017, 237–239.
40 *Malalas* 17.13. See also Hahn 2018, 70.
41 *Michael the Syrian* 2.271.
42 "The Jew": Chronicle of Zuqnin, III and IV.
43 Gerritsen et al. 2008, 260–266.
44 The information was included in a plea of Antioch monks to John of Cappadocia, patriarch of Constantinople. See Uggeri 2014, 869.
45 *Downey, History* 518.
46 *Malalas* 17.12.
47 Brands 2016a, 37; Mordechai 2018.
48 *Malalas* 17.14.
49 Uggeri 2014, 869.
50 Akyuz et al. 2006, 281–293. Ambraseys suggests that the 525 blaze was compounded by a temblor, thus inaugurating a phase of high seismicity which culminated in the events of 526 and following years. See Ambraseys 2009, 183.
51 *Malalas* 17.16. See also Procop. *Bell.*2.14 and *John of Nikiu* 135–136. Chron. Edessenum 11–2; Theoph. 172–173. Guidoboni 1994, n. 203, for a thorough discussion of non-Greek sources.
52 *Michael the Syrian* 93. It should be noted that the Church of Constantine was standing during Khosrow's siege of Antioch in 540. This implies that either the damage had not been that relevant or that the church was swiftly repaired in the aftermath of the catastrophe.
53 The issue is whether the figures of the casualties have any bearing on the overall population's estimate. Michael the Syrian claims that only 1,250 inhabitants survived the quake; see *Michael the Syrian* 93. As for a general assessment of Antioch's demography, see Callu 1997.
54 The lives of Antioch's leaders were not spared by the calamity, either, as various reports attest. Central in many a narrative, however, is the death of the Chalcedonian patriarch Euphrasius. For instance, John of Nikiu reports on the tragic event, claiming that he was "unfitted for the patriarchate"; see *John of Nikiu* 90.30. In his description of damages and casualties, Theophanes places the death of the bishop first: see *Theophanes* 172.30–31. Further, Marcell. Com. 102.19–24 collates the death and accidental decapitation of the bishop with the collapse of the obelisk in the hippodrome in conveying the magnitude of the drama. Late reports like that of the eleventh-century historian George Kedrenos stress the same incident to illustrate the scale of a calamity that, in his words, led to the demise of a city that had flourished for 800 years; see Kedrenos 640–641.
55 *Malalas* 17.16.
56 *Malalas* 17.14. Further, Theophanes reports that Justin greatly invested in the reconstruction of the city, to the extent that Anazarbos changed its name to Justinopolis; see *Theophanes* 171 14–17.
57 *Theophanes* 173. John Lydus, *De Magistratibus* 3.54.4 contends that, overall, a hefty sum of money was mobilized for reconstruction in Antioch. For a general assessment of the overall imperial output toward Antioch, see Saliou 2019, 203.
58 Chronicon Edessenum 10.

59 *Malalas* 17.19, in which the chronicler shows lukewarm interest in discussing the construction of ecclesiastical buildings under Justinian.

60 *Malalas* 14.13. The whereabouts of this "large, well lit, and very beautiful basilica" are not known, except that it was opposite the building known as the *Athla*, of an unknown use.

61 *Theophanes* 177–178:

> The survivors fled to other cities or to the mountains and lived in tents (or cabins). And there was a great and most harsh winter. Those who remained behind all prayed bare-foot, crying out and hurling themselves prostrate in the snow, shouting the *Kyrie eleison*. And it was shown to some God-fearing men in a vision, to say to all the survivors that they should write on their lintels, "Christ is with us. Stop." And when they had done this, the wrath of God ceased. And again the Emperor and his consort gave much money for the repair and reconstruction of the city of Antioch. And the Emperor renamed it Theopolis.

Catherine Saliou poignantly notes that Theophanes, in all likelihood, had access to official records, thus making his information particularly valuable; see Saliou 2019, 201. Further, the description in *Michael the Syrian* II.19 is of interest. He states the town was abandoned for five months and that Justinian demolished the outer wall while building one in the middle of city, presumably the stretch that runs from Mt. Staurin toward the Orontes. The rechanneling of the river is also mentioned, but decades-long building programs seem to be conflated in one murky narrative.

62 On the city increasingly suffering more ills as a punishment from God, see Meier 2007.

63 *TIB* 15, 557. See also *Malalas* 18.29 on the renaming of the city. According to the chronicle, this was accomplished in tandem with the discovery of a written oracle, the ominous text of which read: "And you, unhappy city, shall not be called the city of Antiochus." At the pinnacle of his contempt, the emperor Julian knew exactly how to lash out at the ungrateful folks of Antioch: "Now since this was the (incestuous) conduct of Antiochus, I have no right to be angry with his descendants when they emulate their founder or him who gave his name to the city." See Julian *Mis.* 348 B (transl. by W.C. Wright). The trope of Antiochus I and his alleged knack for incest was one that apparently remained ingrained in local folktales. As for other references to Antioch's name switching to Theoupolis: Steph. Byz. 309.9; Proc. *De Aed.* 2.10.2; *CJ* 1.1.6 and *Theophanes* 178.7.

64 *Chron. 1234*, 194–195 on Justinian's response to the crisis and new city plan.

> When this was brought to the attention of the Emperor, he ordered that the external wall be demolished, and a wall be built in the middle of the city, the most part of the city [thus] being left outside the wall; after this was done, the river was at a distance from the wall. The Emperor also decreed that they should dig [a channel] outside the newly built wall, as a bed for the river, which would [thus] pass near the wall from one part to another. And so, since the river had been obstructed, it moved with force to the side of that wall which had been built with great effort.

65 See *Malalas* 18.29 on the bestowing of 200 litrai to the three cities.

66 Cameron 2012, 151, which argues against Ambraseys 2009, 184, a view grounded in the presentation of the calamity as the beginning of the end for Antioch.

67 Theophanes implies that the 528 earthquake destroyed everything and Justinian's rebuilding was really total. Michael Whitby doubts how much Justinian rebuilt; see Whitby 1989.

68 Mordechai 2018, 27.

69 *Malalas* 18.41.

70 *Malalas* 18.64.

71 Guidoboni 1989, 695. The report on the earthquake is in *Malalas* 18.55; whereabouts and intensity, however, cannot be determined.

72 *Malalas* 18.45; 48. Mayer and Allen 2012, 52–55. On the survival of the church in later centuries and al-Mas'ūdī see Chapter 5, p. 251.

73 *Malalas* 18.49. Of interest is the 386 CE stipulation in *CTh* 9.17.17 whereby the removal, sale, and tampering with bodies of saints was forbidden by law.
74 See p. 130.
75 Brands 2016a, 39.
76 Proc. *Wars*. 2. 8–10.
77 *Downey, History* 534.
78 Shepardson 2015a.
79 Proc. *Wars*. 2.8.1.
80 Proc. *Wars*. 2.8.7.
81 Proc. *Wars*. 2.9.18.
82 Proc. *Wars*. 2.8.23.
83 The site was presumably located near Ctesiphon. Oriental and Greek accounts are in accord. Mirkhond and Tabarī speak at length of a city called al-Rūmiyya in the vicinity of al-Madain, where the Antiochenes were relocated and built streets, baths, hippodromes reminiscent of Antioch. See Rawlinson 1876, 395; De Sacy 1793, 366. Also, Ibn Shaddād, a later medieval source: Ahmad b. Muhammad b. Ishāq al-Hamadānī al Faqih in Kitab al Buldan: he mentions building an Antioch at Madā'in with its markets, streets, and houses. He refers to it as "Zand Husraw." The same place was also referred to as "Bazbahan Husraw." With regard to Byzantine sources, see Proc. *Wars*. 2.8.10; 14.1–2. Ibn Shihna states that each family went to the house that resembled their house as if they went back to Antioch. Lastly, Ball 2000 estimates a population in the order of 30,000 inhabitants.
84 de Goeje's 1885, 115–116.
85 *Michael the Syrian* 206.
86 *Evagrius* 4.29. He witnessed the explosion of the plague when still a "schoolboy." On the assessment of the plague, see Cameron 2012, 114; Horden 2007.
87 Mordechai et al. 2019.
88 Gerritsen et al. 2008.
89 Chrysostom, *Homily on St. Ignatius* 4 (Migne edn, vol. 2, col. 591) tallies the population in the order of 200,000 inhabitants. If slaves, women, and infants are included, a figure of 500,000 inhabitants for the fourth century is realistic. As with the rural districts, the numbers are a matter of guesswork. But settlement density in the Amuq Plain and on the Syrian limestone massif suggests some equally swollen numbers.
90 Proc. *De Aed*. 2.10.1.
91 Proc. *De Aed*. 2.10.2–3 (transl. by B. Dewing and G. Downey).
92 Brasse 2010, 279–280.
93 Ibid., 271.
94 Ibid., 279.
95 Proc. *De Aed*. 2.10.18 (transl. by B. Dewing and G. Downey).
96 Brands 2016a, 44. For a thorough autopsy of the building pre- and post-Justinian, see Brands 2009.
97 *Antioch V*, sectors 19-M and 16-P.
98 While Malalas seems to disregard the ecclesiastical buildings in his narrative of Justinian's rebuilding agenda, Procopius conversely emphasizes the religious scope of much of the program.
99 *TIB* 15, 559.
100 Guidetti 2010.
101 Liebeschuetz 1972, 261.
102 Uggeri 2014, 874.
103 Metcalf 2000, 110–111.
104 Stahl 2018, 230. The late fifth- to sixth-century trends show a low number of local issues, thus suggesting monetary self-sufficiency. The mint closed at beginning of seventh century and resumed only during the Crusader period.

105 Guidoboni 1989, 699–700; Ambraseys 2009, 199. *Life of St. Symeon* 105 describes the event in quasi-apocalyptic terms. Of interest, however, is the intersection between the actual events and the vision of the saint:

> and cities and villages on the coast fell according to the vision he had seen… . However in the north, in the region between Antioch and Laodicea, everything remained standing, only a few towers of city walls, and church walls being damaged: as the saint had said these places did not collapse. And the area from Tyre to Jerusalem and the southern region were likewise preserved, according to Symeon's vision.

106 *Downey, History* 558 on the possibility that the damaged walls eased the job for the Persians assailing the city in 573. See also Guidoboni 1989, 702–703; Ambraseys 2009, 211.

107 *TIB* 15, 561.

108 On the Wondrous Mountain the most authoritative study to date is that of Henry 2015, which merged new research with previous archaeological surveys in the lower Orontes Valley.

109 For a detailed presentation of the monastery and its historical context, see Henry 2015, 20–55.

110 Alpi 2003/2004, on the massacre of Kefr Kermin, an incident that led to the open confrontation of hundreds of monks from each side and several casualties.

111 Sodini 2007.

112 *Life of St. Symeon* 173. Justinian sent Amantius to suppress nonconformists in Antioch, a further attestation that paganism was still present in the city and beyond.

113 *Evagrius* 4.40.

114 *Evagrius* 5.9.

115 See Mayer and Allen 2012, 84, on the identity of the church, often referred to as a martyrium.

116 *Evagrius* 5.17; Guidoboni 1994, n. 227.

117 See n. 6 on Bath F and its inscription. *Levi, Pavements*, 2.

118 *Downey, History* 564.

119 See p. 78.

120 *Downey, History* 565.

121 *Evagrius* 6.7.

122 John of Ephesus 3, 27–34. As for the location of the building, see Chapter 3, p. 153. The motives that led to the construction of the new stadium are a matter of guesswork; it is likely, though, that the structure may have suffered from the earthquakes of the early sixth century. See Humphrey 1986, 459.

123 Brown 1988, 320.

124 Guidoboni 1989, 704–705.

125 *Evagrius* 6.8.

126 *Antioch I*, 107–113.

127 Ibid.

128 Gerritsen et al. 2008.

129 *TIB* 15, 560. Agapius of Hierapolis *Chronicle* 77 reports on the mounting escalation against Jews since the days of the emperor Maurice, with ejections, confiscations of property, and forced hair cutting for public humiliation. The crisis under Phocas, however, took the spiral of violence even further. The Antioch Jews, as in the rest of Syria, were believed to be attempting to kill all the Christians and burn local churches. As a response, many were killed in the cities. Phocas did not take matters lightly, though, and forced the Christians of Antioch, Laodicea, and the rest of Syria to pay new taxes. See Agapius *Chronicle* 81. The account is somewhat reinforced by that of Theophanes, who details the gruesome murder of the patriarch Anastasius and many landowners as well as the attempted negotiation of Bonosus, count of the East. See *Theophanes* 29 and the *Doctrina Jacobi* 40 (Dagron and Déroche 1991, 128). See also p. 387.

130 The Sasanian invasion ravaged through Cilicia and Cappadocia, coming to a halt in the vicinity of the Halys river. See *Theophanes* 299; Agapius *Chronicle* 81; *Michael the Syrian* 117–118; *Chron.* 1234, 127. On Antioch presumably not serving as royal mint during the Sasanian occupation, see Stahl 2017, 230; Foss 1997, 32. The latter's analysis of assemblages ascribable to the Sasanian occupation show a trend of substantial Heraclius emissions, with the exception of two coins of Khosrow II.
131 *Downey, History* 576.
132 Tannous 2014, 33.
133 See Chapter 5 for the discussion.
134 Liebeschuetz 1972, 262.
135 *Evagrius* 3.28. The survival of this practice is noteworthy; all the more recent scholarship tends to consider the phenomenon exhausted at that time. See Gehn and Ward-Perkins 2016.
136 Brasse 2010, 279–280.
137 See p. 211.
138 *Levi, Pavements*, 366, n. 6. Foss 1997, 194, makes a compelling case about Bath F undergoing restoration after the quakes of the 520s, as opposed to other known baths on the Island, to wit, Bath C, destroyed by the earthquake and heavily looted, with limekilns successively installed in ruins, and Bath A, filled with debris and rubble near the Orontes – though some restoration seemingly occurred in the late sixth century. Perhaps its prominent location on flatland west of the Aleppo gate and ease of access to locals and visitors encouraged the reconstruction of Bath F. It was short-lived, though, insofar as a fire may have destroyed the building sometime around 540.
139 Ball 2000, 263–270.
140 Consecrated by Ephraem in 538, rebuilt again after 540 invasion, and had synod of 132 bishops of Syria province.
141 Henry 2015.
142 Patitucci and Uggeri 2008, 29.
143 Column shafts sticking out from the ground had suggested the presence of a pagan temple, to the subsequent disappointment of the archaeologists and inevitable termination of the dig. The church complex superseded a structure destroyed around the time of the emperor Maurice Tiberius (582–602), as a 583 CE coin attests. The three-aisled basilica was equipped with annexes and a decorated chapel. The chronology of the complex is tentatively situated between 969 and 1084, "or between 1098 and 1268." See Downey's report in *Antioch I*, 107–113.
144 Jean Lassus offers a detailed summary of this excavation in *Antioch II*, 5–44 ("L'église cruciforme"), highlighting the annexes around a perfectly cruciform shape of the building with the 25 m long and 11 m wide naves marking the points of the compass and departing from a central square equipped with pillars supporting arches. See also Downey 1938, 45–48.
145 Mayer and Allen 2012, 40.
146 As for the inscription and its popularity in the West, as well as the visual décor of the building, see *Levi, Pavements*, 368–369. For a different perspective and an alternative reading of the liturgical organization of the building, see Mayer and Allen 2012, 58. Settlement in the northern hinterlands of Antioch, near modern Narlica, began in the late first century BCE; see in particular Gerritsen et al. 2008, 259–260.
147 The initial interpretation of the building as martyrium was predicated on the excavators' assumption that the building served a specialized use. Further, they failed to reckon with the addition of a baptistery, a key element for everyday use; see Mayer and Allen 2012, 63.
148 The building was excavated as the Antioch project was coming to a close in 1939. It was located near Seleucia's Market Gate and underwent numerous transformations during the course of its history. Three phases describe the building's life span: a first period from the late fifth century to the 526 CE earthquake. A second phase corresponds to

substantial repairs in the aftermath of the seism (and of that of 528 CE), as well as the addition of new annexes, perimeter wall, *opus sectile* flooring, and a chapel. Lastly, a third phase of gradual abandonment that may have coincided with the seventh century. See *Antioch III*, 35–54; Mayer and Allen 2012, 58–64; Kondoleon 2000, 217–223, for the virtual reconstruction of the building.

149 Mayer and Allen 2012.

150 *John of Nikiu* 90.30.

151 Proc. *De. Aed.* 2.10.

5

ANṬĀKIYA, MOTHER OF CITIES (638–969)

Then by morning we reached Anṭākiya,
   its generous people share its bounty.
They are people of self-restraint and noble affairs,
   whose high morals have always held sway there.
A fortunate city since time immemorial,
   half on the plain and half on the mountain.
Gnats do not enter it and then bite,
   yet it has large mice the size of monitors
It is abundant in bounty and in succulent fruits,
   and figs like necklaces hang from the trees.
Like the stars in the dark before dawn;
   and is impregnable, with many ruins.
In it there is a companion of [sūra] Ya-sin, Habīb,
   and he was esteemed by his Lord.
Now he is in Paradise, gathering its fruits;
   show respect for him, out of pride for the city's Prophet.
A strong city with many vestiges of the past.

– Abū 'Amr al-Qāsim b. Abī Dā'ūd al-Ṭarsūsī[1]

Introduction

Scholars have frequently taken a bleak view of Antioch after the Islamic conquests, arguing that the end of Byzantine rule and its incorporation into the Islamic territories sealed a fate that had already begun a downward trajectory of significant decline and ruin before the conquests.[2] According to those who subscribe to this view, the Islamic conquests were the final nails in the city's coffin, which included the series of natural and human catastrophes that befell the city in the sixth and early seventh centuries, leaving a crippled town that never fully recovered.

Following the Islamic conquests, they maintain, the city remained insignificant, for it is barely mentioned in the Arabic texts. Indeed, this view was supported by the Princeton excavations from 1932 to 1939, which revealed little of the postclassical city. As we will see in this chapter, however, the few historical accounts available to us affirm that the city did not suffer a dramatic loss in population but rather maintained an active economic and religious life. Further, the Princeton excavations revealed significant architectural and material remains. Although Antioch had contracted from its fullest extent in the Roman and Byzantine fourth and fifth centuries, it continued to function as a local urban administrative and economic center for the surrounding frontier province. Moreover, this former capital city was itself a highly attractive prize, alluring as a near-legendary place, its legacy unforgotten. Texts by both Islamic and Christian authors show that Antioch, although reimagined and perceived in new ways, remained strongly connected to its past. Such evidence offers a compelling case for re-envisioning postclassical Antioch and questioning the traditional paradigm. By rereading and reanalyzing the evidence from textual sources and from the published Princeton excavations, we can in fact replace the narrative of Antioch's decline with one of contraction characterized by self-sufficiency and transformation. The consequent methodological and historical revisions to how we understand the city in turn lead to a different conception of space. We are thereby able to increase our knowledge of (1) continuity and change in a major Roman and Late Roman city, (2) the complexity and regional variations of early medieval urbanism, and (3) the role and influence of a frontier town on the periphery of and the borderline between the Islamic and Byzantine Empires.

Debating decline or transformation

Following the series of disasters that befell Antioch between 500 and 638, the Arab conquest delivered a final round of shattering blows to the city, blows from which, some argue, it never recovered. When the disasters of the sixth and early seventh centuries are placed side by side, Antioch and its population appear as a battered ship with a beleaguered crew, barely weathering a succession of calamities and slowly sinking. Indeed, scholars have assumed the city, post-conquest, was a hollowed-out shell: "The city of the Umayyads and their successors seems to have been a place with little of its ancient urban character, but rather a vast field of ruins with occupation on a small scale, often in ancient buildings or streets."[3]

Unlike many other settlements founded by the new Islamic rulers that were commonly adjacent to preexisting cities and other communities – such as the *amṣ ār* (garrison cities like Fusṭāṭ), *quṣūr* (desert castles), and cities like Baghdad and Jerusalem – the Early Islamic settlement at Antioch was not near the Byzantine city; rather, it *was* the Byzantine city. It thereby fits into a model seen in several other comparable cities such as Jarash, Palmyra, Caesarea, and Baysān (modern Bet Shean, classical Scythopolis), which were adapted to suit the needs of a new Islamic community living side-by-side with the established Christian one.[4] These cities were not razed and rebuilt or transformed wholesale but rather were lightly changed while acquiring a few key elements placed in strategic areas: a new mosque in the town center, a new market nearby, and a change in function in the now disused entertainment structures, such as theaters and hippodromes and even baths, to manufacturing use. In all reality, the Early Islamic city, although smaller, would have looked quite similar to that of the sixth-century Early Byzantine period.

One might also question whether it is even relevant or appropriate to describe a city that found itself in the role of *thaghr* (*thughūr*, pl.), or frontier town, astride the newly formed Islamic-Byzantine border between North Syria and Anatolia as having declined. Shifting geopolitical boundaries merely took it out of the race, so to speak. If we proceed from these developments in historiography, we find that current definitions of the transformation of classical, Late Antique, and Islamic cities replace ideas of decline and make possible a new analysis of the materials relating to Antioch.

Three obstacles, however, have prevented the historical record of medieval and Islamic Antioch from being integrated with the city's better-known earlier past: first, the Princeton project was not interested in the later periods; second, it has been assumed that the disasters that befell the city wiped away everything; and third, the city is mentioned infrequently in Islamic sources. Some of the Princeton team were simply not interested in anything Islamic: "The Mohammedan coins among the finds tell little of interest. Few of them can be read beyond the holy ejaculations in the center, the date and place of minting, which are at the edge, being commonly rubbed off."[5] While the archaeologists of the Princeton team were excavating the city of Antioch, Glanville Downey was with them onsite compiling the city's history, which would become his *History of Antioch in Syria from Seleucus to the Arab Conquest*. Downey himself recognized that the history of post-Byzantine Antioch was beyond the scope of that standard and weighty work (and of his scholarly abilities), and he devoted to it only three paragraphs.[6] Nevertheless, by ending Antioch's most detailed historical account with the Islamic conquests, he created an artificial barrier that subsequently has been difficult to breach.[7]

As for the assumption that all the disasters befalling Antioch wiped away everything, little is known of the real effects of the earthquakes, invasions, fires, floods, civil wars, and religious conflict that befell the city in the sixth and seventh centuries and continued into the ninth. Although seismic activity subsided somewhat, more earthquakes struck during the Early Islamic period. Texts, somewhat exaggerated, recount damage to the city, although archaeological evidence of the damage is unclear. An earthquake on February 28, 713, with a likely aftershock on March 10, struck northern Syria and affected Antioch the hardest, causing many tall buildings and private buildings to collapse, including churches and temples, while claiming many lives.[8] The event may have lasted 40 days altogether with its aftershocks, with an intensity between VIII (severe) and X (extreme) on the Modified Mercalli Intensity scale.[9] A second earthquake is in question, as it is known only from a later source, al-Suyūṭī (d. 1505), who said that it destroyed the city in 835 and lasted 40 days, which is similar to the 713 earthquake and so potentially suspect. A third struck on November 24, 847 (or possibly in 846), leaving 20,000 dead under the ruins.[10] Yet another earthquake occurred in 849/850, though the sources provide no further detail.[11] A fifth occurred on December 30, 859, with another likely aftershock on January 29 of the following year. The scholar/historian Ṭabarī (839–923), typically a reliable source and who in Islamic historical narrative fashion relies on a collective of previous reports to verify his monumental work, offers a slightly sensationalist description of this last earthquake, although he was alive when it happened and 20 years old. He wrote that 1,500 homes and 190 towers collapsed.[12] Of those Antiochenes who did not die, many fled the town, while part of Mt. Cassius slid into the sea, the Orontes disappeared for 6 km, and black vapors rose from the sea. Aftershocks were felt for 70 days. Yet despite these earthquakes and the damage they caused, the city continued unabated.

Such disasters are featured in many texts, both Christian and Muslim, during this time; to recognize that they are part of a growing pattern of apocalyptic imagery is not to deny that they occurred or to ignore loss of life and serious damage. Nonetheless, the few but rich descriptions of Antioch and its history after the seventh century until the Byzantine reconquest, suggest a city not destroyed but rather the focus of much reconstruction and transformation with a newly built mosque, two churches foundations, refurbished residential districts with markets and workshop, and repurposed baths, theaters, and hippodromes. Attention to which institutions, monuments, and buildings were selected for rebuilding following each calamity reveals that over time, the priorities of urban planning and space shifted toward plans that were more pragmatic and smaller in scale.

Finally, there is the challenge that the city does not appear as often in texts during the Islamic period as in the Byzantine. One reason is that Antioch was no longer assumed to occupy a privileged position, owing mainly to its new role as a frontier town on the margins of the Islamic intellectual and religious community in the central lands of the first three caliphates – the Rashidūn (632–661), Umayyad (661–749), and ʿAbbāsid (749–969) – of the Early Islamic period. Towns on the Islamic-Byzantine frontier also received little attention in the texts because of a second assumption: that their only purpose was to muster the armies that would raid Byzantine lands. Yet it is possible to gather passing references to the frontier town, even if at times undoubtedly exaggerated or inaccurate.

The Early Islamic conquest and frontier engagements

The written history of Antioch in the Rashidūn and Umayyad periods, during which Islamic territory experienced rapid expansion (Figure 5.1), consists of a patchwork of descriptions from Islamic geographers, most of whom visited the city, and isolated clips from histories tying Antioch into the back and forth of Byzantine and Islamic attempts to hold onto the frontier. Despite the lack of coherent sources, several important descriptions give a sense of both the continuities the city experienced and the transformations it underwent.

The first group of descriptions surrounds the Islamic conquest of Antioch, which was the first long-lasting conquest in the city's history, lasting more than

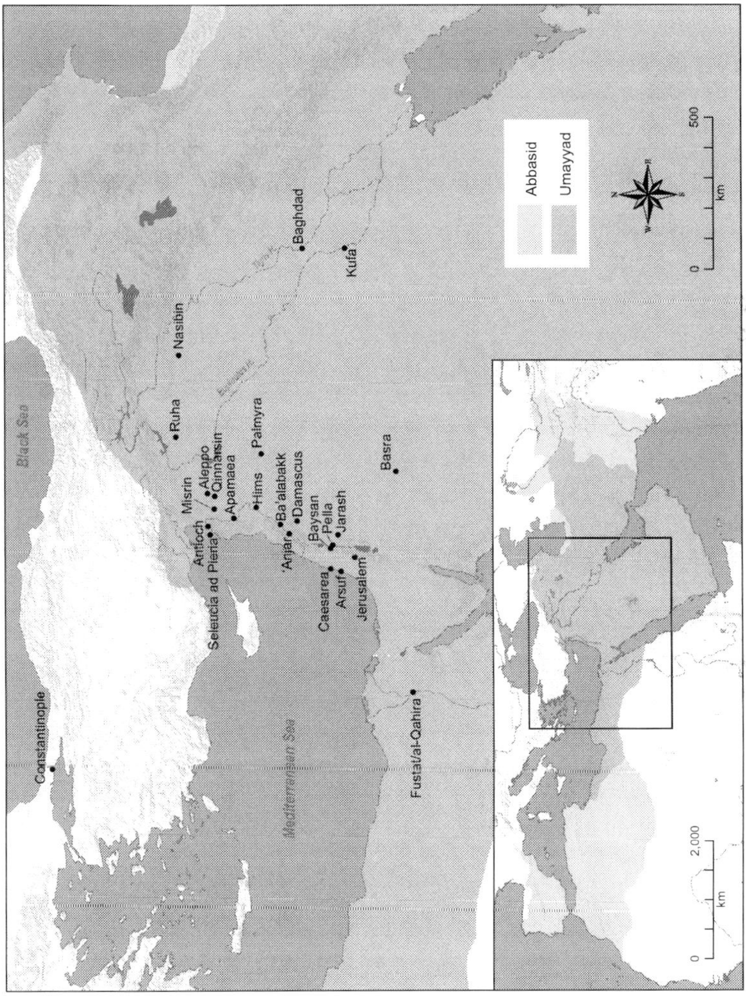

FIGURE 5.1 Map of the Early Islamic conquests

Source: Created by Claire Ebert

three centuries. Although the sources make very little mention of upheaval, this is not a bias of Islamic authors or a consequence of the sometimes generally less strict chronological approach of Islamic accounts as compared with earlier periods. The historians Balādhurī (806–892) and Ṭabarī certainly noted moments in the conquests of other towns when prolonged sieges took place, and Ṭabarī's chronicle proceeds year by year. A poorly known historian, al-Ramlī, whose *Futuḥ al-Shām* (Conquest of Greater Syria) is not extant, is referenced by the mid-thirteenth-century biographer Ibn 'Abd al-Zahir.[13] The earlier historian Ibn Isḥāq (704–c. 767) stated that in the summer of 636, the Byzantine emperor Heraclius (610–641) was camped in Antioch with "assimilated Arabs" (*al-'arab al-musta'riba*) prior to his infamous engagement against the Arabs at the Battle of Yarmūk in August of that year. These were the tribes living in the province of Syria, some independent and some clients, like the Ghassānids.[14] Following his defeat, Heraclius pulled back to Antioch, his headquarters, in September. Arab armies led by Abu 'Ubayda b. Jarrāḥ and Khālid b. al-Walīd under the reign of caliph 'Umar (634–644) surrounded the city on all sides, but mostly concentrated outside the Aleppo Gate and Bridge Gate. The city finally surrendered by treaty in 638.[15] The citizens were given the option to leave the city or stay and pay a tax.[16] Balādhurī writes that the Antiochenes, however, violated the terms, and so the Arab commanders 'Iyāḍ b. Ghanm and Ḥabib b. Maslama and/or 'Amr b. al-'Āṣ, depending on sources, had to reconquer the city and made similar terms. At the request of 'Umar, Abū 'Ubayda established a permanent troop of Muslims in Antioch, who were paid and charged to act as a border patrol, referring to their post as a *ribāṭ*[17]; they were also to receive lands and a stipend *('aṭā')*. Balādhurī relates that lands of Antioch were given as a *qaṭi'a* (land as an estate) from 'Uthmān to some soldiers of Abū 'Ubayda when Mu'āwiya I (b. Abū Sufyān), first Umayyad caliph from 661 to 680, was still governor of Syria. Meanwhile, Ṭabarī says that Abū Hāshim b. 'Utba, Mu'āwiya's maternal uncle made a peace treaty that included Antioch, Cilicia, and Ma'arrāt Miṣrīn.[18]

The Christian sources on the conquest, on the other hand, reflect an expected bias of a bloody conflict. The Byzantine chronicler Theophanes (c. 758–818) further states that 'Umar sent Mu'āwiya as a general and *amīr* and the bishop/historian Agapius of Manbij/Hieropolis, the Miaphysite bishop/historian Gregory Abū al-Faraj or Bar Hebraeus (1226–1286), and the *Chronicle of 1234* add that in 638/9, he took Antioch by siege, plundering the surrounding villages and farms and enslaving people.[19] Meanwhile, the chronicle of the Miaphysite patriarch Michael the Syrian (1126–1199) says that many died and no one escaped and that the armies also went to the Monastery of St. Symeon the Stylite (the Younger) on a festival day and took a large number of men and women. This style of conquering, which included mass enslavement and plundering of land, rarely appears as a common practice by the Islamic armies of the mid-seventh century.

From then onward, Antioch served primarily as a base for expeditions under the caliph 'Umar and his successor 'Uthmān (644–656), who also settled Arab soldiers around the vicinity.[20] During Mu'āwiya I's reign, Balādhurī, as quoted in Ibn 'Abd al-Zahir, gave the same order as 'Umar, that soldiers receive stipends and land and form a permanent garrison. Theophanes states that the caliph ʿAbd al-Malik (685–705) subjugated the city in 686 or 688/9, which he curiously still calls Theoupolis, its sixth-century Byzantine name. This may have been a revolt or a response to a possible Byzantine reconquest in 685; the event is not known from Islamic sources. Theophanes and Michael the Syrian also mention a Byzantine counterattack in the year of a great plague, 694/695, where armies marched to the "valley" of Antioch (the Amuq Plain) and encountered Dīnār b. Dīnār; the result was a massacre of the Greeks, with few escaping. This may be the event Ṭabarī refers to as taking place in 698/699.[21] Another Byzantine counterattack occurred in 698/9 and again around 718/719, with a mention of a southern gate, the Bāb Muslim, that is, the Daphne Gate.[22] Sometime in the first half of the eighth century, Ibn ʿAbd al-Ẓāhir writes that ʿAbbās, the son of the caliph al-Walīd I, burned the city. There is no other reference to this and no explanation as to why, when the city would have been in Islamic hands.[23] The geographer/historian Ibn Shaddād (1217–1285) and Balādhurī both recount a Byzantine attack via the coast sometime after 716/717 (possibly 718/719), with the Byzantines camping around the city and attacking with siege engines. Meanwhile, the Antiochene military played an important role in several campaigns into Byzantine lands. In 705/706, Maslama b. ʿAbd al-Malik, via his commander Maymūn al-Jurjumānī, led 1,000 soldiers into Tyana in Cappadocia. Another campaign of Antiochenes occurred in 716/717 and in 727 under the general Muʿāwiya II (b. Hishām).

Caliph Walīd I b. ʿAbd al-Malik (705–715), meanwhile, gave the territory of Seleucia Pieria on the coast as a *qaṭīʿa* to the troops on the condition that they cultivate it (*ʿammarūha*) and pay a tax of one dinar and one *miand/mudd* (modius or dry liter, about 6.5 kg) of wheat per *jarīb* (the amount from roughly a 40 × 40 m plot of land). Walīd also built its fortress. This is the only mention of an Early Islamic use of this port, which at some point was transferred to the Orontes delta town of Suwaydīya.[24]

Immediately after the Islamic conquest, part of the city's population, likely constituting the majority of the Byzantine elite, left the city, though they had been departing steadily since the sixth and early seventh centuries as part of the urban transformation. Adult citizens who did not evacuate had to pay the same tribute of one dinar (the *jizya* tax) and the same percentage of their agricultural yields as at Seleucia.[25] These terms were used as a model for the surrounding cities. The biographer Yāqūt al-Ḥamawī (1179–1229) states this occurred by the reign of Walīd I. Ibn Shaddād also mentions this during the reign of Walīd, a certain type of land tax (*filṭir*) of a dinar and a modius of grain was levied for each plot of roughly 1,600 m^2 (*jarīb*). A governor was also installed, either Muʿāwiya or Habīb b. Maslama al-Fihrī, appointed by Abū ʿUbayda.[26] Nevertheless, texts indicate that during the short transitional period immediately after the conquest, the city was mostly governed by Antiochene nobles who remained in the city.[27] Of the elite who stayed, most were members of the church.[28] Thus, part of the continuity from the Early Byzantine to Early Islamic periods in the city had much to do with the population that remained, and in particular church leaders, who in some instances became the authority figures for the non-Muslim community in the absence of the Byzantine emperor or his officials. The biographical data on the elites in Antioch is sparse, other than these high religious figures and governors.[29] Elite Greek individuals serving as Roman officials, or of the senatorial or curial class, or major property holders are absent from the sources; church leaders thus appear to have functioned as the major political players.[30]

Administration and local revolts in Antioch

The city's history in the ʿAbbāsid period (749–969 for this region) is also poorly known until the tenth century, although Antioch was by no means a forgotten backwater. This period highlights in particular the Antiochenes' insistence on choosing and approving their own rulers, often local, and rejecting foreign authority. ʿAbbāsid caliphs became more involved in the city and on the frontier, in part to prevent Antioch and its border region from breaking away and becoming autonomous. This process had already begun at the end of the Umayyad period, when anti-ʿAbbāsid sentiment was apparent. During the ʿAbbāsid uprising of the 740s that eventually overthrew the Umayyads in 750, Marwān II, the last Umayyad caliph, firmly ensconced himself in North Syria and North Mesopotamia, making Antioch a refuge. Theophanes writes that it took six years to take him and that Antioch was the last city to fall in Syria, indicating a strong base of support among the population. As so commonly seen, the Antiochenes were not easily subjugated by distant rulers and took agency in their own governance. The governor, ʿAbdallah b. ʿAli, and citizens of the city then rebelled against the new caliph, al-Manṣūr (754–775) in the first year of his caliphate.

It was probably during the caliphate of Hārūn al-Rashīd (786–809) around 787/788, according to Balādhurī, that Antioch became a capital *(qaṣaba)* of the newly apportioned *ʿawāṣim* (literally, "the protectresses"), or rear frontier province not on the front lines whose cities offered a measure of protection and refuge, a category that also included the towns of Qūrus (classical Cyrrhus), Jūma, Bālis (classical Barbalissos), Rusāfa Hishām (Sergiopolis), Tīzīn, and Dulūk (classical Doliche); Manbij (classical Hierapolis) and Raqqa (classical Callinicum) are also said to have served in this role, depending on the sources.[31] The *ʿawāṣim* province was an administrative and political creation designed to break up the unity of the *thughūr* frontier.[32] In reality, there was little differentiation between the *thughūr* and *ʿawāṣim* in this two-tiered system. Ibn Shaddād, a much later source, mentions that the city was governed by the *ʿummāl* (prefects or tax-collectors) in charge of Syria. An interesting story appears in Ibn Shaddād and the even later source Ibn Shiḥna (1402–1485), recounting how Hārūn al-Rashīd wanted to stay in Antioch, as he was fond of the city. But apparently the citizens, as could be expected, were opposed to his settling down, and indeed one elderly Antiochene told the caliph that Antioch would not be become one of his towns. When Hārūn asked him why, he replied, "Because excellent perfume is changed to such an extent that it goes bad and that weapons are rusted there, even if they are made in India." That apparently was sufficient, and Hārūn left.[33]

The role of Constantinople to the ʻAbbāsid caliphate had grown more distant and changed after two attempts to take the city under the Umayyads had failed. Under the ʻAbbāsids, raiding into Byzantine lands had become minimal, ritualized, and symbolic and rarely ventured far. Likewise, there were no serious mounted invasions from the imperial capital into Islamic lands for 200 years. Yet, the caliphs sometimes resorted to indirect pressure through proxy agents, such as rival usurpers and patriarchs. In 821, the caliph al-Ma'mūn (813–833) crowned (or directed the Patriarch Hiob to crown) Thomas the Slav (also known as Thomas of Gaziura), a local and rival to the throne of Constantinople who had good relations with the ʻAbbāsids, in Antioch at the Church of St. Peter, the main church of Antioch in this period. Antioch was thus yet again the stage for an anti-imperial revolt.[34] The city was taken in 877/878 by the Egyptian Aḥmad b. Ṭūlūn. This started as a revolt by Ibn Ṭūlūn against Abū Aḥmad al-Muwaffaq, brother and de facto regent of the ruling caliph al-Mu'tamid (870–892). Ibn Ṭūlūn had come from Egypt to Syria and been appointed governor over its towns, including Antioch, by al-Muwaffaq. The existing governor, the Turk Sīmā al-Ṭawīl, however, naturally resisted. But Ibn Ṭūlūn succeeded in gaining access to the city, aided by a traitor who helped him get through the city wall (a common method of conquering Antioch as seen in the mid-third [see Chapter 3] and mid-sixth centuries [see Chapter 4] and as we will also see in later periods); he thereupon subdued the city via the Aleppo Gate and killed the governor. Holding northern Syria, Ibn Ṭūlūn created a mini-dynasty that continued after his death in 883/4. During the Ṭūlūnid dynasty, several more governors of Antioch – consisting of Ibn Ṭūlūn's sons and grandsons – changed hands in short succession. Under all this administration, Antioch was included under the governance of Aleppo and the *thughūr*. The caliph Muʻtaḍid himself traveled the frontier in November 900 searching for the eunuch Waṣīf, who had fled his master Ibn Abī al-Sāj and asked the caliph for help; he also sought to be promoted to frontier governor. But Muʻtaḍid learned that the rift between the two had been manufactured; in fact the eunuch and master were plotting together to take the region from Baghdad. At this time Muʻtaḍid stayed in Antioch for eight days. The physical presence of caliphs on the frontier and directing activites in and from cities like Antioch is relevant as it belies a certain anxiety or fear of cities on the frontier breaking away from the ʻAbbāsid caliphate and becoming autonomous, as eventually did happen with the Ṭūlūnid and later Ikhshīdid and Ḥamdānid dynasties.

In the tenth century, many provinces on the edges of the ʻAbbāsid Caliphate were already becoming autonomous, as local dynasties emerged and the ʻAbbāsids were unable to control them effectively. Ibn Shaddād recounts from 932 a succession of governors, assassinations, and battles and a rapid changeover of who controlled the region: the eunuch Bisrī; the governor Abū al-ʻAbbās b. Kayghalagh; Muḥammad b. Ṭughj al-Ikhshīd, founder of the Egyptian Ikhshīdid dynasty of governors, followed by his commander the eunuch Kafur; and the ʻAbbāsid senior official Abū Bakr Muḥammad b. Rā'iq. Sometimes the local rulers opposed the caliph, as did Nāṣir al-Dawla b. Ḥamdān of the Ḥamdānid dynasty of governors and *amīrs* against the caliph al-Muttaqī (940–944). The Ḥamdānids fought – with the caliph playing a nominal role on the side of the Ikhshīdids – until 944, when Antioch, Aleppo, and Ḥimṣ (classical Emesa) were ceded to them.

Administratively, Antioch was no longer a capital but under the jurisdiction of one city, then another (Figure 5.2). In the Umayyad period, it was initially part of the *jund* or military province of Ḥims (Emesa). The caliph Yazīd b. Mu'āwiya (680–683) placed Antioch along with Aleppo and Manbij within the *jund* of Qinnasrīn (classical Chalcis); afterward it fell under the administration of Aleppo. Under Hārūn al-Rashīd's apportionment of the *'awāṣim* from the Byzantine-facing *thughūr*, the city shared a regional role of authority, but alternatively with Raqqa and Manbij. Yet throughout the Early Islamic period, unlike Aleppo, Raqqa, and Manbij, Antioch did not have a mint.[35]

Why was Antioch fought over so hard if it was not the chief town of its province or given any elevated administrative status? As we know, Antioch was strategically and economically important because it was the first major urban center reached by travelers after crossing the Amanus Mountains through the Belen Pass from Anatolia and Cilicia into northern Syria, from where roads then led east to Aleppo or south toward Damascus. The scale of trade coming in and going out of the city from the Mediterranean via the Orontes is difficult to assess during the Umayyad period, though it was probably somewhat less than in earlier periods, owing to the strong Byzantine naval presence and the silting up of the river, which thus became unnavigable.[36] The site of Seleucia was no more replaced, by al-Mina/al-Suwaydīyya. We know that the province of Qinnasrīn was heavily involved in vine cultivation, producing a yearly revenue of 420,000 dinars and 1,000 camel loads (*biml*) of raisins (*zabīb*).[37] A tax officer (*ṣahib al-dār*) was also stationed in Antioch and responsible for controlling trade and revenue.[38] As both a trading and a manufacturing center, the city was a terminus of the Silk Road as well as a center of production for luxury textiles – specifically silk weaving, Antioch giving its own name to a certain cover or carpet – and for cotton paper.[39] By the tenth century, citrus (*shajar al-nāranj* and *utruj al-mudawwar*) had been introduced from India and cultivated around the city.[40]

Yet, Antioch's historical reputation and religious power also continued to elevate the city as a tantalizing prize. Antioch appears in the Qur'ān twice, in *sūra* 18:77 (The Cave) and *sūra* 36:13 (Ya-Sin), identified with an unnamed settlement by a consensus of medieval Islamic scholars. *Sūra* 18:77 relates the journey of Moses and al-Khiḍr, his guide, to a *qarya* (village) whose people refused to show them hospitality. Within the town was a wall, perhaps Antioch's legendary wall that was about to collapse, and so Moses and al-Khiḍr repaired it. The accounts of Istakhrī (d. c. 957) and Ibn Ḥawqal (d. c. 978) also mention the Rock (*sakhra*) of Moses in Antioch where he met al-Khiḍr. *Sūra* 36:13 in turn tells the parable of a *qarya* whose citizens at first beat and imprisoned two apostles and then a third, but then a citizen of the town implored its idolatrous people to believe the apostles' message of one God. The citizen was subsequently stoned and became a martyr. Many medieval scholars of *tafsir*, or exegesis of the Qur'an, and historians, such as al-Ṭabarī,

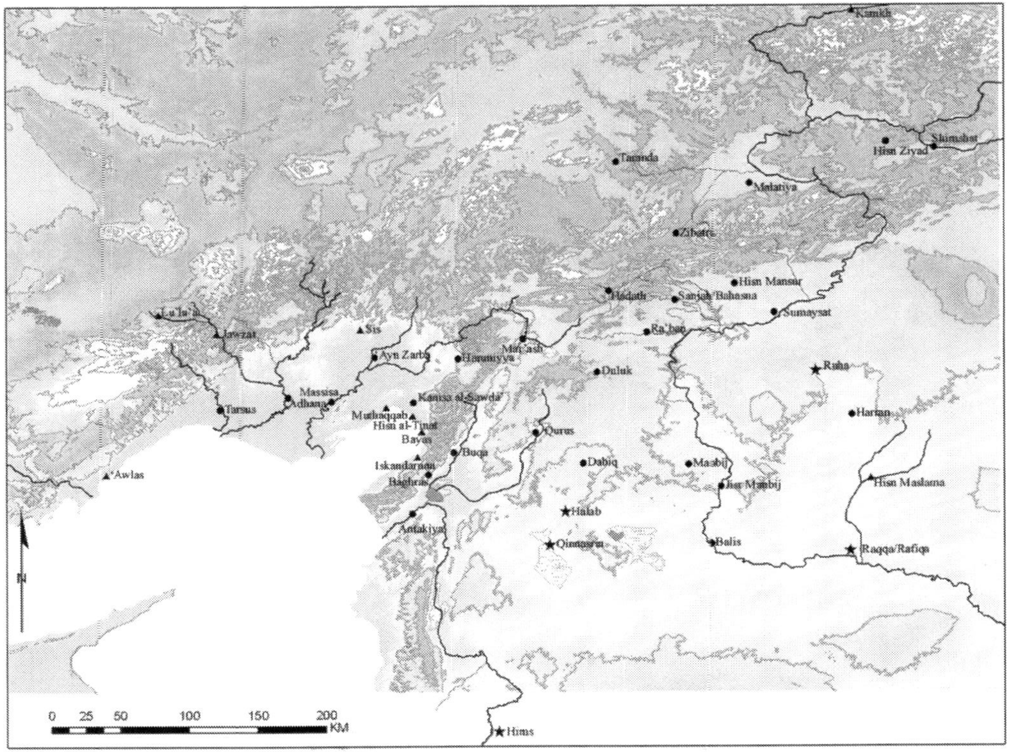

FIGURE 5.2 Map of the *thughūr*, showing Antioch, Aleppo, Raqqa, and Manbij

Source: Created by A. Asa Eger

believed that the town mentioned was Antioch, and that the apostles were Paul and John for the first two, and Simon Peter, Barnabas, or Thomas for the third, while the believer was Habīb al-Najjār, or Habīb the Carpenter, whose mosque and tomb have been the city's primary pilgrimage destination from the Early Islamic period to this day.[41] Interestingly, the verse says that there came running, "From the farthest part/Of the City, a man…" suggesting that he was not an elite or noble living in the city center but rather a craftsman and builder (drawing a parallel with Jesus Christ) who, like others of this profession, lived on the city's edges.[42] The instances may refer to Antioch as a main early center for the teachings of Peter and Paul and the establishment of the first community of Christians. Interestingly, next to Habīb's tomb is that of a figure known as Sham'ūn al-Ṣafā, or Simon the Pure, whom some scholars have identified with St. Peter.[43]

In a *ḥadīth* recorded by Ibn Shaddād, the Prophet Muḥammad saw Antioch on his *mir'āj* or Night Journey, when the archangel Gabriel took him to Heaven to see the people (and places) of the Old and New Testaments:

> We have heard from the messenger of God – May God Bless and Greet him – who said the following: One night I was brought to heaven where I saw a white dome; I had never before seen anything more beautiful. Around it were a number of [other] white domes. I said: What are these domes, Gabriel? He responded to me, these are the *thughūr* of your community. I then said, "What is this white dome that I have never seen anything more beautiful?" He said, that is Antioch and it is the mother of the *thughūr*. Its preeminence above the others is like the preeminence of paradise over other gardens; those that live there are like those who stay at the Ka'ba [*al-bayt al-ma 'ūr*]. All the good people of your community gather there and it is the prison of a scholar of your community. It is a fortress and *ribāṭ*. One day of devotion in this city is worth a year. To those of your community who die there, God promises on Resurrection Day like a recompense of the warriors of the *ribāṭ*s (*murābaṭūn*).[44]

Here, Antioch was the chief city of the frontier, mother of the *thughūr*, and so holy that its citizens were likened to those of Mecca. Thus, the city was an important town not simply in status but in terms of its past and preeminence over all others. In another *ḥadīth* appearing in the fourteenth-century history of Ibn Kathīr, Antioch is the first stop at the end of days in the fight between good and evil:

> The Messenger of God, may God bless him and grant him peace, said: "When the sun rose from the west, *Iblīs* fell down in prostration. He cried out and announced: "Divine one, let me go worship whomever I wish!" He said, "Hell's Angels Assembled to him. They said: 'O, master what is this begging?'" So he said, "Rather, I asked my Lord [Allāh] to watch me *till the time well-known*, but this is the time well-known!" He said: "Then, the Beast of the Earth [*dāba al-ārḍ*] came out of a crack in al-Ṣafā." He said, "The first

step it takes will be to Anṭākiya. [The beast] will come to Īblīs, and then smack him."[45]

Antioch's legacy was also not limited to early texts such as the Qur'ān and *ḥadīth*. The geographer Ibn al-Faqīh al-Hamadhānī (around 903), who composed a compelling list of the top sites to see while traveling the world, included Antioch for its walls. He also mentioned St. Peter's Church as the best building done in marble.[46] Echoing Hamadhānī, the tenth-century explorer/geographer Ibn Rusta repeated this saying, although he disagreed: according to him, Muḥammad b. Mūsī al-Manjjam reported that the Byzantines (*al-rūm*) said that of those built of stone none was finer than the church of al-Ruhā (classical Edessa), and of those built of wood, none was finer than the church of Manbij, and of those built of marble, none was finer than the Qusiyān (Church of St. Peter) of Antioch.[47] Mas'ūdī (896–956), a famous geographer who visited the city toward the end of his life, called Antioch the Mother of the Cities (*umm al-mudun*), as in the *ḥadīth* cited earlier, or City of God (*Madināt Allāh*), from the Byzantine sixth-century renaming of the city to Theoupolis.[48] He also described the city wall as a wonder of the world and, interestingly, remarked on its strong Christian community.

In the poem that opens this chapter, the poet Abū 'Amr al-Qāsim b. Abī Dā'ūd al-Ṭarṣūṣī described the city as a stopping point (*manazil*) on his way from Ṭarsūs in 920–921. He noted its fortified wall, its landscape of ruins and venerable past, its orchards – likened to Paradise – and its association with the Islamic/Christian saint Habīb al-Najjār, the hero of the parable of the town. These Islamic references to the city are not quite like the panegyric of Libanius's *Oration in Praise of Antioch* or the comprehensive history of John Malalas. Yet the texts show that the city was desired as it was strongly connected to its past and that the legacy of this former megalopolis had not been forgotten. On the ground, the older city had not been eradicated or left to fade but was incorporated and transformed into Islamic Antioch, remaining visible both as symbol and reality, much as a palimpsest.

Urban landscape

The archaeological evidence points to general continuity and some reorganizing of space within the city, as well as in social and economic aspects of life. In truth, the Princeton excavators throughout the city paid little attention to the latest phases of occupation, excavating them in arbitrary levels and keeping only the museum-worthy glazed ceramics, coins, and inscriptions. Scholars of the time privileged the Greco-Roman and early Christian world, and excavations of a high-profile site such as Antioch were seen as a way to learn more about this foundation of Western civilization and bring its objects of known provenance to Western museums for study and display. Fortunately, there remain many ceramics, glass finds, and coins from the Byzantine and Islamic medieval periods awaiting analysis in storage at the Princeton University Art Museum and at Princeton's Firestone Library, as well as a few objects at Cornell University, Johns Hopkins University Museum, and the

Fogg Museum in Harvard. Work has already begun on reevaluating the material culture in combination with archives of notes, photographs, and plans of the 1930s excavation, focusing on many of its areas. An examination of Princeton's published excavation volumes (relying on their dating), preliminary reanalysis of the Princeton finds with a deeper focus on sector 17-O (an excavation off the main colonnaded street and in the vicinity of the presumed forum of Valens and heart of the Byzantine city), and limited survey work undertaken in the city make it possible to detect three overlapping zones of occupation and use in the Islamic period. Along the *cardo*, these zones transition from residential to commercial/industrial (and funerary) to agricultural (and funerary), as presented here, with several caveats. These observations depict the city in broad brushstrokes, covering four

TABLE 5.1 Summary of Antioch Excavations

Sector (finds)	*Year*	*Published volume*	*Alternate name*
11-L/M (Hippodrome B/ Stadium, Tower sondage)	1932	I	
9/10-L (Bath A, painted tomb)	1932, 1933	I, II	
House A	1932	I	
10/11-L/M (Bath C, quarry/lime kiln)	1932	I	
7/8-O/N (Hippodrome A/ Circus, cemetery)	1932, 1933, 1934	I, II	
21-K (street, skewed bldg)	1932	I, V	Main Street Dig I
22-K	1934	II, V	Mosque of Habib al-Najjar
21/22-J	1932	V	
Church at Daphne	1932	I	
13-R (Bath F, workshops)	1934, 1935, 1936, 1938, 1939	II, III	Also 13-P
19-M (street, domestic residences)	1932, 1934	II, V	Main Street Dig III Soap Factory
17-N	1934, 1937	II, V	Main Street Dig VI
18-O/P (theater, workshops)	1935, 1936	II	
12/13-F/G (Church of Kaoussié)	1935, 1936	II	
16-O (street, workshops, necropolis)	1936, 1937?, 1938, 1939	II, III, V	Main Street Digs IV, VII, VIII
16-P (walls, cemetery, church)	1936, 1937, 1939	II, III, V	Main Street Dig V
17-O (edge of Forum of Valens, street, market, nymphaeum, workshops)	1937, 1939	III	Also 17-P
DH-27-O (Daphne)	1937, 1938	III	
Narlıca	1938		

centuries; because the excavations and ceramics have been published separately and not linked, the chronology must remain general until further study of the Princeton materials is completed (see Table 5.1).

As shown primarily from excavations along the main colonnaded street, new construction took place on the former *cardo*. In almost every area along the street

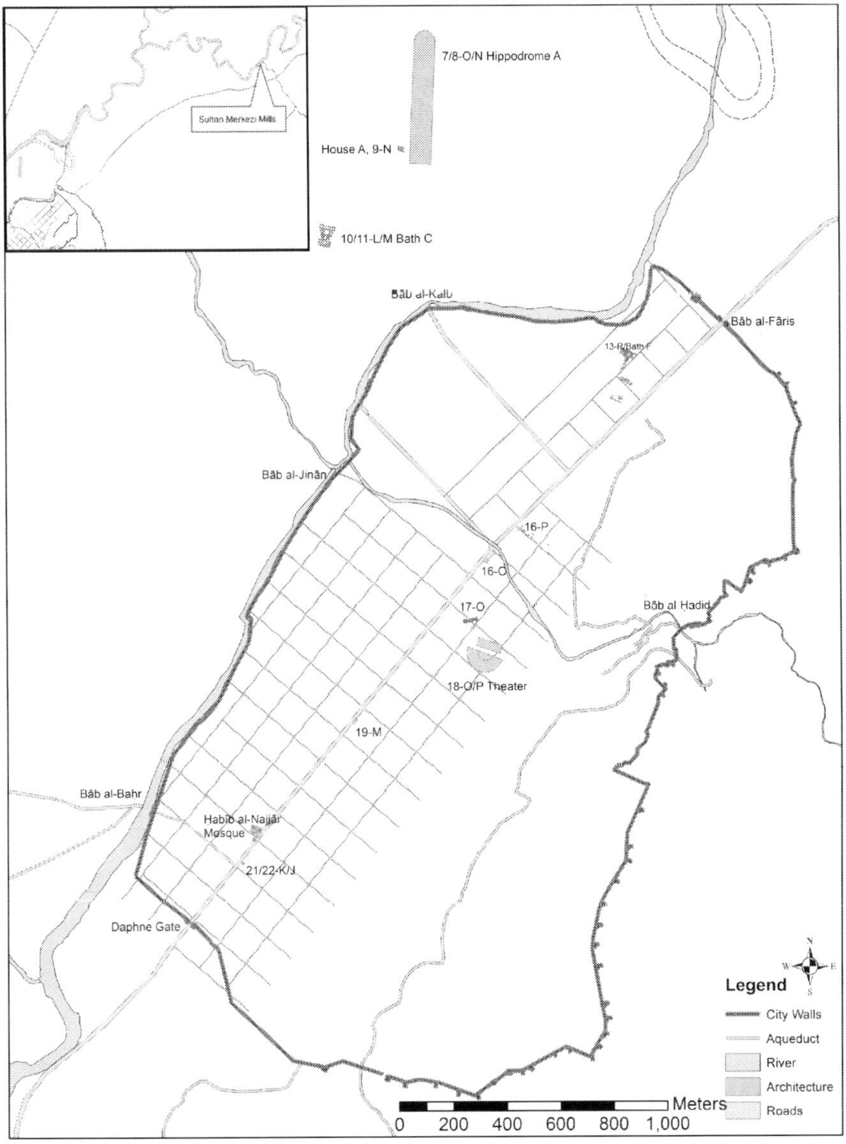

FIGURE 5.3 Plan of Early Islamic Antioch

Source: Created by Steve Batiuk

there were post-Byzantine (whether post-Justinianic or late seventh-century) levels for Early Islamic occupation, often characterized by commercial and industrial use as the street was transformed and encroached upon (see Figure 5.3). The street was again a focus of activity during the mid-seventh-century transition to Islam; analysis of the coins minted between 565 and 668 shows that overall, activity decreased and condensed into areas along the *cardo*.[49] The street was not wholly abandoned; rather, as the excavators noted, in places it shifted west (as in sectors 19-M and 16-P), and it was encroached upon by smaller buildings made of reused materials and constructed after the Islamic conquests, often built directly onto the Justinianic pavement.[50] Kennedy and Liebeschuetz, however, challenged this claim, using contemporary evidence from Jarash, Pella, and Apamaea to argue that the encroachment of buildings onto the colonnaded street had already taken place before the Islamic conquests.[51] The Megalopsychia Hunt Mosaic discussed in Chapter 3 and accounts by Libanius also suggest there were temporary structures built into the street already by the fourth and fifth centuries. Meanwhile, Jodi Magness, reassessing the evidence, contends that the discovery beneath the paved street of post-Justinianic coins of the first half of the seventh century suggests a mid-to-late seventh-century date for the street's reconstruction that argues against "decline," though not necessarily against contraction.[52] Further, the redating of the street would challenge assumptions that the last major reconstruction effort in Antioch took place under Justinian.

While Magness's conclusion is possible, the coin evidence and stratigraphic contexts are problematic and need to be used cautiously. They must also be studied comprehensively before we can determine the date of the street. Colonnaded streets and orthogonal planning are known from the Umayyad period, and parallels occur at other preexisting cities such as Arsūf, Baysān, Palmyra, and Ḥimṣ, as well as new foundations such as 'Anjar.[53]

Meanwhile, the city wall of Antioch probably underwent numerous repairs during the Early Islamic period, though it was apparently never reduced and rebuilt to enclose the contracted city. A section of the wall and gate may have been exposed in a sounding in sector 21/22-H just near the Bridge Gate. This short excavation, reported on May 14, 1937, with only eight workers and a foreman, exposed, at 1.3 m under the modern road, a basalt pavement matching the paved colonnaded street. The pavement was bordered by a substantial thick wall, over 2 m, of ashlar blocks that delimited the city road towards the bridge. An even thicker wall, the city wall, intersected it from the north, and the excavators hypothesized that the bridge may have been flanked by two towers, although no evidence of this was given.[54]

Early tenth-century sources offer insight into the Byzantine and Early Islamic continuity of the physical and religious landscape. Between 744/45 and 750, just prior to the 'Abbāsid takeover, Marwān II undertook work to preserve the city walls. Indeed, Antioch's walls were what the city was best known for after the Roman period. The geographer Mas'ūdī is the best source for information on Antioch during this last century of Ṭūlūnid/'Abbāsid/Ḥamdānid rule between

877 and 896. In particular, he noted the city wall was 12 miles around, with 136 habitable towers and 24,000 embrasures, and he described many of its buildings and, interestingly, its strong Christian community.

The churches in early Islamic Antioch

Only five churches are mentioned during this time, indicating that the overall number had declined from the Early Byzantine period. According to Michael the Syrian, Hārūn al-Rashīd requested that old churches be destroyed. The church of St. Babylas/Kaouissié on the west bank, Constantine's Great Church with its gold cupola on the Island, and the Church of St. Michael the Archangel in Daphne are no longer mentioned. This suggests that the Early Islamic city did not include these areas.

The most important was the Church of St. Peter, often referred to during this period as the Cassianus Church, or sometimes as the cathedral or "large church" (*'etta d-Q'SYN'* or *'etta rabbta*). It is not the cave church called St. Peter today. Cassianus is not a known saint but may refer to an important governor. The Nestorian Christian physician Ibn Buṭlān (fl. 1050s) connected Peter and Cassianus, writing that Peter resurrected a young man after seven days who was the son of Cassianus, a prince of Antioch. He also states that the house was transformed into a church, which apparently held the relic of the right hand (and arm?) of John the Baptist, which was kept in the entrance hall. The relic was later moved by the patriarch Hiob during the night and smuggled to Chalcedon across the Bosphorus from Constantinople, and then subsequently to the palace of Constantine VII in Constantinople in January 956.[55] Mas'ūdī, meanwhile, mentions that St. Peter's was the main patriarchal church in the center of the city and was built in 459. His source is unknown, as is the actual foundation of St. Peter's or the Cassianus Church; the earliest mention from homilies is 513.[56]

The Church of the Theotokos, built under Justinian in 527, was described by Mas'ūdī and later Ibn al-Shiḥna as a round building – one of the wonders of the world in its height, construction, and luxury – that survived, even though in the early eighth century the Umayyad caliph Walīd I removed its marble columns and alabaster or granite by sea for the building of the Great Mosque of Damascus.[57] Still, much of the original church remained.

Michael the Syrian also mentions the Cassianus and Theotokos churches, which functioned as the main patriarchal centers of worship for the Syriac Orthodox (Miaphysite) and Greek Orthodox (Chalcedonian or Melkite Dyothilite) congregations, respectively, following a schism in the Melkite church in the year 839 (or 844/45).[58]

Two other churches were probably built after the early seventh century, since they are not mentioned earlier: St. Paul or Dayr al-Barāghith (Monastery of the Fleas) and St. Barbārā. The Church of St. Paul was built near the Aleppo Gate in the area of the grotto of St. Paul, known in the fourth century to be on the slopes of Mt. Staurin, to honor where the apostle lived and taught. Mas'ūdī and the later Abū al-Makārim note that it was built on the walls of the city above the Aleppo

Gate.[59] Its location is also given in travelers' accounts during the Ottoman period. Pietro della Valle was shown the church in 1625 by locals, though all he was able to see were some poorly preserved ruins. Richard Pococke (1704–1765) mentioned the Church of Sts. Peter and Paul, a quarter way up the eastern hill at the north (near the Aleppo Gate), where little remained but some marble and mosaic. Charles Perry (1698–1780) wrote that St. Paul's Church, which he and many others thought was Constantine's church and also the place where the Crusaders found the Holy Lance, was inaccessible and had only one part of a wall standing. Abraham Parsons (d. 1785) came in through the Aleppo Gate (he states the East Gate) and noted the remains of St. Paul's Church on the left-hand side, whose walls were still standing and strong, though it had no roof or door, nor could anyone around remember a time when it did. Tinco Martinus Lycklama à Nijeholt, a nineteenth-century Dutch orientalist, further commented that St. Paul's Church and monastery was a ruined church near the Aleppo Gate, with some columns consecrated by St. Pelagius. Meanwhile, the Church of St. Barbara is mentioned only by Mas'ūdī and later cited in Ibn al-Shiḥna's work. Originally a virgin of Heliopolis in Syria (Ba'alabakk/Baalbek), she was condemned to death for being a Christian in 255, her own pagan father carrying out the execution (though her historicity has been doubted).

Finally, an anonymous medieval (possibly Middle Byzantine) Arabic description of Antioch of unknown origin and chronology tells about the Church of St. Ashmunit (al-Ashmūnīt), a fourth-century Byzantine church repurposed from a synagogue; this shows the appropriation of an Old Testament Jewish figure as a saint-martyr in the Orthodox Christian tradition within Antioch. Ashmunit was a Jewish woman who, along with her seven children, was supposedly murdered by the Seleucid ruler Antiochus IV during the Maccabean Revolt (167–160 BCE; 2 Maccabees 8) for refusing to eat pork.[60] She subsequently became the center of a local popular cult of the Maccabean Martyrs. The church was located outside the city walls and built over the tombs of the mother and her children in a hidden cave. According to the anonymous source, which interestingly follows Agapius of Manbij (d. 942) almost word for word, it was on the summit of the mountain on the western (southern) side and was also built over the tomb of Eleazar (likely the elderly priest martyred with her). Agapius of Manbij also mentions that the church honored Ashmunit (called Chemouni) and her sons, even though Bar-Hebraeus (1226–1286) states that their bodies were sent to Jerusalem. In the fifteenth century, Ibn al-Shiḥna, referencing Mas'ūdī, said that church also held a dignified holy Christian festival. This church is likely the same as the Church of the Maccabean Martyrs in the *Kerateion* district, though within the city walls, though unlikely to be the Basilica of St. Julian (outside the walls), burned in the late sixth century.[61]

The Christian community of Early Islamic Antioch

The presence of five churches, including two patriarchal churches, attests to the continuity and substantial community of Christians in Antioch during the Early

Islamic period. The texts tell us that the status of the church and its patriarchs was alternately stable and precarious, the latter emphasized more strongly in surviving Greek, Syriac, and Christian Arabic (Melkite) texts. In many instances, the question of whether patriarchs were allowed to reside in Antioch was a matter of which patriarchs the caliphs had close relationships with and wished to appoint. Which Christian doctrine embraced by the patriarchs also played a significant role, as caliphs sometimes deliberately played on the schisms within Christian communities often to advance a patriarch they approved of and could control. The most famous example is the Ḥamdānid *amīr* Sayf al-Dawla and the patriarch Christopher in the tenth century (see Chapter 6), although examples in the seventh and eighth centuries also occurred.

The Miaphysite patriarchs were not allowed to reside in the city, though in the ʿAbbāsid period they visited at times, as seen with George (758–789/90) and Dionysius I of Tel Mahre (818–845). One exception, in 721, was the patriarch Elias (709–723), who, during the reign of caliph Yazīd II (720–724), made a grand entry into Antioch with an entourage of monks and clerics and consecrated a church newly built "by his cares" (i.e., at his own expense).[62] The church was likely that of either St. Paul or St. Barbara, since these were the only newly built churches known. The ceremony was to honor the arrival of a patriarch in Antioch following nearly two centuries after the last Miaphysite patriarch, Severus of Antioch, had fled town in 518.

From the conquest until 742/3, no Melkite Greek Orthodox patriarch of Antioch had been allowed to reside in the city, either, living instead in major cities like Constantinople and Edessa. Theophanes writes that the Holy Church of Antioch was a "widow" for 40 years. Nonetheless, a continuous line of patriarchs still inhabited the position. Finally in 742/3, the caliph Hishām b. ʿAbd al-Malik (724–743) allowed Melkite patriarchs to reside once more in the city when he reinstated his "uncultured but pious" friend, a Syrian monk, who became the patriarch Stephen. Illustrating how Islamic rulers could influence Antioch's religious community, Hishām urged the Antiochenes to accept Stephen if they wanted an actual resident patriarch of Antioch (perhaps understanding their penchant for resisting outside authority figures).[63]

Stephen's tenure was, however, short-lived, and he was soon followed by Patriarch Theophylact (744–750), who enjoyed a close relationship with the caliph Marwān II.[64] Theophylact was a priest from Edessa, appreciated by the Eastern Church, whom Marwān upheld and demanded be honored even by the Arab community, recognizing his spiritual countenance and wisdom. He was followed in turn by Theodore I (750–773), who lasted nearly a quarter century in the position.

Sometimes rival Islamic rulers positioned their appointed patriarchs against each other. Eustathius (839–861/69) became the new patriarch of Antioch with the support of the town's governor (*ʿamla*). But a rival patriarch, Nicholas (839–867) in Aleppo, came to Antioch and challenged Eustathius's position. The latter blocked his entry into St. Peter's Church, yet Nicholas eventually got the governor of Syria to intercede and allow him access, and in the end he was installed. Eustathius, however, was not to be deterred, and he and his followers ensconced themselves in the Church of the Theotokos. From these two churches, both Eustathius and Nicolas tried to win over the Antiochene Arab community by giving them money and gifts from the churches' treasuries.

The Melkite community of Antioch was an important one for northern Syria, and gradually it became more assimilated into Islamic life in the city, adopting the Arabic language.[65] By the beginning of the ninth century, patriarch Hiob or Job (c. 799–c. 838/9) had penned the first Christian homily in Arabic. He and others were among the earliest involved in a translation movement centered around Antioch and the monasteries of the Orontes delta and moving across Greek, Syriac, and Arabic languages. This movement lasted until the thirteenth century. In one example, a certain Maḥfūẓ b. (U)sṭāt copied John Climacus' *Book of the Ladder*, an ascetic treatise written around 600 CE in Greek, from the earlier Arabic translation by Abba Abrami, disciple of Abba Serapion, who collated it with a Syriac translation, and used the Syriac translation to fill in a missing part from the Arabic translation. This all occurred at the Monastery of Our Lady Mary (*Mart Maryam*) at Dafnūnā (Daphne) in 931.[66] Mas'ūdī mentions that the Christian community was able to celebrate holidays and carry out processions through the city and indicates that it held a large, splendid festival procession on January 1 (*kalends*) each year.

Besides dedicating churches, patriarchs also worked to improve social institutions within the city for Christians. Perhaps the most famous of the city's patriarchs in the Early Islamic period, Christopher (960–967), created and funded a school program with food for 12 rich and 150 poor children (including orphans).[67] He also paid the *jizya* tax for the poor, then lobbied the *amīr* Sayf al-Dawla, who was also a friend and patron and responsible for appointing Christopher to his position, for a tax break of 10,000 dirhams per year. Ībrāhīm b. Yūḥannā al-Abrotosbatiar, a native of Antioch from a prominent family, may have been a student in the school program; his literacy was evident later when he wrote Christopher's *Life* in both Greek and Arabic.

In one instance in 913, the 'Abbāsid *wazīr* 'Alī b. 'Isa of the caliph Muqtadir, upon learning that Muslim prisoners of war in Constantinople were being mistreated, asked Elias I, patriarch of Antioch (906/907–934), to mediate, knowing that even Byzantine emperors were subject to the church and proclamations of anathema. Elias, along with his successor, the patriarch of Antioch Theodosius II (936–943), had worked in Baghdad as a secretary (*kātib*) in the caliphal court. The event shows how caliphs used the patriarchs as ambassadors and, at the same time, exploited them as subjects; if their diplomatic attempts failed, they would be held responsible for the lives of the Muslim prisoners. In this way, the caliph in Baghdad kept the Orthodox community of Antioch and other areas in the empire in check.[68]

Caliphs and governors sometimes had even closer relationships with patriarchs than merely appointing them, as well as with other church members. In 838, al-Mu'taṣim (833–842) took the patriarch Hiob with him on his raid of Amorion in far-off central Anatolia.[69] Church members also functioned as physicians for the caliph, for better or worse. Theophanes wrote that in 764/5, ʿIsa b. Mūsa, nephew of both caliphs al-Saffāḥ and al-Manṣūr and the heir apparent, was suffering from headaches and dizziness. Al-Manṣūr sent his own physician, Moses, a deacon of the church in Antioch, to tend to him and give him a sneezing potion. Instead, Moses gave him a numbing drug, causing ʿIsa to slip into unconsciousness. The oath of allegiance was then given to al-Manṣūr's son, who became the caliph al-Mahdi. In the following reign, the patriarch Theodoretus (781–812), responsible for leading a synod to pass an anti-iconoclastic decree, was arrested and deported to Baghdad by Hārūn al-Rashīd. He was later allowed to return after miraculously healing Hārūn's son, and he and his religious community were given tax abatements.[70]

The relationships between caliphs and patriarchs were not always warm. In 756/7, Patriarch Theodore, suspected of supplying information to the Byzantines in Constantinople, was banished to the southern Levant.[71] In 787, Melkite patriarchs from Antioch were not permitted to attend the Seventh Ecumenical Council held in Nicaea. During periods of intolerance toward Melkite Orthodoxy, it seems that the local Miaphysite community was more stable, as indicated by patriarch Elias's consecration of his newly built church in 721. This mostly stable and congenial era of the Christian community in Antioch, however, ended at the end of the Early Islamic period, when the ʿAbbāsid caliphs were no longer able to control the region, and instead Antioch was ruled alternatively by upstart dynasties (like the Ḥamdānids) and local nobles.

The Islamic community

Oddly, less is known about the Islamic community of Antioch during the Early Islamic period. In a departure from his typical descriptions of Islamic cities, Masʿudi neither identifies nor describes the city's Friday mosque, typically in a city's heart, but mentions only its adjacent crypt (al-Dīmās), which lay to its right, built with huge blocks of stone and pierced with windows, possibly dating to the first Persian conquest in 540 (and thought to be a fire temple).[72] The Ulu Camii mosque, the city's main congregational mosque since likely the Saljūq period until today, has no crypt. The Habīb al-Najjār mosque, however, just to its east, does have a crypt (Figure 5.4). The mosque, according to Ottoman *waqf* documents and current Turkish literature and signs, dates to 638 and was built by Abu ʿUbayda, but while this is possible, it remains speculative. The Habīb al-Najjār mosque, meanwhile, is also believed by local Christian tradition to have originally been the Church of John the Baptist. Today, two sarcophagi in a side chamber allegedly house the remains of the Prophet Jonah and John the Baptist. To its left, stairs lead down to the crypt beneath the mosque, which contains a small room with sarcophagi assigned to Habīb al-Najjār and Shamʿūn al-Ṣafā (the Pure). Below this room is another with sarcophagi assigned to the same two individuals. Christensen-Ernst speculates on the name Shamʿūn as perhaps coming from Shim'on or Sam'an, a version of Symeon (which could refer to the younger or elder stylite saint), or

FIGURE 5.4 The Habib Neccar Mosque

Source: Photograph by Canan Karataş, editing by Erik Eger

perhaps an Ismāʿīlī or Nuṣayrī, or possibly even referring to St. (Simon) Peter, but nevertheless a non-Muslim name. Masʿūdī states that also next to the mosque (possibly the main mosque) was a temple built by the Saklābiyūs and the *sūq* of the armorers and lance makers. Sabaeans worshipped at this temple, which may also be identified with the Greek temple dedicated to Zeus Olympius at Epiphaneia but dismantled by Constantine and later, in the Early Islamic period, converted

FIGURE 5.5 21-K, workmen shoring timbers in position, looking north

Source: Courtesy of the Antioch Expedition Archives, Department of Art and Archaeology, Princeton University; Princeton

into a watchtower.[73] Soundings by the Princeton team in sectors 21-K, 22-K, and 21/22-J (Main Street Dig I) along the Mosque of Habīb al-Najjar have revealed at least four medieval levels (Figure 5.5). The lowest of the medieval phases – Level VIII, presumably the Early Islamic layer – rested upon a sixth-century Justinianic or earlier Byzantine public fountain or plaza pavement.[74] Lycklama speculated, likely erroneously, that the Great Mosque (Uu Camii) was formerly the cathedral of St. John and gave an idea of how churches may have looked, with a double range of windows. He noted that in front of the mosque was a large courtyard with ancient remains. Jørgen Christensen-Ernst has noted that a building north of the present-day main mosque, the Ulu Camii, has masonry similar to that in Mas'ūdī's description.[75] In any event, much more work remains to be done on the Early Islamic congregational mosque and others in the city.

Despite the ambiguities surrounding the main mosque during the Early Islamic period, we can assume that Arab settlement within the city would have increased following the Islamic conquest. Arabs were no strangers to the city or region; nomadic and seminomadic pastoral tribes had inhabited the plains and steppe hills of northern Syria well before the Islamic conquests. It is likely that members of these tribes were found among both the Islamic armies and the first settlers of the city. The thirteenth-century biographer Ibn al-'Adīm states that members of the Banū 'Amr b. Fahm and Banū 'Abdallah b. Fahm b. Tanukh settled in the city.[76]

To populate the frontier and destabilize its mainly Christian and formerly Byzantine populations, other nonindigenous minority ethnic groups were also settled in the city. Balādhurī mentions that Mu'āwīya I resettled the Zuṭṭ and Sayābija marsh dwellers hailing from southern Iraq (Baṣra) and around the Persian Gulf (such as al-Baḥrayn) to Antioch and other coastal towns in 669/70.[77] Walīd I did the same during his reign.[78] It is likely that these groups favored the marshy plain of Antioch, where a familiar ecosystem allowed them to live much as they had before their move. But some may have become city dwellers, as evidenced by Balādhurī's mention of a statement by the scholar Abū Ḥafṣ that there was a quarter in the city known as Zuṭṭ.[79] During the 'Abbāsid rise to power in 747–750, the last Umayyad caliph, Marwān II, entrenched himself on the frontier and gathered support not only from surrounding tribes of northern Syria and the Jazira but also from an alliance with Muslim Slavs (Saqāliba) reportedly garrisoned at Antioch by 'Abd al-Malik in 693. Bar-Hebraeus and Michael the Syrian add that there were 7,000 and given women and provisions.[80] These Slavs were deserters from the 692 Battle of Sebastopolis (possibly modern Elaioussa-Sebaste), fought between Justinian II and Muḥammad b. Marwān, the *amīr* of Mesopotamia. Many Slavs deserted the Byzantine armies and defected to the Islamic side, and settled in Antioch and Cyrrhus following the Umayyad victory. The Slavic community as citizens of the city then supported the Umayyads against the rise of the 'Abbāsids. Meanwhile, the Jarājima or Mardaites were a mixed band of insurgents, mostly Christian, living near Antioch in the Amanus Mountains who sometimes were allied with the Byzantines. The Islamic rulers of Antioch employed them as spies and frontier troops, relieving them from paying taxes and allowing them to keep their booty in order to secure their loyalty.

Balādhurī states that Mu'āwīya I, transported Persians, including *asāwira* (cavalry), into Antioch from Ba'alabakk, Ḥimṣ, Baṣra (and Misrān) and Kūfā in 669/70.[81] It is likely that a small community of Persians were already in the city from the time of the first (540) and second (613) Persian conquests, suggested also by the allusion to fire temples, or several temples of Persian construction, that were oriented toward the sun and constellations. Persian settlement increased in the 'Abbāsid period, with the deployment of many eastern Persian Khurāsānī soldiers on the frontier who were sent to Antioch and other frontier towns. Five thousand more were settled in 964, forming a quarter of the city.[82] By the mid-tenth century, the city was thought to have a Persian majority.[83] Nuṣayrī Muslims, or Alawites, a group of Imamī Shi'ā (who believed in the Twelve Imams, also known as Twelvers) started by Ibn Nuṣayr in the mid-ninth century, also made their way to Antioch.

A small scholarly community was also present, and Balādhurī, himself a Persian (though thoroughly Arabized) and one of the most important historians of the Early Islamic period, lived and studied there. He was a companion of the caliph al-Mutawakkil (847–861) and tutor of the caliph al-Mu'tazz (866–869).[84] Meanwhile, Abu Bakr al-Ṣanawbarī (d. 945) was a poet from Antioch, and in 948 or 949 the poet al-Mutannabī worked for Abū al-Ashā'ir, Sayf al-Dawla's cousin and governor of Antioch, and won the attention and favor of Sayf al-Dawla himself with his odes, such as those commemorating Sayf's siege and triumphal entry into Antioch. Yāqūt al-Ḥamawī lists a large group of close-knit scholars and Qur'ān reciters (*ḥāfiẓ*) who lived in Antioch, studying from each another and transmitting one another's works in a genealogy of scholarship in the ninth and tenth centuries.[85] Despite all the military activity, the 940s were intellectually important for Antioch, with al-Mas'ūdī also visiting the city in 943, though his impressions may not have been entirely favorable, citing, among other things, parasites in the city's water supply, the colic and flatulence of the residents, and bedbugs. Despite the lack of creature comforts expected in a border town, the holiness of this city exuded magnetism.

Two main points are suggested by the diverse as well as scholarly populations of Antioch. First, the mix of populations that encompassed different religious and ethnic groups, as well as urban, rural, and settled nomadic people, in many ways characterizes the city as a true frontier town in the Early Islamic period. Indeed, according to Liebeschuetz, and although he is writing through a filter of the fourth-century city, he speaks of Islamic Antioch as comprising polyethnic and poly-religious communities of the city all living in their own quarters, "often divided by walls and gates, possessing their own mosques, baths, and market."[86] Second, the city and its scholarly population did not appear to be seriously affected by political upheaval, despite a nearly four-century-long turbulent period of conquests and successive occupations that began even before the waning of the 'Abbāsid caliphate, with Ṭūlūnid followed by another 'Abbāsid and then Ḥamdānid takeovers.

Residential, commercial, and industrial spaces

The configuration of Early Islamic Antioch is similarly elusive, but evidence of residential, commercial, and industrial spaces off the main *cardo* can be detected in the Princeton excavations. The colonnaded street continued to function as a commercial artery traversing and linking together the city's religious, residential, industrial, and agricultural zones. Chronological examination of coins shows no interruption during or after the Early Islamic conquest; Byzantine coins entered into circulation after the conquest, as attested by finds of many coins of Constans II (641–668) and imitations.[87] Although Antioch was not a mint during this period (rather Aleppo and Qinnasrīn were), it may have minted copper coinage in the early eighth century, but in only a single and, accordingly, rare issue.[88] In the 'Abbāsid period and mainly ninth century, the coin evidence shows some local imitations of Iraqi issues and some imported from Iraq.

The area of 19-M (Main Street Dig III), a soap factory close to the urban core and near the Mosque of Habīb al-Najjār, reveals a residential and domestic sector (Figure 5.6). In one residence, three post-Byzantine occupational and architectural levels consisted of a kitchen with ovens and wells, large walls, and pipes. Level II, better preserved than Level I, was subdivided into three subphases. Level IIa had marble columns in situ, likely spolia. Also in this area, excavators unearthed five Arabic gravestones, two of which dated to the late ninth century, suggesting an

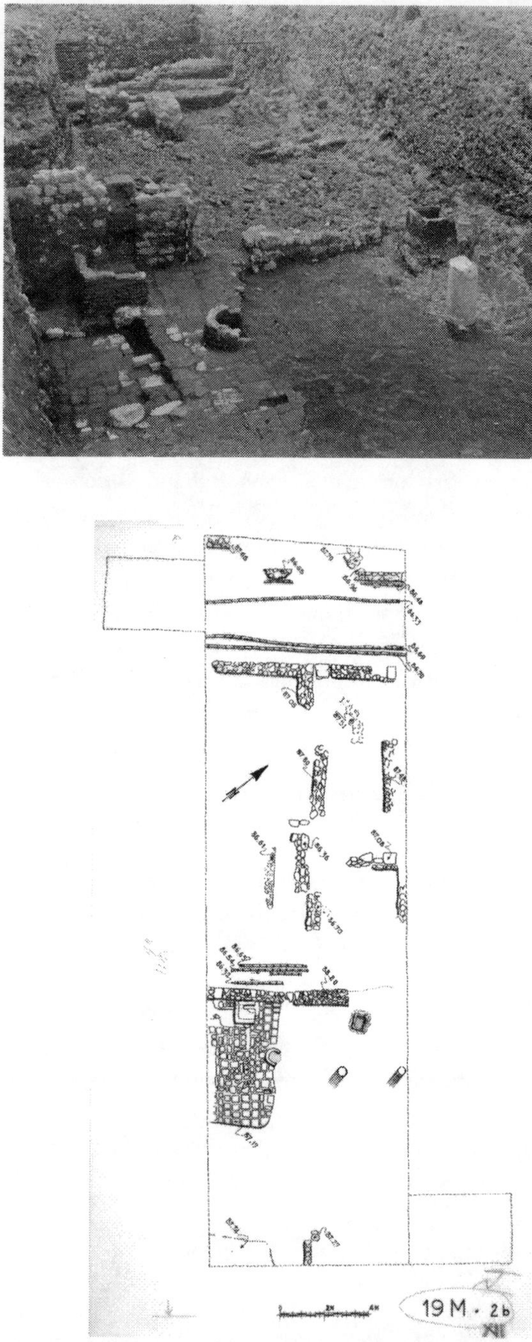

FIGURE 5.6 19-M, Level IIb kitchen, facing north with rectangular wells visible in center and marble flooring; marble columns on the right are from Level IIa

Source: Courtesy of the Antioch Expedition Archives, Department of Art and Archaeology, Princeton University; Princeton

FIGURE 5.7 19-M, Early Islamic gravestone 3861-I73

Source: Courtesy of the Antioch Expedition Archives, Department of Art and Archaeology, Princeton University; Princeton

intramural cemetery. One gravestone was for a man named Hārūn b. al-Khalīl b. 'Abdallah al-Ḥarrānī, who is known, thanks to his father and grandfather's names, which have revealed two more relatives (Figure 5.7).[89] His great-grandfather, Yazīd b. Muhalab (673–720 CE) was the Umayyad governor of the eastern province and later the governor of Baṣra. His great-grandson, Aḥmad b. Hārūn, was a *ḥadīth* scholar alive and working in 999–1000 CE, whose name appears in the bibliographic book *Tar'ikh Baghdad*, mentioning Hārūn b. Khalīl b. 'Abdallah.[90] It is unclear at this time the connection between Hārūn b. Khalīl, evidently a person of some status, and the house in 19-M. The residence in the ninth and tenth centuries may have been a rather wealthy one, given its kitchen with marble columns and paving. Nevertheless, this area, close to but still north of the urban core and near the main colonnaded street, was densely settled in the Early Islamic period; its residential zone had sewage systems and was interspersed with cemeteries.

In sector 17-O, thought to be perched on the edge of the forum of Valens, we can trace the transformation of urban public space as well as continuity (Figure 5.8). Above the *nymphaeum* in Level IV, damaged by the earthquake of 458, and the thick destruction by fire perhaps from the 528 or 528 earthquakes, the courtyard house on the side street of the *cardo*, with its own shops comprising Level III, dates possibly from the sixth century, and it continued well into the seventh. Above it, and entirely new, two well-built courtyard houses with slightly different plans but the same orientation were laid out in the Early Islamic period. The walls were constructed out of well-cut limestone blocks with double facing, plastered white in areas, and with carefully laid and level foundations throughout, suggesting

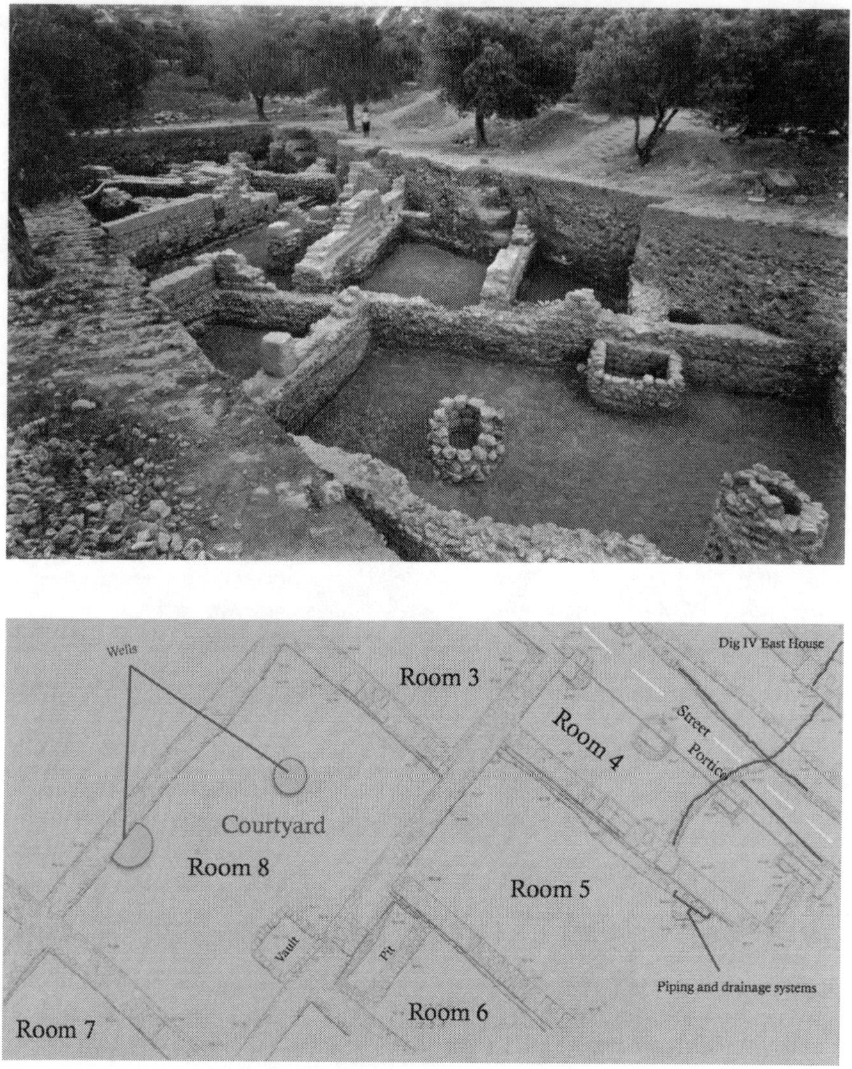

FIGURE 5.8 17-O, Dig III, looking south, central courtyard house

Source: Courtesy of the Antioch Expedition Archives, Department of Art and Archaeology, Princeton University; Princeton; plan altered by Nikitas Tampakis

that the previous house had been leveled and the area cleared for construction all at the same time likely due to the destruction caused by the aforementioned natural disasters. One of the two houses had a kitchen with an oven and a possible dining room, and a storage room with a basalt-lined pit. The courtyard around which these rooms were arranged had two wells and a possible cistern, as well as a possible staircase suggesting an upper level. There was also an elaborate piping system below the foundations and within the walls. This house was inhabited by a fairly well-off middle-class merchant, as attested by the range of materials, large space, and attached shop with a portico on a side street. The shop had a separate entrance, and its finds suggest heavy involvement in the trade and purchase of imported ceramics from the East and the manufacture of mold-made oil lamps. Dating from the eighth century, the buildings continued in use until the tenth. Beginning in the sixth century, any significant open spaces were filled in. The side street (or alley) also had various wells and cisterns encroaching within it. Sector 17-O also was one of the few excavated places that had an overall large number of Early Islamic coins.

Meanwhile, excavations in sector 16-O uncovered an area of workshops and kilns to either side of the Parmenius mountain torrent, further from the city's core but just off the main north-south *cardo* (Figure 5.9). Again, the Early Islamic phases appeared directly over the presumed Justinianic pavements. In 16-O South and 16-O North, Level I revealed a large, well-built wall of cut reused ashlars and two perpendicular walls. There were also *pithoi* (storage containers), the remains of pavement, a marble basin, and a network of terra-cotta pipes, several of which were vertical (perhaps drainpipes). Many pottery wasters, misfired cast-offs, indicating ceramic production, possibly of sphero-conical vessels ("grenades"), were also found. This area, dated to the Early Islamic period, had a domestic or industrial function that continued from the sixth and seventh centuries. North of the stream, 16-P revealed an Early Islamic level consisting of terra-cotta pipes that continued from the early Byzantine period and a wall made of alternating brick and rubblestone. The wall, along with ceramic pipes below it, sat on the edge of and above the Justinianic pavement. Coin evidence shows continuous activity in 16-P during the seventh century, suggesting a commercial function for the space. East of the 16-P main trench, a sounding uncovered a side street composed of a cobbled surface bordered by a wall of large ashlar blocks and a related subterranean vaulted cistern. The street is perpendicular to the main cardo and shows further evidence of orthogonal planning in the medieval period (Figure 5.10). Although Lassus conjectures a tenth- to twelfth-century Middle Byzantine date, the reused ashlar blocks correspond more closely to Early Islamic construction noted around the city (for example, in 17-O). Both pottery-making and burials were located away from the central core of the city and its residential areas.

Changes also occurred to several mainly public structures throughout the city, such as the baths and theaters. Baths continued, although most mentions of them appear in sources dated from the Byzantine reconquest. Istakhrī and Mas'ūdī also discussed the water supply of Antioch, though interestingly they do not mention any conversion of baths to kiln spaces. An apsidal monumental building south of Bath F, in sector 13-R, along the colonnaded street, was partially rebuilt, with smaller walls subdividing the space.[91] This could have been done in the sixth or early seventh century following the earthquakes or the Persian conquest. Islamic pottery dating from the eighth to eleventh centuries was found in the fill 5 m below the surface in this area. A kiln, built inside the building's apse, produced eighth- and ninth-century glazed pottery common all around northern Syria. Interestingly, the highest number of coins in both Umayyad and 'Abbāsid issues of any sector in

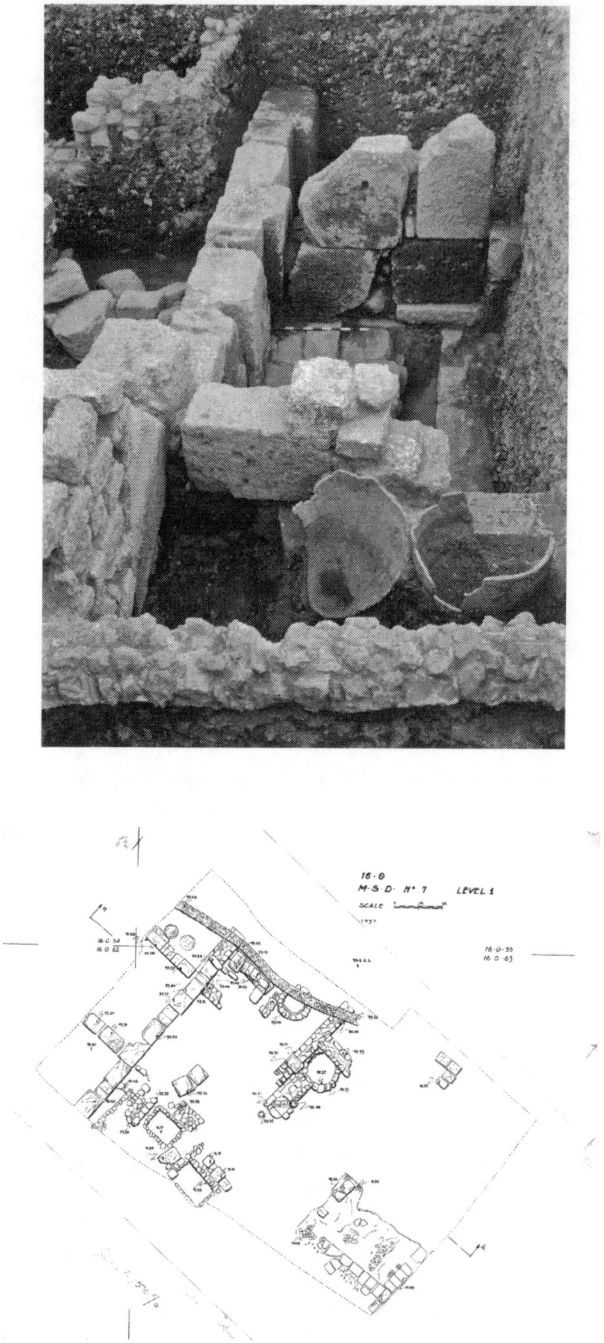

FIGURE 5.9 16–O, Level I, facing southwest with Early Islamic ashlar wall on the left and *in situ pithoi* in the foreground

Source: Courtesy of the Antioch Expedition Archives, Department of Art and Archaeology, Princeton University; Princeton

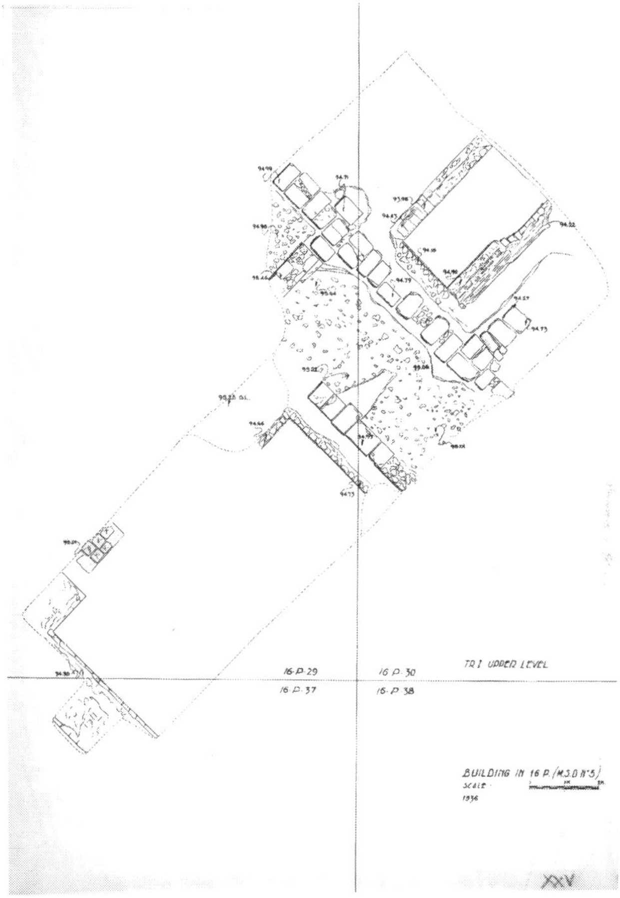

FIGURE 5.10 16-P, medieval phase, facing west

Source: Courtesy of the Antioch Expedition Archives, Department of Art and Archaeology, Princeton University; Princeton

FIGURE 5.11 13-R C3246: excavated June 23, 1934, Umayyad, Damascus mint, 699–709

Source: Courtesy of the Princeton University Firestone Library Numismatic Collection, ex. Peter J. Donald Collection

Antioch was found here, mainly in Bath F just to the north (Figure 5.11). Perhaps the apsidal building and bath at 13-R was transformed into a major commercial center situated at the north end of the market in dialogue with the urban market and merchants entering from or leaving to Aleppo.

The theater (sector 18-O/P) – located between the main street and Mt. Silpius, closer to the center of the city – revealed a similar range of ceramics, as well as many high-end ceramics imported from Iraq, which may suggest a shop, a warehouse for imports, or other commercial use of the space (Figure 5.12). The kilns at the theater and Bath F likely produced wares continuously during the entire Early Islamic period and afterward. Imported Chinese ceramics and imitations of them around Antioch also show the importance of a ceramic trade and local taste.

The buildings in all areas in general were well constructed using large, recycled ashlar walls, sometimes with alternating brick bands; they also had marble floors and reused marble columns. Rather than suggesting that building techniques necessarily deteriorated after the sixth century, they provide evidence that standards were maintained. The transformations at Antioch need not be attributed to the eighth century, however; they may have reflected a longer process in which investment in civic structures, including lavish buildings for public entertainment and bathing, gradually fell, while those spaces were constantly, actively, pragmatically, and innovatively reused, already seen earlier. The old classical buildings of Antioch, such as the theater and baths, clearly were repurposed for industrial use (such as pottery kilns), as apparently happened as well in various other Early Islamic towns within earlier classical cities throughout the Near East, like Jarash and Baysān. Evidence suggests that public institutions such as bathhouses were already transforming by the sixth century, as baths in

FIGURE 5.12 18-O/P, general view, excavation of late walls over what was thought to be the *cavea*. Image number 2720, 5/26/1936

Source: Courtesy of the Antioch Expedition Archives, Department of Art and Archaeology, Princeton University; Princeton

particular were expensive to keep heated, and it was difficult to maintain their connection to the city's water supply. Overall, the excavation results reveal the greater significance of the Early Islamic occupation and production of good-quality local goods such as ceramics.

Green spaces

The geographer/cartographer Muḥammad al-Idrisī (1100–1165) stated that everything anyone needed day to day was within the walls of Antioch. He was referring to a city that had become far more self-sufficient and less reliant on its hinterland. The areas farthest from the central core of the city, including the Island in the Orontes and spaces within and beyond the city walls, had been given over to agricultural use. The Princeton excavations suggest that the Island became a rural area with farms and cemeteries outside the urban core from the sixth and seventh centuries throughout the medieval period. On the Island, which lay north of the medieval city, House A was poorly built in its last phase, with early Kufic inscriptions; it may have been a farmhouse, according to the excavators, who noted its location outside the limits of the reduced city. Eight tombstone inscriptions dated to around the middle of the ninth century to the mid-tenth century were identified in the house and on the west side of the now abandoned hippodrome, whose walls are no longer preserved and became a cemetery.[92] Bath C (sector 10/11-L/M) was used as a quarry after the sixth century and had two kilns to burn marble into lime. Marble burning to produce lime was a valuable recycling practice and used for making building cement. Hippodrome A/Circus (sector 7/8-O/N) likely became a cemetery and yielded eight Kufic gravestone inscriptions dating from the mid-ninth to early-tenth centuries (Figure 5.13). An examination of the numismatic evidence from excavations in the hippodrome and Baths A, B, C, and D shows that Byzantine imperial or local imitation issues ceased with Constans II, while sector 9-N had a mixture of 7.17 percent Umayyad and 4.9 percent Abbāsid coinage.[93]

The area west of the Orontes likely consisted of only agricultural lands, as well. Photos of the cruciform Church of Kaoussié (sectors 12-F, 13-F, G) taken at the time of the Princeton excavations show that the surrounding land remained entirely agricultural with no buildings whatsoever (Figure 5.14). North of Antioch, excavations in sector 20-N on the west bank of the Orontes, 250 m north of the bridge, uncovered a cemetery with a tomb seemingly not buried by meters of alluvium. Two Islamic coins were recovered, but few physical remains were recorded. As for Daphne, the suburb had already faded out after the middle of the sixth century, save for the reference to a monastery of Mart Maryam in 913. In the Umayyad period, Daphne had Umayyad coins, as well, in sector 26-M/N, but not many, only 3.73 percent.

FIGURE 5.13 Hippodrome, Arabic tombstones

Source: Courtesy of the Antioch Expedition Archives, Department of Art and Archaeology, Princeton University; Princeton

FIGURE 5.14 12/13-F/G, general view of the Kaoussié church to the southwest, showing fields and no development. Image number 2078 5/14/1935

Source: Courtesy of the Antioch Expedition Archives, Department of Art and Archaeology, Princeton University; Princeton

In 1998, the Amuq Valley Regional Project found evidence of water mills both just outside Antioch to the northeast on the route into the Amuq Plain and just within the city walls along the same route. Within the city, cut channels in a mountain ravine were discovered that served to contain and make use of the seasonal torrential streams while limiting or screening out colluvial wash (a perennial problem noted by authors of the Byzantine and Islamic periods). At various locations, including the bottom of the channels' course, basalt millstone fragments were found suggesting the energy of the torrents was converted into grinding grain for the city. Very well-preserved mills were also found at Sultan Merkezi (AS 227) outside the city, which were part of a Late Roman/Early Islamic millhouse (Figure 5.15).

The German-Turkish urban survey, undertaken between 2004 and 2009, further recorded many water installations and related buildings, including the Iron Gate across the Parmenius gorge.[94] Although difficult to date precisely, all these excavated and surveyed areas show that the area north of the industrial and commercial areas of the reduced medieval urban core (the former Late Roman city) and west of the Orontes, which Islamic geographers and Christian travelers described as full of gardens, orchards, and mills, was an agricultural-rural and

FIGURE 5.15 Sultan Merkezi mills

Source: Photograph taken by A. Asa Eger in 2002

burial buffer zone. The extended Byzantine city wall, which did not move in to enclose the contracted city, rather protected the farms and grazing lands of Antioch's inhabitants.

Masʿūdī and other tenth-century authors also spoke of cultivated fields, pasturages, trees, mills along the Orontes River, gardens within the city walls, and channels drawing running water off the mountain and supplying it to all the markets, streets, houses, and mosques. This corroborates the archaeological evidence of a contracted city within its larger city walls and empty spaces becoming ruralized. The rural spaces within Antioch, however, were not perceived as markers of decline by Islamic authors. In the Islamic period, gardens and cultivated lands were deliberately put in place and frequently seen not only as pragmatic but also as representing beauty, prosperity, and Paradise, as conveyed in the descriptions of Antioch and the poem by al-Ṭarsūsī that opens this chapter. Accounts and archaeological evidence not only from Antioch but also from numerous other cities such as Naṣībīn (classical Nisibis), Baʿalabakk, al-Qāhira, Kūfa, Caesarea, and Raqqa reveal green or garden spaces with agricultural lands, gardens, orchards, irrigated channels, and water-lifting devices in the heart of the towns and in their abandoned spaces.[95] In Antioch, these lands were easily watered by the Orontes, the Parmenius, and other mountain torrents, and waste water from mosques and baths. The countryside within the city, or *rus in urbe*, denoted by the presence of created green spaces – intramural gardens, orchards, mills, canals, granaries, and other agricultural and pastoral areas – thus represented a dramatically transformed and contracted urban landscape.

Further results from the Amuq Valley survey show that by the Early Islamic period, only about half the number of sites occupied in the Late Roman/Early Byzantine period continued. The earliest and largest of these sites were newly founded agricultural estates located on canals and preexisting sites on the Yaghrā River and in or near marshland. These sites probably constituted consolidated towns or large villages, a continuity of the Byzantine *komai megalai* or *metrokomai*. They were actively involved in agriculture (including rice) and use of wetland resources (such as eels from the Yaghrā and reeds). From the eighth-to-tenth centuries, sites developed on roads as waystations and began filling in the plain, suggesting that nomadic groups were becoming sedentary. While some interaction between city and plain would have taken place, the independent existence of agricultural estates – a feature of the Umayyad period and its elite – and the growth of towns on the plain mark a divergence from town and country. Further, the number of agricultural settlements, reduced by half from the Late Roman/Early Byzantine period, may not have been sufficient to sustain Antioch alone. The intra-urban green spaces of Antioch thus contributed to the city's economy as it shifted from being a "parasite" or consumer city, market-based and dependent on imported products from the surrounding countryside, to becoming a manufacturing center, agriculturally more self-sufficient and less reliant on the hinterland of villages as in Libanius's day.

Conclusions

Antioch in the Early Islamic period was not a city in decline; rather, the textual and archaeological evidence suggests that it was a city transformed, smaller yet more self-sufficient. The city supported modest but vibrant religious and intellectual communities and a more multicultural population than previous periods. Earlier structures were adapted and newer construction took place, and its economy thrived, particularly in ceramic production and imports. Spaces no longer usable for the newly Islamicized city were not simply abandoned but given over to agriculture and industry. Nor did monuments decline; rather, the population of the city shifted. Essentially, Antioch became an administrative and economic center for the central Islamic-Byzantine frontier. Further, Islamic texts show that the town symbolized something far greater; they remembered and extolled its legacy as a pioneer of monotheism and greatness as a strong, fortified ancient capital city. Early Islamic Antioch thus allows for its history to be re-narrated, opening a door into centuries of continued existence and transformation. Passing this threshold into its "afterlife" further allows us to view how a classical and Late Antique city transformed into a medieval one, permitting its use as a model to examine early medieval urbanism throughout the Mediterranean.

Notes

1 Poem on his departure from Ṭarsūs in 920–921, when he stopped at the *manāzil* of Antioch, recorded in Ibn Shaddād and Ibn al-Shiḥna, Ibn Shaddād 1956, vol. 1, part 2. Many thanks to Dr. Raymond Farrin for help with the translation.

2 Using literary evidence and, secondarily, published archaeological material, scholars have argued for a decline by the mid-sixth century caused by natural disaster and plague (Kennedy 1985b, 141–183) – or, as an alternative to decline, stagnation until the tenth century (Foss 1997, 189–269). See also Kondoleon 2000, 4–5. Wickham 2005, 453, 458, 620, 624, 777, views Antioch as one of two exceptions (the other being Gaza) to the process of Byzantine/Early Islamic urban continuity, and therefore argues it was a city in decline. But his assertion mainly reflects a lack of archaeological evidence.

3 Foss 1997, 195.

4 Whitcomb 2011, 65; G. Avni 2011, 301–329.

5 Weber 1934, 80.

6 *Downey, History*, 577–578. See books on Antioch such as F. Cimok 1980, 20, and Demir 1996, 55–57, which reflect and promote the view of Islamic Antioch as an appendix to its history. An exception is Bouchier 1921. Despite opening with remarks that Antioch "resumed its old position as an outpost of European civilization against the hordes of the Far East" and that it experienced the "decay of the caliphate" followed by "the campaigns of the heroic Nicephoros Phocas" (pp. v, x), Bouchier takes a far less negative or judgmental tone as he discusses Early Islamic through Crusader Antioch in its larger Islamic historical context at considerable length (pp. 200–300).

7 Among the only exceptions is Kennedy 1992.

8 Ṭabarī mentions an earthquake in 712/713 in Syria generally. This is mentioned in many sources including Michael the Syrian, Theophanes, Agapius, Chron. 819, *Chron. 1234*, Ya'qūbī, etc. Guidoboni and Comastri 2015, 63; Ambraseys 2009, 224; Guidoboni 1994, 359–360.

9 Forty days may be a trope and not entirely accurate. The following earthquake in 835, as well as an earthquake in 951, also lasted 40 days. See: Mohamed Reda Sbeinati, Ryad Darawcheh, and Mikhail Mouty, "The Historical Earthquakes of Syria: An Analysis of Large and Moderate Earthquakes from 1365 B.C. to 1900 A.D.," *Annals of Geophysics* 48, no. 3 (June 2005).

10 According to Sibṭ b. al-'Ajamī and al-'Umarī (1300–1349) – Ambraseys 2009, 241.

11 Ambraseys 2009, 242.

12 Ṭabarī 2010, 12: 1439–1440, year 245. See also Elias of Nisibis 1910, 99. The notable exception is Ṭarsūs, for which we have the detailed accounts of Ṭarsūsī and al-Muhallabī, preserved in Ibn al-'Adīm, *Bughyat al-ṭalab fī ta'rīkh Ḥalab* 1988; these do at times extol the virtues of frontier fighting. Ambraseys 2009, 244. Abū al-Faraj writes of 90 towers. Demir 1996, 57 mistakes the year and writes 865. Jacquot 1931 in his tourist guide history, though much later, mentions also earthquakes in 716 and 881. It is unknown where he derived this from. Guidoboni 1994, 384.

13 Ibn 'Abd al-Zahir 1976, 315.

14 Ṭabarī 12:132 Assimilated Arabs included those from the tribes of Lakhm, Judhām, Balqayn, Balī, and 'Āmila, affiliated with the Quḍā'a, Ghassān, and Armenians.

15 According to Ibn Abī Yāqūt in Ibn Shaddād. Michael the Syrian says Khālid's armies were the ones to reach Antioch and Aleppo. Many died and no one escaped, etc. Ibn al-Athīr in Ibn Shaddād said it was Abū 'Ubayda who led the forces. An anecdote in the seventeenth-century account by the Ottoman geographer Evliya Çelebi, on the origin of the Albanian people, stated that an Arab shaykh named Jabal-i Alhama, who blinded an Arab *beg* (lord), fled so as to avoid being punished by the same fate. He took refuge with 3,000 of his tribe in Antioch under Heraclius, but during the reign of 'Umar. Çelebi 2000, 64–65, 190–191. Meanwhile, the Syriac sources conflict somewhat on the conquest date. Theophanes and Michael the Syrian state that the conquest occurred

in 637/38, while Agapios (Maḥbūb b. Qusṭanṭīn, Bishop of Hierapolis/Manbij) suggests 636 (Agapius 1912, 476 (216); Theophanes wrote between September 1 637–August 31, 638 – and Yarmūk 634–635 – but this was wrong, as Yarmūk is 636 (*Theophanes* 1982, 38–40), while Khalifa b. Khayyat (d. 854) wrote 637 (Theophilus 2011 118, n. 270). Bar Hebraeus [1932, 94 (101)] states 638 was when Khālid took the country of Antioch. This could reflect a range of years for the conquest, as Balādhurī indicates between 634 and 638. Ṭabarī mentions two accounts: Muḥammad b. 'Umar al-Waqidī (d. 823), who said that Heraclius fled Antioch in September–October 636 and Syria in 636/637, and an *isnad* via Ibn Ḥumayd al-Rāzī (d. 862), Salama b. al-Faḍ al-Azraq (d. 805), and Muḥammad b. Isḥāq (d. 767), who transmitted that Mu'āwiya campaigned in Syria in 641/642, including in Antioch.

16 Bahadır (2013, 194) states that the treaty was to become Muslim or pay *jizya* or leave the city.

17 In Ibn 'Abd al-Zahir's citation of Balādhurī, p. 316.

18 Ṭabarī 14.15.

19 Bar Hebraeus 1932, 94 (101) *Theophanes* 1997, 40.

20 Ṭabarī 18.93. Oddly, Ṭabarī records a winter campaign against Antioch in 668–669 by 'Abd al-Rahmān al-Qaynī, though he is likely referring here to one of the Anatolian Antiochs (such as Antioch in Pisidia), as Syrian Antioch had already been in Muslim hands for 30 years and did not require an extensive campaign to reach, unlike other winter campaigns that were conducted deep into Anatolia.

21 Ṭabarī 22.182

22 Balādhurī 1916, 228. The gate was named after one of a group of resettled people – Persians and people from North Syria (see n. 78) – named Muslim b. 'Abdāllah, father of 'Abdallah b. Habīb b. Muslim al-Anṭakī, was killed at this gate by a stone when he was on the city wall. See also Ibn 'Abd al-Zahir 1976, 316, who adds that the attacker was an *'alj* (infidel).

23 Ibn 'Abd al-Zahir 1976, 317.

24 This account was relayed by an elder (*shaykh*) of Antioch named Ibn Burd, who was a jurist (*al-faqīh*) and possibly a non-Muslim.

25 Abu Ezzah 1980, 51. Interestingly, Ibn 'Abd al-Zahir (1976, 316), who is closely paraphrasing Balādhurī, qualifies that those who paid this tax were *muḥtalim*, meaning sexually mature or pubescent. He must have been using a different version of Balādhurī's text that is no longer extant or interpolated this word.

26 Bahadır (2013, 195); he was also commander in chief of the army of Syria, responsible for distributing tax revenues as salary to city officials, defense, internal security, religious custodianship, public works and construction of markets and mosques.

27 Liebeschuetz 1972, 263.

28 Schoolman 2010, 69, 114–118. Interestingly, there are no Byzantine lead seals from the Early Islamic period in the Hatay Museum in Antakya, suggesting a clear administrative shift or, at the very least, the end of lead seal production until the tenth century; see Cheynet 1994, 469.

29 Sources mainly are Theophanes or *Annals* of Eutychius; see Schoolman 2010.

30 See Schoolman 2010.

31 Or they alternated as capital. For discussion of the difference in sources, see Abu Ezzah 1980, 92. Writing in the middle of the tenth century, Istakhrī and Ibn Ḥawqal stated that Antioch was the capital: Ibn Ḥawqal 1964, 171; Istakhrī 1967; See also Yāqūt 1955–57, 1: 266, 4: 165, 5: 205.

32 Bonner 1996, 87.

33 Ibn Shaddād, al-Mas'ūdī, *TIB* 564; also al-Qalqashandī, but no attribution to Hārūn.

34 Although Thomas was in reality given only bishop and vassal status by the 'Abbāsids, this remains one of the first instances of a coronation in Antioch: Kennedy 2006, art. IX, 137; Treadgold 1988, 229–248.

35 Bone 2000, 247.

36 In the fourth century, a law mandated that the Seleucian fleet be responsible for "clearing the Orontes River" (Pharr, *Theo. Code* 1952, 10.24.3) of obstructions; whether natural (silt) or human (pirates) is uncertain.

37 In Le Strange 1965, 45, *zabīb* is translated "olive oil." This comes to somewhere between 135,000 (298 lbs) to 270,000 kg (595 lbs) of raisins, based on a twelfth-century weight; see Marcinkowski 2003, 18. See also M. Shatzmiller, 2012. "Measuring the Medieval Islamic Economy," www.medievalislamiceconomy.uwo.ca/measures-egypt.html

38 Abu Ezzah 1980, 120.

39 Cheynet 2003, 79–80. For an extensive discussion of textile production and trade in Antioch, see Vorderstrasse 2010, 151–171.

40 Mas'ūdī 1861 – [1930], 2: 438–439.

41 In Acts 11.19–27, several go to Antioch to speak to the Greeks or Hellenes, including Stephen first, then Barnabas, who brought Paul. Peter was also in Antioch. Some think Habīb is Agabus from Acts 11.28, but this is not certain. Qur'ānic commentators disagree over who the apostles may have been. Ṭabarī discusses this episode extensively (1987, vol. 4, 167–169). He dates this erroneously during the reign of Antiochus son of Antiochus (Antiochus II who died in 246 BCE). For further discussion and Qur'ānic commentators, as well as an argument that an unnamed city in sūra 21:11–16 also refers to Antioch, see Frantsouzoff 1999–2000, 399–401. Its impiety may be a reflection of the string of disasters that befell the city in the mid-sixth and early seventh centuries. See also the fourteenth-century Mamlūk historian and exegete Ibn Kathīr, who questions discusses the issue of whether Antioch was the city named and has doubts, 1997, 10, 14, 489.

42 See 'Alī 2008, 1121.

43 Christensen-Ernst 2012, 140; Daftary 2018, 139; Poonawala 2008, 4, 5.

44 Ibn Shaddād 1984, 223–299.19; Ibn al-'Adīm 2016; which he states was transmitted by Kamāl al-Dīn b. al-'Adīm, via Abū 'Amr 'Uthmān b. 'Abdallāh b. Ibrāhīm b. Ṭarṣūṣī (late tenth century), after three seventh-century *ḥadīth* transmitters: Ibn 'Abbās (d. 687), Abū Sa'īd al-Hudrī (d. 682–693), and Abū Hurayra (d. 681). Oddly, however, Ibn al-'Adīm mentions another *ḥadīth* from Abū Hurayra that lists the four cities from Paradise as Mecca, Madina, Jerusalem, and Damascus and the four cities "of fire" as Rome, Constantinople, Antioch, and San'a. Ibn Asākir also mentions this *ḥadīth*, though the latter four cities are "of hell," and Ṭabariyya replaces Rome. Yet a third *ḥadīth* mentions five cities of Paradise (Jerusalem, Ḥimṣ, Damascus, Jibrin [Eleutheropolis in Palestine/Beit Guvrin?], Dhofar [in Oman]) and five of hell: Constantinople, al-Tunna [perhaps Tyana?], Antioch, Palmyra, and San'a. See el-Cheikh 2001. It is unlikely that these *ḥadīth* are authentic, but rather fall into a category of forged *ḥadīth* that showed civic pride (Brown 2017). Still, these three *ḥadīth* show that Antioch retained an importance in "infamy." These should not, however, literally be viewed as cursed or damned cities that were undesirable. Constantinople, in many eschatological accounts, appears prominently as the final prize for Muslims before the end of the world.

45 Ibn Kathīr 1997: vol. 19, p. 259. The Prophet Muḥammad transmitted it to 'Amr b. al-'As and then onto many others. Ibn Kathīr himself writes, following the *ḥadith*, "This is a really strange *ḥadīth*, since he promoted it cunningly." Many thanks to Kyle Brunner for the translation. See also the *Kitāb al-Fitan* (820 CE) by Al-Marwazī, Nu'aym b. Ḥammād 2017, 414. The Amuq valley and Antioch were the locations for many apocalyptic battles; see pp. 257, 261, 265, etc.

46 Al-Hamadhānī 1973, 63.

47 Ibn Rustah 1892, p. 83.

48 Ibn al-'Adīm 1996, 11, writing in the thirteenth century, also wrote that Antioch used to be called Madināt Allah (City of God), Umm al-Mudun (Mother of Cities), and Madināt al-Mulūk (City of Kings).

49 E. Kirkegaard, "The Coins of Constans II from the Excavations at Antioch," paper presented at the International Congress on Medieval Studies, Kalamazoo, MI, May 10–12, 2012 (unpublished).
50 *Antioch V*, 8–10, 65.
51 Kennedy and Liebeschuetz 1988, 66; in his earlier work, Liebeschuetz (1972, 264) still held that despite these constructions, the "regular geometrical street plan of Antioch was maintained to the end of the Byzantine period," ultimately relying on Lassus's conclusion.
52 Magness 2003, 206–209.
53 Foote 2000, 28–32.
54 *Antioch Archives*, Excavator's Diary, May 14, 1937, 45–46.
55 For a treatment by modern scholars, see Kalavrezou 1997; Wortley 2004, 148–149.
56 Mayer and Allen 2012, 52.
57 Mayer and Allen 2012; Troupeau 2001, 319–327; Mas'ūdī, 3: 406–408.
58 *Michael the Syrian* 1963, III.100. Also mentioned by Eutychis Sa'īd b. Batriq, Patriarch of Alexandria (d. 940).
59 Troupeau 2005, 580.
60 In the Eastern Orthodox tradition her name is also Solomonia; other names are Chemouni, Salomee, Semouni, Samuni, or Salumi. For more on the cult of the Maccabean Martyrs, see Chapter 1, p. 66, n. 145.
61 Kennedy 1992, 187, 188; Mayer and Allen 2012, 84, 92.
62 Bouchier; *Michael the Syrian* 1963, II.490.
63 *Theophanes* 1982, 107 (416, *annus mundi* 6234).
64 Schoolman 2010, 116–117.
65 Ibid., 113–115; Kennedy 1986b, 325–344.
66 Treiger 2020, 2, 7–8.
67 Mugler 2019a.
68 Krönung 2019, 72–4.
69 Abu Ezzah 1980, 77.
70 *TIB* 613.
71 *Theophanes* 1982, 119 (430, *annus mundi* 6248). This was ordered by a Salim b. 'Alī.
72 *Michael the Syrian* 1901, 2.490.
73 Mas'ūdī 4: 55–56. The term *saklābiyūs* is unattested elsewhere but perhaps refers to Asclepius. However, the aforementioned temples at Antioch to Zeus Olympius were at Epiphaneia on the mountain, established in the Seleucid period, and at Daphne, established by Diocletian. A temple of Zeus was also part of the forum of Valens. It is noteworthy that Mas'ūdī lists this temple as one of only three ancient Greek temples – the others being the Great Pyramids of Egypt and the Temple of Jerusalem.
74 *Antioch V*, 13–14.
75 Christensen-Ernst 2012, 97. According to a local priest via Christensen-Ernst, the Ulu Camii used to be the Church of the Forty Martyrs. But this is problematic, as there is no attested Church of the Forty Martyrs of Sebaste at Antioch; rather, devotions to them took place at the Martyrium of St. Barlaam located somewhere outside the city walls. See Mayer and Allen p. 50.
76 Ibn al-'Adīm 2016.
77 Balādhurī 1957–58, 230; Abu Ezzah 1980, 49; Athamina 1986, 185–207. Also in Ibn Shaddād 1984, 223–299.25 via Abū Safs al-Shamī via Muḥammad b. Rashīd via Makhul. Curiously. he mentions they also came from Sayābija, which was another group of people, though possibly a misread of this, or possibly also a place where they lived.
78 Ibn Shaddād (1984, 223–299.25) mentions that Muḥammad b. al-Qasim had sent them to al-Hajjāj, governor of 'Iraq, who sent them to Syria.
79 Balādhurī 1957–58, 221.
80 Bar Hebraeus 1932, 104 (112).

81 Balādhurī 1957–58, 120–121; Abu Ezzah 1980, 49; but see Kennedy 2001, 12 and n. 74, who briefly mentions that Persians were settled in the region, though it is unclear whether they were moved to or from the city – though Ibn Shaddād (1984, 223–299.24) states 662–663.

82 Kennedy 1986a, 280.

83 Abu Ezzah 1980, 123–124.

84 Ibid., 16.

85 Yāqūt 1990, vol. 1, 319–320. Yāqūt provides a long list; of these, the first is 'Umar b. 'Alī [etc.], writer of *al-Maqbul* c. 969–970.

86 Liebeschuetz 1972, 263.

87 Foss 1997; Kirkegaard unpublished. Waage, *Antioch* 4.1 109, Figure 97.

88 Schoolman 2010; and see Foss 1997 via Schoolman.

89 Faris, 1938; *Antioch II*, 167–169. Three other gravestones are mentioned; however, they were purchased with no provenance. Two of these mention a Sulaymān b. Muḥammad and a Yūsuf.

90 I am indebted to Dr. Choukri Heddouchi who re-read this inscription and discovered this.

> Al-Khatib Al-Baghdādī, Abuū Bakr, 2002. *Ta'rikh Baghdād*. Bashar Awwad Maruf (ed), 1st ed., Dār Al-Gharb Al-Islamī. vol. 6, p. 435. entry 2934. Also the biographical dictionary of Muḥammad b. Aḥmad al-Dhahabī's (2004–2007), *Siyar 'Alām al-Nubala'*. Heddouchi reads the *nisba* as al-Ḥarrānī rather than al-Jaza'īrī which was the original reading by Faris. The reason, according to Heddouchi is that a crack in the epitaph gives the impression that there is a second letter "ra".
>
> *(Heddouchi, personal communication, 2020)*

91 C. Villani and N. Hastings, "Antioch 13-R: Excavations of 1934–1935," paper written for ART 418, taught by A. Stahl, class on sector 13-R in Antioch, Spring 2019, unpublished.

92 Hitti, 1934, *Antioch I*, 54–57.

93 S. Redford 2002. "Early Islamic Antioch," paper presented at the Third International Congress on the Archaeology of the Ancient Near East, Paris, April 13–19.

94 Brands 2009.

95 See Eger 2014b, 123–127, especially 126, for references to these cities.

6

THE BYZANTINE DUCHY OF ANTIOCH (969–1085)

> I am aware of your desire to destroy this city, how you, the army, are excited and eager to demolish it and ravage it with fire. But a kind of pity for this city has gradually come over me, that the city that is third in the world, on account of the beauty and size of its walls (for you see to what height they rise), and also because of the multitude of its people and the extraordinary construction of its buildings, should be reduced to rubble, like some poor fortress. To me it seems senseless to exhaust the Roman army in the sacking of this city, and to destroy and ravage again what we have subdued with warfare.
>
> – Nicephorus II Phocas, speaking to his army[1]

> I found some lines written by the astrologer who is the nephew of al-Ṣabī on the back of an old book, in the custody of Qādī Abū al-Faḍl (b. Muḥammad) Ibn Abī Jarāda in Aleppo which says: "The narrator spoke of the capture of Antioch at the entrance of the enemy at a certain moment of the night in 358 [968/969]. If his words are exact, Antioch will remain in the possession of the Greeks 119 years." Maḥmūd b. Naṣr b. Ṣālīḥ stopped on these lines when he evoked them in an assembly, but things went on as the astrologer said.[2]
>
> – Ibn Shaddād and Ibn al-'Adīm[3]

Introduction

The return of the Byzantines in the mid-tenth century was a momentous event; after more than 330 years of Islamic rule, Emperor Nicephorus II Phocas (963–969) reconquered the city and placed it under Byzantine control once again. The period of the Byzantine reconquest also offers some of the richest descriptions of the city and the activities of its inhabitants. According to the chronicler Leo the Deacon (c. 920–990s), the Byzantines still regarded Antioch as a great city, indeed third in the world.[4] It was also one of the last cities of the frontier to fall. But unlike the Early Islamic conquest, the Byzantine reconquest, according to textual accounts, was quite brutal, with the Byzantines burning and destroying the city and requiring Muslims to leave. Yet as we will see, the new administration disrupted very little of the city's way of life, for this was not an occupation. Despite serious internal and external challenges, Antioch experienced substantial developments and growth in administration, religious communities, and the economy. Meanwhile, Fāṭimid and Mirdāsid armies attacked and besieged the city, locals rebelled against the imperial government, and the city suffered four earthquakes in rapid succession between 1050 and 1063. But despite these interruptions, Antioch flourished during the Byzantine period, as seen by changes to its architectural landscape and the relationships of the new rulers to the well-established communities already in place. On an ideological level, the retaking of Antioch also carried great symbolic significance to Byzantines, who were fascinated by the *idea* of Antioch, which Nicephorus held up as the third city in the world, even though other Islamic cities greatly overshadowed it.

The reconquest

The details of the reconquest shed light on the material effects of the Byzantine siege of the city. Three sources give a fairly detailed account of the events leading up to its taking and the reconquest itself: the *History* of Leo the Deacon (writing c. 995); *The Life of the Patriarch Christopher*, written in Greek, then translated to Arabic by the same author, Ībrāhīm b. Yuḥannā (c. early 950s–c. 1030) in 1030; and the account by Yaḥya b. Sa'īd al-Anṭākī, a Christian from Egypt who resided in the city.[5] Two later Islamic sources, Ibn Shaddād (1217–1285) and Ibn al-Shiḥ na (d. 1485), referring to an excerpted and previous account by an Ibn Munala that is no longer extant, also discuss the siege, though their details are less reliable.[6] The narrative accounts surrounding the Byzantine reconquest show that the city, ruled by foreign Islamic powers like the Hamdānids (rather than the Umayyads or 'Abbāsids), was generally unstable and that local Muslim nobles running the city had the real power. Furthermore, the relationships between these two groups and the church could be quite complicated, often blurring religious and ethnic divisions.

The Byzantine reconquest of 969 succeeded only after two earlier attempts, in 966[7] and 968 (Figure 6.1). Nicephorus's campaign was part of a new strategy of aggressive reconquest orchestrated in Constantinople.[8] Coming from a military family, he had achieved popularity in the imperial capitol from a string of victories in the east, particularly against Islamic forces along the *thughūr* frontier, which he then celebrated by parading spoils, relics, and prisoners upon his return. His popularity enabled him to rise to emperor in 963. One year later, in 964, after centuries of back-and-forth raiding across the frontier, the Byzantines under Emperor Nicephorus gathered a large army and went on the offensive.

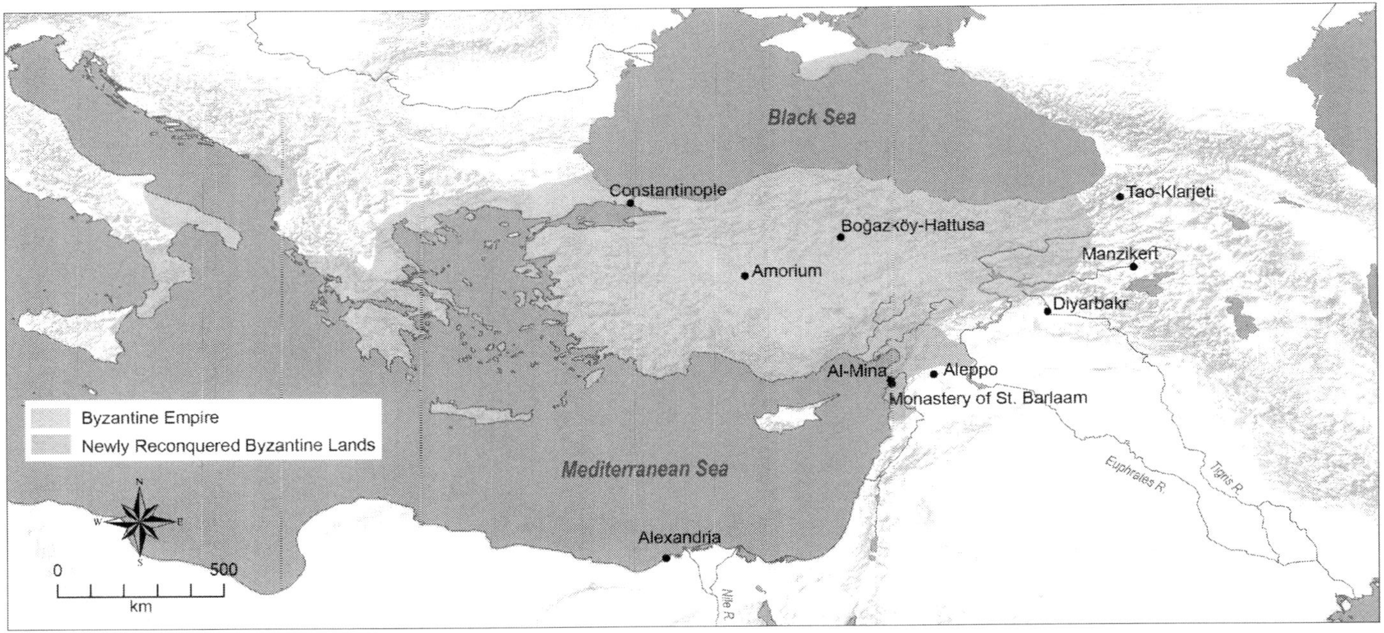

FIGURE 6.1 Map of the Byzantine Reconquest

Source: Created by Claire Ebert

Marching through Cilicia, the emperor took the towns of Tarsus (August 965), Adhana, Maṣṣīṣa (classical Mopsuestia), and Anazarbus. Fleeing before the so-called "White Death," as they called Nicephorus because of his pale skin and aggressive policies, many Muslim residents of Tarsus emigrated to Antioch. However, Nicephorus did not continue and turned back, narrowly avoiding an engagement with Sayf al-Dawla and Khūrāsānī troops. This was due to a drought and famine that struck the region in that year, leading to a shortage of bread and people eating grass and alfalfa:

> I am quitting you not because you are too strong for me or because I am unable to take your city, but because of the scarcity of forage; I am coming back presently, and those of you who would like to migrate elsewhere had best do so before I return; for any whom I find after my return shall be put to death.[9]

Miskawayh (d. 1030), historian and secretary to the Būyid court, custodians of the 'Abbāsid caliphs, also writes that thousands fled the region for the southern Levant. At the same time, the Byzantine conquest, like the Arab one before it, involved a great deal of wheeling and dealing between the upper- and middle-class residents of Tarsus. Surrendering to the Byzantines, they were given gifts and escorted to Antioch by the emperor. Among them was the now-unseated governor of Tarsus, Rashīq 'Abdallāh al-Nasīmī.[10]

At this time, Antioch was still under Hamdānid control, governed by Abū al-'Asha'ir, the cousin of the Hamdānid *amīr* of Aleppo, Sayf al-Dawla (945–967). But the Antiochenes had grown unhappy with the Hamdānids, and the citizens, as well as military who had defected, removed the unpopular governor. In accounts by the contemporary poets Abū Firās and Mutannabī, the Ikhshīdid recently deposed governor of Damascus, Yānis Mu'nisī, in 947 took Antioch by force, surprising Abū al-Ashā'ir as he was returning from the hippodrome.[11] Another mention of an *amīr* of Antioch named Ibn al-Zamān and Ibn al-Zayyāt, probably the same person, is given in the *Life* of the Patriarch Christopher as an authority also over Rashīq when he was in Tarsus, but this name appears nowhere else.[12] This suggests that the area of the old hippodrome, no longer in use, was still known and identified as such.

In 965, the Muslim elite, in typical Antiochene fashion, again rose against their rulers. According to Ibn Shaddād, the tax collector al-Ḥasan b. al-Ahwāzī attached himself to Rashīq, the former governor of Tarsus. Financed by al-Ahwāzī, Rashīq offered 600,000 *dirhams* in yearly tribute to Sayf al-Dawla provided he could be governor of Antioch. Sayf al-Dawla accepted the deal and so appointed Rashīq governor. Antioch, however, already had a military governor (a *ghulām*, or military slave) serving on behalf of Sayf named Abū al-Ṭamāl Fatḥ al-Yamkī, from whom Rashīq would have to gain control of the city. According to an interesting note in Ibn Shaddād, he thereupon told his allies that

> when Fatḥ comes down from the citadel and stands at his door to judge business, one of you will behave badly to someone and submit it to Fatḥ. He will

> decide the dispute. Then, when you stand before him, you will attack him, you will seize [him] and raise your voice. I will then enter, and take possession of the citadel with those who accompany me.

All this came to pass, and Rashīq seized the citadel and city on October 29, 965.[13] This account suggests first (although Ibn Shaddād is a much later source and may be anachronistic here) that there may have been a citadel of some sort before the one built in the Middle Byzantine period and that it was the palace/residence of the governor. And second, it suggests that the governor acted as judge at a location in the city and not the citadel.

Desirous to keep the Byzantines at bay, Rashīq then offered to Nicephorus the tribute he was to have paid to Sayf al-Dawla. The emperor, however, suspicious of the offer, declined, proposing instead that the Antiochenes deliver him the city in exchange for a guarantee that they would be unharmed and protected. He also declared that the Byzantines would build a citadel in the city and station it with a garrison and *strategos* (general). But Rashīq and the Antiochenes refused this counteroffer, confident in their ability and resources to hold out against a prolonged siege.

Al-Ahwāzī then manipulated Rashīq into attacking Aleppo by having a faked letter allegedly from the 'Abbāsid caliph al-Muṭī'read in the mosque in Antioch that granted Rashīq governance over Sayf al-Dawla's lands. Rashīq's troops consisted of Daylamī deserters (Persians from the Alborz Mountains south of the Caspian Sea) from the Hamdānids led by Dizbar b. Uwaynim. On January 31, 966, Rashīq launched his attack against Aleppo, and after many battles gained control of the lower city and then besieged the citadel; three months later, however, he was killed in a skirmish, and his companions fled back to Antioch, among them al-Ahwāzī. Reentering the city, al-Ahwāzī put up Dizbar as *amīr* and governor, making himself his vizier, and inviting Arabs and non-Arabs alike to the city.[14] Those who came were from the Banū Kilāb and the *thughūr*, as well as more Daylamīs. This was a renegade rulership and oppressive against the Antiochenes, and so Sayf al-Dawla sent his chamberlain Qarghūya against Dizbar, but the latter fended him off. Qarghūya then fled to Aleppo, where he was pursued by Dizbar, who captured the city. Sayf al-Dawla marched against him in turn and attacked; routing Dizbar's army, he then took both him and Ibn al-Ahwāzī prisoner and put them to death sometime in January or February 967. He also recaptured Antioch. The Antiochene nobles had to pay dearly with large amounts of money to Sayf al-Dawla, who installed one of his *ghulāms*, Taqī al-Dīn, as governor of Antioch, who later made off with the treasury and went over to the Byzantines.

Meanwhile, Nicephorus had gathered his troops for the first siege of Antioch, telling them, as we have seen, not to destroy or burn the city because its importance and beauty were too great,[15] and on October 23, 966, the siege began. First the emperor tried to surround and starve the inhabitants while launching daily raids and preventing supplies from reaching the city. But keeping with his desire to protect the city from physical harm, he resorted mostly to military display tactics designed to create fear rather than using siege engines outright. Finally, on the eighth day he gave up, and the army withdrew because they were running out of supplies. But although he had failed to take the city, Nicephorus installed the *strategos* Michael Bourtzes,[16] along with Isaac Sachacius Brachamius, to control the region of the Amanus Mountains and with it the northern approach to Antioch.[17]

The two Byzantine sieges that followed were instigated by the murder of the patriarch of Antioch, Christopher (960–967). Previously a Christian scribe from Baghdad, born ʻĪsā, he had moved to Aleppo to the court of Sayf al-Dawla and over time became quite close to the *amīr*. Soon afterward, the citizens of Antioch invited him to become their patriarch; Sayf approved, and ʻĪsā acceded in 960, taking the name Christopher. Christopher worked to alleviate the tax burden and develop religious education in the city. His friendship with the Muslim *amīr* was not, however, well regarded because of the Antiochenes' unhappiness with Hamdānid rule of their city. Fearing fallout from his association with Sayf al-Dawla, Christopher left Antioch during the revolt of Rashiq against Fath and took shelter at Qalʻat Siman, the monastery of St. Symeon the Elder, close to the Hamdānid capital of Aleppo and safer. When al-Ahwāzī was unable to remove him, he instead ordered the seizure of Christopher's house and clergy as well as the houses of other Christians in Antioch. But Sayf al-Dawla, angry at the elders of the city for expelling Fath and handing the city over to Rashīq, arrested them and confiscated their belongings and reinstated Christopher. The patriarch, however, interceded on his opponents' behalf and acted as arbitrator, perhaps out of benevolence, perhaps to avoid association with either political faction. But instead, his arbitration had the reverse effect, angering three Antiochene nobles, possibly the same aforementioned elders – Ibn Mānik,[18] Ibn Muḥammad, and Ibn Diʻāmah – who actually ran the city and had supported the revolts of Rashīq, al-Ahwāzī, and Dizbar. They likely saw their dependence on Christopher to negotiate with the Hamdānids an impediment to their own power.[19] This friendship of patriarch Christopher with a Muslim ruler, despite threats on his life and to his reputation, rather than allying with the Christians or Byzantines, thus illustrates the complexities of Antioch's Christian community, with competing loyalties that often blurred across Christian-Muslim lines.[20]

At this point Sayf al-Dawla died of illness on February 8, 967. When Taqī al-Dīn, the *ghulām* Sayf al-Dawla had placed in charge of Antioch, left the city to attend the funeral, the Antiochenes took advantage of his absence, determined to close their city off to any more Hamdānids. Instead, they gave control to ʻAllūsh, a local warlord and Kurd from the nearby town of Būqā in the Amuq Plain. When a large army of eastern Persian Khurāsānīs, led by Muḥammad b. ʻĪsā, arrived to fight on the frontier against the Byzantines, the city inhabitants and ʻAllūsh welcomed them.

Fearing that any subsequent Hamdānid ruler or representative would be allied with Christopher, Ibn Mānik, Ibn Muḥammad, and Ibn Diʻāmah then tried to stir the Antiochenes to rise against the patriarch as a Byzantine and Hamdānid sympathizer and anti-Muslim conspirator, using an ambiguous *fatwa* (a legal opinion by a jurist) they had procured to bring the Antiochenes and especially the Khurāsānīs on board. The *fatwa* specifically was against those who would conspire against an Islamic *ḥiṣn* or (frontier) fortress.[21] Additionally damning, Christopher likely did communicate with Taqī al-Dīn about if and when he might return to Antioch. Christopher's position was precarious and vulnerable, with his Muslim patron gone. On May 22, 967, Ibn Abī ʿAmr, a Muslim noble friend and possibly neighbor of Christopher, tried to warn him to leave town by the end of the day, as he feared for the patriarch's life. But the patriarch refused, fearing what would happen to the Christian community in his absence, and instead accepted an invitation to Ibn Mānik's home for a meeting in the night. There Ibn Mānik accused him of conspiracy and convinced the Khurāsānīs to attack him. Christopher's head was cut off and thrown in the oven of the bath adjacent to his house, while his body was dragged through the city on a ladder, then thrown out the Sea (Bridge) Gate into the Orontes, a well-rehearsed patterns of disposing of religious enemies. He was found eight days later suspended on a water wheel (*ṭarrāsh*). Ibn Mānik then plundered the patriarch's house and his church – St. Peter's, perhaps adjacent to his residence (*qilāyat al-baṭriyark*) as part of an episcopal complex – taking the relic of the silver-coated palmwood throne of St. Peter, his seat as head of the Church, as well as its treasury of vases, silver, and drapery.[22] It is likely that Christopher's own residence was fairly wealthy to be worthy of being plundered twice, and it had seals (presumably lead) on everything within it. The assassination of the Melkite patriarch proved a flashpoint; when news of Christopher's murder reached Nicephorus, the emperor was determined to try to take Antioch once again.

The Byzantines' second siege began on October 19, 968, though it was not so much a siege as a tactical prelude to the one of 969; it also shows that Nicephorus was still determined to not harm the city itself. Marching toward Antioch, he engaged the Khurāsānī army in Iskandarūna (classical Alexandreia ad Issum, modern Iskenderun) and defeated them; their leader ʿĪsā was taken prisoner, then released by arrangement with the Antiochenes. But then, typical of the Antiochenes, they chased him and the remaining Khurāsānīs out of the city. Nicephorus went on to take Antioch's surrounding towns, destroying "an incalculable number of villages," and built a fortification at Baghrās, the town nearest Antioch.[23] In December 968, he stationed 500 cavalry and 1,000 infantry, commanded by Michael Bourtzes, around the city and at Baghrās, cutting off supply lines. Additionally, he installed the *stratopedarch* or commander-in-chief, the eunuch Peter,[24] in the frontier region along with a large army. Camping near Antioch, Nicephorus employed a scorched earth policy but ultimately withdrew, leaving Bourtzes in charge. Over the next year, Peter commanded Bourtzes to reconnoiter the city, and Bourtzes and some men assessed where the walls could best be scaled and their height and then began constructing siege ladders.

The historians Ibn al-Athīr (1160–1233) and Ibn al-ʿAdīm (1192–1262) add that at the same time, the inhabitants of Būqā (mentioned also as Lūqā) in the Amuq Plain were persuaded by the Byzantines to emigrate to Antioch on the pretext that they were escaping the Greek forces.[25] The story is, however, perhaps suspect, since it is unclear why the people of Būqā would do this, other than wishing to flee the countryside and live as refugees in the city itself in anticipation of being granted protection under future Byzantine rule.

Meanwhile, a black African from Ṭarsūs named al-Zughīlī (or al-Rughīlī or Z'abilī) was visiting from Egypt with a group of others and hosted by the governor 'Allūsh,[26] but turning on the governor, Zughīlī killed him, and he and his associates took over the city.[27] Some Arabic and Syriac sources report that Peter was then contacted by the people of Būqā two months after moving to the city to report they had left a portion of the walls defenseless and that Antioch was powerless and free for the taking. The *Life of Christopher* and Yaḥya al-Anṭākī, however, make no mention of people from Būqā, writing instead that the city was weak from war, the Muslims were not protecting the walls, and the ruler had left the city. Whatever the case, all the pieces were now in place and the timing was right. Internal strife and Byzantine pressure had pushed the city to the breaking point.

On October 28, 969,[28] Bourtzes and Brachamius, disobeying imperial orders not to take the city, entered Antioch at night along with 300 men, with the help of the traitors from Būqā, acting as guards on a part of the city wall near the top of the mountain, a weak point in Antioch's defenses. After the guards abandoned their posts, the Byzantines covertly scaled the walls,[29] and thus, once again, Antioch was taken through an inside job.[30]

The Byzantines took two towers, likely in the vulnerable eastern mountain stretch of the undefended wall, and captured the guards of other towers. Ibn Shaddād and Ibn al-'Adīm add the curious and puzzling event that the Byzantines made the guards recite the *shahāda – allāhū akbar, lā'ilāh'illā-llāh* (God is great, there is no God but God) – or be killed in order to gain their trust and confuse them.[31] Further ignoring Nicephorus's orders not to harm the city, they then set fire "to all four corners of the town," although al-Anṭākī states that the Antiochenes started the fire to separate themselves from the Byzantines. Both may be true. Once in the city, the attackers facilitated the entrance of Nicephorus and his army, including the emperor's nephew John Tzimisces,[32] Peter, and 40,000 men, and Peter put out the fires.[33] Many Antiochenes were killed or captured, although a large number fled via the Garden Gate or Sea/Bridge Gate. Christians were released and allowed to stay.[34] According to one source, male and female youths were deported to Constantinople to be sold.[35] Ibn al-Shiḥna further states that Nicephorus released a large number of elderly men and women. According to Leo the Deacon, Nicephorus, displeased that Bourtzes and Brachamius had burned the city, demoted Bourtzes and placed him under house arrest.[36] Peter, who was put in charge, then asserted complete command over the city, took first choice in the spoils, and rebuilt the vulnerable sections of the walls.[37] He also preserved all the farms and plants of Antioch's gardens.[38] Bourtzes, however, resentful over his arrest and demotion, soon joined with other disgruntled generals back in Constantinople, including Nicephorus's own nephew Tzimisces, in a plot against the emperor's life, and on December 11, 969, Tzimisces murdered his uncle and assumed the imperial throne for himself.

Among the Antiochenes who fled was Ibn Mānik, murderer of Christopher. Found by a volunteer Syrian troop, he was brought back to the city and sold. The Byzantines dismembered his body and tossed it into the Orontes from the bridge of the Sea Gate, where Christopher's body had also been disposed of. Ibn Di'āmah and Ibn Muḥammad were taken as prisoners to Tarsus; the former was drowned in the river while the latter died in prison.

The events of the siege differ considerably from the Early Islamic conquest of the city. They show that by the first half of the tenth century, 'Abbāsid control on the frontier was weak and a series of local dynasties and individuals were vying for control of Antioch. The inhabitants of Antioch wavered back and forth over which ruler to support, often rejecting foreign rulers and upholding local ones. In the city itself, the texts reveal key characters and the population in general in the roles of hero, villain, traitor, and victim. Roles aside, the taking of Antioch, in part as an inside job, and the events leading up to it, reveal a divided city by the mid-tenth century. Embroiled in this turbulent period, the story of Patriarch Christopher reveals that divisions between Christians and Muslims were not so clear-cut, and conflict rarely fell along these lines. Nevertheless, the Byzantine taking of Antioch, although motivated by the desire to create a buffer state on the frontier, also had great symbolic significance. As such, the siege was cast in a propagandistic light, and lines between Christian and Muslim were drawn where they had not been before.

The medieval Byzantine city

Sources

During their 100-year rule, the Byzantines built and renewed Antioch as a new medieval regional capital. But although the city and region were re-Christianized, it did not revert to its past as a Late Antique or Hellenized city. There were no theaters, hippodromes, or bathhouses rebuilt. Neither was the Island with its imperial palace reclaimed. Rather, the only new constructions were a fortification atop Mt. Silpius as well as some churches and renovations to the city wall (Figure 6.4). Cities with separate but adjoining castles became a hallmark of the medieval period.

Most of this early period was under the rule of John Tzimisces and Basil II, stepson of Nicephorus II Phocas, both of whom were dedicated to renewing the city. The richest descriptions of the city and activities of its inhabitants are to be found in the sources dealing with this time. Knowledge of the city from Arabic sources comes mainly from the geographers Istakhrī (850–957) and Ibn Ḥawqal (d. c. 978) and a letter written in 1051 by a visiting Christian physician from Baghdad and later temporary resident of the city between 1055 and 1066, Ibn Buṭlān (d. 1066). This letter was addressed to Hilāl b. al-Muḥassin al-Ṣābī' and preserved by the biographer Yāqūt al-Ḥamawī (1179–1229), as well as by the historian/biographers Ibn al-Qifṭī (1172–1248) and Ibn al-'Adīm (1192–1262), in the latter's *Bughya* (*Bughyāt al-ṭalab fī tārīkh Ḥalab, Everything Desirable about the History of Aleppo*). Another key source in Arabic is a description of Antioch presumed to be written by an anonymous Christian Arab, though even his or her physical presence in Antioch is questionable.[39] The text must date before 1268, the Mamlūk destruction of the city, but after 969, the Byzantine reconquest, as it mentions the citadel, a newly built feature of this period.[40] The text also states that it is based on a Greek source (*Kitāb al-Yunāniyīn*), and it may have been translated into Syriac before Arabic.[41] Yet the text also conflates time, seemingly giving an account of the city as it appeared after its alleged founding by Antiochus, that is, the Seleucid city.[42] Using it as a guide to the urban topography of Antioch must thus be done with great care, since it anachronistically blends not only the city's history but also its buildings. Further, it names several "fantastical" structures, such as talismans for which we know were important parts of the Seleucid and Roman cityscape but not necessarily later. Nevertheless, it does provide much interesting and potentially useful information, and we have included here the account preserved in Codex Vaticanus Arabicus 286 (Figure 6.5). There is also an alternative version at the Bodleian Library (press mark 30, number 870). Some elements are repeated in a similar, likely partially copied account in the Crusader period by the Coptic Orthodox priest Abū al-Makārim (d. 1208); in the Ottoman period by Abdülkadir in his *Kitāb-i Tevarih-i Antakya*, dated to 1671; and in a version of the Codex by the Ottoman geographer Katip Çelebi (Hajji Khalifa) (1609–1657) in his *Cihânnümâ*. These descriptions are the longest medieval accounts of the city and focus on the built environment rather than the religious or political history of Antioch.

Administration

As part of the newly acquired province of Syria, John I Tzimisces (969–976) established Middle Byzantine Antioch as a *kouratoreion*, an imperial estate or treasury, and a *doukaton*, a military province, divided into smaller border *thémata* or themes. The *doukaton* of Antioch included about half the former Islamic frontier, including Cilicia eastward to the Cilician Gates and the coastal plain south to Tartus (Figure 6.2). The harbor of Antioch at this time was no longer Seleucia Pieria but al-Mina (Suetion, Arabic al-Suwaydīya, or the Crusader Port of St. Symeon), another important shift. This territory maximized resources and contained the entire coast, important as a buffer to the Fāṭimid threat. The roughly 18 small border themes, or *strategata*, were based around castle fortifications and located in or near virtually all the main cities of the Early Islamic *thughūr* frontier cities and others farther south into Syria.[43] In this stable landscape, castles, located on strategic high points, were the newest building form, around which settlements were splayed below, a hallmark of the post-tenth century medieval periods.

The Byzantine monk and historian Michael Psellos (c. 1017–c. 1078) characterized the *doukaton* of Antioch as one of the most important of the Byzantine Empire (*archē tōn megistōn*), *he periphanēs kai megalē Antiocheia*. The head of the *doukaton* was the *dux* or duke, a developed role of the *comes Orientes* and *magister*

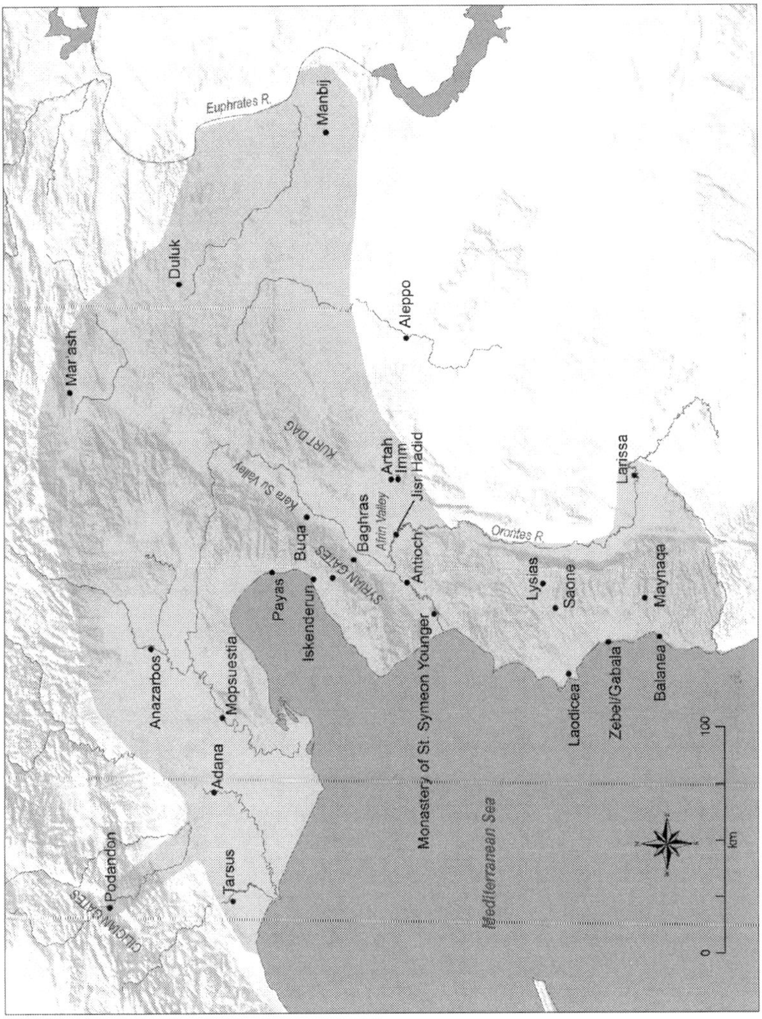

FIGURE 6.2 Map of Middle Byzantine duchy

Source: Created by Claire Ebert

militer per Orientum combined. Under him the governors (*strategoi*), each based in fortifications within the 18 or so *strategata* of the duchy of Antioch, along with a garrison, and other minor administrative officials, such as *taxiarchs*, installed in minor fortresses. Both duke and *strategos* positions were appointments made by the emperor. Many of the dukes of Antioch had short terms in office, on average two or three years, and were appointed to respond to specific military threats, often diplomatically. Some went on to become famous beyond Antioch.[44] Both positions of *dux* and *strategoi* do not, however, imply that the eastern Byzantine frontier of Antioch was a highly militarized province; rather, these positions were mostly ad hoc, and in quiet times these offices and garrisons were demobilized.[45]

In this period officials commonly used lead seals to authenticate private or official correspondence and documents, and these provide material evidence for the continuing importance of the local elites within the duchy of Antioch's administration. The lead seals, some in Antioch's Hatay Archeological Museum, include those of emperors, dukes of Antioch, patriarchs, bishops, and other functionaries (like *hypatoi*, *protonobilissimoi*, *protospatharioi*, and *spatharokandidatoi*).[46] Most were struck between 1060 and 1085, the end of Middle Byzantine rule; those from the tenth or twelfth centuries are rarer. Other seals belonged to members of important families in Antioch.[47] Nevertheless, the evidence for Byzantine administration is sparse, perhaps because the city lacked a *strategos* and paid no tribute; however, evidence for a *strategos* of Antioch named Eustathius Maleinus, the first after the reconquest, comes from a dedicatory inscription on a tenth-century reliquary/eucharist container (*artophorion)* of St. Anastastius the Persian. Furthermore, the local Syrian aristocracy still played an important role, largely in mid-level functionary positions, namely those in the majority Miaphysite/Syriac Orthodox community and in the Chalcedonian Orthodox/Melkite community.[48] One lead seal was for a Slav, Dobromir, a *spatharokandidatos* (mid-level *notarioi* or judge), who perhaps arrived as a soldier. Another lead seal for a *spatharocandidatus* was for a local Arab notable. Lead seals were also found for a female *protospatharia* (wife of a high-ranking general or a provincial governor, *protospatharios*, but by this period more commonly used as a general title of prestige like with Ībrāhīm b. Yūḥannā al-Abrotosbatiar) and a *strategissa* (wife of a *strategos*) from Antioch named Eudokia. Strangely, there is little evidence for the *kommerkiarioi* (officials in charge of trade), which does not necessarily indicate that Antioch was less of a mercantile center. Other positions included *kritai*, the chiefs of the civil administration, one of whom was based in Antioch, the other in Tarsus. *Protonobilissimioi* were also among the highest ranking commanders.[49] The Byzantine armies consisted of Armenian and Frankish mercenaries, as well as two of the imperial *tagmata* (cavalry units), Scholae and Hicanates. The *Escorial Taktikon*, a list of Byzantine offices and titles drawn up in the 970s, records 4,000 garrisons for the duchy of Antioch, although these were not necessarily all filled.[50] The seal evidence, meanwhile, suggests that while the highest positions were approved from Constantinople, these changed hands frequently and were not just handed out to Greeks. The rest of the administrative functionaries and city elite, perhaps in longer-held positions that offered more stability in how the city was run, remained mostly Arabic speaking local Antiochenes.

A new castle

The geographer al-Muqaddasī (945–991) wrote that the city of Diyarbakr (classical Amida, in southeastern Turkey) was like Antioch with its fortifications and outer gates, essentially comparing other city walls as renowned as Diyarbakr to those of famous Antioch. One of these towers was the first one occupied by Michael Bourtzes and his soldiers in their siege of 969 and was called Kalla or Koula, meaning "tower," by the Turks. Many sources commented that it was built, or at least used, for refuge. The city wall and towers were refortified again in 1016. Ibn Buṭ lān stated that the city was immense and had a double circuit wall with five gates (on the plain), a moat (*faṣīl*), and 360 towers in the shape of a semicircle (whose straight side was along the mountain). Four thousand patrol guards were sent from Constantinople, who were changed every two years.

The Codex Vaticanus similarly states there were 365 towers along the city walls.[51] It also mentions that the walls of the city were 4 miles long and 2.5 miles wide (Abū al-Makārim's version says 2), which does not, however, conform with Arab writers such as Idrisī and Mas'ūdī, who state that it was a one- or two-day journey in circumference, 12 miles long. The Codex may be the first source to give such a vast number of towers, two-and-a-half times the actual number, although the stated circumference of the city walls was closer to the actual distance. The Ottoman version by Abdülkadir counted 360 towers, each with two floors. Abū al-Makārim's version, meanwhile, counts only 153 towers; this number deviates greatly from the Codex and is closer to the actual number, though still inflated a bit. The number of towers was likely a conflation but one that permeated sources after this point, one tower for each day of the year. A more accurate number provided by Mas'ūdī and corroborated in Byzantine sources is 136, even though Mas'ūdī's wall length of 12 miles (equivalent to about 13.42 modern US/international miles or 21.6 km using 1.8 km to 1 Arabic mile) was exaggerated. Justinian's walls were about 5.8 miles (9.3 km) in perimeter. These towers and the city wall all predated the Middle Byzantine conquest. Repairs to the walls and towers did take place following the siege of the city, and after earthquakes. This may be what Abū al-Makārim was referring to regarding an earthquake that collapsed 32 towers from the Sea/Bridge Gate to the Aleppo Gate along the Orontes; the towers sank into the river and the river flowed into the city, splitting it in the center, perhaps along the Parmenius. The Codex also highlights two towers in the walls: the Tower of al-Abalāt (perhaps a corruption of al-Abliṭa, "Tower of the Tiles," but this is not certain) on the west slope and the Tower of the Spiral Staircase, or al-Jār, on the summit.

Of the seven gates that are mentioned in the Codex, five were of bronze; three of these five can be identified as the Garden (or Palm) Gate, Aleppo Gate, and Bridge or Sea Gate, possibly also called St. Simeon's Gate.[52] The Gate of St. George and the Dog Gate would have been the other two functional gates, though they are not named. Abū al-Makārim's version states that the gates were of iron with coated panels. Besides the five main gates, there were also two smaller, unidentified gates (totaling seven). One of these smaller two would have been the Iron Gate dam. Another may have been the postern Olive Gate on the eastern portion of the southern wall on the mountain, mentioned in Chapters 4, 9, and 10, this volume. Five bridges were built over the Wadī al-Jashkarūsh (Parmenius), one for an aqueduct and the rest for pedestrians in winter when the water was high. Katip Çelebi's account wrongly states that the Orontes passed through three of the city's gates, which suggests he never visited the city.

The most important new construction in the city, however, was the "amazingly built" citadel (*castellum aedificatum mirabile*) on top of Mt. Silpius, south of the Parmenius mountain stream and the Iron Gate. The question of when the citadel was built remains unresolved, but it was likely by the Byzantines soon after the reconquest by Nicephorus II in 969; it was then repaired during the reign of Basil II in 1000 or 1016. The first act of the Byzantines, recorded by Ibn al-'Adīm in the thirteenth century, after their reconquest was to build a citadel on the mountain.[53] Ibn 'Abd al-Zahir, the thirteenth century biographer of the Mamlūk Sultan Baybars, wrote that it was built by al-Lawn b. al-Faqās.[54] The Bodleian Library Codex states that within the gate of the citadel was a residential street for the dwellings of artisans and engineers.[55] The citadel was never successfully breached, even though the city was besieged by the Fāṭimids four times, as well as by Turkish and Arab tribes. It likely rested on earlier sites, such as the acropolis from the city's earliest Seleucid history.[56]

Ottoman sources provide further description. The surveys of Richard Pococke, Jean-Joseph-François Poujoulat, and Tinco Martinus Lycklama, Western travelers to the city, reveal that the castle was square and had 14 semicircular turrets, seven to the east and seven to the west, including either side of the entrance at the southwest and in the northeast corner. The castle was built and vaulted with many underground rooms and cisterns below, measuring 200 paces in perimeter and built of small cut stones; it also had the remains of a bath. The descriptions of the citadel, however, also assuredly depict it in its final state, after likely renovations in the Crusader period.

Outside the castle, between it and the mountain's summit, was a round reservoir. It measured 50 or 53 paces in diameter and 8 feet deep and was built of stones and brick. The German mathematician and cartographer Carsten Niebuhr (1733–1815) stated the reservoir was 120 feet in diameter, while the British physician and traveler Charles Perry (1698–1780) wrote that it was 135 feet. Francis Rawdon Chesney (1789–1872) noted a circular structure in rock 90 feet in diameter and enclosed with walls 4 feet high in the center of the mountain ridge. He also wrote that the reservoir was built of small cut stones, 70 meters (230 feet) in circumference, and thought it could have watered gardens near the castle. It is not clear which of the structures matches the reservoir mentioned by others, and perhaps there were two.

The citadel, like the one built in Baghrās, are two of the earliest examples representing a new style of architecture and urban planning that was quickly replicated.

It was roughly triangular in shape with the main buildings concentrated on its southern and western sides; the northeast was taken up by the large open bailey (ward or *baqqār*). Its southern wall was interspersed with semi-circular buttress towers, while its western side was not completely fortified, rather using the steep slopes of the mountain itself to limit access (Figure 6.3 and Appendix 1). Upland, strategic, and difficult-to-access fortifications were not a feature of Early Islamic settlements, urban or rural. Likewise, nearly all the known Islamic-Byzantine frontier sites were well-connected walled cities on the plains rather than highland castles.[57] So too were small, fortified enclosures such as Roman and Byzantine *quadriburgia* and Early Islamic *quṣūr*. Such a strategic upland fortification heralded the beginning of a more uncertain period of political instability after the tenth century, where cities needed not only defensible and inaccessible military strongholds but also, more importantly, walled refuges for their population, a process termed *incastellemento*. The citadel represents the transition from a Late Antique or Early Medieval city to a medieval one, and it became a key component of the city's successive sieges, being often the last part of the city to be taken.

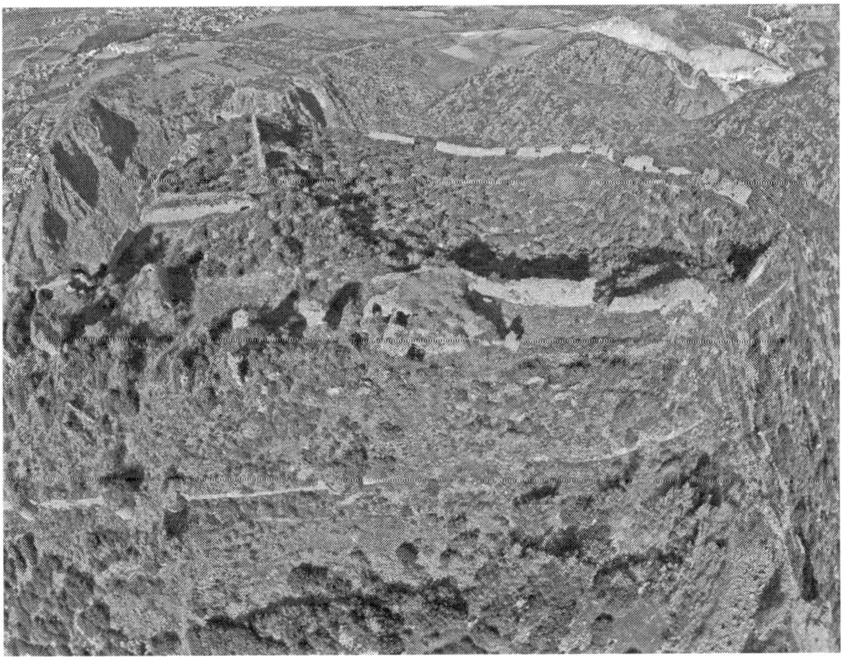

FIGURE 6.3 (a) Middle Byzantine/Crusader citadel on Mt. Silpius, aerial view of the southern half looking north with drone

Source: Photograph courtesy of Hakan Boyacı

FIGURE 6.3 (b) Plan of the Middle Byzantine/Crusader citadel

Source: Created by Steve Batiuk

The Fāṭimid invasions

Politically, the remaining period of Byzantine rule can be divided into four periods marked by internal and external upheaval. Soon after the reconquest, the new Byzantine rulers faced the long-reaching arm of the Shīʿah Fāṭimid caliphs of Egypt, eager to establish themselves and acquire former ʿAbbāsid territory in Syria. According to Ibn Munala in Ibn al-Shiḥna and al-Maqrizī, in 971 the Berber general Ja'far b. Falāḥ, who had already conquered Palestine and central Syria for the Fāṭimids, sent a *ghulām* of the Fāṭimid caliph Mu'izz al-Dīn Allāh named Futūḥ with a huge army to Antioch.[58] But after laying siege for five months, he was unable to take the city, though he caused significant damage, and so returned to Egypt after signing a cease-fire with the Byzantines. The damage was compounded by an earthquake in 972 or 973 in which a large piece of the city wall collapsed, and towers.[59] That summer, John Tzimisces sent 12,000 builders and bricklayers to Michael Bourtzes to repair the wall, along with 136 towers, and restore the city to better than its previous state. This important act of imperial patronage was the largest wall restoration since Justinian and shows that Constantinople regarded Antioch as an important buffer outpost.

In 976, Basil II (976–1025) succeeded Tzimisces and appointed Bourtzes as the first *dux* of Antioch, in part as a response to the Fāṭimid threat. Basil II also continued the renovation program started by Tzimisces and added a cemetery, mausoleum (possibly for himself, with a marble sarcophagus), and monastery.[60] In 992, Fāṭimid armies from Egypt led by the Turkish general Mangūtakīn[61] and some of his companions, including Bashāra al-Qala'ī, Ibn Abī Ramāda, and Mā'ḍid b. Ẓālim, attempted to take the region once again. The general sent an envoy to the *katepano* (a senior military official) of Antioch for diplomatic negotiations; however, the Byzantine official jailed the envoy. The Fāṭimids approached Antioch, burning the outskirts of the city and taking much booty, including an immeasurable number of water buffalo (around 10,000) and cattle. The Antiochenes fired arrows, and the Fāṭimids withdrew but returned a year later, and again in 996 and 998. Meanwhile, Basil II, unhappy with how the envoy was treated, demanded to speak with him directly and freed him.[62] After 993, Basil replaced Michael Bourtzes with the *dux* Damianus Dalassenus. He also sent additional troops to Antioch, led by the *magistros*, or senior administrator, Leo Melissenus, and more in April 995, this time an army composed of Greek, Russian, Bulgarian, and Georgian troops. In the last campaign of 998, the Byzantine garrison clashed with the Fāṭimids at the Garden Gate, and the Antiochene citizens joined in, perhaps as a militia (*'aḥdāt*).[63] Disastrously, however, Damianus was killed, and the Fāṭimids spread throughout the Amuq Plain to Mar'ash.[64] The setback was only temporary, however, as the Byzantines held onto Antioch and quickly reversed their losses.[65] After this, Fāṭimid assaults on Antioch subsided for over half a century.

The Churches of St. Peter and the Theotokos

Aside from re-expanding territory on the frontier, the new Byzantine rulers encouraged the city's re-Christianization and the settlement of its surrounding region. Part of their reason was to reclaim those cities, churches, and relics of historical and religious importance, and legendary and spiritual Antioch featured high on that list. In addition to sparing and preserving the Christian community of Antioch after the conquest, the emperors, notably Basil II, actively settled Christians – including Melkite, Miaphysites, refugee Christians from Egypt and Palestine, and Armenians – and established bishoprics in the area and on the coast.[66] One of these bishoprics was for the Armenians who were garrisoned at Antioch, and the Armenian community of Antioch had its own bishop appointed soon after the reconquest, the Catholicos Ter Xac'ik I Arsaruni (972/973–992). Christians also emigrated from Palestine and Egypt to Antioch from 1012 to 1014 owing to Fāṭimid persecution. Yaḥya al-Anṭākī, himself an émigré from Egypt, wrote that this may have been part of the persecutions under the Fātimid caliph al-Ḥākim (996–1021), who allowed Christians and Jews to go to Antioch and other Byzantine-controlled lands.[67] Melkite Greek Orthodox nobles (*archontes* or *prouchontes*, *ru'asā' al-madīna*), who spoke Arabic, flourished in Antioch and came to hold a majority influence, marking a shift from the previous dominance of the Miaphysites. One of the few inscriptions from Antioch in the Hatay Museum (exact provenance unknown) gives evidence of this multiculturalism and its Arabic-speaking Christian community. The inscription is funerary, dating to 999, however, using the Constantinople calendar system and not an Islamic *hijrī* date. Further, the tombstone is bilingual, dedicated to Basil, a Melkite and "Server of God." Basil is named and his position is given in Greek, while the date of his death and a prayer for forgiveness is in Arabic (Figure 6.4).[68] Ibn Buṭlān as well as the Codex Vaticanus provide the most information on the Christian communities of this period.

The Byzantine reconquest thus represented a re-Christianization of the city, and several churches continued to operate while new ones were built. The sources frequently mention the main church of Antioch, the Church of St. Peter, referred to as the Qusiyān or Cassianus in the Early Islamic period. Byzantine sources state that the church was rebuilt as the Cathedral of Antioch under Basil II. Under Patriarch John III Polites (996–1021), the church was restored based on Justinian's Hagia Sophia in Constantinople, although whether this perhaps could refer to the properties or organization of the church rather than the architectural plan is unclear.[69] Ibn Buṭlān wrote that it was originally the palace of Qusiyān, a king whose son was Futrus or Petros (Peter), chief of the disciples and resurrected. It lay in the center of the city, along with many other elaborately decorated churches with mosaics, colored glass, and colored marble, "more than one can count." He also said that the church was multifunctional; it had a chapel (*haykāl*) 100 paces (*khaṭwa*) long and 80 paces wide (roughly 100 × 80 meters) over which the church was built on columns, and it functioned as a court and school with judges and grammar and logic teachers and students. The church was also equipped with servants who received daily rations, an office (*diwān*) of church expenditures and receipts, and more than ten accountants – the patriarch's administrative offices and treasury. Presumably the church was restored after Ibn Manik's plunders. Ibn Buṭlān also writes that "at one of the gates of this church is a Clepshydra (*finjān*) [water clock] showing the hours. It works day and night continuously, twelve hours at a round, and it is one of the wonders of the world."[70]

The location of the Church of St. Peter, however, remains unknown. From the texts, it seems that its construction was connected with that of the old palace. A Chinese report describing an official visit in 945 says that the clock, an automaton, could be seen coming out of the royal residence. On the upper floor of the second of three large gates, all decorated with precious stones, a large golden scale

FIGURE 6.4 Greek and Arabic bilingual inscription on tombstone, Hatay Museum

Source: Photo taken by Andrea de Giorgi

was suspended in the type of a steelyard weight. Twelve golden balls hung from the horizontal bar, one for each hour. A human figure of gold was "of the size of a man standing upright, on whose side, whenever an hour has come, one of the balls will drop, the dingling sound of which makes known the divisions of the day without the slightest mistake" (Figure 6.5).[71]

It is unlikely there were two such clocks, and perhaps the Chinese account confused the royal residence with the church. The Codex Vaticanus account describes

FIGURE 6.5 "The Castle Water Clock" from al-Jazarī's *Book of Knowledge of Ingenious Mechanical Devices*, 1315. Eastern Turkey or Syria. 14.533

Source: Photograph copyright 2020 Museum of Fine Arts, Boston

the king's palace, which the author calls *balāt*, as also in the center of the city, and in some ways it is quite similar to Ibn Buṭlān's description of St. Peter's Church

> in which are architectural ornaments, and columns of red, white and mottled marble; also in it are specimens of marvelous things, the descriptions of which cannot be portrayed. And it has seven high doors of iron, plated with pure gold; over each door is an idol-talisman, (so that) no cavalry horse of

> the (hostile) army can neigh and charge (against it)… . And outside of it is the court of the judge and the magistrates.

The seven gates of iron echo descriptions of the gates of Antioch itself. Abū al-Makārim's version also resembles Ibn Buṭlān's; he mentions a central palace of marble called Masayla with a spiral staircase, above which was an unknown domed church and seven markets, some roofed, some unroofed. There were houses for the wise men, *diwāns*, and judges. Interestingly, Katip Çelebi's account, which is in the style of the Codex and al-Makārim, writes only of the church, stating that it was in the middle of the city with walls covered in gold and silver and staffed by 100 young men and 500 beautiful girls and 500 monks.[72]

The mention of the clock on a palace also suggests that the church was (re)built after the Chinese visit in 945, and during the Middle Byzantine conquest on or above the marble columns of the palace of the Islamic ruler, which would have been in the center of the city and not on an island (perhaps a *dār al-'imara* or preexisting palace).[73] The Qusiyān church, however, is mentioned throughout the Early Islamic period as the most important church and so predates the Middle Byzantine siege, and it is more likely that the Codex Vaticanus account references old lore of the structure, perhaps that it used to be the royal palace, as Ibn Buṭlān states. Still, it is unusual that Abū al-Makārim's account would describe this most famous church as "unknown." One speculation – based on the details of the clock on an old palace, the church on columns, and the presence of a court of judges and teachers – is that it was built over the old basilica of justice, the Regia.[74] Supporting this speculation is a mention related to the Jewish community in 70 CE of a fire in Antioch that destroyed the four-square market, magistrate's quarters, hall of records, and basilicas. The theory is that this could have been the judicial quarter, housing the Hall of Records (*grammatophylacium*).

St. Peter's was also the home of the Melkite patriarch, housing important relics of the church. The role of patriarch of Antioch was a powerful one in the Byzantine empire. Unlike the Early Islamic period, in the era of the reconquest, the Byzantine emperor appointed nearly all the Melkite patriarchs of Antioch rather than caliphs or the city's local notables. This last group, the regional bishops, often clashed with the imperial capital over influence in selecting the patriarch.[75] Many of these patriarchs came from Constantinople. Following a gap of a few years in patriarchs after Christopher's murder, John Tzimisces appointed the monk Theodore II (970–976) as the Melkite patriarch of Antioch through an agreement with Polyeuctus, the patriarch of Constantinople. One of Theodore's first acts in 970 was to remove the body of the decapitated Patriarch Christopher from the monastery church of Mar Arshāyā outside the city, where the remains had initially been laid for three years, and entomb him in a delicate marble container (*jurn laṭīf*) on a marble table (*mā'ida*) on the west side (possibly narthex) of the Church of St. Peter for a time. *Jurn* should be less a sarcophagus and more a hollowed stone through which liquid is poured for ablutions or even baptism. In this context, the description of the container as delicate or fine, and coupled with this fashion of interring his remains in an elevated visible way, rather than burying him, away from the liturgical focus of the church or the side aisles, but on display for congregants coming in and out of the church, suggests Christopher was placed within a small ossuary and reliquary rather than a tomb.[76] The reliquary would likely not have looked like a small sarcophagus, as Boudier suggests with the fifth-century example from Hūarte in Syria, but perhaps more like a marble version of the Artophorion (container for Eucharist) of St. Anastasius the Persian, used as a reliquary and votive and dated to 969/970 and said to come from Antioch. The silver reliquary's date and provenance come from its inscription dedicated to a certain Eustathios Maleinus, cousin of the Emperor Nicephorus II and proconsul (*anthypatos)*, patrician, and the first *strategos* of Antioch after the reconquest, who would have held office exactly during this translation. It is in the shape of a cross-in-square typical Middle Byzantine church with a dome, external apse, and doors on three side. It is tempting to view the micro-architectural form as a model of what St. Peter's Church looked like at the time; however, this is only speculative, as we have no visual depictions of Antioch's most important church. Further, some have argued that it is a model of the *aedicula* over Christ's tomb in the Church of the Holy Sepulchre in Jerusalem (Figure 6.6).[77]

A procession throughout the city then established Christopher as a martyr and one of the patron saints of Antioch. Patriarch Nicholas II (1025–1030) eventually translated Christopher's body for the third time to within the church treasury, also identified as the House of St. Peter, perhaps a euphemism for the church or perhaps a reference to the micro-architectural church model reliquary.[78] The body was brought alongside a host of relics (*lībsānāt*, a modification of the Greek word) and miraculous transformative liquids (*ḥuyūl*) of the other pantheon of Antiochene saints: St. Ignatius, St. Babylas, St. John the Baptist, the crozier (*shabbūqa)* of John Chrysostom, the collar or corded rope (*minṭaqa*) of Symeon the Elder, the Holy Lance (*al-darba al-karīma al-sayidiya)*, and the throne (*kursī*) and staff (*shabbūqa*) of St. Peter.[79] Patriarch Theodore III (1034–1042) also moved some relics of the ninth-century stylite Timothy from the saint's own village and monastery at Kākhustā, between Antioch and Aleppo, to St. Peter's.[80] Timothy's body was thereafter moved to the chapel (*haykāl*) of St. Domitius in the neighborhood of the Garden Gate, although it is not known when.[81] During this period, Antioch developed continuously as home to the veneration of a host of local saints and martyrs. As a religious center, Antioch remained the focus of its own pantheon, attracting pilgrims and elite alike.

Local rebellions and imperial involvement

Despite the attention Constantinople gave to Antioch during this period, there was much political maneuvering and rebellion between the appointed officials of the capital and the people of the city.[82] A series of local rebellions showed how difficult it was to rule the duchy of Antioch; not only was this typical of a frontier region, but it had also characterized the city throughout its history. In some cases

FIGURE 6.6 Artophorion (reliquary) of St. Anastasius the Persian

Source: Courtesy of Aachen Domeschatzkamme, T15-G-31

the rebellions came from the sometimes divided communities within the city, while in many others, the population, or segments of it, were stirred to protest by individuals rejecting outside authority and manipulating the population in their favor. From this series of local insurgencies, ambitious Byzantines used the powerful office of *dux* and, when possible, the support of the city's citizens to gain local power.

Contributing to the strife was a religiously divided Christian community. Most officials were Melkites, and most residents were Miaphysite Syriac Orthodox. But the religious character of the conflicts may also reflect doctrinally partisan sources.[83]

Furthermore, religious persecutions by Melkites of the Miaphysites and to a lesser extent the Armenians in 983 and again in 1054 and 1076/77 may have reduced the non-Chalcedonian communities significantly.[84] The Melkite patriarch Agapius II (978–995) was a main instigator of the persecutions of 983, getting Constantinople to back him and promising land and wealth to those willing to carry the persecutions out. He was also said to have ravaged the "large church" of the Miaphysites and burned the gospels and liturgical objects, and he also attempted to convert many Miaphysites and Armenians either with gifts and important meetings with nobles or by confiscating lands and banishing some individuals.[85] It is possible he was motivated in this purge more by greed and power than religious fervor. Eventually, however, Agapius was challenged by the Miaphysite patriarch Athanasius IV (986–1002) and removed in 995.

In 1036, a quarrel between the priests of the Miaphysite church and the *archon* (governor) over money led the latter to give money intended for the Miaphysite church to the Melkite church instead; he also asked its patriarch, Theodorus III (1034–1042), to seal up the doors of the Miaphysite church and arrest its priests until they converted. Allegedly, 11,000 Miaphysites joined the Melkite church at this time, and the Melkites burned the Miaphysite church down:

> The priests also became Melkites (*malakiah*), and they left (their) belief, and they went to the aforementioned church (*biya'*), and plundered it and demolished the sanctuary (*haykal*), and they took the Offering (*qurban*) which was in it and cast it into the river, and they demolished the church and dominated over the people and afflicted the majority of them until they become Melkites.[86]

The church in both of these instances may have been the Theotokos Church, used as the main church by the Miaphysite congregation, and possibly rebuilt and repaired. One seemingly rare instance of good relations between the two groups, however, occurred in 1028, when the *dux* was healed miraculously of his leprosy by the Miaphysite patriarch John VII bar 'Abdun (1004–1033).[87]

Some rebellions were about local power, often crossing Christian and Muslim lines. Bardas Sclerus, ally and general of John Tzimisces, who was deposed following the emperor's death, had plans of his own for the imperial throne, and from 976 to 979 he led a revolt against the new emperor, Basil II. He also made alliances with several local individuals on the frontier and succeeded in gaining control of Antioch itself, installing a *basilikos* (civil official) named Kulayb, a Christian Arab who had formerly served the Hamdānids. Bardas next appointed as *magistros* and *shaykh* 'Ubaydallāh of Malatya, an Arab Christian convert who had the support of Antioch's nobles (*ru'asā' al-madīna*). At this time, Agapius, who was originally patriarch of Aleppo, hoped to be selected by the emperor as the new patriarch of Antioch and so convinced 'Ubaydallāh to act against Bardas and support Basil II. As a sign of support, the Orthodox community of Antioch rose up against Bardas Sclerus's general Isaac Brachamius, as well as Armenian supporters of Bardas in the city. In 978, to reward 'Ubaydallāh for taking Antioch from Bardas, Basil II made the *magistros* the new *dux* for life, and Agapius II became patriarch of both Antioch and Aleppo.[88] Kulayb and 'Ubaydallāh, both Arab Christians, represent the Byzantines' support of local authority in the region and the complexity of reasserting Byzantine power in a well-established formerly Islamic city.

Ultimately, however, Bardas's rebellion was defeated by Bardas Phocas, brother of the emperor Nicephorus Phocas, a successful general who had revolted against John Tzimisces and been imprisoned but was restored to power after Basil II came to the throne following Tzimisces's death in 976. Although Bardas Sclerus fled to Baghdad, the peace did not last long, for Phocas installed his own son, Leo, in control of Antioch, but Leo then revolted against the emperor. He also invited Muslims to the city, angering the local population, and so, fearing them, he built a tower on the mountain for a possible retreat. Under orders from his father, Leo also removed Patriarch Agapius from the city by trickery in 989. But that same year, the Antiochenes succeeded in overthrowing Leo and handed him over to Michael Bourtzes.

Meanwhile, the *magistros* Nicephorus Uranus, a close associate of Basil II, was sent to Baghdad to secure custody of Bardas for his return. Eventually he was promoted to *katepano* (second to the *dux*) of Antioch, then *dux* in December 999, a position he may have held until 1011. Between 1005 and 1007, he wrote letters recounting how he put down the rebellion of a local Islamic ruler, al-Asfar.[89]

The confusing political landscape at this time also gave rise to numerous Byzantine/Islamic alliances and internal Byzantine and Islamic defections. For example, Basil II granted asylum and high status to Manṣūr b. Lu'lu, ruler of Aleppo and son of a deposed Hamdānid chamberlain, who himself had been deposed from rule by Arab tribes. In 1016, the *katepano* (called *quṭbān* in Arabic sources) of Antioch gave Manṣūr a residence for his family and servants (amounting to 700 people) in Antioch, estates as *iqta'* (lands given in exchange for service) on the outskirts, a plot in the city, enlistment in the army, monthly stipends from the treasury, and the title of *magistros*.[90] He also gave to Manṣūr's brothers and sons ranks of honor and governorships.[91] Part of this likely stemmed from the Byzantines' failure to take Aleppo, prompting them to resort to a combination of diplomacy, invasion, and manipulation. They were, however, content not to rule the territory directly but to establish a buffer state that was relatively compliant.

In 1030, Emperor Romanus III Argyrus (1028–1034), campaigning against the Mirdāsids of Aleppo – a local Arab Shi'a dynasty of the Banū Kilāb who paid tribute to the Byzantines – stayed in Antioch for a week, directing the construction of siege engines. The campaign, however, was unsuccessful, and his encampment with his army outside Antioch created a drain on its resources. Nevertheless, he also conducted successful diplomatic negotiations with the Banū Ṭayyi' tribe of southern Syria, who agreed to support the Byzantines in the event of a Byzantine campaign against the Fāṭimids. He also negotiated with the Fāṭimids, carried out by the eunuch *katepano* Nicetas of Mistheia, who governed Antioch as *dux* from 1030 to 1032.[92] The emperor's successor Michael IV (1034–1041) then promoted his own brother Nicetas as the new *dux* of Antioch in 1034.[93]

But in that same year, the Antiochenes rebelled against their tax collector (*phorologos*) Salibas, a local Melkite whose impositions were excessive, and killed him, and refused to allow the new *dux* Nicetas to enter the city until he agreed not to punish them. Part of the trouble was blamed on Constantine Dalassenus, son of the former *dux* Damianus, who had held the position of *dux* from 1024 and was accused of stirring up insurrection against Nicetas and his brother. Nicetas, however, put down the rebellion with 100 rebels killed and sent 11 Antiochene leaders responsible for instigating the rebellion to the emperor in Constantinople. After Nicetas's death, Michael appointed another brother, Constantine, as *dux* of Antioch, and also pardoned the 11 rebels and sent them back to the city.

Under the emperors Constantine IX Monomachus (1043–1055), who was born in Antioch in 1000, and Constantine X Doucas (1059–1067), Antioch's military was scaled down, and many were sent to fight on the western borders with Bulgaria. In part this was intended to weaken the influence of the military aristocracy and the potential for uprisings that had been so common in the first half of the century.[94]

Nonetheless, local Antiochene rebellions continued into the century's second half. In 1056/1057, several generals, led by Isaac Comnenus, former *strategos autokrator* (commander of other *strategoi*) of the East under Basil II, and Catacalon Cecaumenus, a *dux* of Antioch who had just been deposed by Emperor Michael VI Bringas (1056–1057), successfully rebelled against the latter, and Isaac ascended the throne as Isaac I Comnenus (1057–1059). At the same time, between 1055 and 1057, the Fāṭimids again advanced under their commander Makīn al-Dawla al-Ḥasan b. ʿAlī b. Mulhim, who plundered the area of Antioch when Catacalon Cecaumenus was still the *dux*.

During the reign of Constantine X Doucas, the eunuch Nicephorus (known as Nicephoritzes, or "little Nicephorus"), who had formerly served under Michael VI, was appointed as *dux* of Antioch. The appointment, though, was a sort of exile to remove him far from the court of Constantinople after he had accused the empress Eudocia Macrembolitissa of adultery. During this time, he instigated conflicts with neighboring Muslim rulers and oppressed the Antiochenes with fees and taxes and land confiscations, while the Orthodox patriarch Aemilian (1074–1078) backed the Antiochenes in resisting him. Finally, Empress Eudocia had Nicephoritzes arrested after her husband's death in 1067 and brought back to Constantinople.[95]

Religious communities and other churches

Following a 70-year period of quiescence, the first of a series of earthquakes struck in 1050, destroying parts of the Church of St. Peter, and the building was further damaged sometime between 1050 and 1054.[96] The descriptions given by

Ibn Buṭlān and Michael the Syrian of damage caused by the two earthquakes provide a great deal of detail of its interior. A huge storm also struck the city on April 13 or May 25, 1050, a Sunday, in the middle of the night. Lightning traveled down a massive silver chain over the altar, breaking it off and melting it. It also struck a mother-of-pearl screen, presumably the chancel, in front of the altar and broke its iron cross and silver crown. A silver-domed cupola wrapped in brocade and suspended on four marble columns covered the altar like a baldacchino; the altar was undamaged. But the marble pavers in front of the altar were hit by lightning, and their mortar cracked, and one marble slab was thrown up, landing on the silver dome above the altar. In the treasury were three wooden stools with a large silver cross inlaid with precious stones on each one. The middle one was preserved, while the ones on either side were smashed. Another feature, a wooden pulley and hemp rope holding a silver tray with bowls for glass lamps, was untouched. Michael the Syrian framed the destruction as punishment for the Melkites owing to their destruction of the newly built church of the Miaphysites; his interpretation that the disaster was divinely wrought is another indication of the tension between the Syriac and Orthodox religious communities.

The earthquake of 1063[97] already mentioned may also have coincided with or caused a fire in the Church of St. Peter. This occurred during a solar eclipse, which, in turn, Melkites in the city interpreted as a divine punishment because the Miaphysite church had become too powerful, with numerous followers and much wealth. According to Smbat, the Miaphysites community had been living a wealthy, luxurious lifestyle, their women adorning themselves in gold on feast days, their children riding to church on the backs of donkeys.[98] In 1054, one of the most senior and wealthy Miaphysite Christians, influenced by Greek Orthodox doctrine, attempted to convert followers of the Syriac liturgy while decrying his own community, leading others to convert as well. In 1076/77, Patriarch Aemilian also joined in and commanded that the Syriac gospels be burned. Apparently, as the gospels were lit, voices emerged from the fire and the gospels remained untouched; it took three tries to finally burn them. Syriac and Armenian sources also reported that the Orthodox patriarch and a mob entered St. Peter's; thereupon the church shook in an earthquake, and fire fell upon it from the sky, burning it as the ground tore apart. The altar split and sank, and a noteworthy gem placed by Constantine, as well as much gold (150,000 pieces), was swallowed up in the quake.[99] Four other unidentified Melkite churches also burned in this fire, but no Armenian or Miaphysite church was harmed.

Smbat writes that the 1063 earthquake also jolted a Roman parade ground where a small bridge had been built over a mountain torrent, possibly referring to the Bridge or Arch of Fishes and the forum of Valens. Here, the patriarch, priests, and deacons had been marching around the city in prayer and had paused at a Roman pavilion. Near the small bridge, the earth swallowed more than 10,000 people;[100] the source states one could hear them cry for 15 days. The bridge over the torrent suggests the Parmenius stream, yet the parade ground suggests the Island's hippodrome or the old Campus Martius on the river's west side. It seems as though parade grounds had moved into the city, perhaps at the northern side. The whole event, told through a Syriac and Armenian filter, suggests that non-Miaphysite and non-Armenian Christians were evildoers who were punished.

The only important church from the Early Islamic period not mentioned by name but known to still be in use in the Crusader period was the Church of the Theotokos, built under Justinian (see Chapter 4). This is the church referred to in passing as the former Temple of Mars, and its use in the Crusader period suggests it was still standing in the Middle Byzantine. This is also likely the church used by the Miaphysite. As noted earlier, the Melkites had allegedly burned down the main Miaphysite church in 1036 over a fight about money. This may be the same event that prompted the temporary closure of the Miaphysite church and the conversion of many of its clergy to Greek Orthodoxy. We have also seen how the Melkite patriarch Agapius II caused severe damage to the "large church" of the Syriacs in 983, as well as the religious tensions in connection with the earthquake of 1063. At this time, the newly built Miaphysite church was confiscated, requiring its congregation to go to surrounding villages to pray. All these events suggest there was only one Miaphysite church, the Theotokos, in the city during the Middle Byzantine period. Its turbulent history may partially explain why the Theotokos church is not easily named or identified in Middle Byzantine sources, as it may have been intermittently closed for repairs.

The Vatican Codex mentions the Church of Ashmunit, which we can assume was still functioning from the Early Islamic period, and it was likely the same place as the Church of the Maccabees/Seven Martyrs mentioned in Abū al-Makārim's version, though listed separately. Abū al-Makārim adds that each year there was a large festival built around the church and a big market. The Church of St. Barbara still served as a site for commemoration and celebration every December 4 on her feast day, with participation by the Melkite patriarch and the *dux*. Both edifices thus survived from the Early Islamic period. Soon after the reconquest in 969, Archbishop Theodore of Seleucia built two new "beautiful" churches, one of which was dedicated to St. John Chrysostom, constructed over the saint's house.[101] This was possibly a chapel 20 feet square, and the saint's house was still inhabited at the time of his visit. The other was the Church of Azkas'utis (*al-azks'awṭs*), an unknown and unclear corrupted name, clarified in another manuscript version with *li-l-ksābtrīghūs*. The latter description possibly could be an Arabized form of the Greek "chief of the angels" (*al-arkistrātīghūs*), suggesting that perhaps it is St. Michael the Archangel.[102] However, this would be the only known reference to a church of St. Michael the Archangel since the sixth century, after which it was assumed the church was abandoned or destroyed. Another possibility is that it was from the Armenian, *Astvatsin* (Mother of God), but built as a new construction, obviously not the same as the Theotokos in the city.[103]

The Vatican Codex also mentions two caves whose associations imply religious function: one on the slopes above the Aleppo Gate called al-Tahakimā or al-Nashakimā, "the impregnable," which is perhaps where St. Peter's grotto is today, the other on the slopes to the southwest called the cavern of Teqlā, a shrine for St. Thecla.[104] According to the text, the Temple of Mars (Ares), next to the mountain, became the Church of the Theotokos or Kanīsā Maryam.[105] The Codex also mentions a nearby bath on the west side of the eastern hill (likely Bath F of the Princeton excavations), north of the Parmenius, possibly in sector 16-O, just inside the Aleppo Gate, as does the Ottoman version. If this description is accurate, it would suggest that the Theotokos was at the Aleppo Gate. It was also near the Arch or Bridge of Fishes, which was a structure over the Parmenius, possibly in sector 16-O. At the head of this church was a spring of hot water; six others were also found in different quarters, to which marvelous virtues were attributed for the cure of various maladies. The dome of the church was a cupola on four arches, and in the later Ottoman version by Abdülkadir, the statue (of Mars, but perhaps of the Virgin) was in gold. According to this text,

> There was, east of one of the bridges of the city [Antioch], called the Fish Bridge, a Temple dedicated to Saturn,[106] and another in the middle of the City dedicated to Mars, which was called the Church of the Virgin.

The location of the Temple of Mars, then, differs in the Ottoman account and was farther from the Aleppo Gate. The description of the Mars temple is similar in the accounts, however: the temple had 120 columns of white marble, 40 doors of yellow copper or brass, gold- and silver-decorated walls, chrysolite floors, a dome on four arches topped with the statue of Mars, and beneath his feet a serpent and scorpion.[107] Interestingly, Ibn al-Shih.na writes there was a statue of the Virgin at the church. Also on a river – likely the Parmenius and not the Orontes – was a *praetorium* (*baṭarim*), or court of justice (*bibinā' muhakimahi*), and causeway (*qāld.r.m*) or castle (*qaṣr*), perhaps on the site of the former theater or forum of Valens.[108]

The Princeton archaeological excavations also revealed a Middle Byzantine church. In sector 16-O, stratigraphically above the Early Islamic level, was the Middle Byzantine level (Level II), consisting of an eleventh-century pavement and cemetery. In 16-P, above the Early Islamic layer, was a later level (Level X) dated to the Middle Byzantine tenth to twelfth centuries, which revealed a small basilica-style, three-aisled medieval church. The church was colonnaded and roofed but not vaulted and, oddly, was oriented north–south with the *cardo* rather than the standard east–west, showing the emphasis on orthogonality in the medieval city. Fragments of a chancel screen carved in relief with simple foliage in a symmetrical pattern led Jean Lassus to speculate that it might be of Umayyad date rather than Byzantine. On either side of the church was a cemetery, containing adults and children buried with grave goods (Figure 6.7). Two Arabic gravestones were uncovered. It can be suggested that neither were in their original location, as one, dating originally between 969 and

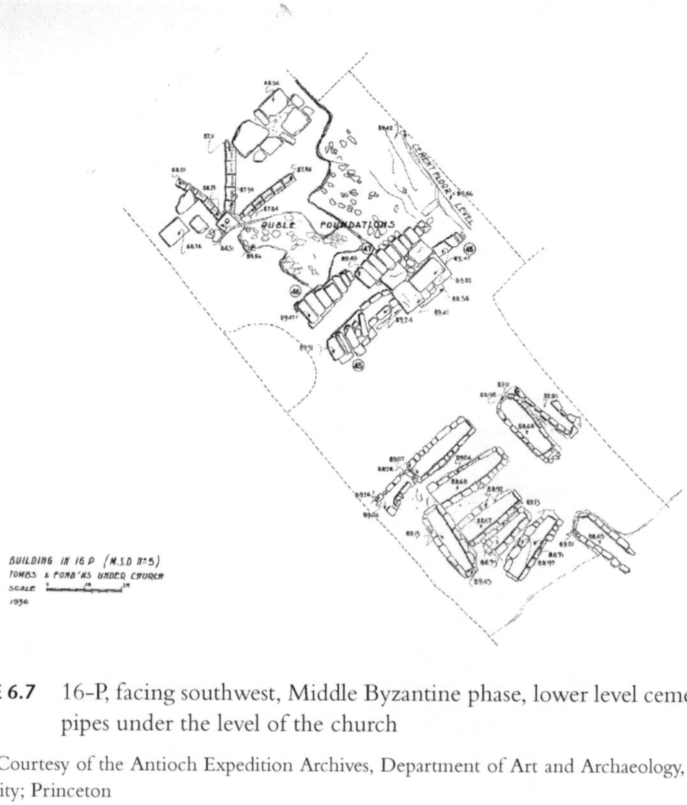

FIGURE 6.7 16-P, facing southwest, Middle Byzantine phase, lower level cemetery and pipes under the level of the church

Source: Courtesy of the Antioch Expedition Archives, Department of Art and Archaeology, Princeton University; Princeton

FIGURE 6.8 16-P, Arabic and Greek inscriptions on tombstone, reused as a well cover, *in situ*

Source: Courtesy of the Antioch Expedition Archives, Department of Art and Archaeology, Princeton University; Princeton

1000, was reused, with Greek written on the back dating to 1042, which was reused as a well cover (Figure 6.8).[109] Meanwhile, a Middle Byzantine coin of Michael IV (1034–1041) was found below one floor level but above another.[110] Both inscriptions and coins date the cemetery to the first half of the eleventh century, though

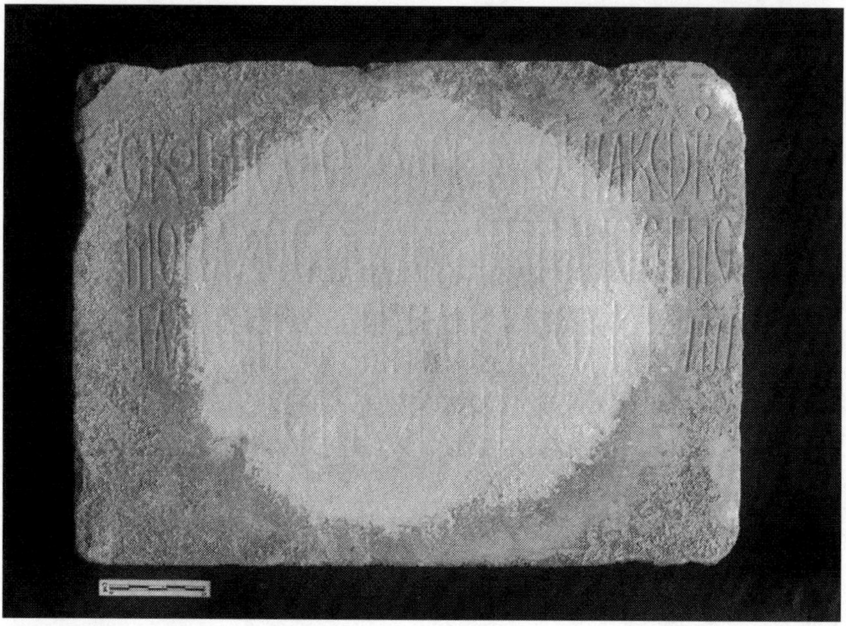

FIGURE 6.8 (Continued)

unfortunately the church cannot be identified. The intraurban cemetery, which may closely date to after the reconquest by Nicephorus Phocas in 969 and have continued to the middle of the eleventh century at least, is exactly contemporary with those excavated at Amorium and Boğazköy-Hattusa in modern Turkey. As Lassus states, the 16-P church and its cemetery, by the roadside, were not isolated, as there was a street to the east, heading towards the mountain among houses.[111]

Glanville Downey also published about a triple-apse basilica found in the suburb of Daphne in sector D-53-J/K dating to the Middle Byzantine period (Figure 6.9). It had three aisles divided with granite columns, traces of wall painting in the apse, and a baptistery in the southern apse, which was identified with the *diaconicon*, or sacristy, and likely a wooden roof. Beneath the floor of later rooms added around the church was a Middle Byzantine coin, also of Michael IV, thereby helping to date it.

Interestingly, the published evidence, though insufficient, preliminarily dates both churches to the reign of Michael IV or afterward, yet the only textual evidence for new church construction points to the two new churches established shortly after the conquest by Archbishop Theodore of Seleucia, including the one to St. John Chrysostom. A possible candidate for the Daphne church is the Monastery of Our Lady of Mart (Mart Maryam) first attested in 931 CE. As such, Daphne was still uninhabited but may have just been home to a monastery removed from the city but in proximity to it. In sector 16-P, the lower pavement upon which the coin was found, however, may represent an earlier level.[112] The presence of the church in 16-P by the tenth century may

FIGURE 6.9 D-53-J/K, Church at Daphne, general view of excavations, looking north

Source: Courtesy of the Antioch Expedition Archives, Department of Art and Archaeology, Princeton University; Princeton

show further intraurban transformation alongside a thriving, continuously used artery and within an industrial and commercial zone of the city.

Mirdāsid invasions

Around this same time, the Mirdāsids, who controlled the Aleppo amirate from 1024 to 1080, attempted to take Antioch on several occasions (Figure 6.10). This coincided with another period of intense seismic activity; in particular, a strong earthquake with an epicenter likely off the Syrian coast occurred in August 1063. In 1062 and 1067, Mirdāsid Arabs and newly arrived Saljūq Turkish armies from the western steppes of Central Asia, led by a Byzantine deserter, Amertices, attacked Antioch in a series of raids. According to the contemporary historian Michael Attaleiates (c. 1022–1080), they devastated a neighborhood of the city and took many citizens as slaves, while many inhabitants starved.[113] But Constantine X had priorities elsewhere, defending the Balkans from the Pechenegs, Anatolia from the Saljūqs, and Italy from the Normans, so it was left up to the local militia and bodyguard of the *dux* Nicephorus Botaneiates to defend the city with an ad hoc militia of locals and guards. Interestingly, in 1065 the Mirdāsid ruler in Aleppo, Maḥmūd b. Naṣr b. Ṣāliḥ (of the chapter's opening quotation by Ibn Shaddād), sent his son Naṣr between these raids to Antioch as a royal captive, where he was met with fanfare and presents.[114]

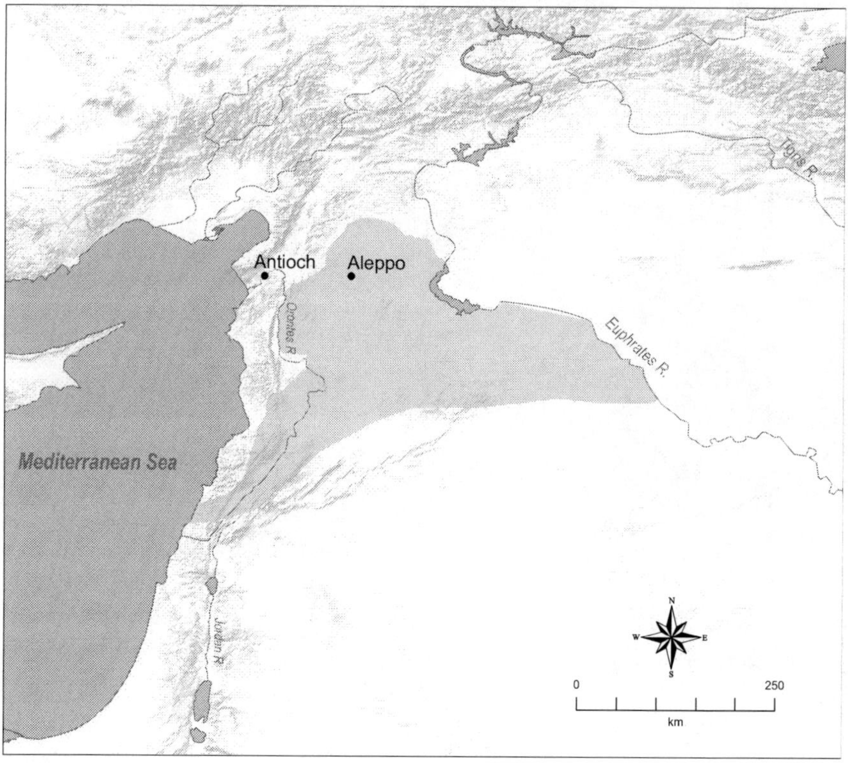

FIGURE 6.10 Map of the Mirdasid Amirate

Source: Created by Claire Ebert

As a result of raids and the earthquake of 1063, Antioch experienced a grain shortage and had to be supplied from the port of Suwaydīyya. In the winter of 1066, Afshīn b. Bakjī, a Turkish amīr and commander for the Saljūq Alp Arslan, together with a large army of Turks, raided and ruined the Black Mountain and Amanus monasteries and stole 40,000 water buffalo from the region of Antioch. He also attacked Antioch in 1067/68 and demanded tribute. The food shortage was so significant that Romanus IV Diogenes (1068–1071) and his army, who came to repel these invasions, were unable to camp outside Antioch in December 1068, since the Amuq farms could not feed the emperor's troops.

That previous autumn, Romanus had besieged the town of Manbij northwest of Aleppo. Peter Libellisius, an Antiochene Melkite and bilingual aristocrat, successfully persuaded the people of Manbij to surrender and as a result was appointed *magistros* by the emperor and then *dux* of Antioch. In 1071, after the disastrous Battle of Manzikert against the Saljūq Turks, Romanus was captured but released with the promise of a ransom, although in Constantinople he was declared deposed and the ransom not paid. The *dux* of Antioch Chataturius, however, sided with Romanus against his junior emperor and successor, Michael VII Doucas (1071–1078). In the ensuing civil war, Michael's army, headed by Andronicus Doucas and the Norman Robert Crispin, defeated the Antiochenes near Tarsus. According to Michael Psellos, this weakened Antioch and allowed Turks and Arabs to attack. Riots provoked by Patriarch Aemilian also occurred in the city after 1071, which tested the new *dux* Joseph Tarchaneoites, who ruled until 1074 and was succeeded by his son, the *magistros* Catacalon.

An Armenian rebellion

During the last quarter of the tenth century, Armenians had been migrating from Armenia to Cilicia and Cappadocia and then to Syria. Their increased presence spurred the creation of an Armenian bishopric in Antioch[115] but also led to ethno-religious tensions. The Armenian Smbat the Constable (1208–1276) stated that the Antiochenes were effeminate and soft, and he called them *peletikk'* (Belted Ones). This trope is reminiscent of Roman imperial historians, who decried Antioch and Daphne as detrimental to moral integrity with its abundant baths, prostitution, decadent way of life (see Chapter 2, p. 117, n. 2). Indeed, Antiochenes were described in Armenian sources as Christian in faith, although they spoke Arabic and sat on the street gossiping like "sick and feeble women."[116] Smbat also stated that the Antiochenes despised Armenians and would shave off the beards of foreigners, take their belongings, and banish them when they came to the city. Though the account seems exaggerated, Smbat and Matthew of Edessa related an incident in that same year of 1064 where an Armenian noble, a visitor from Ani named George Shirakats'i, was treated poorly by the Antiochenes, who took his belongings, shaved his beard, and threw him out of the city. George returned with 500 Turkish horsemen, burned 12 surrounding villages, and killed some inhabitants at the city gate, throwing their bodies into the river. He also took money, silver, and other booty. Smbat also recounted a third incident in that same year, when a caravan from the East brought *tarex* fish to sell in Antioch. The merchants, 80 of them, set themselves up in the market near a customs house (բաժտուն), where they drank wine and watched minstrels dancing. The Antiochenes, stirred up by the minstrels, then beat up the merchants and kicked them out of the city, but the merchants fought back, chasing the citizens to the Church of St. Peter from the unidentified Gate of Sewotoy (of the Blackfoot).[117] These incidents show mounting tensions between the inhabitants of Antioch and Armenians, despite the continuity of trade between these regions and communities.

In 1073, the Armenian separatist leader Philaretus Brachamius, a former *domestikos* (military general) under Romanus IV who was not loyal to Michael VII, tried to take Antioch and the southern part of the duchy of northern Syria, as well as eastern Anatolia and Cilicia, from the Byzantines. City factional riots erupted between followers and enemies of Philaretus, who was allied with Patriarch Aemilian, the old enemy of Nicephoritzes. Isaac Comnenus, older brother of Emperor Alexius I Comnenus (1081–1118) and *dux* of Antioch from 1073 to 1078, thereupon ordered Nicephoritzes to arrest the patriarch and send him to Constantinople, which provoked further rebellion in Antioch to the point where Isaac became trapped in the citadel. At the same time, a Turkish force of the Mirdāsids was approaching from Aleppo, led by Aḥmad Shah, commander of the *amīr* of Aleppo Naṣr b. Maḥmūd's army. Isaac violently suppressed the rioters (some sources say reconciled) and attacked the Turks, but was wounded and captured. The Antiochenes bought his freedom for 20,000 dinars and paid off the Turks to withdraw with another 5,000.

One year later, an earthquake struck the city in 1074, and in 1076 another famine hit; according to the later author Sibṭ b. al-'Ajamī (1415–1479), two loaves of bread or one chicken were sold for one gold dinar.[118] Perhaps connected with the general disaffection of the citizens, the *dux* of Antioch stepped down that same year, replaced by the Armenian prince Vasak Pahlawian, who around 1074 was assassinated while walking down the main *cardo* by two Greek spearmen, who stabbed him in the eye with a dagger. Vasak's troops thereupon assembled in the citadel and rounded up 700 Antiochene Greeks, who were taken to the nearby village of Ap'shun and killed.[119] In the wake of Vasak's murder, his troops gave control of Antioch over to Philaretus Brachamius, who took possession of Antioch in 1079. Smbat as well as Bar Hebraeus and the scholar/historian Anna Comnena (1083–c. 1153) mention that Philaretus was fairly despotic and tyrannical and disliked by Antioch's citizens for his unjustness.[120] As a result, the Antiochenes were partial to the *amīr* of Mosul and ruler of Aleppo, Sharaf al-Dawla Abū Makārim Muslim b. Quraysh (1061–1085) of the Uqaylid dynasty. After 1080, the Byzantines held only tenuous control of the city and paid tribute to Mosul. Philaretus, however, discovered this betrayal, for which he killed 300 nobles of Antioch. Both internal religious conflicts and external invasions and threats by other powers, while significant in shaping the human dimensions of the city, is not reflective in the growth of Antioch, which, in contrast, flourished unhindered during this period.

Monasteries and Scholars

Monasteries in and around the city were also a vital part of the religious landscape (Figure 6.13). The proliferation of monasteries in the region owed in part to the Byzantine re-Christianization and emigration of many Christians to the territory following the reconquest. Ibn Buṭlān likely stayed in a monastery within the city.[121] Georgian, Armenian, and Miaphysite monasteries also appeared on the Black Mountain (Mt. Cassius),[122] the Amanus Mountains, around the city of Antioch, and in and around the monastery of St. Symeon the Younger (Figure 6.14). Monks of different ethnicities could be in the same monastery.[123] Agapius II refounded and rebuilt several Late Antique monasteries, including that of St. Symeon the Younger, 20 km from Antioch.[124] The emperor Basil II also came to Antioch on two occasions, 995 and 999, once secretly with three close associates, to visit a place called Paghts'eak on the Black Mountain and receive baptism, according to Smbat.[125]

Antioch's surrounding monasteries also produced manuscripts. During the period of Byzantine reconquest, a great deal of Christian literature in Greek, Syriac,

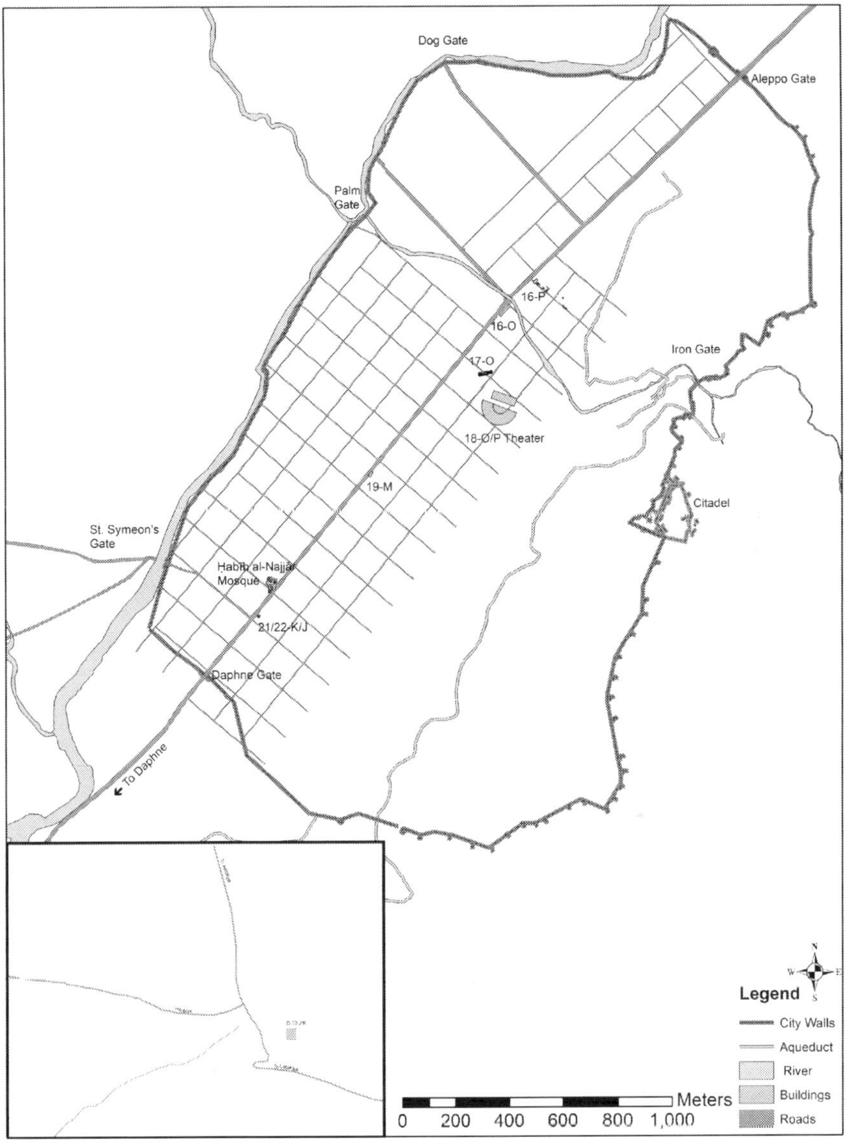

FIGURE 6.11 Plan of Middle Byzantine Antioch

Source: Created by Steve Batiuk

and Coptic was translated into Arabic as part of an intellectual movement comparable to ʻAbbāsid Baghdad in the ninth century. The movement arose mainly out of the Melkite community, by theologians such as ʻAbdallah b. al-Faḍl, a deacon of Antioch; Yānī b. al-Duks, another deacon of Antioch; Antonius, the abbot of the monastery of St. Symeon the Younger; Gregory, the abbot of the monastery of the

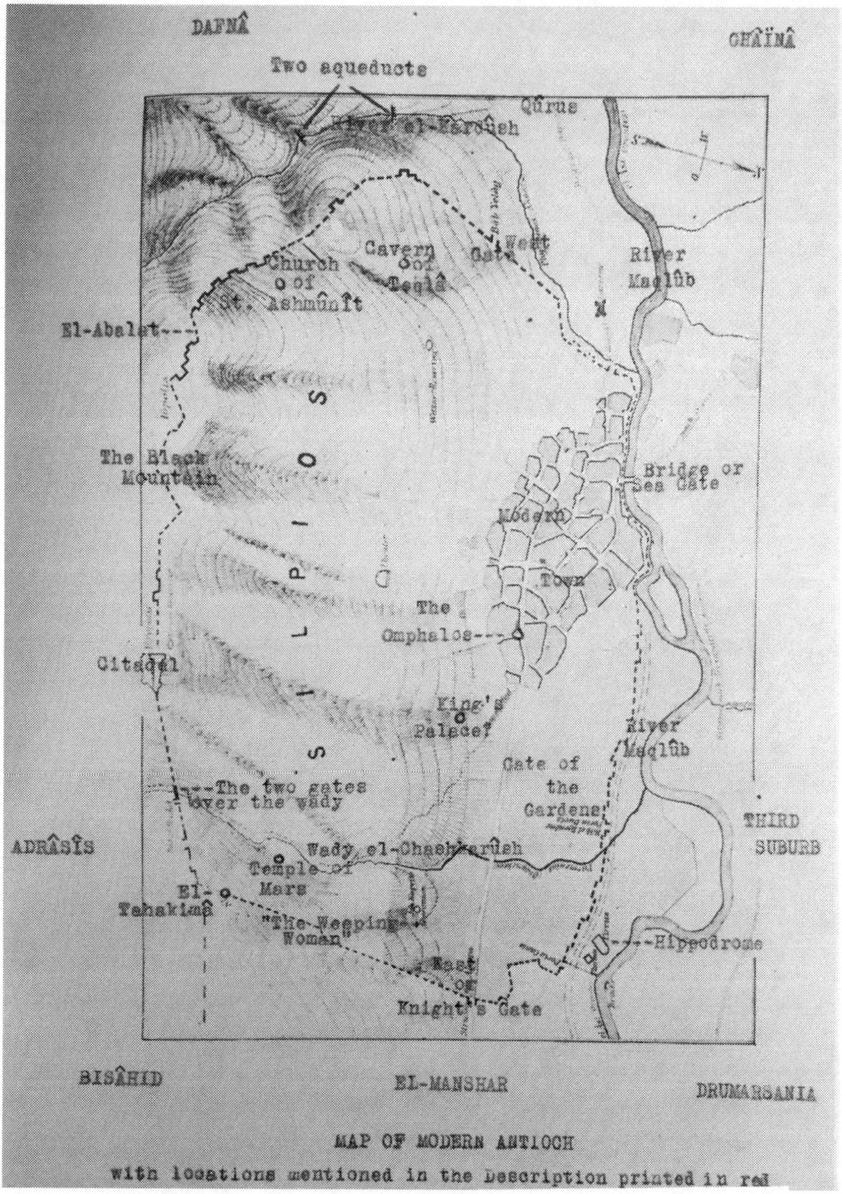

FIGURE 6.12 Map of Antioch by W.F. Stinespring, based on the Codex Vaticanus Arabicus 286

Theotokos Dafnūnā (Our Lady of Mart Maryam in Daphne) known from the early tenth century; Ībrāhīm b. Yuḥannā, author of the patriarch Christopher's life and a *protospatharios* and possibly *kātib al-malakī* (royal scribe); possibly Chariton, the abbot of the monastery of the Theotokos Arshāyā ("the old one"); and a lesser-known priest and monk, Yūḥannā 'Abd al-Masīḥ or John the Catholicos (c. 950–c. 1030s).

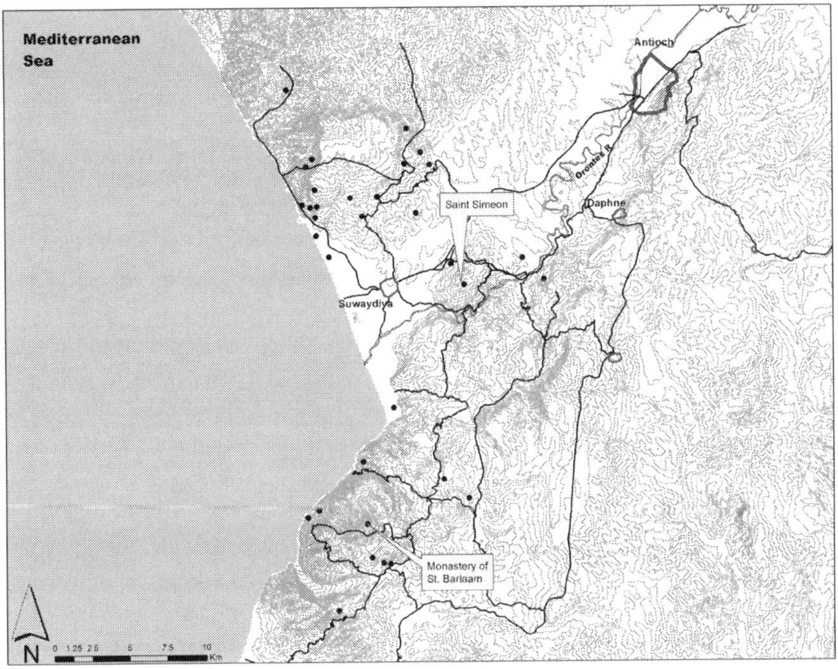

FIGURE 6.13 Orontes delta and the Black Mountain monasteries, based on Djobadze's survey map

Source: Created by Steve Batiuk

FIGURE 6.14 Monastery of St. Symeon the Younger

Source: Photograph by Ayşe Henry

Most of these were all disciples of the patriarch Christopher, and so were all colleagues and connected as a school of translators in the Antioch area. They were culturally inhabitants of a city of the Islamic world, only recently under Byzantine rule, and were therefore products of a mixed Arab-Christian society. For example, 'Abdallah b. al-Faḍl was called, in one of his translations, "the most exalted *shaykh* and most noble deacon," *shaykh* in this period denoting a scholar in the community rather than a tribal chief.[126] Some of these scholars were from prominent families, such as ʿAbdallāh b. Faḍl, whose grandfather served in the high rank of metropolitan bishop, Ībrāhīm b. Yuḥannā, and Yānī b. al-Duks, possibly the son of a *dux*, as his name implies – perhaps Kulayb, ʿUbaydallāh, or Peter Libellisius.

Yūḥannā ʿAbd al-Masīḥ compiled and translated a collection of saints lives and homilies in what is called the Antiochian Menologion (*Kitāb al-Dūlāb* or Book of the Wheel), also at the monastery of the Theotokos Arshāyā.[127] This last monastery, known to be newly built when the patriarch Christopher's body was temporarily interred there, was, according to a manuscript colophon, "west of the city of Antioch, outside the gate known as Bāb al-Fuḍayl [Gate of Excellence]."[128] Based on its direction, this gate is either the Sea or Daphne Gates.

A substantial number of Georgian and Greek manuscripts appeared in the second half of the tenth century, a tradition that continued through the beginning of the thirteenth.[129] Around 1030, many Georgian monks and scholars settled from the Tao-Klarjeti area in southern Georgia and developed their own literary and artistic school.[130] Georgian monks also refounded and reconstructed a chapel, possibly the monastery of St. Barlaam on Mt. Cassius.

Antioch also remained home to a Muslim community, though how robust is unknown from the sources. We know more about individuals who lived in or passed through the city. Scholars, both residents and visitors, created a diverse interfaith intellectual scene. Yaḥya b. Saʿīd al-Anṭākī moved to Antioch from Alexandria around 1015, perhaps to escape the persecutions by the Fāṭimid caliph al-Ḥakīm.[131] The Christian physician Ibn Buṭlān engaged in a medical-philosophical debate with Ibn Riḍwān of Cairo and also mentioned an Ibn Abī Uṣaybiʿa Abū al-Faraj Yaḥya b. Saʿīd b. Yaḥya, who may have been the same as al-Anṭākī.[132] Given the similarity in texts and overlapping stays in Antioch, al-Anṭākī and Ībrāhīm b. Yuḥanna, the biographer of Patriarch Christopher, were likely also within the same intellectual network. A certain Symeon Seth, who lived in the city and was a contemporary of Ibn Buṭlān's, wrote a treatise on diet for the Byzantine emperor Michael VII. Ibn Buṭlān also mentions a chief *qadī* of the city, Shaykh Abū Naṣr b. al-ʿAṭṭār, suggesting an Islamic community with perhaps autonomous institutions within the Byzantine administered city. No Byzantine judges, however, appear on lead seals, suggesting either that the *dux* acted as judge or that the civil court was in another major city and Antioch had more of a military function.[133] The description of the Church of St. Peter with its judges, however, contradicts this argument, though this is based on a single text and could refer to a past judicial precinct. The scholars listed by the biographer Yāqūt al-Ḥamawī included some working in Antioch as late as 970 and perhaps later. Other Muslims, particularly nobles or elite families mentioned in the city, are very few for this period. It is possible that after the reconquest many were sold as slaves or deported by Michael Bourtzes or Peter, or fled to Muslim majority places for refuge.

What of the Early Islamic congregational mosque? Ibn Shaddād and others like Ibn Munala in Ibn al-Shiḥna and Ibn al-ʿAdīm write that the mosque was transformed into a pig stable and then plowed and cultivated as a vegetable garden for the patriarch.[134] This echoes the account by the Persian historian Miskawayh (932–1030) and Bar Hebraeus that the Tarsus congregational mosque became a stable for the

Byzantine emperor.[135] The most likely candidate for the main congregational mosque would be the mosque of Habīb Najjār in the center of the city. The Princeton excavations alongside this mosque in sector 21/22-J discovered pipes and drains and an eleventh-century fountain in Levels VI and VII (Figure 6.18). In nearby 21-K, an eleventh-century coin in Level IV and glazed pottery in the upper levels were found. Whether this supports the account of the Middle Byzantine garden is unknown.

Other buildings

The Vatican Codex mentions some other buildings of note. A circular structure, called a place of learning (*bayt al-ḥikma*), was domed and had an observatory, perhaps serving the aforementioned community of scholars. A place identified as *the Caesarium* of Trajan lay opposite on the east side of Mt. Silpius. This is an interesting anachronistic toponym to emerge during this period of building this old, but perhaps referring to the old theater initially built by Caesar but restored by Trajan who added an apparently spectacular *nymphaeum* and was still standing but used as an industrial space.[136] There was also a treasury. Inside the Aleppo Gate lay a courtyard and possibly barracks called al-Hazārdār, meaning "that which holds one thousand." The inventory mentions many architectural talismans, one of which was of a weeping woman, probably the rock-carved Charonion (see Chapter 1), which Abū al-Makārim wrote was situated above the House of Mars. The aforementioned Tower of the Spiral Staircase, also called the Tower of the Snail/Halazun by Abū al-Makārim, served to ward away vermin from the city, and there were also talismans on each of the east and west gates (Aleppo, and the Daphne or Sea/Bridge Gate to Latakiya). Abū al-Makārim adds a fourth talisman, the central dome of the great market. Ibn Buṭlān also described a hospital (*bimāristan*), whose building he supervised in 1063, where the patriarch himself tended to the sick. The date suggests this may be the hospital established by the wealthy patron Maurus from Amalfi for western pilgrims by 1062.[137] This was presumably located near a bathhouse where lepers bathed, and the patriarch also washed their hair.

The *Life of the Patriarch Christopher* also reveals some topographical information. The author mentions baths operating in certain neighborhoods, as well as a prison. On the slopes of Mt. Silpius and Mt. Staurin were five terraces, the lowest of which had baths and gardens fed by mountain streams. The baths were opulent, with hot rooms that used myrtle wood in the furnaces, likely brought from Daphne. The Vatican codex mentions ten baths in the city, one near the Temple of Mars watered by a mountain torrent. Two aqueducts supplied the city with water from the Bayt al-Mā' (Daphne's suburb); one was called Paulitis or Būlit, and the other was described as "of the cave," in other words, partially tunneled. The name Bayt al-Mā' (House of Water) suggests that there may have been a springhouse over some of the Daphne springs, a possibility depicted in the Peutinger Table's Antioch toponym (see Figure 3.10).

Water channels siphoned the colluvium from the mountain torrents, that is, the Phyrminus (Akakir) and Parmenius, which were a great danger. The Codex and al-Makārim's accounts also mention a spring of water, al-Ardāsīyā, between the two mountains near the Iron Gate. According to the Codex, the Orontes (also called al-Kardūsh, from Hebrew for "the cold") had boats on it, although it remains uncertain whether the river was navigable to the sea, and many accounts mention that it was not. It seems, at least, that boats were used to bring stone from a quarry two days distant. This is perhaps surprising, since stone was plentiful, including on Mt. Staurin and Mt. Silpius, where the Amuq Survey located a quarry in 2001. Stone from abandoned and ruined buildings in the city and from nearby sites must also have been available. The urban survey by Gunnar Brands and Hatice Pamir also recorded spolia from a Muslim cemetery used to repair the Iron Gate.[138] The graveyards were demolished, and it seems as an act of vandalism or to make room for new projects.

Houses and industry

While traveling through the Plain of Antioch to the city, Ibn Buṭlān noted fertile and productive lands – grain and barley under olive trees, and silk and wine production (indicating mulberry orchards and vineyards). The prize resource of the coast was timber – pine, cedar, and oak. The Amanus Mountains provided pitch, and open pit mines or streambeds and alluvial fans provided iron.[139] Antioch was also a producer of ceramics and textiles, and these industries were linked in some cases to residential zones that also had an industrial function.

The archaeological evidence for residential buildings is difficult to interpret but does show continuity.[140] This indicates that the Byzantine siege did not rupture all (or any) parts of the city and that houses remained in use, although whether the families that inhabited them remained the same is unclear. In sector 19-M, the 'Abbāsid period house (Chapter 5) continued into this period. Level IIb was a kitchen with a pavement that included marble flooring and a series of rectangular wells. It was perhaps in one of these wells that an excavator found a cache of intact pottery (Figure 6.15). Judging from the published photograph of the assemblage, it was dominated by Günsenin storage vessels, mainly wine amphorae from the Black Sea region from the late tenth and eleventh centuries, but also contained cooking wares, smaller tablewares, and a single piece of ninth- or tenth-century polychrome-painted maroon and beige lusterware, which are indicative of domestic use. The assemblage, according to the excavators, dates to the Byzantine reconquest because coins dated the houses built over wells to the eleventh century. The third subphase, IIIc, had three round pits and a series of pipes also dated to the tenth to twelfth centuries. The uppermost level (Level I) contained rubblestone walls, carefully aligned, with block headers placed at intervals, four *pithoi* containers, and outside the house a succession of street pavements, including some of packed clay with sewage systems.

Similar to 19-M, along the Parmenius stream, excavators uncovered a Middle Byzantine period house with kitchen and courtyard in sector 17-P (Figure 6.16). The tops of the walls, reworked over time, were 4 m below the surface. The house was just south of a solidly built wall, 1.14 m wide and at least 2 m high,

FIGURE 6.15 19-M, Level IIb, Middle Byzantine cache with some Early Islamic pottery including ninth-century lusterware

Source: Courtesy of the Antioch Expedition Archives, Department of Art and Archaeology, Princeton University and Princeton University Art Museum

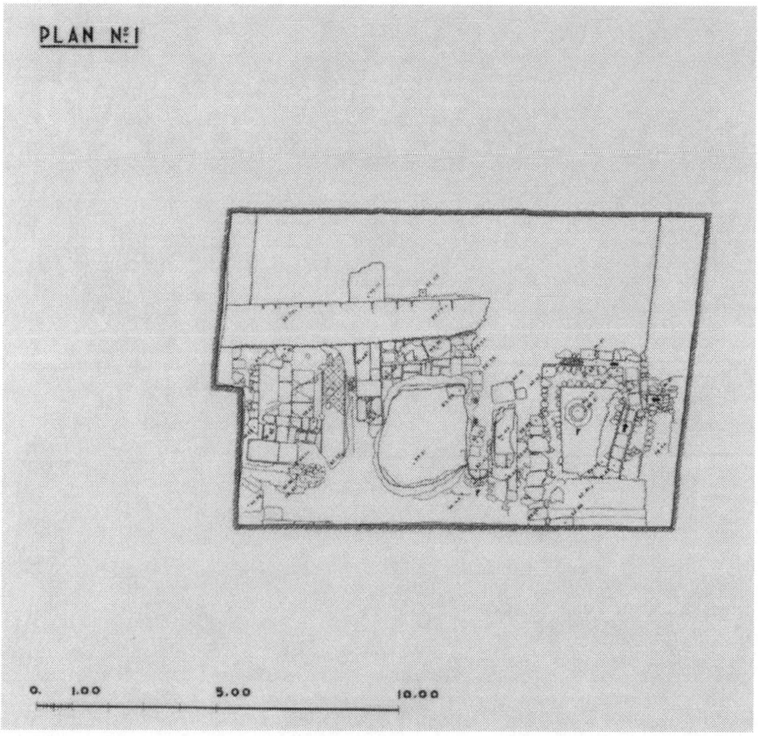

FIGURE 6.16 17-P, Plan 1 and photo, looking north

Source: Courtesy of the Antioch Expedition Archives, Department of Art and Archaeology, Princeton University; Princeton

of large blocks bordering the channel of the Parmenius, likely to protect against flooding.[141] Indeed, during the excavations, the stormy weather caused this mountain stream to flood, making work difficult. A beautiful sgraffito-incised color-splashed bowl with four birds was found here and contemporary with this period (Figure 6.17)

Farther north along the main street in sector 17-O, the upper level (Level I) was a seemingly undifferentiated mass of walls, floor levels, water pipes or drains, and bricks that Lassus called an "unlikely confusion of very late remains" in his notes, but elsewhere, an "urban district." What characterizes this level in relation to the Early Islamic level preceding it was mainly continuity of the courtyard houses as they were renovated. The western, central, and eastern courtyard houses and the narrow alleys continued with mostly rubblestone walls built on the previous walls but following the same orientation. Sections of older walls were patched, new floors were laid of brick or plaster, and internal spaces, such as the courtyards themselves and the shop, were subdivided. The narrow side streets resembled alleys encroached upon by features such as wells. The streets were higher owing to a continuous buildup, suggesting that one stepped down into the houses. This part of the city, however, had changed in function, as residential use took on the industrial attributes of a potters' quarter. The central house still had evidence of a residence with a kitchen (or furnace), latrine, and wells, as well as a well-preserved kiln that likely produced two different types of glazed fineware based on the wasters

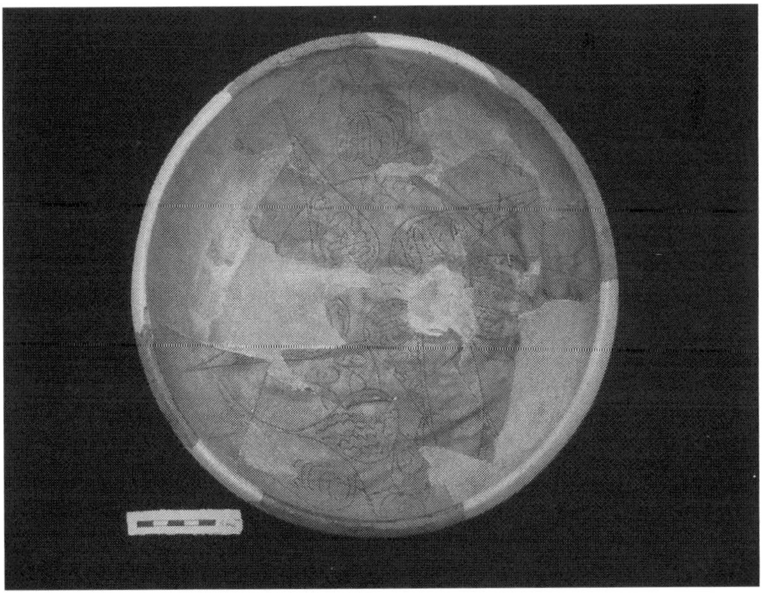

FIGURE 6.17 17-P, sgraffito splashware bowl

Source: Courtesy of the Princeton University Art Museum

FIGURE 6.18 17-O, Level I, Dig II, looking northwest, central courtyard house and kiln

Source: Courtesy of the Antioch Expedition Archives, Department of Art and Archaeology, Princeton University; Princeton

found (Figure 6.18). Exact dates are uncertain for this complex. The tenth-century pottery wasters suggest that production here began at the start of the Byzantine reconquest or even earlier in the Early Islamic period. Production continued up to between the eleventh and thirteenth centuries, while ceramic production peaked in general around the city in the eleventh century.[142] If this is the same neighborhood as the Ostracine damaged in the 458 earthquake, it suggests a potter's quarter that spanned eight centuries.

Among the notable imports and finds that helped date this phase to the Middle Byzantine period were lead seals and material culture from Fāṭimid Egypt and China. In the western house of section 17-O were found two lead seals: one anonymous, likely that of a minor official, and one of a *toumarches* named Christopher dating to the first half of the eleventh century, thus assigning the house to a date after 1050. In the eastern house, a lead seal dating to the second half of the eleventh century of a *kanikleios*, or private secretary to the emperor, dated the floor also from around 1050. The latest coins under the earliest of this level's floors dated to 976, supporting the ceramic evidence that renovations to this neighborhood began soon after the Byzantine reconquest of the city. It would thus be incorrect to assume – because the walls were of rubblestone, earlier houses were subdivided, and inhabitants were living alongside their industry – that these were poor residences and the potter's quarter was a slum.

The presence of three lead seals, as well as Chinese and Fāṭimid imports, raises the question of the association of local nobles involved in this fineware industry or residents. Sector 17-O likely was near a market, perhaps on the main *cardo* of the city. The Vatican Codex mentions seven streets with markets running the length of the city – three uncovered, four covered. These streets must have been main avenues, since the author states that two carts could pass side by side, thus also challenging the notion of a heavily encroached main street. Also, the archaeological evidence suggests commercial trade ties leaning strongly toward the south and the Far East rather than the western Mediterranean. The Byzantines also encouraged free trade between Antioch and Aleppo.

In sector 16-O, at least four wasters of turquoise glazed wares were found. How they relate to the church and cemetery is an interesting question and suggests a kiln in the immediate vicinity, alluding to a certain elevated level of density of space and urban use in the medieval city.[143]

High-end production was not confined to this sector alone or to this industry. Textiles were also produced at Antioch. Texts mention that the city was known for producing a certain type of cover or carpet, and it was known particularly for its silk and silk brocade production throughout this period into the twelfth century and later.[144] A Byzantine silk from Antioch and dating to the tenth century appears in the Cleveland Museum of Art. The silk shows Islamic and Byzantine designs in its decoration, featuring an eight-pointed star with a floriated cross in the center and flanking winged griffins in the corners (Figure 6.19).[145] The finely woven griffin, in white against a green background, is nearly sheer and of Islamic silk design. In this case, either the weavers were manufacturing content for the consumer or a patron, or it was produced around the beginning of the tenth century under Islamic rule and exported to Byzantium. The *dux* Isaac Comnenus also gave Emperor Nicephorus III Botaneiates (1078–1081) textiles from Antioch. This may confirm that Antioch was much more easily connected by small ports and open fertile plains to Armenian Cilicia than to the southern and eastern parts of the principality, at least in the movement of goods.

Shifts in the town

Plotting the anonymous Middle Byzantine bronze coins known as folles indicates that the urban center contracted, as these were concentrated closer to the center of the city.[146] They can be seen in sectors 16-O, 17-O, and 19-M along the main street but are virtually absent from Daphne and Seleucia, thus supporting the inference that the suburb of villas was largely uninhabited and the port had gone out of use. Scott Redford's study of 435 anonymous folles shows similar patterns; most of these were in sectors 19-M, 16-O, 17-O, 17-N, and 22-K, in diminishing rank. We thus see the city contracting away from the Aleppo Gate and Bath-F (sector 13-R) and the Island and down toward the main street in the Middle Byzantine period, thus moving to the core maintained in later periods. The "potters' quarter" of sector 17-O continued evenly until the twelfth century.

FIGURE 6.19 Byzantine silk textile from Antioch

Source: Courtesy of the Cleveland Museum of Art

Some suburban areas, such as Jekmejeh and Narlija, still had some coins as in the Early Islamic period, but in smaller numbers. David M. Metcalf has posited that low numbers of certain categories minted at Antioch and sent to Athens and Corinth suggest that Antioch's Byzantine monetary system was slow to integrate into the rest of the empire, or else that the money flow was interrupted between 1020 and 1050.[147]

While the coin evidence shows that city contracted south of the Parmenius, the excavations also indicated that the Middle Byzantine town continued to extend past the mountain torrent, questioning some claims by scholars that the stream functioned as a northern limit to the town in this period. Lassus writes:

> It seems that after the 12th century, in the entire northern part of the ancient city, all construction disappeared as soon as one deviates a little from the road. There certainly may have been, like nowadays in the olive grove, isolated peasant houses, which we have not had the opportunity to encounter. However, it appears that in the period from the 10th to the 13th century, after the Byzantine reconquest until after the Crusades, the city once again extended to the Parmenius torrent, and even beyond.[148]

Thomas Sinclair mentions that after the 969 reconquest, new parts of city were developed, although his evidence is uncertain, as is the scale to which he is referring.[149] As in the Early Islamic period, rather than a parasitic city receiving all its goods and trade from the hinterlands, numerous tenth-century authors suggest a densely populated, self-sufficient, albeit contracted, settlement.

Ruralization continued

Interestingly, the geographer Istakhrī, although mentioning that Antioch was the most pleasant place in Syria after Damascus, stated that its decline had begun already in the final days of Muslim rule and continued during the Byzantine reconquest. He may have been noting the city's increased ruralization. This process must have started already in the Early Islamic period, as suggested by Peter's sparing of the gardens and farms (*zuru'ah/zaraha*) of Antioch at the time of the Byzantine conquest, alluding to the importance of cultivation within the city walls known from the already-contracted Early Islamic city. Authors of the tenth century and later all spoke of cultivated fields (*mazāri'*), pasturage (*marā'*), trees (*ashjār*), and mills (*ārbiya*) along the Orontes, gardens within the city walls (*basātīn, jannāt al-buqūl*) and on the slopes, and channels drawing running water off the mountain (*miyā tatakharraq*) and supplying it to all the markets, streets, houses, and mosques.[150] The Hajji version of the Codex mentions ten mills on the Orontes with seven mill stones each, while the anonymous account states that in addition to mills, two storehouses (*makhāzin*) were built with vaults over the water channels for more security (and likely to protect from floods) and used as granaries (*ahrā' al-ghalāt*) for farm products.

The Vatican Codex further notes that the local ruler depopulated and destroyed seven towns (*mudun*) and villages (*qarya*) around Antioch and transferred their inhabitants to the city, where they were given residences, shops, gardens, lands, and tax-free status for three years: "No one who had sown seed for himself round about the city or had engaged in any agrarian cultivation was to be hindered in a single detail of that."[151] Although the date of the seven towns' depopulation is unclear, as the account is problematic and condenses the entire history of the city, it likely occurred during the author's time in the Middle Byzantine period.

Evidence from the Amuq Valley survey shows that during the mid-tenth to mid-eleventh centuries, the plain was poorly settled, with about half the number of sites from the Early Islamic period abandoned. There are, however, some exceptions. What villages did exist grew larger. Excavations at the site of Çatal Höyük show a remarkably high number of coins from this period, nearly half of all coins found there. This could point either to a considerable degree of monetization in at least part of the plain or to the presence of a military garrison at Çatal Höyük.[152] Interestingly, Muqaddasī wrote of the Amuq that "in this region villages (*qurā*) are more splendid and larger than most of the cities (*mudun*)."[153]

The century or so of rural decline fits within larger regional archaeological patterns and can be explained by the rise in nomadic and seminomadic groups in the area that formed local, independent tribal dynasties, such as the Mirdāsids, effectively changing the balance of tribes that had largely become sedentary. A transformation of the settled landscape of villages to a more transient and re-nomadized landscape of camps is difficult to pinpoint in the heavily aggraded plains of this frontier region. But then again, it is precisely the accrued level of aggradation from irrigation systems that may have contributed to this transformation in settlement, as demonstrated by increased marshification and the inevitable termination of major canal irrigation systems by the end of the Early Islamic period. The possibility of real decline is indicated by the low number of sites with confirmed occupation, supported by attestations in the historical sources for a period of fragmentation and political instability.

An unstable landscape may also have been a motivating factor for the movement of populations from rural communities to more walled, stable ones, as suggested by the Vatican Codex. The move described in the Codex also gives evidence that, within the city, residents had effectively adopted an urban-ruralized lifestyle, with residences, shops, and cultivated land, and thus were self-sufficient and not dependent on the surrounding agricultural lands, and that this was encouraged by the ruler. All these descriptions indicate that the city consisted of both a contracted urban core and surrounding agricultural lands, which, rather than demonstrating marked decline, contributed to an overall level of self-sufficiency (*wa mā yastaqillā bihi ahlihā min marāfiqiha*).[154]

Conclusion

In the Middle Byzantine period the city of Antioch thrived, without reverting to its Late Antique/Early Byzantine form. Instead, the city was built on the urban form and institutions of an Islamic city that had lasted more than 300 years. Similarly, the Middle Byzantine period did not represent an occupation. The city, as a frontier town and capital of a buffer province, was in many ways run by its diverse population. The symbolic power of this ancient city also gave it a magnetism that continued to resonate throughout this period, attracting conquerors and visitors alike. During this time, Antioch endured significant challenges, starting with

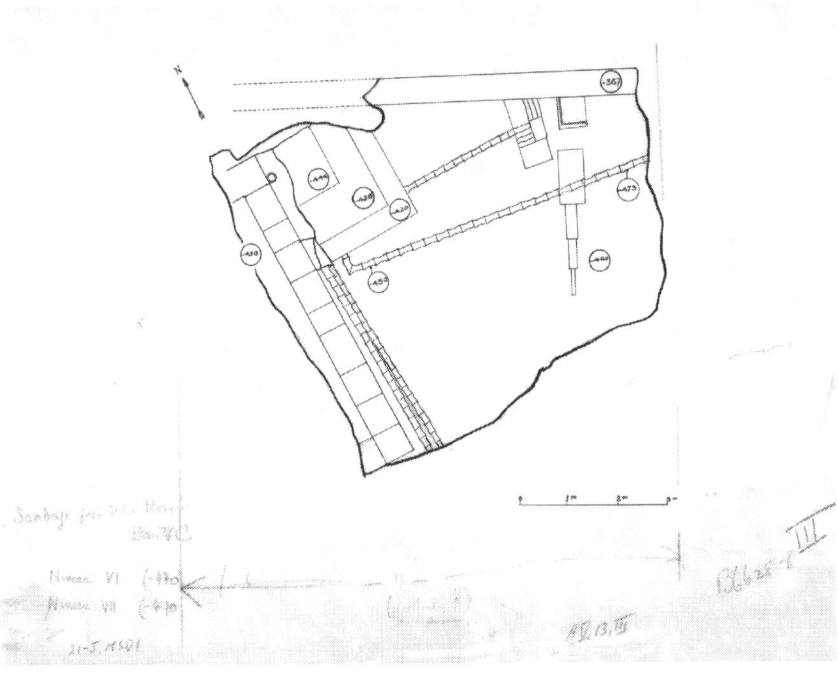

FIGURE 6.20 21-J, corner of Middle Byzantine fountain and pipes cut by later wall, facing north

Source: Courtesy of the Antioch Expedition Archives, Department of Art and Archaeology, Princeton University

the Byzantine reconquest itself, more sieges by foreign armies, local rebellions chafing against Constantinople's occasional overreach, and multiple earthquakes. Yet the city continued to develop. Religious and intellectual communities grew, as did the city's economic role as a manufacturing center and entrepôt, and refurbishment and new construction continued. In some cases, buildings and features such as caves and towers were reused in different ways that often retained an aspect of remembering the city's past, like the talismans. In this way, Antioch remained a palimpsest, a medieval city with a distinct character and urban landscape, shaped by centuries of combined Islamic and Byzantine rule, and consciously expressing its classical foundations and heritage.

Notes

1 Leo the Deacon 2005, Book IV, 123–124.
2 Mahmūd b. Naṣr b. Ṣālīḥ was the Mirdāsid *amīr* of Aleppo (1060–1061, 1065–1075).
3 Ibn Shaddād 1984, 223–299 and Ibn al-ʿAdīm 1996, 211 ff. (our own translation to English).
4 It ranked behind Constantinople and Thessalonike. Leo the Deacon 2005, Book IV, 123–124.
5 Leo the Deacon 2005; Yahya b. Saʿīd al-Anṭakī 1924, 1932, 1957; Zayat, Habib [Ibrāhīm b. Yūḥannā] 1952.
6 Ibn Shaddād 1984; Ibn al-Shiḥna 1990.
7 *Description of Times of Elias Nisibis*, Bar Hebraeus 1932, 171 (189); although 964 mentioned by Yāqūt 1990, 319; Yaḥya b. Saʿid al-Anṭakī 1924, 1932, 1957, 795 (97)
8 For more on Nicephorus and this period, see Kaldellis 2017, 8–12, 43–44.
9 Miskawayh 1921, 217 (203), vol. 2.
10 Yaḥya b. Saʿid al-Anṭakī 1924, 1932, 1957, 796–797.
11 Canard 1951, 587, n. 22 [Abū Firas al-Hamdanī, Diwan, p. 17, v. 13; ed. Dahan, p. 123, v. 218, 153; Mutanabbī, ed. Barquqi, p. 391, cf. Blachere, Mutannabi, p. 118, n. 1] UNC-CH.
12 Canard 1953, 564.
13 This is also recorded in the account of Sibṭ b. al-Ajamī (d. 1479) 1950.
14 Miskawayh [1921, 225 (214)] writes that al-Ahwazī had a brother in Antioch. Further, he was helped and propped up by a Shīʿah of the line of Aftas and had the title of *ustadh* (lit. teacher).
15 Leo the Deacon 2005, n. 42. A prophecy was also circulating that whichever emperor conquered Antioch would die at the same time, Skylitzes 2010, 261 (272).
16 In Arabic sources, Mikhaʾīl al-Burjī.
17 In Arabic sources, Isḥāq b. Bahrām.
18 Originally from Persia. Interestingly, Christopher was able to reduce his debt to 90 percent, which made Ibn Mānik feel as though Christopher was his creditor and so he was beholden to him. Mugler 2019a. Christopher rescued him from prison (perhaps a debtors' prison), Leo the Deacon 2005, 150, n. 54.
19 Boudier 2018, 43–58.
20 See Mugler 2019a for all the information on this episode. Indeed, one can just examine differing accounts of his life and death: Leo the Deacon and Scylitzes mention him briefly, without any nuance that his murderers were Muslims, though they were Antiochenes (Scylitzes), or allusion to Sayf al-Dawla as his assassin (Leo), while the Eastern Christian account of Ibrāhīm b. Yuḥannā shows the complexity of relationships. Scylitzes, though writing a century after the conquest, seems to have used a now missing source, Nicephorus the Deacon, written c. 971.
21 Boudier 2018, 43–58.
22 Yaḥya b. Saʿid al-Anṭakī 1957, 809–810 (111–112).

23 Yaḥya b. Sa'id al-Anṭakī 1924, 1932, 1957, 816 (118).
24 In Arabic sources, al-Turbāzī or Buṭrus al-Āsṭar Tūbadrakh or Abū Yadraḥ.
25 Ibn Shaddād 1984, 223–299.34; Ibn al-'Adīm 1996, 71, 93.
26 Ibn Munala (though written Ibn Mula) in Ibn al-Shiḥna and Yaḥya b. Sa'id al-Anṭakī 1924, 1932, 1957, 822 (124); Ibn 'Abd al-Ẓāhir 1976, 317 says he (and possibly his group) were *al-ṣ'aālīk* (thieves or poor vagrants).
27 Ibn 'Abd al-Ẓāhir states his followers escaped, but he stayed to rule. 1976, 317.
28 Ibn Shaddād 1984, 223–299.34 and Ibn al-'Adīm 1996, 93, state that it was the night of the Nativity, but Ibn Shaddād gives the date of October 28, 969, which indicates a confusion. Bourtzes and Brachamius were also joined by a black servant of Bourtzes (Yaḥya b. Sa'id al-Anṭakī 1924, 1932).
29 The Byzantines killed the Muslim guards, who were sleeping. Al-Anṭākī just stated that the Antiochenes did not expect a raid and so left the walls unmanned at the top of the mountain. Yaḥya b. Sa'id al-Anṭakī 1924, 1932.
30 John Scylitzes 2010, 261 mentions an Aulax who left the portion of the wall undefended after promises and gifts from Bourtzes. He may be the same as 'Allūsh, however. Bar Hebraeus 1932, 172–173 (191) states that it was Christians from the fortress of Lūqā in the neighborhood of Antioch, which must mean Būqā. See *TIB* 566.
31 According to Ibn Shaddād 1984, 223–299.35. Ibn Munala in Ibn al-Shiḥna says that Michael was joined by Isḥāq b. Bahrām and a black slave. Ibn al-'Adīm 1996, 93.
32 In Arabic sources, Yānis b. Shimīshiq or Iwannis Symskai, Ioannes Tzimiskes, the future Byzantine emperor.
33 Leo the Deacon 2005, Book 5, 134. Interestingly, this diverges from Ibn Munala in Ibn al-Shiḥna, who states that the Muslims used fire as a shield as they retreated from the Roman army between the town and mountain (presumably the citadel). This is repeated somewhat in the *Life of Christopher* and Yaḥya b. Sa'id al-Anṭakī 1924, 1932.
34 This policy of not plundering and having the population remain is very reminiscent of Procopius's account of Belisarius's strategies in the sixth century, which Leo the Deacon drew from heavily. Procopius, *History of the Wars,* Book 3, Conquest of Carthage.
35 The totally improbable number of 10,000.
36 Leo the Deacon 2005, n. 42.
37 Interestingly, Michael the Syrian (1963, III.128) states that the Arabs fled and abandoned Antioch when John Tzimisces and Nicephorus arrived, but that the Byzantines took Antioch during the reign of Romanus (presumably II), who ended his reign earlier in 963. He also states this was the period when Abū al-Qāsim died and Faḍl started to reign, although he may be confused, as these are the same person. Abū al-Qāsim al-Faḍl b. al-Muqtadir, son of Muqtadir, known as al-Muṭī', reigned from 946 to 974.
38 Ibn al-Shiḥna. When Peter arrived, he also garrisoned the fortress of Baghrās with men. In the districts, he appointed Tamsīl al-Suryānī and another group with him to raid Antioch's territory.
39 Stinespring 1932, 9–10.
40 Stinespring's argument that the presence of a double wall must date it to the Byzantine reconquest (pp. 24–25) is incorrect, since many Early Islamic cities had double walls. But the manuscript makes no mention Arab or Islamic rule anywhere. This could, however, still place it in the Crusader period. Further, the account by Abū al-Makārim, which resembles this text in many ways and dates to the thirteenth century, makes the dating tenuous. The text was also the basis of Hajji Khalifa's *Jihānnumā* (c. 1650 CE). The manuscripts all need to be examined closely and side by side. The Bodleian, as it refers to the Orontes as the 'Asī and no longer then Maklūb, is likely later than the Vatican, which refers to it as the Maklūb.
41 See the review by Margoliouth 1898, 157–169.
42 Preserved in the Codex Vaticanus Arabicus 286 and a manuscript in the Bodleian Library (870). Both versions, however, are not precisely dated.
43 The main *strategata* included, in Cilicia: Tarsus, Adana, Anazarbos, Mopsuestia and Podandon at the Cilician Gates; in the Amuq Plain: Palatza/Balghāt (which included

the Kara Su and the Amanus Mountains, which also included Payas, the Syrian Gates, and Alexandretta); to the north: Germanikea/Mar'ash; and to the east: Artach (including Jisr Hadid/Siderogephyron, 'Imm on the border of the *doukaton* and the Mirdāsid emirate of Aleppo). Telouch/Duluk, and Hierapolis (Manbij) were also *strategata*. Other newer *strategata* not attested before 1025 were, in the Amuq Plain: Pagrae/Baghras and Zoume/Juma (which included Kurd Dag, Jabal Sim'an, and Afrin); and in the Syrian Jibal: St. Elias, Borze/Barzuya/Lysias in the northern part of the Jabal Ansariyya, and Sezer/Sizara/Larissa. Pagrae was considered a *strategaton* only after the Byzantines had built the castle there above the lower town. To the south were Laodicea (including Jisr al-Shughur and Sahyon), Gabala/Zebel and Balanea/Balaneus, Marakeia/Marakeus, Antares with Antaradus/Tartus (and the island of Arwad/Ruwad).

44 For a list of *duces*: Laurent 1962, vol. 2, 38.

45 Holmes 2002.

46 Most of these lead seals were not excavated but rather purchased by Henri Seyrig (in the 1930s)

47 Cheynet 2006, 21–22, n. 7. Some were Constantinopolitan transplants such as the Eugenianoi, Solomons, and Kataphloroi; others were Antiochene families, like the Marchapsaboi, Antiochitai, and Libellisioi.

48 Cheynet 2006.

49 Ībrāhīm b. Yūḥannā was given this rank, but was also known as a *kātib* (scribe).

50 Cheynet 2006.

51 The length and composition of the walls and towers is inconsistent in the sources. C. Brasse is currently working on a textual and material analysis of the city walls.

52 Demir 1996, 58.

53 Ibn al-'Adīm 1996, 93.

54 Ibn 'Abd al-Zahir 1976, 318.

55 Ibn Shaddād 1984, 223–299.35 states that it was built just after the conquests; *TIB* 652 states at the start of the eleventh century.

56 Chesney (1850, 426) speculates it was on the acropolis, and Pierre Belon (1553) that it was the Palace of Antiochus (mistakenly). Perry (1743) wrote that the castle itself was supposed to include a temple, which he could not find. But he did note a small building with no windows and thought that might be it, dedicated to Mars.

57 Eger 2015.

58 Al-Maqrizi 2009, 94–5; Ibn 'Abd al-Ẓāhir 1976, 318.

59 Al-Maqrizi 2009, 102.; Ibn 'Abd al-Ẓāhir 1976, 318.

60 Ibn 'Abd al-Ẓāhir 1976, 318. The whereabouts of this activity is unclear, whether this occurred in Antioch or elsewhere, although it falls within a description of Antioch.

61 Or Bangutakin or Bengu/Mengu Tegin. Abū Shuja al-Rūdhrāwarī and Hilāl b. al-Muḥ assin 1921, 230 (219), vol. 6.

62 Nicolas Drocourt 2019, 63.

63 *TIB* 567–568.

64 Farag 1990, 44–60.

65 Yaḥya b. Sa'īd al-Anṭākī 1924, 1932; Abū Shuja al-Rūdhrāwarī; Smbat.

66 According to *Michael the Syrian* 1963, III.117–123, this was because the Byzantines were afraid of living in proximity to the Muslims and so settled Christian groups (Miaphysites) who were accustomed to living near them. Yet the Miaphysite had a large population in Antioch already. Dagron 1976, 177–216.

67 Yaḥya b. Sa'id al-Anṭakī 1924, 1932; Czyż, 137.

68 Dagron and Feissel 1987, 457–459.

69 *TIB* 652; Roberts 25–26.

70 Ibn Buṭlān in Yāqūt, translated by Le Strange 1890, 370–371.

71 Hirth, *China and the Roman Orient, Researches into Their Ancient and Medieval Relations as Represented in Old Chinese Records. Leipzig, 1885; blog Clepsydra.* 9E. Wiedeman 1970, 57–68. Al-Jazārī's castle water clock also featured balls dropping and making a cymbal-like sound. *Al-Jami' bayn al-'ilm wa 'l-'amal al-nafi' fi sina'at al-hiyal* ("A Compendium

on the Theory and Useful Practice of the Mechanical Arts"); al-Muradī, *Book of Secrets.* Kowalska, "Namenregister zu Ḳazwīnī's '*Āṯāral-bilād*,'" *RO* 29, 1965, pp. 99–115, 30, 1966, pp. 119–134.

72 Katip Çelebi 2012, 595–597.

73 The fact that the ruler's palace was not on the Island but in the center of the city is more evidence that the Codex dates after the sixth century, when much of the Island was destroyed by the 526 earthquake, and that the Island was out of use.

74 C. Ecclestone, "The Regia" in *The Antiochepedia=Musings upon Ancient Antioch* blog. April 26, 2008. https://libaniusredux.blogspot.com/2008/04/regia.html. Though the presence of one hall of justice is not certain, as this function was carried out at various public buildings.

75 Todt 256–266; Roberts 22–23.

76 Boudier 2018, 43–58. See also Mayer and Allen 2012, 198, on the presence of relics in Antioch and how they were incorporated into devotional and liturgical use and viewed.

77 See Saunders 1982, 216–217; Ousterhout in Evans and Wixom 1997, 461; Angar 2017, 52. The reliquary ended up in Aachen, but it is not known when. Some possibilities include: between 1000–1002 as part of gift exchanges between Holy Roman Emperor Otto III (980–1002) and a Byzantine princess, Zoe Porphyrogenita, daughter of Emperor Constantine VIII, upon their affiancement, or 1081 as part of gifts sent to Henry IV (1050–1106) by the Byzantine Emperor Alexius on his coronation as Holy Roman Emperor. See Franklin 2004, 25–26, n. 81. Magdalino 2019.

78 I am grateful to Brad Hostetler for his insightful comments on the artophorion and the text. See also Hostetler 2009, 17–19

79 See Canard 1953, 568–569 for the translation of *ḥuyūl; shabbūqa* is from the Syriac referring to a branch, staff, stick, or rod. It can also be a bishop's scepter (or crozier). I am grateful to Joshua Mugler and Jack Tannous for their comments. A *minṭaqa,* typically translated as a belt, of St. Symeon the Elder could be the cord of palm leaves he wore tightly under his tunic so it dug into his flesh in an act of mortification and this is mentioned in the Syriac *Life* of the saint (1892, IV.522; I am grateful to Kyle Brunner). Another option is his iron collar that he used to chain himself to a rock, which Evagrius Scholasticus saw in Antioch when Symeon's head was taken out of its reliquary to be sent to the battlefield, see Chapter 4, p. 194. Indeed, the Antiochenes petitioned the emperor Leo to translate Symeon's body from his monastery to Antioch in 459, as after the earthquake of 458, the city was left unwalled, and the presence of Symeon's body as relic would fortify the city for them. Evagrius (2000, 1.13) writes:

> Beside the head lies the iron collar, to which, as the companion of its endurance, the famous body has imparted a share of its own divinely-bestowed honours; for not even in death has Simeon been deserted by the loving iron.

It is worthy of note that, although Evagrius observed the head in remarkable preservation and the belt, only the belt seems present by the time the Patriarch Christopher is brought to St. Peter's in the mid-tenth century. There is no reference to the palm leaf belt as a relic in any source; however, Evagrius' personal observation of the iron collar, which would also last far longer than a palm leaf cord, seems to make the collar the more probable of the two for the relic mentioned in Christopher's *Life*. See also Mayer and Allen 2012, 149–151, 172, 194, 198. I am grateful to Dina Boero for bringing the passage to my attention. It is also interesting to point out that these relics, including St. Peter's throne, must have been recovered from when they were taken by Ibn Mānik. All of these words seem to be fairly uncommon as Arabic words, but all have Syriac counterparts, and some Greek, suggesting Arabic-speaking Christians in Middle Byzantine Antioch may have had their own creole of words or, more accurately, used diglossia or mixed language.

80 Besides those aforementioned, these also included: vestments of the previous patriarchs St. Babylas and St. Ignatius and the right arm and hand of St. John the Baptist. These were all in the treasury of St. Peter's "until our own time," *Life of Christopher*. Relics were removed from Islamic lands after the reconquests and often taken back to Constantinople. Reference to the right hand of John the Baptist, used to baptize Christ, was taken (stolen) by Job the Deacon from Antioch to Constantinople at the behest of Constantine VII in 956. See Kalavrezou 1997; Skylitzes 2010, 236; *TIB* 614.

81 *TIB* 613, in colophon in the life of Timothy. Martyrion of St. Dometius, Mayer and Allen 2012, 68.

82 Todt 2004, 182–184.

83 Cheynet 2006.

84 Matthew of Edessa 1993, II.2 (84–86). D. Weltecke, 2006. "On the Syriac Orthodox in the Principality of Antioch during the Crusader Period," in *East and West*, K. N. Ciggaar and D. M. Metcalf (eds). Leuven: Uitgerverij Peeters, 95–124.

85 M. Czyż, "The Migrations on the Byzantine-Arab Frontier," Unpublished chapter from forthcoming work, *Chosen Aspects of the Byzantine-Arab Frontier during the Reign of the Macedonian Dynasty*, p. 130.

86 Sāwīrūs b. al-Muqaffa 1948, English: 240, Arabic: 108–109; ten Hacken 2006, 197–198. *TIB* 617. See also Troupeau 2005, 578. This was witnessed and recorded by Michael (Mikha'īl) of Damru (Damrawī), deacon, priest, and bishop of Tinis.

87 *TIB* 568, a hagiographic anecdote.

88 Yaḥya b. Sa'īd al-Anṭākī 1924, 1932.

89 McGeer 2008.

90 Beihammer 2012. 157–177; Ibn al-'Adīm 1996, 118.

91 Yaḥya b. Sa'īd al-Anṭākī 1924, 1932.

92 Ibn 'Abd al-Ẓāhir mentions Nicetas as Nīqīṭā, and Ibn al-'Adīm as Naqītā (1996, 140); both give him the title of a *quṭbān* (leader or authority figure) of Antioch.

93 Skylitzes 2010, 373 (395). In the later Mamlūk source of al-Maqrīzī's translation by Quatremere: 1845. *Histoire des Sultans Mamlouks de l'Égypte*. M. Quatremère (transl.) Paris: Oriental Translation Fund. 1.112, passages from Nuwayrī describe the town of Maynaqa in the Jabal al-Rawādif (Amanus Mountains). Here Naṣr b. Musaraf Rawādīfī convinced the Byzantines to build a fortified town, which Nicetas then had to subdue. This demonstrates the continuity of the Jarājima/Mardaite threat and unpredictable allegiance to Antioch since the Early Islamic period.

94 Todt 2000, 455–501.

95 Nicephoritzes would go on to lead the financial administration under Michael VI Doucas, where he was notorious for his corrupt money-making schemes.

96 Ibn Buṭlān in Yāqūt in Le Strange 1965, 372–373, although the *TIB* 653 states the years are 1045–1048.

97 According to Matthew of Edessa, this was in 1053 [1993, II.2 (84–86)]. Ambraseys 2009, 269–270, argues that he was referring to the 1063 earthquake and that the patriarch referred to is actually the Miaphysite Athanasius VI.

98 Smbat the Constable 1980.

99 Sāwīrūs b. al-Muqaffa 1948.

100 Vardan Vardapet Armenian historian corroborates this account; 10,000 people died, including the Melkite Patriarch.

101 *TIB* 658; Wilbrand von Oldenburg 2012, 73, and mentioned in a source of 1207 (Jamil and Johns 2003).

102 See Roberts 26, n. 135 for brief discussion on St. Michael and the contributions by D. Morozov and N. Serikoff on the NASCAS listserv (January 24–25, 2018).

103 For the Mother of God, see Thierry, *Repertoire des monasteres armeniennes*, which mentions an unlocalized church attached to a monastery in the Hatay (entry 278), founded maybe in the tenth and attested in the eleventh century. The *TIB* 5, Kilikien und Isaurien p. 421 suggests it was in the Amanus Mountains. Many thanks to Tasha

Vorderstrasse for this. Canard (1953, 569) suggests it was the name of a specific saint, although he cannot tell which.

104 A martyrium for St. Stephen and St. Thecla is first known from the 526 earthquake, when it was possibly burned shortly before. It is uncertain whether this is the same as the one referred to here.

105 Stinespring 1932, 9–10; Margoliouth 1898, 163. The Temple of Aries was already established by the end of the first century B.C.E.

106 Hajji's version adds that each year a three-day-long feast was held at the Temple to Saturn when an adjacent bath was free. Margoliouth 1898, 162–163.

107 The iconography is reminiscent of a Mithraic temple but could be an astrologically guided representation, as Mars is linked to the constellation of Scorpio. Snakes were also associated with Mars, seen at Thebes. J. Otter (1748), who visited Antioch in 1737, wrote a fairly detailed description, which he attributed to the "Turkish Geographer," who was Ibrahim Effendi, the Director of Printing of Constantinople. From FN 1: A Hungarian who introduced printing and copper-plate engraving in Constantinople in 1729. He printed maps as well.

108 These conflict in each version of the manuscript: the Vatican version: b.ṭ.r.m., Bodleian: court of justice; Hajji: causeway. Margoliouth 1898, 166; Stinespring 1932, 11, 24.

109 Faris, 1938; *Antioch II*, 166.

110 *Antioch III*, 15.

111 *Antioch V*, 119

112 More study of these two buildings is planned by the New Committee on the Excavations of Antioch team.

113 Michael Attaleiates 2012, 16.5–16.6, 16.12 (174–175, 183).

114 Ibn al-ʻAdīm 2016; Ibn al-ʻAdīm 1996, 163; *TIB* 570.

115 Stephen of Taron 1907; see Holmes 2001, 43.

116 Matthew of Edessa 1993, II.79 (148). But in *TIB* 570, this word comes from the Arabic *baladīyūn* or natives, suggesting they were like native Muslim North Syrians in habit and language.

117 Matthew of Edessa 1993, II.79 (148) and Smbat. It is unclear which gate this refers to. Perhaps "of the blackfoot" refers to one of the north or northwestern gates that were encircled by swamp.

118 Interestingly, in 1079 a famine struck the Levant, but the territory of Antioch was spared, and as a result people from all other districts migrated to Antioch.

119 Matthew of Edessa 1993, II.66 (141). Perhaps this is Arabissus, identified with modern Afşin north of Kahramanmaraş. Bar Hebraeus 1932, 226 (254) states that in 1077–1078, Nicephorus Botanicus became ruler of Cyprus and Antioch briefly.

120 Bar Hebraeus 1932, 229 (257), called him Pīlardūs. He took the money from the rulers and divided it among his troops.

121 Sibṭ al-Ajamī 1950.

122 Djobadze 1976, 1986; Thierry 1993.

123 Weitenberg 2006, 79–94.

124 Henry 2015.

125 Smbat the Constable 1980, though this sounds like Armenian propaganda, since following this, Smbat writes, "Thereafter [Basil] was like a father to the land of Armenians"

126 For more information on ʻAbdallah b. al-Faḍl, see the very recently published work by A. Roberts 2020 (p. 7–8 for the quote, p. 14–16). Another intellectual and translator was Symeon Seth (Shimʻān Shaniḥī), who was ʻAbdallah's Greek teacher and a native of Antioch. His Arabic teacher was possibly the poet Abū al-ʻAla' al-Maʻarrī (d. 1057 or 1058) from nearby Maʻarrat al-Nʻumān who visited Antioch, himself studied philosophy at a monastery from monks, and was friends with Ibn Buṭlān.

127 See Glynias 2019, 243–244, Treiger 2017, 2019, 227–238, 2020, 24–26; Mugler 2019b, 180–197. Ibrāhīm b. Yūḥannā was born to a prominent family, and his father was probably a physician.

128 Treiger 2020, 18.
129 Saminsky 2006.
130 Kavtaria 2011, 325–340.
131 Mugler 2019a.
132 Shacht and Meyerhof 1937.
133 Cheynet 2006.
134 Ibn al-Shiḥna; Ibn al-ʻAdīm 1996, 93.
135 Bosworth 1992, 278; Bar Hebraeus 1932, 171 (189), Miskawayh 1921, 225 (211)
136 Or it could refer to baths, the temple, or the house of Trajan.
137 The account by Amatus of Montecassino (1016–1078) in *Historia Normannorum* in, 1892. *Ystoire de li Normant, par Aimé, éveque et moine au Mont-Cassin.*
138 Brands 2009.
139 Redford 2012, 297–310.
140 One of the many challenges with the Princeton archaeological material is that, while a cursory or preliminary look may allow us to differentiate among main periods, it is challenging to separate out the Middle Byzantine from Crusader periods (and Saljūq), in part because of the hasty and arbitrary method of their excavation. But while some of the pottery extends into the Crusader twelfth and early thirteenth centuries, most of the types, as well as coins and some architectural features, seem to reside in the Middle Byzantine period. In fact, there are a lot of Crusader coins, but not as many from the Middle Byzantine period, and the time span is longer; since most of the Crusader period used silver/billon coins rather than the bronze of the Byzantine age, we would expect to see fewer of them from an excavation.
141 *Antioch V* 119.
142 Vorderstrasse 2006, 320–321.
143 *Antioch IV.1*, 101. Turquoise glazed on buff-bodied ceramics are ubiquitous in Islamic lands; however, their production sites are as yet unknown. This evidence strongly suggests Antioch was one producer of the ware.
144 Vorderstrasse 2010.
145 It is dated by parallel to the Byzantine Silk of Siegburg. Underhill 1942, 6–7.
146 Stahl and Glynias 2020.
147 Regarding whether there was a mint, in general, the anonymous folles and the rare ruler-signed bronzes do not have a mint mark and have generally been thought to have all been minted in Constantinople. There has, however, been speculation of regional mints, as well as the idea that the series was introduced at least in part as part of the re-Christianization effort of the re-conquered. Eric Medawar. "Byzantine Administration of the Muslim East in the Tenth Century: Insights from the Numismatic Evidence." Paper presented at the 53rd International Congress on Medieval Studies, Kalamazoo, MI, May 2018.
148 *Antioch V*, 119. Translated from the original:

> Il semble qu'après le XIIe siècle, dans toute la partie Nord de la ville antique, toute construction ait disparu dès qu'on s'écarte un peu de la route. Il a certes pu exister, comme de nos jours dans l'oliveraie, des maison paysannes isolés, que nous n'avons pas eu l'occasion de rencontrer. Par contre il apparait que dans la période qui va du Xe au XIIIe siècle, après la reconquete byzantine jusqu'après les croisades, la ville s'est à nouveau étendue jusqu'au torrent Parmenios, et meme au delà.

149 Sinclair 1990, IV.249.
150 Ibn Ḥawqal 1964, 165; Istakhrī 1967, 62; Idrīsī 1989, II.245. Ibn Buṭlān quoted in Yāqūt 1955–57, i.266–270, translated in Le Strange 1965, 374–375; Stinespring 1932, text 2.13. To this Ibn Shaddād adds open spaces and channeled mountain streams in the vicinity of its city walls: Ibn Shaddād 1956, 2: 354.
151 Presumably these seven towns were the suburbs of Antioch and included, moving from southwest clockwise: Dafnā or Daphne, lying on the west toward the mountain at the Bayt al-Māʼ; Ghāinā or Ghānyā (or Bāshā [perhaps Baṭia from Bottia?]) on the road

to the sea and near the Church of St. John; a village opposite the Gate of the Palm Tree (Bāb al-Nakhl) or Garden Gate in an area of sown fields; Drumarsania (Ṣūrṣā or Gharmardā), which had a theater or hippodrome (this could be the Island); al-Manshar (possibly referring to a "portcullis" or "saw" and near the Aleppo Gate), which had 12 wells and possibly a *qanat*; Bisāhid beyond the eastern mountain along the wall, 330 *qasab* by 280; and Adrāsis/Aṭrashish, a little west of Bisāhid and 254 *qasaba* long.

152 Vorderstrasse 2005a.

153 Muqaddasī 1906, 155: 1–5.

154 See n. 150.

7

THE SALJŪQS

An interlude (1084–1098)

A fire blazed where the red hills come together
Like the forelock of a sorrel horse.
You conquered Byzantine Antioch,
where strongholds had been erected by Alexander,
Your horses trod on its shoulders,
causing the Byzantine women to double over and miscarry their fetuses.[1]

– Yāqūt al-Ḥamawī, *The Dictionary of Countries*

Introduction

The Saljūq period of Antioch is the shortest in its history of occupations, just 14 years. Nevertheless, it remains an important interlude between Byzantine and Crusader control as part of the overall narrative of the city, as well as justification for the Crusader conquest. Archaeologically, it is hard to narrow anything down to such a short period; however, numismatic and textual evidence points to continued, and relatively unchanged, vitality during the Saljūq conquest and occupation.

The Saljūq conquest and 14 years of rule

The Saljūq Empire had been established in 1037 by Turks whose homeland lay near the Aral Sea. From there they had expanded into Persia and eventually Anatolia, most of which they won from the Byzantine Empire in the devastating Battle of Manzikert in 1071. The following year the renowned sultan Malik Shāh I (1072–1092) came to power, under whom the empire reached its furthest extent (Figure 7.1). In 1077, however, Sulaymān b. Qutlumush, a distant cousin of Malik Shāh and son of a defeated competitor for the Saljūq throne, succeeded in carving

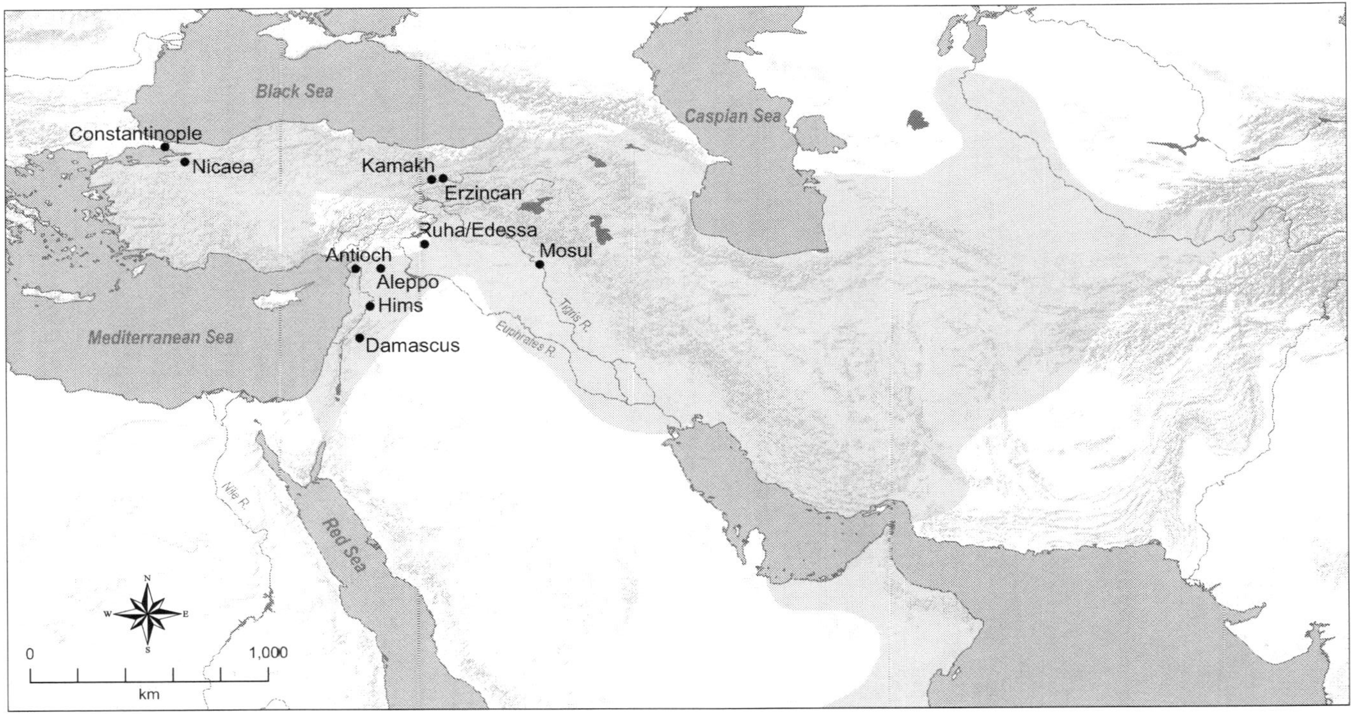

FIGURE 7.1 Map of the Saljūq Empire, 1086

Source: Created by Claire Ebert

out his own independent state encompassing most of central and eastern Anatolia, the Sultanate of Rum, which he ruled until his death in 1086.

By this time, the second half of the eleventh century, greater Syria itself was full of small lordships, each run by a different *amīr*, sometimes allied with one another, sometimes at odds. These included the cities of Aleppo, Edessa, Mosul, Ḥimṣ, and Damascus. At the time, Antioch was still under the control of the local warlord Philaretus Brachamius, but mostly disconnected from the Byzantine Empire as a duchy, though still densely populated and flourishing.[2] The Byzantine hold on Antioch had thus become more precarious as it, too, became a desirable acquisition. In the view of some scholars, the internal feuds between Melkites and Miaphysites in Antioch also gradually weakened the city.[3]

The first Saljūq foray against the city occurred in the summer/autumn of 1075 by a brother of Sulaymān b. Qutlumush, though which one is unknown. Laying siege to Antioch, he demanded 20,000 dinars both as tribute and as surety against further attacks on the agricultural lands around the city.[4] In 1083, the Saljūq *amīr* (later sultan) of Damascus and younger brother of Malik Shāh, Tāj al-Dawla Tutush (1078–1094), also invaded the territory of Antioch briefly but did not stay. Meanwhile, in 1078, the Byzantine emperor Michael VII Doucas (1071–1078) had attempted an alliance with Sulaymān against a challenger, Nicephorus Botaneiates, former *dux* of Antioch, but after initially supporting the emperor, Sulaymān switched sides, and with his support Nicephorus successfully usurped the throne. Two years later, Sulaymān took the city of Nicaea, which he made his capital.

In 1084, the year after Tutush's incursion, Sulaymān decided to go after Antioch itself. His reasons for undertaking the conquest, however, vary widely in the sources. According to Matthew of Edessa, he found the Byzantines of Antioch weak and few in number and the city unguarded, and so decided to attack.[5] Anna Comnena, on the other hand, says that Philaretus had converted to Islam and so his son, Barsama, whom Philaretus had imprisoned, decided to act against his father and asked, ironically, for Sulaymān's help; thus it was Philaretus's defection to Islam that led to Antioch's fall. The historian Ibn al-ʻAthīr (1160–1233) agrees with much of these events.[6] Writing much later in the fifteenth century, Ibn al-Shiḥna, corroborating Anna Comnena's account in part, narrates that the ruler of Antioch had left the city, forcing the people to nominate another. This new ruler, presumably Philaretus, mistreated the Antiochenes and soldiers and imprisoned his own son, who then wrote to Sulaymān, asking him to deliver the city. According to the later Miaphysite bishop/scholar Gregory Bar Hebraeus (1226–1286), Philaretus had left Antioch to go to Edessa and placed either a Turk or a Persian, Isma'īl, in charge of the city, and it was he who imprisoned Barsama; the Antiochenes then rebelled with Barsama's help and that of the local army. Thus, in Philaretus's absence, Sulaymān was easily able to take Antioch and was even preferred by its inhabitants.[7] The connecting theme in all these accounts, however, is that Sulaymān had the support of the local elites, who resisted Philaretus's rule and wanted help in overthrowing him. On the other hand, according to Michael the Syrian, Philaretus was in fact supported as ruler by the people of Antioch and came to fortify the city and fight the Turks.[8] But whatever Sulaymān's reasons for the conquest, Antioch can be seen as an extension in expanding his new Sultanate of Rum, and he chose the precise opportunity, taking advantage of internal tensions within the city between Philaretus and its citizens, to capture it.[9]

Late in the year, Sulaymān quietly left Nicaea with a small army of about 300 knights (*faris*) and some infantry and swiftly made his way south to take Antioch by surprise. Along the way he was joined by a Türkmen named Mencekoğlu Bey.[10] The fifteenth-century source Ibn al-Shiḥna relays a more detailed and slightly different account from Ibn Munala, though Ibn Shaddād and Ibn al-ʿAdīm said the same, that the army, presumably en route to the city, killed all the inhabitants of a village called ʿAmrānīya so they would not betray them.[11]

The sources also differ as to when exactly the attack took place. It may have been the night/morning of Sunday, December 13, or possibly Friday the 11th, though Ibn al-Shiḥna suggests the attack was on a Wednesday, the first of *kānūn al-awwal*, presumably the 9th, while Ibn Shaddād states it occurred one week earlier, on Friday, December 4.[12] In any event, the attackers found Antioch unguarded (and perhaps deliberately so, on account of the invitation to siege) and so entered the city during the night through the Aleppo Gate. Sulaymān's army launched spears attached to ropes at the walls to hang the ropes from the battlements, and some of his men then climbed the ropes up the side of the Aleppo Gate and lifted what seems to have been a harrow or portcullis (*minshār*, literally "saw"). Sulaymān thereupon entered the city with his army. This entry – involving betrayal and invasion in the dead of night – is so characteristic of Antioch conquests. Indeed, the people of the city did not realize what had occurred until alerted by a single cry from the invading Turks. Believing them to be Philaretus's army coming for them, they fought back weakly but were defeated. Some jumped over the city wall and fled to the mountains, while those who remained took refuge in the citadel.

Although writing sometime later in the thirteenth century, Ibn Shaddād, relaying an account by Bahā al-Dīn al-Ḥasan b. al-Khashshāb, a twelfth-century Shīʿī *qadī*, further relates an account corroborated by Bar Hebraeus, Ibn al-ʿAdīm, and Ibn al-ʿAthīr that three days after the conquest, Sulaymān commanded the people to return to their homes and released prisoners, while Ibn al-Shiḥna writes that he gave those in the city protection and let them have their own houses and the slaves they had previously had. Property that was looted was to be sold within the city and not to outsiders, since Sulaymān wished to avoid a massacre of the city's inhabitants or taking more citizens as prisoners. The guarantee of property rights for the citizens also suggests that the Saljūq Turks did not settle in the city, while at the same time it helped prevent an uprising of Philaretus's sympathizers.[13] Another account adds that Sulaymān ordered his men not to marry Christian women.

Several accounts agree that some Antiochenes, mainly sympathizers of Philaretus, took refuge in the castle when Sulaymān conquered the city, suggesting that some were resistant to his help.[14] These were blockaded from receiving food or water until they capitulated. Philaretus's garrison from the citadel, meanwhile, held out and launched an attack but were defeated on January 12, 1085.[15] This illustrates a persistent dynamic that had been introduced with the construction of the citadel: the fortification on top of Mt. Silpius in reality created two cities at odds – the lower town and upper castle. In the course of many invasions of Antioch after the Middle Byzantine period, the besieged often holed up in the citadel, while the besiegers took the city, though sometimes it was the other way around. Ibn al-Shiḥ na includes an eyewitness account by a Melkite Christian named Michael living in Antioch at that time that further shows the division of the city between mountain castle and the town on the plains:

> This relates what the monk and clergyman Mikhāʾīl al-Anṭākī stated, beginning with the report from Yūḥannā the priest of Damascus. He said: Sulaymān b. Qutlumush defeated the great Antiochene city and robbed it from its eastern mountain, named al-Qayshāqīl? on the first day of the first month *kānūn al-awwal* [December], the 8th (?) the year 6593 AM [1085 CE]. Over the course of three days, he placed his rule over the city, as he did not let any of the residents remain except for the side of its mountain in defeat and for its castle. I was that humble one, Michael – the monk and clergyman. It was the third day in the city. I had slipped away in front of them in defeat and I hid in a gloomy house. By God's will, he hid me from their gaze and freed me from them. When night came upon me, I saw the city devoid of its residents. Fear and anxiety followed me as I rebuked myself for my absence, since I did not ascend the mountain along with the city folk. Thus, half-way through the night, I went and climbed up the mountain until I arrived the next day at the castle's gate. While I turned to enter, a group of people from the city set out riding from the castle. There was a company of Turks with them. They had sought aid from Ḥiṣn Artāḥ, and paid them many dinars to help them against Sulaymān – their enemy. Thus, they descended galloping. While I looked over to the right and to the left to enter the castle, I saw them returning in defeat. Suleymān's Turks were subject to them. During that hour and its brevity, they herded whoever was on the wall and the mountain; any man, woman or youth walking around the castle and its sides; and any travelers or mounts similar to that. They took them downhill. I was one of the many prisoners. I had blamed myself for my insensitivity because I remember that very sad incident. For both of my eyes began spilling out courses of hot tears in abundance because they were in terrible pain – nothing like that happened as quickly. After their men herded us on the slope of the mountain, we were confused. We are uncertain and despairing of life. I remember the day in particular. It was the fourth of the month of *kānūn al-awwal* [December]. As far as I know the Antiochenes there had joy, delight, and unbridled happiness. Their clothes were the most splendid of garbs and robes. There were many who, riding upon colts and donkeys, arrive at the temple of the Holy Barbāra and celebrate her yearly memorial with the Patriarch, the churchmen, the governor, and the heads of his state.[16]

Two points are noteworthy concerning Sulaymān's conquest. The first speaks to Antioch's remaining a desirable city to rule, while at the same time it had continued strong for most of the Byzantines' reign; this is revealed by the fact that not until 1084 did a Saljūq lord achieve power there, despite the Saljūqs already holding important cities all over the wider region of greater Syria and the Jazira. And second, Sulaymān made his claim over Antioch in the name of the sultan Malik Shāh, showing that he wished to be recognized as a legitimate Muslim ruler operating within Islamic legal claims of authority as a Saljūq ruler.[17]

Sulaymān's new rule, however, interrupted the yearly tribute Antioch had been making to Aleppo and its ruler, the 'Uqaylid Sharaf al-Dawla Muslim, *amīr* of Mosul and a Shi'ā allied with the Fāṭimids.[18] Sharaf al-Dawla therefore asked Sulaymān to carry Philaretus's debt and continue making payments in the same amount, but he refused, stating that he was not an infidel and not required to pay a tribute and that his sultan would be mentioned in the weekly Friday *khutba* sermon in the mosque and his name minted on money.[19] But Sharaf al-Dawla demanded the tribute anyway, and the two came to blows on June 20, 1085, at a place called Pzah.[20] The victory went to Sulaymān, perhaps because Sharaf's own forces (a larger army) betrayed their ruler and fled, and Sharaf was killed.[21] Ibn Shaddād then writes that on March 31 the following year,[22] Sulaymān was himself killed in fighting by the ruler of Damascus, Tutush, whom the citizens of Aleppo had called upon to help.

Several months later, in December 1085, Sultan Malik Shāh arrived in Antioch, and the city was handed over to him by Sulaymān's vizier and interim ruler, al-Ḥasan b. Ṭāhir al-Shahristānī. Malik Shāh appointed Yāghi Siyān b. Alp, whose daughter was married to Riḍwān, the prince of Aleppo, as governor (likely he gave the city to him as an *iqta'*) and gave him an army to command, while al-Ḥasan b. Tāhir was placed in charge of administrative affairs (the *diwān*).[23] Interestingly, Malik Shāh had no desire to keep the city himself, and in 1092 he tried to negotiate Antioch's return to the Byzantines for an alliance against Abū al-Qāsim, *amīr* of Nicaea, and a marriage between his eldest son and the daughter of Byzantine emperor Alexius I Comnenus. Presumably the deal never went through, and Malik Shāh died that same year. In the next six years, Antioch and its ruler were caught in a constantly moving board of alliances and family feuds over territory fought by members of the Saljūq tribe and other warlords. Some fought alongside Yāghi Siyān and even stayed in Antioch, like Abū Naṣr Shams al-Malik Duqāq b. Tutush of Damascus (1095–1104, nephew of Malik Shāh), along with his *atabeg* (governor subordinate and loyal to him) Zahīr al-Dīn Tughtakīn (d. 1128). Duqaq's brother, al-Malik Ridwan b. Tutush (1095–1113) clashed with his brother after their father's death and, along with his *atabeg* Janah al-Dawlah of Aleppo and Ḥimṣ, r. 1095–1113), went to battle with Yāghi Siyān.

Earthquakes

Two earthquakes are recorded for this brief period of Saljūq rule and corroborated in Arabic and Armenian sources. The main one occurred toward the end of the

Saljūqid reign, on September 26, 1091, an earthquake shook the city, collapsing between 70 and 90 towers to their foundations and pulling down sections of the walls.[24] The area hardest hit was the northwest portion of the city walls between the Sea/Bridge Gate and Aleppo Gate, where 32 towers fell. It also damaged the Theotokos Church (called al-Sayyīda or the Lady). Many people died when their own homes collapsed, and the Orontes channel shifted and flowed through the city's center.[25] Malik Shāh rebuilt the city walls and towers, one of which was described as adorned with equestrian statues of bronze held together with iron chains.[26] According to a seventeenth-century account by the patriarch of Antioch Macarius III Zaim (1647–1672), there were seven bronze statues of horsemen, Turkish in appearance, with chain armor, spears, and shields on a sarcophagus;[27] these, however, were later destroyed by the governor Yāghi Siyān.

Buildings

The accounts by Michael the Syrian, Ibn Shaddād, Bar Hebraeus and Ibn al-ʿAdīm state that Sulaymān took possession of the valuables of the Church of St. Peter and turned it into a mosque on the first Friday after the city's conquest. On the day of the conquest (or four days later, according to another account), the Muslims made Friday prayers in the church, and 110 muezzins called for prayer. A great gathering of people came from all over Syria. Might this have been the first construction of the main congregational mosque today, the Ulu Camii, known in the Mamlūk and Ottoman periods? From the start of the Saljūq occupation, the Melkite Patriarch of Antioch left the city, residing instead in the monastery of Hodegon in Constantinople. Nevertheless, during Sulaymān's rule, Antiochene Christians obtained permission to build (or rebuild) two churches, the Church of the Theotokos (presumably rebuilt after the earthquake's damage) and the Church of St. George, as well as repair any buildings damaged during the conquest. St. George's, not mentioned before this time, was presumably newly built during this period and likely stood near the Daphne Gate, later renamed after it. The eyewitness account by Michael appearing in Ibn al-Shiḥna also suggests that the Church of St. Barbara was functioning at this time and featured a sculpture of her. The continuity of other churches besides St. Peter's and the Christian community is noteworthy and fits the accommodations made to citizens after the conquest, as well as the general continuity favored by the Saljūqs. Virtually no buildings from this period exist today (Figure 7.2); however, the Meydan bath, which continued in use after this period, is reportedly from the Saljūq period, and Saljūq motifs are said to decorate the arched entrance (Figure 7.3).

Numismatics and archaeology

Although the Saljūqs ruled Antioch for only a short period, Sulaymān kept his word and did indeed mint coins in Antioch in the name of his sultan Malik Shāh. Saljūq fulūs minted in Antioch before the Crusader period were excavated in

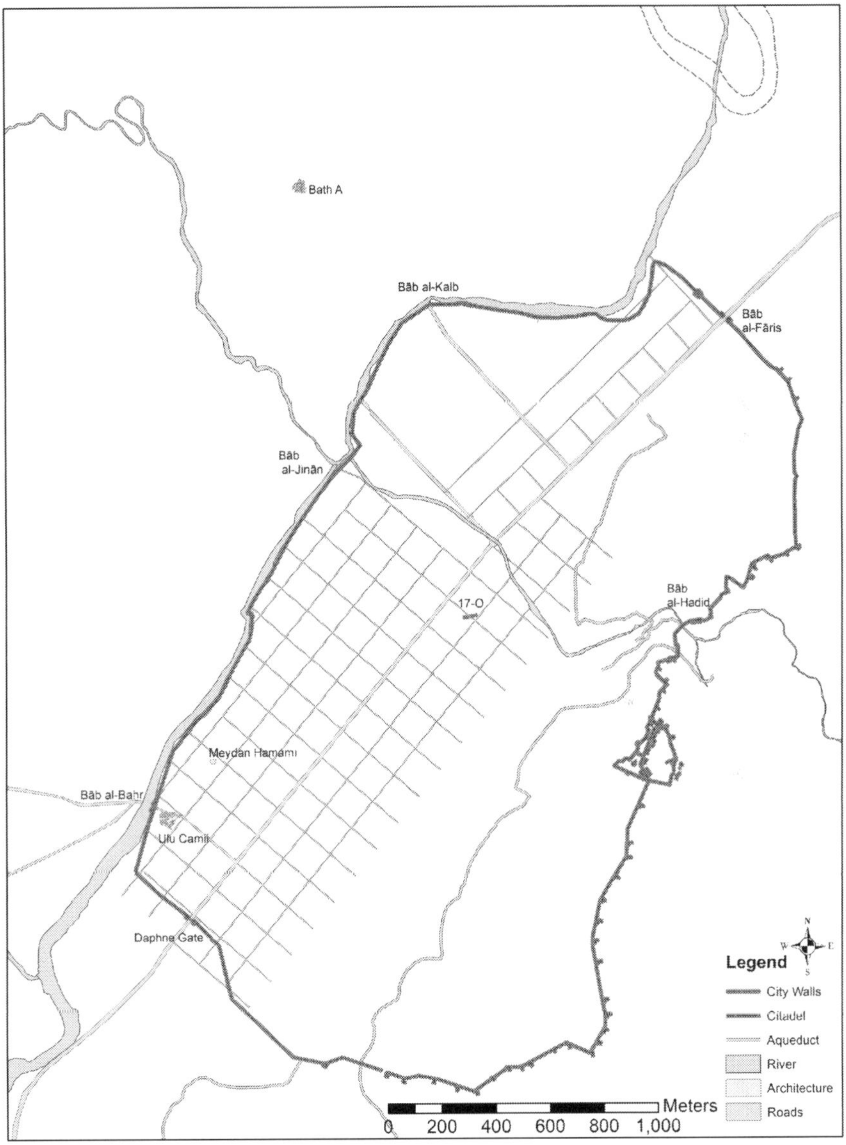

FIGURE 7.2 Plan of Saljūq Antioch

Source: Created by Steve Batiuk

FIGURE 7.3 Meydan Hamam

Source: Courtesy of Zeki Cemali

Corinth, indicating a continuing trade and relationship between the two ports.[28] The Princeton excavations meanwhile revealed a sizable number of Saljūq bronze coins, though most were poorly struck and thin, and differed from mid-twelfth-century figurative bronze Saljūq coins. The largest concentration of Saljūq coins came from Bath A, on the former imperial Island.[29]

At times, these coins were minted over older Byzantine pieces. Yet the most notable features of the Saljūq coins of Antioch are that they depict figures, animals mainly, namely lions, elephants, and cranes, and sometimes plumes and crescents, unusual for Islamic coins. Some coins are also octagonal. All belonged to the mints of Syria, most likely Antioch, many during the years of 1085–1098 under Malik Shah.[30] One bears the name of Riḍwān b. Tutush b. Alp Arslān, governor of Aleppo (1095–1113), while others mention the name of another sultan, Barkyāruk, likely Malik Shāh's son, who ruled 1092–1105.[31] If that is the case, then some of these Saljūq coins date from the subsequent Crusader occupation of Antioch. Sector 17-O was also a main location for these coins (Figure 7.4), three of which were found on the floor of the east courtyard house, two in the well of the central courtyard house, and one seemingly under the kiln, showing that the Level I buildings and pottery production areas continued throughout the Saljūq period and that Saljūq currency was indeed in circulation.

FIGURE 7.4 Saljūq coin from sector 17-O, 8557, Ca379. Obverse (top) shows a border of dots and possible overstriking over an elephant's head. Reverse (bottom) shows a border of dots and the head of a bird (crane) and three round plumage heads, probably overstriking

Source: Courtesy of Princeton University, Firestone Library Numismatic Collection, ex. Peter J. Donald Collection

Conclusion

The Saljūq conquest and 14 years of occupation did little to affect the city and can be seen as an interlude between major periods of Antioch's history. Archaeological evidence shows no dramatic differences, and numismatic and textual evidence point to continuity. The Saljūqs, however, as foreign rulers with little representation among the people of Antioch, were not well loved. Yāghi Siyān's popularity, particularly, is debatable. Their occupation thus opened the door to the arrival of other outside rulers, this time from far to the west.

Notes

1 From Yāqūt's entry on Anṭākiya. Translation by Raymond Farrin, 1990. *Kitāb Mu'jam al-Buldān*, vol. 1, 319. The poem is possibly by al-Abīwardī; see Ibn al-Athīr 2002, 218, for a different version and the attribution.
2 Ibn al-Athīr 2014, 6: 293, 217–218.
3 Cheynet 2003.
4 Sibṭ al-Jawzī 175–6 via Beihammer 2017.
5 Matthew of Edessa 1993, II.78 (147–148).
6 Ibn al-'Athīr 2002, 217.
7 Bar Hebraeus 1932, 229 (257).
8 *Michael the Syrian* 1963, III.173–174.
9 Beihammer 2017.
10 Or Ibn Manjak, Mangujak Ghazī, *amīr* of Kamakh and Erzincan, who brought another 300 knights, although according to Ibn Shaddād, he did not arrive until after the conquest. Ibn Shaddād 1984, 223–299.38.
11 Ibn al-Athīr and Ibn al-Shiḥna both write that Sulaymān came first via ship to the coast, and then his army crossed the Amanus through difficult mountain passes (*maḍā'iq*). This seems unlikely, however, as his army marched from Nicaea and came through the Aleppo Gate. Ibn al-Athīr 2002, 217; Ibn al-Shiḥna 1990; Ibn al-'Adīm 1996, 211.
12 According to Beihammer (2017), the attack occurred on December 1. Ibn 'Abd al-Ẓāhir says the Saljūqs arrived on the 27th of Rajab/November 29 and took the city on December 14, but he has the year wrong (1976, 318–319).
13 Beihammer 2017, 233, n. 187.
14 Beihammer 2017; for example Ibn 'Abd al-Ẓāhir 1976, 319.
15 *TIB* 572.
16 Ibn al-Shiḥna 1984, 212–213: Many thanks to Kyle Brunner for help with the translation.
17 Beihammer 2017
18 Yāqūt 1990, vol. 1, 319.
19 Ibn al-Athīr 2002, 219.
20 Or Qurzahil, but sounds like it could be Buzā'a. See *TIB* 572.
21 Ibn al-'Adīm 1996, 214 writes of a humorous anecdote that just before the battle, Sharaf al-Dawla's companions got together for a meal of watermelon at his cousin's request. His cousin's reasoning was that it is important to go into battle after having eaten because if one were to die, at least they would die stuffed and sated. Sharaf al-Dawla wryly noted that they may all die of his cousin's pessimism first. When Sharaf al-Dawla was finally defeated and stabbed, just before he died, he said to his cousin, "you are the master of all pessimists" (*ya shām al-shawm*) and accused his followers of killing him.
22 Or June 4/5, 1086? or June 13, 1086 in *TIB* 572.

23 See Ibn 'Abd al-Ẓāhir 1976, 319 (although his name there is Baghī Saghān b. Ālb). But in the *Saljūq-nama* of Ẓahir al-Din Nishapurī (2001), Antioch is given as *iqta'* by Malik Shāh to one of his servants, Aqsān.

24 *Michael the Syrian* II:193, 3:183. Michael the Syrian states that in the 1082 earthquake [he gets the date wrong], 86 towers collapsed (3:180). Matthew of Edessa 1993, II.93 (157); Ibn al-Athīr 2002, 250–251. Ibn 'Abd al-Ẓāhir says it was October 6, 1091 (1976, 319).

25 Ibn al-Shiḥna via *Nujūm al-Zāhira* 1990; Ambraseys 2009, 278; Guidoboni 1994, 64–65.

26 *TIB* 653–654.

27 Walbiner 1999–2000, 519. This episode appears in Michael the Syrian; however Michael the Syrian noted that they resembled Crusaders, not Turks. See Chapter 8, p. 400, n. 17.

28 Metcalf 2006, 283–318.

29 *Antioch I*, 80–81, Figure 1.

30 Ilisch 1982. See *Antioch I*, 80–81, Figure 1. No find spots given; Miles, *Antioch IV.ii*, 119–121, numbers 155–156, gives a date range of 1085–1114. Special consideration is given for T. Lankila's study, "Seljuk Coins of Princeton's Antioch Excavations (sector 17-O, 1937)." Unpublished paper, Princeton University, 2012.

31 Miles, 120, but he does not recognize the name with Malik Shāh's son.

8

THE CRUSADER PRINCIPALITY OF ANTIOCH (1098–1268)

> Consider the strength of this city, where it is located, that ravines make it impervious on three sides and on the fourth lies the river and the swamp. Its circuit of walls has no equal anywhere in the world. Fountains flow inside and those who have passed a year since the threats brought by our arrival are able to gather sufficient quantities of other supplies necessary for life. O Antioch, that you had never existed or that we had never come upon you. Our path is to Jerusalem. What is Antioch to us!
>
> – Bishop Adhemar of Le Puy

Introduction

The Crusader history of Antioch is typically dominated by the dramatic events of its siege by the armies of the First Crusade. Indeed, the siege of 1098 is one of a few remarkable events outlined in some detail that is corroborated by authors in Arabic, Latin, Armenian, and Greek. It is usually portrayed, as in the opening quote by the bishop of Le Puy, as a necessary though excessively long engagement, full of destruction and loss of life, and not part of the original goal of reclaiming the Holy Land for Christianity. This speaks to the enduring importance of Antioch as second only to Jerusalem in its perception and symbolism. Beyond the siege, however, the succeeding period of Crusader rule over what became the Principality of Antioch is less well-known, often characterized as a turbulent 170 years of perpetual back-and-forth invasions and occupation by other powers. In addition, during Crusader rule there occurred a frequent number of natural disasters, including some of the most devastating and well-documented earthquakes in Antioch's history, as well as droughts and famine. The siege also reorganized the city's topography and its urban order. Here we will examine how motivations revealed in the siege of Antioch, specifically by the Normans, and later political and military events intersected with the social and religious relationships between the Norman Crusader occupiers and citizens, and how this manifested in the city's changing topography. These threads will be explored and interwoven throughout the chapter as we look at two main questions linking the topography and composition of the population. How did the city look following the siege, and what buildings continued to function, were repurposed or abandoned, or took on multiple functions? And where did the Crusaders live in relation to the rest of the city, and were they or any other communities segregated from the rest?

Below the surface of obvious Christian–Muslim conflict, a whole host of complex processes become clear and can be traced in five periods of Crusader occupation. In the first two periods, that of the siege itself (1097–1098) and the first 25 years (1099–1124), conflict existed among Crusader rulers, some of whom were supporters of the Byzantine Empire while others, like the Normans, were active rivals. The Normans from Sicily, who ruled Crusader Antioch, were the most familiar with coexisting in a formerly Arab and Muslim land. Contrary to some belief, the city and its citizens survived the siege and remained a polyglot, polyethnic, and poly-religious community with many of its original churches intact, though the Crusaders themselves were not fully assimilated. In the third period (1125–1162), a fulcrum of sorts, the Crusaders gradually assimilated into the city's religious, social, and economic life and were no longer segregated, yet relations between rulers and patriarchs began to break down. In the fourth period (1163–1192), the city underwent considerable decline, with a series of natural disasters, little new construction, and ongoing internal feuds between Crusader rulers and patriarchs. Although in the final period (1193–1268) the city recovered somewhat, Antioch experienced a war of a succession, clashes between patriarchs and princes, and local citizens asserting their own wishes over who should rule their town, an Antiochene hallmark we have seen in almost every period so far. Yet older properties around the city were restored and even used by princes as gifts to ease tensions between Crusader rivals. Throughout this history it becomes apparent that the external challengers to the city – Zangids and Byzantines in the third period, Ayyūbids in the fourth, and Armenians in the fifth – did little to affect the composition and topography of the city itself. Despite all the challenges, external and internal, the city survived and continued to thrive as a vibrant, desirable, and heavily visited center.

The siege of Antioch

The siege of Antioch had its origins in the calling of the First Crusade by Pope Urban II, who at the Council of Clermont in France in 1095 called upon the lords and peoples of Europe to answer the plea by the Byzantine emperor Alexius I Comnenus (1081–1118) for military aid against the continuing advances of the Saljūq Turks, who had persisted in making inroads into Byzantine territory following their victory at the Battle of Manzikert in 1071. But Alexius's appeal for help was soon transformed in the West into the goal of reclaiming Jerusalem and the Holy Land from the infidel. The response was overwhelming and, instead of the band of mercenaries Alexius might have expected, by 1097 he had an entire

Crusader army camped outside his doors in Constantinople. Anxious to send them on their way, he undertook negotiations according to which the Crusaders would swear to him an oath of allegiance and agree to return any lands and cities reclaimed from the Turks to him in exchange for food and supplies and passage through his territories.

Along their way to Jerusalem, however, the Crusaders decided to first set siege to Antioch. The Crusader accounts of the siege, celebrated in the Latin West, are particularly detailed, as several of the authors wrote first-hand, eyewitness accounts.[1] But the motivations for taking Antioch are less clear in both primary and secondary sources. The decision to take the city seems not to have been part of the original plan but was made en route. But doubt tinged with regret at the costly siege, particularly in hindsight, led some Crusaders to question whether it had been worthwhile. Some modern scholars have argued that taking Antioch was a strategic necessity to secure the city and thereby have a hold on the northern Levant for communications, supplies, and reinforcements, and to protect the pilgrimage routes.[2] But the Crusaders could also have bypassed the city and, heading south along the Orontes River, reached Jerusalem sooner, with fewer soldier deaths. In the fragmented political landscape of post-Saljūq Syria, however, the taking of its most historically difficult and well-fortified city seems more than just a strategic choice. Antioch represented religiously and symbolically a second Jerusalem as the believed location of the first Christian community and church, and even perhaps a necessary appetizer to further galvanize the Crusaders.[3] Pragmatically speaking, it was also, for its region, a wealthy city, an economic center for production and trade, and home to a community of elites and intellectuals. Further, each of the Crusader lords had his own motivations involving personal power, wealth, alliances, and religious fervor, which, although frequently at odds, manifested in the choice to take Antioch. Once the siege began, it further became clear that the Crusaders, as they became worn down to virtual poverty and starvation, desperately needed to win the city just to survive.

The conquest of Antioch is itself a fascinating event, not only in its deviation from any pure motive of pilgrimage[4] but also in its corroboration in the sources and its dramatic sequence of events, worthy of a big-budget movie – a historically grounded *Lord of the Rings*, so to speak, without the ideological overtones of good versus evil. From the large cast of characters, we can pull out nine Crusader lords who squared off against nine Muslim rulers for control of the city. Sieges and subterfuges, divine intervention, dramatic loss of life – all are part of the story. No wonder, then, that many texts memorialized this siege while its story was told in poetry in the faraway courts of France and depicted in French and English church windows.[5] The accounts of the siege also reveal important processes in the way Crusader Antioch took shape when recounted with an eye to the internal, often quite fragmented, relationships between Crusaders, Saljūqs, and the citizens of Antioch. Finally, the siege reveals the relationship of the city to its landscape while setting the stage for further shifts in the urban topography of Crusader Antioch.

The conquest of Antioch, oddly, gets a fairly balanced and corroborative accounting of events in Arabic sources. Decisions made by Islamic rulers were equally criticized and not always lauded by contemporary medieval Muslim historians, for three reasons. First, Islamic sources demonstrate a profound misunderstanding of who the Crusaders (all called Franks) were and what they were doing; locals had never encountered people from the West before, the only previous Christian raids coming from the Byzantines. Second, at the same time, many of the Turkish rulers were equally foreigners in the Levant. The central Islamic lands at this time were in disarray, the 'Abbāsid caliphs having no real power. In this power vacuum the Byzantines and local Arab warlord dynasties vied for control, eventually being subdued by the arrival of the Saljūqs. But as the Saljūq sultanate disintegrated in the late eleventh century, former Turkish governors, each running their own territory, began carving out fiefdoms for themselves from the major cities of Syria and northern Mesopotamia. And third, the Shi'ī Fāṭimids of Egypt, active in the Mediterranean and Levant, had begun reaching up into northern Syria. Having previously negotiated treaties with the Byzantines, the Fāṭimids proposed cooperation with the Crusaders against the Saljūqs during the siege of Antioch, thinking the Crusaders were simply Byzantine mercenaries gone rogue. Northern Syria was thus a chessboard fought over by poorly understood foreign Crusaders and similarly foreign Islamic rulers. There is therefore no clear, unified Islamic voice in the sources, and thus both Christian and Muslim authors are remarkably, for the most part, in agreement on events.

Although many Islamic accounts, unlike some key Frankish eye-witness reports, typically were written later and after the ideology of *jihād* had taken hold, some of these later Islamic sources still have their use. As typical of Islamic chronicling, they often preserve accounts that appeared in earlier texts (or versions of texts) that are no longer extant. The later author Ibn al-Shiḥna (d. 1485), for example, whose section on the Crusader siege is peppered with extensive quotes from older accounts, begins his description: "We found in all the history books that in the year 490 [1096–1097]. . . ." Although it is not the place of this chapter to assess critically the historiography of individual sources, what is generally agreed upon is the following version of events.

Near the end of July 1097, several Muslim rulers got wind of the approach of the Franks toward Antioch. The Franks had divided into two groups. The main group, comprising the bulk of the army, had come through Mar'ash down into the Amuq Plain via the Kara Su River valley, while a second group, led by Tancred and Baldwin of Boulogne, had crossed the Taurus Mountains at the Cilician Gates (Figure 8.1). These two young lords, independently raiding throughout the Cilician Plain, had taken Tarsus, Maṣṣīṣa, Adhana, Anazarbus, and Iskandarūna, vying for occupation of the towns along the way and in at least one instance attacking each other.[6]

The main Crusader leaders numbered nine, yet not all shared the same motivations for participating.[7] Count Raymond IV (1094–1105) of St. Gilles and Toulouse, from southern Provençal, was the most senior noble with the largest army.

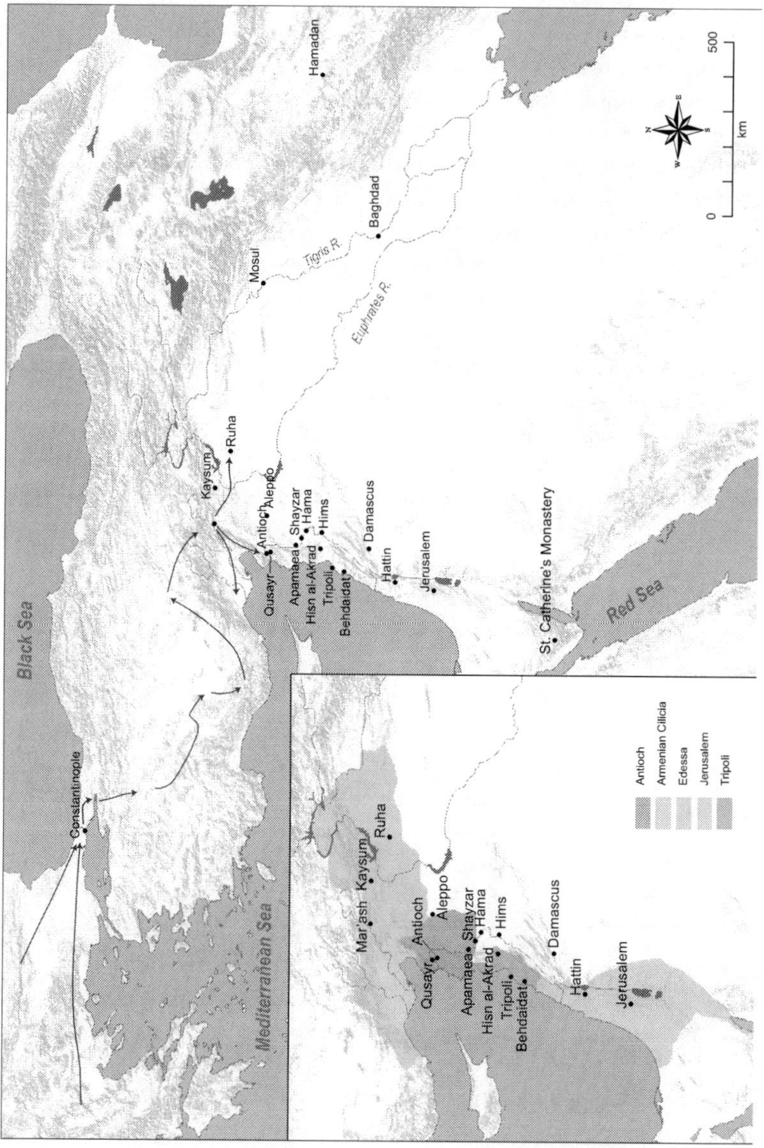

FIGURE 8.1 Map of the First Crusade

Source: Created by Claire Ebert

He may also have had the most religious zeal to visit and liberate the Holy City, and he brought with him his family and the pope's representative Bishop Adhemar de Monteil of Puy-en-Verlay (1082–1098), who acted as a religious reminder, morale booster, and unifier for the Crusaders, as well as an ally with the Melkite Church and the Byzantines. Raymond's desire for power and land, however, became manifest following the conquest of Antioch, as he positioned himself to rule the city.[8] Duke Godfrey of Boulogne and Lorraine (1089–1096, d. 1100) was a major noble from northeastern France who had also rallied a large army. Although his motivations to go on Crusade are less clear, it is likely he had no plan to return to the West.[9] His kinsman, Baldwin[10] of Le Bourg, joined Godfrey as part of his retinue. Also from northern France, the wealthy Count Robert II of Flanders (1093–1111), as well as Duke Robert II Curthose of Normandy (1087–1106), traveled with Stephen II of Blois and Chartres (d. 1102), married to the daughter of William the Conqueror. Robert Curthose, a Norman who had rebelled against his father, William the Conqueror, and tried to seize his brother's inherited lands, had failed in these attempts and ended up impoverished. He likely envisioned the Crusades as a way to increase his status and gain wealth. His brother-in-law Stephen of Blois, meanwhile, saw Antioch as a stop on the way to Jerusalem, and his motivations suggest both religious salvation and financial reward. In a letter to his wife written around March 1098 from Antioch, he wrote:

> We had been continuously advancing for twenty-three weeks toward the home of our Lord Jesus. You may know for certain, my beloved, that of gold, silver, and many other kinds of riches I now have twice as much as your love had assigned to me when I left you.[11]

There was also Hugh I the Great of Vermandois (1085–1101), younger brother of the French king, Philip I, who brought with him an army from northern France.[12] Hugh I and Count Robert II of Flanders appear to have had strong loyalties to Emperor Alexius and no plans to remain in the East. Also joining the expedition was Bohemond,[13] the prince of Taranto (1088–1111), and his nephew Tancred[14] (b. 1075–1112). These two Normans, recently installed in southern Italy with small armies, had already been invested in fighting the Byzantines for nearly two decades, pursuing a policy of encirclement, and so for Bohemond, fighting Byzantium and taking Constantinople may have been a tantalizing reason to join the Crusades. These nine main Crusader figures (not including Bishop Adhemar) were also joined by a Byzantine contingent led by the *megas primikerios* (Grand Commander) and emperor's representative Taticius, a government observer and Turkish eunuch. Accompanying the Crusader host through Anatolia, he was instrumental in giving them advice, having knowledge of how the Byzantines had reconquered Antioch 130 years before.

Upon hearing news of the approaching Franks, Yāghi Siyān, the city's Saljūq governor, mobilized his Turkish troops, numbering about 4,000 to 5,000, to fortify the city,[15] and sent his two sons to ask for aid from nine neighboring *amīrs* and their *atabegs*, all of whom answered the call to fight. Despite their internal rivalries, these lords, whether willingly or pressured, left their lands to fight for Antioch. Among them was Karbughā b. Malik Shāh, the *atabeg* of Mosul, who assumed command of the various Islamic forces.[16] Not all of the leaders, however, came willingly; some were pressured, and thus there was no real, concerted "Islamic front" against the Crusaders, who were seen as just another invading force going after a city, a familiar sight in the unstable landscape of post-tenth-century northern Syria.

Just as the Crusader and Islamic lords had varying loyalties and at times clashed among themselves, similarly the residents of Antioch were not united. The Antiochenes, comprising a blend of religious and ethnic groups, had not fully embraced their Saljūq ruler and his army. Thus, when on September 12, 1097, the Franks took the nearby northern fortification of Baghrās, protecting the Beylan Pass or Syrian Gates connecting Asia Minor and Syria, they quickly defeated the Islamic garrisons at the surrounding fortifications with the help of locals, who revolted and embraced the new Crusader presence. From Baghrās, the Crusaders launched incursions into the surrounding area, securing all the territory in the Amuq Plain around Antioch. In preparation, Yāghi Siyān imprisoned the Orthodox patriarch, John IV Oxeites. Fearing Christian sympathizers in his city, he also ordered the Muslim citizens of Antioch to clean out the moats and ditches and then brought them in at the end of the day; the following day, he had the Christians do the same, but at the end of the day closed the gates, telling them he would let them back in only after he saw how things went with the Crusaders. The Christians thereupon joined the Crusaders in their camp, providing them with useful information about the city.[17] The mention of Christians in the city during the siege belies that this was a total purge, however.

Around October 20, 1097, the Crusaders camped outside the city on the plain, within a mile of its imposing walls. Accounts give a description of wonder and amazement at the city when the Crusaders arrived, which speaks to Antioch's impressiveness at the end of the Saljūq period. The eyewitness account by Raymond of Aguilers, chaplain of Raymond of Toulouse, mentions three (not two) hills along Antioch with a castle on the most northern, another castle on the middle hill called by the Greeks Colax (Mt. Staurin and the citadel, presumably, and the name probably a corruption of *qal'a*), and towers on the third (Mt. Silpius). He wrote that the city "fears the attack of no machine and the assault of no man, even if every race of man should come together against it." An anonymous account from the *Gesta Francorum* (c. 1100–1101), written likely by a vassal of Bohemond, adds that besides the strong citadel, there was a high and broad double wall with 450 towers, which is the most inflated and inaccurate number of towers recorded for Antioch.

The Crusaders then dug a trench between their position and the city. Never surrounding the city totally, they massed only along its river side and pursued a strategy of attrition, building some temporary fortifications and blockading three gates. Between November and April they also built three fortresses. Each leader's camp was distinct and separate (Figure 8.2). Starting north and proceeding counterclockwise, Bohemond and his troops were camped outside the Aleppo Gate. The fortification there, built in late November 1097 and called Tower Malregard, blocked the Aleppo road and defended Bohemond's camp from attack by Antiochenes coming

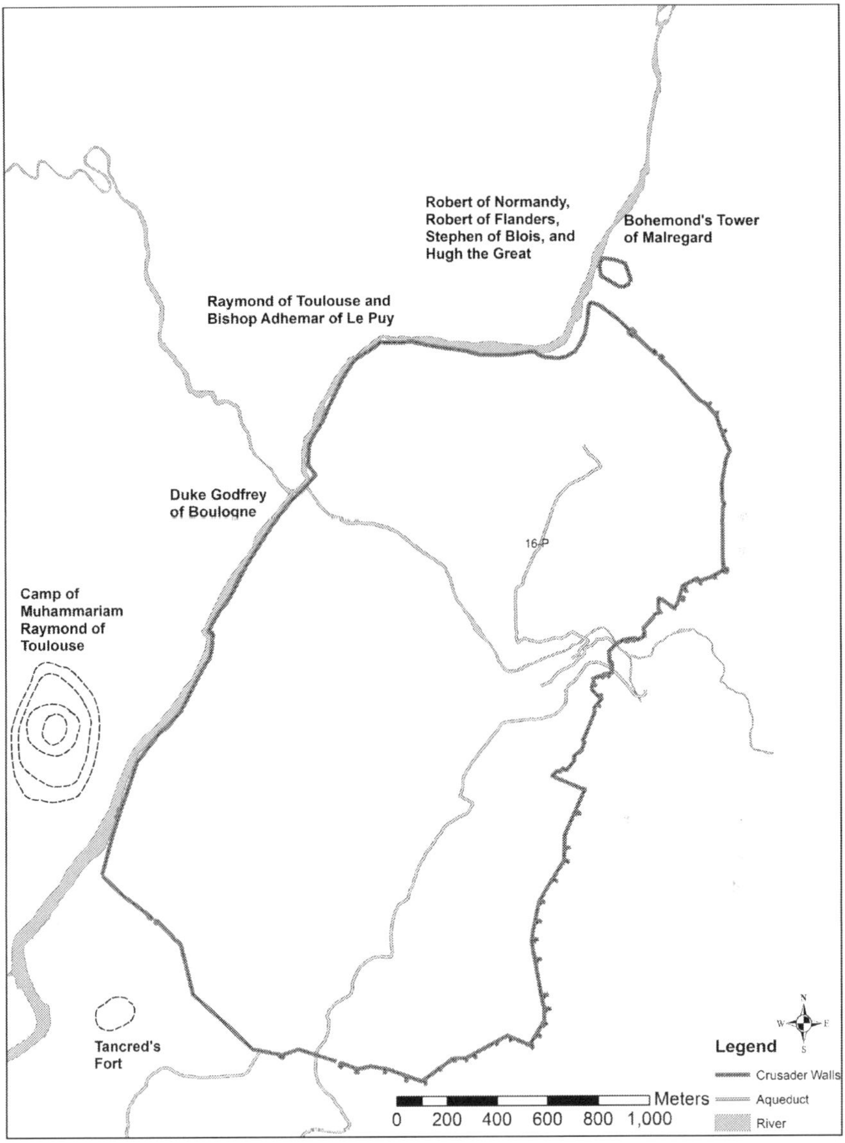

FIGURE 8.2 Crusader camps around Antioch

Source: Created by Steve Batiuk

down from the slopes of Mt. Staurin.[18] Meanwhile, Robert of Normandy, Robert of Flanders, Stephen of Blois, and Hugh the Great camped around the northwest corner of the city between the Aleppo and Dog Gates, while Raymond of Toulouse and Bishop Adhemar of Le Puy set up outside the Dog Gate. This gate, likely created from Justinian's contracted wall and river course alteration, connected the city to the former Island, separated by a relict channel of the Orontes, which, by the time of the siege, was silted and swampy. The archbishop William of Tyre, writing about 70 years after the siege, between 1170 and 1184, mentions that the bridge crossed a swamp. The 1934 excavations revealed one end of the bridge in sector 12-N (Figure 8.3).[19] The Dog Gate, behind the modern municipality building in the neighborhood of Küçükdalyan, was east of the hippodrome, oriented to one of the four porticoed avenues of the *Tetrapylon* of the Elephants.[20] It can perhaps be identified with the disused Tauriane Gate to the now abandoned island and for this reason has no earlier mention.

Duke Godfrey of Boulogne, meanwhile, was camped by the Duke Gate, as it came to be named after him (previously known as Bāb al-Jinān or Garden Gate), located between the wall and river near a bridge made of seized boats.[21] This gate too opened onto swampy terrain. Mentioned specifically in the *Gesta Tancredi*, written around 1112 by Ralph of Caen, another eyewitness and chaplain in Bohemond's army, this wetland along the river hampered the use of siege engines against the city walls: "The sponginess of the ground made the fortification stronger than the hardest of rocks." The swamp resulted in part from the spring at the Aleppo Gate and the annual springtime flooding of the Orontes and would have been mostly confined along the northern and northwestern walls. But it was also a

FIGURE 8.3 12-N, Küçükdalyan Dog Gate 1918, general view of the basalt pavement outside the city wall. Bab el-Kelb: Gate in Justinian Wall

Source: Courtesy of the Antioch Expedition Archives, Department of Art and Archaeology, Princeton University; Princeton

deliberate defense for the city, as noted in the opening quote by the Bishop of Puy, and Yāghi Siyān's orders to dig a moat was presumably intended to spread and deepen the wetland.

Opposite the "middle area" gate or the Sea/Bridge Gate was a small hill in a rocky area extending down the road outside of town. This hill had a wall and a stone temple called a Muhammariam or La Mahomerie – in other words, a mosque. It was also a centuries-old burial ground that continued until the late nineteenth/early twentieth centuries and indicated clearly on the nineteenth-century map of Rey (see Figure 10.9). The *Gesta Francorum* suggests the hill had two mosques and some tombs. It was likely part of Raymond's camp, particularly since he built a fortification there. Tancred, meanwhile, controlled a small castle near the southern or Daphne Gate, where a stretch of wall and tower was still being built and therefore was vulnerable. This was likely an abandoned monastery near the gate, used to bring food to the city, and was referred to as Tancred's Fort once he garrisoned it.[22] An upland area near the river and gate is located just south of the barracks of Ibrahim Paşa that may be its location. These opportunistic structures outside the walls may also have been as much shelters from arrows and wind and rain as fortifications.[23]

Over the next roughly nine months, a prolonged siege of attrition weakened both sides, exacerbated by a particularly harsh, cold, wet, and stormy winter with low agricultural yields and ending with spring floods. The Turkish armies also withheld food, grown undoubtedly in the green spaces within the walls, and prevented the Crusader armies from procuring it as much as the latter prevented outside food from reaching the Turks. Some necessities, such as oil and salt, were smuggled into the city and sold for cheap.[24] Interestingly, the anonymous *Gesta Francorum* account describes an abundant landscape at the start of the siege, full of vineyards, fields of grain, and fruit trees, while Raymond of Aguilers adds that those in the camp could have their pick of the choicest cuts of beef, which they preferred over grain or wine. But by December 1097, the formerly ample supplies of food and fodder around Antioch had been depleted, and the Latin accounts begin to describe desperate searches for food.

Sometime between December 28, 1097, and January 2, 1098, Bohemond and Robert of Flanders and a large force of men left their camps on an unsuccessful quest for food for their troops. They also clashed with Muslim forces coming from Damascus. The night after their departure, Yāghī Siyān, taking advantage of the apparent retreat of two lords and a large host of men from the now unguarded camps outside Antioch, attacked Raymond's men outside the Sea/Bridge Gate and Godfrey's camp at the Duke Gate. Raymond, however, pushed the Saljūq army back to the city, and the Crusaders tried to destroy the Dog Gate to prevent Antiochene troops from emerging. Raymond then had his men build a siege tower to get over the walls, but the Antiochenes burned it. His men then hurled rocks with ballistae (a type of catapult), but the Antioch army destroyed them. Then the Crusaders filled the gate with rocks to seal it.[25] At another point, they also beheaded a large number of Antiochene soldiers, and so in retaliation the Saljūq occupiers killed Antiochene Christians (Melkites, Miaphysites, and Armenians) and threw their heads over the walls; Patriarch John Oxeites was also taken from his prison cell and suspended over the city walls, his feet struck by iron rods.

Interestingly, there is mention of Armenians and Miaphysite Christians in Antioch who sold goods at steep prices to the Crusaders during the siege, indicating that not all Christians were removed from the city by force or trickery and that those that remained did not defect to the Crusader side or flee the city or necessarily oppose Saljūq rule. Rather, the Antiochenes may have been riding out the siege in the relative safety of their walled and well-cultivated city, protecting their homes and obtaining greater access to food, waiting to see the outcome between the Crusader and Saljūq forces. At this point, the Crusaders, having picked the surrounding fields and pastures clean, were forced to eat seeds, herbs, thistles, horses, asses, camels, dogs, and rats during the winter and the following spring rains and floods. Their weapons also rusted, and thus the warning given to the caliph Hārūn al-Rashīd (Chapter 5) came true.[26] Stephen of Blois wrote that

> throughout the whole winter we suffered for our Lord Christ from excessive cold and enormous torrents of rain. What some say about the impossibility of bearing the heat of the sun throughout Syria is untrue, for the winter there is very similar to our winter in the West.[27]

Ralph of Caen specifically refers to the raging winds that made the Crusader camp especially vulnerable. William of Tyre further noted that Muslim forces made the area between the sea and Antioch unsafe and even burned ships and killed crews, leading to a halt in supplies. Some Crusaders, mainly the very poor, but some wealthy as well, deserted.

In February, Taticius and his Byzantine group left for Cyprus to secure supplies but never returned, giving up on the Crusaders' siege but also allowing the Crusaders to proceed with little Byzantine oversight or interference. By March, the Crusaders did finally receive aid from the Byzantines and from Cyprus via the main port at St. Symeon (Suwaydīyya) and also Laodicea, as well as help from local monasteries, and even the Armenian princes of Cilicia.[28] Meanwhile, the Turks ventured out on several occasions via the Sea/Bridge Gate to intercept supply and reinforcement runs.

In one such raid, on March 7, Godfrey killed many Turks, likely between the bridge and Antioch's modern park (Antakya Belediye Parkı). The following day, the Antiochenes ventured out to bury their dead at the site of the La Mahomerie cemetery. The Crusaders subsequently robbed the graves, taking any goods, including garments, gold bezants, bows, arrows, and other objects, then removed the heads from the bodies, throwing the bodies in a ditch and taking the heads back to camp. Beginning around March 10 and over the next four days, the Crusaders built a fortification called the Tower of Raymond, or of the Blessed Mary, in front of the Sea/Bridge Gate at the exact site of this mosque to block any further Turkish raids.[29] The tower was fortified with construction material from the monastery of St. Symeon the Younger near the Orontes delta and tombstones from the La Mahomerie cemetery. This fortification was strategic since it controlled bridge and road access both to the delta and the sea as well as to Alexandretta, and it was also used after the initial conquest to defend the city against Karbughā's army.[30] It also became the main gate by which the Crusaders entered the city. Anselm of Ribemont, count of Ostrevant and Valenciennes in northeastern France and participant in the siege, wrote a letter in July 1098 describing the new fortress as possessing a double moat, strong wall, and two towers, which also had bowmen and men who operated the siege devices.[31]

By the start of summer in 1098, the Crusaders controlled almost all entrances to and exits from the city save the Daphne Gate, which was not completely protected.[32] They also ambushed supply runs by Armenians and Miaphysites bringing provisions to the city. Anselm of Ribemont mentions that Antioch was "supplied to an incredible extent with grain, wine, oil and all kinds of food."[33] But in reality, the Antiochenes at this point were also starving and forced to eat leaves and plants, horses, donkeys, and cats. This may suggest that the green spaces within Antioch were affected by the difficult cold, wet winter or were not sufficient alone to feed the population. Yāghi Siyān meanwhile passed an edict that all citizens must share their grain, sending half the supply to the court. Some accounts state that this affected the wealthy the most since their payments were substantial, and they also had to build catapults and contribute heavy labor. The poor, on the other hand, left the city. At the same time, the Franks were becoming increasingly desperate since they knew that the reinforcement armies of Karbughā and the other Muslim rulers were close to arriving and could pin them against the walls of Antioch, and so they had to hasten the city's capture.

In the end, at the climax of the cinematic unfolding of events, Antioch was taken (and indeed had to be taken) by an inside job, as it had been with the Persians and Byzantines before. An armorer of Antioch named Firuz was in charge of several of the fortification towers adjoining the mountain overlooking a valley, far from the Crusader army.[34] The precise location of the specific tower he was in, however, is unknown, though it may have been in the Phyrminus valley on Mt. Silpius's slopes opposite Tancred's Tower and camp.[35] The tower was near another managed by Firuz's brother, hence the name for the two towers, the Two Sisters, *duo sorores*, as companions to the brothers. Firuz was from an Antiochene family of armorers usually in good accord with the Turkish rulers. But he was also disgruntled over Yāghi Siyān's edict, having been forced to give up his grain and wealth,[36] and so meeting with Bohemond, he struck a deal giving himself money and land in exchange for allowing Bohemond entry into the city.[37] He got Bohemond's attention, according to Ibn 'Abd al-Ẓāhir, by firing an arrow with a piece of paper around it that said, "I surrender the city to you."[38]

According to the Islamic historians Ibn Shaddād, Ibn al-'Adīm, Ibn 'Abd al-Ẓāhir, and Ibn al-Furāt (1334–1405), Bohemond, keeping this insider betrayal a secret, proposed to the other Crusader lords a competition that whoever was the cleverest in taking the city within ten days should become its ruler. All agreed but Raymond of Toulouse. According to Smbat the Constable, Firuz killed his brother in the night to protect the secret, and on the night of June 2, when it was Bohemond's chance to siege, he allowed a group of Crusaders, led perhaps by Bohemond himself, to come in through a window and occupy the city. At dawn local Christians opened the western Sea/Bridge Gate or Daphne Gate and northern gates,[39] and thus the Crusaders finally took Antioch on June 3, 1098 (Figure 8.4).

What followed was massive destruction. Over the next three days, many citizens – men, women, and children – were killed or taken prisoner as the city was pillaged and destroyed. Ibn Qalānisī, a contemporary to these events, wrote that "the number of men, women, and children, killed, taken prisoner, and enslaved from its population is beyond computation."[40] Numbers vary, of course, and some enumerate a massacre of 10,000 Antiochenes, including Melkite and Armenian Christians, since much of the takeover happened at night, making it difficult to discern Christians from Muslims among the integrated and mixed populace.[41] Turks meanwhile also pretended to be Christians. Whatever the number, several eyewitness sources agree that they killed

> all the Turks and Saracens [Arabs] whom they found there except for those who fled up to the citadel… all the streets of the city on every side were full

FIGURE 8.4 Siege of Antioch in miniature, KAO_253v-afb

Source: Courtesy of the National Library of Netherlands

> of corpses, so that no-one could endure to be there because of the stench, nor could anyone walk along the narrow paths of the city except over the corpses of the dead.[42]

Accounts also mention that the Crusaders used fire within the city to rout out the Turks, and the fire, of course, burned homes and churches. Ralph of Caen reports that Bohemond permitted Robert of Flanders to burn the area near Yāghi Siyān's palace; the fire, whipped up by the winds, destroyed a large number of churches and houses (some sources say 2,000), though St. Peter's and the Theotokos Church were spared. Many citizens, fleeing to the citadel, entrenched themselves behind its walls, of whom few escaped. Yāghi Siyān himself fled the city toward Aleppo, leaving behind his family and possessions, but soon was captured and beheaded by an Armenian woodcutter, who sent the head back to the Crusaders. Some sources also detail battle in the city, describing how Turks coming from the citadel gates were met by Crusaders on another height opposite the citadel and guarding the path down to the fortress.

The day after the city's capture, a huge army of Persian and Turkish reinforcements led by Karbughā began to arrive, but just too late.[43] Raymond of Aguilers states that the Crusaders held onto La Mahomerie for three days while it was besieged by the Muslims; then, before surrendering it, Robert of Flanders set it on fire so that it could not be used against the new Latin rulers. Now the tables were turned, and it was the Muslims who had the besieged and diminished Crusader troops in Antioch encircled. Blockading the city, the Muslim armies also took over the citadel from the still present Turkish troops and Antiochenes taking refuge there.

For nearly two weeks the Crusaders in Antioch were afflicted by hunger and famine, since the city's food supplies were already depleted. According to the *Gesta Francorum*, bread sold for a gold bezant (one solidus), an egg was two solidi, and a rooster went for between eight and 15 solidi. The Crusaders (and Antiochenes) were forced to eat carrion, leaves, thistles, and their own horses, as well as the hides of donkeys, water buffalos or cattle, and camels, essentially reducing themselves to an infantry army. In response to a rain of Turkish arrows from the citadel into the lower town, the Crusaders also built a wall between the citadel and city on the slopes of the mountain to the south, presumably during the change of hands as Karbughā took command of the citadel and regarrisoned it, although there is no physical evidence of this as yet.[44]

Frankish sources at this point depart from the accounts given in Islamic ones. Here they assume there was an actual concerted anti-Crusader Islamic front. But the amassing of so many Muslim leaders together was not a defense of Islam but of territory, since those involved were all *amīrs* of northern Syrian and Mesopotamian cities. They were not, however, all unified. Karbughā, who was in the citadel, told the other eight *amīrs* not to invade the city or pick off Crusaders breaking out of it in small numbers, since he wanted an all-out standoff with both sides arrayed on the plain in formal battle formation. But there was discord among the Muslim armies, especially between Arabs and Turks, as they disagreed with this strategy, and several *amīrs* took their troops and left.

At their bleakest hour, Frankish sources (and surprisingly some Islamic ones) attribute the final Crusader victory to a holy artifact – the Holy Lance, said to have pierced the side of Jesus while he was being crucified. According to the sources, a priest, Stephen of Valence, had a vision of Jesus, Mary, and Peter in the Church of Saint Mary (the Theotokos) who promised the Crusaders help. At the same time, Peter Bartholomew, a low-level monk, saw a vision of St. Andrew, who told him that the Holy Lance was buried in the Church of St. Peter and, if found, would insure victory (some hagiographic and liturgical sources of the tenth and eleventh centuries also state that the church held this relic).[45] After three days of fasting and repenting, the Crusaders found the Lance on June 14, though no two sources agree on where.[46] There were, however, skeptics. Ralph of Caen stated that the Lance had been deliberately planted by Peter Bartholomew and served to give Raymond of Toulouse, its discoverer, justification for taking ownership of the citadel, royal palace, forum, bridge, gates, and the city's defense. Bohemond also suspected deceit, as did Bishop Adhemar.[47] This may be supported by the Middle Byzantine *Life* of the Patriarch Christopher, which certainly does indicate that the Holy Lance was in a treasury of sorts along with other relics in the House (Church) of St. Peter, although this may have all been taken by the Saljūqs, and why it was buried seems strange. The episode in any case illustrates some of the infighting between Crusader rulers and even religious skepticism. Nevertheless, as a powerful relic, the Lance must have boosted morale, and so did contribute to the Crusaders' victory (Figure 8.5).[48]

The final battle for Antioch, on June 26, is often depicted as a quick bloodbath and rout, as the Crusaders emerged from the city, led by Raymond of Aguilers bearing the Holy Lance, and forced a great retreat of Turks and Arabs, who left behind all their possessions in their flight. The Crusaders took spoils, provisions, money, furnishings, horses and mules, and weapons from the attackers' camps, while killing many of them. The *Gesta Francorum* mentions the appearance of St. George himself riding a white horse and coming to aid the Crusaders.[49] The citadel was surrendered by Aḥmad b. Marwān, commander of Karbughā's troops, to Bohemond in exchange for his life and the lives of his family, who were given safe-conduct. Aḥmad and those remaining were among the first converts to Christianity.[50] Bohemond, who throughout the siege until the end emerged as a skillful commander, now took control of the citadel, thereby cementing his rule over the city.

After the conquest, several of the main buildings and parts of town were divided up among the various Crusader lords. Raymond of Toulouse, Bohemond's main rival, held the former palace of Yāghī Siyān, as well as the forum and Sea/Bridge Gate and quarter closest to this area along with the area he had controlled outside the gate. That the palace was in the city and likely near the Sea/Bridge Gate indicates that the Saljūq ruler had not resided in the citadel. Bohemond had earlier set fire to the palace because he wanted Crusaders to direct their efforts toward the

FIGURE 8.5 Lance of Antioch, *Histoire d'Outremer* or *Livre d'Eracles, a history of the Crusades* in French, based on Guillelmus, Archbishop of Tyre (b. 1130, d. 1190). Royal MS 15 E 1 f. 98v

Source: Courtesy of the British Library

citadel (while sabotaging the holds by other Crusaders on the city). In retaliation and to improve his own chances of ruling the city, Raymond tried to provoke the citizens of Antioch to riot against Bohemond.[51] But while, as we have seen, the Antiochenes never turned down a chance at revolting against a ruler, Bohemond proved to be the more popular of the two Crusader lords, and with Taticius and the Byzantine delegation gone, there was little counterclaim. Six to nine months later, the other Crusader lords and their retinues set off for Jerusalem, with Raymond also deciding to turn his aspirations there. Eventually, Bohemond expelled the counts Godfrey of Bouillon and Robert of Flanders from the city as well, and by May/June 1100, he had become the sole ruler of Antioch. Many scholars believe he saw Antioch as his from the start,[52] in defiance of the Crusaders' promise to the Byzantine emperor Alexius that any lands reclaimed from the Turks would be returned to the Byzantines. In any event, Bohemond elected to rule from Antioch and not accompany the Crusaders further to Jerusalem.

Crusader archaeology

Although virtually no material culture remains from the conquest itself, the Princeton excavators found a small hoard of 19 Western silver deniers in the vicinity of the hippodrome. These deniers represent the various places of origin of the Crusader armies, including Poitou, Chartres, Le Mans, Lucca, Valence, Melgueil, and Le Puy (Figure 8.6). They are thus a purse of money matching almost precisely the Western mints that the chronicler Raymond of Aguilers listed as "our money" when explaining a transaction of gold Islamic *dinars* and their Western equivalents.[53] Further, its location at the hippodrome site provides a small clue, though hardly anything substantial, that during the siege the Island was in Crusader hands, indeed part of the Crusader camp.

Unfortunately, we know little else about the archaeology of Crusader Antioch; the Princeton team barely focused on the city's Crusader remains. The slow process of teasing out the architecture and material culture using their method of arbitrary stratigraphy makes it difficult to differentiate the Crusader occupation from the general Middle Islamic strata of the eleventh to fourteenth centuries (Figure 8.7). Two churches, however, were uncovered that act as a chronological entryway to the study of Crusader Antioch. On the Island of the former Roman/Byzantine imperial palace in the Orontes, north of the medieval city, excavation of Bath A (III or sector 9/10-L) – a third-century bath soon abandoned – revealed medieval pottery and a middle Byzantine coin (1034–1041) in its uppermost stratum.[54] An Arabic inscription on marble also covered the mosaic floor. Much of the pottery was Port St. Symeon ware, characterized by a mixture of Frankish, Byzantine, and Islamic elements of the twelfth to fourteenth centuries and uncommon in the Antioch excavations. The building was possibly destroyed by earthquake and fire, then used as a quarry and cemetery. Its later phase consisted of a rock-cut tomb with stairs leading to a chamber with a vaulted ceiling (Figure 8.8). Inside were wall paintings of a Virgin with nimbus seated on a cushioned throne, and the inscription was in Latin (Figure 8.9). The painted tomb thus dates to the Crusader period and may have included a church, though its precise date and historical identification remain uncertain.[55] The Middle Byzantine church in the suburb of Daphne (sector 53-K), about which Glanville Downey wrote, was enlarged with an attached chapel with

FIGURE 8.6 Crusader Coin 9491. Penny, Chartres. C1040m. Sector 9-N-SE 5/4/32, from hoard; obverse (top) and reverse (bottom)

Source: Courtesy of Princeton University, Firestone Library Numismatic Collection, ex. Peter J. Donald Collection

wall paintings, and monastic buildings dating to the Crusader period (Figure 8.10). The church had substantial rooms outside on two sides, including one storeroom and possibly a second. The outer rooms of the monastery were of different construction and described as Crusader style.[56] The presence of a monastery outside

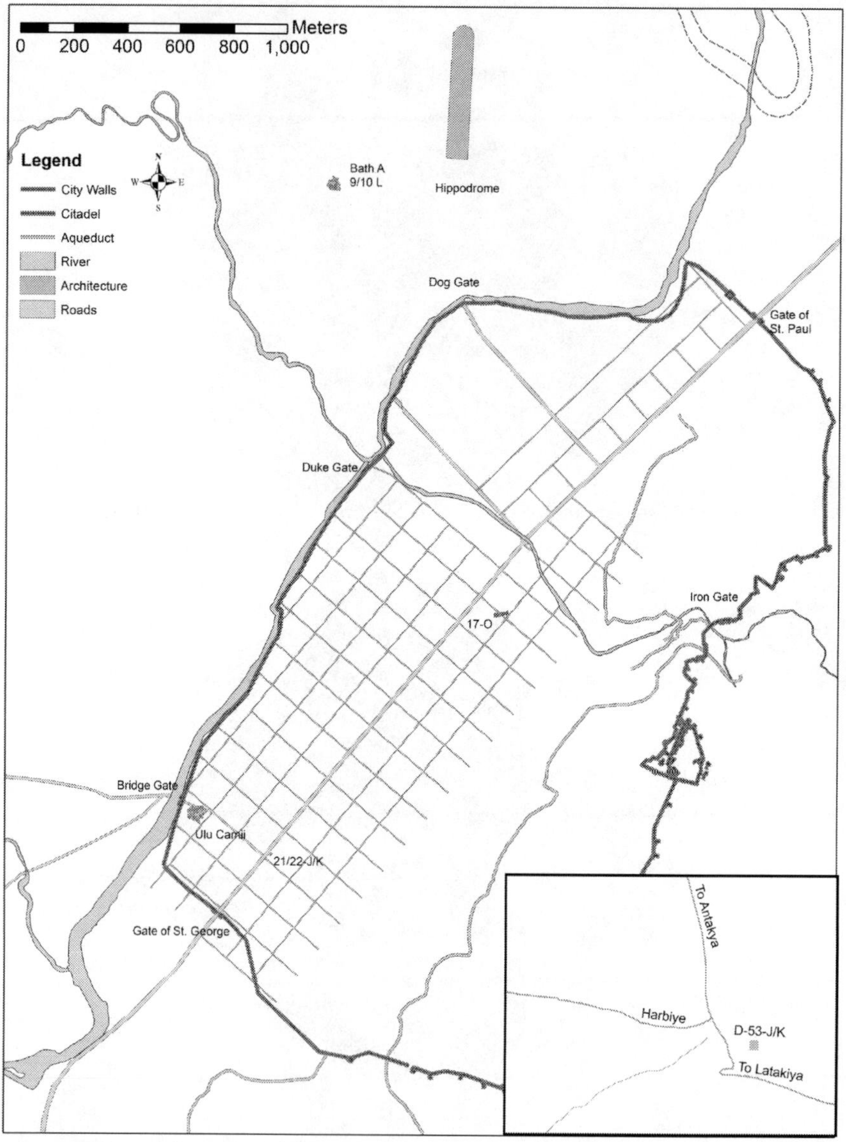

FIGURE 8.7 Plan of Crusader Antioch

Source: Created by Steve Batiuk

FIGURE 8.8 10-L, Bath A, 864. Detail of Tomb 1 entrance after digging

Source: Courtesy of Antioch archaeological archive

FIGURE 8.9 10-L, Bath A, 865. Detail of interior frescoes of tomb, right half of north wall

Source: Courtesy of Antioch archaeological archive

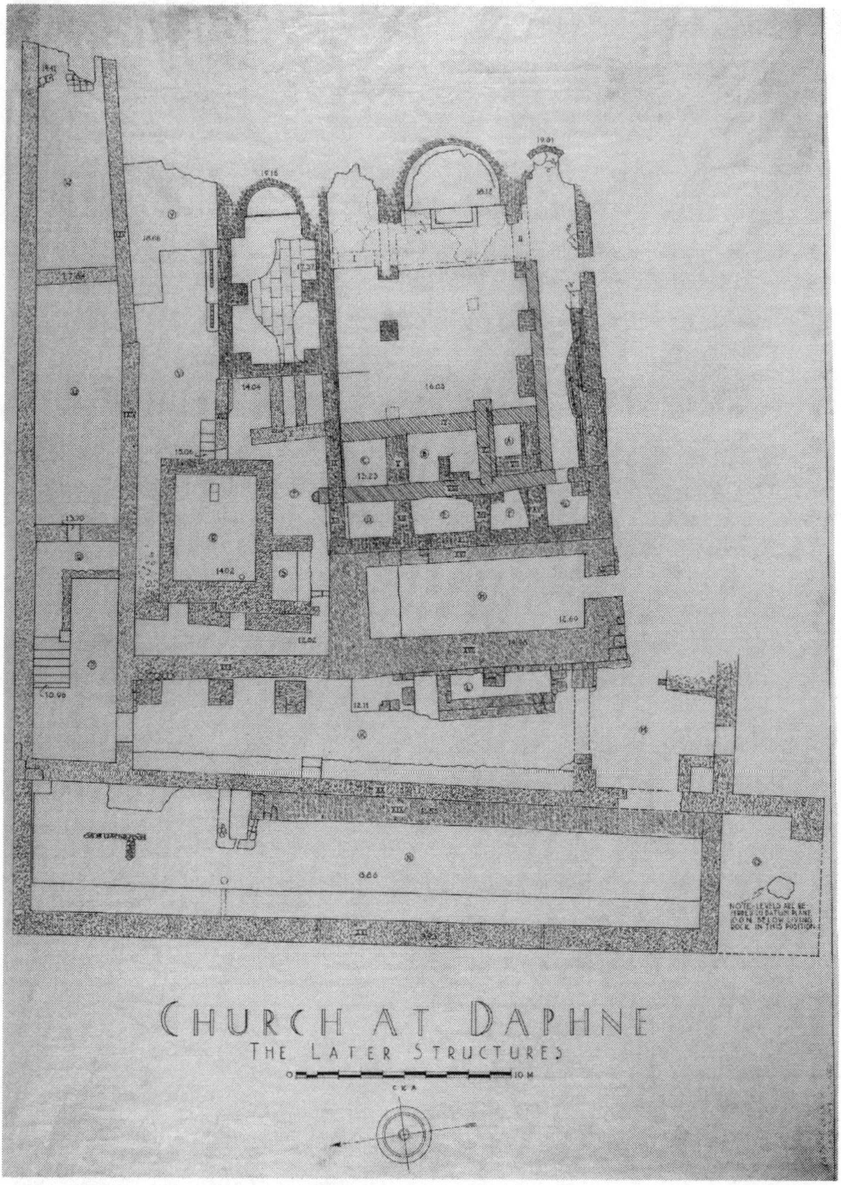

FIGURE 8.10 D-53-J/K, church at Daphne, early plan 842. *Antioch I*, plate XVII

Source: Courtesy of Antioch archaeological archive

the walls of Antioch also suggests that Daphne was not significantly inhabited and certainly no longer a suburb of the city. The monastery itself was built over a fourth-to-sixth century rectangular building of undetermined function, although the intermediate phase can possibly be identified with the Monastery of Our Lady of Mart (Mart Maryam), known since 931 and in the Middle Byzantine period.

These two churches are the only physical signs of the Crusaders' occupation of the city. Yet they were not aberrations. A close examination of the built environment, communities, and economies of the city show that Crusader Antioch continued as a vibrant and popular city, despite the prolonged traumatic events of its siege, invasion, and foreign occupation.

After the conquest: the first 20 years (1099–1124)

Antioch now became the capital of a Norman principality, with Bohemond I as its prince. For the Normans, this must have been a worthy enough prize to delay for nearly a year committing countless lives and provisions toward the larger intended goal of the Crusades: the taking of Jerusalem. Here we will address the following questions: what did the city look like after the grim events of the nine-month siege, and how was it revived by the new Norman rulers? And how did the Norman Crusaders establish rule over the varied communities within the city?

Topography

Ralph of Caen, in recounting the Crusaders' first arrival in Antioch, reports that the city had magnificent churches, a line of columns of Parian marble, pavements looking like crystal, wood made of Lebanese cedars, marble from the Atlas Mountains, glass from Tyre, gold from Cyprus, and iron from England. The furnaces baked bricks, and temples were covered in lead from Amathonta in Cyprus. The anonymous account from the *Gesta Francorum* described the city as possessing many churches, 360 monasteries (likely an exaggeration, like the tower motif), a patriarch, and 153 bishops. The sources suggest that the city had an active Christian community throughout the Saljūq period. Indeed, from all available accounts, we have references to 25 churches, both preexisting and newly built in the Crusader period. Still, some accounts say that they required restoration, carried out by Bishop Adhemar, since several had been converted to mosques or stables and had their possessions plundered and their paintings destroyed.[57]

The main church continued to be St. Peter's, rededicated and redecorated as the seat of the new Latin patriarch after the Saljūqs had used it as a mosque. Albert of Aachen writes that the Turks covered over the images of Jesus Christ and the saints with plaster and scratched out their eyes, "blinded as if they were living people."[58] Ibn al-Athīr described the church as a great building when the Crusaders were searching for the Lance.[59] A further detail suggests that in the south sacristy stood the throne for St. Peter.[60] Many important Crusaders were to be buried there, including Bishop Adhemar, Tancred, Raymond of Poitiers (Prince of Antioch from 1136 to 1149), and Frederick I Barbarossa of the Third Crusade, who was buried in a marble sarcophagus.[61]

Fulcher describes several other churches that were well built: "Although these had long been under the Turks, yet God, knowing all things beforehand, saved them intact for us, so that at some time or other He would be magnified by us in them." Walter, a Crusader who became chancellor of Antioch, also states there were many other churches. Ralph of Caen describes an existing Church of St. James during the city's conquest. The Church of St. Andrew appeared to Bishop Adhemar in a vision in which he instructed Peter Bartholomew, the monk who had the vision of the Holy Lance, to give up one of his vestments to the church.[62]

Raymond of Aguilers mentions an earlier mosque that stood on the site of Church of St. Peter:

> I arose, therefore, and followed him [St. Andrew] into the city, dressed in nothing except a shirt [i.e., as a penitent]. And he led me into the church of the apostle of St. Peter through the north gate, which [the church] the Saracens had previously made a mosque (*quam antea Sarraceni maumariam fecerant*).[63]

This seems to indicate and corroborate the Syriac and Arabic sources that the Saljūqs did indeed convert St. Peter's Church into a mosque, which the Crusaders reverted back to a church. The text of Raymond of Aguilers mentions another interesting church dedicated to St. Leontius. In it were supposedly the relics of Leontius, as well as Cyprian, Omechios, and John Chrysostom, which Peter Desiderius was directed, also in a vision by St. George, to carry to Jerusalem. Instead, he, along with Raymond IV and others, find relics of St. George and some of the blood of the Virgin and St. Thecla in a little ampule.[64] The church of St. Leontius, evidently important enough to house all of these important relics, ought to be his martyrium, mentioned by Malalas in Daphne as built over a synagogue and by Severus and located at the top of the main road to Daphne upon entering the suburb. Leontius is the martyred Roman soldier (d. c. 73) who became a patron saint of Syria. It is curious to note that the Church of John Chrysostom, built in the Middle Byzantine period on the slopes of Mt. Silpius, did not house his relics. Furthermore, which relics these were of his are a question, as his relics were translated to Constantinople on January 27, 438, a celebrated day. St. Cyprian, not mentioned in earlier texts, is likely Cyprian of Antioch, martyred under Diocletian in 304. Downey speculated that the church of 53-K, which we hypothesize as the Monastery of Mart Maryam, may be the martyrium of St. Leontius. Indeed, a rectangular structure of unknown function dated to the fourth to sixth centuries lay below the church. However, the church itself is dated to the Middle Byzantine period, and not to the sixth century, when texts say the martyrium was dedicated. Second, although near the main road, it is not as one enters Daphne from Antioch, but rather as one leaves Daphne on the way to Latakiya.

Rather than holing up in the castle, living apart from the population of the lower town, the Crusaders received properties within the city, given out to them seemingly in piecemeal fashion. A charter in the *Cartulaire General de l'Ordre des Hospitalliers de S. Jean de Jerusalem* recounts how Roger of Salerno, regent of Antioch at the time, approved and confirmed in writing on June 4, 1118, all gifts to the Jerusalem Hospital in the realm of Antioch. These included six or more houses in the city's walls,[65] with one piece of land and a certain dwelling in Antioch's square going to Lord Gerard, grandmaster of the Hospital of Jerusalem from 1099 to 1118. Walter the Chancellor's account also mentions courtyard houses as markers of class and wealth; the largest of these were those closest to the mountain at its base and were taken over by the Crusaders on a first come, first served basis. The documents suggest that the Crusaders were interspersed throughout the town and had to acquire property legally.

The establishment of new quarters for Genoese, Amalfitans, and Pisans shows a mercantile sector also taking root, although not all of these were merchants. On July 13, 1098, less than three weeks after the conquest, Bohemond gave a *fondaco* (a hostel for foreign merchants) to the Genoese in exchange for their loyalty, a grant that also included the Church of St. John, a well or fountain, and 30 neighboring houses in the square near the church; this was reconfirmed by Bohemond II in 1127 and Bohemond III in 1169.[66] Later, the quarter acquired a hospital and marketplace. This effectively established for them a quarter with extraterritorial jurisdiction while also helping establish Bohemond's authority in Antioch so soon after the conquest.[67] Two years later the Genoese received part of the street on which the Church of St. John was located. There was also an Amalfitan hospice, presumably in the quarter in which they resided mentioned in the eleventh century. As a gesture of thanks for supplying ships to the Crusaders, Tancred, in 1108, gave the Pisans a quarter in the center of the city that included the parish of Saint Savior, and in 1170 Bohemond III gave them land to build a house.[68] Venetians also had rights to a *fondaco*, mentioned in 1140, 1153, 1167, and 1183.

Ruling over a diverse city

A resonating theme appearing in many primary sources throughout this period is Antioch's composition as an ethnically and religiously mixed polyglot city. Walter the Chancellor could hear, during the earthquake of 1114, "voices of different nations, Latins, Greeks, Syrian Jacobites, Armenians, strangers, and pilgrims." How did the Normans rule over such a beleaguered yet diverse city? While we can speculate over whether the Crusader occupation of Antioch involved a heavy dose of subjugation of the majority local population, at least in the first 20 or so years,[69] the Norman Crusaders were, more than any other Crusading group, the most familiar with ruling over a non-Latin and predominantly Muslim society.[70] Their experience came from their occupation of Islamic Sicily, which Bohemond's father, Robert Guiscard of Hauteville, and uncle Roger I, subjugated between 1060 and 1091. In Sicily, the Normans not only cooperated with their Muslim subjects but patterned their own administrative, economic, and social structures strongly on existing Islamic models already in place. They also hired language interpreters and advisors on Islamic law and custom.[71] The adaptable precedent of Sicily thus greatly frames the context of Bohemond's style of rule and that of his successors in such a well-established, ethnically and religiously diverse city.

Following the departure of most of the Crusader armies, Bohemond found himself the master of a sizable city, with the approximately 3,000 Crusaders who remained.[72] In this first period of Antioch's Crusader occupation, the structure of rule established was a composite. The ruler of Antioch was the prince, under whom several other high officials served, including the constable, marshal, chamberlain, butler, seneschal, chancellor, castellan, and viscount.[73] The castellan was at the head of the citadel. The chief administrator was the vicecomes or sheriff. Some Byzantine offices still existed, however, such as the duke of Antioch (*dux Antiochiae*), based on the Middle Byzantine *dux*, since the Principality of Antioch was modeled after the duchy, though he was now second-in-command. Both types of officials worked closely together. Aside from the hierarchy of offices under the Prince of Antioch, in practice the patriarch held an important position and was arguably the second most powerful personage. Throughout the Crusader occupation of Antioch, various patriarchs frequently took charge of affairs, at times clashing with the prince.

There was also a rising class of Antiochene nobility, both greater (*maiores*) and lesser (*minores*). A council of landholders existed, involved in matters such as diplomacy and princely marriage, as did a herald, and offices of the *praetor* (chief judge), *praeco* (messenger), and *iudex* (also a judge), in continuation from the Middle Byzantine period and even earlier Islamic models.[74] Several *ru'asa* (local nobles or heads of community) are also known, such as Theodore Sophianus (Tādrus b. al-Ṣaffī) and George, likely both eastern Arabic speaking Christians from Antioch. The rulers of Antioch also demanded tribute from surrounding areas such as Aleppo and Shayzar, which led to alliances with other Islamic rulers, as well as conflict between Crusader lords in an exploitative and opportunistic power system; this resembled the *ṭa'ifa* system of city-based "party kings" occurring at exactly the same time in Spain.

Still, the first 20 years of Crusader occupation did not go smoothly. Unlike the rulers in Middle Byzantine period, the Crusaders probably did not assimilate into Antiochene society, nor did the city recover from the conquest until about the 1120s. In one instance, as related by Walter the Chancellor, in June 1119, after Roger of Salerno, regent to the young Bohemond II, was defeated and killed at the Battle of the Field of Blood (Ager Sanguinis, about 70 km east of Antioch at Sarmadā), non-Latin locals revolted, and the Latin patriarch Bernard of Valence, in charge of organizing the city's defense, disarmed non-Crusaders and gave them a nightly curfew.

Coexistence was often tense, since after 1100 Antioch had in effect two patriarchs – one for the Melkite Church, one for the Latin. One provision of the terms of conquest was that the Latins could have their own church but had to acknowledge the existing Melkite Church and its hierarchy. At first, the question of whether to appoint a Latin patriarch was met with hesitancy. The Crusaders, perhaps at the request of Bishop Adhemar,[75] reappointed the Melkite patriarch John IV Oxeites, imprisoned during the siege, to head the Greek Church. This was an uneasy move, however, since Bohemond feared that an Orthodox patriarch would help pave the way for a Byzantine reconquest. Shortly after Adhemar's death on August 1, 1098, from an outbreak of disease in the city, the Crusaders, in agreement with Pope Urban II, deemed non-Latin churches as heretical. Subsequently, after Bohemond was captured in 1100 by the Artūqids, Tancred, serving as regent, evicted John IV Oxeites and installed the first Latin patriarch, Bernard of Valence (1100–1135); he also chased out other Melkite bishops from the large churches. Bernard thereupon established St. Peter's Church as the center of the Latin Patriarchate of Antioch, with a full hierarchy of administrative positions and clergy. This episode implies the sporadic existence of a Melkite patriarch in Antioch, while suggesting that Bohemond I, despite his initial trepidation, may have been the ruler most amenable to coexistence of the churches, while subsequent rulers cared very little. The role of the Melkite Church and its continual use as leverage in the Middle Byzantine and Crusader periods is in fact a recurring theme, as the fate of the church hung in the balance, its survival continuously a term of peace negotiations between Crusaders and Byzantines, such as the 1108 Treaty of Devol (where Bohemond submitted to Emperor Alexius I Comnenus) and later treaties with John II Comnenus and Manuel I Comnenus.

Conflicts between the Miaphysites and Latins also occurred, with a few periods of good relations, such as when the Latin patriarch Aimery of Limoges (1139–1196) installed the Miaphysite patriarch Michael I in St. Peter's in opposition to the Melkite patriarch Athanasius I Manasses. Here we also see tensions among the non-Latin churches, and negotiations between Armenians, Miaphysites, and the Byzantine church occurred fairly often. Of the various religious groups, non-Latin Christians held an inferior rank and were subject to their own customs and laws.[76] To that mix we can add, at least before the Crusader conquest, the Arab and Turkish (i.e., Saljūq) communities as well. Despite claims that all Muslims were killed or enslaved, we do have sporadic textual references to existing citizens. A *qadī*, or Muslim judge, existed in the Principality of Antioch at Jabala, though none are known specifically at Antioch.

Various scholars passed through Antioch and stayed there, writing, studying, and teaching, suggesting that a small intellectual community remained not even 30 years after the siege. We have mentions of several academic exchanges and cross-community interactions. Adelard of Bath (1080–1152), a scientist from England, stayed in Antioch learning Arabic and purchasing manuscripts to bring home. His mention of the 1114 earthquake gives us a time frame for his visit. At nearly the same time, Stephen of Pisa translated Arabic texts into Latin as well, such as the *Kitāb al-Malakī* by ʻAlī ʻAbbās al-Majusī and some *materia medica* in 1127. Indeed, Antioch was a center, possibly a school even, for Latin literary works and works translated into Latin (such as those of the Christian physician Ibn Buṭlān and the popular tale of *Khalīla wa Dimna*) which subsequently were brought to Europe.[77]

Earthquakes and other disasters

The twelfth century also experienced significant earthquakes, on top of periods of drought, famine, and food shortage, beginning in the first 20 years. But while destructive and harmful to the city's communities and topography, these did not fatally affect Antioch. During Roger of Salerno's reign as regent from 1112 to

1119, the city was ravaged by the first major earthquake of this period, on November 29, 1114. It was likely preceded by one on August 10 centered in the Bay of Iskenderun and another on November 13 centered in the Cilician Plain, which caused houses in Antioch's suburbs to subside. The November 29 earthquake, with an estimated surface-wave magnitude of 6.9, struck the city and entire Syrian frontier region to Ḥarrān during the night and was reported by 25 sources, Latin and Arabic alike. Walter the Chancellor provided a first-hand account, corroborated also by Ibn al-Adīm, of the chaos and destruction of collapsed walls, towers – particularly one tower of the Aleppo Gate – and other buildings, both in the city center, the upper district (*aqaba*), and suburbs. In the suburbs was evidence of sliding or liquefaction of the ground. People of all faiths and ethnic groups flocked to the Church of St. Peter for refuge and prayer and lived in tents or homes in the streets, squares, gardens, and thickets of Antioch, while some moved out of the city to the Amuq Plain. All in all, however, this was not the most destructive of Antioch's earthquakes, as partly attested by the fact that St. Peter's Church withstood the quake and was used as a safe place.[78]

At the time of the quake, Roger of Salerno was absent from the city on an expedition against the Saljūq Bursuq b. Bursuq, *amīr* of Hamadān. In an example of how the offices of the prince, *dux*, and Latin patriarch worked together, Roger communicated with his second-in-command, Ralph Akkon, the *dux* of Antioch, and they agreed to repair only the city's defense system – that is, its walls and towers – in 1115. The patriarch Bernard took command of the rebuilding efforts but used only clergy and monks from the Latin Church to rebuild the fortifications and defend the walls, since he distrusted the Antiochenes and prohibited them from helping or bearing weapons. Yet they were also asked to donate what money they could for the repairs.

A significant drought in 1117 was described as caused by intense winds that dried the wheat at the moment of its maturity, and in 1119 a swarm of locusts drove people to St. Peter's for shelter. There is reference to another, smaller, earthquake in 1123/24 that dried up the water and caused gardens to wither, but presumably it did no major structural damage.[79]

Norman consolidation of the city

While Bohemond worked to secure good relationships within the city, he was still surrounded by potentially hostile neighbors; he also had only a short time to enjoy his rulership, being defeated by the Artuqid Sūqman and captured by the Dānishmand Malik Aḥmad Ghazī Gümüştekin in August 1100. Searching for a new ruler, the citizens of Antioch initially asked Baldwin I of Edessa if he would assume lordship of the city, but he refused; eventually they persuaded Tancred, Bohemond's nephew, to become regent for his uncle, until Bohemond was ransomed and returned to Antioch in 1103. Meanwhile, Emperor Alexius sent letters to Bohemond demanding he hand over the city as part of the Crusaders' sworn agreement with him, but he refused. Leaving the city to Tancred the following year, he returned to Europe to raise another army against the Byzantines and continue their long-lasting feud.[80] Determining to take the offensive against Alexius, he set siege in 1107 to the Byzantine military stronghold of Dyrrhachium on the Adriatic but was eventually forced to surrender, and in September 1108, he signed with the Byzantines the Treaty of Devol/Deabolis. As recounted in Anna Comnena's *Alexiad*, under the terms of the agreement, Bohemond would compel Tancred to surrender Antioch and other towns to the Byzantines: "With regard to Tancred, my nephew, I shall wage relentless war against him unless he is willing to abandon his hostility to Your Majesties and relax his grip on the towns which belong to you."[81] Bohemond would then rule them as vassal of the Byzantine emperor, given the title of *dux* of Antioch only until his death, at which point the city would return to the Empire: "When these towns are recovered, with his [Tancred's] consent or otherwise, it will be I who become their master, holding them on your behalf."[82] It is telling that allowances are made for a Latin to hold the Byzantine position of *dux* of Antioch, albeit under the aegis of the Byzantines. In addition, the patriarch of the city would be a Melkite cleric appointed by the emperor: "For in future, the throne of Antioch will be occupied by such a man; he will carry out all the duties of an archbishop, the laying on of his hands and the other business of the church, according to the privileges of this see."[83] Bohemond, however, never returned to Antioch, retreating instead to Apulia, where he died six months later.

Tancred, meanwhile, rejecting the treaty's terms, refused to turn Antioch over, instead remaining until his death in December 1112 as regent for Bohemond's young son growing up in southern Italy.[84] Thereupon the city passed to Tancred's nephew Roger of Salerno (1112–1119), who continued to act as regent until June 1119, when he was killed and his army annihilated by Najm al-Dīn Ilghazī b. Artūq, the ruler of Aleppo, at the Battle of the Field of Blood.[85] Four years prior, Roger had been victorious over Aqsunqūr and Zangī, and apparently brought 3,000 Turkish prisoners, except children and the elderly, who they burnt, back to Antioch.[86] At this point the regency passed to King Baldwin II of Jerusalem.

The prosperity of the countryside

From the late eleventh to early fourteenth centuries, during the Middle Islamic period, settlement in the Amuq Valley reached its second highest peak after the Late Roman era. With textual evidence indicating a countryside denuded of agriculture during the Crusader siege and ravaging of the landscape during the Mamlūk siege in 1268, we can perhaps limit the greatest period of this peak from roughly 1100 to 1250. The later Middle Islamic occupation in the Amuq Valley and surrounding uplands was represented by a variety of sites, including small field scatters that probably identify farm sites, larger villages, tell sites, and castles. The patterns of consolidation traced in the Early Islamic period had advanced even further where newer and dispersed settlements shifted toward conglomerate villages (some made up of groups of farms) and small towns, recombining a similar process of pre-Hellenistic nucleation with already dispersed sites in a new pattern of "nucleated dispersal." In some cases, villages grew to the level of importance of cities, advancing the system of equalization of cities and towns found in the Late Roman and Early Islamic periods. Unlike the Early Islamic period, however, there were no discernable canal-building projects. Agriculture was probably practiced in extremely localized fields around sites with a heavy emphasis on nomadic pastoralism. Industry, including ceramic and glass production, was also present.

Another noticeable characteristic was a return to occupying large, multiple-period tells, which had formerly been inhabited until the Hellenistic period. Often villages would incorporate tells as a defensible high point, which was walled and offered refuge for villagers and their livestock from raids such as by the Zangids and Ayyūbids. The fact that many of these sites are found in the plain near villages and towns and not exclusively along a borderline emphasizes their protective potential rather than their military nature. Newly founded sites tended to be fortified upland castles built in this period. This combination of lower towns with tells or fortified mountain settlements appear to be of a single type, self-sufficient to a point, and were in effect part of a contemporary process known pervasively in the western Mediterranean as *incastellemento*. The reasons are to be found in a combination of a politically and economically unstable landscape and adaptive strategies to changing environmental and economic conditions. These show a shift to subsistence strategies that were more immediate and protected, differing greatly from the large-scale, economic entrepreneurial markets of the Roman and Late Roman periods or the continuing extensive maintenance of irrigation networks in the Early Islamic.

An interesting economic resource can be found in various Crusader charters of the time. Relatively early charters (before 1114) detail an annual supply of eels from the swampy Antioch Plain, soon after the Crusaders occupied and drained it of its resources to feed their starving Crusader armies. The best sources for these were the Lake of Antioch and a small lake to the northeast called Buḥayra al-Sallūr ("Lake of the Catfish") or al-Jirrī ("Lake of the Eel").[87] This taste for eels, not mentioned as part of the Antiochene diet previously, was not limited to survivalist needs but was well-regarded enough to send an annual shipment to monasteries in Jerusalem.[88]

Crusaders, Byzantines, and Zangids (1125–1162)

On September 27, 1126 (or possibly mid-October), an 18-year-old youth arrived from Italy claiming to be Bohemond I's heir and son, Bohemond II. Baldwin II recognized his right to rule, and Bohemond married Baldwin's daughter Alice and became Prince of Antioch.[89] During his rule, Turkish raids were a constant threat, owing in part to Count Joscelin I of Edessa, who did little to keep the territory safe, but Bohemond also scored significant victories against various Muslim rulers in the area. His invasion of Cilicia in February 1130, however, proved his undoing, for its ruler sought help from the Dānishmandid *amīr* Gümüştekin Gazi II, son of Bohemond I's captor, who defeated and killed him in battle. His head was embalmed and sent as a gift to the ʿAbbāsid caliph in Baghdad. Some scholars consider Bohemond II's reign as marking the zenith of Antioch under the Crusaders, after which the city was beset by many calamities, internal and external, entering into a sort of survival mode.[90]

Topography

Despite the external challenges during this period, we have more information on the churches of Antioch, including those already existing and those Crusader structures newly built and integrated within the city. We know that St. Peter's was rededicated under the authority of the Latin patriarch. A property confirmation of Prince Raymond for the Holy Sepulchre in Jerusalem in April 1140 lists five churches of Antioch, including St. Menas (formerly Beruti), St. Peter, St. Leonard, Sts. Cosmas and Damian (known since Justinian's time), and St. Symeon, presumably the Elder. St. Leonard, dedicated as it was to Bohemond I's patron saint, was probably a new building, perhaps to honor Bohemond's release from the Dānishmandids.[91] Saints Cosmas and Damian and St. Menas were older Eastern saints, and St. Symeon was closely associated with Antioch from the Byzantine period. The Church of Sts. Cosmas and Damian was a Justinianic construction, and the martyrium of St. Symeon the Elder was also mentioned in the Byzantine period, though not at all in the Early Islamic period, and perhaps was not functioning then.

Two more churches included the Miaphysite churches of St. George/Mar Gewargius and St. Bar Sawma. The basilica Church of St. George is referred to in the Saljūq period and perhaps was located in the southern part of the city, near the Daphne Gate,[92] which began to be referred to as the Gate of St. George in the Crusader period, by which point Daphne was barely inhabited. Pococke wrote that it was halfway up the southwest hill opposite the aqueduct and below the Iron Gate, and rather difficult to access.[93] Elsewhere, St. George appears as a monastery gifted to the evicted Jerusalem patriarch Daibert by Bohemond I and lying before the gates of Antioch, perhaps at or near Tancred's Fort. The Abbey of St. George, perhaps the same structure, was given in 1140 to the Austin (Augustinian) canons.

Sometime in the 1150s, a Crusader named Henry and his wife, Elisabeth, made successful prayers to the Miaphysite saint Bar Sawma for the healing of their child; as a result, Basil Bar Soumana, bishop of Edessa and Kaysūm, along with the Franks, who also embraced the saint's cult, built a church to him in the garden of a house of Henry and Elisabeth. The church was then consecrated in a ceremony of Latin nobles, Armenians, Miaphysites, and Franks with a procession (but no Greeks).[94] That it was newly constructed fits with the historical record, which does not indicate its existence prior to the Crusader period.

The Theotokos Church – along with St. Peter's the only other Byzantine church mentioned by Mas'ūdī as still in use – became the center for both the Melkite and Miaphysite churches and gave liturgies in either Greek or Syriac. The German Wilbrand von Oldenburg, a canon of Hildesheim cathedral who made a pilgrimage to the Holy Land in 1211 and visited the city in November of that year, said that the circular church "of the Syrians" was near St. Peter's and decorated lavishly with a painting of the Virgin Mary.[95] He added that the local Christians believed that if the painting was moved, rain would fall.

For St. Paul's Church, known since the Early Islamic period, Wilbrand states that either on Mt. Silpius or Mt. Staurin stood a wealthy monastery (Benedictine since 1108) to St. Paul with an underground chapel and gilded frescoes, said to be the cave where St. Paul rested and wrote some of his epistles. Abu al-Makārim and the Codex Vaticanus describe the Church of Paul the Apostle (Būlus) as large and located in the city wall above the St. Paul's Gate (perhaps on a second story) and near a spring. Also above the church was a tower called the Hindering One (al-Māni'), and beneath that was a cave, likely the location of the grotto church of St. Paul mentioned by Wilbrand, which may be the same grotto known today as the St. Peter's Church (see Chapter 10). The church of St. Paul near the Aleppo Gate was likely not a cave.

Several baths were also in operation, as evidenced by their names and ownership. The geographer al-Idrisī, who visited the city in 1154, mentions baths on Mt. Silpius. The *balnea Tancredi*, mentioned by sources in 1134 and 1140, were restored as luxurious baths and may have existed since Tancred's rule, while the *balnea dicta Omar* mentioned in 1140 suggests a Muslim owner. The Knights Hospitaller possessed two baths, one dated also to 1140 and one in 1186 owned by Brother Renard de Margat. Further evidence of working baths in Antioch is provided by mention of the Byzantine emperor Manuel Comenus (1143–1180), on his first stay in Antioch in 1159, visiting the baths and enjoying them.[96]

The Crusaders begin to lose control

Bohemond II left behind a 2-year-old daughter, Constance (1128–1163), but no son, and upon his death a struggle ensued between his wife, Alice, and her father, Baldwin II, over possession of the city and the regency of Constance. To that end, Alice tried to forge an alliance with 'Imād al-Dīn Zangī, the *atabeg* of Mosul and lord of Aleppo, that would allow her to keep possession of Antioch. As a Greek Orthodox, she also was sympathetic to the return of the Melkite patriarchate in Antioch, though her mother's side was of Armenian origin. Although she barricaded the city against her father and the Antiochenes recognized her as regent, some of the nobles allowed Baldwin II, Joscelin I, and Fulk of Anjou, Baldwin's son-in-law and acting bailiff of the city, to enter through the Duke and Aleppo Gates. Alice was then removed from the citadel and banished from the city, and following Baldwin's death in August 1131, Fulk became regent. In 1135, Alice made another play for Antioch, seeking a marriage alliance for Constance with Manuel Comnenus, son of the Byzantine emperor and heir to the throne, but Fulk sent for Raymond of Poitiers, younger son of Duke William IX of Aquitaine, as a husband for Constance instead.[97] Bringing in a non-Norman ruler was in fact a deliberate act to break Norman hegemony over the principality and northern Syria.[98] The new patriarch, Ralph I of Domfront (1135–1139), persuaded Alice to allow Raymond into the city by convincing her that his intention was to marry her, but Constance was then secretly taken from the palace to St. Peter's Church, where the patriarch married Raymond to her instead. Raymond thus became Prince of Antioch, thereby foiling Alice's second attempt to take the throne.

Meanwhile, the Byzantine emperor, John II Comnenus (1118–1143), already engaged in a long war with the Normans, had to respond to the Norman Crusader occupation of Antioch, perhaps in part because of the Norman bloodline's continuation via Constance (the bloodline of Norman rulership over Antioch was maintained matrilineally). In August 1137, John came at the head of 100,000 men to take the city, gaining Cilicia in the process. Camping outside, he blockaded the inhabitants and then attacked. In response, Raymond made an agreement that Antioch would swear allegiance to the Byzantines for a sum of money, but only if the emperor was able to take Aleppo, Shayzar, Ḥimṣ, and Ḥamā successfully as well – a seemingly unachievable condition. The Byzantines agreed, however, on condition that Raymond would reestablish a Greek patriarch in Antioch and evict the Latin one. Joined by Raymond and Count Joscelin II of Edessa, the Byzantine emperor led the attacks, though Raymond and Joscelin proved poor allies, wanting him to fail. Nevertheless, John succeeded in taking the cities (though not the citadel of Aleppo) and thereupon made a triumphal entry into Antioch in April 1138, where he was welcomed by large, mixed crowd of "Italoi, Assyrioi, and Hemeteroi [people]."[99] The emperor praised the city for its piety and devotion to Christianity, but then, typical of the rebellious Antiochenes, Joscelin stirred up a riot of Crusaders and Armenians, forcing the emperor to depart (though other accounts say he was called back to Constantinople). In 1142, John returned and moved into Antioch but then died in a hunting accident the following year, thus securing a 16-year suspension in the Byzantine challenge to the Norman-Aquitanian hold over the city. An interesting point is that John Comnenus sought to reclaim Antioch for the Byzantines, even as other parts of Anatolia and Cappadocia, closer to Constantinople, were in Saljūq hands, thus testifying again to the city's historical, religious, and ideological power.[100]

The fall of the County of Edessa in 1144 to the Zangid ruler 'Imād al-Dīn Zangī subsequently made Antioch's region more vulnerable to Zangid attacks[101] while also prompting the Second Crusade (1147–1149), led in part by Louis VII of France. In March 1148, Louis and his wife, Eleanor of Aquitaine (and Raymond's niece), arrived together with their forces in Antioch, but rumors soon began swirling that Eleanor and her uncle had become engaged in an incestuous affair (largely discounted by modern historians). Eleanor in any event wanted to stay and join her uncle in his fight against the Zangids, but Louis compelled her to leave with him for Jerusalem instead. Late in 1148, Raymond defeated Nūr al-Dīn Zangī at Ḥiṣn al-Akrād (Crac de Chevaliers), but in June the following year he was in turn defeated by Nūr al-Dīn while his army was destroyed at the Battle of 'Ināb (or Fons Muratus). Raymond's head was cut off and sent to Baghdad, though his body was buried in the vestibule of St. Peter's Church. Because his son with Constance, Bohemond III, was too young, his widow ruled the city in his place, along with

Patriarch Aimery, who was involved in government affairs, defense, and recruitment of troops.

Nūr al-Dīn, now camped with his army outside the walls of Antioch, which was emptied of its soldiers, commenced negotiations to accept the city's surrender. The townspeople gave him gifts, while the Syriac community disagreed over whether to hand the city over to him. Nūr al-Dīn then posted a detachment to guard the city and prevent anyone from entering and declared himself master of both Antioch and Aleppo, taking booty from all the surrounding fortresses. He did not, however, try to take Antioch itself, whether because its defenses were too formidable and he feared Byzantine or Crusader retribution, or whether he had his sights set on Damascus and did not wish to expend significant resources on holding Antioch.[102]

In 1153, Constance married a French knight, Raynald of Châtillon, who thereupon became Prince of Antioch and served as regent for Bohemond III.[103] The relationship between the princes and patriarchs of Antioch was at times strained, particularly in this period, as exemplified by the conflicts between Raymond and Patriarch Ralph of Domfront, and Raynald and Patriarch Aimery, who held the office longer than any other patriarch, over 50 years. Raymond had Ralph's house plundered in advance of the reestablishment of a Greek patriarch, as demanded by John II Comnenus. Some patriarchs wielded power in the absence of a prince, such as Patriarch Aimery, who ruled in place of Constance after her husband Raymond's death. Part of this conflict had to do with the rich assets of the Church, the presence of a treasury, and control of it in releasing funds. Raynald had the patriarch beaten up and forced to spend a day on a rooftop with honey on his head to attract bugs so as to coerce him to fund an expedition to Cyprus (Figure 8.11).

Early in 1156 Raynald, angry that the Byzantine emperor Manuel had failed to pay a promised sum of money, invaded Byzantine Cyprus together with the Armenian prince Thoros II of Cilicia, and for three weeks they ravaged the island, plundered its riches, and maltreated its inhabitants, leaving behind a devastated wreckage and returning with lots of booty and prisoners (including bishops and governors) for ransom.[104] Enraged, the Byzantine emperor invaded and conquered Cilicia and then headed for Antioch. Knowing he could not defeat Manuel, Raynald made a humiliating submission to the emperor at Maṣṣīṣa, with a rope around his neck, walking crownless on foot to show humility and holding the bridle of Manuel's horse. The emperor forgave him only after Raynald agreed to become his vassal, thereby effectively ending Antioch's independence, and to accept a Greek Orthodox patriarch in the city. On April 12, 1159, Easter Sunday, the Byzantine emperor, wearing full armor, made a triumphal entry into Antioch. A royal residence was prepared filled with gold and silver vessels, furniture, and clothes, and the gates of the city were decorated. The Latin patriarch Aimery welcomed the emperor with his clergy bearing crosses and gospels. The walls were hung with the imperial banner at the summit of the citadel, and soldiers lined the way into the city from the gates. As the emperor entered on horseback, trumpets were blown and he was

FIGURE 8.11 Patriarch of Antioch smeared with honey on tower, 1232–1261, *The Histoire d'Outremer*, French translation of *Historia rerum in partibus transmarinis gestarum* by William of Tyre (d. 1185). Yates Thompson MS 12 f. 120r

Source: Courtesy of the British Library

presented a crown with precious stones. Behind him walked Raynald and Baldwin of Jerusalem, also uncrowned. The entourage went to St. Peter's, then to the palace. Manuel thereby created a lavish spectacle of the Byzantines' visual might and the Crusaders' subjugation to dazzle the citizens of the town, coupled with gifts to win over the rest of the Latin elite.[105]

In November 1161, Raynald was captured and imprisoned by Majd al-Dīn Abū Bakr, governor of Aleppo and second in command to Nūr al-Dīn, while on a raiding expedition, and so once again Constance ruled without a husband. But her determination to rule Antioch on her own and prevent her son, Bohemond, still a minor, from ever ascending the throne caused a scandal among the citizens, and so they called upon Baldwin III of Jerusalem, who, coming to Antioch, proclaimed the young Bohemond the rightful ruler and appointed Patriarch Aimery to run the principality until Bohemond should come of age. But Constance appealed to Emperor Manuel, who supported her claim in exchange for marriage to her daughter Maria, and on Christmas Day, 1162, the two were married. Nonetheless, when Bohemond reached the age of maturity the following year, the Antiochene nobility forced Constance from the city, and her son ascended the throne as Bohemond III (1163–1201).

During these years – sometime between August 9 and September 7, 1157 – another serious earthquake struck near Antioch, part of a series of high-intensity shocks between 1156 and 1159 in the region, and for Antioch measuring VIII (severe) out of XII on the Modified Mercalli Intensity Scale, with a surface-wave

(Rayleigh) magnitude of 7.2.[106] Although this earthquake was not widely documented, some texts state that the city walls were damaged and much of Antioch was destroyed and its population annihilated.[107] According to seismologist Nicholas Ambrasey, however, there is no evidence for most of the city being destroyed or for a significant loss of life, so this is likely an exaggeration or else refers to the wider principality and not the city itself.[108] The Egyptian encyclopedist al-Qalqashandī (1315–1418) stated that the quake affected citadels in other Syrian cities as well, including Ḥamā, Shayzar, Ḥimṣ, Ḥiṣn Akrād, and Tripoli, and that markets and castles all collapsed.[109]

The Crusaders' mint

It is not until this period that Crusader coinage from Antioch began to be minted. The earliest coins were modeled after Middle Byzantine bronze folles rather than their own silver deniers or Islamic currency,[110] perhaps because of Armenian and Ayyūbid coins in circulation around the area. Saljūq coins also continued to circulate. The exact beginning of Crusader minting, however, is unclear.[111] The earliest issues of Frankish coinage appeared around the 1120s, some 20 years after the conquest. From the 1130s or 1140s onward until the reign of Bohemond IV (1201–1216, 1219–1233), silver was predominantly used, and deniers of silver-copper alloy were minted in Antioch in large quantities, though the source of silver at the time is unclear.[112] The location of the mint is also unknown, though one possibility is the citadel. The currency of the denier was strong, suggesting Antioch was wealthy, primarily through long-distance trade; however, the billon deniers of France and Italy had a range limited to the city and principality and surroundings. A hoard of Antioch deniers was found at Kinet (al-Tīnāt/Canamella), a small Templar fort and port close to the city. Michael Metcalf has suggested that one reason for the prolific minting of billon deniers was to pay the Templars, who guarded the northern approaches to the principality. He and others also maintain that, like other Outremer coinages, the silver for deniers came from Europe; in this way, raw material (bullion) from the mines of Bohemia traveling east and manufactured goods returning west anchored the economy in a pan-Mediterranean system. It is not known whether gold bezants were minted in Antioch, though gold Byzantine *hyperpyra* (*perperi* in the West, which replaced *solidi*) and Islamic dinars were still accepted and referred to as bezants.[113]

Crusaders and Ayyūbids (1163–1192)

Following the reigns of Raymond and Raynald, the Zangid incursions, and the reassertion of Byzantine imperial authority, the Principality of Antioch weakened considerably. During these next few decades, earthquakes, food shortages, and the third external challenge to the city after the Zangids and Byzantines, namely the Ayyūbid threat to the city, greatly diminished Antioch's power.

Topography, communities, and the economy

At this time we have a brief but useful description of the city. William of Tyre, writing between 1170 and 1184, mentioned that water came from Daphne at specific times of the day. Benjamin of Tudela, a Jewish traveler from Spain, visiting between 1165 and 1170, mentioned the city wall and a well at the summit of the mountain managed by an inspector, who channeled the water in 20 underground channels to the homes of the city.[114] A small community of Jews, headed by three rabbis, still lived in the city, encompassing ten families, all involved in glass-making. Benjamin's brief insights suggest that the aqueduct and water tunnels was still functioning, there remained a community of Jews, albeit greatly diminished, and the city produced glass, a major manufactured product from the Levant exported to the Mediterranean and the East.

In August 1163 an earthquake struck, the only documentation for which are letters sent to King Louis VII written by Bertrand of Blanquefort, Grand Master of the Templars, as well as King Amalric I of Jerusalem and Bohemond III.[115] Each letter mentions the damage vaguely as shaking and collapse of fortifications and loss of life. Another major earthquake hit on June 29, 1170, hypothesized to be a 7.7 energy magnitude and moment magnitude scale, 7.3 in surface-wave magnitude, and IX (violent) out of XII on the Modified Mercalli Intensity Scale, with its epicenter around the Ghab Valley of the Orontes, south of Antioch.[116] Many sources mention the quake's destruction, which affected half the city. A section of the west wall along the river collapsed, as did many houses, and cracks appeared and filled with water. Most notably, St. Peter's Church fell, its dome collapsing while about 50 congregants, clergy, and the Melkite patriarch Athanasios I were underneath, all of whom perished. Many other churches were damaged, including the Church of St. Mary (presumably of the Latins) and the altar of the Church of Sts. Cosmas and Damian. Michael the Syrian and Bar-Hebraeus state that the "church of the Greeks" was also destroyed. This should have been the Theotokos; however, the same authors also write that three Miaphysite churches were preserved – the Theotokos Mother of God, St. George, and St. Bar Sawma – thus suggesting the Theotokos was no longer being used by the Melkites.[117] Following the death of the Greek patriarch, the Latin Patriarch Aimery returned to Antioch from Qusayr/Cursarium, his fortified manor home outside the city.[118] Like in the previous earthquakes of this period, the patriarch spearheaded the rebuilding efforts, which, however, were only partial and limited mainly to the walls and churches, owing to lack of funds: "Even today, and with much work, vast sums of money, continual care and tireless devotion [the Antiochenes] have been unable to restore it even to a mediocre standard," wrote William of Tyre.[119] We can assume that St. Peter's Church was rebuilt, as it continues to be used throughout the Crusader period.

Food shortages caused by earthquake lasted from 1170 to 1174. As recounted by the Muslim courtier Usāma b. Munqidh (1095–1188), writing around 1183, a second food shortage returned in 1177/1178, while famine struck nearly all the Middle East, and people flocked to Antioch as Patriarch Aimery distributed wheat and other grain at the price of one gold dinar for a *kayla* of wheat.[120] In May 1178, a bad flood resulting from heavy rains engulfed homes, public buildings, people, and animals, and pooled within the city walls. But in the following year the lack of rain caused a fire to spread around St. Peter's Church and destroyed buildings, houses, and battlements. The pilgrim John Phocas, who visited the city on his way to the Holy Land (c. 1185), described it as poor under the rule of the Crusaders, perhaps slower to recover from these disasters. Yet he still noted the strong city walls and numerous springs and still functioning aqueducts, including the spring of Castalia in Daphne. The Princeton excavators noted continuous repairs to two aqueducts from Daphne and suggested, based on later buttressing and thick travertine deposits, that the later aqueduct was in active use in the medieval period and the one mentioned by William of Tyre, Benjamin of Tudela, and John Phocas.[121]

A brief anecdote provides a glimpse into the continued diverse nature of the city, with Crusaders and Muslims interacting both amicably and with hostility. Usama b. Munqidh mentions that one of his men visited a Crusader knight who had come on the initial 1098 siege and was now retired and living in a home in Antioch. Entertaining Usāma's man, the knight served him local food cooked by Egyptian women (with no pork), claiming that he himself had adjusted to this style of eating. The knight then later defended and protected this man in a confrontation in the market against a group of Franks. For Usāma, the point was that the older "first wave" of Crusaders were more acclimatized to life in Islamic society and open to such friendly relationships than those who had arrived more recently.[122]

The principality weakens

In 1164, Nūr al-Dīn attacked a fortress within the Principality of Antioch, but when Bohemond III and his allies pursued him, he handed them a sound defeat, capturing Bohemond and other Christian commanders. He did not, however, continue on to attack, since the Zangid sultan was concerned that Manuel Comnenus might intervene to take over the city, and he preferred a weak Crusader state as neighbor over the emperor. He was quoted in Ibn al-Athīr as saying,

> The city is an easy matter but the citadel is strong. Perhaps they will surrender it to the Byzantine emperor because its ruler is his nephew. To have Bohemond as a neighbor I find preferable to being a neighbour of the ruler of Constantinople.[123]

He also eventually released Bohemond for a ransom.

Shortly thereafter, in 1165, Bohemond went to Constantinople to ask for funds, but in return he had to restore the Greek patriarch Athanasios I Manasses to St. Peter's. In 1177, he also married a Byzantine princess, Theodora Comnenus, niece of Manuel I, to strengthen his alliance with the emperor, but then shortly after Manuel's death in 1180, he divorced her, and then illegitimately married Sybil, an Antiochene woman of poor repute. Bohemond's divorce caused Patriarch Aimery to excommunicate him for adultery; in retaliation, he attacked the patriarch, forcing him and the clergy to flee to Qusayr/Cursarium, and plundered the churches and monasteries of Antioch. King Baldwin IV and the Latin patriarch of Jerusalem had to intervene and mediate, and Bohemond was required to return the church's property.

The momentous victory of Salaḥ al-Dīn (Saladin, 1174–1193) – founder of the Ayyūbid dynasty and first Ayyūbid sultan of Egypt and Syria – over the Crusader Kingdom of Jerusalem at the Battle of Hattin[124] in July 1187 and his subsequent capture of Jerusalem itself in October left Antioch as one of the last Crusader strongholds, and the Ayyūbid threat now became more immediate. In July of the following year, Salaḥ al-Dīn launched his invasion of northern Syria, taking the Templar fortresses of Darbassāk and Baghrās along the way to Antioch. Camping outside the gates, he effectively had the city surrounded and blockaded, using mangonels, and the Antiochenes surrendered on September 26. But because his own army was tired and weakened, Salaḥ al-Dīn concluded a temporary truce with Bohemond III to spare Antioch in return for the release of every Muslim prisoner, while Bohemond was left with only the city and the port of St. Symeon.[125] Salaḥ al-Dīn put one of his *amīrs*, 'Alam al-Dīn Sulaymān b. Jandar, in charge. After seven or eight months (from October 1188 to May 1189), the truce would end, at which point the city would be turned over to Salaḥ al-Dīn with no resistance if no reinforcements had arrived by then. Around this time, Raynald, who was freed from prison, returned to Antioch to serve Bohemond with a group of 14 people, and they were all given properties in the center of the city. At that point little was left of the principality, and its agricultural lands had already been taken. Bohemond now made appeal to the Holy Roman Emperor, Frederick I Barbarossa, to come to his aid, offering him suzerainty over Antioch in return.

The following year, in June 1190, Frederick VI of Hohenstaufen, Duke of Swabia and son of Barbarossa, arrived in Antioch with 40,000 troops and the body of his father, who had just drowned in the Göksu River in Cilicia on his way to succor Antioch, reconquer the Holy Land, and liberate Jerusalem in the Third Crusade (1189–1192). The duke had hoped to bury his father's body in Jerusalem, but attempts to preserve it in vinegar had failed. Meanwhile, his troops were soon dying, diseased with dysentery, "looking as though they had been exhumed from their graves"[126] and suffering from the food shortages caused by the raids destroying the countryside and instability of the hinterlands. Bohemond thus opened the city to the Germans and gave them whatever they wanted. In the city, Barbarossa's body was boiled a long time to remove the flesh, which was then laid to rest in the Church of St. Peter in a marble coffin, though his bones were taken to Jerusalem at the end of August 1190. Ibn 'Abd al-Ẓāhir, Ibn al-'Adīm, and Bahā' al-Dīn b. Shaddād, however, say that the Germans conquered Antioch's castle by strategy and treachery and forced Bohemond to provision the army and move his treasures to the citadel before leaving for Palestine.[127] The Germans must in any case have further depleted already weakened granaries.

Indeed, this whole period was difficult for Antioch. Most of the 1180s were filled with famine, disease, and locusts. Food costs rose – in late summer 1188 a bag of flour sold for 12 dinars, while in 1190 it went for 96. In 1192, another food shortage occurred, owing in part to a famine and an embargo by Salaḥ al-Dīn. Smbat describes it as a terrible calamity, and by spring, people were eating grass in the fields like sheep.[128] Eventually, Bohemond III met with the Ayyūbid ruler in his tent and received three months of food (or a 20,000 dinar pension) in exchange for Salaḥ al-Dīn's control of the city. Unsurprisingly, there was little reconstruction in the city at this time, aside from some unspecified amount following the earthquake of 1170, including St. Peter's Church.

Crusaders and Armenians (1193–1268)

This final period of Crusader Antioch was the most trying for the city and principality, for it involved a war of succession pitting rulers and princes and heirs against one another, setting churches in conflict, and splitting churches from rulers. The period is also characterized by the external threat of the Armenians and their attempts to annex the city.

Topography

Although historical narratives of the city in this last period paint a picture of an already beleaguered town rife with internal and external conflict, nevertheless many wonderful, though not all reliable, descriptions of Antioch were written during this time. For example, the biographer/geographer Yāqūt, writing between 1224 and 1228, said that Antioch was one of the most esteemed and honored lands (literally: "lords and mothers of the region," *wa hiya min ā'yān al-balād wa āmhātihā*) and known for its beauty, fresh clean air, sweet water, large production of fruits, and prosperity and wealth.[129]

Several other accounts provide micro-details of the relationships between communities and the topography of the town. The richest text is Abū al-Makārim's, written around 1200. Abū al-Makārim, a Coptic priest, made use of earlier Arabic works, including the Codex Vaticanus Arabicus (see Chapter 6). The manuscript is, however, problematic, since it gives a sensationalized and sometimes incorrect account of buildings and many talismans.[130] For example, it mentions that Simon Peter built a church in the city in the first year of the reign of Claudius, the Qusiyān/Cassianus, which was atop a mountain on the east side and was formerly a synagogue. But the Qusiyān, mentioned in many sources throughout Antioch's post-Roman history, was never described as being on a mountain and was never formerly a synagogue. Because Abū al-Makārim's account is also remarkably similar to, and likely based on, the Vatican Codex text, thought to date to the Middle

Byzantine period, the features mentioned here will be those not found in the Codex which are in Chapter 6.

Abū al-Makārim mentions eight other churches to which other authors allude but do not always identify.[131] These include the Church of St. Thomas/Mārī Tūmā, where the fifth-century martyr Jacob (sometimes James) the Persian was buried along with his relics. The St. Thomas to whom the church is dedicated is possibly the monk who died and was buried in Antioch in 542. A Church of St. Thomas is known from the tenth-century Agapius of Manbij to have been present in the 470s.[132] A different version of Abū al-Makārim's account mentioned a separate Church of St. James the Intercessor, the martyr Persian identified also as Jacob whose Feast Day is November 23. In this version, his body was located in al-Bahnasa in Egypt.[133] The Church of the Martyr Sūsinīyūs (Susinius) was originally a house that someone named Aristochus built, then lived in, that later became a church after Susinius' body was transferred there. The saint's Feast Day is April 21. The Church of Luke (Lūqā) honored the evangelist/doctor/artist who was from Antioch and buried there in a marble sarcophagus suspended on four marble pillars but whose body was later transferred to Constantinople. His Feast Day is October 18. The Church of the Apostles, or al-Hawāriyīn, was built by the Greeks, then renewed and called by them al-Hazardar.[134] This may suggest that the *Palaia*, or Old Church, also called the Apostolic Church and Antioch's oldest, had been rebuilt, but this would be the only reference to this church being restored. Abū al-Makārim also mentions the Church of Saint Andronikos/Andrunīqūs, one of the 70 Disciples, whose Feast Day is May 17. Abū al-Makārim described the church's walls as glistening with a perfumed oil more pleasant than Indian nard (spikenard or muskroot), sweeter than honey, and more healthy than medicine, by the miracles it manifests in healing the sick, the helpless, and those afflicted by unclean spirits.[135] Other churches included the Church of Yūḥannā al-Maylī/al-Mīlī, a church on the Garden/Duke Gate (perhaps St. Domitius), and the Church of John the Evangelist on the summit of the mountain to the east (north). Likely outside the city were the Church to the Forty Martyrs[136] and the monasteries of Dayr Aqbunias/Ammonios and of Thecla, which was a cave hermitage. Additionally, he mentions 700 Armenian monasteries on the Black Mountain, each with a round fortification and tower and cells for monks and a bishop that could hold up to 400 monks.

Abū al-Makārim also states that after Antiochus (he does not specify which one), the Greeks built within the Aleppo Gate a palace for the king and 1,000 houses for his high personnel and soldiers. Here the reliability of his account must be called into question, since he is now talking about Seleucid history. According to him, the house of the wise men was covered by a dome 100 cubits high with images of the heavens, stars, and constellations; perhaps this was the *Mouseion*, or Temple of the Muses, built by Antiochus IV and repaired by Marcus Aurelius.[137] There was also a hall of wisdom. Elsewhere he mentions a pillar with a serpent. A canal outside the city walls was 17 cubits wide and deep. One tower on the west side at the foot of the mountain was called Inhibat in Hebrew, and another on the west side was called Karus, also built upon a massive rock. He further enumerates seven large streams that flowed into the city bringing water in a canal, and refers to the Valley of Khaskarout (Parmenius), with a gate and iron window (the Iron Gate) that controlled floods and had a bridge over it. He also mentions a source of mountain water called the Well of Būlit, perhaps the same as the one mentioned by the Vatican Codex and Benjamin of Tudela which was partially tunneled. Outside the citadel was a watchtower.

We have more documentation on residential houses in this period from the account of Wilbrand von Oldenburg, who described two turreted walls, water-mills, orchards and gardens, and water that came to houses in underground channels. He also stated that the interior walls of houses and palaces were decorated and "shone like gold," even though the exteriors were unappealing. Below the citadel at the foot of Mt. Silpius was a cell where Mary Magdalene stayed doing penance, and nearby a small chapel where St. Margaret spent her final moments before her death. On the lowest hill (the third) of Mt. Silpius in the southeastern part of the city wall was a Church of St. Barbara, known in the Early Islamic period, and he also mentions the Church of St. John Chrysostom from the Middle Byzantine period. The former may be the church from which, according to Abū al-Makārim, you could see the city.[138] Wilbrand also corroborates Abū al-Makārim's tomb/church of Luke, adding that it was at the bottom of the mountain and built over the house of St. Luke. He refers to the presence and importance of St. Peter's, corroborating that it was rebuilt after the earthquake of 1170. Wilbrand also comments on the same polyethnic and poly-religious mixture of the Antiochenes and includes among them the "Saracens."

A third account is a wonderful document written in March 1213 that details a real estate transaction related to one of the Hospitallers' houses also mentioned in a Latin deed of 1207.[139] In that deed, a certain John of Cursalt, a Latin deacon of St. Peter's, became a beneficiary of the Church of Our Lady of Shabūba (Holy Virgin),[140] a property owned by the abbey of St. Mary of Josaphat, a Latin shrine-church in Jerusalem held since at least March 1182. The property (named a *gastina*, or land that has buildings in disrepair and is abandoned or partially occupied) was next to the House of the Hospital, and along with it was an oratory in honor of the Mother of God, the Theotokos, similarly in terrible shape and lacking a roof, suggesting it had not been the focus of any rebuilding since the earthquake of 1170. John was given the property to hold for the rest of his life with the intention of repairing the church, building a house, planting an orchard, and recovering the church's possessions. But failing to refurbish it, instead, six years later he tried to lease it to a Greek Orthodox priest with the Arabic name al-Mawādd li-Illāh, also offering to assist financially in its renovation in return for his name being commemorated in the church. The priest, however, wanted it in his own name. After some deliberation, a new priest of the St. Mary Church in Jerusalem entrusted another priest of the local Antiochene chapter of St. Mary Latin Church to facilitate the transaction detailed in the document, where the property would go to Mawādd in perpetuity in exchange for two dinars per year coming to the ruined church, one in cash, one in kind, under the condition that he had to begin repairs immediately, though he had two years rent remitted to help restore the chapel. Interestingly, the contract was written in Arabic (since that was spoken by the Greek Orthodox) and used an Arabic legal term (*dīmūs*, from the Greek *demosion* and meaning yearly rent as a perpetual lease), Arabic currency, and the Greek term *nomikos*, or notary. Some lines at the beginning and end are in Latin, and the deed was made with a Latin translation in duplicate (notarized and approved by four witnesses), witnessed, and sealed in wax.

The document also provides topographical details. The property was bordered to the east by an open road, to the west by an open space and neglected estate, a large baked-brick building (*gh.mādh.n*), which could possibly refer to a building or house not on a public road, or even a brick-maker's kiln or ruin.[141] To the south was a house and garden of Yani al-Kamīlarī (John the Camel Driver) and the garden of Yarā b. M.r.k.lāym (or Yarī b. Mardala), and to the north an open road and land of al-Sitt Dām Akās (the Lady Dame Agatha), now in the hands of the scribe Rumānūs (Romanos). The northern side also had a gate allowing entrance into the property. Although its exact whereabouts are unknown, it was likely near the round church of St. Mary, the Theotokos, in the city's northeast, near the slopes of Mt. Staurin, and also near the Churches of St. John Chrysostom and St. Mary Latin. Thus, among the neighbors of this Latin-owned property, leased by a Greek cleric and now containing a Melkite church, were Latins and individuals of Greek/Syriac/Arabic background. The document also shows, during a time of heightened strife between the Latin and Greek communities and patriarchates in Antioch, and between the Hospitallers and rulers, a fascinating and amicable business deal between a Latin and a Greek (John was presumably Latin), although neither party spoke the other's language. Further, it provides evidence for the constantly changing nature of the city, which comprised actively used and inhabited buildings alongside abandoned and ruined properties.

Giving out properties as gifts was a way to increase Latin ownership and involvement within the city, as well as to cement alliances. Its piecemeal fashion also negates any idea of a segregated community. For example, the aforementioned site was very likely to be the same old *gastina* next to the Hospital mentioned in another source as a gift given by Bohemond III in September 1194 to the Hospital. Both properties were on a public road, with a wall in common. Interestingly, the holding of properties by the Church or other individuals and institutions outside the city is not unique to this period. We have the example of the *martyrium* of St. Peter in Rome donated a public bath in Antioch by Constantine. The symbiotic relationship allowed for the bath to be continuously run and paid for and in return provide funds for the church.[142]

In 1238, the Miaphysite patriarch Ignatius III had a patriarchal residence constructed in the upper part (the northern area near the Aleppo Gate) of the city with a domed church, two lofty cupolas, monastic cells, and gardens. A Church of St. Ignatius is already known from the Byzantine period, since he was an early and important martyr, celebrated December 20. Abū al-Makārim says this is the church where Ignatius was buried, and there were also hidden there the five books of the Torah, the tomb of Ezra, the garment of Moses, fragments of the Tables, the stick of Joshua that split the Jordan River, the knife of Jephthah, and the key to the Ark. These are then two different buildings – one a private residence/church to the Crusader patriarch and one to a Byzantine-period saint.

Another document mentioning a church/monastery is from 1262 in the Codex Vaticanus Syrus 21, originally written in 1041. Its colophon mentions a monk named Gabriel from the monastery of St. Domitius at the Church of Paraskevi (*al-Kanīsā al-Jamī'a*) in Antioch.[143] This could refer to the chapel of St. Domitius in the neighborhood of the Garden Gate where St. Timothy rested, mentioned in the Early Islamic period. The unnamed church at the Garden Gate in Abū al-Makārim might also be the same place. The Arabic text describing the church as a "congregational church" interestingly suggests an adjacent church for the masses, rather than a monastic church.

Antioch's intellectual life continued through the early thirteenth century right up until the Mamlūk conquest of 1268. Bar Hebraeus, the Syriac Orthodox bishop, arrived with his father, Aaron, a physician, and studied there from 1243, as did the Miaphysite Theodore of Antioch, who studied Syriac and Latin and who served at the court of the Holy Roman Emperor Frederick II (1220–1250).[144] We can also add a compendium of laws, the *Assises of Antioch*, compiled during the rule of Bohemond IV sometime in the first quarter of the thirteenth century and translated into Armenian around 1250. The inter-connected tradition of manuscript translation and copying across Greek, Syriac, and Arabic in the Antioch area persisted in the last days of Crusader Antioch. The late tenth-century Antiochian Menologian was copied in this period by a scribe, Jawān b. Dimitrī b. Yūḥannā b. Ḥamza of Antioch, who collaborated with three other Antiochenes, one Kyr Simeon b. al-Buṭayṭa al-Anṭākī, who was at the monastery of Mār Mūsā on Mt. Sinai, and Abā Tūmā b. Hilāl at the monastery of Our Lady (Theotokos) Arshāyā, and a deacon and monk, Ghrīghūrī b. Yūḥannā, working from the monastery of Saint Shamūnīth (Ashmūnīt).[145] This also suggests that the Church of St. Ashmunit, if the same structure as the one mentioned outside the city walls on the mountain in the Early Islamic and Middle Byzantine period, was still functioning, as a monastery.

Although hardly mentioned in this last period of Crusader Antioch, it is possible that the mosque of Habīb al-Najjār was still active, and its tomb definitely so, as noted by several authors who visited. The Kurdish historian Bahā' al-Din spent several days in the city, paying a visit to the tomb of Habīb al-Najjār during the siege of Baghrās in September 1188. It is noteworthy that even during a siege, Bahā' had to go into the enemy city to pay respects at this important tomb. Ibn al-Shiḥna states that the adjacent crypt (al-Dimas) mentioned by Mas'ūdī was now known as al-Bornos (the Helmet?). On the crypt's right was a great mosque built with regular baked brick (*ājurr al-'adī*) and stones. Yāqūt also noted that the tomb of Habīb al-Najjār was visited by pilgrims. The guide by the Persian traveler al-Harawī (d. 1215) to pilgrimage sites also mentions the tomb, stating that formerly the mountain had been a place of worship and attracted pilgrims from far away. Ibn al-ʿAdīm also mentions the shrine of ʿAwn b. Urmiyā (Jeremiah) and ʿĀdh b. Sām (Shem) b. Nūḥ (Noah) in Antioch.[146]

At the site of the mosque of Habīb al-Najjār, the Princeton excavations uncovered levels dating to this period. In sector 21/22-J, the uppermost levels contained drains and pipes running under the most recent buildings. Jean Lassus noted an astonishing 4 m of deposition between the post-Byzantine reconquest layer and the Mamlūk destruction layer of 1268. Such accumulation over 300 years speaks to intense episodes of flooding and/or deliberate filling. In the 1934 excavation diary for sector 22-K, the excavators recorded a large quantity of glazed "Turkish and Arabic pottery." An interesting observation is that most of the Port St. Symeon pottery, a hallmark of the Crusader period for this region, of which there was little overall, came from sector 22-K. Although no kilns were explicitly mentioned, these presumably would have been associated with an excavated building consisting of two parallel walls and small rooms between them in Level I. The smallest of these rooms had a jar in situ in the northeast corner (Figure 8.12).

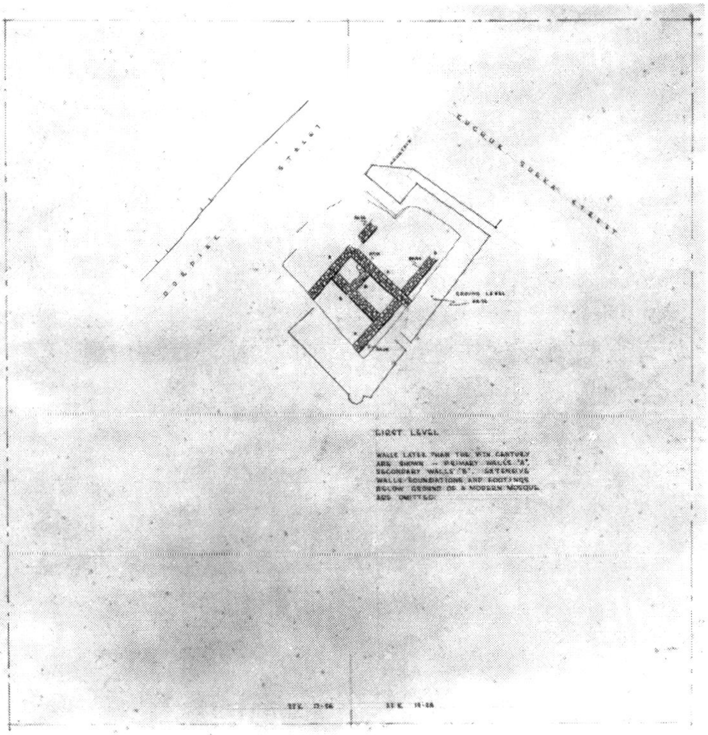

FIGURE 8.12 22-K, Level I building, facing northeast with *in situ* jar visible in the far right (northeast) corner of the small room on the left

Source: Courtesy of the Antioch Expedition Archives, Department of Art and Archaeology, Princeton University; Princeton

FIGURE 8.12 (Continued)

Atypical of the Byzantine reconquest phase of the city, the later wall in sector 21/22-J and building in sector 22-K were not orthogonally oriented, a feature that may suggest their close association with the continuing (or former) mosque oriented toward Mecca.

The War of Antiochene Succession

That the city appears as still vibrant and diverse stands in counterpoint to the political narrative of events in this last period, which was characterized by a war of succession, in particular with the Armenian Kingdom of Cilicia. In the late 1180s, Bohemond III had compelled Cilician Armenia to recognize him as its suzerain in exchange for protection. In 1194, however, the Armenian prince Leon II (1187–1198; king 1198–1219) lured Bohemond and his wife and son to the fortress of Baghrās on the ruse of making negotiations but took them captive instead and forced Bohemond to turn Antioch over to him.[147]

Unlike 55 years earlier, when the Antiochenes, Armenian and Latin alike, had welcomed the Armenian patriarch, the citizens now resisted the advances of the Armenian forces, nor would they tolerate the permanent residence of an Armenian archbishop in the city. The city's Melkite and Latin inhabitants now made an alliance in the form of a commune and, arming themselves on the Sea/Bridge

Gate, fought off the Armenians. The Latin patriarch Ralph II (1193–1196) acted as leader for this commune, which was effectively a governing body. To replace Bohemond temporarily, his eldest son Raymond IV, Count of Tripoli, was declared ruler of Antioch. Eventually, Bohemond was released provided he would cede Cilician Armenia back to Leon and his son Raymond would marry Alice, Leon's niece. In 1201, upon the death of his father, Bohemond IV (also called Le Sire or al-Asīr (the captive) and the One-Eyed) became the new prince, aware that his right to rule was already challenged by the 3-year-old Raymond-Rupen, posthumous son of his elder brother Raymond IV, who had died in 1198, and Alice. While most Melkites in the city and some Latins, including the Templars, were anti-Armenian and so opposed the young claimant, most Latins, including the Latin patriarch Peter of Angoulême (1196–1208) and the Hospitallers, supported Raymond-Rupen in taking the throne.

Shortly after Bohemond III's death in 1201, Leon set siege to the city, thus inaugurating the so-called War of the Antiochene Succession, a series of clashes lasting from 1201 to 1219, but was soon forced to withdraw. Since Leon had no heir, his great-nephew Raymond-Rupen[148] was his hope for his dynastic succession and plans of expansion, which included Antioch. Although he tried to buy the Templars' support, they refused, and in November 1203 Leon tried again to take the city, even getting through the Daphne Gate. But although the patriarch helped negotiate a peace treaty, the Antiochenes and Templars, with the help of the al-Malik al-Zahir, son of Salaḥ al-Dīn of the Ayyūbids from Aleppo, soon chased Leon and his army out of the city. Attacking yet again in August 1204 and breaking a truce, Leon raided the Amuq villages and destroyed the rural areas (*rustāqiha*) near the city, taking livestock (*mawāshiha*), but still was unable to take Antioch. The attack on the hinterlands, however, caused a food shortage, inflation, and famine in the city once again, and al-Malik al-Zahir supplied Antioch with crops (*ghalā'*). Eventually, in 1206, Leon and Bohemond IV forged an eight-year truce, facilitated in part by the Ayyūbid Sultan. Leon was to return what he took from the raids, including all Muslim captives, and swear to not have any more intentions on taking Antioch.[149]

But conflict over whether the city would have a Latin or Melkite patriarch then ensued. Pope Innocent III's legate Peter of Capua, while in Antioch, had overruled the authority of Patriarch Peter by making appointments and taking lands. Refusing to comply, Peter was excommunicated, and Bohemond removed him as patriarch for his support of Raymond-Rupen. Bohemond and the Antiochenes then plundered the treasuries of St. Peter's Church and enthroned a Greek Orthodox patriarch, Symeon II, in 1208, causing Innocent and Peter to unite against him.[150] Peter, excommunicating Bohemond's retinue, tried to evict him by instigating another invasion by Leon and accepting Raymond-Rupen as the rightful prince of Antioch in St. Peter's Church, prematurely reneging on the ceasefire. But Bohemond and the Templars, from their base in the citadel, defended Antioch and, expelling Armenians from the city, imprisoned Peter with nothing to drink but the oil from his lamp, and he soon died in prison. Those Latin Antiochenes who supported Raymond-Rupen fled to Cilicia, though some remained, including the seneschal of Antioch and mayor of the commune. In 1212, the 14-year-old Raymond-Rupen led an army into the region of Antioch, destroying villages, fields, and orchards, and the Armenians took spoils of 100,000 *byzantinici*. In 1213, John of Brienne, the king of Jerusalem, sent troops to help Antioch, but in the following year he forged a diplomatic alliance with Leon by marrying his daughter.

In December 1215, Leon attacked Antioch again now that the eight-year truce had expired, though without success. But the following February, while Bohemond was away in Tripoli, Leon came again, this time sneaking into Antioch by night through the Aleppo Gate and taking possession of the city with the help of the seneschal and other nobles, whom he won over with gifts and promises. Entering with his troops, he seized the gates and guard towers and stationed soldiers in the streets. In the morning, the people saw their city had been taken, though no one was harmed and nothing was stolen. The citadel, controlled by the Templars, resisted capture for a few days but then surrendered to Leon and was given to Raymond-Rupen; the Hospitallers, allies of Raymond-Rupen, then took control of it, and Raymond-Rupen released its Muslim prisoners. The Latin patriarch Peter III of Ivrea (1209–1217) and nobles then took King Leon and the 18-year-old Raymond-Rupen to St. Peter's Church, where the patriarch crowned the young man as Prince of Antioch. The formerly banished Armenians were invited back and their properties restored. The Antiochenes, however, came to hate Raymond-Rupen, who was also no longer on good terms with his great-uncle Leon, without whose help he found it difficult to hang on to the city, and in 1219 Antiochene noblemen rose up against him and helped Bohemond retake it, forcing Raymond-Rupen to leave. (Interestingly, a hoard was found in Antioch consisting of 844 billon deniers of Bohemond IV and one of Leon. The appearance of a unique billon coin of Leon has suggested to one scholar that he forged the coin in hopes of annexing Antioch.)[151]

Bohemund IV continued to rule until his death in 1233, when his son Bohemund V took over as Prince of Antioch and Count of Tripoli until 1252. But because he resided mainly at Tripoli, Antioch was run primarily by the commune.[152] Upon his death, his son, Bohemond VI (1252–1275), inheriting both thrones at age 15, chose to return to Antioch. By this time, the Armenian claim to the city had subsided somewhat, and Bohemond VI even married the daughter of the Armenian king, Hetoum I. In 1263/64, Hetoum went to Antioch for pleasure, taking with him a doctor, archbishop, priests, deacons, and gold and silver objects from his father's treasury to give to the poor and donate to sanctuaries in memory of the deceased. The Armenian Smbat the Constable states that as he entered the city, its citizens responded with joy. He visited the churches of St. Paul and St. Peter and other sanctuaries.[153]

But Antioch's relative peace with its western neighbors at this time was offset by intimidations from two rising major powers: the Mamlūks and the Mongols. The Mamlūks, allying with local *amīrs*, began raiding around the countryside. More immediate, however, was the Mongolian threat and the arrival of the Mongol Ilkhānids after their conquest of Baghdad in 1258. In 1260, Bohemond VI preemptively submitted to the Mongols, as did his father-in-law the Armenian king. Antioch was now a Mongol protectorate, one of six administrative districts in the province of Syria under the jurisdiction of Mongol Aleppo, which Bohemond and Hetoum helped the Mongols seize from the Ayyūbids; in return, they restored to Bohemond various towns taken by the Muslims. Because the Mongols were also making alliances with the Byzantines, Bohemond was also compelled to replace the Latin patriarch with a Greek Orthodox one, Euthymius (1260–1263). This Mongol alliance proved to have severe consequences, however, as meted out by the Mongols' enemy the Mamlūks, who defeated them in the Battle of 'Ayn Jālūt in September 1260. Bohemond VI's reign, and indeed the whole chapter of Crusader Antioch, would end abruptly eight years later with the Mamlūk capture of Antioch in 1268.

An international trading city

In contrast to the political war of succession of the thirteenth century, there was at this time a decided economic commercial boom.[154] We can attribute this to truces between the Franks and Ayyūbids, the Crusader conquest of Cyprus in 1191 by King Richard I of England, and the spread of Italian trading colonies. Indeed, we have no reason to assume there was not economic continuity and active manufacturing and trade in exported goods. Additionally, the Greek Orthodox patriarch Euthymius sponsored and promoted international artistic projects connecting Syria, Egypt, the Mongol Empire, and Italy, while often acting on behalf of the Byzantine Emperor Michael VIII. These projects included icons at St. Catherine's Monastery in the Sinai, a wall-painting program at the Church of Mar Tādrus (St. Theodore) at Behdaidat in northern Lebanon, and a *pallium* (ceremonial robe) gift by the Michael VIII to the Genoese.[155] The patriarch also invested in local merchants from Damascus, Acre, and Ayas, although merchants had their own trading consortiums and functioned privately.

Texts from the last three-quarters of the twelfth century, when Antioch was undergoing many tribulations, mention glass and iron production.[156] Glass was produced by the Jewish community, as commented by Benjamin of Tudela, while Idrisi mentions iron, which was extracted from the Amanus Mountains and forged into swords and knives. The main items produced in the city for export, however, were textiles and ceramics. Tasha Vorderstrasse's study shows that Antioch was a center of textile production in the Crusader period, run by the Melkites as artisans and intermediaries of trade, and produced several cloths widely known and sought after.[157] Cotton from Antioch appears in Genoese records and was given a tariff, and the Venetians traded linen from Antioch. Antioch textiles appear on paintings such as those in Mar Tādrus and St. Catherine's and in English and Vatican church treasury inventories of 1295. The accounts of the Clerks of the Wardrobe in Scotland mention the cloth, as do French literary texts. Antioch textiles were also sold closer to home, in Acre. A 1209 inventory from Antioch lists textiles from St. Peter's Church in the form of vestments, and a source mentions Hospitallers sending Antiochene cotton to their Grand Master. The twelfth-century geographer from Grenada al-Zuhrī, though possibly making use of a ninth-century work, mentions the production of a specific red brocade with white on the reverse called *siqlāṭūn*. The red dye may have come from madder root, which was known in the Orontes region.[158] Another production may be of a "diasper" contrasting pattern of black with gold brocade and ermine. Red and black stripes were also attributed to Antiochene style. Idrisī mentions that plain/monochrome cloth was manufactured in Antioch, as well as watered silk and two other types of cloth (*al-Iṣbahānī* and *al-Tasatturī*). Meanwhile, William of Tyre mentions the city's large quantities of silk.[159] Antioch may have also been a market for textiles made in other parts of the Islamic Middle East. Other plain brocades called *'Attābī* (perhaps named after a Baghdad quarter), *Destuwā'ī*, and *Iṣfahānī* could be obtained there, according to Istakhrī, Ibn Ḥawqal, and Idrisī.

Pottery production likely enjoyed the same long-lived artisanal tradition in Antioch. Antioch pottery of the Crusader period tells an interesting story. Inhabitants used imported Byzantine pottery (43 percent of the pottery found) and Raqqa frit ware (17 percent), but Port St. Symeon is rather rare in the city, and proto-mailoica, with a tin glaze, nonexistent. Thus it appears the Crusaders did not bring ceramics with them, nor did they reproduce the types of the West. In fact, Northern and Western Europe had no glazed pottery at this time; only Italy produced glazed tablewares, which were not exported. Port St. Symeon ware, dating from the late twelfth to early fourteenth centuries and once attributed to the Crusaders, and therefore believed to come from the principality, was in fact produced before and after the Crusader period and is found over a wide geographic range. It was likely made at several sites and exported from Cilician Armenia and Antioch. Yet these wares are almost completely absent from the Princeton excavation material. There are several examples of Zeuxippos ware, a glazed fineware produced only in a small handful of centers found in Cyprus, the Haifa region of Palestine, near Ephesus in western Anatolia, and Sparta and northern Greece (Figure 8.13).[160] Their presence indicates interregional and international trade. On the other hand, yellow glazed gouged champlevé, often decorated with Islamic motifs and pseudo-calligraphy – excavated in association with the continuing potters' quarter house-kilns such as in sector 17-O – was used in Antioch but is not generally seen in the surrounding region; instead, it is encountered in the Aegean and Byzantine world (Figure 8.14).

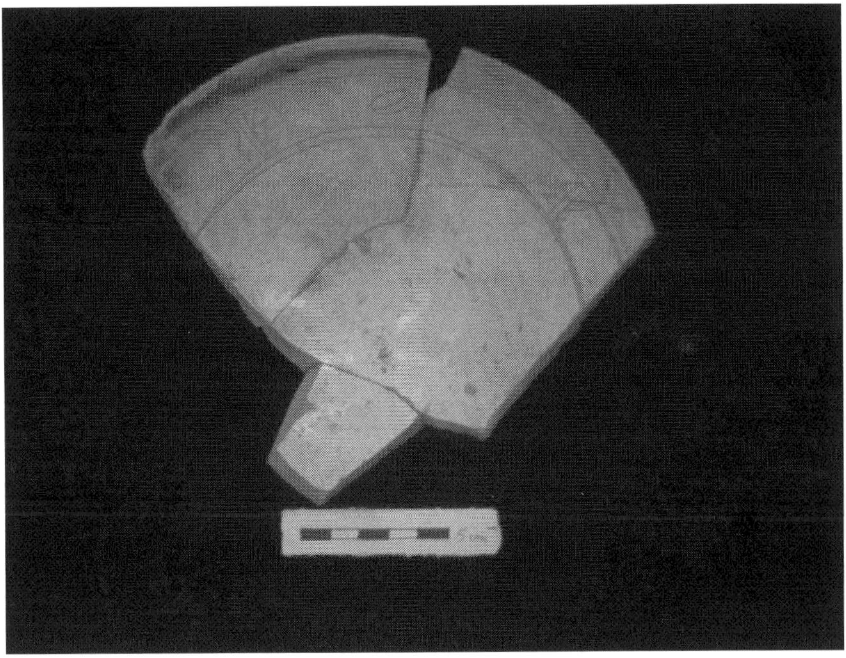

FIGURE 8.13 Zeuxippos ware plate, Antioch box 045-A4p RCH 7272?

Source: Courtesy of the Princeton University Art Museum

This suggests, first, a twelfth-century date for the champlevé production and second, that Antioch not only produced local ceramics but also manufactured wares for export, but only to non-Islamic lands in the central (and perhaps western) Mediterranean. Italian merchants and their markets drove the tastes for Western consumption.[161]

At the potter's house and workshop in sector 17-O, the presence of Saljūq/Ilkhānid white ware suggests the owner was a person of means, perhaps of a well-established Islamic or Christian family predating the Byzantine reconquest, as does the presence of seals of the period. At that time the port was still al-Suwaydīyya (St. Symeon), as indicated by Yāqūt, who noted that it was two parsangs from Antioch and that it was where Crusader ships offloaded goods to Antioch via pack animals.[162] Idrisī, in the mid-twelfth century, also refers to al-Suwaydīyya as a *furḍa* or small port. The sector 17-O evidence highlights Antioch as an international trading city, even producing wares for the world market more so than its own hinterlands. In addition, the results affirm that certain communities, industries, and spaces were long-lived from before and during the Crusader periods, calling into question how much of city life was in fact disrupted by the Crusader siege and providing evidence of a still-thriving city.

FIGURE 8.14 Fragments of champlevé ware, Antioch box 053-D2, D3p

Source: Courtesy of the Princeton University Art Museum

Conclusion

There is no more famous siege of Antioch throughout its history than the one led by the Crusaders. Their siege, however, was but one blow to the city, struck by a wave of external invasions from Zangids, Ayyūbids, Byzantines, and Armenians at this time. Internally, the Crusader period was marked by several clashes in the succession of rulers and conflict between the Latin, Melkite, and Miaphysite churches, between patriarchs and princes, and between locals and Crusaders. A wave of calamitous and powerful earthquakes, accompanied by droughts and famine, also scarred the city, a precursor to the Mamlūk conquest of the following period. Nonetheless, the city, as we have seen in previous periods, remained prosperous, desirable, and an important destination for many. Indeed, the Crusader siege, arguably unnecessary for the larger goal of taking Jerusalem, illustrates how powerfully the idea of taking Antioch, the first city of Christianity, had endured. But while the siege showed the continued defensive strength of the city's fortifications and inhabitants, the Crusader occupation that followed was accepted, at least on some levels. This is largely because its rulers were the Normans from Sicily, familiar with ruling over a multiethnic and religiously diverse, formerly Islamic-ruled polity. The archaeological and textual evidence further shows that following the siege, the water-supply system of Antioch, bringing water via aqueduct from Daphne, still continued to function. Buildings continued in use, and many took on multiple functions, while some older properties were renovated and used as gifts to help ease tensions between the Crusaders and local inhabitants. New construction, however, took place only for the first 60 years or so. Although the Crusaders were not segregated within the city, at the same time it took a while for them to fully integrate. In the meantime, many of the medieval city's economic, religious, and social institutions continued unaffected. Indeed, Christians of all stripes, Muslims, and Jews alike visited and venerated Antioch as a holy place in its own right, brimming with saints and relics.

Notes

1 For example, *Gesta Francorum* 1962; Raymond of Aguilers 1968; William of Tyre 1943; Fulcher of Chartres 1941; Peter Tudebode 1974.
2 Asbridge 2004, 156–157.
3 Pope Urban II, in his call for the Crusade, even refers to the city and St. Peter. See Riley-Smith 1982.
4 France 1994, 1, 196.
5 Meuwese 2006, 337–355; for example, on Suger's basilica of St. Denis in the stained glass window and in the Antioch chamber of Westminster Palace. Henry III also commissioned images of the city.
6 France 1994, 193–194.
7 France 1994, 11ff.
8 Asbridge 2004, 244–245. Raymond was also known, in Arabic sources, as Salfīs, Gundsanjīl, and Sanjīl (the Count of St. Gilles).
9 In Arabic sources, Gondoffer, Kandafrī, Kundufī, and al-Qumās. Godfrey was at first joined by his younger brother Baldwin I of Boulogne, though Baldwin disengaged on his own expedition and was not involved in the siege. Baldwin I became Lord of Edessa in February 1098, elevating his social position and making a small state for himself, setting aside the larger goal of retaking Jerusalem. See also C. Tyerman, 2011. *Chronicles of the First Crusade*. London: Penguin, 376.
10 In Arabic sources, Bardwīl/Baghdawayn.
11 Munro 1896, 4: 5–8.
12 Michael the Syrian also mentions Rajīl (Roger) of Salerno, Gosselin (Joscelin I of Courtenay, first cousin of Baldwin II), Galeran of Le Puisset (count of Toulouse). *Michael the Syrian* 1963, III.183.
13 In Arabic sources, Bimand or Baymand or Maymūn [monkey].
14 In Arabic sources, Tanjarī.
15 Estimates of numbers are notoriously unreliable and inconsistent from source to source. For example, the Antiochenes numbered 100,000, their militia consisting of 5,000 Turks, according to Stephen of Blois, or 16–17,000 according to Raymond of Aguilers (who also says there were 100,000 Crusaders). Four thousand seems a reliable estimate; France 1994, 223–224.
16 Yāghī Siyān's two sons were Shams al-Dawla and Muḥammad. Karbūqā b. Malik Shah, mentioned in the text, was *atabeg*-general of the sultan Barkyāruq b. Malik Shāh of Baghdad and prince of Mosul. The eight other Islamic rulers consisted of *amīrs* and their atabegs: Abū Naṣr Shams al-Malik Duqāq b. Tutush and his *atabeg* Zahīr al-Dīn Tughtakīn, Al-Malik Ridwan b. Tutush and his *atabeg* Janah al-Dawlah of Halab and Hims, and four other leaders: the Turkmen Artuqid *amīrs* Mu'ain al-Dawla Suqmān b. Artuq of Mardin (r. 1091–1098), his brother, Shams al-Dawla Sulaymān b. Il-ghāzī b. Artuq (Amisoliman) of Sumaysāṭ (d. 1124), Arslantaş the prince of Sinjar, and the Arab

leader al-Watthab b. Maḥmūd, also answered the call for troops. Not all of these leaders came willingly; some were pressured.

17 *Michael the Syrian* 1963, III.183 records a further curious detail. He notes that while the Crusaders were still "besieging" Constantinople in 1097, an earthquake shook Antioch. A vast subterranean house was revealed under a tower that had collapsed, in which were found large bronze sculptures of men that resembled Crusaders on horses with swords and spears but also in iron chains. Yāghi Siyān, not knowing what they were, determined they were idols from the city's past and had them all smashed. An old woman then told him they were talismans placed by Byzantines under the tower to ward off the Crusaders from taking Antioch. Yāghi Siyān, willing to put them back together, asked if it would help, but the woman told him no, the damage was done. In response, he killed her. This prophetic episode by a Syriac source is telling in that it shows Eastern Christian fear of the potential fury of these Western Christians once unleashed on their city. MacEvitt 2015, 260–275. 47. It is also remarkably similar to the one mentioned in Chapter 7, p. 347, nn 25 and 27.

18 Christensen-Ernst 2012, 101. The *Gesta* (2002, 30) states that the castle was built on top of Mt. Malregard, suggesting that it was on a height (hill).

19 *Antioch II*, p. 3.

20 J. Leblanc and G. Poccardi, 1999. "Étude de la permanence de tracés urbain et ruraux antiques à Antioch-sur-l'Oronte," *Syria* 76: 91–126, Christensen-Ernst 2012, 138. See Chapter 3, p. 134 in this volume.

21 According to Christensen-Ernst (2012, 138), the Duke Gate was close to the crossroads of 119.Cadde and Nehir Caddesi, where there is a wall fragment; the wall would have run parallel to Istiklal Caddesi and Şehit Osman Durmaz Caddesi.

22 Asbridge 2000.

23 Recent excavations by Shimon Gibson and Rafi Lewis in Jerusalem have uncovered the remains of the ditch dug as a defensive measure against siege towers outside the city walls and a nearby house reused by the Crusaders during the siege. The ditch and reuse of the house date very closely to the time of the city's siege in July 1099, just months after Antioch was taken, and these results are likely a good parallel to the situation at Antioch, especially since the Crusader army and its leaders were the same and coming fresh from their experience there. A. Borschel-Dan. July 15, 2019. "First Evidence of Crusader Siege from July 15, 1099 uncovered at Old City walls." *The Times of Israel*. www.timesofisrael.com/first-evidence-of-crusader-siege-from-july-15-1099-uncovered-at-old-city-walls/

24 Ibn Qalānisī 1932, 43.

25 d'Ault-Dumesnil 1852 *Dictionnaire historique, géographique et biographique des Croisades, embrassant toute la lutte du Christianisme et de l'Islamisme, etc. coll. Cxcvi. 1042*. Paris.

26 Interestingly, the *Gesta* (2002, 51) repeats this when Karbughā camps outside the Crusader-occupied town and laughs at the state of the Crusader weaponry.

27 Munro 1896, 4: 5–8.

28 For more on the port, see Vorderstrasse 2005b. For Armenian princes helping, Matthew of Edessa 1993 II.114 (167).

29 Peter Tudebode 1974, 53.

30 France (1994, 254, n. 53) speculates whether this is where the roundabout, old Museum, and cinema are today.

31 Krey 1921, 157–160, 161–167.

32 Asbridge 2004, 196.

33 Munro 1896, 2–5.

34 Alternately described as Armenian in Muslim sources but Turk (or converted Muslim Armenian) in Christian accounts (and an officer of the city), His name appears quite differently in sources in a beguiling number of ways as Firuz, Pirus, Ruzye, Ruzbah, Barzuya, Zarrād, Ge'org, Arjarz, perhaps as his identity was kept secret.

35 France 1994, 264–265, deduces it should be at the southeast corner of the fortification walls. Bar Hebraeus (1932, 234, 264) says it was on the side of a ravine called the Kashkarūf which is the Parmenius gorge.

36 Reputedly he was also upset that his wife was having an affair with a Muslim.
37 Another account names Emirfeirus, Yāghi Siyān's notary, as Bohemond's informant and a traitor, Beihammer 2017, 42 In Ibn Qalānisī (d. 1160), *Mudhayyal Ta'rik Dimashq*, the armorer sold the tower to the Crusaders, Ibn Qalānisī 1932, 45. *The Damascus Chronicle of the Crusades*. H.A.R. Gibb (transl.). London: Luzac, A.H. 491 (December 9, 1097 to November 27, 1098).
38 Ibn 'Abd al-Ẓāhir 1976, 320.
39 Asbridge 2004, 209.
40 Krey 1921, 153; Ibn Qalānisī 1932, 44.
41 In Qalqashandī – 100,000 persons (1987, vol. 4, 185).
42 *Gesta Francorum* 1962, 47–48. Also Albert of Aix (Aachen), 2007, iv, 23 who wrote between 1102 and 1130s.
43 *TIB* 575: June 8, 1098.
44 France 1994, 276. A much later yet brief episode of Ibn al-Furāt, perhaps following Albert of Aachen's account, held that the Crusaders were so desperate that they sent Peter the Hermit and his interpreter Herluin to negotiate with the Muslims for safe conduct to leave and determine the fate of the city through a duel, and at one point came out and scored a small victory against the Muslims. Another account states that Karbughā replied that the only way the Crusaders would be allowed to depart was through battle. See Asbridge 2004, 230–231.
45 *TIB* 575.
46 Matthew of Edessa stated it was on the left-hand side of the church in front of the altar [1993 II.121 (171)], Vartan said it was on the right, Ralph of Caen said it was under the altar, Smbat says it was in a reliquary in front of the altar, Fulcher said it was in a pit, and Ibn al-Athīr in a corner. Michael the Syrian (1963, III.184) said that it was Tancred who found it along with nails from the cross, which they used to fashion a cross, and the tip of the lance. Bar Hebraeus [1932, 235 (265)] said that in a "certain place" within the church, the Crusaders found splinters of the cross that they fashioned into a cross, as well as the head of a spear. Ibn al-Athīr, interestingly, offers the Muslim viewpoint – that the Lance was a ruse designed to bolster morale and was planted ahead of time by a monk (Peter Bartholomew, presumably).
47 Unsurprisingly, there are several Lances. Christensen-Ernst 2012, 104: the Lance was also perhaps carried by Otto III in 996 on his way to Italy at the head of an army (and perhaps the one held today in Vienna's Imperial Treasury). Another has been in Constantinople since the seventh century and was given, in 1492, by the Ottoman Sultan Beyazit II to Pope Innocent VIII. See Norwich 1992, 254 n. 3. France (1994, 18) sees Peter Bartholomew as representative of the lesser knights who had no claims to lands, already taken by the main lords, but who wished to assert themselves in battle and acquire booty.
48 See also Morris 1984, 33–46. This lance may be the one kept in the Armenian cathedral at Etchmiadzin (Norwich 1992, 254 n. 3).
49 Lapina 2015, 38.
50 Ibn al-'Adīm refers to a house (*dār)*, a hostel of sorts, that Aḥmad b. Marwān and his men stayed in when they surrendered the castle. He and Walter the Chancellor also refer to the houses around the Aleppo Gate as belonging to the "upper" quarter, which also negates ideas of a fully contracted city south of the Parmenius.
51 Asbridge 2004, 258, 261.
52 Asbridge 2004, 242–243.
53 Stahl 2018, 30 of Outremer. Raymond of Aguilers 1968.
54 It also had a coin of Saljūq fabric but Christian imagery, which could be seen as transitional from Byzantine to Saljūq or Saljūq to Crusader, to be published by E. Medawar, "A New Seljuk Rum Coin for Antioch? The Search for Turkic Political Identity in the Eleventh Century," forthcoming.
55 Vorderstrasse 2015, 79–92.

56 Djobadze wondered if it was the Middle Byzantine Kastana/Castalia spring or Tskarotha. Brock speculates on the Mar Georgios/Beth Mayya. Nasrallah suggested that perhaps it was the Theotokos of Daphne. *Antioch I*, 107–113.

57 *TIB* 655.

58 A Latin source describes a "magnificent fresco of Christ" as its centerpiece, which was untouched during the Saljūq occupation, apparently on account of its power. Asbridge 2004, 246. Albert of Aachen 2013, 177, vol. 1, Book 5.

59 Krey 1921, 293, n. 5.

60 When the Miaphysite patriarch Michael I was enthroned there briefly in 1168–1169, he occupied the seat of St. Peter in the south sacristy of the church. *TIB* 623–624. This may be corroborated in Wilbrand von Oldenburg's account (2012, 72), which details St. Peter's Church in the center of the city and includes a detail that inside was a room where St. Peter was chained to a chair. If this were taken by Ibn Manik (see Chapter 6), presumably it was returned.

61 Tudebode (1974, 72) says that a knight named Arvedus Tudebodus was buried in front of the church's western door.

62 *TIB* 655.

63 Original translation in Krey 1921. Original Latin text: Raymond d'Aguilers (Hugh and Hill 1969), 69, but modified. The translation of "*antea*" as spatial, "before which the Saracens had built a mosque," is incorrect. I am grateful to Rick Barton and Kate Sheeler for fine-tuning this translation. This was translated as the mosque having been converted into a church in: Skottki 2015, 295, n. 1276: "Die groβen Kirchen hätten sie in Moscheen ungewandelt."

64 Original translation in Krey 1921; Raymond d' Aguilers (Hugh and Hill 1969). Interestingly, there is a relic of St. Leontius in the Church of the Holy Sepulchre in Jerusalem. On the Crusader passion of obtaining relics from the east (and the relic market), see Hahn 2015, 193–214; Krueger 2010, 12–13, see Wortley 2006, 631, on the removal of relics from Constantinople by the Crusaders during the Fourth Crusade.

65 Cahen 1971, 285–292.

66 Constable 2003, 225–226; see also Byrne 1928, 139–140.

67 Paul 2010, 554.

68 Müller 1879, 3, no. 1, pp. 15–16; no. 13.

69 Asbridge 1999, 305–325.

70 See Edgington 2006, 247–260.

71 In one instance, in 1060 in Sicily, the local Muslims, "wished to demonstrate their fidelity to the Duke [Robert Guiscard]. And, in order to avoid suspicion, both the Christians and the Saracens who lived there armed themselves against the Pagans of Sicily." In another, Robert Guiscard sent Peter the Deacon as ambassador to the *amīr* of Palermo, "who could understand and speak very well, just like a Saracen." See Johns 2002, 31–33.

72 France 1994, 15.

73 See Buck 2014, Chapter 3.

74 Asbridge 1999.

75 Asbridge 2004, 246.

76 Weltecke 2006.

77 D'Angelo 2017, 77–88; Burnett 2000. 1–78.

78 Ambraseys 2009, 282–283 and Figure 3.10.

79 *TIB* 656.

80 Todt 2000. Ibn al-Furāt states that Bohemond was defeated and captured by al-Dānishmand in August 1100 and ransomed himself for 100,000 dinars (Albert of Aix says 100,000 bezants). He was released three years later and in 1104 sailed to the West. Meanwhile, the Saljūq Qilij Arlsān b. Sulaymān from Anatolia reached the city in July or August 1103.

81 Anna Komnene 1969. *The Alexiad*. E.R.A. Sewter (trans.) Penguin, p. 389.

82 Ibid., 389.

83 Ibid., 392.
84 Though Ibn al-Furāt says Sept. 6, 1112.
85 Asbridge 2012, 302.
86 Bar Hebraeus 1932 248 (280–81).
87 Also called Buḥayra al-Yaghrā (modern Gölbaşı). The Lake of Antioch and Buḥ ayra al-Sallūr have often been confused, as the latter can firmly be identified as the small lake northeast by association with its location along the Yaghrā River, near the site of Yaghrā (modern Jisr Murat Paşa; Hellenistic Meleagrum), known for its ample fish resources, and also near ʿAyn al-Sallūr, mentioned in Islamic sources, and Casal Sellorie and the fishery of Agrest in Crusader texts. Yāqūt i.516, iii.762 in: Le Strange 1965, 72; Balādhurī 1916 *228* (148). The location of this hydronym has been clearly asserted by Jacquot 1931, 169–170, and Dussaud 1927, 436–438 and nn 3–4. Regarding the identification of the attendant site of Yaghrā, see also Eger 2014a, 58–64.
88 Asbridge 1999; Burgtorf 2006, 217–246.
89 Bohemond II's name in Arabic sources is Baghdwīn bī al-Qaḍiya.
90 Buck 2014, 2–3.
91 *TIB* 656.
92 As observed by the French orientalist Louis Alexandre Olivier de Corancez (1816).
93 Pococke 1745.
94 *TIB* 623; *Michael the Syrian* 1963, III.303–304; Weltecke 2006.
95 Wilbrand von Oldenburg 2012, 72.
96 Ciggaar 2006, 265.
97 Prince Raymond, in Arabic sources was known as al-Ābrans (the Prince).
98 Buck 2014, 69–73.
99 The panegyrical oration for the Emperor John II, *Logos eis ton aoidimon basilea kyr Iōannēn ton Komnēnon*. Nicephorus Basilaces 1977, 120–124.
100 See Maciej, Conclusion, 149.
101 Buck 2014, 36.
102 Buck 2014, 41; Bar Hebraeus 1932 275 (314); Ibn Qalānisī 1932, 293–294.
103 Prince Raynald, in Arabic sources, was known as al-Ābrans Ārnāṭ.
104 Bar Hebraeus 1932 284 (325)
105 See Jones and Maguire 2002, 116–117.
106 Guidoboni et al. 2004a, 105–127.
107 These texts are Bar Hebraeus 1932, 285 (326), "the greater part of Antioch… was destroyed," Ibn al-Athīr, Kamāl al-Dīn, and *Chron. 1234*.
108 Ambraseys 2009, 303–311, Figure 3.11
109 Qalqashandi 1987, vol. 1, 523. Elsewhere Aleppo was also mentioned.
110 Stahl, from forthcoming "Coinage" article in the *Cambridge History of the Crusades* [check the Metcalf Oxford Catalogue, 2nd edition; for details III.9–10].
111 For example, coins with Tancred's name may have been minted either when he ruled as regent when Bohemond was prisoner from 1101 to 1103 or during his own reign from 1104 to 1112. Some Bohemond I coins may have been minted under Bohemond II. See Stahl 2020.
112 Stahl 2020. The first couple of attempts at minting deniers were unsuccessful.
113 Metcalf 2006, 313.
114 Benjamin of Tudela 1907, 26–27.
115 Guidoboni 1994, 172–173.
116 Guidoboni et al. (2004b, 11); Ambraseys 2009, 316–325, Figure 3.12, Guidoboni 1994, 189–210.
117 Michael the Syrian (1963, III.339) may be giving us more of a biased account of things, rather than conveying a miracle. Michael the Syrian visited in 1168/69 and several other times as patriarch. Smbat the Constable, however, says that the Theotokos church was destroyed, killing many people (1980, 35).

118 The site and its vicinity are currently being surveyed by Ayşe Henry.
119 William of Tyre, RHC, xviii/971–973 (Latin).
120 Morony 2000, 160.
121 *Antioch II*, 54.
122 Usāma b. Munqidh 2008, 153–154.
123 Ibn al-Athīr 2007, 148 (304); Buck 2014, 46.
124 Hattin is where Raynald of Châtillon, widower of the now deceased Constance, finally met his end after his capture and execution by Salaḥ al-Dīn. According to many accounts, Salaḥ al-Dīn told Guy of Lusignan, the now widely cited and famous adage: "A king does not kill a king." In Ibn al-ʿAdīm 1996, 408–409: "It is not the habit of kings to kill kings" (*lam tajri ʿādatu al-mulūk ānahum yuqaṭalūn al-mulūk*).
125 See Ibn al-Athīr 2007, 353 (19). A number of scholars posit that some of Salaḥ al-Dīn's allies in fact tried to prevent him from securing Antioch, since it would have given the sultan greater strength. Buck 2014, 56.
126 Ibn al-Athīr 2007, 375 (49). Ibn al-ʿAdīm goes further to say that they spread an epidemic in the city and filled Antioch with their own tombs. 1996, 420.
127 Ibn ʿAbd al-Ẓāhir 1976, 445. This comes from a letter preserved in a book that discusses the incident and was known by Salaḥ al-Dīn.
128 Smbat the Constable 1980, 67.
129 Yāqūt 1990, vol. 1, 316.
130 Indeed, no study has yet explored the relationship of the two.
131 Troupeau 2005, 579–582.
132 There was also a Church of Thomas the Apostle in Seleucia Pieria, Mayer and Allen 2012, 110–111. For the martyrium: Ibid., 109–110.
133 Troupeau 2005, 579–580.
134 Hazardar is a strange name. In the Codex it says "holding a thousand." It appears in Ṭabarī (1992, vol. 36, 109) as a place near Baṣra and in Balādhurī in the same area as a castle in 1924, 81 (359), see n. 3 – which states *hazārdar* means "1,000 doors".
135 He is most likely Saint Andronicus of Pannonia, a first century Christian mentioned by Paul in Romans 16:7 who was martyred.
136 *TIB* 657, from a handwritten manuscript. This could also be identified with the Martyrium of St. Barlaam, outside the city walls.
137 See Chapter 1, p. 165, n. 133. C. Ecclestone, 2008. "The Museion," in *The Antiochepedia: Musings upon Ancient Antioch* blog. April 27, 2008, https://libaniusredux.blogspot.com/2008/04/museion.html
138 *TIB* 657. See Chapter 1, p. 65, n. 134 in this volume.
139 Cahen 1971, 285–292; Jamil and Johns 2003, 157–190.
140 *Shabūba* may be referring here to young lady or virgin.
141 Jamil and Johns, 185–185. *Ghumdān* alludes to the famous pre-Islamic palace in Yemen but also means a scabbard or sheath and denotes something concealed or hidden (hence off the main road).
142 Poccardi 2009, 281–287.
143 *TIB* 659. The Arabic, "congregational church," is an interesting usage and suggests that this was a main church at the time.
144 Kedar and Kohlberg 1995, 164–176.
145 Treiger 2017, 215–252. Fourteen years earlier, it seems that Jawān b. Dimitrī copied texts out of the church of our Lady al-ʿAmmāriyya. This may be the same as the village mentioned during the Saljūq conquest of Amrānīya, or perhaps refers to Amorion (ʿAmmurīyya) in central Anatolia.
146 Via Harawī 2004, 49, n. 28.
147 Ibn Shaddād (1984, 223–299.52–57) also recounts this later but calls Bohemond III, Nusayr.
148 Ibn Lāwn in Arabic sources. Ibn al-ʿAdīm (1996, 445) notes that he was a descendent of Bardas in the tenth century. This is correct in that he was the great-great-grandson of Bardas Phocas.

149 Ibn al-'Adīm 1996, 445–446.
150 This is one possible time that the Artophorion Reliquary of St. Anastasius the Persian may have been taken out of Antioch and ended up in Aachen, Germany.
151 Stahl, *Antioch I*. Bedoukian; there is little basis for this.
152 In Arabic sources, Sadd.
153 Smbat the Constable 1980, 111.
154 Redford 2012.
155 Hunt 2019, 127–137.
156 Redford 2012.
157 Vorderstrasse 2010.
158 Heyd 1923, I, 179. The madder is said to have replaced murex as a source of reddish dye, especially after 1204; Jacoby 2004, 197–240.
159 William of Tyre 1943, 1: 260–297.
160 A production center has also been identified in Venice. The Antioch examples have still to be studied and their production origin is unknown at present (İnanan 2010, 115–128; Berto and Gelichi 1997, 85).
161 Redford 2012.
162 Yāqūt 1990, vol. 1, 318.

9

A MAMLŪK ENTREPOT (1268–1516)

> This Turk, Bībars, who will seize power, will be bad [for the Christians]. He will take your own city, Antioch, Peter,… he will reduce the churches to ruin and massacre the priests and monks.
>
> – *Testament of Our Lord Jesus Christ*, 263[1]

> The God that gave you Antioch, took it back from you.
>
> – Ibn ʿAbd al-Ẓāhir, *The Radiant Gardens*[2]

Introduction

Nearly all secondary and many primary source accounts agree: if ever there was a period of decline in the history of Antioch, it was after 1268, when the Mamlūks destroyed the city, forever sealing its fate as a small town. Yet, as we have seen, the city had previously been destroyed, whether by war or natural disaster, time after time and nonetheless recovered. Thus it is worth asking just how accurate or exaggerated these accounts might be. Although textual sources describe the conquest in great detail, there are few accounts of life in Mamlūk Antioch in the fourteenth and fifteenth centuries. Similarly, this period has among the least amount of archaeological evidence for material culture published so far. Art historical studies and of existing buildings and legal religious endowment documents, however, have challenged the perception of decline within the city. While Antioch may have been at its smallest both physically and by population, it was by no means forgotten or in decline; rather, it maintained its importance and was renewed, primarily as a center for religious communities and commerce.

Under the Mamlūks' nearly 300-year rule, it appears they had no interest in maintaining Antioch's status as an important administrative center. This may have been partly because, by the end of Crusader occupation on the eve of the Mamlūk conquest, Antioch was already in part a shell of its former self after the crippling earthquakes and invasions of the twelfth century. And yet the city continued to have an important role to play in trade and commerce. According to Fuat Şancı, who has made close study of the city's historical buildings, around six of the 27 mosques and *masjids* (neighborhood mosques) examined were pre-Ottoman Mamlūk, and possibly five others, and four of five baths were also Mamlūk.[3] Art historical analysis of architectural styles and study into the patrons and names also offer insight where documents are lacking. Although some buildings have direct evidence of their Mamlūk origins, we are also lacking the foundation stories of many. Şancı's study has in turn been supported by Enver Çakar, who has studied sixteenth-century *waqf* documents.[4] *Waqf* or the plural, *awqāf*, were religious endowments that tied together public and private institutions, economies, and social structures of the city and stimulated construction and renovation of buildings. To the aforementioned evidence, we can add a *waqf* document from 1359 describing the endowments of the mosque of the Mamlūk Sultan Ḥasan, which was being built in Cairo. Among these were many urban and rural properties in greater Syria, including Antioch, a town in a state of renewal, replete with many Islamic buildings, including more than two dozen mosques, three *zāwiyas* (pilgrimage tomb-shrines), three bathhouses (*ḥammāms*), and five *khāns*. This description includes a detailed tour of the properties of the Mamlūk state. Given the combination of these sources, our understanding of Antioch in the Mamlūk period should in fact be one of growth and re-Islamicization and thus needs to be completely revised. The new city was distinctly an Islamic one, reformulated from the ruins of the old, replete with its own institutions, and relatively unchanged, providing a template for the next 600 years. Yet, its character, history, and legendary spiritual significance were not erased; rather they were its raison-d'être.

Rise of the Mamlūks

The institution of Turkic slave soldiers, upon which the Mamlūks were based, had its origins in the ninth century, when the 'Abbāsids of Baghdad first created a slave army (*mamlūk* meaning "slave" in Arabic) by purchasing boys from non-Muslim peoples and then raising them in the Islamic faith and training them as soldiers. But although they were slaves, they held a favored status above ordinary slaves and even citizens and soon came to dominate the military. The use of these slave soldiers spread throughout the Muslim world, and the power they enjoyed allowed them at times to usurp control from established rulers. Under the Ayyūbids of Egypt, the Mamlūks became increasingly powerful, until in 1250 they overthrew their masters and established the Mamlūk Sultanate centered in Cairo (Figure 9.1). Among their key achievements was their defeat of the Mongols at 'Ayn Jālūt in 1260, a historical turning point that prevented the Mongols from incursions into the Levant, Arabia, and Egypt, and their final expulsion of the Crusaders from the Levant at Acre in 1291 and Ruad in 1303, thus putting a permanent end to the Crusaders' presence in the Holy Land.

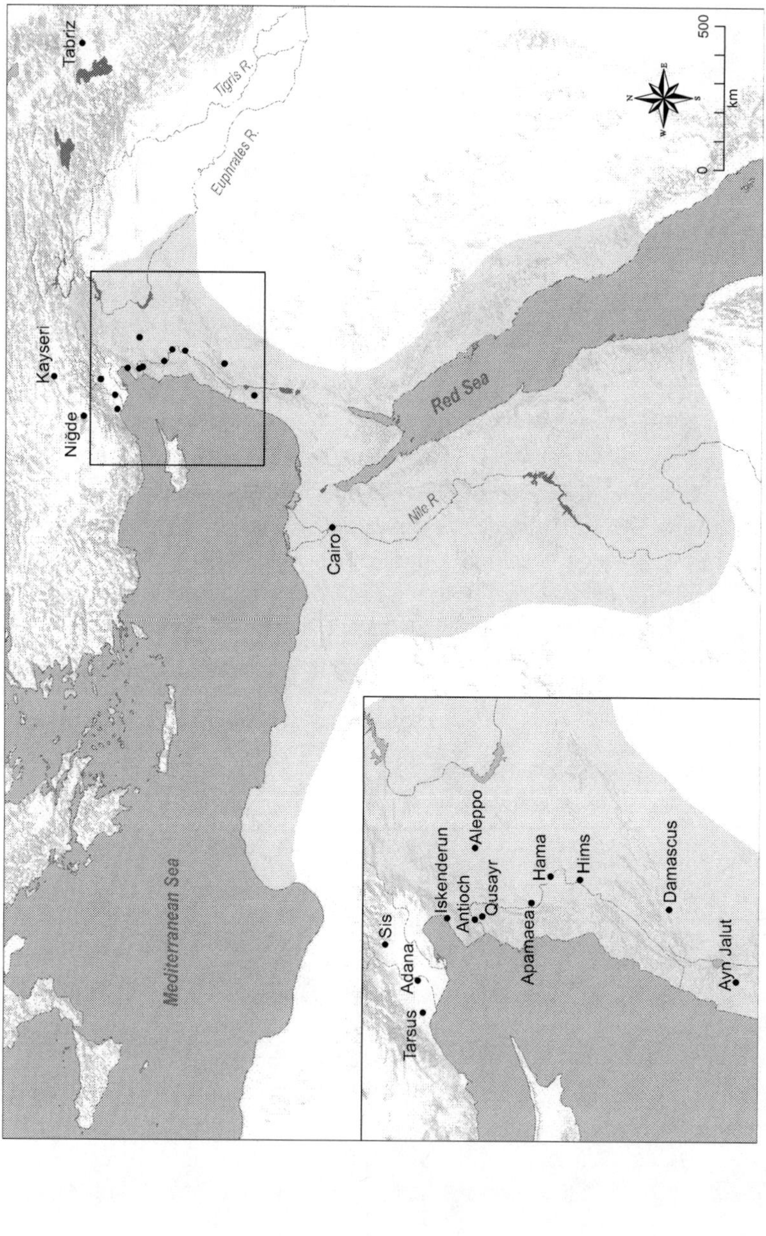

FIGURE 9.1 Map of the Mamlūk Sultanate

Source: Created by Claire Ebert

The destruction of Antioch

The lion's share of references to Antioch in the Mamlūk period comes during the rule of al-Malik al-Ẓahir Rukn al-Dīn Baybars, sultan of Egypt and Syria from 1260 to 1277 and one of the victors against the Mongols at 'Ayn Jālūt; these detail his conquest of the city and subsequent terms and treatment of its inhabitants and buildings. According to Abū al-Fidā' (1273–1331), historian and governor of Ḥamā, as early as June 1262, Baybars sent three generals against Antioch. Marching on the city, they devastated its territory and blockaded the town[5] and also took the port of Suwaydīyya, burning ships, seizing cargoes, and taking prisoners before returning to Cairo. These earlier raids may have been to weaken Antioch's military potential and show Mamlūk displeasure at the Crusader and Mongol alliance.[6]

With respect to the 1268 conquest itself, sources offer various versions on the details, but curiously most do not dwell on it significantly.[7] Baybars took the city as he had taken others in Syria along the coastal region, following a route by which he had captured Damascus, Ḥimṣ, Ḥamā, and Apamaea, as well. Although the date of conquest in Christian sources varies somewhat, nearly all Islamic sources write that Baybars arrived on the first day of Ramadan (a common day to start an invasion) in the year 666 AH (May 15, 1268), a Wednesday, and by Saturday he had taken the city. The fourteenth-century Egyptian historian Ibn al-Furāt goes into more detail, writing that Baybars's strategy consisted of deploying three armies: one to the port of Suwaydīyya (St. Symeon), led by Badr al-Dīn Bilik Khazindār (the treasurer); one to Darbassak in the northern part of the Amuq Plain, led by 'Izz al-Dīn Ighan; and Baybars's own army, led by an advance guard commanded by Shams al-Dīn Aqsunqur al-Rūmī (*ustadh al-dār* or Master of the House), which went north up the Orontes Valley to Antioch. The first army at the port burned all the ships and took all of the merchandise.[8] Baybars himself camped west of the town on the flanks of the mountains, presumably in the Amanus foothills.

Most sources agree that the Antiochenes sought capitulation and terms from the Mamlūks but disagree on Baybars's response. Ibn 'Abd al-Ẓāhir (1223–1293), a contemporary and most famous of the biographers of Baybars, and later Ibn al-Furāt (1334–1405) stated that the Constable of Antioch, Simon Mansel, was the emissary, who asked permission from Baybars to warn the Antiochenes of the impending invasion, leaving his own son as hostage.[9] Yet the Sunni scholar Badr al-Dīn al-'Aynı (1360–1451) states that Simon was taken prisoner and not allowed to warn the town, while Ibn Shaddād, who served under Baybars in Egypt and wrote a biography of him, and Ibn 'Abd al-Ẓāhir corroborated that Baybars did not permit any treaty, but that priests and monks now came out for three days of talks. Non-Muslim accounts like *Les Gestes des Chiprois* state that Baybars gave the Franks an opportunity to leave, but they did not respond.

On Saturday morning at dawn, Baybars announced his invasion and waited for the priests and monks to reenter the city before surrounding it and the citadel. As the Mamlūks were scaling the walls near the citadel and descending into the city, citizens were heading up to the citadel, where a large group took refuge (8,000 men, not including women and children). The fourteenth-century Coptic historian Mufaḍḍal b. Abī al-Faḍā'il and the *Gestes des Chiprois* both state that Baybars posted *amīrs* at each gate to monitor the population and prevent any Franks from leaving with their possessions, though some of the town's leaders, including the governor, bailiff, and seneschal, managed to flee at night into the mountains.

In the ensuing takeover, it appears that most of the city's inhabitants were killed – according to some sources, every man. Bar Hebraeus wrote, "they slew all the males therein, and they destroyed the famous churches, and they took captive women, and sons, and daughters, and they left it a heap of ruins and a desert place until this day."[10] Although numbers of killed or captured are generally unreliable and often exaggerated, in this case there is some agreement. Ibn 'Abd al-Ẓahir and Ibn al-Furāt cite a number of 100,000 killed, according to a Mongol representative (*shaḥna*) of the Ilkhānid ruler in the city who had been there since 1260, while Badr al-Dīn al-'Aynī states that most of the more than 100,000 citizens were killed or captured. Ibn Shaddād and Mufaḍḍal both estimate 40,000 killed, although 100,000 seems to be the agreed-upon number for the population itself.[11] The *Gestes des Chiprois* meanwhile states that 17,000 adult men were killed and 100,000 women and children taken prisoner.[12] Whatever the truth, according to Thomas Madden, it "was the single greatest massacre of the entire crusading era."[13] Most Armenians, however, were spared and allowed to go to Cilicia.

Those citizens holed up in the citadel suffered from expected conditions of overcrowding and lack of water and food, leading to many deaths. During the night, the vizier and *wālī* (governor) escaped. On Sunday, the day after the city's seizure, they asked for mercy, and descending into the city wearing their best clothes and carrying flowers, they were taken prisoner by the various princes in Baybars's army. Ibn 'Abd al-Ẓāhir and Ibn al-Furāt state that Baybars demanded a tribute of one dinar or bezant per person, which was the same tribute imposed by the Mongols and collected by their representative in town, but the Antiochenes refused. One dinar was given for each inhabitant of the lower town, according to the Mongol representative; those taking refuge in the citadel or in the neighboring towns and countryside received nothing. Among those taken captive, boys were sold for 12 dirhams and girls for five, and spoils and booty were divided. According to Badr al-Dīn al-'Aynī, a portion of the booty not distributed among the soldiers was set aside for building a mosque in al-Ḥasaniya, presumably a neighborhood in Cairo.

The citadel was then handed over to Badr al-Dīn Khazindār and Badr al-Dīn Baysarī al-Shamsī.[14] Simon Mansel, the constable, was freed along with his family and relatives and went to Sis, the capital of Armenian Cilicia, taking with him the *Assises of Antioch*, the collection of laws compiled under Bohemond IV, for Sempad, brother of the Armenian king Hetoum I. Some of the iron from the gates and lead of the churches were also taken. Ibn Shaddād states that at first Baybars forbade his soldiers from plundering anything; rather, he distributed booty among the *amīrs* and troops according to their rank, which Ibn 'Abd al-Ẓāhir details and

Mufaḍḍal and al-Maqrīzī, writing a century later, corroborate.[15] He also installed a troop of Turkmen to guard the Amuq Plain. Ibn 'Abd al-Ẓāhir, Ibn al-Furāt, and Badr al-Dīn al-'Aynī then write that Baybars burned the citadel and the fire spread throughout the city.[16] This is, however, a strange detail, and questionable, since he had just granted the citadel to two *amīrs*. The citadel was mentioned by the Arab geographer al-Dimashqī (1256–1327) around 1300, there is no evidence of fire today, and the citadel is quite far above the town for the fire to have spread easily downslope. Thus, it is likely that the two chroniclers actually meant the palace. Accounts also state that the city's walls were demolished, and all churches, palaces, and villas were burned. But undoubtedly this is as an exaggeration and part of the usual conquest narrative tropes, used also in the Crusader conquest of Antioch. In this case, it likely stemmed from an infamous letter written from Baybars to Bohemond VI.

The letter, written in Arabic and appearing in several sources,[17] contains perhaps one of the most compelling descriptions of the siege. Baybars addresses it to *Count* Bohemond (insultingly not addressing him as prince), who was in Tripoli at the time of the conquest. This was apparently how Bohemond first learned the news.[18] Baybars stated that the siege began at the start of Ramadan. Troops from the city tried to engage but were defeated, and the military commander (constable) was taken prisoner. The account is peppered with colorful language of victory, each boast greater than the previous in a way that seems deliberately provocative: "the churches and crosses overthrown [also: swept from the face of the earth]; the leaves of the sacred gospels scattered; the sepulchers of the patriarchs trodden down" and "bodies accumulating on the edge of the sea like islands." He further wrote that women were sold in groups of four for one dinar, and trees and fields were cut down and wood used for building catapult frames and wooden entrenchments to shelter the troops from missiles shot from the walls.

It is perhaps from Baybars's letter and subsequent accounts that Antioch's fate appeared to be over, taken from Baybars's own words. Yet we can also take a step back and understand this account for the purpose it was meant to serve, namely, hyperbole in order to strike fear:

> If you had seen your palace burning in the flames, and the very dead burning in the fire of this world before they could be that of the other, certainly your soul would have exhaled itself away in sighs; your tears, by their abundance, would have extinguished the devouring fire... you know now what to expect; you need not apply to any other to inform you of the truth.

Although we cannot know the extent of damage, we can assume that buildings such as the palace and the Churches of St. Paul and St. Peter (the only two specifically named) were burned (though Badr al-Dīn al-'Aynī, citing Baybars's letter, says the churches were abandoned), people were killed and captured, and treasure was looted. Many monasteries on the Black Mountain were also depopulated and possibly destroyed. Djobadze, in his survey of the region, noted that the Monastery of St. Barlaam had signs of fire throughout.[19] It is likely, however, that the patriarchs of Antioch (Melkite, Latin, and Miaphysite) were all absent at the time of the conquest.[20] Baybars invokes *sūra* 36:13 of the Qur'ān, the parable of the town, reframing its interpretation of apostles arriving to bring the true faith to Antioch as the Mamlūks bringing Islam to Crusader Antioch, connecting his invasion with seventh-century Islamic conquests and the legendary status of the city itself.[21] Baybars did not, however, stay in Antioch but continued on his campaigns. He also settled Turks in the plain to offset the Armenians. A letter by Bar Hebraeus in early 1283 confirms some of this and adds that the Church of Antioch and its dioceses were in desolate condition.

Antioch under the Mamlūks

References to the city of Antioch itself after the Mamlūk conquest are quite patchy. Yet, some visitor accounts give us an indication of how the city fared after the conquest in the last quarter of the thirteenth century and beyond, into the fourteenth and fifteenth centuries. The few mentions of the city in historical accounts suggest that Antioch's administrative importance was dwindling, perhaps because for the Mamlūks it was a border town, far from their heartland in Egypt and under the control of Aleppo. And yet, out of the ashes, the Mamlūks reformulated a new city that was to set the standard until the nineteenth century.

In Ibn Faḍl Allāh al-'Umarī's *Masālik al-Absar fī Mamālik al-Amṣār* (The Ways of Discernment into the Realms of Capital Cities), an administrative geography written around 1337/1338, Aleppo receives a discursive description while Antioch does not; instead, it is mentioned in passing as one of Aleppo's 23 subdistricts and described simply as a "great and famous city."[22] The Egyptian historian Shihāb al-Dīn al-Nūwayrī (d. 1333) makes no mention of the city at all in his 33-volume, 9,000-page encyclopedia *Nihāyat al-arab fī funūn al-adab* (Ultimate Ambition in the Arts of Erudition), a compendium of information on the cosmos, the natural world, human nature, and the history of the world. In *La Fleur des histoires de la terre d'Orient* (Flower of the Histories of the East), written in 1307 by the Armenian nobleman and historiographer Hetoum of Corcyrus (and younger brother of the Armenian king Hetoum I), Antioch gets cursory mention as one of the two great cities (along with Aleppo) in the third province of Syria.[23]

Yet, Badr al-Dīn al-'Aynī states that Antioch at the time of the conquest was large, with 12 miles of ramparts, 130 towers, and 24,000 battlements. The accounts of Ibn Shaddād and the geographers al-Dimashqī and Abū al-Fidā', meanwhile, all discuss the city prior to 1268, suggesting that perhaps the city had indeed been greatly altered and was not now worthy of much discussion. Fourteenth and fifteenth century maps by Western travelers are more idealistic than real (Figures 9.2, 9.3, 9.4) Still, some accounts mention a small number of new buildings and a town still inhabited, though contracted and ruralized. These accounts also refer to a significant population of pastoralist Turkmen living in

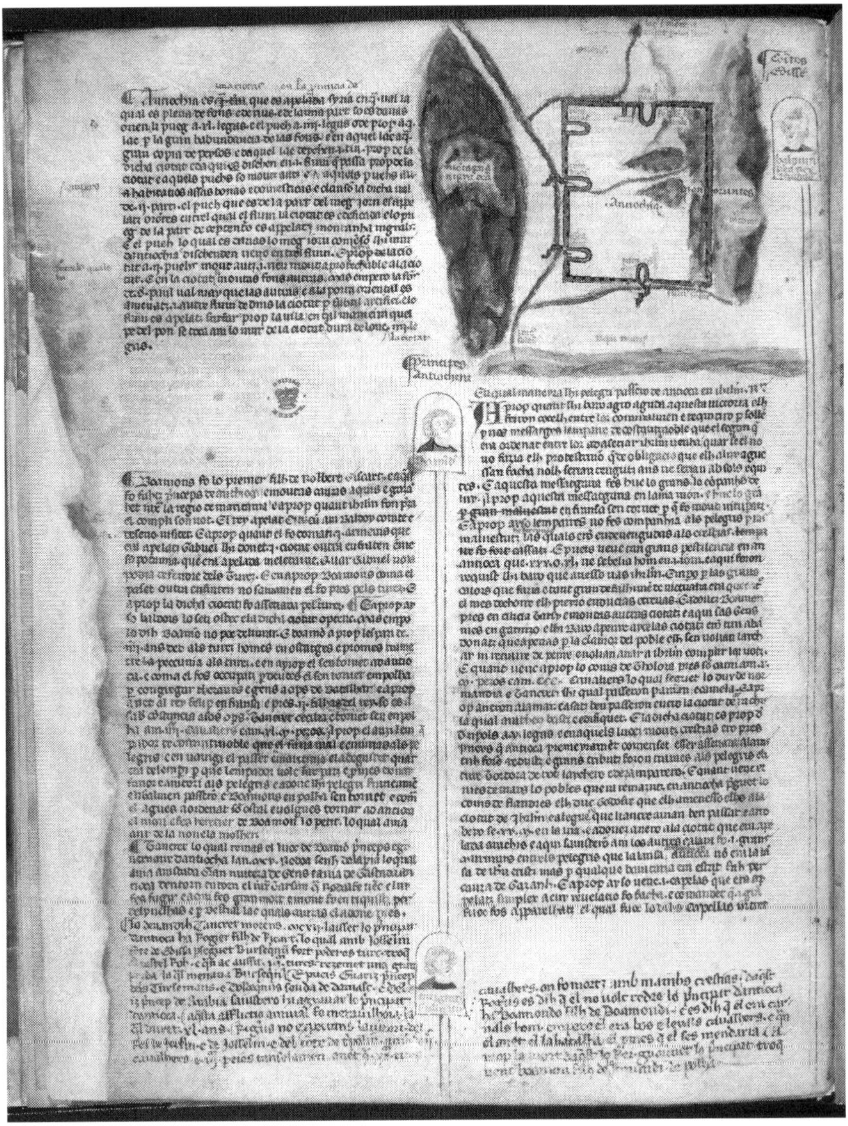

FIGURE 9.2 Antioch from *Compendium gestarum rerum (A Universal History from the Creation of the World to the Death of the Emperor Henry the Seventh)* by Paul of Venice (Paulinus Venetus), 14th century, Egerton MS 1500 f.47v

Source: Courtesy of the British Library

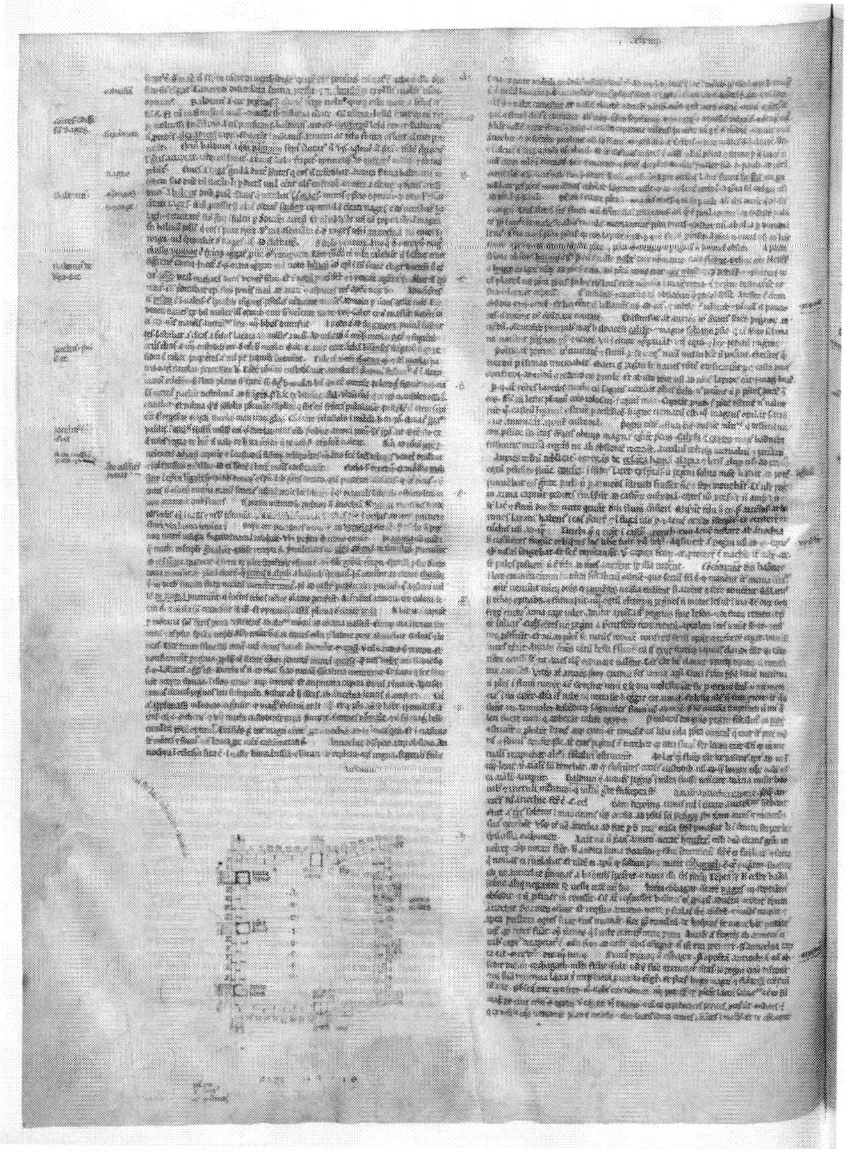

FIGURE 9.3 Antioch from *Chronologia magna* by Paul of Venice (Paulinus Venetus), fourteenth century (1328–1329), 4939 fol. 98v

Source: Courtesy of Bibliothèque Nationale de Paris

and around the city and the continued importance of the textile industry to the town's economy.

Ibn 'Abd al-Ẓāhir gives a brief history and description of Antioch in his biography of Baybars, *al-Rawḍ al-Zahir fī sīrat al-Malik al-Ẓahir* (*The Radiant Gardens in the biography of al-Malik al-Ẓahir*), a play on Baybars's title, *al-malik al-ẓahir* (the

FIGURE 9.4 "Darstellung der Stadt Antiochia 1465," from *History of the First Crusade* by Robertus Monachus, Stiftsbibliothek, Cod. Sang. 658, p. 131

Source: Courtesy of St. Gallen

Ascendant King). He states that there is a lake and on its river are mills, ships (*al-murākib*) that bring goods and produce to it.[24] Although describing its foundation, by the king Asūkhash (a corruption of [al-]Seleucus), we might wonder whether in al-Zahir's day in the mid-thirteenth century, the river was navigable and this statement was based on his own observation. He further writes that the city was built with 153 towers, seven gates (five large ones and two small ones), a place for money (*al-ādar*), shops, and seven channels or embankments (*'awādī*) that drain to the river. He describes the Iron Gate in the Parmenius valley (al-Khashkarūt) as a gate, bridge for people to cross the valley, and dam which controls the flow into the city via two subterranean channels: al-Būlīṭ (known from the Vatican Codex) and al-'Āwiya. The description on the water supply of the city closely matches that of the Abū Makārim (d. 1208) (see Chapter 8) and the Vatican Codex (see Chapter 6), which seem to have been sources for his account. Most interestingly, he calls the Sea Gate the "Gate of Mercy" (*Bāb al-Tarḥīm*), a rare word with religious connotations.[25]

Al-Qalqashandī offers one of the more extensive accounts of the city, calling it old and magnificent, built by King Antiochus and named after him, with a great city wall of stone that had no rival in the world. He cites two earlier works also stating that it was 12 miles in circumference with 24,000 battlements (*shurufāta)* and 136 towers.[26] He further provides information about the water, not only its distribution but also its quality. The waters of the Orontes flowed to the city's houses, buildings, and the congregational mosque, but it also calcified (*yustahajara*) in the sewer drains (*majārīhi*) with such hardness that not even iron could break it, and drinking it caused waves of intestinal pain (*rīyaḥ al-qūlanj*). From this description, it is unclear whether the spring-fed aqueduct from Daphne was still working or how the mountain streams figured into the water-supply system. Further, throughout Antioch's history, water was never supplied from the Orontes, but mountain streams and sewerage were discharged into the river. This is known as early as the days of Polybius who wrote how the Orontes siphoned all of the city's refuse (see Chapter 1). It is no wonder why people became sick from drinking it. Regarding the city's non-Muslim community, Qalqashandī notes that the Christians had a patriarchal seat, and as for its legendary status, he states rather definitively that the city alluded to in *sūra* 36 was Antioch, and that the man who came running from its farthest point was Habīb al-Najjār, whose tomb was a famous pilgrimage site. He also wrote that here weapons rusted and the scent of perfume vanished, taken from the anecdote of Hārūn al-Rashīd and the elderly Antiochene (Chapter 5).[27] Qalqashandī further quotes Ibn Ḥawqal as saying that Antioch was the most touristic (*ānzahu)* place in the region of greater Syria after Damascus.

Despite his overall neglect of the city, Baybars did sponsor some building activity there. Al-Dimashqī, writing around 1300, says that the only monument really left was the tomb of Habīb al-Najjār, which was on the slopes below Mt. Silpius. (He also says that the citadel was still in use, thus also calling into question its destruction by fire during the conquest.) Although no foundation inscription is present, the *madrasa* of the Habīb al-Najjār mosque has an inscription giving the first part of Baybars's honorific title, al-Malik al-Ẓahir, suggesting that the building dates back at least to between 1268 and 1271.[28] If al-Dimashqī is correct, it would indicate that this mosque in its more current form was built or else renovated from an older structure during Baybars's reign. The Ulu Camii (mosque) also dates from Baybars's rule to 1271 based on a square-gridded 16-letter inscription or chronogram that uses a system of numerology that assigns numerical values to the letters (*abjad*).[29] Ibn Shaddād's biography of Baybars mentions that he built a mosque over a church in Antioch;[30] according to Şancı, the Ulu Camii is the likeliest candidate for this conversion, which he says would have been originally the Saljūq mosque turned into a church by the Crusaders.[31] Meanwhile, the Ağca Mosque, largely of Ottoman construction, has lion-head decorations on waterspouts near the roof, which are pre-Ottoman decorative features. Şancı further notes parallels in the Karatay Han and the Sivas Sultan Han around Kayseri and the Alaaddin Mosque in Niğde, among other places. These were thirteenth-century Saljūq buildings, but he hypothesizes that the Ağca example is late thirteenth century, attributed to Baybars, as the lion was his symbol and appeared on many of his buildings.[32] The Kürt Fakih Mosque, whose patron and early history are unknown, further has a minaret feature very similar to Ağca's. The Cündi Ḥammām (bathhouse) was also established by Baybars (but perhaps on earlier remains), as evidenced by an endowment deed detailing how to administer the baths.[33] The Baysari Ḥammām was possibly named after Baybars's brother-in-law or "milk brother" Badr al-Dīn Baysarī (Bı'seri), who participated in the conquest of the city, and can be attributed to Baybars's reign.[34] A third bath, the Saka or Saqqā, known primarily as a sixteenth-century building, may have also been built in the Mamlūk period, based on its Mamlūk-style dome construction.[35] The state of the surviving churches is unknown. There were no active patriarchs in the city that we know of. After the conquest, the Greek Orthodox patriarchate was absent from the city for 100 years, while the Miaphysite patriarchate went to Damascus.[36] Baybars, recognizing the special religious status of Antioch as an Islamic Qur'ānic city, thus re-Islamicized the city by sponsored building or renovation to its two main mosques, possibly two lesser mosques, and two of its baths.

After Baybars's death in July 1277, his son al-Sa'īd Baraka took control of Antioch the following month then transferred it to al-Malik al-'Ādil Sayf al-Dīn Salāmish in August 1279. Three months later, al-Manṣūr Qalāwūn took over the city, later assigning it as part of a treaty as an *iqta'* (land gifted in exchange for service) to the *amīr* Shams al-Dīn Aqsunqur al-Ashqar, along with other cities, which is how it remained at least until the date of Ibn Shaddad's writing, as late as 1285.[37] Qalqashandī wrote that Antioch was one of 12 states, or *wilayāt*, under the *na'īb* (chief official) of Aleppo and was associated with the *niyaba* of al-Qusayr, suggesting that it may have had its own *na'ib* in Qusayr as a subregion of Aleppo.[38] It also had 12 subdistricts, including the port Suwaydīyya. The *walī* of the 12 subdistricts might sometimes be a soldier or prince (*amīr al-'ashara* or Commander of Ten [Mamlūk horsemen], a fairly low rank). During this period, it is possible that the

Sofular Camii, known by its earlier names as the Sheikh Kasim Camii or Erdebili Camii, was originally built, although its first patron is unknown.[39] Several of its features are Mamlūk, including its minaret, which is of the Syrian style, eight sided, and squat, with a pavilion or umbrella-type top, identified by Şancı as Mamlūk. Indeed, this minaret style, visible in about eight mosques today, is one of the signatures that these buildings are pre-Ottoman Mamlūk.

On August 8, 1303, Antioch was struck by another earthquake, causing unspecified damage, according to the fourteenth-century Egyptian historian Ibn al-Dawādārī.[40] Al-Dimashqī wrote that in 1319, parts of the city were damaged by high winds that also "swept away" the monastery of St. Symeon and 300 olive trees. In 1326 the Berber Moroccan scholar and explorer Ibn Baṭṭūṭa (1304–1369) visited the city, where he spent time with the *shaykh* of the Habīb al-Najjār mosque, the pious and venerable Muḥammad b. ʻAlī, over 100 years old but incredibly strong. He was carrying wood into the city on his shoulders to his garden in his home.[41] Ibn Baṭṭūṭa reported that the city wall, formerly unrivaled in its strength, was still in ruins after Baybars's assault. Yet he also commented the city was densely populated, with beautiful buildings, abundant water, and many trees, and was overall a large and noble town. Next to its main feature, the tomb of Habīb al-Najjār, was a Sufi *zāwiya* school run by the aforementioned *shaykh*, who gave food to all who came. In May/June 1335 most of the city was burned, as well as Ḥamā, although little else is known about the cause or rebuilding.[42] Antioch was now a small, heavily contracted town. It may be during this period that the Sarimiye mosque, known as an Ottoman mosque, was originally built.[43] The Mahremiye Mosque, also from the Ottoman period, has similarities in elements of the minaret and may be contemporary.

A 1359 *waqf* document illustrates that Antioch was a growing town, full of mosques, bathhouses, and markets.[44] The *waqf* was for the monumental Mosque of Sultan Ḥasan, built in Cairo between 1356–1363 and begun under the rule of Sultan Ḥasan (r. 1354–1361) but never completed. As half of the city inside and outside of the wall (12 shares) contributed to the Cairo mosque's endowment, the document contains an account of a state visit to Antioch 15 years prior. The description of the city was written by the historian Ibn Habīb, who joined the *amīr* Sharaf al-Dīn Mūsā on a tour of the northern lands of the Mamlūks in 1343–4 in order to inspect properties that belonged, or were tied to, the state treasury (*bayt al-mal*). Interestingly, revenues and values are not listed, only property ownership. This tour was ordered by Sultan al-Kāmil Shaʻbān (r. 1345–1346). Just several years after the tour, between 1348–1349, the Black Death plague struck the city of Antioch, perhaps by sea, as it was spread up and down the Levantine coast. Its effect on the city is not known with any detail, but many of its population fled northwards to Anatolia, leaving its districts depopulated. These lands, having declined in value, were acquired by state and also contributed to the *waqf* of the Mosque of Sultan al-Ḥasan, which was never completed.[45]

The *waqf* document states that the city, namely the Muslim enclave (*ʻimara islamiyya*), was a contracted settlement in the southwest quarter of the city within the larger walls, which were intact but had parts ready to collapse. Between the Islamic town and the walls were extensive swaths of ruined (*kharab*) and denuded (*'atala*) lands given over to mulberry trees and other orchards and gardens among crumbling Christian (*rumaniyya)* buildings including the unidentified Church of al-Finān[46] and the Church of al-Sayyida (presumably the Theotokos) and a rich home called the Dār al-Zīr. The omission of the citadel suggests it was not rebuilt or reoccupied. There were four main gates in use and connected to main routes in and out of the city, and some minor gates. The four main gates were the Aleppo Gate, Garden Gate (previously Duke Gate), Sea/Bridge Gate, and Daphne Gate (called Qaṣr, referring perhaps to the nearby castle of Qusayr/Cursarium). Four other gates are mentioned, including the Bāb Bāshūra (Gate of the Tower) to the south and the Bāb al-Ḥur (Gate of the Free or Noble) on the river side. The former may identify with a postern gate at Tower 9 on Justinian's southern refortified city wall, mentioned by Emmanuel Guillaume-Rey in his 1850s map that was east of the Daphne Gate on the slopes and called the Olive Gate (see Figure 10.9). The towers on the southern wall would have been likely better preserved. The Bāb al-Ḥ ur was perhaps the same as the Dog Gate. The Bāb al-Aqmayn is written in Ibn Kathīr as Bāb Qamayn or Qamīn. Its meaning, Gate of the Furnace (*qamīn*), suggests a bath, which is reinforced by the fact that the Ḥammām al-Saqqā was just south of it. As this bath was to the north of the enclave, this suggests that the gate was likely just north of it and that perhaps this enclave was encircled and demarcated somehow from the rest of the now ruralized city. The last unidentified gate is the Bāb al-Arb'aīn (Gate of the Forty), which is near the market. It is likely that it refers and leads to a shrine to the Forty Martyrs, originally derived from the Forty Martyrs of Sebaste but adapted into Islamic tradition to denote 40 companions of the Prophet Muhammad who died. One is known from the Crusader period outside the city walls that may have actually been within St. Barlaam (see Chapter 8). The description of the gate may suggest one inside the city, and if so, may refer to the Ulu Camii, which local lore states used to be a Church of the Forty Martyrs (see Chapter 5). The valley east of the city, presumably the Parmenius valley, is called the Spring of Thieves ('Ayn al-Ḥarāmiyya).

The document mentions what lay beyond each gate, as well. Outside the Aleppo Gate was land owned by the state treasury, and beyond it were five lands or villages – M'ashuqa, Iṣṭabiya, Baṭriya, Karīḥ, and the village of al-Sitūn – all near the Orontes. M'ashuqa retained its name, as known from the Princeton excavations (Machouka, sector 9-U/V/W), less than 1 km beyond the city wall. In addition there were olive and mulberry orchards owned by the state treasury, a tower called Burj Kūmayn (Tower of the Two Mounds, perhaps what was left of the Crusader Malregard Tower?) a market called the Sūq al-Balad (Country Market), and three ruined olive presses (*m'aṣara)*. Outside the western Garden Gate, there were private orchards and a mill on the Orontes, the Bustān al-Abyaḍ (White Garden), Bustān al-Ziyāda (the Other Garden), and Ibn al-Ṣābūnī mill, presumably used for soap manufacture and run by a family of soap makers. This mill was connected to a water-wheel (*nā'ūra*) and ruined bathhouse (*ḥammām*). Interestingly, the text speaks of a building in the middle of the Orontes called *maṣṭaba al-Sitt*, which may translate in this case to the hippodrome of the lady.[47] As the *waqf* account hardly mentions any ancient buildings of the city, this (1) may indicate that the surveyor and writer of the account recognized that the ruins of the classical hippodrome were indeed identifiable as a hippodrome and (2) calls into question, perhaps, whether Antioch's famous royal Island, assumed to be no longer as such by the fourteenth century by the redirection of the Orontes channel, was still recognizably, or at least referred to, as still an Island. There also is reference to an island in the river, not necessarily the same one, with mulberry trees. Also, in this western area was a reference to a River of the Beehive Workshops (*al-'assālāt*), although it is unclear what additional river is being referred to here. Beyond the southern Daphne Gate were orchards of fig trees and vineyards near a valley with a bridge. Some vineyards belonged to Sunqur. There was a dilapidated mill and orchard of saplings belonging to *amīr* Naṣr al-Dīn Muḥammad b. al-Shujā'and Bahādir b. 'Aynu.

The small Islamic enclave, in the southwest part of the city, may have been a quarter the size of the classical city, but the *waqf* document enumerates many buildings and emphasizes that the Muslims renewed it (*istajadaha*), in contrast to the rest of the city within the walls. The Arab community was led by a local head, Ṣārim al-Dīn, the *na'ib al-'arab*. It had two congregational mosques – an unnamed one called the Great Mosque (*jamī'a al-kabīr*), which can be assumed to be the Ulu Camii and described as populous (*m'amur*), and the Mosque of Habīb al-Najjār, attached to a shrine-tomb (*maqām*). In addition, there were 35 *masjids*, even though the text says 23 newly added by the Muslims, all named after individuals who presumably were their patrons: Hājj 'Abdullāh al-Qalānisī, 'Abd al-Raḥman al-Maghribī, Abī Bakr al-Fawāl, Aḥmad al-Batwānī, Aḥmad al-Ḥalabī, Hājj Aḥmad b. Ḥasan, Hājj 'Alī al-Dakhsūrī, Akhī 'Alī, Shaykh 'Alī al-Sarmantī, 'Alī al-Banā, Hājj Bākī, Dār al-Bartar, Baysarī, Faqīh al-Naṣrāt, Fāris and Shaykh Khalīl, Hājj Khalīl (possibly the same as the previously mentioned), Shaykh Khamīs, Hājj Ḥasan, Faqīh Ḥusayn, Qadī Jamāl al-Dīn Wardī, Maḥmūd al-Jashārī, Maḥmūd al-Jābī, Marwān al-Kurdī, Shaykh Mūsā, Marāwātiya, Shujā'a al-Dīn, Sirāj, Salama, Faqīh Ṣāliḥ (Ibn) Sāṭlamish, Faqīh Sa'īd, Yūsuf al-Barānī, Yūsuf al-Qarmī, and the Masjid dedicated to the Almighty God (Lillah Ta'alī). Around some of the mosques and *masjids* were small vegetable gardens that were leased (*hakūra*). There were also two pilgrimage shrines (*zāwiyas*), the Zāwiya of Akhī Aḥmad and the Zāwiya of 'Adawiya. In total, this is a remarkable number of religious buildings given the reduced size of the city after the Islamic conquest. By contrast, throughout the Early Islamic and Saljūq periods, we know of only one or two mosques. There were also *qadīs* and *faqīhs*. The post-Crusader city had become firmly Islamicized.

There were three other bathhouses besides the ruined one, the aforementioned Baysarī, Ibn al-Saqqā (or Saqqā), and Dār al-Batrar, as well as seven *khāns*, each named after a person, likely the patron – Maḥmūd, Shujā'al-Dīn, Kīshī, Ibn Ṣāliḥ, 'Alī al-Jām'a, Fakhr al-Dīn (the *qadī*), and Qarāsunqur (an *amīr*).[48] There was a prison located in a tower (*burj al-ḥabs*) and jail (*sijin*); whether they were different places or the same is unclear. The most detailed description, however, concerns the large commercial district (*haḍara*) of the city, centered between and north of the two congregational mosques and on the western side of the city near the river, where they are today. This included a large central area (*maydān*),[49] central slaughterhouse (*maslakh*), bakery (*al-furn*), oil press (*m'aṣara*), tannery (*madbagha*), dye workshop (*maṣbagha*), place for harvested crops ('*arḍa*), and a granary (*qaṣṣāra*).[50] The market consisted of several streets, each dedicated to specific commodities. The Merchant's Market (*Sūq al-Tijār*) was the largest, with 27 shops on either side, located just west of the mosque. Other markets included the goldsmiths/jewelers (*ṣāgha*), the cobblers (*āsākifa*), cotton weavers (*qaṭānīn*), butchers (*qaṣābīn*), carpenters (*najārīn*) (with a wholesale market or *qayṣarīya*), reed mat-makers (*ḥaṣriyīn*), spice/perfume dealers (*'aṭṭārīn*), cooks (*ṭabbākhīn*), butter makers (*shammānīn*), milk sellers (in the courtyard of dairy shops, *sāḥa al-laban*), blacksmiths (*ḥādadīn*), makers of travel equipment or horse tack (*muraḥilīn*), barley dealers (*sha'ārīn*),[51] and Hājj Khālid's market, an unknown individual. This last market had two sitting areas (*maq'adayn*). The markets were overseen by an inspector (*muḥtasib*) named Sharaf al-Dīn who, himself, owned a lot of commercial property, although another is named, Aḥmad al-Muḥtasib. Of course, there were many merchants and traders, including a veterinarian.

Perhaps most importantly, the names given as owners, patrons, and founders of markets, mosques, and *khāns* show not only a significant number of middle-class private citizens but suggest their influential role in renewing and running the town. There are about 123 names listed, which when placed alongside a reference to 300 houses in 1432 (mentioned later) seems quite extraordinary, as it suggests, on a basic level, that roughly half the town not only owned property but were investors in property throughout the town beyond their own homes. Six of these property-owners were women. About 26 of these bore the title Hajj, indicating they made the pilgrimage to Mecca, while four were considered *faqīh* (Islamic jurists), and five had the title of *shaykh* (a scholar or a religious, perhaps Sufi, leader). The *qadī*, or chief Islamic judge, was Fakhr al-Dīn'Uthmān, patron of a *khān*; a prayer caller (*mu'adhadhin*) was Aḥmad. There were also three mentioned *amīrs*, Mamlūks likely appointed and not local: Aḥmad, Naṣr al-Dīn Muḥammad b. al-Shujā', and Shams al-Dīn Qarāsunqur (al-Manṣūrī), ruler (*na'ib*) of Aleppo from 1282–3, and also patron of a *khān*. Further, most of the names are Arabic, and few suggest Mamlūk (Turkic) individuals, indicating that Mamlūk patronage in the city was minimal and also raising the probability that many were long-standing old Arab residents of the city who lived during its Crusader occupation. There are virtually no discernible Christian or Jewish names, though this is not so surprising, as this is a document detailing Islamic religious endowments. Lastly, Antioch, although greatly reduced, was an entrepôt frontier town with a wide range of goods bought and sold, all of which helped pay for the extensive religious buildings around the town.

During the expansion of the Turco-Mongolian Timūrid Empire under its founder Timūr (or Tamerlane the Great, 1336–1405), Antioch was spared and protected, much as it had been by the Mongols. In 1401, Timūr, though not targeting Antioch specifically, sent an army of 5,000 men under Mirza Sultan

Ḥusayn from Ḥimṣ to the Orontes toward Antioch. Part of his motivation was to ensure that local Dulkadırlı and Köpeklü Türkmen did not try to raid or take the city for themselves, thus indicating he was invested in protecting it.[52] The armies, however, were unable to approach the city because of "great waters, sloughs and marshes."[53] Although unsubstantiated, Evliya Çelebi states that Timūr did enter Antioch and gazed upon the tomb of Habīb al-Najjār and found it to be very fresh.[54] Üzerli and Gündüzlü Turkomans also tried to control Antioch during the fifteenth century.[55] Early in the century an earthquake struck the city in a wave of three shocks on April 29, 1407, which damaged houses and claimed lives.[56] The following year on December 29, 1408, another earthquake struck, though no specific damage is mentioned.

Among the earliest Western descriptions of Antioch is that furnished by Bertrandon de la Brocquiere (c. 1400–1459), a Burgundian secret agent of Philip the Good, Duke of Burgundy, who in 1432/1433 made a pilgrimage to Rome, the Holy Land, and Constantinople, vividly recounted in his *Le Voyage d'Outremer*. Visiting Antioch in 1432, he called it the capital of Turcomania and Armenia, describing it as a very considerable town that had once been very flourishing, with handsome walls in good repair but no more than 300 houses. The city and region's ruler was Ramedang (Ṣārim al-Dīn Ībrāhīm Bey Ramazanoğlu, d. 1416), whom Bertrandon describes as a good, rich, and valiant man feared even by the Ottoman sultan (Murad I). The latter, wishing to destroy Ramedang, conspired with a Karaman (of the Karamanid/Karamanoğullları *beylik* or principality) trusted by Ramedang and brother of his wife. One day while they were eating, the Karaman had him arrested and turned him over to the sultan, who put him to death and took over Turcomania, giving part of it to the Karaman. The Ramazanids (Ramazanoğullları) were a small Turkmen dynasty that lasted two centuries and ruled Adhana, Iskandarūna, and parts of northern Syria. Their rule ended during the reign of the Ottoman Sultan Sulaymān I (1520–1566), the sultan turning them into pashas. This reveals the precariousness of the area in the fifteenth century – mostly a frontier region under Turkic *beylik*s facing the Mamlūk territories to the south – and the Mamlūks' tenuous hold at this time. This instability was also compounded by still depopulated rural districts, also mentioned by Bertrandon as having occurred during the Black Death.[57] While sedentary communities of farmers and villagers fled and were more susceptible to the plague, pastoralists were likely less affected, being less tied to urban areas. In this period, they controlled the city.

Bertrandon also goes into obsessively great detail on the sheep and goats of Antioch, stating that their ears were long and hanging, typical of Syrian species, and whiter than others, with long, large, and fat tails.[58] Most of the population was Turcoman or Arab (perhaps descendants of the Turks settled by Baybars) with their grazing animals – camels, goats, cows, and sheep, the handsomest he had ever seen. They took advantage of the Orontes River, giving evidence for the city's contraction, ruralization, and pastoralism. Curiously, Bertrandon mentions that water buffalo were used not only as pack animals but also as riding mounts. His descriptions speak to the Turkmen pastoralist population of the area and their stimulation of the already well-known textile industry associated with Antioch into the fifteenth century. Around 1300, Rashīd al-Dīn (1247–1318), the well-known historian and physician, asked his son, who was governor of Qinnasrin, to send 50 camlet (wool/*ṣūf* or goat hair) weavers to Antioch as well as to Sis, Tarsus, and Tabriz, perhaps in efforts to improve their economic production. Inventories of churches in Britain from the late thirteenth/early fourteenth centuries mention specific textiles from Antioch, which possibly were obtained from the city after the Mamlūk conquest.[59] A colony of Italian merchants was part of this textile industry.

Some 30 years after Bertrandon's visit, Basil the Merchant, arriving from Aleppo in 1465/1466, described the city favorably and even surprisingly: immense and as great as Constantinople but no longer an imperial ruling city, and under the control of the Muslims, as was Constantinople now as well, having fallen to the Turks in 1453.[60] He stated it was situated on seven hills (part of the trope that all great cities like Rome, Constantinople, and Jerusalem were built on seven hills) with seven gates. He was able to see the ancient walls in the city banded with iron on houses and covered with lead. The bridge was preserved with four arches, and he wrote that in the middle of the bridge was a gate of iron and flanking towers with arrow slits. Basil also mentioned that the city had many Christians but they still were a minority, along with people of other religions, and that in the center of the city was the Church of St. Sophia, though it is unclear which church he was actually referring to.

On October 9, 1477, the Mamlūk Sultan Qāi'itbāy toured the northern parts of his territory and the Mamlūk-Turkmen frontier to assess his lands and towns and implement necessary repairs. His chronicler, Ibn Jī'ān, noted that Antioch still had strong fortifications and enormous walls 12 miles long with 136 towers and 24,000 crenellations. The city was rich with shops and had many people, most of whom were Turks, whom he called uncivilized. Most houses had gables covered with thatch called *burda*. He also mentioned the tomb of Habīb al-Najjār. Just three years earlier, renovations had been made to the Mosque of Habīb al-Najjār, as noted by an inscription between one of the doors to the courtyard and minaret. Above all, Ibn Jī'ān noted the city's ruralization and self-sufficiency, "so that the whole city with its crops, its fields, its properties, and its river [likely alluding to the Parmenius] lies within the walls" (see Figure 5.15).[61]

Archaeology of the Mamlūk period

In contrast to the city's growth, the settlement evidence from the Amuq Valley Regional Project survey suggests that the plain entered a serious decline in the fourteenth century, after the end of the Crusader period. This would tend to support the accounts of contemporary European travelers who came to the region, although the decline may not have been as serious as their laments for the fate of Antioch might suggest. One reason for the downturn in settlement may be that the region was no longer a focus of Mamlūk attention, apart from extracting heavy taxes. The textual evidence suggests powerful Turkmen pastoralists who inhabited the plains and were independent from urban areas. But the potential resulting increase in nomadic settlement in the area would be difficult to observe in the survey data. Only a few coins have been found in the area, and there is a distinct lack of pottery that can be definitely dated to this period. It is possible that the fact that Middle Islamic types continued to be produced after the Mamlūk conquest of the Frankish territory hampers recognition of the pottery of this phase. Thus, it remains a possibility that many of the sites discussed in the previous period continued to be inhabited, probably into the fourteenth century.

In the town, there are few physical remains at present that we can attribute to Mamlūk Antioch, including both architecture and material culture. This is due to sedimentation and areas excavated. Jean Lassus alluded to a Mamlūk layer of destruction in sector 21/22-J, which is the only evidence found of actual destruction caused by human conquest in the city's archaeological record. The excavations suggest that during the Mamlūk period, silt and sediment accumulated in parts of the city to a depth of several meters. For example, the two most recent levels in sector 17-P of a house with kiln, attributed to the Middle Byzantine period, were covered by 4 m of sediment (Figure 9.5).[62] This would have buried most of the ancient and even medieval structures, with the exception of the walls and hippodrome. The city's sedimentation indicates that its rulers did little to put into place protective measures against flooding from the Orontes and Parmenius following the city's conquest. Assuming the *waqf* document detailing the contracted

FIGURE 9.5 17-P, general view of Level 1 excavations, looking west, 4104

Source: Courtesy of the Antioch Expedition Archives, Department of Art and Archaeology, Princeton University; Princeton

town surrounded by fields of ruins and gardens is correct, then very few sectors excavated by Princeton actually fall in this area. With the exception of 21/22-J/K, most of the ones we have seen important in the Early Islamic and Middle Byzantine periods, such as 17-O, 17-P, 16-O, 16-P, 13-R, and even 19-M, would have been outside the Mamlūk enclave; the Princeton team hardly dug within the Mamlūk town (Figure 9.6).

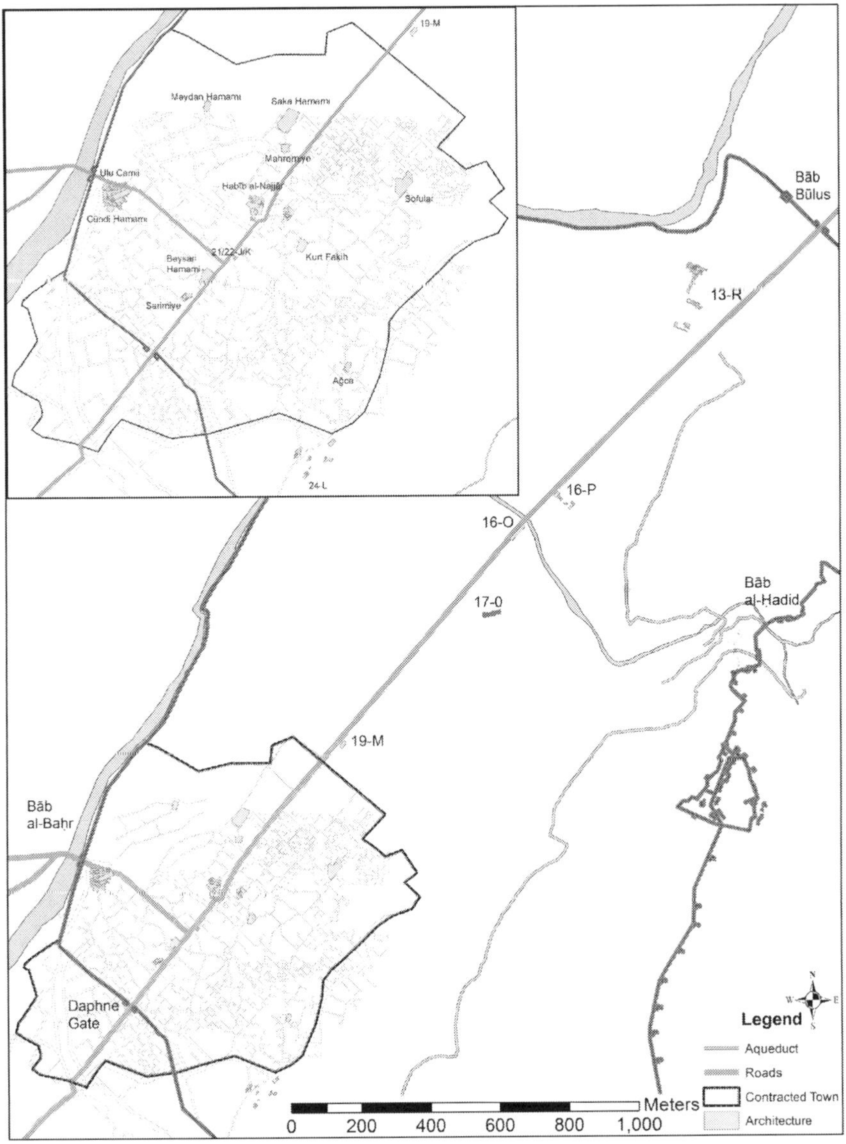

FIGURE 9.6 Plan of Mamlūk Antioch

Source: Created by Steve Batiuk

FIGURE 9.7 Coin from Mamlūk coin hoard, 8643; reverse (bottom) and obverse (top)

Source: Courtesy of Princeton University, Firestone Library Numismatic Collection, ex. Peter J. Donald Collection

Although the Mamlūks, unsurprisingly, did not establish a mint in Antioch, a large hoard of about 300 unpublished Mamlūk coins – mostly dirhams but some fulūs – was excavated from the cemetery area in sector 24-L in the city's southeast, on the border of the Mamlūk enclave. Mostly from the mint of Aleppo, they have legible dates going up to about 1398 and may have been buried in anticipation of Timūr's assault on the city (Figure 9.7).[63] Associated with this hoard were 25 tripods under a cement floor, which would have been used in pottery production.

Some had green or brown glaze residue. A sherd of black painted turquoise underglaze (Raqqa ware) was found in the same context and is contemporary. This assemblage suggests the presence of pottery production on the city's edge during the fourteenth century in the Mamlūk period.

Conclusion

Antioch under the Mamlūks decreased in physical size and population and was relatively insignificant administratively. In part, its extensive destruction during the conquest was a strategic movement to remove any remaining Crusader presence permanently and seal off the coast from easy incursions. Yet Antioch was also a frontier town. Far from Cairo, it received fewer benefits and less infrastructure, patronage, and attention than other Mamlūk towns and fortifications farther south, though it remained a buffer against expansionist Turkic regimes. Although the boundaries of the Mamlūk frontier extended farther north, the town's surroundings were strongly of Turkmen nomads. Because of this local pastoralist population, the area's economy remained centered on textile production and trade. Antioch was not, however, forgotten. The town boasted between six and eight mosques and four *ḥammāms*, not a small number for a town with around only 300 houses. Further, several of these buildings were established by the Sultan Baybars himself, who sought to re-Islamicize the city that he recognized as holy. Antioch was now decidedly reimagined in the wake of the Mamlūk destruction; it became a medieval Islamic town. Its complex and intertwined system of religious endowments linking spiritual and eonomic institutions was to be the template for the Ottoman city.

Notes

1 Apocryphal/apocalyptic tale of the *Testament of Our Lord Jesus Christ*, addressed to the Apostle Peter. See Graff 1944; Debié 2005, 111–146.
2 Ibn ʻAbd al-Ẓāhir 1976, 313.
3 F. Şancı, 2006. "Hatay İlinde Türk Mimarisi I," PhD diss., Ankara University, Ankara.
4 E. Çakar, 2015. "16. Yüzyılda Antakya Vakıfları (1550 Tarihli Evkaf Defterine Göre) [The Waqfs of Antioch in the 16th Century]," *Vakıflar Dergisi* 43 (June): 9–39.
5 Abu al Fidā' 1872.
6 Amitai-Press 2009, 54.
7 An example is Grigor of Aknerts'i or Gregory of Akner (2003, 15.10), who writes:

> Now during these days the sultan of Egypt came against the city of Antioch which he took and demolished to its foundations, mercilessly destroying and enslaving to the point that it is impossible to relate what the foreigners did to the believers in Christ.

8 Ibn ʻAbd al-Ẓāhir 1976, 132, 307.
9 In Ibn ʻAbd al-Ẓāhir 1976, 307, he is called *kandāṣṭabl*.
10 Bar Hebraeus 1932, 448 (525). This is his last mention of the city in his chronicle. His last year of his history, for when he claims the city was in ruin, is 1297.
11 *TIB* 590.
12 "Les gestes des Chiprois." 1906, 3.641.
13 Madden 2006, 181.

14 Al-Maqrīzī 1837–1845, 53 (343).
15 Al-Maqrīzī 1837–1845, 53–54 (343); Ibn 'Abd al-Zahir 1976, 323–324.
16 Ibn al-Furāt 1971; Badr al Din al-'Aynī 1887; Ibn 'Abd al-Zahir 1976, 324.
17 Troadec 2013, 107–125, including also Ibn 'Abd al-Ẓāhir 1976, 309–313, whose version of the letter toggles back and forth between hyperbolic boasting and a more sequential and subdued narrative of events.
18 Reinaud 1827, 65–93; Mufaḍḍal 1973.
19 Djobadze 1976, 108; Djobadze 1986, 6.
20 *TIB* 630.
21 As Baybars himself had no legitimacy as an Islamic ruler, he acquired this status by referencing people and places that were part of the Islamic "cultural memory" of greater Syria. This is a good example. For more, see Troadec 2014–15, 113–147. This letter is also part of pseudo-*futūḥ* literature, reviving the spirit of the Islamic conquests during the Crusades. Donner 1991, 53.
22 Al-'Umarī 2017.
23 Hetoum 1988, 18, line 13; Hayton 1906 supplies more detail referencing the Crusader siege.
24 Ibn 'Abd al-Ẓāhir 1976, 314.
25 Ibid., 316. This word seems to be only found in *tafsir* (Qur'ānic exegesis) literature. Thanks to Kyle Brunner.
26 This duplicates Mas'ūdī's description and is corroborated in Middle Byzantine sources, though Qalqashandī refers to two other works. Ibn Kathīr (1997, vol. 17, 476) also describes Antioch at the time of Baybars's conquest as 12 miles with 136 towers and 24,000 battlements.
27 Qalqashandī 1987, vol. 4, 133–134, no attribution to Hārūn.
28 Tekin 1993, 52.
29 However, this is still quite unusual and rare for a Mamlūk period inscription based on its style, and looks Ottoman, according to Doris Behrens-Abouseif, personal communication.
30 Ibn Shaddād 1983, 358.
31 Şancı 2006, n. 79.
32 Ibid., 159.
33 Sahillioğlu 1991, 230–231.
34 See Rifaioğlu 2018b for this and other *ḥammāms* of this period. It is possible that the Meydan Hamamı goes back even earlier to the Saljūq period, although Şancı 2006, 342, does not agree.
35 Şancı 2006, 350.
36 Ibn Kathīr 1997, vol. 18, 715 mentions a certain Bashāra known as Mīkhā'īl who was recognized as patriarch of Antioch. This may be the Miaphysite patriarch Michael II (born Barsoum, d. 1312).
37 Ibn Kathīr 1997: vol. 17, 571.
38 *TIB* 591; al-Qalqashandī says he was told this by some secretaries (*kutāb*) of Aleppo; 1987, vol. 4, 236/7.
39 Şancı 2006, 62.
40 Ibn al-Dawādārī, *Kanz al-Durar* via Guidoboni 1994, 348, 361.
41 Ibn Baṭṭuṭa 1962.
42 Ibn Kathīr 1997, vol. 17, 375.
43 Attributed either to Ṣārīm al-Dīn b. Şaybanī, ruler of Baghrās under Malik Naṣr (1299–1341), or to Ṣārīm al-Dīn Ībrāhīm Bey Ramazanoğlu, ruler of the Ramazanids from 1378 to 1383, Şancı 2006, 151. Şancı suggests Ṣārim al-Dīn b. Şaybanī is the likelier of the two. However, the 1350 *waqf* mentioned others with the same name; it may be attributed to Ṣārim al-Dīn, head of the community (*na'ib al-'Arab*), Ṣārim al-Dīn Ibrahim al-Badāwī, or Ṣārim al-Dīn al-M'utī.
44 I am indebted to Doris Behrens-Abouseif for bringing this text to my attention and for sharing her presentation on it with me. H. N. al-Ḥarithy (ed. and annot.) 2001. *Kitāb*

waqf al-Sulṭān al-Nāṣir Ḥasan b. Muḥammad ibn Qalāwūn ʿalā madrasatihi bi-al-Rumayla [The Waqf Document of Sultan al-Nāṣir Ḥasan b. Muḥammad b. Qalāwūn for his complex in al-Rumaila]. Beirut: Das Arabische Buch. The *waqf* exists in two copies in the Dar al-Wathā'iq al-Qawmiyya in Cairo: (n. 40/6, on original parchment but partial only; and n. 365/85, bound and more complete).

45 M. Dols, 1977. *The Black Death in the Middle East*. Princeton University Press, 62: He writes on p. 174:

> In the case of Antioch, the horses of the dead fugitives returned, and the people who had remained in the city followed the horses back to their dead colleagues. The survivors took what the others had abandoned and came back to the city, only to be overtaken by plague themselves.
>
> *(Taken from al-Maqrīzī (d. 1442), 1971)*

46 Which church is indicated is unknown. *Finān* in modern Arabic usage refers to "artist." It is interesting that a relatively little-known church, such as that of St. Luke, who was also known as an artist and patron saint of artists and from Antioch, and first definitively mentioned by Wilbrand von Oldenburg in 1211, should be one of the two main churches remembered in this description. The expected church, alongside the Theotokos, to be remembered is rather St. Peter's (al-Qusiyān). One other possibility is that al-Finān is a scribal error for al-Qusiyān.

47 The word *maṣṭaba* means a bench or even more specifically benches of a mosque; however, in Mamlūk chronicles and *waqf* accounts, it can refer to a hippodrome (and more specifically, then, the seats of the hippodrome). Behrens-Abouseif 1981, 169.

48 Perhaps Shams al-Dīn Qarasunqur, the *na'ib* of Aleppo

49 A *maydān* in this period usually referred to a hippodrome or polo ground, but could be a park. It is difficult to see where this would be in the contracted urban Islamic enclave of fourteenth-century Antioch, with the exception possibly along the river bank. The old hippodrome was outside the city, as mentioned in n. 47 and as reinforced separately in the Ottoman period when travelers visit the ruins of the hippodrome, which are clearly not associated with the market and bath known as Maydan/Meydan. The meaning of *maydān* as a central square is more modern. See Behrens-Abouseif 1981, 169–170.

50 The term *ʿarḍa* as a place for crops is undetermined but assumed, based on reference to harvests being there. The term *qaṣṣāra* is suggested, as the document gives the term *qaḍāra*, which is not an Arabic word and assumed to be a scribal error (Doris Behrens-Abouseif, personal communication).

51 But in the early twentieth century, this market of the same name made goat-hair bags and tents.

52 Yücel 1989, 110.

53 Cherefeddin Ali 1723, 203, Chapter 28.

54 Çelebi 1999, 38 (36).

55 Sümer 1963, 1–112.

56 Karabacak et al. 2010, 172–182; Akyuz et al. 2006, 281–293.

57 Dols 1977, 165.

58 Bertrandon de la Broquière 1892. *Le Voyage d'Outremer*. Ch. Schefer. Paris: Ernest Leroux, 83–88.

59 See Vorderstrasse 2010, 169.

60 Basil the Merchant 1889, 255.

61 Devonshire 1922, 1–43. Some watermills on the Orontes, such as those at Sultan Merkezi to the north of the city, found on the Amuq Survey, also date to this period.

62 But sector 21/22-J had 4 m of sediment which accumulated in the Saljūq and Crusader periods. Lassus was able to date this to before the Mamlūk conquest not by pottery but by encountering a destruction layer assumed to be Mamlūk.

63 Not in published reports of Miles coin catalogue in Princeton's *Antioch II*, 2.

10

OTTOMAN ANTAKYA (1516–1918)

> The more I wandered through the narrow paved streets the more delightful did they appear. Except the main thoroughfare, which is the bazaar, they were almost empty… . The shallow gables covered with red tiles gave a charming and very distinctive note to the whole city, and shuttered balconies jutted out from house to house.
>
> – Gertrude Bell, *The Desert and the Sown*

Introduction

Antioch's least understood era, though rich in texts, is the period under Ottoman rule, from 1516 to 1918. This 400-year time span, though lacking much in the way of Ottoman sources and archaeological evidence, remains full of accounts from the many travelers who visited the city. From these reports we can piece together the city through their various descriptions while carefully stepping around the often quite overt orientalist filter these travelers saw through. Moreover, combining the evidence from Ottoman records and travelers' accounts with physical remains allows us to establish a link between the assumed destruction of Antioch by the Mamlūks and its evident survival to the present day. This link can more specifically be understood as one of continuity, connecting an important period in the life of the city with its past and its future. This continuity must, however, be tempered. Following the Mamlūk conquest, Antioch was much smaller physically, with a reduced population, but nevertheless remained an important trading entrepôt and production area operating within far-ranging networks of commerce; it was also a religious and educational center, and its history and legend made it an important destination for many travelers and place of abode for its residents. Although as a sleepy town it did not feature in any major historical events during the Ottoman era, by the end of the period, in the nineteenth and early twentieth centuries, we can begin to observe the city's modernization and "Westernization" as it was transformed and rebuilt out of a medieval city to its present-day role as capital of the province of Hatay in Turkey.

Antioch under the Ottomans

Antioch finally came into Ottoman possession in 1516 in the course of the Ottoman Empire's dramatic expansion in the fifteenth and sixteenth centuries (Figure 10.1). In May 1453, the Ottomans brought to an end the 1,000-year reign of the Byzantine Empire when Sultan Mehmet II (1451–1481) conquered Constantinople. Then, in August 1516, Sultan Selim I (1512–1520) dealt the Mamlūks, under Sultan al-Ghūrī (d. 1516), a heavy blow at the Battle of Marj Dabiq just north of Aleppo, thereby gaining all of Syria, which Selim put under the control of his grand vizier, Yunus Paşa (d. 1517). The following year the Ottomans took Egypt as well, thus also putting an end to the Mamlūk Empire. Located along military routes, Antioch was a key stop for Ottoman forces on their way to conquer the Mamlūks and spread their power to the southern Levant, Arabia, Egypt, and North Africa. Likewise, the city served as a stopping point for pilgrims on the annual *hajj* pilgrimage to Mecca from Anatolia and Istanbul, and for merchants as well. Its economic importance increased after Iskenderun (Alexandretta) became the main port of Aleppo, replacing Tripoli in the mid-sixteenth century, thereby making Antioch the main halfway stop on this important commercial corridor. At first Antioch was part of the *beylerbey* (province) of greater Syria, or Shām, beginning in 1522. Then it became a *kazā* (subdistrict) under the *sanjak* (district) or *paşalık* of Aleppo and was eventually run by an *ağa* (general officer) and *qadī* (Muslim judge). Between 1516 and 1581 it wavered in status between *kazā* and *sanjak*. Its first governor was Bıyıklı Mehmed Paşa (d. 1521). During this early period, the pastoralist Doğancıoğlu Türkmen, who inhabited the Amuq Valley and region of Antioch, still carried a certain amount of power over the city. Twenty years after its absorption into the empire, Sultan Süleyman the Magnificent visited the city in December 1536, staying but one night on his way back to Istanbul, as opposed to the eight days he spent in Aleppo, thus giving some idea of the relative importance of the two towns in the eyes of the Ottoman court at this time.

We know little of the people and society in Antioch in this period. The well-known Syrian Christian Dāwūd al-Anṭakī (1535–1599), author of many medical works, was from al-Fū'a, a Shī'a village near the town, though he lived mainly in Cairo. He also wrote love poetry in his *tazyīn al-aswāq*, where he makes reference to a Christian monk, Nicholas, who lived on the mountain in Antioch in the church of al-Brtzfa.[1] Shaykh (Şeyh) Ahmed Kuseyri, from a nearby village, also had an influential following in the city, where he lived and taught in the Sufi Halvetī order.

Among the few Turkish Ottoman accounts is the incredibly important *waqf* (religious endowment) register of Aleppo in 1550, one of the few remaining such documents, which includes a substantial section on Antioch. The detailed description,

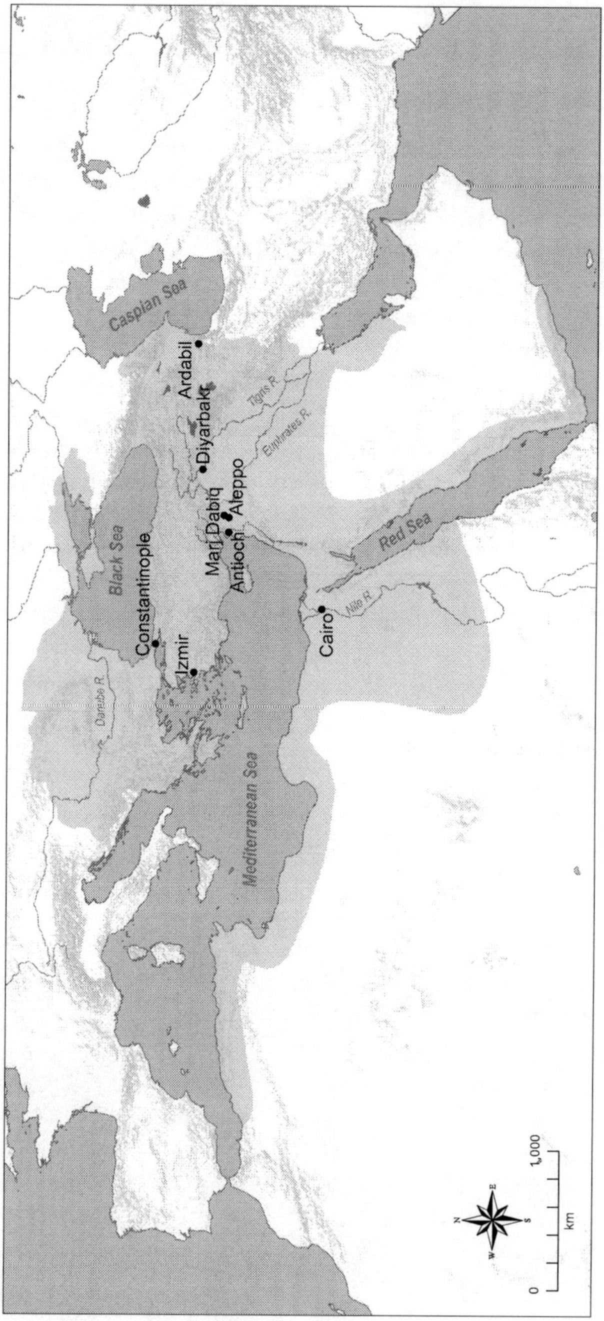

FIGURE 10.1 Map of the Ottoman Empire

Source: Created by Claire Ebert

which gives information on buildings, the economy, people, and administrative structures, reveals a large number of public religious and educational institutions enmeshed and interconnected very deeply into the city's social and economic life through the *waqf* system from the time of the Mamlūk occupation and beginning of the Ottoman period. In addition, there are five tax registers (*tahrir defteri*) from the sixteenth century on the district of Antioch that corroborate and add to our socio-economic view of the city. Among other details, these describe the city's administrators. Besides a governor, there was a *qadī* who wielded some power, as well as a city steward and stewards for each neighborhood, who were responsible for food and lodging services to inhabitants, visitors, and soldiers. An officer (*şubası*) was in charge of security and tax collection, under whom there was a police chief of sorts (*asesler*). Finally, there was a market inspector (*muhtesib*) who set prices.

Another account is the description by the explorer Evliya Çelebi in his *Seyāhatnāme* (Book of Travel) (see Appendix 2).[2] Çelebi visited the city in 1648, when Antioch was one of six *sanjaks* under Aleppo. Yunus Paşa appointed Bıyıklı Mehmed Paşa, the *beylerbey* (commander in chief) of Diyarbakr, as the new governor, and İskefserizade Rami Ali Efendi was made the *qadi*. He added that the city was run by 300 officials, a *muftī* (Islamic jurist) for each of the four *madhhabs* or schools, janissary general, deputy magistrate, and superintendent of municipal inspectors, as well as a garrison and officer in the citadel. It also had 20 cannons.

Just how independent Antioch was from Aleppo is unclear. The Spanish soldier and explorer Alī Bey al-Abbāsī (Domingo Francisco Jorge Badia y Leblich), who visited between 1803 and 1807, stayed in the house of the governor al-Hajj Bekir Ağa, whom he said was dependent on the *paşa* of Aleppo. But just a few years later, in 1809, the French orientalist Louis Alexandre Olivier de Corancez stated that Antioch, governed by an *ağa*, was independent of Aleppo's *paşa* and paid an annual tribute to Istanbul directly rather than Aleppo. British traveler James Silk Buckingham, on the other hand, wrote in 1816 that the governor of Antioch was the *mutsellem*, or subject, of Aleppo and had 50 to 60 personal guards.

In 1831, the Ottoman governor of Egypt, Mehmed Ali Paşa, seeking to establish his own empire, rebelled against the Ottomans and sent his son İbrahim to invade Syria. The following year İbrahim's army of Egyptians delivered several major defeats to the Ottomans, and İbrahim took over as governor of Syria, administering from Antioch. At this time he carried out an active program of dismantling Antioch's city walls for building materials.[3] In 1841, however, he was forced to withdraw from Syria after the European powers, worried about the potential collapse of the Ottoman Empire, compelled Mehmed Ali Paşa to agree to the 1840 Convention of London, which among other terms confirmed his rule over Egypt but forced him to give up Syria.

Ottoman foundation chronicles

A rather specific category of Ottoman texts concerning Antioch are chronicles describing the city's foundation. One in particular, the *Kitāb-i Tevārih-i Antākkiya* by Abdülkādir, who is otherwise unknown but likely hailed from the city, dates to 1671 (noted in Chapter 6). Another, *Tevārih-i Antākkiye*, was written by Edirneli Nazmī around 1585–1586. The anonymous Codex Vaticanus Arabic account and the Crusader period account by Abū Makārim also fit within this category of texts and were most likely the basis of these later Ottoman sources. The text by Abdülkādir describes a city founded by Antiyahuṣ (Antiochus) at a place near the Nehr-i Maklūb (Orontes) River and is fairly fantastical, with demons and demon kings, sorcerers, and wizards. The accounts do mention buildings. There was a church called Kadis Ism (Holy Name), presumably Catholic, and below it another church with the throne of Balqis (the Queen of Sheba). Alexander the Great's throne was also there somewhere in a cave in the mountains before it was taken to the Dome of the Rock. This cave, possibly al-Ashmūnīt, held the knife Abraham nearly used on his son Isma'īl.[4] The account also links to the Qu'rānic parable of the town of Habīb al-Najjār, his martyrdom, and tales of Jesus's disciples. Habīb al-Najjār was buried beneath the stone in the space between the mosque's gate and the *madrasa* (Islamic religious school), together with Ukeyl b. Urmiyā ('Uqayl, son of Jeremiah) and Sām b. Nūḥ (or rather Shem, son of Noah), details perhaps taken from Ibn al-'Adīm's work (see Chapter 8). Abdülkādir also includes a quotation from *a ḥadīth* on the *mi'rāj* (Muḥammad's ascension to heaven) about the holiness and reverence of this "mother of cities" (mentioned in Chapter 5):

> Antakya is the mother of cities (*şehirlerin anasıdur*). Its merits are more than those of other cities (*Anın fazilesi gayri şehirlerden ziyadedür*). It is equal to the Firdaws paradise, which has more merits than other paradises. To dwell in it means to dwell in the Ka'aba (*Beytü'l-Ma'mūr*).[5] The chosen ones (*ahyār*) of your community (*ümmet*) dwell there. One day's worship (*ibadet*) there is equal to one thousand days of worship. Whoever from your community dies there, he shall be given the excellence of those who are firm [in their allegiance to God] (*murābıt*).[6]

The seventeenth-century Ottoman geographer Kātip Çelebi wrote a geography, the *Cihānnümā*, also based on the Codex Vaticanus, that includes a short description of Antioch similar in style to this genre. The buildings mentioned in these texts, however, cannot be considered helpful in establishing any topography but rather testify to the enduring memory of this historical city and the legacy of the Codex Vaticanus account.

Evliya Çelebi also provided a foundation account, dating the city's origin to sometime before Noah's Flood and its rebuilding, after the flood, to Japheth, Noah's son. Early on, he mentions that a large citadel (*kal'a*) was built that acted as a refuge for the people of the city but was eventually conquered, and also lists the city among the greatest whose walls are built on mountains that reach up to heaven. He also stated that the city was called Dār-ı cāhim and Dār-ı Kayāsıra (The Land of Hell and the Land of the Caesarea), and that the origin of the name Antakya was from An-Takyanus, or the throne of Takyanus who restored the walls. Constantine burned all of the statues of Takyanus and built churches. In its heyday, during the

Byzantine period, it boasted 70 great churches richly decorated, but totaling all churches, monasteries, and Christian houses of worship, there were 600. Çelebi's account of the foundations and early history of the city, like most of these Ottoman chroniclers, is thus steeped in legend and myth with a very loose peppering of history.

Orientalism and the city

Many descriptions abound from Western travelers to Antioch, starting mainly in the eighteenth century and continuing until the early twentieth. Travelers to the city often commented not on the city's politics or administration but on its sights, sounds, and people. It is with these that the perception of Antioch as a town in decline really began, as Westerners, eager to see this city so renowned in Roman, Byzantine, and Crusader history and so important for "Western" civilization, came away disappointed. French travelers in particular – such as Jean de la Roque, a journalist who initially visited the Levant in 1689 and published his experience in 1722 – were obsessed with tracing their own heritage through the Crusader occupation of Antioch, even though the city was ruled mostly by Normans from Sicily.[7] These travelers were chagrined to find a greatly reduced, albeit typical, Middle Eastern town, dilapidated in their eyes. Since travelers frequently used one another's texts as guides, their views of the city can be traced over time. In 1625 the Italian composer and ethnographer Pietro della Valle wrote a brief description:

> Today, Antioch is still inhabited by a few communities that either dwell among the ruins or in habitations that they made for themselves within the gardens that cover the city, for almost no ancient house or building outside the walls is still standing.[8]

Charles Perry, a British physician and traveler who published an account of his travels in 1743, encapsulated the orientalist view quite succinctly: "Antioch, though formerly a magnificent and renowned City, is now a wretched scurvy Hole."[9] Five years later, in 1748, Alexander Drummond, a Scottish consul, visited and was disappointed, commenting that the city he saw was very different from that described by de la Roque.[10] George Robinson, visiting in 1832, wrote, "Alas! The 'defenced' city, she that ranked third amidst all the provinces of Rome, now lies stretched 'silent and in darkness,' a mass of undistinguishable ruin, lifeless, yet beautiful in death."[11] British general and explorer Francis Rawdon Chesney, who together with the surgeon and traveler William Francis Ainsworth visited the city from May to October 1835, commented that scarcely anything remained of Antioch.[12] The following year, the British artist William Henry Bartlett and British traveler John Carne wrote in an account filled with orientalist critique:

> Is this Antioch, the queen of the East, the glory of the monarch, the joy of the evangelist? Brought down even to the dust, she shall no more be called the lady of kingdoms. On every side is the silence of ruin and the dimness of

> despair: yet how beautiful and exulting is the face of nature: *she* sitteth not solitary, with the tears on her cheek, but dwells, as of old, in her loved valley of the Orontes.[13]

In 1895, Swiss researchers Max van Berchem, an Islamic epigrapher and historian, and Edmond Fatio, an architect, upon visiting Antioch called it a small town and left feeling despondent.[14]

The search for Antioch and subsequent lamentation over its decline is in fact a major obstacle to using Western descriptions during the Ottoman period: it is difficult to assess Ottoman Antioch objectively if all accounts relate it to its past. Ironically, what travelers today love about the city – its Ottoman-period buildings, its bustling Middle Eastern maze of markets, its spicy Syro-Turkish cuisine – left Western travelers in the Ottoman period, with few exceptions, unimpressed, with little willingness to enjoy what they found. So, too, few commented on the religiously and ethnically diverse communities, especially the Muslim inhabitants. When they were drawn to the "oriental" city, it was as a Western male in a harem: "I see all these cities of the Orient like a circle of young women among whom I was invited to choose," in the words of the Comte de Volney, who visited between 1783 and 1785.[15]

For Europeans, the Muslims were to blame for Antioch's decline, as it was under "Muslim" custodianship that the city had contracted into a village, relatively unimportant in the Ottoman Empire. Johannes Aegidius van Egmond, a Dutch emissary to Naples who journeyed to the Levant in 1720 and published his account in 1759, wrote that the city was a large assemblage of ill-built houses of one floor and few remains, since, as he said, its conquerors destroyed everything.[16] The Comte de Volney devoted one page to Antioch, mentioning that it was a ruined town, "a spectacle of misery and disorder," and was in its past much better. Corancez's account has the usual anti-Muslim rhetoric, stating that as soon as the Muslims conquered the city, they ruined it out of hatred.[17] In 1840, William McClure Thomson, an American Protestant missionary, published his itinerary to Antioch, steeped in bigotry. He stated the town was now miserable, with little trade, wealth, or political importance, much of which he attributed to the period after the Mamlūk conquest, since the Muslims occupying the city loved to destroy rather than build.[18] Maurice Barrès, a French writer and politician, in 1914 lamented what he could not see: the Church of St. Peter, the Theotokos (which he called the Rotunda), the Church of St. John Chrysostom, the Church of Sts. Cosmas and Damian, the churches of Saint Mesme (Maximus) and Simeon. He wrote that all of these had been Islamicized or buried by sediment, yet "the Arabian color has peeled off and allowed us to see a substance kindred to ours." Unfortunately, his remark encapsulated the view of many of these travelers. Ironically, whatever buildings he did see were all churches built after the Islamic conquests and likely influenced more by local medieval (and Islamic) styles than the earlier Byzantine ones.[19]

Accounts were also steeped in thinly disguised racism toward the contemporary Muslim population. In August 1816, British Consul-General John Barker met Lady Hester Stanhope, British explorer and early archaeologist, in Antioch. He wrote that "the rabble at Antioch have the reputation of being extremely uncivilised, uncouth, and... 'fanatical'" and that "no European before Mr. Barker's arrival had ever been allowed to ride through town," a canard repeated by Lieutenant-Colonel Paul Jacquot in his tourist guide of 1931.[20] Bartlett and Carne further wrote that the Antiochenes were unlike others in the region and not civil or kind but bigoted, and that strangers rarely stayed in the town. The Abbot Émile Le Camus, who visited the Catholic Mission there and whose account was published in 1890, echoed the sentiment that the town felt like a tomb and wrote of the "fanatical guardians of relics" at the Mosque of Habīb al-Najjār.

Wolffgang Aigen, a seventeenth-century German merchant, wrote perplexingly in 1661 that Christians were not allowed to live in the city.[21] Richard Pococke, a bishop and anthropologist who visited twice in 1738, provided the first lengthy description of the site, along with a map and illustrations. While incredibly useful for his descriptions, several of his statements – for example, that no Christians lived in Antioch until 50 to 60 years before his visit owing to Baybars's conquest – were complete orientalist falsehoods, as was Aigen's assertion. This notion was repeated in 1868 by the Dutch orientalist Tinco Lycklama, who said there were no Christians in the city before the seventeenth century.

Despite the overwhelming orientalist critique, some positive depictions are to be found.[22] For instance, the French traveler and naturalist Pierre Belon, visiting around 1548, praised the city walls and said there was no city in France that could compare. He also was taken by the variety of goods sold in the market and the surrounding types of trees, plants, and wildlife. The Swedish orientalist Jean Otter in 1737 (who interestingly includes translated descriptions of Abū al-Fidā' and Ibn Ḥawqal) called the town "passably great and pretty." Buckingham, in 1816, while giving a neutral description, questioned the reliability of Volney's curt description as, he noted, Volney seems to have never visited the town. Women travelers such as Emily Beaufort (Lady Strangford), who traveled to the area in 1858/1859, and Gertrude Bell, who visited in 1905, were also more charitable and less judgmental overall. So, too, were the accounts of Ottoman travelers, such as Evliya Çelebi in the mid-seventeenth century, who called it "truly a prosperous town in a fertile valley," and even that in 1807 of the Spanish Alī Bey al-'Abbāsī, who presented as a Muslim.[23] Beaufort wrote that "the people are somewhat fanatical, but thrifty and industrious," and also stated that after the Persian destruction in the early seventh century, the city was "once more rebuilt by the Saracens."[24] Bell, who documented scenes of daily life with photos, wrote in a letter to her parents that "Antioch is like the pantaloon whose clothes have grown too wide for his lean shanks... . But you must not think that it is not one of the loveliest places in the world, because it is."[25] As she also expressed in the opening quotation to this chapter, she was charmed by the city and its red tiled houses with balconies, its bazaar, and its quiet side streets.

Earthquakes

One year after Sülayman's visit, an earthquake struck the city in 1537, and another in 1615, but no more information is known of their effects. Pococke described an earthquake on September 25, 1738, that damaged the city's wall, some houses, and surrounding villages. Another struck in 1755, and inhabitants left their homes for 40 days, but little damage occurred. It is unclear whether this is the same earthquake (the duration matches somewhat) as the one that struck that year from August 13 to October 9, where for 56 days and nights tremors were felt; descriptions do not mention any depopulation of the town. On November 25, 1759, an earthquake destroyed one or two old houses, a *khān* (wholesale market and/or hostel for traveling merchants), and part of the market, while also killing several people.

Then on August 13, 1822, the largest quake in five centuries, felt over much of southeastern Anatolia, struck the area, measuring 7.4 on the surface-wave magnitude scale, with estimates of destruction at Antioch and Aleppo ranging from VIII (destructive) to X–XI (intense to extreme) on the Modified Mercalli intensity scale.[26] Travelers wrote that it left half the city in the dust and the other half in ruins and destroyed a majority of homes but not the city wall. The city's inhabitants fled the town and camped in the plain,[27] while aftershocks continued for two-and-a-half years. Another occurred on January 1, 1837, for which the ground reportedly moved a long time.

Another major earthquake occurred on April 3, 1872, measuring 7.2; this one flattened much of the city, damaging two-thirds of its buildings and destroying four mosques, along with 1,960 of the city's 3,000 houses, while another 894 were uninhabitable and 149 spared. A similar proportion of Antioch's other buildings were damaged or destroyed, including *khāns*, mosques, churches, shops, and factories. Also damaged were estates outside the city, including one owned by a Scottish national. The quake also destroyed the Spanish consulate, though none of those of other European countries. Deaths, however, were low compared to many earlier quakes, between 500 and 600, with 400 to 800 injured,[28] the result of much of the population fleeing to the plains after the initial shock. Gertrude Bell expressed her sadness at the destruction caused by this earthquake to the castle, city walls, and ancient buildings.

Further earthquakes occurred on February 9, 1873; May 3, 1874; August 21, 1875; November 9, 1875; and in February 1893. An earthquake centered around Malatya was also felt in Antioch on March 2, 1893, with surface waves of 7.2, and another struck on January 13, 1894. The effects of these quakes in Antioch, however, were hardly described and assumed minimal.

State of the classical and medieval structures

During the Ottoman period, only the core of the city was the focus of building, as the city had contracted significantly already in the preceding Mamlūk period (Figure 10.2). The northern half was full of ruins. Abraham Parsons in 1722 noted that the ruins of the old city also extended halfway up the mountain.[29] Yet what is often surprising is that some travelers remarked on next to nothing of antiquity in the town, as if they had not ventured around enough or were kept from looking at specific ruins. In 1599, the Sherley brothers, Sir Robert, Sir Anthony, and Sir

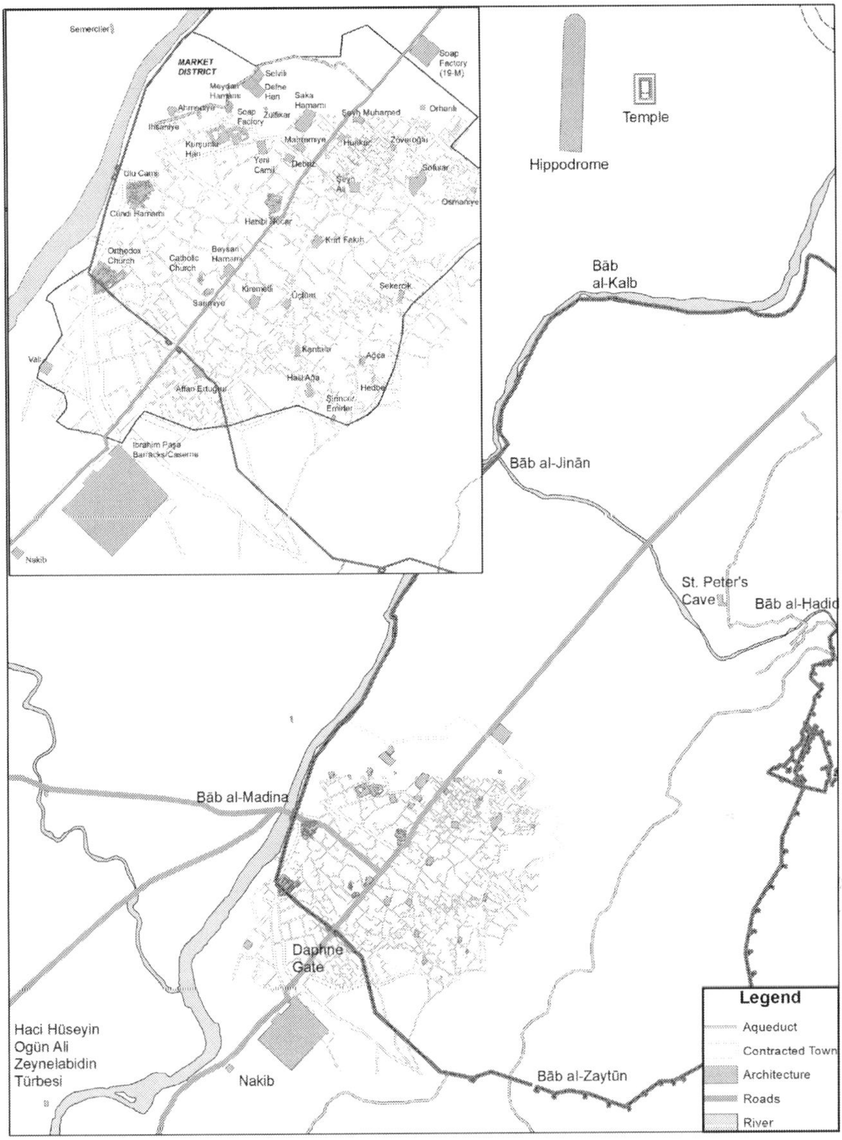

FIGURE 10.2 Plan of Ottoman Antioch

Source: Created by Steve Batiuk

Thomas visited the city, where they lodged at the house of two Janissary brothers. Curiously, they wrote that the Janissaries gave them permission to walk freely about the town but accompanied them for protection. They also commented that the city was ruined and decayed and only the walls were left. This suggests that their hosts showed them only the walls and nothing else, since at the end of the sixteenth century there were surely other things to see.[30] It is doubtful much had changed in the 50 years since Pierre Belon had visited in the mid-sixteenth century, when he noted much more. The only thing in town on which Perry commented in 1743 was the spring-fed fountain on the left as one entered via the Aleppo Gate.

Yet many remains of classical and medieval churches, palaces, and other structures were to be found around the city. Aside from the travelers' narrative accounts, visitors began to produce maps of the town, make etchings and drawings, and take photographs. The best-known illustrator was the French painter, archeologist, and antiquary Louis-François Cassas, who visited Antioch between 1784 and 1787 and published six engravings of the city. His and other etchings are quite detailed, showing the blend of new and old monuments in the city yet evoking the common orientalist trope of a ruined ancient city interspersed lightly with exotic natives. Nevertheless, the etchings bring life to the city, often showing ruins no longer visible today (Figure 10.3).[31]

Visitors' maps are also problematic yet still useful. Some were far from reality, while others were surprisingly close, offering details about where certain topographic features lay and their relationship to one another. They often differed, however, on the course of the Orontes and the location of the city walls. Further, some maps included features visible to travelers at the time that are now long gone. One of the earliest sketch plans, by Pietro della Valle, who visited in August 1625, shows a basin behind the Aleppo Gate, near a tower and the main colonnaded street (Figure 10.4). Karl Otfried Müller published a map in his *Antiquitates Antiochenae* in the 1830s, which, though not very accurate, was very influential since it served as the basis for the planning and early mapping of the Princeton excavations (see Chapter 1, p. 53, Figure 1.15). Poujoulat's map illustrates well the small urban core amidst the larger older city that was uninhabited (Figure 10.6). Richard Förster's map of 1898, also less than accurate, followed the map made by engineer Josef Cernik for the Baedeker travel guides (Figure 10.5). Among the elements he showed on the Island were the ruins of the hippodrome and the Island bridge, as well as the Church of St. John.

Many of the maps – like those of Richard Pococke (Figure 10.7), Carsten Niebuhr, and Emmanuel Guillaume-Rey – also show the relationship of the city walls and gates, the contracted city and main streets, and fields covering much of the "empty" space. One advantage of these maps is that many were made before İbrahim Paşa held the city in the 1830s and went around exploding walls and buildings for stone. Taken with caution, the maps are thus useful documents. Pococke and those who came afterward show effort in producing more detailed and accurate representations of the urban plan and surroundings. Pococke in particular attempted to link monuments to historical events from the Crusades rather than focusing on classical monuments. For example, he identified the Tower of (Two) Sisters and showed the ruined monument called the Prince (L, fifth-century, ruin 1), which he thought was an imperial palace, as well as three churches (N, O, and P). The German Niebuhr, a mathematician and cartographer and member of the

FIGURE 10.3 Etchings by Louis-François Cassas from *Picturesque Travels in Syria, Phoenicia, Palestine and Lower Egypt, Volume 1.* 1798. Object ID M23730.1.#, The Aleppo Gate (bottom – outside the walls)

Source: Courtesy of the Harvard Museums of Art

FIGURE 10.3 (Continued) The Aleppo Gate (top – inside the city), The city walls (bottom)

FIGURE 10.3 (Continued) The Iron Gate (top), The city walls and aqueduct looking to Daphne and Mt. Cassius (bottom)

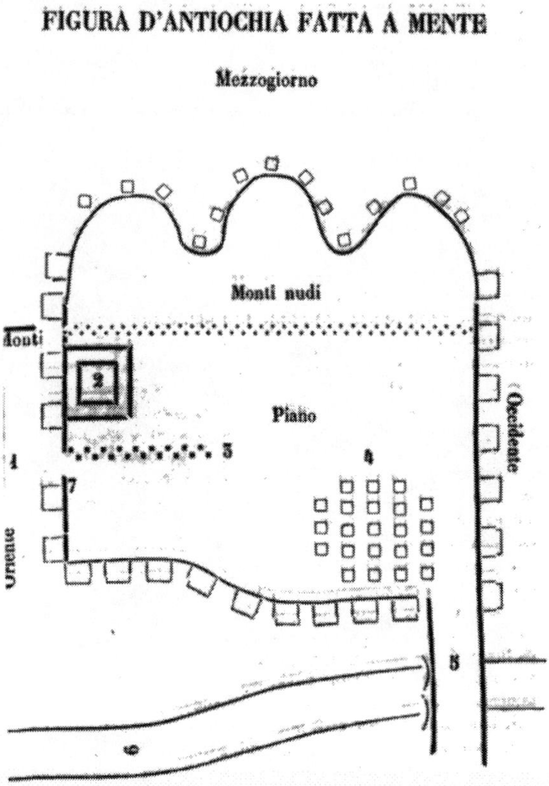

FIGURE 10.4 Map of Antioch by Pietro della Valle, based on the memories of his 1625 visit

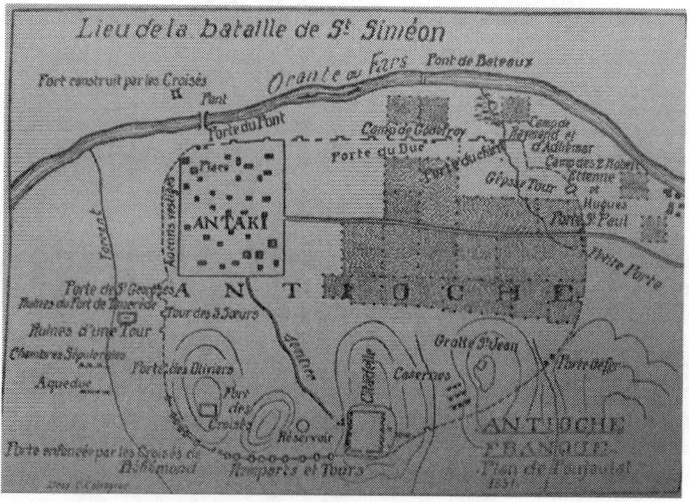

FIGURE 10.5 Plan of Antioch by Poujoulat, 1831

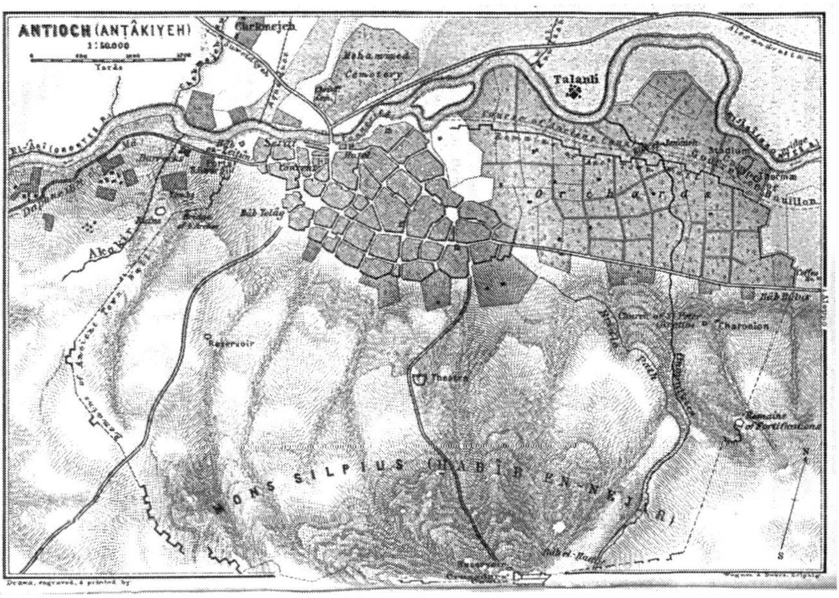

FIGURE 10.6 Plan of Antioch, Baedeker Guide, 1912

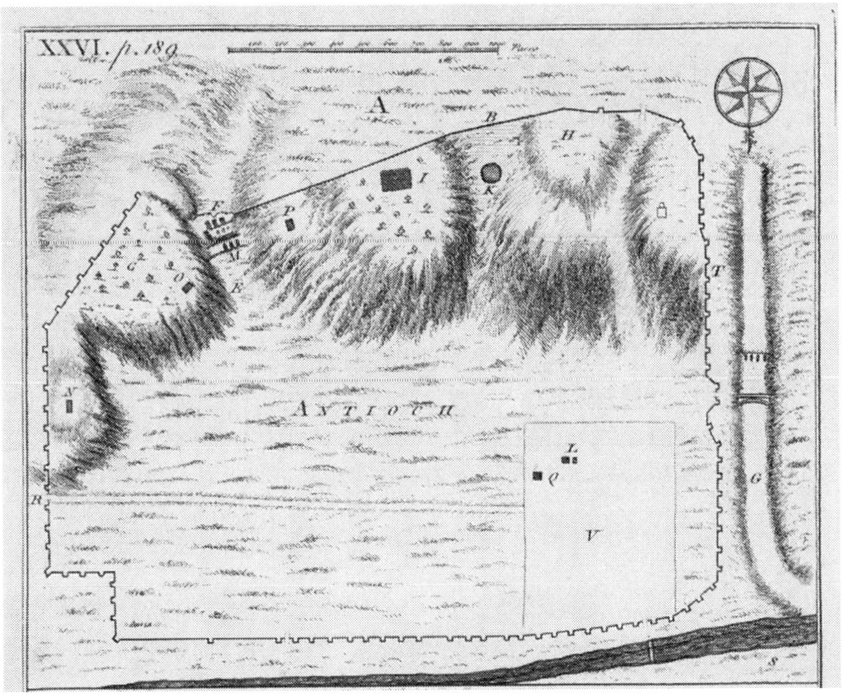

FIGURE 10.7 Plan of Antioch by Pococke, 1745

Danish expedition to the Orient (1761–1767) who visited in late June 1766, produced a map published in 1774 (Figure 10.8).[32] The French Emmanuel Guillaume-Rey, an archaeologist and cartographer, created a map that was the most precise and detailed from the 1850s, illustrating a bit of the landscape with forest, gardens, and fields as well as five mosques and other contemporary features of the Ottoman city (Figure 10.9). He also showed the fountain near the St. Paul Gate, a common feature and starting point for entry and exploration of the city.

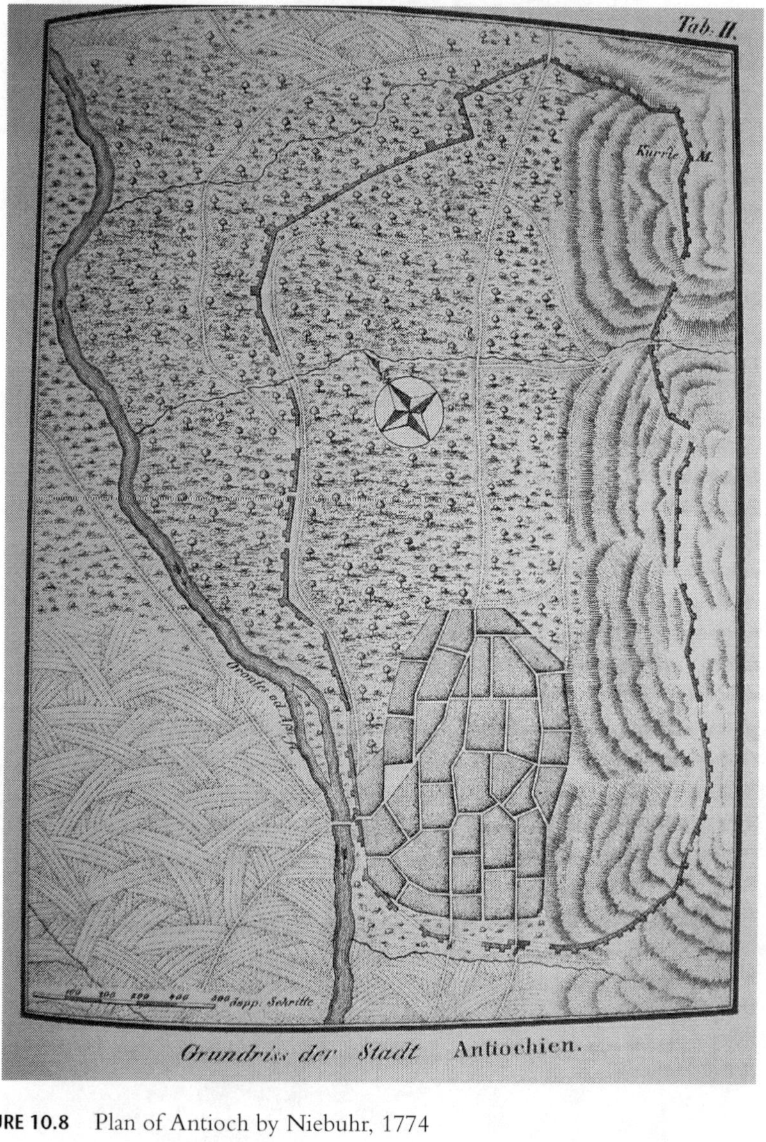

FIGURE 10.8 Plan of Antioch by Niebuhr, 1774

The city's walls and towers

The most reliable account of Antioch's walls and towers is the 1550 *waqf* charter of Aleppo, which states that Antioch was indeed fortified by a city wall but that parts of the wall were damaged from a history of earthquakes and war. The citadel had 14 towers. Traveling to the city at the same time, Pierre Belon superlatively praised the town's *intact* walls, devoting some time to them and comparing them to those of Constantinople or Nicomedia; he even wrote that the feat of enclosing mountains had no parallel, even in Europe (except perhaps Lyons). Çelebi stated that the walls were 12 miles (presumably Arabic miles) or 44,000 paces and took 12 hours to walk around and were the highest he had seen in his travels, surpassed only by Constantinople and Baghdad. The city walls were the most common subject for etchings, as seen in those by Bartlett, Cassas, and Rousset (Figure 10.10). As usual, the number of towers always varied, and the largely inflated number of 365, matching the days of the year, continued as a trope. The length of 10 to 12 miles was also a trope and also incorrect, even in conversion from the Arabic mile to the modern mile, which would be 11 to 13.42 miles. Ainsworth and Chesney gave the most accurate estimation of wall length – 7 miles – the actual length being about 5.7 modern miles, or 7.2 miles at its greatest extent under Theodosian II, and enclosing an area of 4.37 or 6.06 km^2 respectively, or 437/606 ha (see Appendix 1). The heights also varied from account to account, but 30 to 50 feet for the walls and 50 to 80 feet for the towers is the most accurate, with differences accounted for by the terrain, the lowest heights being nearer to the river. Wall thicknesses also varied, but were on average 10 to 15 feet on the slopes and 20 to 22 feet on the river.[33] Çelebi writes they were 20 cubits on the mountainside. Corancez noted that the towers were built close together, on average 70–80 paces apart, so that even if earthquakes brought down parts of the wall, the towers would still be defensible. Ainsworth and Chesney also correctly noted that the walls and towers were all of different ages (Figure 10.11).

Buckingham by 1816, and later Ainsworth and Chesney, gave the most detailed description of the walls, seemingly those of Justinian's constructions (see Chapter 4). The interiors of the towers, which were mostly stone with brick banding (typical Byzantine construction) and square (though at least one was round, thought to be Crusader built) had three to five floors, and chambers arched with tiles in mortar, and arrow slits on brick arches. The highest floor had a stone platform, while a small cistern was the lowest level. Niches of the doors and windows were also tiled. On the inner front of the city wall, a projecting cornice made of an overhang of longer upper stones allowed passage from tower to tower as a parapet on top of the wall, wide enough to support even wagons and horses from the city to the citadel. As the wall negotiated slopes, the parapet formed steps. The best-preserved sections of the walls and towers, including the parapet, were in the southwestern quarter of town. There on the architraves of one of the southern doors one could see a Maltese cross (suggesting a Crusader

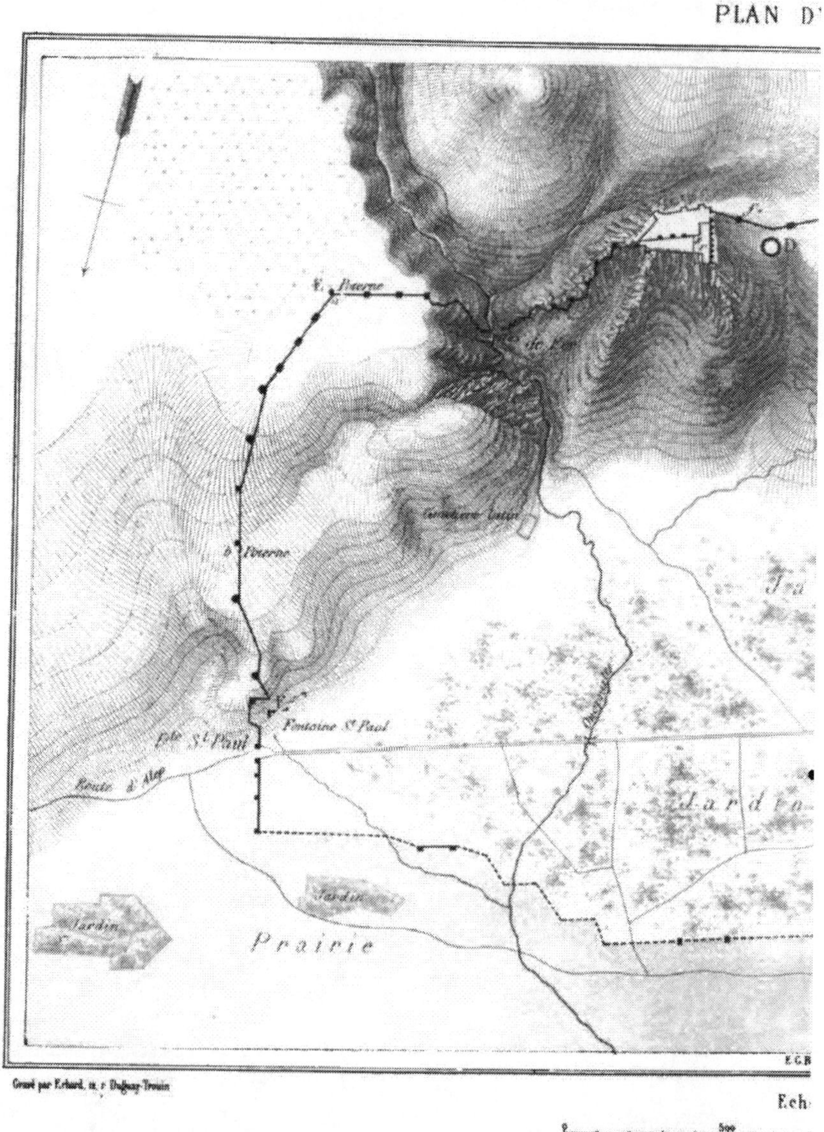

FIGURE 10.9 Plan of Antioch by Rey, 1850s

embellishment, not Byzantine, as other travelers had thought and which Buckingham discounted). The French historian and journalist Jean Joseph François Poujoulat, writing shortly before İbrahim Paşa's arrival, said there were eight surviving towers in good condition with Maltese crosses in relief on the outside and bands of

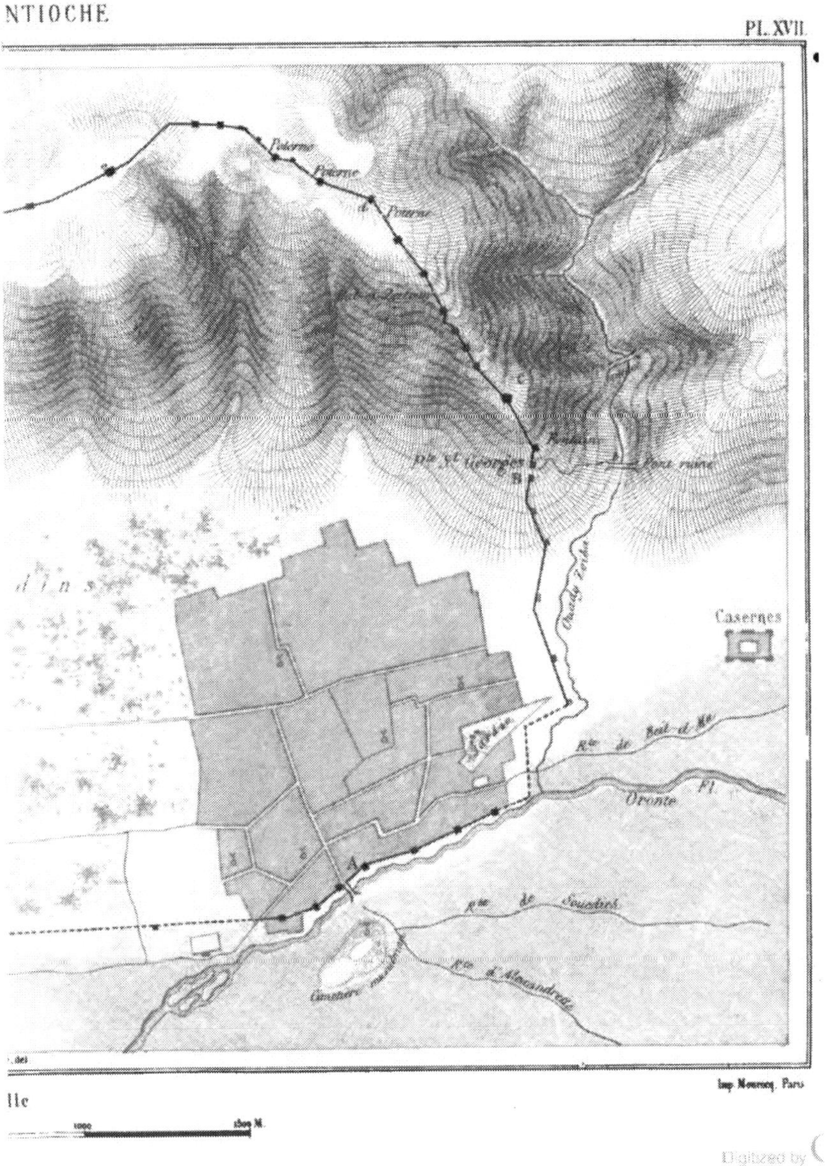

FIGURE 10.9 (Continued)

small crosses inscribed on the insides.[34] Interestingly, the architrave, which usually consisted of one large stone, was made up of five: two end ones each 5 feet long, and three central ones each 1 foot long, and "being dove-tailed into each other in the Turkish and Arabian manner."[35]

FIGURE 10.10 The western walls of Antioch, 1841 engraving by J.H. Le Keux after a drawing by W.H. Bartlett from *La Siria e l'Asia minore illustrate* by G. Briano, 1841

Tower of Antioch.

FIGURE 10.11 North Tower by W. Ainsworth, 1842

Both Ainsworth and Chesney relayed a Greek inscription, discovered by a resident European, on one of the city's north towers; as translated by Ainsworth, it read: "Sunk to ruin by time and tumult/____ Medon had hastily built/____ with haste and difficulty of the army of the _____/the tower." This tower may in fact have been part of the Dog Gate. The inscription has recently been retranslated as: "God the Protector has caused an army in speed and the inhabitants with labour to build the tower that due to age and martial uproar had leaned upon its destruction."[36]

By the mid-eighteenth century, the walls had holes in places caused by earthquakes. Many of the towers had since become stables or trash pits. Lycklama stated that eight towers had been preserved, suggesting that Ibrahim Pasha's demolitions did not destroy the towers but only the walls.

City gates

Çakar, in his article on the 1550 *waqf* document, states that there is confusion as to the number of gates but enumerates eight gates in use: the Aleppo Gate, the Duke Gate, the Dog Gate, the Bridge Gate, the Olive Gate, the Iron Gate, the Süveydiye Gate, and the St. George or Daphne Gate. It is unclear why the Süveydiye (Suwaydīyya) and Bridge (Sea) Gates are listed separately, as they are the same. The Olive Gate, noted by Rey on his map as *east* of the Daphne Gate on the slopes of the mountain, should correspond with the postern gate in Justinian's southern wall near Tower 9. This may be the same as the Gate of the Tower in the fourteenth-century *waqf* document. The main gate used was the Sea/Bridge Gate, yet by the seventeenth century the Aleppo Gate had become the primary gate by which one entered the town. In Çelebi's time, the gate was 15 or 20 cubits high. Many travelers – like Jean Otter as well as Parsons and Buckingham – noted there were many ruins here, mostly unornamented, and on either side of the gate. Along the slopes of the mountain were many caves, tombs, and springs. Poujoulat, who visited Antioch between 1830 and 1831, wrote that the Aleppo Gate had a perfectly preserved tower outside, accessible by a low door with a domed roof and six large embrasures. The gate itself was over 30 feet high and 12 feet wide. He also noted three large plane trees. Lycklama's measurements of the gate itself were even larger: 12 m (39 feet) by 4 to 5 (13 to 16.4) m; he also wrote that it was seemingly unaffected by the earthquake that struck the city in 1822.

The Sea/Bridge Gate – also called Bab el-Medine (Gate of the City), Bab al-Jisr, and Bab Suwaydīyya – lay outside the city walls and was the best preserved, having been rebuilt.[37] Engravings show that it had four arches, although Parsons wrote, oddly, that it had three (Figure 10.12). It was 60 yards wide and had part of a wall and parapet to each side. Thomson stated that the bridge was paved all over with green stone; perhaps this was serpentine from the nearby Amanus Mountains. It was also wide enough to accommodate three packed camels side by side. Parsons said that the Bridge Gate was closed from sunset to sunrise, and that each man coming or going on horseback and with a loaded animal paid a toll in or out. This

FIGURE 10.12 "Antioch in Syria" engraved by E. Finden after a picture by J.D. Harding and Las Casas, in *Landscape Illustrations of the Bible*, 1836

is verified from the mid-sixteenth century, where the *waqf* charter states that the toll to enter was 10,000 *akçe* (an Ottoman silver coin), rising to 12,000 by 1584. In the 1872 earthquake, the bridge was cracked; it was also described as fortified with a parapet wall that fell off (Figure 10.13).

The same "Turkish/Arabic" style seen on the architraves of the towers was also observed on the southern Daphne Gate – probably also called the Bab Jelag – to the city. The doors were absent but visible from an upper socket for pivots in the bottom of the architrave and square sills for the inner bars, and thus was a double door. The Aleppo Gate also was built in this way. Ainsworth and Chesney both mentioned four Islamic-style arched entrances (perhaps the two of Buckingham's Aleppo and Daphne Gates, and two others, perhaps the Bridge and Dog Gates). The Olive Gate, close to the Daphne Gate and in the southwest, also was fairly well preserved. The Duke Gate (or Garden Gate) in Corancez's time was intact and had houses built up around it. By the mid-nineteenth century, however, the Duke Gate was a ruined mound lying beneath orchards, and Förster noted in 1898 that the Dog Gate had been dismantled and used to build İbrahim Paşa's barracks.[38] During and after the 1872 earthquake, most of the city walls and the main Orontes bridge were damaged, and the quake destroyed the Daphne and Aleppo Gates.

FIGURE 10.13 "On the Orontes" by J.A. Johnson, *Harper's New Monthly Magazine* 45 (August 1872): 395, 45.267

Churches and palaces

As we have already witnessed, often the descriptions of ruins are confusing or misidentified and require some sorting out. Although de la Roque wrote that nothing of the city's past was really visible, particularly none of the grand public structures, he still described some surprising objects. Along the town's southern side, he described a sumptuous hexagonal structure. This was a palace with vast ruins occupying almost the entire hill on which it was built. He also noted some fairly well-preserved parts of porticoed galleries raised on marble Corinthian columns. To the building's side was a temple, also on the mountain, but that rose in the center of the city. De la Roque also said that the Christians of Antioch could see still the ruins of St. Peter's basilica (which he called the Church of Constantine, though it would not have been the Domus Aurea on the Island), and also noted the ruins of a church on a precipice south of the center of town.

Pococke, although touring the city in only one day, must have had an incredibly full and productive one, since he saw a great deal. He, too, observed that little remained of ancient buildings, except for the front of a large building called the Prince, which he believed was the imperial palace and speculated appeared to be fourth to fifth century based on architecture and the same masonry style as the House of John Chrysostom. It is unclear, however, what these structures were. Perry stated that near the Latakia Gate was a large building, possibly the palace of Seleucus, though which gate this was – whether the Bridge/Sea, or Daphne Gate – is uncertain. Although Drummond could not see the hexagonal building mentioned by de la Roque, he did note a square brick building in the middle of town, which he thought was now a harem or *seraglio*. This could be what Ainsworth and Chesney mentioned oddly was a building with a square basement. Evliya Çelebi's 1648 account mentioned eight large mansions, including one named Ketaağaç Paşa Sarayı with many rooms and a gate with an iron chain. Around 1834, Francis Arundell, an English antiquarian and clergyman, also referred to eight palaces when describing the city, as well as its citadel, the well-built houses on the Orontes River, and the city's commercial activities and baths (Figure 10.14).[39] These "mansions" or "palaces" referred to were probably the *havş* or *khāns* strewn around the city discussed in the next section as part of the medieval Islamic city and not classical remains.

FIGURE 10.14 Citadel by G. Bell, 1905, C_072

The Island

The abbot Le Camus mentioned a network of ruined walls between the colonnaded street on the Island and the river. He also identified the ruins of the hippodrome and temple, and speculated on two tumuli as possibly being the nymphaeum and the Octagonal Church.[40] Beaufort described, for the first time it seems, the hippodrome and a temple, although she did not identify them as such.[41] The former structure, she noted, comprised 13 masses of solid masonry buttresses, 14 feet high and 15 feet wide, all built on a long foundation wall. She hypothesized that these buttresses supported an aqueduct for water. One hundred yards away was the temple, which she described as accessible on three sides, with 14-foot-high walls, 12 feet thick of hard cement. The northern (northeastern) end had a detached wall, as did the others. She hypothesized incorrectly, however, that this was a theater for sea fights, which was instead in Daphne. Lycklama also visited the hippodrome, which he correctly identified, although he thought the temple to be a fortification.

Cisterns and aqueducts

During the Ottoman period, it appears as if the Daphne aqueduct, although noted by travelers, was no longer functioning and part of the ruined landscape. Water was supplied from the mountain streams, the spring at the Aleppo Gate that was channeled into the city, and from the water-wheels on the Orontes. Within the walls Belon noted immense cisterns, which he compared with those of the palace of Philippi in Macedonia. He also described copious fountains with water coming from the mountain.[42] Pococke noted that water came out of the mountain and was carried in channels of stone alongside the hill, which became aqueducts suspended on brick arches. He also noted several mills on the channel. Drummond stated that by the Damascus Gate was an aqueduct of five arches, though it is unclear which gate this was, perhaps the Daphne Gate. Buckingham further wrote of two ancient bridges over the Phyrmenius torrent, likely referring to aqueducts; one had four arches and was full of calcite travertine deposits with modern repairs and was used as a road, and both were Roman (Figure 10.15, Figure 10.16, Figure 10.17).

Nearly every traveler entering the city first passed through the Aleppo Gate and commented on the spring of excellent water. Pietro della Valle, in his early sketch plan, included the gate, to the left of which upon entering was a pool or open cistern surrounded by large trees and filled by a mountain stream and holding fish. On the right was a tall tower and large vaulted chamber. De la Roque noted a large basin and canal of quarried stone revetted in marble, measuring 100 × 200 paces. The canal was divided into compartments and accompanied by an aqueduct on arches; water arrived from a variety of sources, some subterranean. Jean Otter, who visited in the 1840s, also mentioned a subterranean canal that brought hot water to houses and baths, called the Canal of Paul (the Būlit mentioned in the Middle Byzantine and Crusader periods). Pococke also noted aqueducts and the

FIGURE 10.15 Aqueduct and Iron Gate by G. Bell, 1905, C_069

springs around the east gate, the Bab Bulus (Gate of Paul or Aleppo Gate), which he surprisingly thought was "Bablous," related to Babylon. The adjacent fountain, 'Ayn al-Ṭawīl (Long Fountain), was shaded by a large plane tree and café, where Muslims played chess and checkers. Le Camus adds that a Latin cemetery was there and the aqueduct had three levels and ancient canals in red brick that watered terrace gardens.

FIGURE 10.16 Aqueducts, *Encyclopedia Britannica*, 1902

FIGURE 10.17 Antioch, postcard, 1900

Katip Çelebi's version of the Ottoman foundation chronicle mentions that the ruler had a house built at the head of the aqueduct with his likeness there, and two statues, one of a king and one of a queen. Several later travelers also wrote that at the head of the aqueduct, a little beyond the Iron Gate, were two figures in bas-relief: the king and the queen, perhaps referring to Constantine and his mother Helena or Septimius Severus and his wife Julia Domna. The sculpture has since been destroyed or disappeared.

The Ottoman city

Despite the focus on the town's historical remains and the orientalist filter applied by most Western travelers, it is possible to learn a great deal about the Ottoman city. Detailed Ottoman records, mainly tax and *waqf* registers and census counts, though not extensive, have been preserved for Antioch.[43] Further, each observation, description, or census of the town provides a small snapshot of the city throughout this period. By organizing its transformation chronologically under several broad categories (population, public buildings, economy and natural resources, and neighborhoods and houses), we can chart the city as it moved from the small medieval town recovering from the Mamlūk conquest to a rebuilt, modernized, and more Europeanized provincial capital.

As depicted on all maps and mentioned in most accounts, the Ottoman town of Antioch was condensed, about one-fifth or one-sixth the size of the ancient city, with most of the space north of the city up to the ancient city walls filled with trees. Parsons wrote in 1772 that the Ottoman city was 1.5 miles long, a quarter the size of the old city, compared to the 3 miles from the east to west gates. From the east gate to the town was 1.25 miles, and from the west gate to town was half a mile. The city was still confined, even until 1931, to the east side of the river, while the west side was dominated by gardens, cemeteries, and a few buildings – two schools and a power plant.

The population of Ottoman Antioch remained quite diverse in character, a hallmark of the city since its foundation. Pierre Belon stated in 1553 that Syrian Arabic was the official language. Not long afterward, Turkish became the official language of the Ottoman period in the city, but inhabitants also spoke Arabic, Armenian, and Greek, reflective of the population, which also continued to include a small Jewish community. We have a sizable number of censuses for Antioch that allow us to track the rise and fall in demographics in the sixteenth century and the nineteenth and early twentieth centuries (Tables 10.1, 10.2). From the mid-eighteenth

TABLE 10.1 Population of Ottoman Antakya (Antioch), 1526–1589

Date	*Households (average 6 people)*	*Bachelors*	*Households of imams*	*Total*	*Total with garrisoned soldiers*
1526	1,002	131		6,143	6,493
1527	1,006	131			
1536	1,165	255	30	7,443	7,793
1537	1,196	265			
1550	1,056	393	24	6,896	7,246
1552	1,087	395			
1570	1,047	384	23	6,666	7,016
1571	1,074	387			
1584	1,008	539	28	6,755	7,105
1589	1,064	511			

TABLE 10.2 Population of Ottoman Antakya, 1803–1909/19

Date	*Total population*	*Christians*	*Jews*	*Egyptian troops*	*Armenians*	*Alawites*
1803–1807	18,150	3,000	150			
1813	9,500					
1816	10,000	1,150	20			
1822	12,000					
1830–1831	4,000					
1835	5,600			6,000		
1838	6,000					
1840	9,000			4,000		3,000
1850	10,000		3,000			
1867	9,904	1,096	33			
1868	11,000	650				
1880	17,500	2,500	250			
1889	16,818	3,000				
1890–1891	23,550	3,500	266		3,784	6,000
1895–1896	23,550					
1906 or 1913	28,000	4,000				
1909 or 1931	36,000	5,000			1,000	

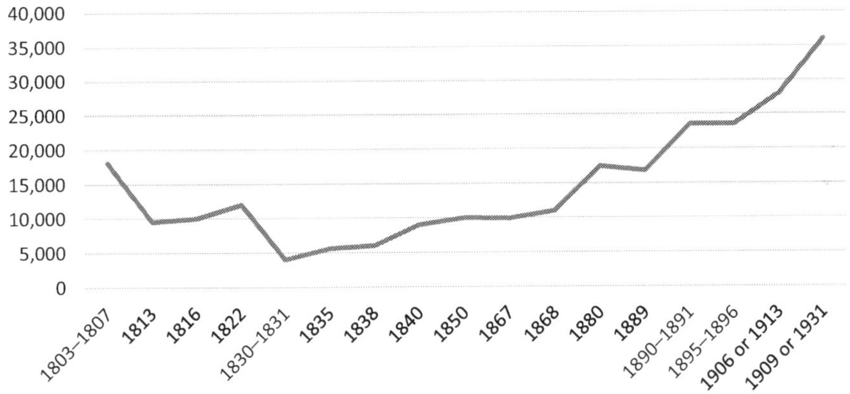

FIGURE 10.18 Total population of Antioch, 1803–1909 or 1931

century onward, Antioch surpassed the population attributed to the Seleucid city. The average minority population in the nineteenth century was about 10 percent Christian and .25 percent Jewish. A book of engravings by William Henry Bartlett and Thomas Allom mentioned there were very few Jews in the city, "in a wretched state" with no synagogue.[44] Despite several drops in population in the nineteenth century, by the start of the twentieth century the total population had grown significantly. These drops were potentially caused by the effects of two earthquakes and an epidemic. Although the effects of each disaster were completely varied, some dramatically changing the face of the city while others were hardly felt, resilience was always a constant feature.

Public buildings

The Ottoman town retained its strong medieval character as a contracted yet dense Islamic city with typical public buildings: the *hamam* (bathhouse), *bedesten* (covered market), *madrasa* (school), *han* (*khān*, wholesale market doubling as hostel), *ribāṭ* (quasi-religious hostel), *camii* (main mosque), and *masjid* (neighborhood mosque). Abdülkadir in his Ottoman foundation chronicle exaggerated that the city was built up with 20 baths, 30 *tımarhane* (hospitals), and 100 caravansarays or roadside inns. On the other hand, de la Roque stated in 1688 that a century had passed since Istanbul had decreed or sponsored any repair or building programs in Antioch for the castle or houses of Turks, Greeks, Armenians, and Jews. Both views are extreme and incorrect. De la Roque's view is typical of the Western-dominant perspective that often denigrated anything Ottoman. He was not aware of the complex system of *waqf* religious endowments. Other early descriptions are more realistic. The 1550 Aleppo *waqf* register is incredibly detailed, naming not only all the main public buildings but where they were located in the city, who was employed to work in them, and how they were funded, often naming other places in the city not mentioned elsewhere that provided the endowments. The large number of religious and educational institutions in a small town, as Antioch had become, highlights its continued importance, long after the Mamlūk conquest.

To focus first on the more secular buildings, the *waqf* mentions two *hamams*: the central Meydan (Maydān) bath and an unnamed one. It is likely that the unnamed bath in the 1550 charter is one of the other two Mamlūk-period baths, probably the Mamlūk-founded Cündī or Saka (Saqqā), while a third Mamlūk bath was renovated after 1550. The Meydan bath was repaired by Jafer Ağa, a sixteenth-century noble, while the Cündī bath became part of Sinan Paşa's *waqf*. The Saqqā Hamam, Mamlūk originally, was endowed in 1573 by Sokullu Mehmed Pasha. It is possible that the Beyseri (Baysarī) bath was not operational although still standing. By the seventeenth century, there were five *hamams*: besides the Meydan, Cündī, Saka, and Beyseri baths, a new bath – the Yeni – was built likely in 1676 by an architect named Ahmed Ağa and sponsored by a Mustafa Bey. Three or four of the five were thus pre-Ottoman but had enjoyed long, continuous use.

Two points can be made here. At least three of these baths were renovated with funds from the Ottoman court in Istanbul. Jafer Ağa, who sponsored the Meydan bath repairs, was the chief white eunuch and gatekeeper (*kapı ağası*) of the Gate of Felicity in Topkapı Palace in Istanbul, the gate that separated the public from private spaces of the Ottoman court; he also founded other buildings in Antioch and Istanbul, such as a *madrasa* near Hagia Sophia. At this time, these court eunuchs were often Arab, and it is possible that he hailed from Antioch. Hadım Sinan Paşa was originally Bosnian, a eunuch who served as grand-vizier for Sultan Selim I in 1516–1517 and was instrumental in the conquest of Syria over the Mamlūks.[45]

Sokullu Mehmed Paşa, originally a Christian janissary from the Balkans, served as grand-vizier under Sultans Sülayman and Selim II (1565–1579). The second point is that interestingly the number of bathhouses in the city remained constant from the thirteenth to seventeenth centuries, even as the city grew. This may have been the result of water supply issues and lack of favorable spaces in the city. But minor baths also appeared, Çelebi wrote that there were also small unnamed *hamams* located on the interior face of the city walls along the river and watered by it. There is also a note in 1703 of a bath in the citadel fed by water that was carried by the river in containers (*dolap*).

The city also had places to stay for travelers to town or passing through and for the poor. The 1550 account writes of eight *havş* institutions, which were very cheap enclosed rental spaces, often for the poor, comprising either one house of three to 36 rooms or two to eight houses, all surrounding a courtyard containing wells and toilets that were shared. Three that are mentioned by name include the Ibn-i Eyne Bey, Kara Mercümek, and Hacı Hüseyin. In the sixteenth century, Dāwūd al-Anṭakī's father 'Umar, who was a wealthy merchant, built a *ribāṭ* outside the city for travelers and provided it with daily deliveries of food.[46] This was perhaps where Pietro della Valle resided in 1625 when he wrote that he stayed in a place near St. Paul's Church, which would have been near (or outside) the Aleppo Gate. It is not mentioned in the *waqf* of 1550, and so perhaps it was not funded by or did not pay for religious endowments, or else was built after 1550. The Kurşunlu Han, built around 1660 by Köprülü Mehmed Paşa, grand-vizier under Mehmed IV, was intended to house the imperial procession making pilgrimage to Mecca with gifts (*surre alayı*). The building contained a *masjid* and fountain (*çeşme*). It was originally built, however, in 1569, sponsored by Sokullu Mehmed Paşa or Jafar Ağa and paid for with lead (*kurşun*) from the Balkans. There was also the Yeni Han from the sixteenth or seventeenth centuries. These buildings are likely the eight "palaces" and "mansions" mentioned by Western travelers.

The religious buildings in the city included educational institutions, places of worship, and shrines, tombs, and other holy places. These all received money via the *waqf* system from a complicated combination of shops, *hamams*, rents from homes, mills, gardens, and orchards, both in the city and from its surrounding districts and villages. After paying the salaries of employees, such as *imāms*, Qur'ān readers, and teachers, there was often little money left, which was used for annual expenses of candles, oil, rugs, mats, and renovations.

The 1550 *waqf* account also discussed buildings where education took place. The main ones were the Kapıağası Jafer Ağa Muallimhane, a teacher training school founded by the sixteenth-century noble; the Fārisiye Madrasa, perhaps located near the Aleppo Gate; and the Gāziliyye Berrāniye Buk'ası.[47] The *muallimhanesi*, mentioned by Çakar as the only *waqf* building founded in the Ottoman period by 1550, primarily used its *waqf* funds to pay its teachers, who taught at all levels. The Fārisiye Madrasa was also called Ibn Sāhibü'l Bāz, after its founder Fāris b. Sāhibü'l Bāz, who was leader of the Doğancıoğlu Türkmen. The *madrasa* received its endowments from the weavers' (*çulha*) and perfume and spice markets ('*aṭṭār*) of the city. The Gāziliyye

Berrāniye Buk'ası was not quite a *madrasa* but was an educational institution, almost like a college. Its teachers were paid less as compared to those who worked in a *madrasa*. This one was built by a certain Ömar ('Umar) (b. Yakūb b. Aḥmad b. Manṣūr al-Anṭākī). Its endowments came from 11 shops and two bakeries, and this school continued into the eighteenth century. The tax registers also refer to two more schools: the Gülbaviye and Hariciye *madrasas*.

The following century, Evliya Çelebi enumerated 40 primary schools for small children and three Qur'ān schools or *madrasas*. Other places also had secondary roles as locations where schooling took place. Anecdotal evidence shows that young Dāwūd learned the Qur'ān in his father's *ribāṭ* from a Shaykh Muḥammad Sharif, as well as math, science, and Greek, indicating these spaces also functioned in multiple ways. Both from the 1550 account and that of Çelebi, it is clear that mosques, *masjids*, and other holy places such as Sufi lodges and shrines (*zāwiya)* also functioned as schools. In the *waqf* document, the Mağrıbiye Zaviye, seemingly connected with Sufis from North Africa and Spain, was located in the Meydan next to the Habīb al-Najjār mosque and was endowed partially by a house in the Maslaba neighborhood. Tax registers also mention the Fenk Zaviye, perhaps connected to or paid for by a village in the Amanus Mountains of the same name. Çelebi counted nine *tekkes* (Sufi lodges), two of which were dedicated to Habīb al-Najjār, one in town and one on the slopes. He writes that *faqir* dervishes guarded the tomb, likely those from the *tekke* (Mağrıbiye Zaviye) Central Asia and those of the Naqshbandiya sect, the Özbekiyye Tekkesi Camii or Özbekhan, was located at the entrance to the city at one end of the main bridge, likely at the Bridge Gate. It was mentioned in 1730. The tax registers also mention the Zeynelabidin Meşhed (a *meşhed* or *mashhad* was a religious shrine and tomb). This must be the Haci Hüseyin Ogün Ali Zeynelabidin Türbesi today, interestingly just on the other side of the river in the cemetery area for the city. Tombs for an İnal Eşfer, in charge of stables for the Mamlūks, and his brother or father, Kansu, in the Meydan neighborhood, were still mentioned in the 1550 account. Endowments were used to pay for readers of the Qur'ān.

In the sixteenth and seventeenth centuries, there were five mosques and 23 *masjids*. Accordingly, between 1536 and 1584, the tax registers indicate the number of *imāms* fluctuating between 23 and 30. Main mosques were typically located in markets. The main two were the pre-Ottoman mosques of Habīb al-Najjār and the Camii-i Kebir, or Great Mosque, also known as the Ulu Camii, which was located near the main market (Figure 10.19).[48] The Habīb al-Najjār mosque comprised two separate *waqf* endowments – one for the mosque and one for the tomb (*makam* or *maqām*) beneath it. The *makam* also had a soup kitchen (*imaret*), which prepared food daily for the poor, students, and pilgrims. The mosque's foundation is not entirely known, but it was built over an earlier religious building dating to the last quarter of the thirteenth century, so from the time of the Mamlūk sultan Baybars. The later building was reconstructed, possibly in the sixteenth century, and had a broad plan, with the main visitor door southeast on the courtyard and a tall minaret with a wooden balcony. A room on either side of the minaret's base

FIGURE 10.19 "The Great Mosque at Antioch, Turkey" from *Syria, the Holy Land, and Asian Minor, Volume III* by John Carne; artist: Henry Adlard, 1841

had a tomb to St. John (Yaḥya/Yūḥannā) and St. Paul, although these were not the main tombs. Stairs went down four meters to the *makam* – the tombs of Habīb al-Najjār and Şem'un Safā (Simon Peter). The tomb attracted many people, Christian and Muslim alike, who went for healing and help with fertility. Çelebi wrote that only Habīb al-Najjār's head was in the subterranean tomb (which he called a *tekke*), but that his body was in the citadel (*kale*), lit by candles. Some of the endowment money of the mosque came from orchards and gardens within the city walls of Antioch. Most of the *makam*'s endowment revenue went to the soup kitchen and, among other places outside the city, came from one orchard within the city, one grain mill endowed in 1525/1526 by Hatim b. Yusuf al-Hamravī, four shops in the market, and, unlike any other place in the city, from donations by visitors to the religious site. A mention in a 1720 document states that the *waqf* also paid for a person in charge of cleaning public toilets (*kennası*) in the Meydan.

The *waqf* account further states that the Ulu Camii, dating to 1271 and in the neighborhood of the same name, was the oldest mosque, rather than the Habīb al-Najjār mosque (Figure 10.20). It is not, however, mentioned in a *defter* (register) from 1536 because before that year it was privately owned by two brothers, Ali and Ahmed, sons of Osman, who were also known as Cündī. There may be a connection between them and the *hamam* and mill of the same name, in operation during this time. Half of the mosque's endowments came from within the city from shops and rents from fields. The *waqf* account said that this mosque was in a terribly dilapidated condition and recommended that it use its remaining funds, after paying its staff, for renovations. Today, the mosque has a rectangular plan whose shortest sides are east and west. The doors on these short walls are arched and ornamented. The courtyard is paved with stone and has an ablution area. The minaret, repaired several times, including by Sokullu Mehmed Paşa, is in the Ottoman style with a pointed top and a balcony. Sokullu Mehmed Paşa's repairs, dating after the 1550 *waqf*, were then necessary interventions in the building's preservation and maintenance. There was also an associated *madrasa* called Ahmed Ağa.

The other three mosques were the Şeyh Alaüddin, Eredbilī, and Yunus Fakih. The Şeyh Alaüddin (b. Şeyh İbrahim el-Halvetī) or Şeyh Ali Mosque, connected with the Sufi order of Halvetī, was in the Sofular/Sofiyan-i Şeyh Ali Halvetī neighborhood where the adherents of the order lived. It is named after Şeyh Ali, the uncle of Şeyh Ahmed Kuseyr (b. 1470), who was from the village of Zerbenu near Antioch, moved to the city to learn, became a *shaykh* in 1520, and died in Antioch around 1549. Its original plan is lost after so many renovations, but at some point it became a complex or *külliye*. There was no foundation inscription found, but the oldest dates to 1580. The building is fairly plain, with cut stones. There is a stone-paved courtyard with ablution fountain and a *madrasa* of six study rooms. Of its many sources of endowments, two in the city were small urban gardens or *hakūre*, one called Ibn-i Seffāh and one in the Maslaba neighborhood. The Erdebili Mosque, called later Sofular, was in the same neighborhood, although at one point called Şeyh Kasim and likely pre-Ottoman built in the Mamlūk period. Şeyh Kasim was a religious leader from Ardabil in Iran on the western shore of the Caspian Sea.[49] Most of its endowments came from 17 shops in the market. The Yunus Fakih Mosque does not exist today but was in the Habīb al-Najjār neighborhood. Part of its endowments from within the city came from the Semā shop (*dukkan*) and a mill called the Beyt ul-Mā, which must refer to the spring in Daphne. A fourth mosque, Şeyh Ali, is also mentioned in the tax registers of the sixteenth century.

The *masjids* were neighborhood mosques, usually one per neighborhood, and sometimes named after the neighborhoods in which they were located. These included Maslaba (Maslaba neighborhood, partly endowed by a small garden called Hanya), Sarı Mahmud (Sarı Mahmud neighborhood, also endowed by the Kara Mercümek *havş* and Hacı Hüseyin *havş* and two weaving shops), Gazioğlu (Hayyak area), Hümmāreoğlu (Süveyka neighborhood), Şenbek (Şenbek neighborhood),

FIGURE 10.20 Ulu Camii: (top) entrance from the street; (bottom) minaret and courtyard

Source: Photo taken by Canan Karataş

Kastel (Kastel neighborhood), Mukbil (Mukbil neighborhood, receiving part of its endowment from three shops and lasting until the end of the seventeenth century), Şuğurluoğlu (Debbūs neighborhood), Nu'man (Mahsen neighborhood), Ağıloğlu (Şirince neighborhood), Hamamcıoğlu (Henārik area linked to a wool comber's shop), Şeyh Necm (Henārik area), and İmran (İmran neighborhood). The Meydan *masjid*, in the Meydan neighborhood, is today located on İstiklal Caddesi and Meydan Hamam Caddesi, near the Meydan *hamam*. It has a courtyard with an ablution fountain, and on the north side is a *madrasa* with rooms for study. In the courtyard is a curious round, kiosk-type building, a *muvakkithane*, for those who decide the prayer times. Below the minaret, the door leading into the courtyard is decorated with an ornamented arch. This *masjid* experienced many renovations and, along with the *hamam*, became a small interdependent complex, or *külliye*. Its endowments came from shops in the Meydan market and three homes. The following *masjids*' whereabouts are unknown: Ibn Sûfî, Ibn Ruteyl (at the start of the Sük'ü Semanin (butter-maker's) market), Kubbelü (receiving endowments from the Ibn-i Eyne Bey *havş* and the Kara Mercümek *havş* and one weaving shop), Şam, Şeyh Ahmed Şenbek (perhaps also in the Şenbek neighborhood), Şeyh Haliloğlu, Şırşır Saray, and Debbâğa (perhaps in the Helvani Market, as it was endowed by the shops of this market and a tannery *han*, or *tabakhane*). The Mahremiye mosque was possibly part of the Sokullu Mehmed Paşa *waqf* of the second half of the sixteenth century, as it was built in close proximity to the Sokullu Han and Saka Hamam. The Nakib and Kantara mosques are *manzume* or complexes whose buildings were not all built at the same time. Parts of these mosques were likely built in the early sixteenth century, if not earlier. The Nakip mosque, if it is to be identified with the Nakib Camii today, would have been located outside of the city, in front of the Daphne Gate. The Yeni Camii, connected by inscription to the Halvetī order, could also date to the sixteenth century or earlier. The Kiremitli mosque had a sixteenth-century type minarets. All these mosques share architectural features both with one another and to Habīb al-Najjār and Sarimiye, possibly built in the first half of the fourteenth century under the local Ramazanid dynasty but with some sixteenth-century features.[50] The İhsaniye (Ağa) Mosque was founded by Şeyh İhsan b. Ahmed Kuseyr, noted in a 1602 inscription, though architecturally the mosque is sixteenth century.

No fewer than four mosques (Sofular/Şeyh Kasım, Şeyh Ali, Yeni, İhsaniye) in the city and a neighborhood (Sofiyan-i Şeyh Ali Halvetī) were associated with the fifteenth-century Sufi order of Halveti. Şeyh Ahmed Kuseyr, his uncle Şeyh Ali, and his son İhsan were all honored with mosques. The Şeyh Ahmed Kuseyr Camii, containing his tomb and his father's, Şeyh Abdo, was outside the city in the village of Şenkoy, dated to the sixteenth century or perhaps earlier, to 1464. The subdistrict (*nahiye*) was also named after Şeyh Kuseyr.

The Ağca *masjid* was a Mamlūk mosque mentioned in the seventeenth century that became a *camii* mosque around 1864 and was in the Hayyāk area. Other documents name this as the Tut (probably Dut) neighborhood. Today it survives in the Çağılık neighborhood on Dutdibi Street in the southeast part of the city on the slopes of the mountain. It has a rectangular plan and two prayer halls. The building was built in a depression, and so one entered from the street and then climbed up stairs. The roof is pitched rather than domed. There is an inscription from 1842 mentioning renovations.

In the eighteenth century, the city expanded to the southern districts. The old Mamlūk and early Ottoman structures were mostly gone, through earthquakes and lack of renovations, or else renamed.[51] The city in many ways underwent a significant transformation. New *waqf*-based public buildings were built. Mosques were established on Kurtuluş Caddesi (the classical and medieval north–south *cardo*), each in its own new district. In 1703/04 the grand vizier, Moralı Hasan Paşa, endowed a *külliye*, a typical Ottoman feature of cities, which was a complex that included a mosque, *imaret* (soup kitchen), school, and *hamam* for the use of pilgrims en route to Mecca.[52]

By the nineteenth century, however, the number of mosques was down to only 12 to 14, as corroborated by several sources, indicating that many had shut down over the previous 150 years. The Scottish army officer John Macdonald Kinneir stated in 1813 that the city had 12 mosques with minarets visible on the skyline, half of which were white with a blue pointed top and round shaft, with close galleries in the Ottoman Turkish style, and also domed; the other half had the lower and thicker octagonal or polygonal shaft minarets and umbrella/pavilion top of the Mamlūk Syrian Arab style. We can identify the various mosques based on photographs by Clém Thévenet appearing in the *Iskenderun ve Mülhakatı Albümü* commissioned by Sultan Abdülhamid II (1876–1909) about three-quarters of a century later, as well as newer studies.[53] This album, however, although written after the 1872 earthquake, does not contain mosques built after this date. Those mosques visible today with the Syrian (Mamlūk) style minarets have later inscriptions (whose earliest dates are provided here in parentheses) indicating renovations and include the Yeni (1702, commissioned by Mehmed son of Ali), Sarimiye (1718), Mahremiye (1720), Kantara (1750), Nakip (Nakibzade, commissioned in 1762 by Mehmed Efendi), Kiremitli (1842), Şekercik (1867), Habīb al-Najjār (1858), Sofular (rebuilt after 1872), and Kürt Fakih/Tufaki (commissioned by Haci Hasan Kürt Fakih in the 1800s, before 1846). The Yeni mosque was linked to the Halvetī order as a *makam* (tomb and *tekke*) of Ahmed Zühre and, later, Muhammad Zühre in 1752. Both Kantara and Kiremitli were on the same street and repaired in 1847, likely owing to a disaster, possibly a fire. While it is very likely that many of these correspond to the mosques mentioned in the mid-fourteenth century Mamlūk *waqf*, they have all been renamed. Of the Ottoman minaret style, these include the Ulu Camii (1705, minaret), Şeyh Muhammad Mosque (1718, but minaret renovated), İhsaniye (Ağa) Mosque (1710, *madrasa* sponsored by Abu Bakr Ağa), Halil Ağa (1729, founded by its namesake), Şeyh Ali (1899), and Ahmediye Şıh Ahmed (1842, minaret from 1941 and not original).

Several mosques have no clear minaret information, such as the Şirince/Emirler mosque (1793), Zoveroğlu *masjid* (1800), Zülfikar mosque (1824), and Selvili mosque and *külliye* (between 1812 and 1853, founded by Mustafa, son of

Abdullah). Most of these mosques were built in the eighteenth and nineteenth centuries except the Meydan, which was renovated after the earthquake in 1878 and its minaret in 1884, and the Şeyh Ali (Şeyh Alaüddin) mosques.[54] Another exception may be the sixteenth-century Gazioğlu *masjid*, not mentioned in the previous list, which was called the Abdullah Gazi Camii in the eighteenth century and its endowment enlarged by a Yeğen Mehmed Ağa in 1750 with more shops. It is not preserved today or else has been renamed.

In Buckingham's description of 1816, two other mosques were actually tombs but used for prayer. Apart from these, he stated there were no public buildings of any beauty. Several fountains included the 'Ayn al-'Umra (Fountain of Life), which had 1,000 nails driven between the stones. Because its waters were purported to be medicinal, anyone using it would drive in a nail as an offering of gratitude. Near the southern gate was a new fountain built by Jazzar, the last *paşa* of Acre, with an Arabic inscription in marble. There was also a cave in town where barren women went to become fertile or for help with producing breast milk. On the west bank of the river Bartlett and Carne described a cemetery, which Poujoulat included on his map. Cemeteries also were placed in gardens within the city.

Following the 1822 earthquake, Poujoulat noted only three mosques and *hamams*, a gross miscalculation, while George Robinson in 1832 recorded ten to 12 mosques. Ainsworth and Chesney gave related accounts, and Ainsworth, who revisited Antioch in 1839, referred to the previous descriptions of Captain William Allen (who described the city as miserable), Poujoulat, Pococke, and the German explorer Otto Friedrich von Richter. Apart from the 14 mosques noted by Ainsworth and Chesney in 1835, they also mentioned several baths and *madrasas*. In 1868, Lycklama stated there were 15 mosques in the city, as well as five or six public baths, not in good shape, and about the same number of mediocre markets.

The first Turkish encyclopedia *Kamūs'l Â'lām* (Universal Encyclopedia), published in 1889 and authored by the Albanian Sami Frashëri (Şemseddin Sāmī), also stated that Antioch had 14 mosques, some *madrasas*, a secondary school, and some *hamams*.[55] The French geographer and orientalist Vital Cuinet, however, described more precisely in 1890/1891 a significant number of mosques (24), 28 *masjids*, and ten *madrasas*. His count of two *tekke*s for Sufis, five *hamams*, and 117 public fountains (*sabils*) suggests that these categories of public buildings and structures remained constant.[56] An Ottoman survey in 1895/1896 confirmed the exact same numbers. Thus, in the last decade of the nineteenth century the number of mosques appears to have nearly doubled.[57] While some discrepancy is likely, and the *Kamūs-l 'Alām* may have been using outdated numbers, we can only presume that in between there was a flurry of building activity in the city after all the destruction of the 1872 earthquake. Some that we know were built soon after the 1872 earthquake, often on empty lots, included the *masjids* of Semerciler (1873), Hünkar (1873–5), Uçtum (1876), Debruz (between 1872 and 1911), Hedbe (possibly), and Ali Çavuş. Three were commissioned by Sultan Abdülhamid II in 1895: Orhanlı, Osmaniye (interestingly with a Mamlūk/Syrian style minaret), and Affan Ertuğrul (with an Ottoman minaret). From the mostly standing remains it seems that by 1900 there were about 37 mosques. The discrepancies in numbers of mosques from the mostly material evidence and visitors' accounts likely stem from those that were still standing and those now gone, as well as those with minarets and those that may have had none.

The city also had an active Christian community of both Armenians and Melkites, although the status of Antioch's churches, long part of the urban landscape, was far less evident. Evliya Çelebi mentions in his time seven well-kept monasteries, chapels, and churches. Katip Çelebi, also writing in the seventeenth century, curiously mentions two clocks on the doors of the church in the middle of the city.[58] These buildings may all be pre-Ottoman, as several travelers wrote that before the nineteenth century, no churches in the Ottoman city had been newly built or even repaired. In fact, the community was not allowed to build a new church or repair an existing one without a money payment. Buckingham stated in 1816 that Christians had a hard time building a church, although they had money and permissions from Constantinople, since local fanaticism prevented them. Jacquot further said that around 1840 the population hanged a Greek priest from the sycamore trees near the Aleppo Gate when he wanted to build a church.[59] The Christian community thus resorted to using much older buildings in disrepair. For example, in 1772, Parsons (and, slightly earlier, Perry) wrote that the Greek population still used the unroofed St. Paul's Church and raised a canopy during service, and that it was the only active church in the city. What was left of this church was wiped out in the 1872 earthquake, although a *firman* (decree) was issued to allow its rebuilding. A wooden church in the southwestern Christian neighborhood of Jneyne, apparently visited by a priest from Latakia in 1790, was also destroyed and rebuilt after this earthquake.

The most frequently mentioned church, however, was what is today known as the cave church of St. Peter and popularly associated with the apostle and first Christians, but which at the time was identified with the Church of St. John. Further, it is clear that the cave church of St. Peter was not an Early or Middle Byzantine church but rather was used mainly out of necessity as no new churches were built or old ones repaired. Pococke mentioned this latter church of St. John toward the Iron Gate, hewn out of the rock as a grotto with no altar but still used. During Sunday services, the Greek population brought an altar and also buried their dead around it. This was likely the same place that Poujoulat later mentioned as a small cave that may have been a primitive church of St. John where Christians worshipped at the foot of the mountain. George Robinson, in 1832, also wrote that because Christians could not have a church within the city walls, they used a grotto for their services. Alī Bey noted on the steep slope of the mountain just west of the Aleppo Gate a building cut into the mountain, a door, and two windows, which may be the same structure. Beaufort meanwhile mentioned in 1858/59 the remains of the Church of Sts. Peter and Paul at the summit (it is unclear what she was referring to), and the ancient Church of St. John, the cave church, as recently purchased by the French for a cemetery, where the wall came down from the Iron

Gate to the plain. This latter church was built into the mountain, with two pillars as a portico and a small well by the altar. The grotto had been excavated and still had traces of color paint on the walls.

This may also be the church referred to during brief visits, in 1652 and 1663, by the Orthodox Patriarch Macarius III b. al-Zaʿīm (1647–1672) when he participated in church liturgies and masses, sending a Bible to the Mar Yuhanna Church (St. John's) and providing evidence for an active Christian community.[60] From its location, it appears to be the cave church of St. Peter today. In their illustrated account, Bartlett and Carne mentioned the cave where Christians were forced to worship at night half a mile from the town (i.e., the grotto), the walls of which were 60 feet high. Lycklama, who visited in 1868, was given a tour by Father Ludovico, head of the Capuchins. He described the grotto of St. Peter as having a small, square open space enclosed by a wall, accessed by wooden stairs, and decorated with columns supporting the vault. There was also a cemetery, left of the grotto, where Father Basilio Galli of Navarro was buried after being assassinated by Turks while playing the organ in his church in 1851.[61] Lycklama believed this church to be the cathedral of St. Peter. Father Ludovico had restored the sanctuary and colonnade and raised an altar of white stone. Work on the façade was done in 1863 under orders from Pope Pius IX and paid for, in part, by Napoleon III.[62] To the left of the altar was a door to a small underground sacristy and a secret passage into the mountain, now filled in. This grotto church was unharmed in the 1872 earthquake. It was in fact likely during the Ottoman period, and perhaps as a result of the lack of churches in the city, that the cave church first began to become important, having apparently been given to the Christians by the Muslims in 1580. But it was only after the French consul of Aleppo purchased the cave in 1856 and then handed it over to the Catholic Church that evidently the cave began to be strongly associated with St. Peter and the early Christians, rather than St. John.[63]

Pococke further wrote that the church of St. George was used by the Armenians, yet Corancez said that the same church was owned by the Greeks at the time of his visit, to the exclusion of other sects. At the end of the sixteenth century, the Sherley brothers commented that Christians paid a yearly tribute to the Turks to keep a lamp burning over the tomb of St. Lawrence, the first mention of this saint in Antioch. Patriarch Macarius also mentioned a monastery of the king (*Dayr al-Malik*) located at the gate of Antioch as well as that of Arshaya or St. Arsenius, which he erroneously said was dedicated to the fourteenth-century archbishop of Tver in Russia, although we know of this monastery from the tenth century. Bartlett and Carne also mentioned "some remains of a church, said to be that of Chrysostom" and various tombs, as did Ainsworth and Chesney. Lycklama wrote that the only church remaining was one of the schismatic Greek churches, presumably Orthodox (perhaps the Church of St. John Chrysostom?), which was remarkable for its mosaic paving, sculpted wooden choir, and altar ornamented with tableaux (icons) from Russia. There were a few other simple chapels, badly decorated. Lycklama also added that during his visit there were four Christian patriarchs – a Latin, Melkite, Maronite, and Miaphysite – and he also observed a caravan of Anglican missionaries. In 1846, an Italian priest, P. Basile, established a Capuchin mission from which a Christian community grew in 1851, with more missionaries and homes in 1860. In the 1872 earthquake, a church and hospice of the Capuchins, made of wood of antiquity, was also heavily damaged and rebuilt in stone.[64] Among the collapsed buildings was the recently built Greek cathedral and an American Protestant church, while four members of the Christian community were killed. Ancient and medieval stones were used in the rebuilding.[65]

The earlier constrained situation of the Christian churches had obviously changed by the late nineteenth century. Cuinet mentioned in 1890/1891 three churches (including the Orthodox Church of St. Peter and Catholic Church of St. Peter). A photo album commissioned by Sultan Abdülhamit II in the last quarter of the nineteenth century included photographs of an Armenian church, Greek Orthodox church, and Greek Orthodox school. There was also a picture of a ruined church of St. Batras (St. Peter?) outside the city. Dating the building of churches to the second half or even last quarter of the century would align with this shift, which also agrees with population figures, which nearly doubled during this span of 18 to 22 years. The concentration of Christian religious spaces to the north of the city near the Aleppo Gate and grotto suggests that the Christian community lived in this part of the town. The Jewish community, while present, must have been quite small; Buckingham wrote that Jews used a small room in the house of their leader. Ainsworth and Chesney in 1835 were the first to note a synagogue, while Cuinet in 1890/1891 also mentioned its existence.

Prior to the establishment of hotels, travelers stayed in caravansarays/*khans*, like Parsons in 1722, who stayed in a cotton *khan* by the east gate, or else in private homes. Usually Westerners stayed in Christian homes. If they had means and influence, they stayed in the house of the governor, like the Spanish Muslim Ali Bey in 1807, or else in the homes of consuls, like Emily Beaufort in the English consul's home in 1858/1859 or the German orientalist Carl Eduard Sachau in that of the German consul in 1880. Pococke stayed in 1738 with a merchant under the protection of the English consul. These instances also show the presence of these consulates in the city.[66] Gertrude Bell was taken around by the vice-consul (a Jew from Damascus) and met with M. Poton, a French merchant and his wife, and Refa'it (Rifat) Ağa, one of the town's wealthiest citizens and an antiquities collector who lived in a beautiful home. Buckingham in 1816 stayed in the house of a young Christian merchant named 'Abd al-Massiah (al-Masīḥ), who was suspicious of him but cordial, while Bartlett and Carne stayed in the house of the wealthy Christian Girgius Adeeb. They preferred to stay in a local's home rather than a caravansaray, suggesting the latter buildings were more rudimentary and uncomfortable.

As for Daphne, by Ottoman times it was largely an uninhabited field of ruins. De la Roque wrote in 1688 that nothing there was left. Barker stated in 1816 that in Daphne, called Dwaire or Bayt al-Ma' (see Chapter 6), there was a spring called Sghaibo but no trace of the Apollo temple. Robinson, however, wrote that above the springs was an ancient ruin with a structure built over it and using its materials, which he speculated was a Christian church covering the Apollo temple. Perhaps, this was the monastery-church that Downey excavated in sector 53-K. Chesney noted the aqueducts and other ruins coming from Daphne 2.5 miles southwest of the town (including the Fountain of Zoiba), and one mile further the amphitheater, and the mills and Bayt al-Ma', while Thomson in 1840 stated that the road between Antioch and Daphne was filled the entire way with granite columns and other ruins.

As noted, İbrahim Paşa had used explosives to obtain stones from the ruins and city walls – these he used to build himself a palace and massive barracks on the Orontes. It is likely this was the most extensive destruction of any surviving classical or medieval remains and a main reason why little is visible today of the city's medieval monuments. In his first visit in 1835, Ainsworth noted İbrahim Paşa's mansion and barracks built out of stones of the walls, but on his second visit in 1839 he wrote that the barracks were still incomplete. He also said that İbrahim had sold the palace to Muḥammad (Mehmed) Ali Paşa and it was now converted to a military hospital. Emily Beaufort, visiting 20 years later, stated that the palace and barracks, which had never been finished, were now being dismantled for roofing by the English consul, who had gained permission for a barracks for the Land Transport Corps at the start of the Crimean War. Le Camus noted in 1890 porphyry paving between the barracks and palace on the line of the colonnaded street.

The economy and natural resources

Nearly every traveler's account discusses the city's ruralization, the contracted modern town, and the large spaces in the northern section composed of earlier ruins and enclosed by the walls from antiquity. Volney also said that the contracted town was walled, though no one else did. The large, empty spaces, given over in the medieval periods to agriculture, were evidence for these travelers of a ruined, destroyed, and miserable city. This ruralization continued throughout most of the Ottoman period. Many authors described and depicted in maps this northern half of the city as full of fruit trees growing over the ruins. These orchards included figs, olives, pomegranates, walnuts, and apricots. Alī Bey described this part of the city as full of small urban or "kitchen" gardens. The area between the Orontes delta and the city and on the slopes was cultivated with most of the mulberry trees for the silk industry. Black and white poplars lined the river, and there were also sycamore trees. Belon in the mid-sixteenth century fixated on the city's vegetation, which he described as a forest of a kind unparalleled in Europe. He observed large numbers of *Celtis australis* (hackberry or nettle tree) that grew nearest the mountain and large plane trees near the gates (like the famed one near the Aleppo Gate). Also growing all around the city's gardens were sugar cane and colocasia tubers (*qulqas* in Arabic). The mountains were covered in oaks, purslane, or eastern strawberry trees (*Arbutus andrachne)*, lavender (*Lavandula stoechas*), and hedge-nettle (*Stachys*). The feeling of a forest was echoed by Lycklama, who wrote that the only beauty was in the trees – elm, plane, and some palms – that filled the empty spaces and surrounded houses to such a degree that from a high point the city appeared green. Instead of a forest, Poujoulat likened Antioch to an "oriental" cemetery with cypress trees, under which small fountains and cafés could be seen. Many of the city's open spaces were given over to gardens, fields, and orchards, and some of these were taxed for religious endowments. In 1550 there were 3,949 olive trees recorded, mainly used to produce olive oil for soap manufacture. On the river, *nā'ūras* (waterwheels) 60 feet in diameter dispersed water into channels built on brick piles or on ruins in the town and gardens (Figures 10.21 and 10.22). These waterwheels also fed mills along the river for grain or olive oil. The sixteenth-century accounts enumerated eight mills: Sābūniye (for the olive oil soap milling, was known since the mid-fourteenth century as Ibn Ṣābūnī), Ibn Cündī (perhaps near the *hamam* of the same name), Rikābiye, Sultaniye, Ibn Mu'allā or Mevla, Ibn-i Özeriye, Meşre'a, and Cedid (the newest one). The Zer'ūniye mill was already no longer operational in 1536, and another mill is referred to called Arguniye. There were also dams of reed stakes (weirs) to raise the water for the mills and trap fish. On the opposite side of the river grew irrigated vegetable gardens of all kinds. The *waqf* account also states there were nine *hakūre* gardens, meaning small urban gardens, perhaps near to mosques or baths, that could be rented out to individuals.

The Amuq Plain also provided important agricultural goods, including grain, cotton, tobacco, citron and orange orchards and other fruits, sugar cane (though for local consumption only, not for sugar processing), and eels from the lake, still preserved and exported (especially during Lent for Christians). Parsons in the late eighteenth century wrote that the eels were more than 3 feet long and were still an export, salted and dried and sold all over Syria. By 1895/1896, 250,000 eels were being caught annually and shipped to Cyprus, Egypt, and Beirut. The Nusayris (Alawites), who lived in villages, were mainly in charge of tobacco production, which was exported. Corancez wrote that the city included territory enclosing part of the Amuq Plain below the Orontes River and down to the Orontes delta. Interestingly, he also commented that the rest of the Amuq Plain, controlled by Turkmen who lived in round huts and tents in camps, were in conflict with the *ağa* of Antioch, which made travel and trade via caravan challenging. Belon also noted in the Amuq Lake white storks on their migratory patterns across the Levant, as well as pelicans, tufted ducks, smew ducks, and a golden-eye, canvasback northern pintail.

From the Amuq Survey data, the Late Islamic II period (sixteenth to nineteenth centuries) shows a pattern in the plain of a limited number of small settlements. An insight into how the Amuq Plain was viewed in sixteenth-century Ottoman court circles is provided by a drawing in a manuscript written by Nasuh Matrakçı chronicling the first Persian campaign of Sultan Süleyman in 1534–1536. This manuscript contains a number of pictures representing towns, villages, and the countryside. Because the overall manuscript is quite accurate from a topographical point of view, it is possible the artist was trying to depict the ancient mounds in the Amuq Valley. What is remarkable, however, is that the manuscript drawings show

FIGURE 10.21 Waterwheel at Antioch, Turkey, American Colony, Photo Dept., 1898–1930

FIGURE 10.22 Waterwheel and cemetery, Grigord Collection, 1858–1859, R.14 (PP22.01)

no sign of any settlement either around the lake or by the bridge over the Orontes. But the evidence from Ottoman tax registers shows, in agreement with the Amuq Survey data, that the region was not quite so empty. In the sixteenth century, the number of villages in the district of Antioch grew from 27 to 55 while the number of fields decreased, likely becoming new villages.[67] In the Amuq Plain, peasants largely worked lands owned by others and then received proceeds from their labor after the taxes on the profits had been taken. The types of products they would have grown included wheat, barley, lentils, broad beans, millet, oats, vetch, chickpeas, olives, grapes, fruit, garden vegetable produce, and most importantly, rice, which is mentioned in both plant (*çeltik*) and processed (*pirinç*) forms. Of the animals raised in the plain, there were cattle, water buffalo, sheep and goats, and bees.

In the first half of the sixteenth century, the city had a horse market, slave (male and female) market, butchery, tannery, a *başhâne* (place that sold heads of animals), fishmongery, and textile, linen, and dye markets. Some of these, such as the butchery, tannery, and textile and dye markets, and even a shop-owner which sold animal heads (*rawwās*), were known already since the Mamlūk era. Textile production and commerce was the main economy of the town's markets, especially from the second half of the sixteenth century. This is evident by the significant raising of taxes on textile and dye shops and silk loomers from 1550 to 1584. Taxes were applied to raw cloth, plain oil, molasses, honey, figs, rice and cereal in bulk, silk looms, and all goods coming into the city via land. Snow was even brought from the mountains to cool foods and was in high demand. Soap was exported to Adana, Kayseri, and Sivas. There was also a *meyhane* (tavern), a *bedesten* with 101 shops inside and two outside, and a *han* called Han-i Sebil, given as a *waqf* by Jafer Ağa in the Dörtayak (Debbūs) neighborhood, with 28 rooms on the first level and 22 on the upper level, with two shops. This may have been later transformed into the Çelenkoğlu Sabun Hanesi, built before 1862, although the patron named was Hasan Bey b. Abdülmuin. There is also a reference to a different building – the Sokullu Han and Bedesten,[68] sponsored by Sokullu Mehmet Paşa and built before 1574 – which was mentioned by Evliya Çelebi and became a soap factory (*sabunhane*) in 1845.

In the sixteenth century, the city had several markets and about 200 shops, as detailed in the *waqf* document. Besides the main market (Suk-i Antakya), there were the market of sweets/desert makers (Suku'l Halvani) with sellers of cookies and *künefe* (still the pride of Antakya today), the market of perfumer and spice vendors (Suku'l Attarin, also known since the Mamlūk period), and the area of bakers (Uncular Meydan). Agricultural products included those of the plain and town: wheat, rye, barley, bread, wine, tobacco, sugar cane, fruit, vegetables (such as eggplant and okra), and licorice. In the Meydan of the city, grain would arrive to be weighed by the measurer (*keyyal*). It could then go to one of the mills on the river and on to the bakers. Belon thought poorly of the local bread, which he said was badly cooked and badly leavened, but was his only critique of Antioch. Çelebi specifically mentioned noteworthy products of white "camel's tooth" or large-grained wheat, cotton, sugar cane, lemons, and oranges, but unlike Belon praised the city's *çakıl* bread (Figure 10.23).

Both *waqf* documents and travelers like De la Roque wrote that there were in the markets guilds for craftsmen, who were grouped on streets each devoted to an industry. Guild leaders were often called *shaykhs*, and there were recorded *shaykhs* for the guilds of perfumers/spice merchants, carpenters, tanners, weavers, and wool combers (*hallaç*). These also indicate those businesses that had the most numbers of shops. By the end of the seventeenth century and first half of the eighteenth century, there were guilds with shaykhs for blacksmiths, loomers, tailors, jewelers, dyers, gardeners, furriers, saddle makers, shoemakers, barbers, hat makers, weavers of blankets and *aba* (coat) makers, water carriers, and bowyers (who made bows). The neighborhood of Çullāhan in the Hayyāk area was likely an area of the weavers' shops (*çulha*). Seventeenth- and eighteenth-century *waqf* documents mention many more markets as well, including the Külahçılar (cone hats), Tahtānī (lower market), Uzun (long market) in the Hümmāre neighborhood, Muytab for weavers of wool, Najjar (near the mosque), Sipahi (for the military), Öküzvāt (bulls), and Şiʿār (also known in the Mamlūk period). Çelebi wrote that the economic infrastructure of the city was supported by 350 uncovered shops, nine *hans* for bachelors and traders, and the aforementioned wooden *bedesten* for luxury goods.

The variety of merchants and artisans selling all kinds of goods in the market suggests that the city was already a bustling, vivacious, and colorful entrepôt and center for production in the sixteenth and seventeenth centuries. Among those businesses not already mentioned were rope makers, sellers of scarves and turbans, printed cotton shops, ceramic shops, reed mat makers (known since the Mamlūk period), towel shops, felt shops, sword shops, coppersmiths, smoking pipe makers, coffee sellers, fermented barley drink (*boza*) shops, kebab shops, dried chickpea vendors, horseshoe makers, wooden furniture makers, lathe operators, musical instrument shops, iron solderers, thrift shops, sellers of small wares or haberdashers, butcher shops, and even an architect. Intermingling in these areas were porters to facilitate the movement of goods around the city and garbage men. These merchants were not only Muslim but also Christians and Jews (*bazirgan).*

The markets also contained mineral and metal goods. Corancez stated that Antioch was rich in coins and gemstones (carnelian, agate, and jasper); of ancient coins, there were Kufic and Arab specimens that, "to the contrary of received general opinion, present diverse figures of people and animals," perhaps referring to the Saljūq coins of Rum. This observation also seems to suggest an economy of looted antiquities.

Despite the great variety of goods made and sold in the markets, the markets were variously commented on as rich or poor, though the negative observations were tinted by the same European orientalist views of the town's character. For example, Ainsworth noted that although cultivation was to be found all around the town within the walls, the town itself remained impoverished and was not prosperous, while Corancez stated that the Muslims had been unable to revive the city's commerce because they were unskilled, unlike Jews and Christians. Nonetheless, Belon said in 1553 that the city's market was well-stocked with all manner of provisions, shops, druggists, and craftsmen, similar to Damascus, while two centuries

FIGURE 10.23 Grain market by G. Bell, 1905, C_073

later van Egmond wrote that one could buy anything in the market. Volney noted that the city was still an entrepôt for European traders and better than Aleppo. Certainly, Antioch's markets were not as large or robust as Aleppo's; nevertheless, there was a thriving local manufacture and export business that could not have been run solely by Jews and Christians. By the end of the Ottoman period, the market districts (Meydan, Haraparası, Yeni Camii, Akbaba, and Ulu Camii) cut through several neighborhoods along the river and took up a quarter of the town. Like in the previous period, this district lay between the Ulu Camii and Habib Neccar Camii and stretched north, occupying the northwest corner of the contracted city. Looking at the street names today in this area, still the market district, we see that the long east–west street markets perpendicular to the river framed the district (Meydan to the north, Tijaret in the center, Uzun in the south), with the small north–south side street markets devoted to the specific commodities. Within these districts were the *hans*, many of which were turned into soap factories. A 1710 census also showed 1,161 tradesmen working in the city, which included shoemakers, tailors, jewelers, builders, butchers, bakers, saddlers, grocers, tin makers, coppersmiths, gardeners, watchmakers, perfumers, and tanners.[69]

Surprisingly, early-twentieth-century Western guidebooks stated that timber and licorice from the area were exported to the United States and maize to Europe. Textiles of silk, cotton, and leather were a main commodity and both produced and sold. Goat and camel hair products, such as saddlebags from the Türkmen nomads, were also sold. On the east riverbanks were tanneries and shoe manufacturers; these produced horse-riding gear (saddles, bridles, and martingales), which were famous, red and yellow leather shoes, and also raw leather. The city's main industries were cotton weaving and raw silk production for export (Figure 10.24). These industries also took place in the suburbs of Daphne and Samandağ at the Orontes delta. Parsons in the late eighteenth century wrote that most silk was exported to England. Specific garments included coats (*abas*) that were colorful but whose colors did not hold, according to Corancez. The *Kamūs'l 'Alām* stated that silk shirts, coarse cloth, *çarşaf* (women's outer robes), Tripoli shawls, and *maşlah* (sleeveless open cloaks) were produced. Blue-dyed cloth was exported and worn by lower classes in Marseilles. These were also worn by locals, where the fashion included red shalloon trousers for men with yellow boots and slippers and long robes, and black veils for women. The 1872 earthquake, however, hurt silk manufacture, as the city lost half of its silk industry and European traders left for Aleppo's markets.[70]

Besides silk and cotton, the other two main industries were olive oil and soap. These were linked, since soap was made of olive oil (and sometimes laurel) and exported along with textiles. There were also woodcarvers, goldsmiths, metalworkers, and potters producing a coarse pottery. In 1880, the main exports were silk and wheat, and Antioch was a main center of soap production, one of two in Syria; according to the *Kamūs'l 'Alām*, 12,000 to 15,000 tons of soap were being produced every year by 1895/1896.[71] But in that same year, grain had to be purchased from Aleppo, since not enough could be cultivated. Other goods were imported as well. Kinneir noted that coffee, sugar, and salt were imported from Egypt and cotton from Izmir, providing a range of local and imported cotton clothing.

The noted Ottoman statesman and historian Ahmed Cevdet Paşa wrote in his memoirs (*Tezakir*) that in 1867 Antioch had 1,000 shops, eight *hans*, and other buildings.[72] Vital Cuinet counted in 1890/1891 some 1,451 shops, 35 warehouses, 20 *hans*, one pharmacy, 25 bakeries, five watermills, nine soap factories (including Siddik Müftu, Sefa Dağlı, Şeyhoğlu, and Aselci), and 13 silk

FIGURE 10.24 Turkish and Syrian workers at a silk factory in Antioch, c. 1900–1920, Meadeville, PA: Keystone View Company (1513 71)

Source: Courtesy of Kheel Center, Cornell University

factories. The Ottoman survey in 1895/1896 gave the same numbers save for three more warehouses and one more silk factory. The presence of so many soap and silk factories confirms the main concentrated industries of the city. The population jump and building boom in mosques and other buildings between 1867 and 1890 are further confirmed by the number of *hans*, which suggests a growing economy.

Streets, neighborhoods, and houses

In 1661, Wolffgang Aigen commented that Antioch's streets were broad and large but unclean. The streets that came to typify the Ottoman city, however, were narrow and winding, with raised sidewalks for foot passengers, a deeper narrow passage for animals, and a central gutter to siphon off water (Figure 10.25). This change in street style and street grid would have been gradual. The average width of Antioch's streets was between 2.6 and 3.25 m. These narrow streets, similar to the side streets of sector 17-O and other sectors of the Late Antique and medieval city excavated by Princeton, stand in contrast to the colonnaded streets in antiquity, which were 30 m wide. Shallow water channels called *ariks* ran down the center – 6–10 cm deep and 60–90 cm wide – and were similar to those excavated in the side streets. These were important owing to the city's flooding from the mountain torrents. The streets were paved with marble blocks, and travelers interpreted the raised parts of the streets to either side as sidewalks.

In the sixteenth century, the number of neighborhoods (*mahalle*) grew from 21 to 24, although the 1550 *waqf* account lists only 11 but makes reference to two

FIGURE 10.25 Antioch street by J. D. Whiting, c. 1930–1940 (Photographs of Lebanon, Turkey, and Syria Archive (Lot 13856-G, reproduction number: LC-DIG-ppmsca-18437)

Source: Courtesy of the Library of Congress

more and two areas. New neighborhoods appeared, while some changed names or grew in size and were subsequently divided. Neighborhoods were important units, not only for tax and *waqf* purposes, but because they cultivated social cohesion, security, and unity among their residents, focused around the neighborhood mosque as a community center and place of prayer.[73] Additionally, each neighborhood had a steward (*kethüdası*). These neighborhoods included new ones after the Ottoman conquest: Dörtayak, Haraccı or Harami Bekir, and Hallabünnemli (Basaliye). These were among the most populated and so changed names or were subdivided. Between 1550 and 1570, Dörtayak grew from 38 to 114 houses and so became subdivided into Dörtayak and Debbūs. Dörtayak may have originally included Harami Bekir, which after 1570 was no longer mentioned. Hallabünnemli (Basaliye) became Maslaba, which became Ma'beliye after 1536. Some larger neighborhoods were connected to smaller ones. These included Kastel, connected to Şirince (Pınar), Mahsen, Mukbiloğlu, Paşaoğlu, and Sarı Mahmud; (Ibn) Şenbek, connected to Camii Kabir, İmranoğlu, and Saha; Ma'beliye, connected to Meydan; Süveyka or İbn Hümmāre, connected to the aforementioned Dörtayak; and Sofular or Sofiyan-i Şeyh Alī Halvetī, connected to Mescit-i Şeyh Hamza or Bıçakçılar (knife-makers). This last neighborhood was also that of Şeyh Kasım Camii (al Ma'ruf Sofiyan-i Erdebilī), which alongside the neighborhood of Habībünneccār (Habīb al-Najjār)/Keşkekoğlu was the most populated. The 1550 document lists two areas not mentioned elsewhere: Hayyāk/Dikişçi and Henārik. Some neighborhoods were part of these areas, such as the second most populated in 1526, Çullāhan (weavers), and Kanavāt, which replaced it as the second most populated between 1536 and 1584. Some others are less known – Gülbek/İbn-i Seb and Tab-i Çullāhan – and some were established later like Debbūs (from Dörtayak) and Zeytinoğlu. Most of these are likely known by different names today, except Şirince, Sofular, Camii Kabir (as Ulu Camii), and Meydan.

De la Roque wrote in 1688 that the city had 45 quarters or neighborhoods in the center, 27 of which were Muslim. Greeks, Armenians, and Jews lived in neighborhoods on the edge, as well as Shī'a (Alawites), who had quarters to the north and south of the city and were a poor minority. Two of these new districts in the seventeenth century were established to the east on the mountain slopes, while in the eighteenth century expansion was to the south. New mosques appeared for each new district, such as the Şeyh Muhammad Mosque in 1724 on Kurtuluş Caddesi, built roughly over the ancient cardo.[74] A 1766 census counted 2,500 houses in the city. The first mention of a neighborhood, Selāmet (today Cumhuriyet), on the west side of the river was made in 1838 by M. Georges Robinson.

The Belgian geographer Jacques Weulersse, who studied the neighborhoods in 1935, characterized them into three types – the Turkish quarters (in the center), the Christian (Greek), and those of the Alawites, a Muslim Arab-speaking sect found mainly in the northern Levant (i.e., the region of Antioch, Syria, and Lebanon).[75] After the Ottoman – Russian War in 1877–78, the first neighborhood on the west bank of the Orontes was built as a refugee area for Circassians, an ethnic group from the North Caucasus and mainly Sunni Muslim, and called Muhacirin Osmaniye (Ottoman Immigrants) or Yeni Mahalle (New Neighborhood). By 1900, there were about 3,500 houses in the city.

Turkish scholar Ataman Demir has today enumerated 35 districts, seven of which on the west bank of the Orontes (Kanatlı, Cebrail, Akevler, Emek, Cumhuriyet, Elektrik, and Armutlu) began in the nineteenth century. The old town neighborhoods include Kışla-Saray, Kantara, Güllübahçe, Dutdibi, Zenginler, Biniciler, Ulu Camii, Kocaabdı, Akbab, Şeyhalı, Yeni Camii, İplikpazarı, Meydan,

Barbaros, Haraparası, Orhanlı, Sofular, Fevzipaşa, Gazipaşa, Kuyulu, and Şehitler, which do not exactly correspond to the districts in Weulersse's map of 1934. The districts of Bağrıyanık, Kardeșler, Aydınlıkevler, Karaalı Bölüğü, Havuzlar, Şirince, and Bedevi-Sümerler near the slopes of the mountain consist of illegally built houses of rural migrants. Those buildings currently designated historic for preservation purposes include 25 mosques, six *masjids*, three *hans*, four *hahamams*, seven *türbe* (tombs), 23 *sabils*, one *bedesten*, four soap factories, one church, one synagogue, and 24 other structures, as well as 190 houses. These were registered in 1975 and updated in 1985.

Jean Chesneau, a clerk of Gabriel d'Aramon, who was the French ambassador to the Ottoman Empire under kings Francis I and Henry II, detailed the ambassador's journey in December 1549, one year after Belon's visit, at the time of Süleyman the Magnificent.[76] He stated that the houses of Antioch were sparse and dilapidated and inhabited by Turks, Armenians, and a few Jews. Pococke wrote that the houses were "ill-built," low, and built on bad foundations, and consisted of one story with flat roofs supported by light rafters and thin roof tiles. During the 1755 earthquake, a Mr. and Mrs. Barker, sleeping in an upper room in a house on the river, were awakened as part of the old city wall against which the house was built gave way, and their own house's walls fell outward while they fell to the first floor. In 1772, Abraham Parsons wrote there were 40 to 50 houses remaining outside the western gate. Carsten Niebuhr also noted that the houses were very poor. Some houses had pitched roofs with roof tiles, which he thought may have been introduced by Europeans with the Crusades. Volney wrote in 1783–1785 that houses were made of mud and thatch, although this seems odd since there were certainly enough stones, tile, and brick around. These observations were tempered somewhat, however, in the late seventeenth century by Çelebi, who commented on the large, wealthy homes along the river.

In the nineteenth century, Antioch's houses were all similarly described as small, mostly two stories high, and of light construction owing to earthquakes (Figure 10.26). They were built of cut stone with the upper story of wood and sometimes a wooden frame filled with sun-dried bricks, and featured a central courtyard shaded by a fruit tree. The outer walls were high, and small, arched windows and doors faced west to catch the sea-borne Orontes breezes. They also had a pent or pitched roof and red tiles. Lycklama and Poujoulat noted that building materials, such as stones, columns, and capitals, were actively taken from ancient buildings and used as material in homes. According to the 1836 account of Bartlett and Carne, the house of the Christian Girgius Adeeb was built on the city wall and comprised a building for his family (*haremlik*) and a building for offices, all arranged around a courtyard with a well. After the 1872 earthquake, inhabitants were allowed to use stones from the city wall to reconstruct their homes.

The Antiochene houses, many of which are inhabited or preserved today, have been the subject of several studies.[77] They were of Syrian style – courtyard houses with little departure from similar houses 1,000 years or older in the city. Only

FIGURE 10.26 An Ottoman Antioch house at No. 5 Kara Ahmet Çk. off Kurtuluş Cadd. between the Ertuğrul Affan Camii and the Catholic Church

Source: Photograph taken by Zeki Cemali

in the late nineteenth/early twentieth centuries were these houses replaced by closed, central hall houses. They are thus helpful in envisioning what some of the excavated courtyard houses, such as those in sector 17-O of the medieval periods, may have looked like above their foundations. The courtyard houses featured a narrow entrance from the street, often a side street ending in a dead end. The exterior of the house was an undecorated wall 3 m high, blocking the view into the home, typical of Islamic residences. The entrance had two doors and a corridor 2 to 3 m long, 1.5–2 m wide. Often there were two doors, an inner and outer. In some cases, the passage between the doors had a cylindrical wooden cupboard allowing the women of the house to receive deliveries without going outside. In some houses there was a small door within the larger door. The entrance opened onto a stone-paved courtyard (*havuş*) that featured a well, sunken marble pool (*burke*), and fruit trees (pomegranate, orange, lemon, olive, and grape), which helped provide shade. Often in one corner was a stone platform (*seki* or *livan*), raised 40 to 50 cm off the ground and frequently decorated, where guests were received and which was roofed. Around the courtyard were niches, often decorated, for lamps (*fanus takası*), which also functioned as family shrines. Some niches were partially covered with decorated wood and could hold other objects, while some were larger for mattresses and pillows and covered with a cloth curtain. Above the windows were smaller windows with carved, decorated rosettes and other patterns above, letting in light and called *kafa penceresi/tepe penceresi* (or *kuş takasi/kuş penceresi*). In the corner of the courtyard was a bathroom on a lower level. The rooms (*oturma evi*) were all in a row on one side, usually facing south, and opening to the courtyard. A main room in an *iwan*-style (*selamlik*), open on its courtyard side, was often for meetings and receiving guests and ornamented with rooms to either side. The first floor was built of ashlars, often reused from ancient or medieval buildings, and redressed at times.

A staircase from the courtyard provided access to a long, wooden balcony and an upper gallery row of rooms, usually for sleeping, storage, pantry, and drying clothes. The upper levels were built of lath and plaster, with windows facing the courtyard and bay windows facing the street. These windows were shuttered, allowing one to view outside but not in. The houses were gabled or hipped roofed with red tiles. Rooms were often decorated with built-in, carved wooden shelves that were decorated and sometimes painted, marble-tiled floors, and coffered or paneled ceilings. The more elite houses featured painting on the walls and ceilings. These details of nineteenth- and early-twentieth-century houses thus differed significantly from the earlier, more dilapidated descriptions, though to be sure, older unrenovated tenament style homes were peppered throughout the city's neighborhoods, much as they are even today.

Ottoman reform and defeat

Around the time that Mehmed Ali Paşa was forced to withdraw from Syria, the Ottoman Empire, under Sultan Abdülmecid I (1839–1861), began implementing a comprehensive series of political, social, legal, military, and economic reforms. Known as the Tanzimat ("reorganization"), these were intended to halt the empire's decline and strengthen it against both internal and external threats by modernizing the Turkish state and bringing it in closer alignment with Western principles and practices, yet within an Islamic framework. Patterned after the Napoleonic Code of France, the reforms included centralizing the empire's administration under the sultan with a system of provincial representative assemblies, guaranteeing civil liberties and legal and social equality for all citizens throughout the empire regardless of race or religion, establishing a system of secular schools, including the empire's first modern universities, modernizing the military, and reorganizing the civil and criminal codes. These reforms were designed to undermine internal nationalist movements by uniting all peoples within the empire – whether Turks, Greeks, Armenians, Jews, Kurds, Alawites, or Arabs – under a single Ottoman identity and to alleviate strife between Muslims and non-Muslims, thereby forestalling European intervention in the empire's affairs.

Reflecting the Ottoman Empire's turn to the West, Antioch's urban landscape began exhibiting Western influences both in building and planning and in foreigners residing in the city. A new quarter, the Hamidiye (after Sultan Abdülhamid), south of the bridge, was built with Western European-style buildings of iron and brick and large public facing doors, including hotels, mansions, and coffee-houses along the river.[78] People enjoyed resting along the Orontes, which was 100–150 feet wide at the bridge and flowed at a rate of 3 miles per hour.[79] There was also a regular "Arab Orchestra" that performed on the banks of the river. Vital Cuinet counted in the 1890s three hotels and 14 coffee houses, as did an Ottoman survey. Influenced by Western styles of administration, by around 1850 a government office building (*hükümet konağî*) had been built in Daphne near the Christian quarter, while in Antioch an office of the governor (*kaymakam*) had replaced a previous one[80] and a government palace had been built on the sultan's land. The new Palace Road (Saray Caddesi) connected the government palace and office building to the Great Mosque. New buildings, restaurants, and shops built along this road also helped create new social spaces in parts of the city.[81] Restrictions on church building were removed, and Christian communities petitioned to build and repair places to congregate.[82] In about 1855, the Capuchin Order of the Catholic Church built a church after obtaining permission.

In the end, however, the Tanzimat reforms only partially succeeded in modernizing the Ottoman Empire, and ultimately they failed altogether in their purpose of saving it. By the mid-1870s, Sultan Abdülaziz (1861–1876), who retained almost unlimited power, had begun pulling back on the reforms, which also faced strong opposition from religious leaders and the upper classes as well as the majority Muslim population. A few decades later, the outbreak of World War I in 1914 sounded the empire's death knell after it sided with the Central Powers of Germany, Austria-Hungary, and Bulgaria; following their defeat in 1918, the empire was partitioned into separate political entities, including what became the French Mandate for Syria and the Lebanon and the British Mandate for Palestine. It was Antioch's fate to fall under the French mandate and in particular the district called the Sanjak of Alexandretta, where heading further into the twentieth century the city faced a deeply uncertain future.

Conclusions

The descriptions of Western travelers, filtered through an orientalist lens, are to be taken with a grain of salt. Indeed, placed side by side with Ottoman census records, the accounts show two very different ways of seeing a city – one as a shell of its past self, and one as a gradually developing provincial town. We can, however, make two observations and two criticisms. First, Antioch began to be rebuilt as an Islamic city after 1268 and continued throughout the Ottoman period, although as a small border town. As a palimpsest, vestiges of the Crusader and earlier medieval iterations were visible in the Ottoman city. At the same time, the changes that did occur to its buildings, walls, and other spaces – whether reused or utilized as talismans, or abandoned, or both, as in the case of towers becoming trash pits – would have been part of the overall transformation of any city. A main criticism is that the Ottomans made virtually no effort to preserve any sort of cultural heritage. This is partly understandable: while the Ottomans did pursue archaeological research, it was linked to establishing legitimacy within the Anatolian landscape, and Antioch had little to do with grounding this mythic background. A second criticism is that the Ottomans failed to put in place any sort of anti-flooding infrastructure throughout this period. Finally, the second observation is that, despite the despair spilt by Western travelers over Antioch with its few remains, dilapidated character, and unfriendly citizens, the travelers continued to come, even after reading the negative descriptions by others of the city; Antioch was, and to this day remains, an important tourist destination. In 1931, Paul Jacquot published his guidebook to the city, *Antioche, centre de tourisme*. One year later, the Princeton team began its seven-year-long project. Antioch, with its legendary ties to antiquity, early Christianity, and the Crusades, was still for Western audiences too irresistible to avoid or merely read about; it had to be seen with one's own eyes.

Notes

1 Al-Antaki, *Tazyīn al-aswāq bi-tafṣīl 'ushshāq*. II 77. The church is connected with Luke.
2 E. Çelebi, 1999. *Seyahatnāmesi*, Book III. Topkapı Sarayı Kütüphanesi Bağdat 305 Numaralı Yazmanın Transkripsiyonu – Dizini. S. A. Kahraman and Y. Dağlı (eds). Yapı Kredi Yayınları. 34 (32)–39 (38).
3 Other Ottoman-period local nobles did similarly in other cities, sometimes using the spolia to legitimize themselves as inheritors of the ancient past. For example, see Neumeier 2017, 311–337.
4 Islamic tradition commonly holds Isma'īl to be the son almost sacrificed by Abraham rather than Isaac.
5 Qur'ān 52: 4
6 From Abdülkādir, *Kitāb-ı Tevārih-i Antākiyya* on the Prophet Muḥammad's *mir'āj*, as explained to him by the Archangel Gabriel upon viewing the city. This manuscript is at the Orientabteilung at the Staatsbibliothek zu Berlin (National Library) and filed as ms. or. oct. 2896. Many thanks to Necati Alkan for sharing his unpublished "Legendary Chronicles of Antioch," which is a translation and commentary, with me.
7 Açikgoz 2016, 1–17; J. de la Roque, 1722. *Voyage de Syrie et du Mont-Liban.: contenant la description de tout le pays compris sous le nom de Liban & d'Anti-Liban, Kesroan, &c. ce qui concerne l'origine, la créance, & les moeurs des peuples qui habitent ce pays: la description des ruines d'Heliopolis, aujourd'huy Balbek, & une dissertation historique sur cette ville; avec un abregé de la Vie de monsieur de Chasteüil, gentilhomme de Provence, solitaire du Mont-Liban; & l'histoire du prince Junés, maronite, mort pour la religion dans ces derniers temps*. Paris: Chez André Cailleau.
8 della Valle 1843; see De Giorgi 2016, 1.
9 Perry 1743.
10 Drummond 1754.
11 Robinson 1837, 338.
12 Ainsworth 1842.
13 Bartlett et al. 1838–1838, 19.
14 Berchem and Fatio 1914–1915.
15 Volney 1787.
16 Van Egmond also said the city had 360 convents, several churches, and 150 bishops under a patriarch, two walls, and a staggering 450 towers. Presumably he was talking about what the city had in its past and embellishing a great deal. Van Egmond van der Nijenburg 1759.
17 de Corancez 1816.
18 W. M. Thomson, 1885. *The Land and the Book; or Biblical Illustrations drawn from the Manners and Customs, the Scenes and Scenery of the Holy Land: Lebanon, Damascus and Beyond Jordan*. New York: Harper & Bros.
19 M. Barrès, 1923. *Une enquete aus pays du Levant*. Paris: Plon-Nourrit.
20 Barker 1876; Jacquot 1931, 311, vol. 2.
21 Aigen 1980.

22 Including Belon 1553; Otter 1748; Kinneir 1818; Buckingham 1825.
23 Ali Bey 1816.
24 Beaufort 1861.
25 Bell 1907.
26 Sbeinati et al. 2005, 376, 379.
27 Neale 1854, described it 25 years later. Lycklama 1872–75; Ambraseys 2009, 632–625.
28 Ambraseys 2009, 766–767.
29 Parsons 1808.
30 Sherley et al. 1825.
31 Cassas 1798.
32 Niebuhr 1837.
33 Pococke 1745. Forty yards east of the bridge was the largest part of the ancient wall, 120 paces long with two arched apertures, 12–16-foot-long stones. This was possibly the wall that van Egmond described as a piece of strong brick wall with apertures/windows and thought was possibly a church or palace.
34 See. J. F. Michaud and J. J. F. Poujoulat, 1841. *Correspondance d'Orient, 1830–31*. Brussels: N.-J. Gregor, V. Wouterset Cie.
35 Buckingham 1825, 561.
36 Christensen-Ernst 2012, 138.
37 Volney 1787 wrote that the Bridge Gate was in ruins.
38 Le Bas and Waddington 1850, Incr. III, 1. N2712.
39 Arundell 1834.
40 Abbot Le Camus 1890, 76–79.
41 Beaufort 1861, 312, 313.
42 Belon 1553.
43 For a good summation, see Demir, *Antakya through the Ages*.
44 Pelle and Galibert 1848.
45 Şancı 2006, 334, fn 188.
46 N. A. Ziadeh 1999–2000, "al-Antāqi and his Tadkhara," *ARAM* 11–12: 503–508.
47 Demir 1996.
48 Sahillioğlu 1991.
49 Probably Mu'īn al-Dīn 'Alī Ḥusaynī 'Arabī Tabrizī Kasim-i Anwar (1335–1433). Hanif 2002, 231–232.
50 Dedeoğlu 2018.
51 Çakar 2015.
52 Elker 2006, 18; Demir 1996, 103; Rifaioğlu 2014, 21–288. See also Yakit 1992, 315.
53 Dedeoğlu 2018.
54 There seems to be confusion over whether this mosque, originally sixteenth century (1571), was the Şeyh Aleüddin or Şeyh Ali mosque, which had a *türbe* to the daughter of Şeyh Ahmed b. Ahmed in 1580, no longer extant.
55 Şemseddin Sāmī, 1889–1898. *Kamūs'l 'alām: tarih ve coğrafya lūgati ve tabir-i esahhiyle kāffe-yi esma-yi hass-yi camidir*. Istanbul: Mihran Matbaası.
56 V. Cuinet, 1890–1895. *La Turquie d'Asie, géographie administrative Statistique descriptive et raisonnée de l'Asie Mineure*. Paris: Ernest Leroux.
57 See the work by Kara 2005, especially 89–94.
58 Sahillioğlu 1991.
59 Jacquot 1931, 311, vol. 2.
60 *TIB* 591; Walbiner 1999–2000, 509–521. He did, however, establish a new saints' calendar including only saints connected to the Patriarch of Antioch.
61 He was assassinated by two men in the pay of the Turkish governor Omar Effendi. His body was apparently removed by Turks. It is thought that "schismatic" Greeks also had a hand in this.
62 Zambon et al. 56.
63 Ibid.; Christensen-Ernst 2012, 175–176.
64 Weulersse 1940.

65 Karabacak et al. 2010, 172–182; Akyuz et al. 2006, 281–293.
66 Ambraseys 2009, 732.
67 Gündüz and Gülcü 2009, 289–323.
68 Dedeoğlu 2018, 8.
69 Sahillioğlu 1991.
70 Ambraseys 2009, 733.
71 Rifaioğlu 2018a, 33.
72 Cevdet 1953.
73 Gündüz and Gülcü 2009.
74 Rifaioğlu 2014, 274.
75 J. Weulersse, 1934. "Antioche. Essai de géographie urbaine," *Bulletin d'Études Orientales* 4: 27–79.
76 Chesneau 1887.
77 E. Fındık, 2006. "An Ottoman House with Wall paintings in Antakya: The Kuseyri House," *Chronos* 13: 151–180; M. Akpolat, 2006. "The Traditional Ottoman-Period Houses of Antioch," *Chronos* 13: 117–149. See also Demir 1996, 232–339.
78 Weulersse 1940; Demir 1996.
79 Here Buckingham (1825, 559) criticized Volney for never having actually been there since, as he states, the Orontes was too rapid. Buckingham was about the only person to say that the river was to the northwest, not the north.
80 Within the governor's house was a cupola or round building with thick walls, possibly a church. Van Egmond 1759.
81 Rifaioğlu 2014, 274.
82 Capar 2017, 198–202.

11

A FRONTIER TOWN ONCE MORE (1920–2020)

> Surely the Sanjak shall be forever in spirit an Arab country and a part of Syria by name and origin.
>
> – Adhib Ishak, Secretary of the Antioch Expedition[1]

Introduction

The last days of the Alexandretta Sanjak and, in general, of Antioch under the Syrian Mandate were witnessed by a group of American and French observers who had stakes in the unfolding events. Since the Spring of 1932, a team of archaeologists, historians, and art historians, under the direction of Charles Rufus Morey of Princeton University, had relentlessly worked in Antioch and its vicinity seeking to unravel the great riches of the ancient city (Figure 11.1). How their story wound up being entangled in the momentous events of the late 1930s and the ushering up of a "new" Antakya is the subject of what follows.

Antakya in 1932

"Sièges, pillages, et tremblements de terre expliquent suffisamment ces ruines et le site de la ville leur enfouissement profond."[2] Thus wrote Jacques Weulersse in 1934, an authoritative observer of the history, customs, and social configuration of the city. Just like many other voices that had preceded him, he decried the loss of the ancient city, deeply buried by sieges, looting, and earthquakes. Rhetoric aside, his lucid account on Antakya during the days of the Syrian Mandate is instrumental in understanding the social fabric of the city and, ultimately, the momentous events of the late 1930s.

FIGURE 11.1 The Committee for the Excavations of Antioch and its Vicinity posing with local officials. Sitting at the center, C.R. Morey. Second line, fourth from left, Richard Stillwell. Next to him, W.A. Campbell. Third from right, J. Lassus

Source: Courtesy of the Antioch Expedition Archives, Department of Art and Archaeology, Princeton University; Princeton

Antioch had 45 neighborhoods in the 1930s, each defined by a religious or ethnic group that clustered together in larger districts. These groups comprised the Turks, Christians, and Alawites, who all lived in their own segregated communities. Where one district met another, a neighborhood split apart in some cases into two religious/ethnic groups, though under the same name. This was accomplished by attaching an extra name to the neighborhood: either "Islam" for the Sunni Turks, "Khristiyan" for the Greek Orthodox, or "'Arab" for the Alawites. These subdivided but shared neighborhoods were located at the edges of their own districts. They formed internal borders.[3] For example, the neighborhood of Mukbil straddled the southern border of the Turkish district and northern border of the Christian district. As such, there existed both a Muqbil Islam and Muqbil Khristiyān.

More than half the neighborhoods, 27, were Turkish, constituting about two-thirds of the inhabitants of the city and about 2,150 houses. The Turkish neighborhoods occupied the center of the city. Weulersse classifies these into three groups based on wealth. Aristocratic neighborhoods had riverside real estate and bordered the commercial district, and all resided west of the old *cardo*, Kurtuluş Caddesi. One of these neighborhoods took its name after a noble family, 'Umrān.

The middle-class neighborhoods stretched east, across the old *cardo* towards the foothills of the mountains. Finally, the poorest neighborhoods could be found on the easternmost peripheries on mountain slopes, where houses were ruralized with courtyards, gardens, and trees. Three of the four neighborhoods possessed the name "Būlūkī," a Turkish word suggesting a military company. It is possible that these soldiers, essentially unattached bachelors, initially settled in these poor neighborhoods.

At the start of the twentieth century there existed two Christian groups – the Armenians to the northeast and the Orthodox to the southeast. By 1930, the Christian neighborhoods remained only in the south and comprised seven neighborhoods, about 600 houses. The northern Armenian neighborhood disappeared after the genocide in 1909, although the empty Dört Ayak church remained. An Alawite community replaced the Armenian one in this neighborhood. The Orthodox community inhabited some of the oldest and poorest neighborhoods of Antioch, such as Sarı Maḥmūd (known since the sixteenth century) and Janīne or Jnayne (Garden), a completely internally oriented enclave with residences facing a central church, almost like a fortress within the larger city. Perhaps owing in part to the Tanzimat Reforms in the mid-nineteenth century, socioeconomic dynamics allowed the Orthodox Christian community to gain wealth and power by commandeering the silk industry of Antioch and its trade, indeed all trade with the West. The most modern and rapidly populated neighborhoods of Ward and Hamidiye, located along the Orontes south of the Bridge Gate and built in the European style with brick and iron, developed as Christian communities in the last quarter of the nineteenth century. Hamidiye featured the governor's palace, a prison, and banks.

The Turks considered the Alawites of the city as peasants from the hinterlands, living on the edges of the city, near the Aleppo Gate and at the southern edge. These neighborhoods resembled suburbs. Fairly insular, they were described by Weulersse as villages within the city. In keeping with Alawite tradition, women dispensed with the veil and frequently wore brightly colored clothing. No mosques existed in these quarters. Rather, unobtrusive *ziyāras* or shrines to holy men (*shaykhs*) abounded, usually possessing a simple enclosure with a tomb inside. Like the talismanic markers of the Middle Byzantine city, Alawites would go to these places for blessings and often make specific requests depending on a certain *ziyāra*. Some *ziyāras* would be particularly good for blessings for children, others for praying to heal the sick, for demonic possession, and to grant fertility to women. This practice resembled saint worship in Christianity, and it is likely for this reason that some syncretic practice took place on the part of Orthodox women, who would also visit these *ziyāras* for blessings and healing. These saints also protected the neighborhoods themselves. The Jadide neighborhood had *ziyāras* to Shaykh Ḥasan, Shaykh Muḥammad al-Qadim, and Shaykh Muḥammad al-Riḥani. The Maḥsan neighborhood had shrines dedicated to Shaykhs 'Alī and 'Isa, Shaykh 'Awn, Shakyh Khiḍr, and Shaykh Hamza. This last tomb, to Shaykh Hamza, comprised the only substantial monumental structure of the group. Other *ziyāras* dedicated to Shakyh

Shahid, Khiḍr al-Jibb, Shakyh Gharib, and Shakyh Muḥammad Dalatī may have been located in the appropriately named and long-lasting neighborhood of Sofular to the north, known since the Ottoman period.

The barracks stood at the southern end of the city, set apart from its urban plan and unincorporated. It is worth noting that by 1934, the west bank of the Orontes remained still largely undeveloped. At the center of the city on the west bank loomed the main municipality building, museum, and *lycée* located in a "free" zone. Additionally, two quasi-rural neighborhoods of Muhajirīn Osmaniye and Yeni Mahalle sprang up as refuges for Circassian immigrants.

Several of these neighborhoods give toponymic and hydronymic information based on their names. For example, nearly all the easternmost neighborhoods on the slopes of the mountain are named after water sources. Qanawat (canals) straddled where the Parmenius gorge entered the city; Kuyu (wells) Būlūkī and Shirinje (or Şirince, freshwater spring), to the center and south along the mountains, similarly are named after water. These, side by side with the ancient aqueducts, canalized mountain streams, and springs, point to the *longue durée* of the city's water supply. Qasṭal (possibly derived from the mythical Castalia spring in Daphne) took its name after an ancient public fountain fed by a *nuri'a* water wheel, both defunct in the 1930s. The center of the city was not the neighborhood of Shaykh Muḥ ammad, formerly called Dörtayak (meaning crossroads) in the Ottoman period, but does align with sector 17-O, the assumed crossroads of the Byzantine city, where the forum of Valens is assumed to have been, though this name existed long before the Princeton excavators arrived. Was this ancient topographical information embedded in the local lore of the city's inhabitants century after century? The neighborhood of Sāḥa, meaning a plaza or courtyard, suggests one of note there. The last toponym of the neighborhood of Qanṭara (meaning bridge or arch), known since the Ottoman period, featured, according to Weulersse's observations in the 1930s, a ruined ancient monument, which corresponds with the remains of the putative theater in sector 18-O.

In the 1930s, Antioch still boasted a bustling commercial district, set apart from the residential areas. This district cut across from the bridge of the Orontes towards the slopes of the mountains. Weulersse lists 29 different markets, each surrounding blocks that featured *hans* and mosques. Although he suggests that the market/*han*/mosque combination in the commercial district of Antioch is recent (late-nineteenth century),[4] many of these markets in fact are a direct continuation of the Mamlūk and Ottoman commercial district. What is interesting and potentially can be projected into earlier periods, however, is that one religious or ethnic group monopolized the production and trade of a specific commodity and, as a result, dominated that bazaar.

First, of the few (ten) mosques listed by Weulersse (only those in the commercial district), half are known earlier than the late nineteenth century. One is already known from the Mamlūk period in the thirteenth century – the main Ulu Camii (or Jāmi' al-Kabir); one from the sixteenth century – Maydān; two are eighteenth century Ottoman buildings, including the Ağa (İhsaniye 1710), Mahremiye (1720);

and one is mid-nineteenth century, Ahmediye (Ahmediye Şıh Ahmed 1842). The others may have been from this Sanjak period or renamed and rebuilt earlier buildings and are mostly named after markets or *hans*, including Selvili (cypress), Samerji (saddlebag makers), Yemenji (slipper makers), Khān al-Raṣāṣ (lead-roofed), Jadid (new), and Shaykh Muḥammad (rebuilt in the 1930s).

Mosques in the commercial district connected to *hans* and were located side by side. Yet the *han/mosque* model is not recent. The *han* model also persisted in the Mamlūk and Ottoman periods, although nearly all the ones listed in the 1930s have different names than ones known earlier.[5] *Hans* still functioned as institutions for the production and wholesale distribution of specific commodities with second floors that doubled as hostels, where the *han* owners rented rooms out to tenants. Many *hans* in Antioch became soap factories, still the main export of the city, exemplified by the fact that there the amount of these buildings nearly doubled from 1890/91, although only ten were operational. Their export trajectories still reached similar markets in northern Syria and Anatolia, including Ankara, Amasya, Diyarbakı, Mardin, Mosul, and Van. The output boasted about 330 tons of soap per year on average. As in the Mamlūk and Ottoman periods, wealthy and notable families owned these *hans* and could also act as private bankers. Weulersse writes that soap manufacture and trade contributed to the prosperity of the town only in the nineteenth or early twentieth century. However, as we have seen in the previous two chapters, the Mamlūk and Ottoman *waqf* documents show soap manufacture since the fourteenth century and important throughout the Ottoman period.

Of the bazaars, 11 of these markets existed since the Mamlūk period. These include the merchants' market (Suq Tijjār), still among the wealthiest and run by Turks, while the main grain market occurred at the Suq al-Maydān, with mostly Turkish and Christian vendors and some Alawites. Markets with Mamlūk origins included the reed mat market, a local specialty likely sourced from the Amuq marshes (Hashirji, with Alawite women vendors); the blacksmith and iron-workers markets (Suq al-Bayāṭra, run by Turks; and Suq al-Ḥaddādin, run by Alawites); spice/perfume merchants (Suq al-'Aṭṭārin, run by Turks, Christians, and some Jews); goldsmiths (Suq Kuyumji, run by Christians); the carpenters and furniture maker market (Suq al-Najjārīn, run by Turks); the shoemakers' market (Suq Kundraji, run by Turks); the market of weavers of goat hair bags, covers, and tents (Suq al-Sha'ārin, run by Alawites); and the market for saddle bag makers (Suq al-Samerji), located near the mosque of the same name. A market for flour millers is suggested by the neighborhood name Daqīq (meaning milled flour). The tannery market, called Eski Dabbāgha, was, in the 1930s, abandoned and replaced by new tanneries on the Orontes outside the city. Indeed, most of the fourteenth century Mamlūk markets still existed in some form in the early twentieth century.

The ten or 11 markets still in existence and known since the sixteenth and seventeenth centuries – that is, during the Ottoman period – included the makers of wool coats, one of the specialties of Antioch (*'aba*, at the Suq al-'Abāji, run by Turks and some Christians); the makers of fur hats and caps (Suq al-Lebbādin); the coppersmiths at the Suq al-Naḥḥāsīn run by Alawites; tinsmiths at the Suq

Tanakeji; the markets for lathe operators, Suq Kharrāṭīn (mainly Alawite and some Christians); a thrift market that sold all manner of fabrics, used garments and shoes, mirrors, perfumes, knives and scissors (just called "the Suq"); sellers and peddlers of junk and small items (Suq Basṭaji, mostly Turk); the market for silk and embroidery (Suq Qazzāzīn, run by Christians); and the market of knife and other cutlery makers (Suq al-Sakkākīn, Alawite). The long market (Uzun), known by the same name as the Suq al-Tawil, housed all the butchers, confectioners, and bakers (mainly Alawite); and greengrocers (Turks) as the general food market of the city. Apart from these, it is possible that the main general market in the Ottoman period was the Suq al-Jum'a (Friday Market) in the early twentieth century.

Of the other markets mentioned without explicit reference in the Ottoman period, we can assume that the Suq al-Yemenji, market of slippers, existed previously, as part of typical Ottoman dress. Interestingly, in the 1930s, this was the largest market, with more than 24 vendors, all Turkish. Another carpenters' market, for agricultural implements, probably also hailed from the Ottoman period. Weulersse observed a market for bucket makers (Suq Dalwatīn, run by mainly Alawite and some Christians), and a wood market, near the Ağa Mosque. A market of small animals (sheep and goat) stretched along the Orontes near the bridge and old cemeteries.

The more recent markets included another greengrocer area besides the Maydān; a *suq* at the Bridge/Sea Gate (Bab al-Medine) mainly used by Alawite villagers in the Amuq; and a market that sold mostly European clothes, run by Armenians while they were part of the population prior to 1909.

The commercial district model of blocks containing specific markets paired with *khāns* and mosques can be traced to Ottoman tradition (if not earlier). Indeed, half the mosques and more than two-thirds of the bazaars of Antioch were not a product of the late nineteenth/early twentieth century but rather evolved from the urban transformations and planning that took place from the thirteenth and fourteenth centuries onwards. This supports the view that the urban identity of medieval and modern Antioch initiated after the Mamlūk conquest in 1268 and slowly developed as a heavily commercial entrepôt specializing in silk and soap and an Islamic (Sunni and Sufi) religious town studded with holy places. The increasing socioeconomic influence of its Christian community and subsequent Western European influence, however, was a feature of the late nineteenth and early twentieth century (Table 11.1).

A trove of information about the city at this most critical juncture is to be found Paul Jacquot's three-volume *Antioche: Centre de Tourisme*, published in 1931.[6] Jacquot, a French lieutenant-colonel stationed in Antioch during the early 1920s, dabbled in archaeology and wrote about life in the city. In particular, his lucid description of Antioch's ethnic signature and infrastructure are of interest. According to him, the city's population stood at 35,000, of whom 23,000 were Sunni, 8,000 were Alawite, and 4,000 were Christian. Forty-two mosques, one synagogue, and four churches (Catholic, Greek Orthodox, Capuchin, and Armenian Gregorian) catered to the city's religious needs. Schools were also prominent: one

TABLE 11.1 Old and Contemporary Neighborhoods in Antakya

Ottoman	*Sanjak (1934)*	*Modern*
	Orkhānīye	Orhanli
Dörtayak	Dört Ayāk Armīnī (Christian/Arab, 30 households)	
Sofular/ Sofiyan-i Şeyh Alī Halvetī	Ṣūfīlar Arab (Arab, 105 households)	Sufilar
Sofular/ Sofiyan-i Şeyh Alī Halvetī	Tābi'Ṣūfīlar Islām (Turkish, 63 households)	Sufilar
Kanavāt	Qanawāt 'Arab	
Kanavāt	Qanawāt Islām (Turkish, 125 h.)	Aydinlikevler
Meydan	Maydān (Turkish, 215 households)	Meydan
	Shakyh Muḥammad/Dört Ayāk Kabīr/ Orkhaniye (Turkish, 170 households)	
Bicaklilar	Sakkākīn	
	Jamāliye (Turkish, 50 households)	
	Shaykh 'Alī (Turkish, 107 households)	Şeyhalı
	Aq Bābā (Turkish, 50 households)	Barbaros or Akbab
	Rakābiye (Turkish, 75 households)	Iplikpazari
	Daqīq (Turkish, 85 households)	Yeni Camii
	Koja 'Abdī (Turkish, 180 households)	Kocaabdi
Debbus	Darbūs (Turkish, 70 households)	
	'Umrān (Turkish, 70 households)	
	Kūyū Būlūkī (Turkish, 65 households)	Kardeşler or Kuyulu
	Awrūj Būlūkī (Turkish, 70 households)	Şehitler
Şenbek (Ibn Şenbek)	Shanbik (Turkish, 100 households)	
Ulu Cami	Jami'Kabīr (Turkish, 120 households)	Ulu Cami
Kastel	Qasṭal (Turkish, 30 households)	Zenginler
Mukbil (Mukbiloğlu)	Muqbil (Turkish, 20 households)	
Saha	Sāḥa (Turkish, 30 households)	Gazipaşa
	Qanṭara (Turkish, 230 households)	Kantara
Tut	Tūt Dībī	Çağılık or Dutdibi
	Kara 'Alī Būlūkī (Turkish, 70 households)	Karaali Bölüğü
Sirince	Shirīnje (Turkish 90 households)	Sirince
	Jinjī Būlūkī (Turkish, 65 households)	
Kastel	Qasṭal Khristiyān (Christian, 50 households)	
Mukbil	Muqbil Khristiyān (Christian, 30 households)	
	Janīne (Christian, 50 households)	Gullubahçe (possibly)
Mahsen	Maḥṣan Khristiyān (Christian, 80 households)	
Sarı Mahmud	Ṣāri Maḥmūd Khristiyān (Christian, 85 households)	
	Ward (Christian, 145 households)	Gullubahçe Kişlasaray (possibly)

(*Continued*)

TABLE 11.1 (Continued)

Ottoman	*Sanjak (1934)*	*Modern*
	Ḥamīdiyye (Christian, 160 households)	
Mahsan	Maḥṣan 'Arab (Arab)	Fevzipaşa
	Jadide (Arab)	
	Kūnlik Khristiyān (Christian, 28 households)	
Sarı Mahmud	Ṣāri Maḥmūd (Arab)	
	Kuaykhat (Arab)	
Muhacirin Osmaniye	Muhājirīn Osmāniye (Circassian)	
Muhacirin Osmaniye	Yeni Maḥalle (Circassian)	

lycée with 400 students, four Christian schools, one Alawite, one female Turkish school, six primary schools, and one British primary school. Three hospitals and the bazaar with a staggering 170 shops also fell under his radar. The temporary Museum, later the fulcrum of much activity,[7] was a repository of stunning antiquities found in Antioch and its environs under the direction of Dr. Basile Khoury, who was more of a private collector than a museum professional. The city's businesses were also listed in Jacquot's text: silk, oil, soap, and drapery. Local entrepreneurs exported soups, cocoons, fish, wool, olive oil, cotton, laurel oil, tar, pitch, and untanned skins. Small local industries also dotted the streets: silk, soap (11 places), tanneries, shoemakers, boilermakers, cutlery, rugs, and embroidered cotton. Jacquot was, moreover, perfectly cognizant of the city's ancient and complicated legacy: his section on history was given the heading "La Tragique Histoire d'Antioche." He also offered a gripping overview of the most conspicuous monuments in the region of Antioch, compiled during the years of the French mandate. Among the buildings he mentioned were the remains of the hippodrome and the various Roman roads on which he traveled. He even went so far as to suggest a location for the site of ancient Antigonia on the left bank of the Orontes and identify aqueducts that may, in fact, have been water mills: "aqueduc qui capte les eaux de la montagne." The guidebook that grew out of his touring also focused on archaeological itineraries and the natural amenities of the region. It was also peppered with advertisements for tours. Overall, it was a time of great excitement in the city, and the authorities of the French Mandate sought to exploit the growing interest in orientalism, archaeology, and exotic travel that still loomed large in Europe (Figure 11.2).[8] In that vein, Jacquot's publication was intended as the portal to unique wonders.

Some of Jacquot's remarks, however, also convey the nuisances of what apparently involved living in a multiethnic community. As he wrote:

> Or that we spend the night, but especially in Antioch, a compact and collected city, commanded by a dozen minarets, and traveled by noisy guardians of the night, armed with canes and whistles – and that they use it! – the

FIGURE 11.2 The Parliament building and the Roman bridge over the Orontes

Source: Photographs of Lebanon, Turkey, and Syria Archive (Lot 13856-G, reproduction number: LC-DIG-ppmsca-18437

prayer of muezzins, at growing dawn, awakens, by the way, innumerable cocks, and therefore it is better to rise to admire the west, dotted with dawn or plumes of vapors, the admirable silhouette of Mt. Cassius, unless one prefers to cradle one's reverie to the acute groaning of the great water-wheels, or to the rapid rattles of wind-turbines, which the wind of the Orontes torments without pause. In the evening, one may be annoyed by the barbarian orchestra of a native concert strengthened in honor of a noted dancer or a Persian magician! "Gramophone, piano, nothing is missing, there is Turkish, Jew, Armenian, pseudo-French, there is the light singer and the woman with a voice" (Tharaud). It is sometimes funny, because there is the audience and it is so good, so fresh in the "Luna Park" of Antioch, all at the edge of the Orontes in the gardens.[9]

The league of nations, the Sanjak, and the end of independence

Such was Antakya's microcosm that had to reckon with the momentous days of the Sanjak. Much has been written on the eclipse of the Ottoman Empire, the crises that ensued at local levels, as well as on the geopolitical overhaul implemented by the League of Nations in the aftermath of World War I. As noted, Antioch and its territory were not exempt from the reconfiguration of the former Ottoman provinces, being incorporated into the Sanjak of Alexandretta, a swath of land straddling the Mediterranean coast and the Orontes River valley.[10] Measuring approximately 4,345 km^2, it tallied some 150,000 inhabitants. Administratively and politically, the Sanjak was under the jurisdiction of the French Mandate for Syria yet gained full independence in 1921, pursuant to the Franklin-Bouillon Agreement of October 20, 1921. This treaty, stipulated in Ankara, established the Sanjak's right to self-determination with the *placet* of France and Turkey.[11] As for the Sanjak's population, its ethnic signature was one of remarkable diversity, as befitted the tradition of the region. Turks, Sunni Arabs, Alawis, Armenians, Kurds, Circassians, and Jews created a concoction that, despite minor squabbles, had held well together during the last centuries of the Ottoman Empire. The city of Antioch also bristled with life.

The size of the city's Turkish population, however, was an issue because of two conflicting estimations. On the one hand, Turkish reports firmly asserted that Turks in the region were in the majority, as seen in Weulersse's report; on the other, French authorities assessed the Turkish community in more modest terms, somewhere on the order of 37 percent of the population, thus by no means dominating the non-Turkish constituency (see Table 11.2).[12] This was no mere discrepancy in numbers; in the years following the Antioch agreement, Turkey was to mount a most effective political campaign on these grounds, leading ultimately in 1939 to its full acquisition of the Sanjak.[13]

TABLE 11.2 The 1924 Demographic Composition of the Sanjak, According to the French Government

Ethnicity	*Population*	*Percentage*
Turks	47,445	37.1
Alawites	36,968	28.14
Shias	26,763	20.96
Arabs	14,482	11.31
Others (Armenians, Circassians, Jews, and Greeks)	2,228	1.72
Total	127,886	

Source: Yerasimos 1988

Overall, this has been a most controversial page in history, with no consensus reached establishing the rights and the wrongs of the parties involved. That Turkey, despite the agreements of 1921 and 1923, never acquiesced in accepting the loss of the Sanjak is well known. Because of its position and economic potential, the district was especially tantalizing for the authorities in Ankara. The newly discovered oil wells in Arzouz (Arsuz), the position of the port of Alexandretta, and, lastly, the untapped potential of the Amuq Plain, in particular, made control over the Sanjak desirable. Moreover, the rhetoric of a "forty-century-old Turkish land"[14] added a populist touch essential to coopting the masses into the project. How the Turkish Republic, still in its infancy, successfully orchestrated the wholesale acquisition of the Sanjak in overt violation of the League of Nations' provisions, however, needs to be underscored. In particular, a key provision in the Sanjak's charter mandated that no foreign power was to interfere or tamper with its administration. Equally central was the recognition of the Turkish minority and its cultural autonomy. This settlement was further confirmed by the Treaty of Lausanne in 1923, which established the borders of the Turkish Republic, stipulated the exchange of populations with Greece, and prescribed no further claims on the former provinces of the Ottoman Empire. In practical terms, France was the guarantor, thus safeguarding its interests in the region. Put simply, French authorities ensured that such resolutions were in place, treating the district, however, as a legitimate extension of Syria.

No sooner had the Lausanne treaty been signed, however, than a shrewd Turkish propaganda machinery began to embrace the cause of the Turks in the Sanjak. But it was the Franco-Syrian agreement of 1933 – which de facto mapped out France's gradual disinvestment from the mandate and, in its intentions, paved the road to Syria's sovereignty in the Sanjak, to become effective in the next three years – that precipitated the crisis that shortly ensued. The demographic argument in particular became paramount. Through a savvy operation of political interference and mobilization of Turks in the region, the Turkish president, Mustafa Kemal Atatürk, made clear to the people of Turkey that their brothers in the Sanjak would not be left alone. In 1934, the Turkish People's Party in Antioch became the voice of irredentist demands. Though limiting their activism to the press, they functioned as proxies to spread awareness about the prospects of a fully Turkish Sanjak.[15] Confident in its fast-growing political clout, Turkey began mobilizing Turks, moving them into the Sanjak by offering incentives and opportunities while also boosting Turkish census figures, thereby altering the registration system for the ensuing parliamentary elections. The situation deteriorated in 1938, with Antioch becoming the locus upon which the political manifestations of various ethnic groups, together with League of Nations' envoys, ambassadors, and military leaders, converged. Sectarian violence also wreaked havoc both within and outside the city, as Antioch had witnessed for centuries in the past. But this time major changes lay ahead of the great turmoil.

At that juncture, France had to reckon with closer, more concrete threats endangering the sense of concord that the League of Nations had sought to enforce.

Specifically, with Germany increasingly flexing its muscles and Italy enlarging its holdings in the eastern Mediterranean, the issue of the Sanjak became secondary. The control of the Dardanelles and Bosphorus straits, still under Turkey, was also a central concern in British politics at a time of heightening tension. All in all, Turkey became a key interlocutor, while the Sanjak of Alexandretta turned into an expendable entity. It is fair to say that France – with the blessing of Great Britain – turned a blind eye to the realities of the Sanjak, its constituents, and those stipulations that had previously cemented the district's inviolable independence. Thus, in 1938 France practically handed over a territory to Turkey without having the authority to do so.[16]

Arguably, Antioch was the place where these politics played out and where a mix of anxieties and tensions unfolded. The city's long boulevards became once again a locus of the heated political debates and predicaments of the day. And, as mentioned, this situation gathered steam before the very eyes of a distinguished group of scholars, mainly American and French, who had undertaken to excavate the city beginning in 1932.

The chronicles of the archaeologists

As early as 1927, Charles Rufus Morey of Princeton University had established the Committee for the Excavation of Antioch and its vicinity. From the outset, the enterprise received support from both the university and the intellectual voices of the day.[17] Substantial fundraising underpinned the operations and ensured the feasibility of a project not modest in its aims. The Antioch of the fourth century CE, with Constantine's Octagonal Church, the hippodrome, the forum of Valens, and the great imperial palace, were but some of the targets the project set out to explore. Of course, Morey molded the agenda in ways that matched his interests; a scholar of classical visual traditions in the East, he owed much of his interest in Antioch to Howard Crosby Butler, the trailblazing archaeologist who had explored the monuments of classical and post-classical Syria in the early 1900s. Despite the Great Depression of 1929 and some anxiety about the political realities of Syria, Morey firmly held the helm of operations until 1931, when the project was poised to begin. A permit had been clinched, a *partage* plan of sharing with the Musées de France was achieved, and Princeton was poised to serve as the powerhouse for study of the excavated materials. The Louvre Museum became a key partner with Princeton in the financing, excavation management, and division of the collections. Jean Lassus, representing the French institution, in the following years stood out as one of the most capable archaeologists in the field.

As preparations were under way, however, the situation grew less rosy, for American donors kept pulling out of the project's funding plan. In the early 1930s, the American economy was in a nosedive, yet Morey did not flinch. Instead, he succeeded in involving the Baltimore Museum of Art and the Worcester Museum of Art in the roster of sponsoring institutions. The former was represented by Robert Garrett, a Princeton alumnus who had been a member of Butler's expedition and gained fame as the gold winner of the shot put at the first modern Olympics in 1896. The latter was represented by its director, Robert Taylor. Decisions and roles about the team of archaeologists in the field ensued shortly thereafter. In particular, the Committee for the Excavation of Antioch and its Vicinity voted Princeton Professor George W. Elderkin as general director of the excavation, Clarence Fisher of the American School in Jerusalem as field director, and W. A. "Sandy" Campbell of Wellesley College as assistant field director.

By the time the team reached Antioch, all aspects of the expedition had been overseen, from banking to logistics. The one area where the archaeologists had not sufficiently planned was, ironically, field strategy. With no previous knowledge of the site and essentially relying on the texts of Libanius and Malalas, as well as on the 1839 map by Karl Ottfried Müller,[18] the team encountered ecological realities they had not foreseen, with a great deal of the city buried beneath the sediments of the runoffs from Mt. Silpius and Mt. Staurin. Nor was the plan to open simultaneous excavations from the Island to Daphne, and later all the way to Seleucia Pieria, any more rewarding, with continuous mobilization of the work force and limited inspection of archaeological contexts. Land lease contracts, internal feuds, and overall limited engagement with the local community compounded the slow progress of the operations.

Indeed, the archaeological exploration of Antioch was perhaps the last great excavation of modernity, conducted as it was by a regimented system of a handful of supervisors and hordes of local workers, a format that had characterized most excavations in the Middle East, especially Egypt, in the early twentieth century. Admittedly, encouraging results were achieved as early as season one in 1932, with a panoply of baths, a temple, and the hippodrome brought to light on the Island. Yet the palace of Diocletian and the Church of Constantine, to name but two targets, were nowhere in sight. Nor did the excavators ever achieve an understanding of Antioch's ancient topography, with the program of "street digs" having to reckon with meters of layering and sediment burying the eastern tracts of the ancient city. Were it not for Antioch's treasure trove of tessellated pavements, the project would have shortly plummeted into catastrophe. An unflagging hunt for mosaics, fueled by local villagers' tips, thus generated the dividends the sponsoring institutions had so adamantly expected. The exquisite – albeit now greatly dispersed – collection of Antioch mosaics was assembled mostly by the project's "mosaic crew," a group of specialists who were in charge of lifting pavements, with modest or no attention to archaeological context, especially during the 1934–1938 campaigns. At that juncture, the political tensions in the Sanjak, and not least in Antioch, were becoming increasingly palpable, further complicating the activities of the excavations.

Some of the American archaeologists went so far as to assemble detailed analyses of the League of Nations' provisions and current political climate in and around the city. One of the expedition's notable members, Donald Wilber, for instance, penned a succinct history of the Sanjak describing some of the events that framed its political and institutional transformations. For most, his major contribution to the Antioch excavations lay in drawing the signature map of the ancient city in tandem with Glanville Downey.[19]

Wilber also extolled the new state of affairs in the aftermath of the Franco-Syrian treaty "with its promise of complete independence." But much of his enthusiasm quickly subsided as events took a different turn. As he vividly described the deteriorating situation:

> But no sooner than the elections for the new parliament were over breaks occurred in this united front. Muslims attacked Christians and outbreaks took place in Beyrouth and smaller towns. The spirit of agitation spread to the Sanjak even before the elections. At Antioch one party supported the four candidates of the nationalistic bloc and favored union with Syria. Another declared for the pan-Arab movement and began wearing the "feisalia" or trench caps which are the traditional headgear of Iraq. The Christian minorities sought a solution from France or the League. The Turks, with the largest minority, favored a union with Turkey and waged the most active as well as the most vicious campaign. Gangs of small boys were sent out on the streets to shout slogans and throw stones at whomever they pleased. The Turkish leaders placed a boycott on the elections with a result that only a handful of the 40,000 inhabitants of Antioch cast votes to elect the national candidates. A few days after the election, on December 1st [1936], an unruly and menacing mob appeared before the house of one of the new deputies and demanded that he resign his new post. Soldiers gathered to disperse the crowd and succeeded after a burst of machine gun fire from an armored car had mowed down several of the demonstrators. Thus martial law was proclaimed in Antioch and even such a drastic means seems insufficient to preserve order, for on January 10th a new riot caused the death of one person and the wounding of several others. The Sanjak remains in a state of siege. Picked troops under a specially selected French commander patrol the Turkish frontier. Representative groups from the smaller minorities gather every morning to send frantic wires of appeal to the League of Nations.[20]

More and more, descriptions of events appeared in the expedition's field diaries and notebooks. In particular, as the project was enlarging its radius of explorations, increasing riots among ethnic groups were reported in villages outside of Antioch. While duly noting the scientific progress of the operations, daily activities, acquisitions, and visits of colleagues/officials in their field diaries, the archaeologists also became particularly keen to comment on the political events in Antioch. Further, the journal for Wednesday, June 25, 1938, reads as follows: "Incidents of minor violence occurred in various districts, and in Rihanie [modern Rehanlı], where Turks and Arabs live in closer proximity, there was a serious riot."[21] Interestingly, it was noted in the same daily entry that

> le Capitaine Gacon of the Services Speciaux [i.e., the French Secret Service in the Mandate] revealed that in case of a prolonged and serious riot of the

> Turks, it was the plan of the French Army to bomb the Turkish quarter in which we live. Accordingly, he requested that either McEwan (Amuq Valley Projects-Oriental Institute) or I [Fisher] have a telephone installed so that we could be warned a half hour before the bombardment began. It was decided to put the phone in McEwan's home, which was done immediately.

Behind much nonchalance, the directors of the excavations were making plain that France intended to prevent the Turks in the Sanjak from causing any more stir. What transpires in this and many other accounts, however, is a sense of discomfort as to the possibility of a Turkish takeover. Neither the local French authorities nor the Princeton archaeologists ever feigned enthusiasm for the Kemalist movement and the nationalistic undertones of Turkish propaganda. Nevertheless, they proceeded to sit and talk with all representatives of the parties involved, invariably being reassured that the project would continue to be sustained by whatever coalition was in charge. Looking ahead, members of the excavations wrote in 1937:

> Expedition work in Antioch and its vicinity shall never be interrupted and can be run on [an] easier and safer basis in the future, as the local government now is more friendly with the Arab population whom we work with more. Both the Turks and the Arabs have smart leaders now and are on very good terms and shall continue on [a] friendly basis with the Expedition. We generally have business connections with the three famous leaders of the public in Antioch.[22]

The archaeologists' hope of continuing fieldwork in harmony with current and future powers also triggered a great deal of diplomatic activity. During the month of May 1938, they held meetings with members of the anti-Turkish groups as well as with the consul general of Turkey and the leader of the Kemalist party in Antioch. Because of the nature of the investment, and the major stakes involved in the Antioch excavation, the archaeologists kept fully abreast of the local political situation, occasionally checking with the US consulate in Beirut and the Department of State to examine all options on the table. On May 28, the latter informed Morey that

> your desire to take any measure possible on behalf of your organization in the field is entirely understandable and, while no one, of course, can guarantee that unfortunate incidents in a disturbed area will not occur, you may be assured that we shall render whatever assistance we may.[23]

In the days ahead, the group would indeed resort to the help of the American consulate general in Beirut. But political tension was not the only source in anxiety. Much was brewing in Ankara's government offices, with officials and their media decrying the indiscriminate loss of archaeological treasures in Hatay. In short, Atatürk's intelligentsia was well aware of the work of the Antioch Committee; foreseeing an upcoming closing on Hatay, they were mapping out ways to come to terms with the Americans. The recommendation for the group was thus to stay neutral and not to engage in local politics. In a recent analysis, James Goode poignantly notes:

> Unfortunately, everything they did was political. Some saw them as treasure hunters; others believed they favored one side or the other in the increasingly vocal struggle for control of the Sanjak. The casual observer might caution them to keep their distance, but that was well-nigh possible. And to make matters worse, the archaeologists did not always understand just how political their activities really were. The records are full of sincere statements, disclaiming any interest in local affairs; yet, to do archaeology in the Middle East in those years, amid the swirl of nationalist movements, was to enter the vortex.[24]

The crescendo of sectarian violence increasingly took the upper hand in the daily entries. On May 30, 1938, it was written:

> The rioting and disorders continue. M. and Mme. Lassus had the unpleasant experience of seeing an Arab, whom we all knew, killed by a Turkish mob; an Armenian, attacked at the same time, escaped by jumping into the Orontes and swimming to safety.[25]

The following day, news began to spread that France had agreed to hand over the Sanjak to Turkey, to the bewilderment of the French authorities in Antioch and the Princeton archaeologists. Disquiet loomed large in the chronicles of the following days, with the expedition mostly left to its own devices, exploring the best course of action between a new deal with the incoming powers or a swift evacuation. The tension became palpable amid rumors of possible Italian military options from Rhodes against the Turks, and England's enticing Turkey into the French–British alliance by means of a generous loan and promise of occupation of the Sanjak.[26] By the first week of June, it became clear that the expedition would have to evacuate Antioch, and all French and American archaeologists – excluding Lassus and Campbell – headed to Beirut. Despite conflicting reports of martial law and closed borders, the few remaining members brought several operations in Seleucia, Daphne, and near the Parmenius to a halt. The June Field Report reads:

> Civil disturbances became so serious that it seemed advisable to confine work areas near the field headquarters; and so, the excavation was resumed along the Main Street and in 13 R. By June 6th the political situation seemed so grave that an emergency division was held and the Staff sent to Beirut. Then followed the difficult period of evacuating the antiquities to Beirut where the haven kindly granted by President Dodge of the American University proved a god-send.

With the Moroccan troops of the mandate still patrolling the city and borders, Antioch was now gearing up for the arrival of the Turkish army. The Turkish general Âsım Gündüz, in particular, officially requested that the excavation's headquarters be turned into barracks for the soldiers. Only high-tier diplomacy prevented the act of dispossession.[27]

On July 5, the Turkish army occupied Alexandretta; on July 7, at 10:30 a.m., they entered Antioch, thus bringing the Sanjak's independence to a close. As for resuming the excavations for the following year, obtaining a permit and wiring the funds proved more difficult than expected. But the relationship with the local government also became "increasingly cordial."[28] With the usual zest, fieldwork began in the spring of 1939; the sector 15-M and 13-R excavations sought to glean the east–west artery of traffic and a bath partially explored in 1935, respectively, while more mosaics were lifted at Daphne. No meaningful results, however, were obtained, and the reports of alarm from Europe took a big toll on the team's hopes and aspirations. After much negotiation with the newly appointed Turkish authorities, the antiquities made it out of Antakya and made it to Beirut, where they were promptly shipped to the United States.[29] Shortly thereafter the Antioch excavations disbanded, and the promise to revive the project after the war was never kept.

At that point fully integrated into the Turkish Republic, Antioch and the Hatay District signaled on the one hand the confidence of the Turkish state and, on the other, the souring of Turkey's relationship with the Syrians, who to this day have yet to accept the loss of the Sanjak. Decades of diplomatic efforts have not succeeded in mending the controversy,[30] nor is it likely to be brought up in the near future as long as Syria remains entangled in a most tragic civil war. All the same, the memories of the days of the Sanjak still survive thanks to a few visible relics of 1930s Antioch. The Ottoman houses along Hürriyet Caddesi, with their overhangs and exquisite stone décor, as well as the austere building that now accommodates the Council for the Arts (Kültür Sanat Merkezi), so heavy with modernist accents, powerfully conjure up the voices, rallies, and popular mobility of those days.

Of course, the city has changed dramatically in the decades that have followed. A new archaeology museum, elegant hotels, shopping malls, roads, and modern infrastructure have signaled heavy government investments and a sense of Turkish pride. Today Antioch buzzes with life, and tourists from around the world, whether drawn by its antiquities or its religious history, flock to the city's center. In its relentless growth, the city now tallies 35 districts, seven of which are located on the expanses west of the Orontes, which is an area that has developed only in the last 50 years.[31] The flavor of old Antakya, however, still survives in the sectors between the river and the mountains (Figure 11.3), with the long bazaar (Uzunçarşı) serving as the visual centerpiece of a bygone era.

With much urban expansion and development under way, however, the antiquities remain in danger. The city plans of 1948 and 1957, while seeking to ameliorate transportation and the general infrastructure, showed no interest in protecting Antioch's heritage. In 1970, a blast pulverized the last remaining Roman bridge on the Orontes to make way for a now inadequate concrete structure. More recently,

FIGURE 11.3 View of Antakya in 1932

Source: Courtesy of the Antioch Expedition Archives, Department of Art and Archaeology, Princeton University; Princeton

stone quarries have been carving out extended gaping holes on the slopes of Mt. Staurin, endangering, if not destroying, entire stretches of Antioch's fortifications. Conservation efforts are now seeking a better deal for Antakya's past (Figure 11.4),[32] and one can only commend the preservation of a vast bathhouse under a newly erected five-star hotel in an area that may be near the elusive forum of Valens. But the story of modern Antakya, after 1939, is for others to tell in more detail.

Conclusions

The landscape around the city has also changed in fundamental ways. In the late 1960s the great lake of the Amuq was drained as part of an extensive reclamation plan.[33] Diversion projects have also manipulated the waters of the Kara Su, Afrin, and Orontes Rivers, while extensive tobacco and cotton plantations have added a widespread sense of an engineered landscape. The hinterlands are now even better integrated thanks to new roads and amenities, not least a new stadium for the local soccer team Hatayspor.

Meanwhile, Antioch's perennial environmental issues still harm the community with punctual incidence; the spring 2019 flood of the Orontes and the destruction of an entire quarter, Bağrıyanık Mahallesi, caused by torrential rains, are powerful reminders of this community's endemic vulnerability. For all these changes and ills, however, Mt. Silpius, the Amanus, and the Orontes continue to contemplate the

FIGURE 11.4 A celebration of King Suppiluliuma of Tell Tayinat in Antakya, 2018

Source: Courtesy of Elif Denel

miracle of a city that sparkles with buildings, exudes a unique vitality, and continues the legacy of its extraordinary and compelling past.

Notes

1 "Ishak's Report," one of several documents compiled by the archaeologists on the history and politics of the Sanjak. *Antioch Archives*, 1938 Correspondence.
2 Weulersse 1934, 27.

3 Qasṭal, Muqbil, Maḥsan, Sarı Maḥmūd to the south; Ṣufilar, Qanawat Dört Ayak to the north.
4 Weulersse 1934, 70.
5 Of those named by Weulersse were Ḥurriyet Khan, Khan al-Baladiya (Municipality) for fruits and vegetables, Rif'at Ağa Khan, Khan al-Raṣāṣ (Lead-Roof Khan), Suduklu Khan, Khan al-Tutun (for tobacco), Khan al-Ṣabūn (for soap), Rif'at Efendi Khan, Mardros Ağa/Jābra Khuri Khan, Yeni (New) Khan, Bazar Khan (for large animals – mules, horses, cows), and the As'ad Ağa Khan.
6 Jacquot 1931. The first volume focuses on region. Touristic guide to Sanjak of Alexandretta. Routes, hotels and restaurants, food. The second volume has a brief history, description of the city, and plans for some tours, p. 6, which are mainly historical, one around the Ottoman town, one in the suq.
7 Rifaioğlu 2014, 279.
8 Ibid., 278, on the establishment of first, second, and third degree archaeological areas of interest within Antakya's city limits.
9 Jacquot 1931, 15.
10 Shields 2011.
11 Sanjian 1956, 379.
12 On the demography, zoning, and ethnic clustering in the city, see Weulersse 1934.
13 Shields 2011, 246.
14 Yerasimos 1988, 207.
15 Yerasimos 1988, 206.
16 Sanjian 1956, 382.
17 De Giorgi 2016, 30.
18 Müller 1839, see Figure 1.15.
19 Other than being intellectually involved in the quest for Antioch, Wilbur also had a knack for providing the US government with fresh intelligence on political crises in the Middle East. During World War II, he served with the OSS, precursor to the CIA, and afterward became a leader in CIA activities in Iran, including the 1953 coup d'état against Mohammad Mosaddegh, Iran's first democratically elected prime minister, in favor of the Shah of Iran, Mohammad Reza Pahlavi, thus setting the stage for the Iranian Revolution of a quarter century later.
20 *Antioch Archives*, a Statement by Donald Wilber.
21 *Antioch Archives*, Diary of the 1938 operations.
22 *Antioch Archives*, Political Crisis at Antioch.
23 *Antioch Archives*, Letter of May 28, 1938.
24 Goode 2004, 61.
25 *Antioch Archives*, Diary of the 1938 operations.
26 *Antioch Archives*, Diary of the June 1, 1938, operations.
27 *Antioch Archives*, Diary of June 30, 1938.
28 *Antioch Archives*, April 2–May 15, 1939. Summary of Events.
29 Goode 2004, 63. Of course the Antioch team operated under terms that the Turks would have never approved. The honoring of the old stipulations with the French Mandate, however, in the end enabled the shipment of a sizable portion of antiquities.
30 Sanjian 1956, 383–394.
31 Demir 2004, 226.
32 Rifaioğlu 2014.
33 After heavy rains, the lake formed again in January 2019, flooding vast properties as well as the Hatay airport.

APPENDIX 1

Mapping the walls of Antioch

Stephen Batiuk, Andrea U. De Giorgi, and A. Asa Eger

In every period, Antioch's legendary attractions, confirmed by its visitors and biographers over two millennia, were its city walls and ample water supply. These are not negligible. The former enabled the city to endure sieges and invasions and rebuild time and time again. The latter was, simply put, a wondrous luxury for a Middle Eastern town. However, tracing the walls and water systems of Antioch is riddled with difficulty. At least 17 maps, from the fourteenth to twenty-first centuries, exist, mainly drawn by Western travelers to the city. The concern to illustrate the city plan of Antioch for each of the epochs that we have brought into focus is central in the book. In that vein, most chapters are correlated with an image of the city that features monuments, known archaeological features, and 1932–39 Princeton excavation sites. Prime above everything we have chosen to emphasize, in accordance with the main argument of the volume and departure from every other map of Antioch, is the transformation of the city over time, and so have not reduced the city to one plan and privileged one period in which to show Antioch. We have produced ten plans of the city. In so doing, we have harnessed a wealth of sources from modern archaeological surveys to historical accounts to early travelogues and lithographs. In particular, we owe it to Gunnar Brands and Ulrich Weferling to have considerably furthered our understanding of Antioch's topography[1] and moved the discourse away from Wilber and Downey's iconographic, widely duplicated and accepted, but inaccurate 1963 map (Figure 1.8). Brands and Weferling's work, as well as the study of the city walls by Brasse,[2] are key to the definition of an image of the city. Weulersse, Leblanc and Poccardi, Uggeri, and Hoepfner have also provided us with key solutions, for instance, in the analysis of the island and riverbeds.[3] Remote sensing, however, using aerial photographs from the 1930s (courtesy of the Princeton Visual Resource Archive), Corona satellite imagery acquired from 1958–1972, SRTM digital elevation data acquired in 2000, and modern DigitalGlobe satellite imagery, enabled us to visualize hitherto unseen features and propose new solutions for poorly known sectors of the city, as for instance the southern sections of the fortifications and their intersection with the Phyrminus gorge and the northern channel of the Orontes. All legacy imagery was imported into ESRI ArcMap (10.7.1) GIS Software and was georeferenced using the DigitalGlobe imagery based on known chronologically consistent features such as churches, mosques, the hippodrome and temple, and other structures, including bridges and roads.

Many features have been lost to modern development, and the imagery is of different resolutions, which adds to the difficulty of georeferencing the legacy data. The past phantom form of Antioch still lingers in its historic district (the Mamlūk, Ottoman, and Mandate town), with its older houses and seemingly labyrinthine streets. These passages are less random than may seem and follow at times the classical *insulae*. The *cardo*, the backbone of the city in every period, survives clearly to this day and is key to assembling the plan of the city regardless of imagery and resolution. However, despite the difficult challenges of resolution and modern construction, an iterative approach was taken, with Corona imagery[4] being re-rectified based on the DigitalGlobe for the city plan of each period. As all three imagery sources (aerial photography, Corona photos, DigitalGlobe imagery) were of different resolutions, the geo-rectification of the aerial photos were referenced based on features visible in both, as some features were visible in the Corona due to modern development and sprawl of the city only in the last 40 years, and other features were only visible in the modern DigitalGlobe imagery because of its higher resolution. All imagery was layered with the available GIS data that has been collected by the Computational Research on the Ancient Near East (CRANE) Project and Tayinat Archaeological Project[5] over the past 20 years. The plans in this volume, based on remote sensing, geo-rectification, and digitization in GIS, were all produced by Stephen Batiuk. The layering of this data served as the base for the published maps and the following analysis.

Features such as paleochannels of the Orontes River and Phyrminus gorge were identified through discolorations in the soil, the result of infilling of channels with abandoned channel accretion that retains water differently than the surrounding soils. Geomorphic features identified in both satellite and SRTM digital elevation models data provided additional constraints in identifying possible courses of paleochannels. Essentially, the topography dictated possible locations of paleochannels and other features. Features such as roads were mapped by known historical roads and pathways, or by mapping older roadways in Corona imagery, aerial photos, and maps. Before the introduction of mass earth-moving machines, road locations were dictated by geography. By looking at older roads in relation to ancient and medieval settlements – for example, in the plan of the Orontes delta region (Figure 6.13), which most notably used the monasteries recorded by Djobadze[6] – but also settlements identified in the Orontes Delta Survey, published by H. Pamir,[7] a good estimation of ancient roadways could be developed.

The various features were mapped and layered in the GIS, and then their identification and chronological placement was done in extensive discussion between the three of us (the authors and Steve Batiuk), and consultation with ancient literary descriptions and other historical data. The whole process was consultative and continuous, with each of us providing valuable insight in interpreting and understanding the mapped features.

The compression of several historical layers within single, inert maps, of course, is a danger that any survey of ancient topography has to reckon with. We leave to the reader to wed the visual transformation and evolution of Antioch's fabric with the background of our narrative. Occasionally, the picture gets fairly convoluted. The enceinte and its many defensive systems are a good case in point: the mesh of masonry styles and sudden shifts in orientation make their analysis a thorny issue, as shown repeatedly in the book. However, we have decided to illustrate discrete fortifications and the gates of the city against the background of the most immediate previous defensive systems, thereby conveying a sense of urban transformation. Further, our tracing of walls and features is grounded in firm evidence, whether documented by material remains or remote sensing and supported by textual accounts. When plausibility was the only option at our disposal, we have resorted to the analysis of the terrain topography and the geological configuration of the area, especially in the highland districts. Simply put, these maps are a visual transposal of historical, archaeological, and geological data. For instance, with the Hellenistic city wall (Figure 1.9), surrounding Antioch's first small incarnation (whose area was roughly 3.88 km^2/388 ha), we followed the evidence of the earliest dry-laid polygonal walls as presumably built by Seleucus, subsequently superseded and expanded by Antiochus IV to include the upland settlement of Epiphaneia and extending the northern wall of the city farther toward the Amuq Plain (5.23 km^2/523 ha in area, 11.3 km/7.03 miles in length). We do not have any concrete evidence to suggest that the island was fortified under Antiochus III, apart from a small stretch of wall to its north, which may be the location of the predecessor of the Romanesian Gate, the city's Late Antique portal to the Amuq Plain. The existence of a gate, presumably located in the southern districts, is attested for the year 246 BCE in the Gourob Papyrus; whether it was the Bridge Gate or the Daphne Gate is a matter of guesswork.[8] The line of fortifications along the Orontes is another puzzling issue; we suggest, however, that the early settlement and its four nuclei, each with its own perimeter, seized sectors where the propinquity of the river and the "cardo" offered suitable settlement opportunities. For the southwestern wall, fragments of walls were visible in the 1930s aerial photos that stopped at the town's edge. The remainder could be approximated based on the medieval road system of the city, which in all probability is reflective of the earlier system. An angular road system, in line with the newly identified wall fragments, probably represents the path of a road that would have run along the face of the wall (as is seen with the Theodosian and Justinian reconstruction phases), allowing us to approximate its position.

The Roman fortification wall (Figure 2.11) of Tiberius in the first century C.E., in our opinion, may have not been more than an enhancement of these Hellenistic walls incorporating Antiochus IV's expansion and bounding the island to the south by the Parmenius gorge (5.23 km^2/523 ha in area, 11.3 km/7.03 miles in length). What is more, the location of the Sarı Mahmud (24-K) and Mnemosyne (24-K/L) *necropoleis*, in use already in the first two centuries of our era, as attested by funerary marble slabs, have provided us with the yardsticks that safely position the limits of the city walls, so as to necessarily keep these burial grounds outside the city limits.

Also, at stake is the definition of the great expansion under Theodosius II during the Late Roman period in the first half of the fifth century CE (Figure 3.23), one which led to the addition of the Jewish Kerataion neighborhood in the southern quarter. The crux, of course, is whether Theodosius I or II were behind the project, with the conflicting accounts of John Malalas and Evagrius. As noted already by Downey,[9] the prefect of the *praetorium* Chuzon, the man who recommended that a new enceinte be built, is known to have retained that capacity under the mandate of Theodosius II, thus safely assigning the new walls to first half of the fifth century. In archaeological terms, the Phyrminus gorge offers the southernmost limit of this development, while the fortifications on Mt. Silpius, expanded with a new larger circuit wall laden with towers and occasionally reminiscent of the walls of Constantinople with their layers of red brick with a core of mortared rubble, are suggestive of their agency. In short, the city under Theodosius II was at its peak extent and enclosed the largest area (6.06 km^2/606 ha in area, 11.6 km/7.2 miles in length), longer and larger than the Theodosian II city walls of Constantinople, which measured about 5.4 km^2 and 5.7 miles in length.

Lastly, and crucial for the subsequent epochs, is the "shrinking" of the city operated by Justianian following the devastating earthquakes of 526 and 528 in the mid-sixth century CE, with the cutting off of most of Theodosius II's plan, the abandonment of the Island, and the carving of a new channel for the Orontes (Figure 4.7). As already noted by Leblanc and Poccardi, we posit that the river side of these defenses follow what may be reasonably referred to as the channel of Justinian, a straight course from the Parmenius gorge south to the Orontes, which was used as a moat by the new southeastern stretch of wall. Only a narrower channel, similar to the Parmenius, can be suggested, based on the remote sensing data. This narrower river channel is difficult to understand at first, but when one factors in the historical earthquakes that could have created an uplift and centuries of recorded droughts,[10] one could posit a diminished flow for the Orontes, which would make the observed width logical.

Justinian's city walls were more regularized and the plan of the city more rectangular than previously, and they used the southern part of the larger Theodosian mountain wall but cut out the walls around Epiphaneia, previously strengthened by Tiberius. The area was larger than the Seleucid city but smaller than the Antiochus IV, Tiberian, and Theodosian (4.37 km^2/437 ha in area, 9.3 km/5.77 miles in length). We also assert that the southern wall of the city, like the northern wall, was brought in closer to the center of the city to form a new line, and this dating is supported by architectural features like the conspicuously large Tower 1, an example of his sixth-century construction. What is more, towers along the Silpius defenses, as noted by Brasse, were each provided with cisterns, supporting Procopius' claim.[11]

All of these changes are corroborated by Procopius' description of the city in *On Buildings*:

> In ancient times its circuit-wall was both too long and absolutely full of many turnings, in some places uselessly enclosing the level ground and in others the summits of the mountain, and for this reason it was exposed to attack in a number of places. But the Emperor Justinian, contracting this wall as would best serve the need, carefully remade it so as to guard, not the same districts as before, but only the city itself. As for the lower part of the circuit-wall, where the city was dangerously spread out (since it lay in a soft plain and could not be defended because of a superfluity of wall), he changed its course by drawing it inward as much as possible, it having gained protection by being compressed. And the River Orontes, which had flowed past the city, as it formerly was, in a winding course, he thrust over so that it ran in a new bed, hugging the circuit-wall. He did this by winding the stream round again by means of an artificial channel as near the wall as possible. In this way he both relieved the city of the danger arising from its excessive size and recovered the protection afforded by the Orontes.[12]

Stephen Batiuk, Andrea U. De Giorgi, and A. Asa Eger

It is Justinian's plan that was retained throughout all successive periods, from Early Islamic to Middle Byzantine to Saljūq and Crusader. In the Mamlūk, Ottoman, and Mandate periods, while Justinian's enceinte remained, the inhabited portion of the city was greatly reduced. The citadel, built and incorporated into the city wall during the Middle Byzantine period and key to the medieval history of Antioch, has been replanned, replacing Sinclair's architectural plan which has a number of inaccuracies.[13] The revised plan uses GIS satellite imagery, information from Brands' and Weferling's survey and some information that can still be obtained, Sinclair's plan as well as the drone image (see Figure 6.6).

As with all things pertaining to the materiality of Antioch, paramount questions remain: the geological evolution of the Island, the shifting of the Orontes' riverbed, and the exact placement of several gates and bridges are but some outstanding problems. Nevertheless, we are confident that our presentation of Antioch's topography will offer a new platform for discussion in the years ahead.

Notes

1 Brands 2016a; Brands et al. forthcoming.
2 Brasse 2010
3 Weulersse 1934; Leblanc and Poccardi 1999; Uggeri 1998; Hoepfner 1999.
4 Corona imagery was sourced from the University of Arkansas Corona Digital Atlas Project (https://corona.cast.uark.edu/). The imagery, when downloaded, was roughly georeferenced, and the tiles which covered Antakya had significant error, being off by over 330 m, and needed to be re-rectified.
5 www.CRANE.utoronto.ca; https://tayinat.artsci.utoronto.ca/
6 Djobadze 1986.

7 Pamir 2005.
8 See the discussion of the document in this volume, Chapter 1, p. 64, nn 92 and 93.
9 *Downey, History* 452.
10 Climate data seems to suggest a period of drier conditions (and droughts) lasting until 470 or perhaps the mid-sixth century. This may also account for the narrowing of the Orontes channel and low flow of the river, but at present this is mere speculation. Justinian's implementation of cisterns in each tower do suggest a stopgap measure to augment water supply, however. See Izdebski et al. 2016 (especially 205, and Figure 8).
11 Brasse 2010, 279–280; Procopius 1940, II.102.
12 Procopius 1940, II.102.
13 Sinclair 1990, IV.246–247.

APPENDIX 2

Evliya Çelebi's *Seyahatnamesi*

Translation by Peter Klempner

E. Çelebi. 1999. *Seyahatnāmesi*. Book III. Topkapı Sarayı Kütüphanesi Bağdat 305 Numaralı Yazmanın Transkripsiyonu – Dizini. S. A. Kahraman and Y. Dağlı (eds). Yapı Kredi Yayınları. 34 (32)–39 (38).

Features of city of the land of hell and the old center of the throne, the Antakıyya (Antioch) Citadel.

It has been given a particular name in every language since it is a very old town, and it is a beautiful city. Some say İntâkiyye, others İntakya, and others say Ayn-ı takıyye; others Entakiyye, others Antakıyya, and some say Antekya, but the most common, however incorrect, is Antakıyya and İntakiyye. Though in Coptic they say Cebsinân (?), in Arabic they say [...], and in Greek they say [...]. In Persian they say Ân-tâkiyye. It is a very old city. Before Nûh's (Noah) Flood, Sürid Hakîm built a small and tidy city, but because the people did not know Islam in the time of the Prophet Idris, all of the people were wiped out in torment, whipped by fiery winds like the torture of hell. After the flood, Yâfet (Japheth) son of Nûh, peace be upon him, rebuilt it, settled here for a while ***[22a]***, and the children of his children spread over the land, but as the Prophet Nûh also did not come to the faith, Allah the Creator struck down these people with furious fire, which is why many historians call this city the Land of Hell and the Land of the Caesars.

Later, [...] built a large citadel, rose in rebellion against the Prophet Süleyman, and took refuge with all the people in the citadel. The Prophet Süleyman waged war against the citadel with the people, jinns, wild beasts, and birds, and in the end, the Prophet Süleyman conquered this citadel and enslaved the padishah together with his people. Because Takyanus (Decius) took the throne later in the time of the Prophet […], they say Antakıyye is a corruption of An Takyanus.

{Description of the affairs of Denklayanuş, that is King Takyanus

They called these the caesars of Rome in olden times. Since they possessed the cities of Erzurûm and Sivas and Kayseriyye (Caesarea) and Konya, they would say the Caesar of Rome. If a few kings gathered, they called them *kayâsıra* (caesars). Takyanus, however, was a king of Rome, and the centers of the throne were the cities of Rome and Antakıyya. He became an aberrant king in the Alexandrian year of 595 (879 CE), as is described in the incontrovertible verse of the Companions of the Cave [1],رجما بالغيم ويقولون سبعة وثامنهم و كلبهم and it is written in all books of exegesis that seven or eight Companions of the Cave fled due to his cruelty. He came on İskenderiyye (Alexandria) with their possessions, through trickery slaughtered the vizier rebelling against him, took possession of İskenderiyye, and wreaked havoc on the country of Egypt, as Buhtunnasr (Nebuchadnezzar) had. From there he went to the land of Persia, put his vizier in command, and waged a great war against Shapur Shah. He slayed Shapur Shah and sent everyone in his family and all of his treasure off to Takyanus. He restored the Antakıyya Citadel even more with this booty. In the end, he reigned for 20 years. His gums receded and his teeth fell out, and he died from his tyranny. His rogue of a son Karnibal became king in his place, and when he died two years later, it was the end of the caesars in this place. The state was destined for the Christian people. Kostantin (Constantine) the Great became king and committed to the sacraments of the Prophet İsa (Jesus). It was Konstantin, the first Christian king, who destroyed all of Takyanus' idols, burned all of his statues in flames, and in their place built churches, but after Takyanus}, the descendants of Buhtunnasr destroyed Antakıyya and it passed into the hands of many kings and into the hands if the dynasty of caesars when the caliphate of Holy Omer (Umar) conquered holy Qudüs (Jerusalem). Hâlid b. Velîd (Khālid b. al-Walīd), Esved b. Mikdâd (Miqdād b. al-Aswad), Ebû Ubeyde ibn Cerrâh (Abū 'Ubayda b. Jarrāḥ), and many other similar, preeminent companions came and waged great battles. Some having conquered and some having not conquered, they returned to Medina. Finally, in the year […], Hârûnu'r-Reşîd (Hārūn al-Rashīd) of the Abbasid dynasty came with Seyyid Battâl Ca'fer Gâzî[2] and three times 100,000 soldiers and waged great battles, conquered, and put all the infidels to the sword. Prince al-Ma'mūn came to power when Hârûnu'r-Reşîd returned to Baghdad and died, and then infidels again overran the Antakıyya Citadel. In the end, his Excellency Nûreddîn eş-şehîd (Nūr al-Dīn), king of Şâm (Damascus), conquered it from the hands of the infidels. After he passed away, Yûsuf Selâhaddîn (Salaḥ al-Dīn Yusuf), while sultan of Egypt, overran Qudüs, Tarabulus of Şâm, and the Frankish infidels in Antakıyya. {The Turkmen dynasty was five people in all and one of them was Emîr Kerboğa. He came with an army as big as the seas to rescue Antakıyya Citadel from the infidels, but was defeated by the hand of the warring Franks and, because of his disgrace and in an effort to preserve his honor, he stepped down from the throne of Haleb (Aleppo), and in the year 495 [1102 CE], he died in the city of Hoy (Khoy) while on the way to the half of the Persian realm that is Isfahân, and was buried there.} Then Yûsuf Selâhaddîn came from Egypt with soldiers like the seas and conquered Qudüs, Tarabulus of Şâm, and Antakıyya, which stayed in the hands of the Egyptian kings until the time of Sultan Gavrî (Ghūrī), who was from the Circassian kings of Egypt. When Sultan Selîm I was battling the Persians, Sultan of Egypt Gavrî was aiding the Qızılbaş. When Sultan Selîm was defeated on the Çıldır Plain because of the aid Gavrî lent the Persians, a wind of opportunity blew over Sultan Selîm upon order from the Almighty, and as 'İsmâ'îl Shah fled in defeat, 40,000 elite Egyptian soldiers were put to the sword. Sultan Selîm returned victorious and said, "It is obligatory to kill the men who pretend to be Muslims and aided the Qızılbaş," and with a *Bismillah*, proposed a holy war after receiving noble fatwas from Kemâlpaşazâde Ahmed Efendi. He sent envoys to Gavrî in Egypt the following year, and when Sultan Selîm got news that his envoys had been murdered by Gavrî, he received another fatwa of credence and testimonium. He first destroyed the king of Mar'aş, Sultan Alâüddevle (Bozkurt of Dulkadir), in the Göksun Highlands with more soldiers than the land could carry and put 40,000 unruly Turkmens to death. He sent Alâüddevle's misfortunate head and the heads of 70 of his closest chiefs to Gavrî Khan in Egypt, and said, "Be prepared for your time!" Gavrî met Selîm Khan in Mercidâbıq (Marj Dabiq) with four times 100,000 men and, in the place where the Holy Prophet Dâvûd (David) fought against King Câlût (Goliath), there was a battle between Selîm and Gavrî, at the end of which Gavrî fled forlorn to the Citadel of Haleb with 700 vile Circassians. Sultan Selîm went in pursuit, gave notice, conquered Heleb, and handed the key to this Antakıyya to Yunus Paşa. The people of the province came to Selîm Khan, who now ruled Haleb, with many times 100,000 gold and gifts, and presented their gifts with prayer and praise. Bıyıklı Mehemmed Paşa became governor of Antakıyya, and it was incorporated into the province of Haleb. This conquest of Antakıyya took place in the year 922 [1516 CE]. The Haleb governor, still held by the House of Osman at present, is a noble jurisdiction from the voivodship administration at the padishah's pleasure with 300 men connected to it and a commission of 300 *akçe*. A commission of several times 500 is granted to the many mullahs as gratuity. There is a sheikh ul-Islam from each four denominations, a nakîbü'l-eşrâf (naqib al-ashraf),[3] chamberlain of the army, janissary commander, city deputy, constabulary official for public order, citadel guard, and [...] men of the citadel. Because it is an inner province, it has a sufficient number of armories and 20 damaged cannons, small and large.

Features of the grand, old Antakıyya Citadel: Great citadels and old buildings have been built over the many 1000 years God Almighty has adorned the face of the earth with the sons of Adam, but by command of God, for the first time, the sons of Adam built the first exemplary structure, the pyramids in Egypt, with the teachings of the Prophet ***[22b]*** Idris in the time of the rule of Sürid and Kalimon. After the flood, the city of Cûda was built in the Armenian realm, then in the land of Hâsân in Egypt, the city of Arîş (Arish), the city of Balîs, the city of Ahmîm (Akhmim), the city of Elvâhât (el-Wahat), the city of Asvân (Aswan), the city of Sûdân, the city of Menufiyye (Menoufia), and the city of Antakıyya. This is also one of the great buildings. One is the mother of the world, Kâhire (Cairo) in Egypt. One is paradise-like Baghdad in Iraq. One is Haleb in Iraq-ı Arab. One is Iraq-ı Dadyan[4] in the foothills of the Elburz Mountains looking out to the Kipchak Steppe. Another great city is Ahlat. Another is the fortress of Macedonia, that is the walled city of Kostantiniyye (Constantinople), whose first founder was the Prophet Süleyman, but this Antakıyya Citadel was built before Islâmbol (Istanbul, i.e. Constantinople), and the Prophet Süleyman waged war on Antakıyya and conquered it. As such, one of the old and great works is the Antakıyya Citadel whose grand walls were built on five tall and great mountains. The citadel's walls on the mountain to the east are mountains that stretch to the vault of heaven. It is a large citadel, with half of it then built down to the west, all the way to lowlands at the banks of the great Âsî (Orontes) River. With this reckoning, half of the citadel is on high keystone mountains. The other half was built down the slopes of the mountain. Reckoning in miles, the citadel is 12 miles. Every mile is 4,000 paces. With this reckoning, the citadel is 44,000 paces all around from top to bottom, which takes 12 hours to walk slowly. Yet the fortress of Islâmbol is 47,000 paces, and with an architect's cubits, the face of its walls come to 87,000 *arşin* [about 37 miles, or 60 kilometers]. After this, paradise-like Baghdad is also a great citadel. It has 24,000 crenellations and is 27,000 paces. After that is this great Antakıyya Citadel. Smaller than this is the citadel in Egypt, and smaller the citadel in Şâm, and then Haleb, and then smaller the Kefe Citadel on the Island of Crimea, and the Salonika Citadel in Rumelia, which is equivalent to Kefe. After these, all other citadels are smaller than that of Antakıyya. I have never seen a citadel with walls, towers, and bastions as high as those of the Antakıyya Citadel. The walls on the mountain to the east are at a height of 80 imperial cubits, but on the side of the banks of the Âsî River, they are 20 because it is lowland and the walls are one level. Other than these, there are many levels of towers and bastions climbing up the mountain from the Haleb gate and Şâm gate, making a total of [...] large towers. In olden times, Takyanus had his drums sound from each of these towers, the interiors of which are all divided into five floors. The width of the walls facing the mountain are each 20 cubits. This citadel was built with such massive and large hewn stones that each one is the size of Mengerûsî's elephants. And the adept master cleaved the stones together with Ferhad's chisel so one would think the citadel is one solid wall. There is a total of [...] gates. First of all, the Haleb Gate, which faces north, is a wide and tall gate 20 cubits high. Pure water of life wells from the stones on the inner face of the gate and the Bridge Gate to the west is a sturdy gate that crosses the Âsî River with a large [...] arched bridge. And

There are five high mountains at the east side of the citadel and, because the walls on these mountains are 80 cubits high, the sun touches the city below two hours later. May all know that because the sun takes two hours to appear from the side of Habib-i Neccâr on the mountains in the east of the city, and because the mountains are high, the sun rises over the city below in two hours.

The features, names, and number of neighborhoods:

The features and number of grand mansions, houses, and buildings: In all, there are eight large mansions. First of all, Keteğaç Paşa Mansion in the city below has a quite sumptuous chamber, many small rooms, and a gate with an iron chain. Once, Ketağaç Paşa even struck the chain with a sword and split it in two, and it is still hung on the door as it was no feat of man. Thus, they call him Ketağaç Paşa, and *ketağaç* means sword. Most often, the fine houses are along the Âsî River. ***[23a]***

The features and number of the mosques of the city of Antakıyya: In all, there are [...] mihrabs and Muslim houses of worship.

Features of the masjids of Antakıyya:

Praise of the madrasahs and dârü'l-hadîs:[5] Although there are no special stone masonry places of study or dârü'l-hadîs as there are in Islâmbol and other cities, all of the sciences are taught in seven places and in mosques and in masjids. In particular, Ders-i âm[6] [...] Efendi is one who is a scholar well-versed in the sciences [...]

Features of Quran methods classes and primary schools: There are Quran methods classes in three places where is taught *seb'a*, *aşere*, and *takrîb*,[7] and correct recitation, however there is no specified fee for the students and the sheikhs are volunteers. In all, there are 40 primary schools and reading schools for small children. Many of them have holiday dress and gift bags donated to them by the foundation and they are well-maintained schools.

Features of the illustrious dervish lodges: In all, there are nine dervish lodges. Firstly, there is the Lodge of the Remains of Habib-i Neccâr in the city below, and its dervishes are prosperous. It is in low-laying land. There is also a Lodge of Habib-i Neccâr on the mountain, which takes an hour to climb to and looks out over everything.

Features of the appeasing baths: All [...] are small baths. All of them are on the inner face of the walls of the citadel running along the Âsî River and are baths with pleasant air and water. The waters are drawn from the Âsî River with water wheels and are the water of life.

The features of inns: In all, there are nine inns for traders and bachelors. Firstly, in the market is [...] inn,

Features of the market bazaar and shops: In all, there are 350 shops. The stone structures are not covered and they are not very fancy. However, all items of value are available. [...] [...] [...] [...] [...] [...] [...] [...] [...] [...]

Praise of the beloved and beloveds: Since it is the cusp of the border of renowned Arabia, there are beauties with gazelle eyes lined in eye liner, with bright faces, sweet words, and comely faces. When the pashas enter the city, all the women wrap up in white skirts and ululate as in Yemen.

Features of the city's water, air, and climate: Since it is in the third climate, its air and water are sweet and soft. According to the science of the astrolabe, the latitude of the city is [...] and longitude is [...] hours and degrees and [...] minutes.

The state of pure water and sources of flowing life: Since there are high mountains to the east of the city, several springs of paradise and sources of pure water flow into the citadel. Clear and sparkling yellow water even flows on the inner face of the Haleb gate and {runs into} the Âsî River.

Description of the lauded produce, foods, and beverages: First of all, there is white large-grained wheat, white bread baked on stones, cotton, lemons, oranges, and sugar cane, and the gardens and orchards arranged along the Âsî River are all connected to and watered by water wheels.

Features of the Arabian border: The western side of this city is the land of Rum. The city is the beginning of the land of Arabia and is on the border with Iraq-ı Arab, that is, the city of Halep. It is, however, not a sacred place. They apparently say it is one of the cities of the lands of hell. [...] [...] [...] [23b]

Features of the building complexes of Antioch: The just king by the name of Bî'atü'l-Kassân who made this city prosperous in the time of the Prophet Yahya [John the Baptist] converted to the faith of the Prophet İsa. He ruled in the city for 100 years, built 70 great churches. There were in all 600 churches, monasteries, and Christian houses of worship within the citadel. Each of the exquisite buildings of the great churches and monasteries had jewels and gild, crystal, colored quartz, carved stone, clouded marble and porphyry, and yellow jade. Most of them were razed on the night of the prophet's [Muhammad] birth and there are still the ruins of the buildings and seven well-kept monasteries, chapels, and churches.

Features of the Âsî River of Antakkıya: In the thinking of the historian who wrote *Tuhfe* (The Gift), the birth of this river happened in the time of the Prophet Muhammad. The city of Hamâ was waterless, and from the Jewish people there was a Jew named İzâ'îl (Izael) who made and prepared a water wheel, but there was not a trace of a drop of water. "I think I need to bring the Nile to this city, make it flow in these deserts and develop them," he said to those asking questions. He finally arrived in Egypt, and recited an incitation as he took four bottles of water from the Nile: "Toward the road to Hamâ," and as he went, a part of the River Nile immediately split off with this Jew and came all the way to the city of Menzile [Manjil?]. From there it came through the plain of the city of Yafa [Jaffa?], and in that plain, from Askalân it arrived at the Island of Kıbrıs (Cyprus), and there was a narrow path in the sea. All of the caravan people from the city of Askalân and the land of Hâsân and the city of Arîş (Arish) and the city of Tabaristan and the city of Filistîn (Palestine) and all the land and sea merchants from the city of

Kefirnâhûn (Capernaum), that is the city of Sıfit (Safed), would go to the island of Kıbrıs on this road. As the River Nile magically passed through the city of Menzile, and in that place, {when this conjuror struck one of the bottles to the ground, by command of Allah, the Nile boiled up and became a great lake} and sunk the road to Kıbrıs, so when going to the fortress cities of Arîş and Gazza and Askalân and Yafa and Teyme, there is a great lake. This lake is visible while passing on the Arîş side when going from Şâm to Egypt. {After that, the conjuror struck another bottle to the ground, and to show His creation, God the Creator made the Lake of Lot [Dead Sea] in proximity to the city of Remle, and these incidents have been written in all trustworthy books.} After that, as the River Nile came underfoot of the Jew, {the conjuror again struck another bottle to the ground in the place of Lake Mine, and with command from the Ever-Living and All-Powerful, brought forth the fresh water of Lake Mine from that place} and the lake is still fresh water. Then, the River Nile was again beneath the ground and the water of the Nile the Jew brought with magic in the bottle went to the place he went to, up to Gülbîn Mountain, where it stopped. Then the prophet [Muhammad] said, "Come help, O Ali! The River Nile had magically left the Holy Land and wants to devastate Rum,[8] come help!" When the Messenger commanded Holy Ali, Ali immediately mounted Duldul and caught up with the Jew at the foot of Gülbin Mountain, and as he killed the Jew there, the fourth of the bottles on his breast was broken on Gülbin Mountain, and by command of the Almighty, the Nile water was poured to the ground, and with a resounding, "yâ Allah!" from the boulders of Gülbin, a large river flowed to the west and Holy Ali said, "O Âsî River, all rivers tend toward the presence of Allah and flow to the qibla. Why do you flow to the west? Turn, flow back, you are rebellious."[9] By command of the Ever-Living and All-Powerful, the river took to speech and said, "O Ali, by command of God, I water Hımıs (Homs) and Hamâ and several cities as I come here, and when I visit Habib-i Neccâr in the city of Antakıyya, then from there let me flow toward the qibla." Then Holy Ali said, "Turn, if not I will split you in two with my vanquishing Zulfiqar." The river said, "If you strike, you will make one part of me flow as blood and one part of me as pus, and up until Judgement Day, the servants of Allah will not be able to get benefit from me." Holy Ali said, "May your name be rebel.[10] May the sons of Adam see benefit from you and find drink." Holy Ali drank at the foot of Gülbin Mountain and watered Duldul, and they call where he prayed "the Place of Ali." Hazret Ali commanded the river in the beginning. The Jew he killed also lays in that place. {However, about this killed Jew, the Jewish people say he is a prophet. They say the River Nile came from Egypt with his miracle and claim that he came in the time of Holy Moses.} Even if they brought this river with magic, then it is another of God's secrets. This river forms a small lake at the foot of Gülbin. From there it goes to Hımıs and Hamâ and Antakıyya, flowing west, then it pounds the wall of the citadel on the side of Antakıyya facing the qibla and is crossed by a great [...] arched bridge, and waters all of Antakıyya's gardens and orchards, prostrates its necessary vow and oath in the land of Habib-i Neccâr, and then just below Antakıyya, coming back under the command of the Almighty, flows straight to the qibla [...] in the land of [...] sanjak, in a place named [...] flows into the Mediterranean sea, and is a river of sweet, pure water. Many historians have written that the river came in this way from the land of Egypt. Allah willing, it is written it also flows in its place in the city of Hamâ.

Features of the pilgrimage sites of the perfected saints of Antakıyya: First of all is the honor of virtuous devotees, the ascetic's trove of treasures, the center of the circle of miracles, the lead pillar of heavenly sainthood, the chief companion, the most precious companion, the hidden secret, the fore of pious virtue, Habib-i Neccâr [Habib the Carpenter]. He has reached the excellency of Holy Yahya and the Holy Messiah. At some times they say Holy İsa, *peace and blessings upon him*, was the chief of the apostles from the caliphs of the holies. Many say they are prophets, but some dispute it and say Luqman and Hizr (Khiḍr) and İskender and this Habib-i Neccâr are not prophets.

Tales of Habib-i Neccâr: He was the light of the eye of the founder of Antakıyya written above, the king by the name of Bî'atü'l-Kassân, and beloved by him. Like his father, he also converted to faith in the Holy Messiah and became a believer and disciple. The wisdom of God came as he laid in wait for death, and following the command, "Return to your Lord!" he headed for God and was buried in Antakıyya. Holy Habib-i Neccâr came to this city of Antakıyya seven years later and, when he invited all the people to the religion of the Messiah, all the city folk wanted a miracle from Habib-i Neccâr, and they said, "Our king had a just son named Yavhîd. He has been dead for seven years. Restore him to life and all of us will convert." Habib-i Neccâr immediately went to the prince's tomb and prayed, "By Allah's permission, rise," and when he did, by God's command the freed prince was rescued from the hopelessness of the tomb, and when he was alive, he live seven more years and all the people of Antakıyya were honored with Islam. The prince was so just in those seven years and made great monasteries and churches and gave much charity, and while building and making the city of Antakıyya prosperous, because of the carpentry Habib-i Neccâr did to provide himself with a livelihood, they call him Habib-i Neccâr. He became the head of carpenters at that time, but in the time of the Holy Prophet, it was Ebü'l-Kâsım Abdülvâhid en-Neccârî (Abu al-Qasim Abd al-Wahid an-Najjar). In the presence of the prophet, he gave faith to Selmân-ı Pak (Salman the Pure, Salman the Persian] and became the forty-second pir.[11] [Ibn] Zübeyr (al-Zubayr) built another gate for Great Mecca with the edict of his holiness so that pilgrims would enter through one and exit through another. Later, Yûsuf Haccâc-ı Zâlim (al-Hajjāj b. Yūsuf) came and with great persecution waged great war {in Mecca}, and when his holiness defeated ibn Zübeyr, he asked, "Why did you have another gate built in Mecca?" Haccâc-ı Zâlim hanged his Excellency [ibn] Zübeyr in the year [...] and Zübeyr's tomb is in the great cemetery. When the head of carpenters, Ebü'l-Kâsım, was wanted to be hanged because he also built a gate, Ebü'l-Kâsım fled on a ship from Cidde (Jeddah) to Habeş (Habesh), and later passed to the ever after in Asvân, but Habib-i Neccâr was the old head of carpenters. When {Habib-i Neccâr} showed the miracle of reviving the prince {by the name of Yavhîd in the city of Antakıyya} who was dead, the denialists saw it and, in the end, martyred Habib-i Neccâr seven years later and tossed his blessed head from the height of the mountain. They descended [...] stairs in a dug-out cave in the city below and it was buried in a dervish lodge full of light. It is still a place of pilgrimage for all Muslims and Christians.

The pilgrimage site of Habib-i Neccâr: His blessed body is buried in a cave tomb in an excursion spot within the citadel on an escarpment stretching to the vault of heaven. They say Timur looked it over and found it to be very fresh. Since his martyrdom, the oil lamp on top of his blessed tomb has never extinguished, praise Allah. The fakir dervishes keep the lamp burning. After his martyrdom, when he was dead, the revived prince also died and was buried within the citadel, below and near Habib-i Neccâr.

{The Site of King Yavhîd and King Bî'atü'l Kassân}: All the Christian peoples say they are their kings and come with devotional offerings, but one day I saw that they said this freed prince is the resurrected Holy İsa and that this holy verse gives definite evidence. They said to look at the exegesis of the verse {Sūra Ya-Sin, verse 13}

واضرب لهم مثلا اصحب القرية اذ جاءها المرسلون[12]

And that is the end of it

After visiting and looking around the Antakıyya Citadel and doing prayers for the 1,058th blessed Ramadan in the [...] mosque within the bazaar, the horn of travels was blown and for eight hours passing well-kept villages, again in the direction of the qibla,

The lodging place of the town of Zanbakıyye: It is truly a prosperous town in a fertile valley with gardens, orchards, lilies, and 300 houses. It is a [...] administration in the Antakıyya district. Its ground is covered with fig trees. In this town ***[24b]***, Cânpolâdzâde Alî Paşa gave a grand feast for Murtezâ Paşa – such that a padishah had not given a king. Even though Murtezâ Paşa and Alî Paşa's 6,000 soldiers in all and so many townsfolk and others ate, 1,000 large copper dishes remained filled to the brim with delectable foods. He gave the pasha three Arabian mares as gifts and Murtezâ Paşa Alî Paşa gave sable pelts and a jeweled dagger as gifts. From here, again in the direction of the qibla, in [...] hours,

The lodging place of the bridge of lightless perception: This place is in the land of Haleb, on the banks of the Asî River, and there is a small inn in an area with greenery, but it is a pitiless place. God the Creator destined the charitable to improve the pilgrims' road so it may be safe and secure. From here, again in the direction of the qibla, in six hours passing through land sometimes rocky and sometimes reedy and marshy,

Notes

1 Quran, *sūra* Al-Kahf, verse 22: "guessing at the unseen, and they will say there were seven, and their dog, the eighth."
2 The character of Seyyid Battâl Ca'fer Gâzî in Ottoman folk literature is based on the historical figure 'Abdāllah al-Baṭṭal (d. 740 CE) who was a commander under the Umayyads in the Arab-Byzantine Wars and known with the *nisba* al-Anṭākī (of Antioch).
3 The naqib al-ashraf was a post in the Ottoman government and other Islamic states denoting the head or leader of the community of descendants (*ashrāf*) of the Prophet Muhammad, established in order to maintain their privileged position in society.
4 A city in Daghestan.
5 Schools where *ḥadīth* is taught.
6 A title for those who provide lessons to the public in mosques.
7 *Seb'a*: the seven recitations of the Qur'ān, *Aşere*: the ten recitation of the Qur'ān, *Takrib*: A method in the teaching of Qur'ānic recitation by limiting the transmitters and lines of transmitters to two.
8 That is, Asia Minor, Anatolia.
9 Rebel, rebellious: *âsî*.
10 See n. 9.
11 A type of religious leader.
12 Qur'ān, *sūra* Ya-Sin, verse 13: "And set forth for them a parable, for example the story of the people of the city when the messengers came to them."

BIBLIOGRAPHY

Abbot Le Camus. 1890. *Notre voyage aux Pays Bibliques*, Tome III. Paris: Letouzey et Ané, 76–79.

Abdul Massih, J. 2009. "La fortification polygonale et les Mosaïques d'une maison romaine à Cyrrhus (Nebi Houri). Notes Préliminaires," *Syria* 86: 289–306.

Abu al Fidā'. 1872. "Tiré des annales d'Abou'l-Feda," in *Recueil des Historiens Croisades, Historiens orientaux 1*. Paris: Imprimerie nationale.

Abu Ezzah, A. M. 1980. "The Syrian Thughūr," PhD diss., University of Exeter, Exeter.

Abu Lughod, J. 1989. *Before European Hegemony: The World System A.D. 1250–1350*. New York: Oxford University Press.

Abū Shuja al-Rūdhrāwarī and Hilāl b. al-Muḥassin. 1921. "The Experiences of the Nations," in *The Eclipse of the 'Abbasid Caliphate: Original Chronicles of the Fourth Islamic Century*, H. F. Amedroz and D. S. Margoliouth (eds and trans.). London: Oxford.

Açikgoz, Ü. 2016. "*À La Recherche de l'Espace Perdu*: Architecture, Urban Fabric, and French Travelers to Antioch (1784–1914)," *Architectural Histories* 4 (1): 1–17.

Agapius of Manbij. 1912. *Kitab al-Unvan. Histoire Universelle*. A. Vasiliev (trans.). Second Part, Fasc. 2. *Patrologia Orientalis*, vol. 8. Paris: Firmin Didot, 399–550.

Aigen, W. 1980. *Sieben Jahre in Aleppo, 1656–1663: ein Abschnitt aus den "Reiss-Beschreibungen" des Wolffgang Aigen*. A. Tietze (trans.). Vienna: Verlag des Verbandes der wissenschaftlichen Gesellschaften Österreichs.

Ainsworth, W. F. 1842. *Travels and Researches in Asia Minor, Mesopotamia, Chaldea, and Armenia*. London: J.W. Parker.

Akpolat, M. 2006. "The Traditional Ottoman-Period Houses of Antioch," *Chronos* 13: 117–149.

Akyüz, H. S., Altunel, E., Karabacak, V., and Yalçıner, C. 2006. "Historical Earthquake Activity of the Northern Part of the Dead Sea Fault Zone, Southern Turkey," *Tectonophysics* 426 (3–4): 281–293.

Albert of Aix (Aachen). 2013. *History of the Journey to Jerusalem*. S. Edgington (trans.), vol. 1, Books 1–6. Burlington, VT: Ashgate.

———. 2007. *Historia Ierosolimitana*. S. Edgington (trans. and ed.). Oxford: Oxford Medieval Texts.

al-Dhahabī, Muḥammad b. Aḥmad. 2004–2007. *Siyar 'Alām al-Nubala'*. Beirut: Manshurat Muḥammad 'Alī Bayḍun, Dār al-Kutub al-'Ilmīyah.

al-Hamadhānī. 1973. *Abrégé du Livre des Pays*. H. Masse (trans.). Damascus: Institut Français de Damas.

'Alī, 'Abdullah Yūsuf (trans. and comment.). 2008. *The Meaning of the Holy Qur'ān*. Beltsville, MD: Amana Publications.

Ali Bey. 1816. *The Travels of Ali Bey, in Morocco, Tripoli, Cyprus, Egypt, Arabia, Syria, and Turkey, between the Years 1803 and 1807. Written by Himself.* Philadelphia, PA: M. Carey.

Al-Khatib Al-Baghdadi, Abu Bakr. 2002. *Tarikh Baghdad*. Bashar Awwad Maruf (ed.), 1st edn. Beirut: Dār al-Gharb al-Islāmī.

Alkım, U. 1969. "The Amanus Region in Turkey: New Light on the Historical Geography and Archaeology," *Archaeology* 22: 280–289.

Al-Maqrizi. 2009. *Towards a Shi'I Mediterranean Empire: Fatimid Egypt and the Founding of Cairo. The Reign of the Imam-caliph al-Mu'izz from Taqī al-Dīn Aḥmad b. 'Ali al-Maqrīzī's Itti'āẓ al-ḥunafā' bi-akhbār al-a'imma al-Fāṭimiyiīn al-khulafā'*. Shainool Jiwa (trans.). New York: I.B. Tauris Publishers.

———. 1837–1845. *Histoire des Sultans Mamlouks de l'Égypte*. M. Quatremère (trans.). Paris: Oriental Translation Fund.

———. 1971. *Kitāb as-Sulūk li-ma'rifat duwal al-mulūk*. Cairo: Maṭba'at Dār al-Kutub.

Al-Marwazī, Nu'aym b. Ḥammād. 2017. *Kitāb al-Fitan. "The Book of Tribulations": The Syrian Muslim Apocalyptic Tradition*. D. Cook (ed. and trans.). Edinburgh: Edinburgh University Press.

Al-'Umarī, Ibn Faḍl Allāh. 2017. *Egypt and Syria in the Early Mamluk Period*. D. S. Richards (trans.). New York: Routledge.

Allen, P. and Hayward, R. 2004. *Severus of Antioch*. London and New York: Routledge.

Alpi, F. 2012. "Le paysage urbain d'Antioche sur l'Oronte dans les sources syriaques anciennes," in *Les Sources de l'histoire du paysage urbain d'Antioche sur l'Oronte*, C. Saliou (ed.), vol. 8. Paris: Université Paris, 149–157.

———. 2007. "Maison païenne et chrétienne: représentation de l'habitat domestique à Antioche chez quelques auteurs tardo-antiques (IVe–VIe S.)," in *From Antioch to Alexandria. Recent Studies in Domestic Architecture*, K. Galor and T. Waliszewski (eds). Warsaw: Institute of Archaeology, 37–50.

———. 2003/4. "Sévère d'Atioche et la massacre de Kefr Kermin," *Tempora* 14 (15): 135–152.

Amatus of Montecassino. 1892. *Ystoire de li Normant, par Aimé, éveque et moine au Mont-Cassin*. Abbé O. Delarc (ed.). Rouen: A. Lestringant.

Ambraseys, N. N. 2009. *Earthquakes in the Mediterranean and Middle East: A Multidisciplinary Study of Seismicity up to 1900*. Cambridge: Cambridge University Press.

Amitai-Press, R. 2009. *Mongols and Mamluks: The Mamluk-Ilkhanid War, 1260–1281*. Cambridge: Cambridge University Press, 54.

Angar, M. 2017. *Byzantine Head Reliquaries and their Perception in the West after 1204. A Case Study of the Reliquary of St. Anastasios the Persian in Aachen and Related Objects*. Wiesbaden: Harrassowitz Verlag.

Aperghis, M. 2001. "Population – Production – Taxation – Coinage: A Model for the Seleukid Economy," in *Hellenistic Economies*, Z. H. Archibald, J. Davies, V. Gabrielsen, and G. J. Oliver (eds). London and New York: Routledge, 69–102.

Archi, A., Pecorella, P. E. and Salvini, M. 1971. *Gaziantep e la sua Regione. Uno Studio Storico e Topografico degli Insediamenti Preclassici*. Roma: Edizioni dell'Ateneo.

Arundell, Rev. F. V. J. 1834. *Discoveries in Asia Minor; Including a Description of the Ruins of Several Ancient Cities, and Especially Antioch of Pisidia*. London: Richard Bentley.

Asbridge, T. 2012. "The Significance and Causes of the Battle of the Field of Blood," *Journal of Medieval History* 23: 301–316.

———. 2004. *The First Crusade: A New History*. New York: Oxford University Press.

———. 2000. *The Creation of the Principality of Antioch, 1098–1130*. Rochester, NY: Boydell Press.

———. 1999. "The 'Crusader' Community at Antioch: The Impact of Interaction with Byzantium and Islam," *Transactions of the Royal Historical Society* 9 (December): 305–325.

Asutay-Effenberger, N. 2007. *Die Landmauer von Konstantinopel-Istanbul: historisch-topographische und baugeschichtliche Unterschungen*, Millenium Studien 18. Berlin: De Gruyter.

Athamina, K. 1986. "Arab Settlement during the Umayyad Caliphate," *Jerusalem Studies in Arabic and Islam* 8: 185–207.

Austin, M. M. 1981. *The Hellenistic World from Alexander to the Roman Conquest*. Cambridge: Cambridge University Press.

Avni, G. 2011. "'From Polis to Madina' Revisited – Urban Change in Byzantine and Early Islamic Palestine," *Journal of the Royal Asiatic Society* 21 (3): 301–329.

Aydın, M. and Saliou, C. 2020. "Vespasian, Antoch on the Orontes, and Dipotamia in the Greek Version," *ZPE* 216: 120–128.

Badr al-Din al-'Ayni. 1887. Extracts from *'Iqd al-Jumān fī ta'rīkh ahl az-zamān* [*The Necklace of Pearls concerning the History of the People of the Time*]. Recueil des historiens croisades historiens orientaux 2.1.

Bagnall, R. and Frier, B. W. 1994. *The Demography of Roman Egypt*. Cambridge: Cambridge University Press.

Bahadır, G. 2013. "The Transformation of the Socio-Political Structure in the Beginning of the Islamic Reign in Antioch," *International Journal of Social Science* 6 (7): 185–204.

Baird, J. 2018. *Dura-Europos*. London: Bloomsbury Academic.

Balādhurī. 1957–58. *Futūḥ al-Buldān*. Beirut: Dār an-Našr li-l-Ğāmi'īyīn.

———. 1924. *Kitāb Futūḥ al-Buldān*, Part II. F.C. Murgotten (trans). New York: Columbia University.

———. 1916. *Futūḥ al-Buldān*. P. K. Hitti (trans.). New York: Columbia University.

Ball, W. 2000. *Rome in the East. The Transformation of an Empire*. London and New York: Routledge.

Balty, J. C. 2004. "Antioche, centre d' art sous Séleucos I Nicator," in *Antioche de Syrie. Histoires, images et traces de la ville antique*, Topoi Orient-Occident Supplément 5, B. Cabouret, P. L. Gatier, and C. Saliou (eds). Lyon: Jean Pouilloux.

———. 2000. "Tetrakionia de l'époque de Justinien sur la grande colonnade d'Apamée," *Syria* 77: 227–237.

———. 1994. "Grande colonnade et quartiers nord d'Apamée à la fin de l'époque hellénistique," *Comptes-rendus des séances de l'Académie des Inscriptions et Belles Lettres* 138 (1): 77–101.

———. 1988. "Apamea in Syria in the Second and Third Centuries A.D.," *JRS* 78: 91–104.

———. 1981. *Guide d'Apamée*. Brussels: Centre belge de recherches archéologiques à Apamée de Syrie.

Balty, J. and Balty, J. C. 1981. "L'Apamée antique, Géographie politique et administrative d'Alexandre à Mahomet. Actes du Colloque de Strasbourg, 14–16 juin 1979," in *Travaux du Centre de Recherche sur le Proche-Orient et la Grèce Antique*, vol. 6. Leiden: Brill, 41–75.

———. 1977. "Apamée de Syrie, archéologie at histoire," *Aufstieg und Nedergang der Römischen Welt* 2 (8): 103–144.

Barker, J. 1876. *Syria and Egypt under the Last Five Sultans of Turkey: Being Experiences, during Fifty Years, of Mr. Consul-General Barker. Chiefly from His Letters and Journals.* Edward B. B. Barker (ed.). London: Samuel Tinsley.

Bar Hebraeus. 1932. *The Chronography of Gregory Abū'l Faraj the son of Aaron, the Hebrew Physician commonly known as Bar Hebraeus being the First Part of his Political History of the World.* E. A. W. Budge (trans.), vol. 1. London: Oxford University Press.

Barrès, M. 1923. *Une enquete aus pays du Levant.* Paris: Plon-Nourrit.

Bartlett, W. H., Purser, W., and Carne, J. 1838–1838. *Syria, the Holy Land, Asia Minor, &c. Illustrated.* London: Fisher, Son & Co., 19.

Basil the Merchant. 1889. "Pèlerinage du marchand Basile, 1465–1466," in *Itinéraires Russes en Orient, traduits pour la Société de l'Orient Latin*, B. Khitrowo (trans.). Geneva: Imprimérie Jules-Guillaume Fick.

Bassett, S. 2005. *The Urban Image of Late Antique Constantinople.* Cambridge: Cambridge University Press.

Batiuk, S. 2007. "Ancient Landscapes of the Amuq: Geoarchaeological Surveys of the Amuq Valley 1999–2006," *JSMS* 2: 51–57.

Bay, C. 2018. "Pseudo-Hegesyppus at Antioch? Testing a Hypothesis for the Provenance of the Excidio Hierolymitano," *Babelao* 8: 97–128.

Beaufort, E. 1861. *Egyptian Sepulchres and Syrian Shrines, Including Some Stay in the Lebanon at Palmyra, and in Western Turkey.* London: Longman & Co.

Becker, L. and Kondoleon, C. 2005. *The Arts of Antioch: Art Historical and Scientific Approaches to Roman Mosaics and a Catalogue of the Worcester Art Museum Antioch Collection.* Worcester: Worcester Art Museum.

Behrens-Abouseif, D. 1981. "The North-Eastern Extension of Cairo Under the Mamluks," *Annales Islamologiques* 17: 157–189.

Beihammer, A. 2017. *Byzantium and the Emergence of Muslim – Turkish Anatolia ca 1040–1130.* New York: Routledge.

———. 2012. "Muslim Rulers Visiting the Imperial City: Building Alliances and Personal Networks between Constantinople and the Eastern Borderlands (Fourth/Ten-Fifth/Eleventh Century)," *Al-Masaq* 24 (2): 157–177.

Bell, G. 1907. *Syria: The Desert & the Sown.* London: William Heinemann, Ltd.

Belon, P. 1553. *Les Observations de plusiers singularitez et choses memorables, trouvées en Grece, Asie, Iudée, Egypte, Arabie, & autre pays estranges.* Paris: G. Corrozet.

Benjamin of Tudela. 1907. *The Itinerary of Benjamin of Tudela.* Marcus Adler (trans.). New York: Philipp Feldheim, Inc.

Benjelloun, Y., et al. 2015. "Characterization of building materials from the aqueduct of Antioch-on-the-Orontes (Turkey)," *Comptes Rendus Geoscience.* http://dx.doi.org/10.1016/j.crte.2014.12.002

Bergjan, S. and Elm, S. (eds). 2018. *Antioch II. The Many Faces of Antioch: Intellectual Exchange and Religious Diversity, CE 350–450.* Tübingen: Mohr Siebock.

Berto, G. and Gelichi, S. 1997. "'Zeuxippus Ware' in Italy," in *Materials Analysis of Byzantine Pottery*, H. Maguire (ed.). Washington, DC: Dumbarton Oaks, 85–104.

Bertrandon de la Broquière. 1892. *Le Voyage d'Outremer.* Ch. Schefer (ed.). Paris: Ernest Leroux.

Boehm, R. 2018. *City and Empire in the Age of the Successors. Urbanization and Social Response in the Making of the Hellenistic Kingdoms.* Berkeley, CA: University of California Press.

Bone, H. 2000. "The Administration of Umayyad Syria: The Evidence of the Copper Coins," PhD diss., Princeton University, Princeton, NJ.

Bonner, M. 1996. *Aristocratic Violence and Holy War.* New Haven, CT: American Oriental Society.

Borschel-Dan, A. 2019. "First Evidence of Crusader Siege from 15 July 1099 Uncovered at Old City walls," *The Times of Israel*, July 15. www.timesofisrael.com/first-evidence-of-crusader-siege-from-july-15–1099-uncovered-at-old-city-walls/

Bosworth, C. E. 1992. "The City of Tarsus and the Arab-Byzantine Frontiers in Early and Middle 'Abbāsid Times," *Oriens* 33: 268–286.

Bouchier, E. S. 1921. *A Short History of Antioch, 300 B.C.–A.D. 1268*. Oxford: Basil Blackwell.

Boudier, M. 2018. "Le mémoire des Patriarche dans l'Église melkite: le cas de Christophore d'Antioche (Xe siècle)," in *Les Vivants et Les Morts dans les Sociétés Médiévales*. XLVIIIe Congrès de la SHMESP, Jerusalem, 2017. Paris: Éditions de la Sorbonne, 43–58.

Bouffartigue, J. 2009. "Julien entre biographie et analyse historique," *AnTard* 17: 79–90.

Bowersock, G. W. 1994a. "Roman Senators from the Near East: Syria, Judaea, Arabia, Mesopotamia," in *Studies on the Eastern Roman Empire*, G. W. Bowersock (ed.). Goldbach: Keip Verlag, 141–160.

———. 1994b. "The Search for Antioch," in *Studies on the Eastern Roman Empire*, G. W. Bowersock (ed.). Goldbach: Keip Verlag, 411–427.

———. 1994c. "Hadrian and Metropolis," in *Studies on the Eastern Roman Empire*, G. W. Bowersock (ed.). Goldbach: Keip Verlag, 371 401.

———. 1978. *Julian the Apostate*. Cambridge: Cambridge University Press.

———. 1973. "Syria Under Vespasian," *JRS* 63: 133–140.

Braidwood, R. J. 1937. *Mounds in the Plain of Antioch*. Chicago, IL: The University of Chicago Press.

Brands, G. 2018a. "Eine Artemis in Antakya. Mit einem Anhang von Ulrich Elferling," *Jahrbuch des Deutschen Archäologischen Instituts* 133: 259–288.

———. 2018b. "Preservation, Historicization, Change: Antioch A.D. 350–450," in *Antioch II. The Many Faces of Antioch: Intellectual Exchange and Religious Diversity, CE 350–450*, S. P. Bergjan and S. Elm (eds). Tübingen: Mohr Siebeck, 13–33.

———. 2016a. *Antiochia in der Spätantike. Prolegomena zu Einer Archäologischen Stadtgeschichte*. Berlin and Boston, MA: De Gruyter.

———. 2016b. "Kastalia und Pallas. Zum Megalopsychia-Mosaik aus Daphne," *Ist Mitt* 66: 256–291.

———. 2009. "Prokop und das Eisene Tor. Ein Beitrag zur Topographie von Antiochia am Orontes," in *Syrien und seine Nachbarn von der Spätantike bis in die islamische Zeit*, I. Eichenr and V. Tsamakda (eds). Wiesbaden: Reichert Verlag, 9–20.

Brands, G., Pamir, H. et al. 2009. "Hatay Yüzey araştırmaları 2007. Antakya, Samandağ, Yayladağı ve Altınözü," *Araştırma Sonuçları Toplantısı* 26: 1–12. Ankara.

———. 2008. "Hatay Ili, Antakya ve Samandağ yüzey araştırmalası," *Araştırma Sonuçları Toplantısı* 25: 393–410. Ankara.

———. 2007. "Asi deltası ve Asi vadisi arkeolojisi projesi. Antakya ve Samandağ," *Araştırma Sonuçları Toplantısı* 24: 397–418. Ankara.

Brasse, C. 2010. "Von der Stadtmauer zur Stadtgeschichte. Das Befestigungssystem von Antiochia am Orontes," in *Aktuelle Forschungen zur Konstruktion, Funktion und Semantik antiker Stadtbefestigungen*, J. Lorentzen, F. Pirson, P. I. Schneider et al. (eds). *Byzas* 10: 261–282. Istanbul: Ege Yayınları.

Brennan, T. C. 2000. *The Praetorship in the Roman Republic*. Oxford: Oxford University Press.

Bridgland, D. R., Westway, R., Romieh, M. A., et al. 2012. "The River Orontes between Syria and Turkey: Downstream Variation of Fluvial Archives in Different Blocks," *Geomorphology* 165–166: 25–49.

Brinkerhoff, D. M. 1970. *A Collection of Sculpture in Classical and Early Christian Antioch*. New York: New York University Press.

Brody, L. R. 2011. "Yale University and Dura-Europos: From Excavation to Exhibition," in *Dura Europos. Crossroads of Antiquity*, L. R. Brody and G. L. Hoffman (eds). Chicago, IL: The University of Chicago Press.

Brody, L. R. and Snow, C. 2015. "The Gerasa City Mosaic: History and Treatment at the Yale University Art Gallery," in *Age of Transition. Byzantine Culture in the Islamic World*, H. C. Evans (ed.). New Haven, CT and London: Yale University Press, 20–29.

Brown, P. 1988. *The Body and Society. Men, Women, and Sexual Renunciation in Early Christianity*. New York: Columbia University Press.

———. 1971. "The Rise and Function of the Holy Man in Late Antiquity," *JRS* 61: 80–101.

Brown, J. 2017. *Hadith: Muhammad's Legacy in the Medieval and Modern World*. London: Oneworld, 75.

Bru, H. 2011. *Le pouvoir imperial dans les provinces syriennes. Représentations et celebrations d'Auguste à Constantin (31 av. J.-C.–337 apr. J.-C.)*. Boston, MA and Leiden: Brill.

Buck, A. 2014. "On the Frontier of Latin Christendom: The Principality of Antioch, ca. 1130-ca. 1193," PhD diss., Queen Mary University of London, London.

Buckingham, J. S. 1825. *Travels Among the Arab Tribes, Inhabiting the Countries East of Syria and Palestine, Including a Journey to Bozra, Damascus, Tripoly, Lebanon, Baalbeck, and by the Valley of the Orontes to Seleucia, Antioch, and Aleppo with an Appendix*. London: Longman.

Burgtorf, J. 2006. "The Military Orders in the Crusader Principality of Antioch," in *East and West in the Medieval Mediterranean I: Antioch from the Byzantine Reconquest until the End of the Crusader Principality: Acta of the Congress Held at Hernen Castle in May 2003*. OLA 147, K. Ciggaar and M. Metcalf (eds). Leuven: Peeters, 217–246.

Burnett, C. 2000. "Antioch as a Link Between Arabic and Latin Cultures in the Twelfth and Thirteenth Centuries," in *Occident et Proche-Orient: Contacts scientifiques au temps des Croisades*, B. van den Abeele et al. (eds). Turnhout: Brepols, 1–78.

Burns, R. 2005. *Damascus. A History*. London and New York: Routledge.

Burrell, B. 2004. *Neokoroi: Greek Cities and Roman Emperors*. Leiden: Brill.

Burton, G. 2002. "The Regulation of Inter-Community Relations in the Provinces and the Political Integration of the Roman Empire (27 BC–AD 238)," in *Oikistes. Studies in Constitutions, Colonies and Military Power in the Ancient World. Offered in Honor of A.J. Graham*, V. Gordman and E. W. Robinson (eds). Leiden: Brill, 113–128.

Butcher, K. 2004. *Coinage in Roman Syria. Northern Syria, 64 BC–AD 253*. London: Royal Numismatic Society.

———. 2003. *Roman Syria and the Near East*. Los Angeles, CA: Getty Publications.

———. 1988. "The Colonial Coinage of Antioch-on-the-Orontes c. AD 218–253," *The Numismatic Chronicle* 148: 63–75.

Butcher, K. and Ponting, M. 2009. "The Silver Coinage of Roman Syria under the Julio-Claudian Emperors," *Levant* 41 (1): 59–78.

Byrne, E. H. 1928. "The Genoese Colonies in Syria," in *The Crusades and Other Historical Essays Presented to D.C. Munro*, L. J. Paetow (ed.). New York: F. S. Crofts, 139–182.

Cabouret, B. 2004. "Pouvoir municipal, pouvoir imperial au IVe siècle," in *Antioche de Syrie: Histoire, images et traces de la ville antique*. Topoi Orient-Occident Supplément 5, B. Cabouret, P.-L. Gatier, and C. Saliou (eds). Lyon: Jean Pouilloux, 117–142.

———. 1999. "Sous les Portiques d'Antioche," *Syria* 76: 127–150.

———. 1994. "L'oracle de la source Castalie à Daphnè près d'Antioche," in *Eukrata. Mélanges offerts à Claude Vatin*, M. C. Amouretti and P. Villard (eds). Aix-en-Provence: Publications de l'Université de Provence, 95–104.

Cahen, C. 1971. "Un document concernant les Melkites et les Latin d'Antioche au temps de Croisades," *Revue des études byzantines* 29: 285–292.

Çakar, E. 2015. "16. Yüzyılda Antakya Vakıfları (1550 Tarihli Evkaf Defterine Göre) [The Waqfs of Antioch in the 16th Century]," *Vakıflar Dergisi* 43 (June): 9–39.

Callot, O. 2013. "Les pressoirs du Massif Calcaire: une vision différente," in *Villes et Campagnes aux rives de la Méditerranée ancienne. Hommages à George Tate*. Topoi Supplément 12, G. Charpentier and V. Puech (eds). Lyon: Jean Pouilloux, 97–109.

———. 1984. *Huileries antiques de la Syrie du Nord*. Paris: Paul Geuthner.

Callu, J. P. 1997. "Antioche la grande; la cohérence des chiffres," *Mefra* 109: 127–169.

Cameron, A. 2012. *The Mediterranean World in Late Antiquity 395–700 AD*. London and New York: Routledge.

Canard, M. 1953. "Review: Une Vie du Patriarche Melkite d'Antioche, Christophore (†967)," *Byzantion* 23: 561–569.

———. 1951. *Histoire de la dynastie des Hamdanides de Jazira et de Syrie*. Algiers: Imprimeries la typo-litho et Jules Carbonel reunies.

Caner, D. 2020. *Wandering Begging Monks. Spiritual Authority and the Promotion of Monasticism in Late Antiquity*. Berkeley, CA: University of California Press.

Capar, A. 2017. "A Portrait of an Ottoman City and Its Inhabitants: Administration, Society, and Economy in Ottoman Antakya (Antioch), 1750–1840," PhD diss., University of Arkansas, Fayetteville, AR, 198–202.

Casana, Jesse. 2007. "Structural Transformations in the Settlement Systems of the Northern Levant," *American Journal of Archaeology* 111 (2): 195 221.

———. 2004. "The Archaeological Landscape of Late Roman Antioch," in *Culture and Society in Later Roman Antioch*. Papers from a Colloquium. London, December 15, 2001, I. Sandwell and J. Huskinson (eds). Oxford: Oxbow, 102–125.

Cassas, M. 1798. *Voyage pittoresque de la Syrie, de la Phénicie, de la Palestine et de la Basse-Égypte*. Paris: Imprimerie de la République.

Casella, M. 2016. "La vocazione centripeta. Una divergenza ideologica tra Libanio e Temistio di fronte alla prospettiva costantinopolitana dei buleuti di Antiochia," *Historika* 6: 205–242.

———. 2010. *Storie di ordinaria corruzione. Libanio, Orazioni LVI, LVII, XLVI*. Messina: Di.Sc.A.M.

Çelebi, E. 1999. "*Seyahatnāmesi*. Book III. Topkapı Sarayı Kütüphanesi Bağdat 305 Numaralı Yazmanın Transkripsiyonu – Dizini." S. A. Kahraman and Y. Dağlı (eds). *Yapı Kredi Yayınları* 34 (32), 39 (38).

Cevdet, A. 1953. *Tezākir: yayınlayan*. C. Baysun (ed.). Ankara: Türk Tarih Kurumı Basımevi.

Chapot, V. 1907. *Séleucie de Piérie, Mémoires de la société nationale des Antiquaires de France – Tome 66*. Paris.

Chausson, F. 1997. "Les Egnatii et l'aristocratie italienne des IIe–IVe siècles," *Journal des savants* 211–331.

Cherefeddin Ali. 1723. *The History of Timur-Bec, Known by the Name of Tamerlain the Great, Emperor of the Moguls and Tartars: Being an Historical Journal of his Conquests in Asia and Europe*. Petis de la Croix (trans.), vol. II. London.

Chesneau, J. and Schefer, C. 1887. *Le Voyage du Monsieur d'Aramon escript par Jean Chesneau. Publié et annoté par M. Ch. Schefer*. Paris: Ernest Leroux.

Chesney, F. R. 1850. *The Expedition for the Survey of the Rivers Euphrates and Tigris Carried on by Order of the British Government in the Years 1835, 1836, and 1837*, vol. 1. London: Longman, Brown, Green, and Longmans.

Cheynet, J.-C. 2006. "The Duchy of Antioch during the Second Period of Byzantine Rule," in *East and West in the Medieval Mediterranean I: Antioch from the Byzantine Reconquest until the End of the Crusader Principality: Acta of the Congress Held at Hernen Castle in May 2003*. OLA 147, K. Ciggaar and M. Metcalf (eds). Leuven: Peeters, 1–16.

———. 2003. "Basil II and Asia Minor," in *Byzantium in the Year 1000*, P. Magdalino (ed.). Leiden: Brill.

———. 1994. "Sceaux byzantins des Musées d'Antioche et de Tarse," *Travaux et Memoires* 12: 391–478.

Christensen-Ernst, J. 2012. *Antioch-on-the-Orontes: A History and a Guide*. Lanham, MD: Hamilton Books.

Christof, E. 2001. *Das Glück der Stadt. Die Tyche von Antiochia und anderen Stadttychen*. Frankfurt am Main and New York: P. Lang.

Chrubasik, B. 2016. *Kings and Usurpers in the Seleukid Empire*. Oxford: Oxford University Press.

Clarke, G. 2015. "The Jebel Khalid Temple: Continuity and Change," in *Religious Identities in the Levant from Alexander to Muhammed*, M. Blömer, A. Lichtenberger, and R. Raja (eds). Turnhout: Brepols, 143–155.

Clarke, G., et al. 2002. *Jebel Khalid on the Euphrates. Reports on the Excavations 1986–1996*. Sydney: Meditarch.

Ciggaar, K. N. 2006. "Adaptation to Oriental Life by Rulers in and Around Antioch: Examples and Exempla," in *East and West in the Medieval Mediterranean I: Antioch from the Byzantine Reconquest until the End of the Crusader Principality: Acta of the Congress Held at Hernen Castle in May 2003*. OLA 147, K. Ciggaar and M. Metcalf (eds). Leuven: Peeters, 261–282.

Cimok, F. 1980. *Antioch on the Orontes*. Istanbul: A Turizm Yayınları.

Cohen, Getzel M. 2006. *The Hellenistic Settlements in Syria, the Red Sea Basin and North Africa*. Berkeley, CA: University of California Press.

Constable, O. 2003. *Housing the Stranger in the Mediterranean World: Lodging, Trade and Travel in Late Antiquity and the Middle Ages*. Cambridge: Cambridge University Press.

Cribiore, R. 2007. *The School of Libanius in Late Antique Antioch*. Princeton, NJ: Princeton University Press.

Crook, J. A. 1995. *Legal Advocacy in the Roman World*. Ithaca, NY: Cornell University Press.

Cuinet, V. 1890–1895. *La Turquie d'Asie, géographie administrative Statistique descriptive et raisonnée de l'Asie Mineure*. Paris: Ernest Leroux.

Cumont, F. 1934. "The Population of Syria," *JRS* 24: 187–190.

Ćurčić, S. 1993. "Late Antique Palaces: The Meaning of Urban Context," *Ars Orientalis* 23: 67–90.

d'Angelo, E. 2017. "A Latin School in the Norman Principality of Antioch?" In *Peoples, Texts and Artefacts*, D. Bates, E. d'Angelo, and E. Van Houts (eds). London: University of London Press, 77–88.

d'Ault-Dumesnil, E. 1852. *Dictionnaire historique, géographique et biographique des Croisades, embrassant toute la lutte du Christianisme et de l'Islamisme, etc. coll. Cxcvi. 1042*. Paris.

Dabrowa, E. 2020. *Camps, Campaigns, Colonies. Roman Military Presence in Anatolia, Mesopotamia, and the Near East. Selected Studies*. Wiesbaden: Harassowitz Verlag.

———. 1998. *The Governors of Roman Syria from Augustus to Septimius Severus*. Bonn: Habelt.

———. 1986. "The Frontier in Syria in the First Century AD," in *The Defence of the Roman and Byzantine East. Proceedings of a Colloquium Held at the University of Sheffield in April 1986*, P. Freeman, and D. Kennedy (eds). Oxford: BAR, 93–108.

———. 1980. *L'Asie Mineure sous les Flaviens*. Krakow: Gdańsk.

Daftary, F. 2018. *Ismaili History and Intellectual Traditions*. New York: Routledge.

Dagron, G. 1979–1984. "Entre village et cité: la bourgade rurale des IVe-VIIe siècles en Orient," *Koinônia* 3: 29–52. Reprinted in *La Romanité chrétienne en Orient. Héritages et mutations*. London: Variorum Reprints, 29–52.

———. 1976. "Minorités ethniques et religieuses dans l'Orient Byzantin à la fin du Xe et au Xie siècles: L'immigration Syrienne," *Travaux et Memoires* 6: 177–216.

Dagron, C. and Déroche, V. 1991. "Juifs et Chrétiens dans l'Orient du VIIe siècle," *Travaux et Mémoires* 11: 17–273.

Dagron, G. and Feissel, D. 1985. "Inscriptions inédités du Musée d'Antioche," *Travaux et Mémoires* 9: 421–461.

Dauer, A. 1996. *Paulus und die christliche Gemeinde im syrischen Antiochiakritische Bestandsaufnahme der modernen Forschung*. Weinheim: Beltz Atenäum Verlag.

de Corancez, O. 1816. *Itineraire d'une partie peu connue de l'Asie Mineure*. Paris: Chez J.-M. Ebehrard, Chez Antoine.

De Giorgi, A. U. 2019. "*'Til Death Do Us Part*. Commemoration, Civic Pride, and Seriality in the Funerary Stelai of Antioch on the Orontes," in *Funerary Portraits in Greater Roman Syria*, M. Blömer and R. Raja (eds). Turnhout: Brepols, 27–44.

———. 2015. "The Princeton Excavations in Antakya, 1932–1940," *JRA* 28: 873–876.

———. 2016. *Ancient Antioch: From the Seleucid Era to the Islamic Conquest*. Cambridge: Cambridge University Press.

———. 2007. "The Formation of a Roman Landscape: The Case of Antioch," *JRA* 20: 283–298.

de Goeje, M. J. 1885. *Mukhtaṣar Kitāb al-Buldān by Ibn al-Faqīh al-Hamadhānī*, vols. 1–5. Leiden: Brill, 2013.

de la Roque, J. 1722. *Voyage de Syrie et du Mont-Liban: contenant la description de tout le pays compris sous le nom de Liban & d'Anti-Liban, Kesroan, &c. ce qui concerne l'origine, la créance, & les moeurs des peuples qui habitent ce pays: la description des ruines d'Heliopolis, aujourd'huy Balbek, & une dissertation historique sur cette ville; avec un abregé de la Vie de monsieur de Chasteüil, gentilhomme de Provence, solitaire du Mont-Liban; & l'histoire du prince Junés, maronite, mort pour la religion dans ces derniers temps*. Paris: Chez André Cailleau.

De Sacy, S. 1793. *Memoires sur les antiquités de la Perse*. Paris: Louvre.

Debié, M. 2005. "Les apocalypses apocryphes syriaques: des textes pseudoépigraphiques de l'Ancien et du Nouveau Testament," in *Les Apocryphes Syriaques*, M. Debié, A. Desreumaux, F. Jullien, and C. Jullien (eds). Paris: Geuthner, 111–146.

Decker, M. 2001. "Food for an Empire: Wine and Oil Production in North Syria," in *Economy and Exchange in the East Mediterranean During Late Antiquity. Proceedings of a Conference at Somerville College, Oxford, 29th May 1999*, S. Kingsley and M. Decker (eds), Oxford: Oxbow, 69–86.

Dedeoğlu, M. 2018. "Hatay Cami ve Mescitlerinde Taş Süsleme," MA thesis, Selçuk University, Konya.

della Valle, P. 1843. *Viaggi di Pietro della Valle, il pellegrino, descritti da lui medesimo in lettere familiari all'erudito suo amico Mario Schipano, divisi in tre parti cioè: la Turchia, la Persia, e l'India*. Brighton: Gancia.

Demir, A. 2004. "The Urban Pattern of Antakya: Streets and Houses," in *Antioche de Syrie: Histoire, images et traces de la ville antique*. Topoi Orient-Occident Supplément 5, B. Cabouret, P.-L. Gatier, and C. Saliou (eds). Lyon: Jean Pouilloux, 221–238.

———. 1996. *Antakya through the Ages*. Istanbul: Akbank.

Descœudres, J. 2002. "Al Mina across the Great Divide," *Mediterranean Archaeology* 15: 49–72.

Devonshire, R. L. 1922. "Relation d'un voyage du sultain Qâitbây en Palestine et en Syrie," *Bulletin de l'Institut Français d'Archéologie Orientale* 20: 1–43.

Dey, H. W. 1976. *Materials for the Study of Georgian Monasteries in the Western Environs of Antioch on the Orontes*. London: Secrétariat du CorpusSCO, 108.

Djobadze, W. 1986. *Archaeological Investigations in the Region West of Antioch on-the-Orontes*. Stuttgart: Franz Steiner Verlag.

Dobbins, J. J. 2000. "The Houses at Antioch," in *Antioch: The Lost Ancient City*, C. Kondoleon (ed.). Princeton, NJ: Princeton University Press, 51–62.

Dodgeon, M. H. and Lieu, S. N. C. 1991. *The Roman Eastern Frontier and the Persian Wars, AD 226–363: A Documentary History*. London and New York: Routledge.

Dols, M. 1977. *The Black Death in the Middle East*. Princeton, NJ: Princeton University Press.

Donner, F. 1991. "The Sources of Islamic Conceptions of War," in *Just War and Jihad: Historical and Theoretical Perspectives on War and Peace in Western and Islamic Traditions*, J. Kelsay and J. T. Johnson (eds). Westport, CT: Greenwood Press, 31–69.

Downey, G. 1963. *Ancient Antioch*. Princeton, NJ: Princeton University Press.

———. 1961. *A History of Antioch in Syria: From Seleucus to the Arab Conquest*. Princeton, NJ: Princeton University Press.

———. 1959. "Libanius' Oration in Praise of Antioch," *Proceedings of the American Philosophical Society* 103 (5): 652–686.

———. 1951. "The Economic Crisis at Antioch under Julian the Apostate," in *Studies in Roman Economic and Social History in Honors of Allan Chester Johnson*. Princeton, NJ: Princeton University Press.

———. 1938. "The Gate of the Cherubim at Antioch," *The Jewish Quarterly Review*, New Series 29: 167–177.

———. 1937. "Q. Marcius Rex at Antioch," *Classical Philology* 32: 144–151.

———. 1932. "The Church at Daphne," *Antioch* 1: 107–113.

Drake, H. A. 2011. "Religious Violence and Political Legitimacy in Late Antiquity," *The Journal of American Academy of Religion* 79 (1): 193–235.

Drocourt, N. 2019. "Arabic-Speaking Ambassadors in the Byzantine Empire," in *Ambassadors, Artists, Theologians: Byzantine Relations with the Near East from the Ninth to the Thirteenth Centuries*. Mainz: Verlag des Romisch-Germanischen Zentralmuseums, 57–70.

Drummond, A. 1754. *Travels through Different Cities of Germany, Italy, Greece, and Several Parts of Asia, as Far as the Banks of the Euphrates: In a Series of Letters. Containing an Account of What Is Most Remarkable in Their Present State, as Well as in Their Monuments of Antiquity*. London: W. Strahan.

Dunbabin, K. M. D. 1989. "Baiarum Gratia Voluptas: Pleasures and Dangers of the Baths," *Papers of the British School of Rome* 57: 6–46.

Dussaud, R. 1927. *Topographie historique de la Syrie antique et médiévale*. Paris: Geuthner.

Edgington, S. 2006. "Antioch: Medieval City of Culture," in *East and West in the Medieval Mediterranean I: Antioch from the Byzantine Reconquest until the End of the Crusader Principality: Acta of the Congress Held at Hernen Castle in May*. OLA 147, K. Ciggaar and M. Metcalf (eds). Leuven: Peeters, 247–260.

Eger, A. 2015. *The Islamic-Byzantine Frontier: Interaction and Exchange Among Muslim and Christian Communities*. New York: I. B. Tauris.

———. 2014a. "Patronage and Commerce at the Twilight of Mamlūk Rule: Two New Fifteenth Century Inscriptions from the Amuq Plain, Turkey," *Journal of Islamic Archaeology* 1 (1): 55–73.

———. 2014b. "(Re)Mapping Medieval Antioch: Urban Transformations from the Early Islamic to Crusader Periods," *DOP* 67: 95–134.

———. 2012. *A Gazetteer of Towns on the Islamic-Byzantine Frontier*. Istanbul: Ege Yayınları.

Eilers, C. 2003. "A Roman East: Pompey's Settlement to the Death of Augustus," in *A Companion to the Hellenistic World*, A. Erskine (ed.). Malden, MA: Blackwell Publishing, 90–102.

el-Cheikh, N. M. 2001. "Byzantium through the Islamic Prism from the Twelfth to the Thirteenth Century," in *The Crusades from the Perspective of Byzantium and the Muslim World*, A. Laiou and R. Mottahadeh (eds). Washington, DC: Dumbarton Oaks, 53–69.

Elias of Nisibis. 1910. *La Chronographie d'Elie Bar-Sinaya Metropolitain de Nisibe*. L.-J. Delaporte (trans.). Paris: H. Champion.

Elker, S. 2006. "Kitābelerde (Ebced) Hesabının Rolü," *Vakıflar Dergisi* 3: 17–25.

Ellis, S. 2007. "Late Antique Housing, an Overview," in *Housing in Late Antiquity. From Palaces to Shops*, L. Lavan, L. Özgenel, and A. Sarantis (eds). Leiden: Brill, 1–22.

Erdkamp, P. 2002. "The Corn Supply of the Roman Armies During the Principate (27 BC–235 AD)," in *The Roman Army and the Economy*, P. Erdkamp (ed.). Amsterdam: Gieben, 47–69.

Erol, O. and Pirazzoli, P. A. 1992. "Seleucia Pieria: An Ancient Harbour Submitted to Two Successive Uplifts." *International Journal of Nautical Archaeology* 21 (4): 317–327.

Evans, H. and Wixom, W. 1997. *The Glory of Byzantium: Art and Culture of the Middle Byzantine Era, A.D. 843–1261*. New York: Metropolitan Museum of Art.

Evliya Çelebi. 2000. *Seyahatnamesi*. R. Dankoff and R. Elsie (trans.). Leiden: Brill.

Farag, W. 1990. "The Aleppo Question: A Byzantine – Fatimid Conflict of Interests in Northern Syria in the Later Tenth Century A.D," *Byzantine and Modern Greek Studies* 14: 44–60.

Faris, N. A. 1938. "Kufic Inscriptions," in *Antioch on the Orontes II. The Excavations. 1933–1936*, R. Stillwell (ed.). Princeton, NJ: Princeton University Press, 166–169.

Fatouros, G. and Krischer, T. 1992. *Libanios, Antiochikos (or. XI). Zur heidnischen Renaissance in der Spätantike*. Vienna: Verlag Turia & Kant.

——— 1985. "Deux Listes de Quartiers d'Antioche Astreints au Creusement d'un Canal (73–74 Après J.-C.)," *Syria* 62: 77–103.

Feissel, D. and Gascou, J. 1989. "Documents d'Archives Romaines Inédits du Moyen Euphrate," *Académie des Inscriptions et Belles Lettres: Comptes Rendus des Séances de l'Annèe 1989*: 535–561.

Festugière, J. 1959. *Antioche païenne et chrétienne: Libanius, Chrysostome et les moines de Syrie*. Paris: De Boccard.

Filipczak, P. 2017. "Antioch on the Orontes: The Topography of Social Conflicts (4th-7th cent. AD)," *Syria* 94: 325–345.

Fındık, E. 2006. "An Ottoman House with Wall paintings in Antakya: The Kuseyri House," *Chronos* 13: 151–180.

Foote, R. 2000. "Commerce, Industrial Expansion, and Orthogonal Planning: Mutually Compatible Terms in Settlement of Bilad al-Sham during the Umayyad Period," *Mediterranean Archaeology* 13: 25–38.

Foss, C. 1997. "Syria in Transition, A.D. 550–750: An Archaeological Approach," *DOP* 51: 189–269.

France, J. 1994. *Victory in the East: A Military History of the First Crusade*. New York: Cambridge University Press.

Franklin, C. V. 2004. *The Latin Dossier of Anastasius the Persian: Hagiographic Translations and Transformations*. Toronto: Pontifical Institute of Medieval Studies.

Frantsouzoff, S. A. 1999–2000. "Antioch in South Arabian Tradition: (Remarks on Some Commentaries to the Qur'anic Verses 21:11–15 & 36:13/12–14/13/)," *Aram* 11–12: 399–407.

Fulcher of Chartres. 1941. *Fulcher of Chartres: Chronicle of the First Crusade*. M. E. McGinty (trans.). Philadelphia, PA: University of Pennsylvania Press.

Garnsey, P. 1988. *Famine and Food Supply in the Graeco-Roman World*. Cambridge: Cambridge University Press.

Gascou, J. 1977. "Klèroi aporoi (Julien, *Misopogôn*, 370d-371b)," *B.I.F.A.O.* 77: 235–255.

Gatier, P. L. 2016. "Géographie mythologique de l'Oronte dans l'antiquité," in *Le Fleuve Rebelle*, D. Parayre (ed.). *Syria* IV Suppl., 249–269.

Gawlikowski, M. 1992. "Les temples dans la Syrie à l'époque hellénistique et romaine," in *Archéologie et Histoire de la Syrie*, J. M. Dentzer and W. Orthmann (eds). Saarbrücken: Saarbrücker Druckerei und Verlag, 323–346.

Gehn, U. and Ward-Perkins, B. 2016. "Egypt, the Near East, and Cyprus," in *The Last Statues of Antiquity*, R. R. R. Smith (ed.). Oxford: Oxford University Press, 109–119.

Gerritsen, F. A., De Giorgi, A., Eger, A., et al. 2008. "Settlement and Landscape Transformation in the Amuq Valley, Hatay. A Long-Term Perspective," *Anatolica* 34: 241–314.

Gesta Francorum et aliorum Hierosolymitanorum: The Deeds of the Franks. 2002. R. M. Hill (ed. and trans.) Oxford: Clarendon Press.

———. 1962. R. M. Hill (ed. and trans.). London: Nelson.

Gibbon, E. 1776. *The History of the Decline and Fall of the Roman Empire*, vol. 1. New York: Fred de Fau & Company Publishers.

Glynias, J. 2019. "Homiletic Translation in Byzantine Antioch: The Arabic Translation of a Marian Homily of Patriarch Germanos I of Constantinople by Yānī ibn al-Duks, Deacon of Antioch," in *Patristic Literature in Arabic Translations*, B. Roggema and A. Treiger (eds). Leiden: Brill, 241–275.

Gnoli, T. 2013. "La Fortuna di un'immagine: Antiochia," in *Polis, urbs, civitas: moneta e identità. Atti del convegno di studio del Lexicon Iconographicum Numismaticae (Milano 25 Ottobre 2012)*, L. Travaini and G. Arrigoni (eds). Bologna: Quasar, 89–101.

Goilav, A. M. 2014. "Proposal for the reconstruction of the Golden Octagon," in *Les sources de l'histoire du paysage urbain d'Antioche sur l'Oronte*, C. Saliou (ed.). Paris: Université Paris 8, 159–178.

Gonzales, J. 1984. "Tabula Siarensis, Fortunales Siarenses, et municipia civium romanorum," *ZPE* 55: 55–100.

Goode, J. 2004. "Archaeology and Diplomacy in the Republic of Turkey, 1919–1939," in *Turkish-American Relations. Past, Present, and Future*, M. Aydin and Ç. Erhan (eds). New York and London: Routledge, 49–65.

Graff, G. 1944. *Geshichte der christlichen arabischen Literatur*, vol. 1. Vatican City: Biblioteca apostolicana vaticana.

———. 1990. *The Cities of Seleucid Syria*. Oxford: Clarendon Press.

Grifor Aknerts'i. 2003. *History of the Nation of Archers*. R. Bedrosian (trans.). Long Branch, NJ, 15.10. https://archive.org/details/GrigorAknertsisHistoryOfTheNationOfArchers-mongols/mode/2up

Guidetti, F. 2010. "Urban Continuity and Change in Late Roman Antioch," in *Urban Decline in the Byzantine Realm, ed. B. Forsén, Proceedings of the Conference (Helsinki, 25 September 2009)*, special issue of *Acta Byzantina Fennica*, n.s., vol. 3, 81–104.

Guidi, I. 1897. "Una descrizione araba di Antiochia," *Atti della Reale Accademia Nazionale dei Lincei. Rendiconti* 6: 137–161, Serie 5.

Guidoboni, E. (ed.). 1994. *Catalogue of Ancient Earthquakes in the Mediterranean Area up to the 10th Century*. Rome: Istituto Nazionale de Geofisica.

———. 1989. *I Terremoti prima del Mille in Italia e nell'area mediterranea*. Bologna: SGA.

Guidoboni, E., Bernardini, F. and Comastri, A. 2004a. "The 1138–1139 and 1156–1159 Destructive Seismic Crises in Syria, South-eastern Turkey and Northern Lebanon," *Journal of Seismology* 8: 105–127.

Guidoboni, E., Bernardini, F., Comastri, A. and Boschi, E. 2004b. "The Large Earthquake on 29 June 1170 (Syria, Lebanon, and central Southern Turkey)," *Journal of Geophysical Research – Solid Earth* 109: 21.

Guidoboni, E. and Comastri, A. 2015. "The Earthquakes of Aleppo and the Region of the Dead Cities," in *The "Dead Cities" of Northern Syria and their Demise*, T. Riis (ed.). Kiel: Ludwig.

Gündüz, A. and Gülcü, E. 2009. "XVI. Yüzyılda Antakya Nahiyesi (1526–1584)," *Mustafa Kemal Üniversitesi Sosyal Bilimler Enstitüsü Dergisi* 6 (12): 289–323.

Habicht, C. 1992. "Ἀντιόχεια ἡ πρὸς Δάφνηι," *ZPE* 93: 50–51.

Hahn, C. 2015. "The Sting of Death Is the Thorn, But the Circle of the Crown Is Victory Over Death: The Making of the Crown of Thorns," in *Saints and Sacred Matter: The Cult of Relics in Byzantium and Beyond*, C. Hahn and K. Holger (eds). Washington, DC: Dumbarton Oaks, 193–214.

Hahn, J. 2018. "Metropolis, Emperors, and Games," in *Antioch II. The Many Faces of Antioch: Intellectual Exchange and Religious Diversity, CE 350–450*, S. P. Bergjan and S. Elm (eds). Tübingen: Mohr Siebeck, 53–71.

Haines, R. C. 1971. *Excavations in the Plain of Antioch. Vol. 2. The Structural Remains of the Later Phases: Chatal Hoyuk, Tell al-Judaidah and Tell Ta'yinat*. Chicago, IL: The University of Chicago Press.

Haldon, J. 1990. *Byzantium in the Seventh Century*. Cambridge: Cambridge University Press.

Haldon, J. and Brubaker, L. 2011. *Byzantium in the Iconoclast Era, c. 680–850*. Cambridge: Cambridge University Press.

Hanif, H. 2002. *Biographical Encyclopaedia of Sufis: Central Asia & Middle East*. New Delhi: Sarup & Sons. 231–232.

Harawī. 2004. *A Lonely Wayfarer's Guide to Pilgrimage: 'Alī ibn Abī Bakr al-Harawī's Kitāb al-ishārāt ilā m'arifat al-ziyārāt*. J. W. Meri (trans.). Princeton, NJ: Darwin Press.

Harrison, T. P. and Denel, E. 2017. "The Neo-Hittite Citadel Gate at Tayinat (Ancient Kunulua)," in *The Archaeology of Anatolia: Recent Discoveries (2015–2016)*, vol. 2, S. Steadman and G. McMahon (eds). Newcastle upon Tyne: Cambridge Scholars Publishing, 137–155.

Harrison, T. P., Denel, E., and Batiuk, S. 2018. "Tayinat Höyük Araştırmaları, 2016," *Kazi Sonuclari Toplantisi* 39 (Cilt 1): 563–571.

Harvey, S. A. 2000. "Antioch and Christianity," in *Antioch: The Lost Ancient City*, C. Kondoleon (ed.). Princeton upon Tyne: Princeton University Press, 39–50.

Henck, N. 2007. "Constantius and the Cities," in *Wolf Liebeschuetz Reflected. Essays presented by his Colleagues, Friends, & Pupils*, J. Drinkwater and B. Salway (eds). London: Institute of Classical Studies, 147–156.

Hennecke, E. and Schneemelcher, W. 1965. *New Testament Apocrypha*, 2 vols. Philadelphia, PA: Westminster Press.

Henning, J. (ed.). 2007. *Post-Roman Towns, Trade and Settlement in Europe and Byzantium*, 2 vols. New York: de Gruyter.

Henry, A. 2015. "The Pilgrimage Center of St. Symeon the Younger: Designed by angels, supervised by a saint, constructed by pilgrims," PhD diss., University of Illinois, Urbana-Champaign, IL.

Herrmann, P. 1965. "Antiochos der Grosse und Teos," *Anadolu* 9: 29–160.

Hess, Richard S. 2002. "The Bible and Alalakh," in *Mesopotamia and the Bible*, Mark V. Chavalas and K. Lawson Younger, Jr. (eds). Sheffield: Continuum, 209–221.

Hetoum [Hayton]. 1988. *A Lytell Cronycle*. G. Burger (ed.). Toronto: University of Toronto Press.

———. 1906. *La Flor des Estoires des parties d'Orient*. Recueil des historiens des croisades: documents arméniens 2. Paris: Imprimerie nationale.

Heyd, W. 1923. *Histoire du Commerce du Levant au moyen-age*. Leipzig: Otto-Harrassowitz.

Hirth, F. 1885. *China and the Roman Orient, Researches into Their Ancient and Medieval Relations as Represented in Old Chinese Records*. Leipzig: L Georg Hirth.

Hitti, P. K. 1934. "Kufic Inscriptions," in *Antioch on the Orontes I. The Excavations of 1932*, G. Elderkin (ed.). Princeton, NJ: Princeton University Press.

Hoepfner, W. 2004. "'Antiochia die Große'. Geschichte einer antiken Stadt," *Antike Welt* 35 (2): 3–9.

———. 1999. "Antiochia die Große," in *Geschichte des Wohnens. 5000 v. Chr. – 500 n. Chr. Vorgeschichte – Frühgeschichte – Antike*, W. Hoepfner (ed.). Stuttgart: Wunsterot Stiftung, 472–491.

Holleaux, M. 1906. "Remarques sur le papyrus de Gourob," *Bulletin de Correspondance Hellénique* 30, 330–348, repris dans Id., Études d'épigraphie et d'histoire grecques (éd. L. Robert), III, Paris (1942), 281–310.

Hollmann, A. 2003. "A Curse Tablet form the Circus at Antioch," *ZPE* 145: 67–82.

Holmes, C. 2002. "Byzantium's Eastern Frontier in the Tenth and Eleventh Centuries," in *Medieval Frontiers: Concepts and Practices*, D. Abulafia and N. Berend (eds). Burlington, VT: Ashgate, 83–104.

———. 2001. "'How the East was Won' in the Reign of Basil II," in *Eastern Approaches to Byzantium*, A. Eastmond (ed.). Burlington, VT: Ashgate, 41–56.

Hoover, O. D. 2007. "Chronology for the Late Seleucids at Antioch (121/0–64 BC)," *Historia: Zeitschrift für Alte Geschichte* 56 (3): 280–301.

Horden, P. 2007. "Mediterranean Plague in the Age of Justinian," in *The Cambridge Companion to the Age of Justinian*, M. Maas (ed.). Cambridge: Cambridge University Press, 134–160.

Horden, P. and Purcell, N. 2000. *The Corrupting Sea: A Study of Mediterranean History*. Malden, MA: Blackwell.

Horster, M. 2013. "Coinage and Images of the Imperial Family: Local Identity and Roman Rule," *JRA* 26: 243–261.

Hostetler, B. 2009. "The Art of Gift-Giving: The Multivalency of Votive Dedications in the Middle Byzantine Period," MA thesis, Florida State University, Tallahassee, FL.

Houghton, A. and Lorber, C. 2002. *Seleucid Coins. A Comprehensive Catalogue. Pt. 1. Seleucus through Antiochus III*, 2 vols. New York: The American Numismatic Society.

Houghton, A., Lorber, C. and Hoover, O. 2008. *Seleucid Coins. A Comprehensive Catalogue. Pt. 2. Seleucus IV through Antiochus XIII*. New York: American Numismatic Society.

Howgego, C. J. 1982. "Coinage and Military Finance: The Imperial Bronze Coinage of the Augustan East," *Numismatic Chronicle* 142: 1–20.

Hugh, J. and Hill, L. 1969. *Le "Liber" de Raymond d'Aguilers*. Paris: Librairie Orientaliste Paul Geuthner.

Hull, D. 2008. "A Spatial and Morphological Analysis of Monastic Sites in the Northern Limestone Massif, Syria," *Levant* 40 (1): 89–113.

Humphrey, J. 1986. *Roman Circuses: Arenas for Chariot Racing*. Berkeley, CA: University of California Press.

Hunt, L.-A. 2019. "The Byzantine Emperor Michael VIII (1261–1282) and Greek Orthodox/Melkite-Genoese Cultural Agency in a Globalised World: Art at Sinai, Behdaidat, of the *pallio* of San Lorenzo in Genoa, and in Mamluk Egypt," in *Ambassadors, Artists, Theologians: Byzantine Relations with the Near East from the Ninth to the Thirteenth Centuries*, Z. Chitwood and J. Pahlitzsch (eds). Mainz: Verlag des Römisch-Germanischen Zentralmuseums, 127–137.

Ibn ʿAbd al-Ẓāhir, Muḥyī al-Dīn al-Saʿdī ʿAbd Allāh. 1976. *al-Rawḍ al-Zāhir*. Riyadh: [publisher not identified].

Ibn al-'Adīm. 2016. *Bughyat al-Ṭalab fī Tārīkh Ḥalab [The History of Aleppo]*. Al-Mahdi Eid al-Rawadieh (ed.). London: al-Furqān Islamic Heritage Foundation.

———. 1996. *Zubda al-Ḥalab min Tārīkh Ḥalab [The Cream of the History of Aleppo]*. Beirut: Dār al-Kitāb al-'Alamīyya.

———. 1988. *Bughyat al-ṭalab fī ta'rīkh Ḥalab*. Damascus: S. Zakkār.

Ibn al-Athir. 2014. *The Annals of the Saljuq Turks: Selections from al-Kamil fi'l-tarikh of 'Izz al-Din Ibn al-Athir*. New York: Routledge.

———. 2007. *The Chronicle of Ibn al-Athīr for the Crusading Period from al-Kāmil fī'l-ta'rīkh. Part 2. The Years 541–589/1146–1193. The Age of Nur al-Din and Saladin*. D.S. Richards (trans.). Burlington, VT: Ashgate.

———. 2002. *The Annals of the Saljuq Turks. Selections from al-Kāmil fī'l-Ta'rīkh of 'Izz al-Dīn Ibn al-Athīr*. D. S. Richards (trans. and annot.). New York: RoutledgeCurzon.

Ibn al-Furāt. 1971. *Ayyubids, Mamelukes and Crusaders. Selections from the Tārīkh al-duwal wa'l-muluk*. U and M. C. Lyons (trans.). Cambridge: Heffers.

Ibn Baṭṭutṭ. 1962. *The Travels of Ibn Battuta, A.D. 1325–1354*. C. Defrémery and B. R. Sanguinetti (trans.). Cambridge: Hakluyt Society.

Ibn Ḥawqal. 1964. *Kitāb ṣūrat al-ārḍ*. Beirut: Manshūrāt Dār Maktabat Al-Ḥayā.

Ibn Kathīr. 1997. *Al-bidāya wa al-nihāya*. Jizah: Hajar.

Ibn Qalanisī. 1932. *The Damascus Chronicle of the Crusades*. H. A. R. Gibb (trans.). London: Luzac.

Ibn Rustah. 1892. *Kitāb al-A'laq al-Nafisa*. M. J. de Goeje. BGA 7. Leiden: Brill.

Ibn Shaddād. 1984. *al-'Alāq al-Khaṭīra fī Dhikr Umarā' al-Shām wa'l-Jazīra*. A.-M. Edde (trans.). Damascus: Presses de l'IFPO.

———. 1983. *Tarīkh al-Malik al-Ẓāhir*. Bibliotheca Islamica 31. Beirut: Orient-Institut der Deutschen Morgenländischen Gesellschaft.

———. 1956. *al-'Alāq al-Khaṭīra fī Dhikr Umarā' al-Shām wa'l-Jazīra*. Damascus: Manshūrāt Wizārat al-Thaqāfah.

Ibn al-Shiḥna. 1990. *The History of Aleppo, Known as ad-Durr al-Muntakhab by Ibn ash-Shihna*. Tokyo: Institute for the Study of Languages and Cultures of Asia and Africa.

———. 1984. *al-Durr al-muntakhab fī ta'rīkh mamlakat Ḥalab*. A. M. al-Darwīsh (ed.). Damascus: 'Alām al-Tarāth.

Idrīsī. 1989. *Kitāb nuzhat al-mushtāq fī ikhtirāq al-āfāq*. Beirut: 'Ālam al-Kutub.

Ilisch, L. 1982. "The Seljuk Copper Coinage of Antakya – Summary," in *IV. Milletlerarası Türkoloji kongresi: Unveröffentlichte Tischvorlage*. Istanbul: Edebiyet Fakültesi.

İnanan, F. 2010. "Anaia-Kadikalesi: A New Zeuxippus Ware Production Centre," in *Proceedings of the International Symposium "Trade and Production through the Ages," Konya, 25–28 November 2008*, E. Doksanaltı and E. Aslan (eds). Selçuk: Selçuk University, 115–128.

Isaac, B. 1990. *The Limits of the Empire*. Oxford: Oxford University Press.

Istakhrī. 1967. *Kitāb masālik al-mamālik*. Leiden: Brill.

Izdebski, A., Pickett, J., Roberts, N. and Waliszewski, T. 2016. "The Environmental, Archaeological and Historical Evidence for Regional Climatic Changes and Their Societal Impacts in the Eastern Mediterranean in Late Antiquity," *Quaternary Science Reviews* 136: 189–208.

Jacoby, D. 2004. "Silk Economics and Cross-Cultural Artistic Interactions: Byzantium, the Muslim World, and the Christian West," *Dumbarton Oaks Papers* 58: 197–240.

Jacquot, P. 1931. *Antioch centre de tourisme*. Paris: Comité de tourisme d'Antioche.

Jalabert, L. and Mouterde, S. J. 1950. *Inscriptions Grecques et Latines de la Syrie*. Paris: Geuthner.

Jamil, N. and Johns, J. 2003. "An Original Arabic Document from Crusader Antioch (1213 AD)," in *Texts, Documents and Artefacts, Islamic Studies in Honour of D.S. Richards*, C. F. Robinson (ed.). Leiden: Brill, 157–190.

Johns, J. 2002. *Arabic Administration in Norman Sicily: The Royal Dīwān*. Cambridge: Cambridge University Press.

Jones, A. H. M. 1998. *The Cities of the Eastern Roman Empire*. Oxford: Oxford University Press.

Jones, C. 2000. "The Emperor and the Giant," *Classical Philology* 95 (4): 476–481.

Jones, L. and Maguire, H. 2002. "A Description of the Jousts of Manuel I Komenos," *Byzantine and Modern Greek Studies* 26 (1): 104–148.

Kalavrezou, I. 1997. "Helping Hands for the Empire: Imperial Ceremonies and the Cult of Relics at the Byzantine Court." in *Byzantine Court Culture from 829 to 1204*, H. Maguire (ed.). Washington, DC: Dumbarton Oaks Research Library and Collection, 53–79.

Kaldellis, A. 2017. *Streams of Gold, Rivers of Blood: The Rise and Fall of Byzantium, 955 A.D. to the First Crusade*. New York: Oxford University Press.

Kalleres, D. 2015. *City of Demons*. Berkeley, CA: University of California Press.

Kara, A. 2005. *XIX. Yüzyılda Bir Osmanlı Şehri Antakya*. Istanbul: IQ Kültür Sanat Yayıncılık.

Karabacak, V., Altunel, E., Meghraoui, M., and Akyüz, H. S. 2010. "Field Evidences from Northern Dead Sea Fault Zone (South Turkey): New Findings for the Initiation Age and Slip Rate," *Tectonophysics* 480 (1–4): 172–182.

Kasher, A. 1982. "The Rights of the Jews of Antioch on the Orontes," *Proceedings of the American Academy for Jewish Research* 49: 69–85.

Katip Çelebi. 2012. *Kitâb-i Cihânnümâ*. Bulent Özükan (ed.). Istanbul: Boyut Publishing Group.

Kavtaria, N. 2011. "The Iconography and the Ornamental Decoration of the Canon Tables of the 11th Century Georgian Manuscripts from the Black Mountain (Antioch)," in *Anadolu Kültürlerinde Süreklilik ve Değişim Dr. A. Mine Kadiroğlu'na Armağan*, A. Ceren Erel Bülent İsler, N. Peker, and G. Sağır (eds). Ankara: Rekmay, 325–340.

Kedar, B. Z. and Kohlberg, E. 1995. "The Intercultural Career of Theodore of Antioch," *Mediterranean Historical Review* 10: 1–2, 164–176.

Kelly, G. 2018. "Ammianus, Valens, and Antioch," in *Antioch II. The Many Faces of Antioch: Intellectual Exchange and Religious Diversity, CE 350–450*, S. P. Bergjan and S. Elm (eds). Tübingen: Mohr Siebeck, 137–162.

Kennedy, H. 2006. "Byzantine-Arab Diplomacy in the Near East from the Islamic Conquests to the Mid-Eleventh Century," in *The Byzantine and Early Islamic Near East*. Burlington, VT: Ashgate.

———. 2001. *The Armies of the Caliphs: Military and Society in the Early Islamic State*. New York: Routledge.

———. 1992. "Antioch: From Byzantium to Islam and Back Again," in *The City in Late Antiquity*, J. Rich (ed.). London and New York: Routledge, 181–198.

———. 1986a. *The Prophet and the Age of the Caliphates*. New York: Longman.

———. 1986b. "The Melkite Church from the Islamic Conquest to the Crusades: Continuity and Adaptation in the Byzantine Legacy," in *The 17th International Byzantine Congress: Major Papers*. New Rochelle, NY: Aristide D. Caratzas, 325–344.

———. 1985a. "From Polis to Madina: Urban Change in Late Antique and Early Islamic Syria," *Past and Present* 106 (1985): 3–27.

———. 1985b. "The Last Century of Byzantine Syria: A Reinterpretation," *Byzantinische Forschungen* 10: 141–183.

Kennedy, H. and Liebeschuetz, J. H. W. G. 1988. "Antioch and the Villages of Northern Syria in the Fifth and Sixth Centuries A.D.; Trend and Problem," *Nottingham Medieval Studies* 32: 65–90.

Kinneir, J. M. 1818. *Journey Through Asia Minor, Armenia, and Koordistan in the Years 1813 and 1814: With Remarks on the Marches of Alexander and Retreat of the Ten Thousand*. London: J. Murray.

Klein, H. A. 2006. "Sacred Relics and Imperial Ceremonies at the Great Palace of Constantinople," in *Visualisierungen von Herrschaft*, F. A. Bauer (ed.), *Byzas* 5: 79–99. Istanbul: Ege Yayınları.

Kleinbauer, W. E. 2006. "Antioch, Jerusalem, and Rome: The Patronage of Emperor Constantius II and Architectural Inventions," *Gesta* 45 (2): 125–145.

Kokkinia, C. 2008. "Grain for Cibyra: Veranius Philagros and the 'Great Conspiracy'," in *Feeding the Ancient Greek City*, R. Alston and O. Van Nijf (eds). Leiden: Brill, 143–158.

Komnene, A. 1969. *The Alexiad*. E. R. A. Sewter (trans.). New York: Penguin Books.

Kondoleon, C. (ed.). 2000. *Antioch. The Lost Ancient City*. Princeton, NJ: Princeton University Press.

Kontokosta, A. H. 2018. "Building the Thermae Agrippae: Private Life, Public Space, and the Politics of Bathing in Early Imperial Rome," *AJA* 123 (1): 45–77.

Kosmin, P. 2014. *The Land of the Elephant Kings: Space, Territory, and Ideology in the Seleucid Empire*. Cambridge, MA: Harvard University Press.

———. 2011. "The Foundation and Early Life of Dura-Europos," in *Dura-Europos: Crossroads of Antiquity*, G. Hoffmann and L. Brody (eds). Chestnut Hill, MA: McMullen Museum of Art.

Kraeling, C. H. 1968. "A New Greek Inscription from Antioch on the Orontes," *AJA* 64: 178–179.

———. 1932. "The Jewish Community at Antioch," *Journal of Biblical Literature* 51 (2): 130–160.

Kramer, N. 2004. *Gindaros. Geschichte und Archäologie einer Siedlung im nordwestlichen Syrien von hellenisticher bis frühbyzantinische Zeit*. Rahden: Verlag Marie Leidorf GmbH.

Krey, A. C. 1921. *The First Crusade: The Accounts of Eyewitnesses and Participants*. Princeton, NJ: Princeton University Press.

Krueger, D. 2010. "The Religion of Relics in Late Antiquity and Byzantium," in *Treasures of Heaven: Saints, Relics, and Devotion in Medieval Europe*, M. Bagnoli et al. (eds). New Haven, CT: Yale University Press, 5–17.

Krönung, B. 2019. "The Employment of Christian Mediators by Muslim Rulers in Arab-Byzantine Diplomatic Relations in the Tenth and Early Eleventh Centuries," in *Ambassadors, Artists, Theologians: Byzantine Relations with the Near East from the Ninth to Thirteenth Centuries*, Z. Chitwood and J. Pahlitzsch (eds). Mainz: Verag, 71–83.

Kunkel, W. 1953. "Der Process der Gohariener vor Caracalla," in *Festchrift Hans Lewald*, H. Lewald, M. Gerwig, and A. Simonius et al. (eds). Basel: Helbig & Lichtenhahn, 81–91.

Laflı, E. and Christof, E. 2014. "New Hellenistic and Roman Grave Reliefs from Antioch," in *Uluslararası çağlar boyuncax Hatay ve çevresi arkeolojisi sempozyumu bildirileri. 21–24 Mayıs 2013 Antakya [The Proceedings of the International Symposium on the Archaeology of Hatay and its Vicinity through the Ages. 21–24 May 2013 Antakya]*, A. Özfirat and Ç. Oygün (eds). Antakya: Mustafa Kemal Üniversitesi Yayınları, No. 52, 161–181.

Laflı, E. and Meischner, J. 2008. "Hellenistische und römische Grabstelen im Archäologischen Museum von Hatay in Antakya," *Jahreshefte des Österreichischen Archäologischen Instituts in Wien* 77: 145–183.

Laniado, A. 2002. *Recherches sur les notables municipaux dans l'empire protobyzantin*. Paris: De Boccard.

Lapina, E. 2015. *Warfare and the Miraculous in the Chronicles of the First Crusade*. University Park, PA: Pennsylvania State University Press.

Lassus, J. 1972. *Les Portiques d'Antioche*. Princeton, NJ: Princeton University Press.

———. 1938. "Une villa de plaisance à Daphne-Yakto," in *Antioch-on-the-Orontes. The excavations 1933–1936*, R. Stillwell (ed.). Princeton, NJ: Princeton University Press.

———. 1934. "Le mosaïque de Yakto," in *Antioch-on-the Orontes. The Excavations of 1932*, G. W. Elderkin (ed.). Princeton, NJ: Princeton University Press.

Laurent, V. 1962. "La Chronologie des Gouverneurs d'Antioche sous la seconde domination Byzantine (969–1084)," in *Mélanges Université de Saint-Joseph*, 2 vols. Beirut: Université Saint-Joseph, 38.

Lavan, L. (ed.). 2001. "Recent Research in Late Antique Urbanism," *Journal of Roman Archaeology* Supplementary Series 42.

Lavan, L., Özgenel, L. and Sarantis, A. (eds). 2007. *Housing in Late Antiquity: From Palaces to Shops*. Leiden: Brill.

Le Bas, P. and Waddington, W. H. 1850. *Voyage archéologique en Grèce et en Asie Mineure: fait par ordre du gouvernment pendant les années 1843 et 1844*. Paris: Firmin-Didot frères, fils, et cie.

Le Rider, G. 1999. *Antioche de Syrie sous les Séleucides. Corpus des monnaies d'or et d'argent. I: De Seleucos I à Antiochos V*. Paris: Mémoires de l'Academie des Inscriptions et Belles Lettres.

Le Strange, G. 1965. *Palestine under the Moslems: A Description of Syria and the Holy Land from A.D. 650–1500*. Khayats Oriental Reprints 14. Beirut: Khayats.

———. 1890. *Palestine under the Moslems*. London: Committee of the Palestine Exploration Fund.

Leblanc, J. and Poccardi, G. 2004. "Leblanc Jacques, Poccardi Grégoire. L'eau domestiquée et l'eau sauvage à Antioche-sur-l'Oronte: problèmes de gestion," in *Antioche de Syrie. Histoires, images et traces de la ville antique*. Topoi Orient-Occident Supplément 5, 239–256.

———. 1999–2000. "Note sur l'emplacement possible du stade olympique de Daphneé (Antioche-sur-l'Oronte)," *Aram* 11–12: 389–397.

———. 1999. "Étude de la Permanence des Tracés Urbains et Ruraux Antiques à Antioche-sur-l'Oronte," *Syria* 76: 91–126.

Leo the Deacon. 2005. *The History of Leo the Deacon: Byzantine Military Expansion in the Tenth Century*. A.-M. Talbot and D. F. Sullivan (trans.). Washington, DC: Dumbarton Oaks.

Lenski, N. 2002. *Failure of Empire. Valens and the Roman State in the Fourth Century A.D.* Berkeley, CA: University of California Press.

Leriche, P. 2007. "Le città dell'Oriente ellenistico," in *Sulla via di Alessandro. Da Seleucia al Gandhara*, V. Messina (ed.). Milan: Silvana, 83–91.

"Les gestes des Chiprois." 1906.3.641. *Recueil des Historiens des Croisades: Document arméniens 2*. Paris: Imprimerie Nationale.

Levi, Doro. 1947. *Antioch Mosaic Pavements*. Princeton, NJ: Princeton University Press.

Lewis, N. 1968. "Cognitio Caracallae de Goharienis: Two Textual Restorations," *TAPhA* 99: 255–258.

Leyerle, B. 2018. "Imagining Antioch, or the Fictional Space of Alleys and Markets," in *Antioch II. The Many Faces of Antioch: Intellectual Exchange and Religious Diversity, CE 350–450*, S. P. Bergjan and S. Elm (eds). Tübingen: Mohr Siebeck, 255–279.

Liebeschuetz, J. H. W. G. 2006. "Malalas on Antioch," in *Idem, Decline and Change in Late Antiquity: Religion, Barbarians and their Historiography*. Aldershot: Ashgate (Variorum Collected Studies), 143–153.

———. 1972. *Antioch. The City and the Imperial Administration in the Later Roman Empire*. Oxford: Oxford University Press.

Lopez, R. 1976. *The Commercial Revolution of the Middle Ages, 950–1350*. New York: Cambridge University Press.

Lycklama à Nijeholt, T. M. 1872–75. *Voyage en Russie, au Caucase et en Perse, dans la Mésopotamie le Kurdistan, la Syrie, la Palestine et la Turquie, exécuté pendant les années 1866, 1867 et 1868*. Paris: A Bertrand.
Ma, J. 1999. *Antiochos III and the Cities*. Cambridge: Cambridge University Press.
MacEvitt, C. 2015. "True Romans: Remembering the Crusades among Eastern Christians," in *Crusades and Memory: Rethinking Past and Present*, M. Cassidy-Welch and A. Lester (eds). New York: Routledge, 260–275.
Madden, T. 2006. *The New Concise History of the Crusades*. New York: Rowman & Littlefield.
Magdalino, P. 2019. "Review of Byzantine Head Reliquaries and their Perception in the West after 1204: A Case Study of the Reliquary of St. Anastasios the Persian in Aachen and Related Objects," *Byzantine and Modern Greek Studies* (April): 139–141.
Magness, J. 2003. *The Archaeology of the Early Islamic Settlement in Palestine*. Winona Lake, IN: Eisenbrauns.
Mahaffy, J. P. 1893. *The Flinders Petrie Papyri with Transcriptions, Commentaries, and Index. Part II*. Dublin: Academy House.
Mahaffy, J. P. and Gilbart Smyly, J. 1905. *The Flinders Petrie Papyri with Transcriptions, Commentaries, and Index. Part III*. Dublin: Academy House.
Mancinetti Santamaria, G. 1983."Le concessioni della citadinanza ai Greci ed Orientali nel II e I sec. a.C.," in *Les Bourgeoisies municipales italiennes aux IIe et Ier siècles av. J.-C.*, M. Cébeillac-Gervasoni (ed.). Paris: Jean Bérard, 125–136.
Marcinkowski, M. I. 2003. *Measures and Weights in the Islamic World*. Kuala Lumpur: International Institute of Islamic Thought and Civilisation, International Islamic University of Malaysia.
Margoliouth, D. S. 1898. "An Arabic Description of Antioch by I. Guidi," *Journal of the Royal Asiatic Society* (January): 157–169.
Mas'udī. 1861/1930. *Murūj al-dhahab wa-ma'ādin al-jawhar* [Les Prairies d'Or]. C. Barbier (ed., text, and trans.), 9 vols. Paris: Imprimerie Impériale.
Matthew of Edessa. 1993. *Armenia and the Crusades, Tenth to Twelfth Centuries. The Chronicle of Matthew of Edessa*. A. E. Dostourian (trans.). New York: University Press of America.
Mattingly, D. J. 1988. "Oil for Export? A Comparison of Libyan, Spanish and Tunisian Oil Production in the Roman Empire," *JRA* 1: 33–56.
Mayer, W. 2003. "Antioch and the West in Late Antiquity," *Byzantinoslavica* 61: 5–32.
———. 2001. "Patronage, Pastoral Care and the Role of the Bishop at Antioch," *Vigiliae Christianae* 55: 58–70.
Mayer, W. and Allen, P. 2012. *The churches of Syrian Antioch (300–638 CE)*. Leuven: Peeters.
McAlee, R. 2010. *The Coins of Roman Antioch: Supplement No. 1*. Lancaster and London: Classical Numismatic Group.
McCormick, M. 2002. *Origins of the European Economy: Communications and Commerce AD 300–900*. New York: Cambridge University Press.
McGeer, E. 2008. *Sowing the Dragon's Teeth: Warfare in the Tenth Century*. Washington, DC: Dumbarton Oaks.
McKenzie, J. and Reyes, A. T. 2013. "The Alexandrian Tychaion, a Pantheon?" *JRA* 26 36–52.
McNicoll, A. 1997. *Hellenistic Fortifications from the Aegean to Euphrates*. Oxford: Clarendon Press.
Mecella, L. 2018. "La *Istoria* di Pietro Patrizio e il sacco di Antiochia del 253 d.C. Conflitti sociali in città sotto assedio nel III secolo d.C.," *Mediterreaneo Antico. Economia, Società, Culture* 21 (18): 577–600.
Meier, M. 2007. "Natural Disasters in the Chronographia of John Malalas. Reflections on Their Function – An Initial Sketch," *The Medieval History Journal* 10: 237–266.

Meischner, J. 2003. "Die Skulpturen des Hatay Museums von Antakya," *Jahrbuch des Deutschen Archäologischen Museums* 118: 285–384.

Menegazzi, R. 2012. "Creating a new language: the terracotta figurines from Seleucia on the Tigris," in *Mega-cities & Mega-sites. The Archaeology of Consumption & Disposal. Landscape, Transport & Communication*, vol. 1, Proceedings of the 7 ICAANE: The 7 International Congress on the Archaeology of the Ancient Near East, R. Matthews and J. Curtis (eds). Wiesbaden: Harrasowitz, 157–167.

Metcalf, W. E. 2006. "Six Unresolved Problems in the Monetary History of Antioch, 969–1268," in *East and West in the Medieval Mediterranean I: Antioch from the Byzantine Reconquest until the End of the Crusader Principality: Acta of the Congress Held at Hernen Castle in May 2003*. OLA 147, K. Ciggaar and M. Metcalf (eds). Leuven: Peeters, 283–318.

———. 2000. "The Mint of Antioch," in *Antioch. The Lost Ancient City*, C. Kondoleon (ed.). Princeton, NJ: Princeton University Press, 105–111.

Meuwese, M. 2006. "Antioch and the Crusaders in Western art," in *East and West in the Medieval Mediterranean I: Antioch from the Byzantine Reconquest until the End of the Crusader Principality: Acta of the Congress Held at Hernen Castle in May 2003*. OLA 147, K. Ciggaar and M. Metcalf (eds). Leuven: Peeters, 337–355.

Meyer, M. 2006. *Die Personifikation der Stadt Antiochia. Ein neues Bild für eine neue Gottheit*. Berlin and New York: De Gruyter.

Michael Attaleiates. 2012. *The History*. A. Kaldellis and D. Krallis (trans.). Boston, MA: Harvard University Press.

Michael the Syrian. 1899–1963. *Chronique de Michel le Syrien*. J.-B. Chabot (ed.), vols 1–4. Paris: E. Leroux.

Michaud, J. F. and Poujoulat, J. J. F. 1841. *Correspondance d'Orient, 1830–31*. Brussels: N.-J. Gregor, V. Wouterset Cie.

Miles, G. C. 1952. "Islamic Coins," in *Antioch on the Orontes IV. Part Two. Greek, Roman, Byzantine, and Crusader Coins*, D. Waagé (ed.). Princeton, NJ: Princeton University Press (2).

Millar, F. 2002. *The Roman Republic and the Augustan Revolution*. Chapel Hill, NC: University of North Carolina Press.

———. 1993. *The Roman Near East. 31 B.C.–AD 337*. Cambridge: Cambridge University Press.

———. 1971. "Paul of Samosata, Zenobia, and Aurelian: The Church, Local Culture and Political Allegiance in Third-Century Syria," *JRS* 61: 1–17.

Miskawayh. 1921. "*The Concluding Portions of the Experiences of the Nations.[Tajārib al-Umam]*." D. S. Margoliouth (trans.), vol. 2, in *Eclipse of the 'Abbasid Caliphate*, H. F. Amedroz and D. S. Margoliouth (ed. and trans.), vol. 5. London: I. B. Tauris.

Mordechai, L. 2018. "Antioch in the Sixth Century: Resilience or Vulnerability?," in *Environment and Society in the Long Late Antiquity*, A. Izdebski and M. Mulryan (eds). Leiden: Brill, 25–41.

Mordechai, L., Eisenberg, M., Newfield, T., Izbeski, A., Kay, J., and Poinar, H. 2019. "The Justinianic Plague: an Inconsequential Pandemic?" *PNAS* 116 (51): 25546–25554.

Mordechai, L. and Pickett, J. 2018. "Earthquakes as the Quintessential SCE: Methodology and Societal Resilience," *Journal of Human Ecology* 46 (3): 335–348.

Morony, M. 2000. "Michael the Syrian as a Source for Economic History," *Hugoye: Journal of Syriac Studies* 3 (2): 141–172.

Morris, C. 1984. "Policy and Visions: The Case of the Holy Lance at Antioch," in *War and Government in the Middle Ages, Essays in Honour of J. O. Prestwich*, J. Gillingham, and J. C. Holt (eds). Totowa, NJ: Barnes and Noble Books, 33–46.

Morvillez, E. 2007. "À propos de l'architecture domestique d'Antioche, de Daphne et Séleucie," in *From Antioch to Alexandria. Recent Studies in Domestic Architecture*, K. Galor and T. Waliszewski (eds). Warsaw: University of Warsaw, 51–78.

———. 2004. "L'architecture domestique à Antioche dans l'Antiquité tardive: conservatisme ou modernité?," in *Antioche de Syrie: Histoires, images et traces de la ville antique*. Topoi Orient-Occident Supplément, 271–287.

Mufaddal, 1973. *Histoires des sultans mamlouks*. Turnhout: Brepols.

Mugler, J. 2019a. "A Martyr with Too Many Causes: Christopher of Antioch (d. 967) and Local Collective Memory," PhD diss., Georgetown University, Washington, DC.

———. 2019b. "Ibrāhīm b. Yūḥannā and the Translation Projects of Byzantine Antioch," in *Patristic Literature in Arabic Translations*, B. Roggema and A. Treiger (eds). Leiden: Brill, 180–197.

Müller, G. 1879. *Documenti sulle relazioni della cittá toscane coll'oriente Cristiano e coi turchi*. Florence: M. Cellinie.

Müller, K. O. 1839. *Antiquitates Antiochenae*. Göttingen: Libraria Dieterichiana.

Munro, D. C. 1896. *Letters of the Crusaders. Translations and Reprints from the Original Sources of European History*, vol. 1. Philadelphia, PA: University of Pennsylvania.

Muqaddasī, 1906. *Aḥsan al-taqāsīm fi ma'rifat al āqālīm*. Leiden: Brill.

Najbjerg, T. and Moss, C. 2014. "The History of Antioch on the Orontes in the Greco-Roman Period," in *Antioch on the Orontes: Early Explorations in the City of Mosaics [Asi'deki Antakya: mozaikler şhrinde ilk araşımalar]*, S. Redford (ed.). Istanbul: Koç Universitesi, 23–35.

Neale, F. A. 1854. *Evenings at Antioch with sketches of Syrian Life*. London: Eyre and Williams.

Neumeier, E. 2017. "Spoils for the New Pyrrhus: Alternative Claims to Antiquity in Ottoman Greece," *International Journal of Islamic Architecture* 6 (2): 311–337.

Newell, E. T. 1918. *The Seleucid Mint at Antioch*. New York: The American Numismatic Society.

Newson, P. 2016. "The Carchemish Region between the Hellenistic and Early Islamic Periods," in *Carchemish in Context*, T. J. Wilkinson, E. Peltenburg, and E. Barbanes Wilkinson (eds). Oxford: Oxbow, 184–202.

Nicephorus Basilaces. 1977. *Niceforo Basilace: Gli encomī per l'imperatore e per il patriarca: testo crit., introd. E commentario*. Naples: University Cattedra di Filologia Bizantina.

Niebuhr, C. 1837. *Reisen durch Syrien und Palästina, nach Cypern und durch Kleinasien und die Türkey nach Deutschland und Dänemark. Mit Niebuhr's astronomischen Beobachtungen und einigen kleineren Abhandlungen*, vol. 3. Copenhagen and Hamburg: Möller.

Noreña, C. F. 2016. "Heritage and Homogeneity in the Coinage of Early Roman Antioch," in *Beyond Boundaries. Connecting Visual Cultures in the Provinces of Ancient Rome*, S. Alcock, M. Egri, and J. F. D. Frakes (eds). Los Angeles, CA: Getty Publications, 294–306.

Norman, A. F. 2000. *Antioch as a Centre of Hellenic Culture, as Observed by Libanius*. Liverpool: Liverpool University Press.

Norwich, J. J. 1992. *Byzantium: The Apogee*. New York: Alfred A. Knopf.

Ogden, D. 2017. *The Legend of Seleucus. Kingship, Narrative and Myth Making in the Ancient World*. Cambridge: Cambridge University Press.

———. 2011. "Seleucid Dynastic Foundation Myths: Antioch and Seleucia-in-Pieria," in *Seleucid Dissolution: The Sinking of the Anchor*, K. Erickson and G. Ramsey (eds). Philippika 50. Wiesbaden: Harrassowitz, 149–160.

Olivier, J. and Parisot-Sillon, C. 2013. "Les monnayages aux types de Cléopâtre et Antoine. Premiers résultats et perspectives," *Bulletin de la Societé Française de Numismatique* 68 (9): 256–268.

Osborne, J. Harrison, T., Batiuk, S., Welton, L., Dessel, J. P., Denel, E., and Demirci, Ö. 2019. "Urban Built Environments of the Early First Millennium BCE: Results of the Tayinat Archaeological Project, 2004–2016," *Bulletin of the American Schools of Oriental Research* 382: 261–312.

Otter, J. 1748. *Voyage en Turquie et en Perse, avec un relation des expéditions de Tahmas Kouli-Khan*. Paris: Freres Guerin.

Pamir, H. 2019. "Antakya Hipodrom ve Çevresi Kazıları 2018 Yılı Çalışmaları," *Kazı Sonuçları Toplantısı Cilt* 41 (2): 349–370.

———. 2017. "An Underworld Cult Monument in Antioch: The Charonion," in *Overturning Certainties in Near Eastern Archaeology, A Festschrift in Honor of K. A. Yener*, Ç. Maner, M. T. Horowitz, and A. S. Gilbert (eds). Leiden: Brill, 543–559.

———. 2016. "Antakya hipodrom ve çevresı kazısı," *Kazı Sonuçları Toplantısı Cilt* 36 (3): 271–294.

———. 2014a. "Archaeological Research in Antioch on the Orontes and Its Vicinity: 2002–12 /Antakya ve ÇevresindeYapılan Arkeolojik Araştırmalar: 2002–12," in *Antioch on the Orontes. Early Explorations in the City of Mosaics. Asi'deki Antakya. Mozaikler Şehrinde İlk Araştirmalar*, Scott Redford (ed.). Istanbul: Koç Üniversitesi Yayınları, 78–127.

———. 2014b. "Recent Researches and New Discoveries in the Harbours of Seleucia Pieria," in *Häfen and Häfenstadte im östlischen Mittelmeerraum von der Antike bis in byzantinische Zeit. Neue Entdeckungen und aktuelle Forschungsansätze [Harbors and Harbor Cities in the Eastern Mediterranean from Antiquity to the Byzantine Period: Recent Discoveries and Current Approaches]*, S. Ladstätter, F. Pirson, and T. Schmidts (eds). Istanbul: Ege Yaınları, 177–198.

———. 2005. "The Orontes Delta Survey," in *The Amuq Valley Regional Projects. Vol. 1. Surveys in the Plain of Antioch and Orontes Delta, Turkey, 1995–2002*. Chicago, IL: Oriental Institute Publications, 67–98.

———. 2004. "Eine Stadt stellt sich vor: Seleukia Pieria und ihre Ruinen," *Antike Welt* 35 (2): 17–21.

Pamir, H. and Yamaç, İ. 2012. "Antiokheia ad Orontes Su Yolları," *Adalya* 15: 33–64.

Parlasca, K. 1982. *Syrische Grabreliefs hellenistischer und römischer Zeit: Fundgruppen und Probleme*. Mainz am Rhein: Philipp von Zabern.

Parsons, A. 1808. *Travels in Asia and Africa; including a journey from Scanderoon to Aleppo, and over the desert to Baghdad and Bussora...* . London: Longman, Hurst, Rees, and Orme, Paternoster-Row.

Patitucci, S. and Uggeri, G. 2008. "Antiochia sull'Oronte nel IV secolo d.C," in *XXII Atti del Simposio Paolino. Paolo tra Tarso e Antiochia*, L. Padovese (ed.). Archeologia/Storia/Religione. Rome: Pontificio Ateneo Antoniano, 7–42.

Paul, N. L. 2010. "A Warlord's Wisdom: Literacy and Propaganda at the Time of the First Crusade," *Speculum* 85 (3): 534–566.

Pelle, C. and Galibert, L. 1848. *Voyage en Syrie et dans l'Asie mineure. D'après les dessins pris sur les lieux par W. H. Bartlett, Thomas Allom, etc.* London and Paris: Fisher.

Pellizzari, A. 2015. "Testimonianze di un'amicizia: il carteggio fra Libanio e Giuliano," in *L'Imperatore Giuliano. Realtà storica e rappresentazione*, A. Marcone (ed.). Florence: Le Monnier, 63–86.

———. 2012. "Terme e bagni pubblici e privati nella corrispondenza di Libanio," in *Les sources de l'histoire du paysage urbain d'Antioche sur l'Oronte. Actes des journées d'études des 20 et 21 Septembre 2010*, C. Saliou (ed.). Paris: Université Paris 8, 69–80.

Perry, C. 1743. *A View of the Levant: Particularly of Constantinople, Syria, Egypt, and Greece*. London: T. Woodward.

Peter Tudebode. 1974. *Historia de Hierosolymitano itinere*. J. H. Hill and L. L. Hill (trans.). Memoirs of the American Philosophical Society 101. Philadelphia, PA: American Philosophical Society.

Pharr, C. (trans.). 1952. *The Theodosian Code and Novels and the Sirmondian Constitutions*. Princeton, NJ: Princeton University Press.

Piejko, F. 1990. "Episodes from the Third Syrian War in a Gurob Papyrus, 246 B.C.," *Archiv für Papyrusforschung* 36: 13–27.

Poccardi, G. 2009. "Un bain publique d'Antioch, propriété de Saint-Pierre de Rome (*Liber Pontificalis*, XXXIIII. Sylvestre, 19)," *Syria* 86: 281–287.

———. 2001. "L'Île d'Antioche à la Fin de l'Antiquite. Histoire et Problème de Topographie Urbaine," in *Recent Research in Late-Antique Urbanism*. L. Lavan (ed.). *Journal of Roman Archaeology Supplement* 42. Portsmouth, RI: Journal of Roman Archaeology.

Pococke, R. 1745. *A Description of the East and Some other Countries. Vol. II. Part I. Observations on Palestine or the Holy Land, Syria, Mesopotamia, Cyprus, and Candia. Book the Second of Syria and Mesopotamia*. London: W. Bowyer.

Pollard, N. 2000. *Soldiers, Cities, & Civilians in Roman Syria*. Ann Arbor, MI: Michigan University Press.

Posamentir, R. 2008. "Ohne Mass und Ziel? – Anmerkungen zur Säulenstrasse von Anazarbos," in *Festschrift für Haluk Abbasoğlu anläßlich seines 65. Geburtstages*, I. Delemen et al. (eds). Istanbul: Ege, 1013–1033.

Potter, D. S. 2004. *The Roman Empire at Bay AD 180–395*. London and New York: Routledge.

Poonawala, I. K. 2008. *Ismaili Literature in Persian and Arabic*. London: Institute of Ismaili Studies.

Procopius. 1914. *History of the Wars*. Volume I, Books 1–2 (Persian War). H. B. Dewing (trans.). Cambridge, MA: Loeb Classical Library, 48.

Procopius. 1940. *On Buildings*. Cambridge, Mass: Harvard University Press/Loeb.

Pucci, M. 2019. *Excavations in the Plain of Antioch III. Stratigraphy, Pottery, and Small Finds from Chatal Hoyuk in the Amuq Plain*. OIP 143. Chicago, IL: Oriental Institute.

Qalqashandi. 1987. *Ṣubḥ al-a'shā fī ṣinā'at al-anshā*. Beirut: Dār al-Kutub al-'Ilmīyah.

Rawlinson, G. 1876. *The Seventh Great Oriental Monarchy*. London: Longmans.

Raymond of Aguilers. 1969. *Le "Liber" de Raymond d'Aguilers*. J. Hugh and L. Hill (trans.). Paris: Librairie Orientaliste Paul Geuthner.

———. 1968. *Historia Francorum qui ceperunt Iherusalem*. J. H. Hill and L. L. Hill (trans.). Philadelphia, PA: American Philosophical Society.

Redford, S. 2014. *Antioch on the Orontes: Early Explorations in the city of Mosaics*. S. Redford (ed.). Istanbul: Koç Üniversitesi Yayınları.

———. 2012. "Trade and Economy in Antioch and Cilicia in the Twelfth and Thirteenth Centuries," in *Trade and Markets in Byzantium*, C. Morrison (ed.). Washington, DC. Dumbarton Oaks, 297–310.

Reinaud, M. 1827. "Histoire des Guerres des croisades, sous la règne de Bibars, sultan d'Egypte, d'après les auteurs arabes," *Journal Asiatique* 11 (August): 65–93.

Remijsen, S. 2010. "The Introduction of the Antiochene Olympics: A Proposal for a New Date," *GRBS* 50: 411–436.

Rey-Coquais, J. P. 1978. "Syrie Romaine de Pompée à Dioclétien," *JRS* 68: 44–73.

Ridgway, B. S. 2000. *Hellenistic Sculpture II: The Styles of ca. 200–100 B.C.* Madison, WI: University of Wisconsin Press.

Riedel, M. 2012. "Syriac Sources for Byzantinists: An Introduction and Overview," *Byzantinische Zeitschrift* 105 (2) (November): 775–801.

Rifaioğlu, M. N. 2018a. "The Role of Production in Shaping the Architectural Character of an Ottoman Soap Factory in Antakya (Antioch)," *Journal of Architectural and Planning Research* 35 (1): 25–46.

———. 2018b. "Memluk Dönemi Hamam Yapılar: Antakya Beyseri Hamamı Özelinde Yapısal-Mekânsal-İşlevsel Çözümleme," *Megaron* 13 (4): 545–558.

———. 2014. "The Historic Urban Core of Antakya under the Influence of the French Mandate, and Turkish Republican Urban Conservation and Development Activities," *Megaron* 9 (4): 21–288.

Riley-Smith, J. 1982. "The First Crusade and St. Peter," in *Outremer: Studies in the History of the Crusading Kingdom of Jerusalem Presented to Joshua Prawer*, J. Prawer, B. Z. Kedar, H. E. Mayer, and R. C. Smail (eds). Jerusalem: Yad Izhak Ben-Zvi Institute.

Rinaldi, G. 2015. "Antiochia nel secolo quarto. Interazioni tra pagani e cristiani e note prosopografiche," *Studi e materiali di storia delle religioni* 81 (1): 21–69.

Ristvet, L. 2014. "Between Ritual and Theatre: Political Performance in Seleucid Babylonia," *World Archaeology* 46 (2): 256–269.

Roberts, A. 2020. *Reason and Revelation in Byzantine Antioch: The Christian Translation Program of Abdallah ibn al-Fadl*. Oakland, CA: University of California Press.

Robinson, G. 1837. *Three Years in the East, Being the Substance of a Journal Written During a Tour and Residence in Greece, Egypt, Palestine, Syria, and Turkey in 1829–1830, 1831, and 1832*. London: Henry Colburn.

Roussel, P. and De Visscher, F. 1942. "Les Inscriptions du temple de Dmeir," *Syria* 23: 173–200.

Sahillioğlu, H. 1991. "Antakya," *Türk Diyanet Vakfi İslam Ansiklopedisi* 3: 230–231.

Saliou, C. 2019. "Reconstruire Antioche?" *In Reconstruire Les Villes*, E. Capet, C. Dogniez, M. Gorea et al. (eds). Turnhout: Brepols, 197–214.

———. 2018. "Libanius' Antiochicus, Mirror of a City? Antioch in 356, Praise and Reality," in *Antioch II. The Many Faces of Antioch: Intellectual Exchange and Religious Diversity, CE 350–450*, S. P. Bergjan and S. Elm (eds). Tübingen: Mohr Siebeck, 35–52.

———. 2016. "Malalas and Antioch," in *Die Weltchronik des Johannes Malalas. Autor- Werk-Überlieferung*, M. Meier, C. Radki, and F. Schültz (eds). Stuttgart: Franz Steiner Verlag: 59–76.

———. 2013. "La Porte des Chérubins à Antioche sur l'Oronte et le développement de la ville," *Anatolia Antiqua* 21: 125–133.

———. 2012. "Les sources antiques: esquisse de présentation générale," in *Les sources de l'histoire du paysage urbain d'Antioche sur l'Oronte. Actes des journées d'études des 20 et 21 Septembre 2010*, C. Saliou (ed.), vol. 8. Paris: Université Paris, 7–16.

———. 2009. "Le palais impérial d'Antioche et son contexte à l'époque de Julien. Réflexions sur l'apport des sources littéraires à l'histoire d'un espace urbain," *Antiquité Tardive* 17: 235–250.

———. 2006. "Statues d'Antioche de Syrie dans la 'Chronographie' de Malalas," in *Recherches sur la "Chronique" de Jean Malalas. 2*, S. Agusta-Boularot, J. Beaucamp, A. M. Bernardi et al. (eds). Paris: Monographies du Centre de Recherche d'Histoire et Civilization de Byzance, 69–95.

———. 2000. "À propos de la ταυριανὴ πύλη: Remarques sur la localisation présumée de la Grande Église d'Antioche de Syrie," *Syria* 77: 217–226.

Saminsky, A. 2006. "Georgian and Greek Illuminated Manuscripts from Antioch," in *East and West in the Medieval Mediterranean I: Antioch from the Byzantine Reconquest until the End of the Crusader Principality: Acta of the Congress Held at Hernen Castle in May 2003*. OLA 147, K. Ciggaar and M. Metcalf (eds). Leuven: Peeters, 17–78.

Şancı, F. 2006. "Hatay İlinde Türk Mimarisi I," PhD diss., Ankara University, Ankara.

Sanjian, A. 1956. "The Sanjak of Alexandretta (Hatay): Its Impact on Syrian-Turkish Relations (1939–1956)," *Middle East Journal* 10 (4): 379–394.

Saradi, H. 2006. *The Byzantine City in the Sixth Century: Literary Images and Historical Reality*. Athens: Society of Messenian Archaeological Studies.

Saunders, W. B. R. 1982. "The Aachen Reliquary of Eustathius Maleinus, 969–970," *Dumbarton Oaks Papers* 36: 211–219.

Sauvaget, J. 1934. "Le Plan de Laodicée-sur-Mer," *Bulletin d'études orientales* 4: 81–114.

Sawirus b. al-Muqaffa, 1948. *History of the Patriarchs of the Egyptian Church Known as the History of the Holy Church*. Volume II, Part II. Aziz Suryal Atiya, Yassa 'Abd al-Masih, and P. H. E. Khs.-Burmester (trans. and annot.). Cairo: Publications de la Société d'Archéologie Copte.

Sbeinati, M., Darawcheh, Ryad and Mouty, Mikhail. 2005. "The Historical Earthquakes of Syria: An Analysis of Large and Moderate Earthquakes from 1365 B.C. to 1900 A.D.," *Annals of Geophysics* 48 (3): 386.

Scheid, J. 1990. *Le Collège des frères Arvales. Étude prosopographique du recrutement*. Rome: l'Erma di Bretschneider.

Schoolman, E. 2010. "Civic Transformation of the Mediterranean City: Antioch and Ravenna 300–800 C.E.," PhD diss., UCLA, Los Angeles, CA.

Şemseddin Sāmī. 1889–1898. *Kamus-ül alām: tarih ve coğrafya lugati ve tabir-i esahhiyle kāffe-yi esma-yi hass-yi camidir*. Istanbul: Mihran Matbaası.

Seyrig, H. 1938. "Le cimitière des marins à Séleucie de Piérie," in *Mélanges syriens offerts à M. R. Dussaud: secrétaire perpétuel de l'Académie des inscriptions et belles-lettres*. Paris: Geuthner, 451–459.

Shacht, J. and Meyerhof, M. 1937. *The Medico-Philosophical Controversy Between Ibn Butlan of Baghdad and Ibn Ridwan of Cairo. A Contribution to the History of Greek Learning Among the Arabs*. Cairo: Egyptian University.

Shatzmiller, Maya. 2012. "Measuring the Medieval Islamic Economy," www.medievalislamiceconomy.uwo.ca/measures-egypt.html

Shaw, B. 1990. "Bandit Highland and Lowland Peace: The Mountains of Isauria-Cilicia," *Journal of the Economic and Social History of the Orient* 33 (2): 199–233.

Shepardson, C. 2015a. "Meaningful Meetings: Constructing Linguistic Difference in and around Antioch," in *Syriac Encounters. Papers from the Sixth North American Syriac Symposium. Duke University, 26–29 June 2011*, M. Dorfler, E. Fiano, and K. Smith (eds). Leuven and Bristol: Peeters, 79–90.

———. 2015b. "Between Polemic and Propaganda: Evoking the Jews of Fourth-Century Antioch," *JJMJS* 2: 147–182.

———. 2014. *Controlling Contested Places. Late Antique Antioch and the Spatial Politics of Religious Controversy*. Berkeley, CA: University of California Press.

Sherk, R. K. 1969. *Roman Documents from the Greek East. Senatus Consulta and Epistulae to the Age of Augustus*. Baltimore, MD: Johns Hopkins University Press.

Sherley, A., Sherley, R., Sherley, T., Manwaring, G., and Cooper, R. 1825. *The Three Brothers; or, the Travels and Adventures of Sir Anthony, Sir Robert, & Sir Thomas Sherley, in Persia, Russia, Turkey, Spain, Etc.* London: Hurst, Robinson, & Co.

Sherwin-White, A. N. 1983. *Roman Foreign Policy in the East. 168 B.C. to A.D. 1*. Norman, OK: University of Oklahoma Press.

Sherwin-White, S. and Kuhrt, A. 1993. *From Samarkhand to Sardis. A New Approach to the Seleucid Empire (Hellenistic Culture and Society, Number 13)*. Berkeley and Los Angeles, CA: University of California Press.

Shields, S. 2011. *Fezzes in the River. Identity Politics and Diplomacy in the Middle East on the Eve of World War II.* Oxford: Oxford University Press.

Sibṭ b. al-'Ajamī. 1950. *Les Tresors d'Or.* J. Sauvaget (trans.). Beirut: Institut Français de Damas.

Sinclair, T. A. 1990. *Eastern Turkey: An Architectural and Archaeological Survey*, vol. IV. London: Pindar Press.

Sitz, A. M. 2019. "Beyond Spolia: A New Approach to Old Inscriptions in Late Antique Anatolia," *AJA* 123 (4): 643–674.

Skottki, K. 2015. *Christen, Muslime, und der Erste Kreuzzug.* New York: Waxmann.

Skylitzes, John. 2010. *John Skylitzes: A Synopsis of Byzantine History, 811–1057.* J. Wortley (trans.). Cambridge: Cambridge University Press.

Sodini, J. P. 2007. "Saint Syméon, Lieu de Pèlerinage," *Les Cahiers de Saint-Michel de Cuxa* 38 (2007): 107–120.

Smbat the Constable. 1980. *La Chronique Attribuée au Connétable Smbat.* G. Dédéyan (trans. and annot.). Paris: Librairie Orientaliste Paul Geuthner.

Stahl, A. M. 2020. "Coinage and the Crusades," in *The Cambridge History of the Crusades*, Jonathan Phillips and Thomas Madden (eds). Cambridge: Cambridge University Press.

———. 2018. "The Denier Outremer," in *The French of Outremer*, L. Morreale and N. Paul (eds). New York: Fordham University Press, 30–43.

———. 2017. "New Archaeology from Old Coins: Antioch Re-examined," in *European Archaeology as Anthropology. Essays in Memory of Bernard Wailes*, P. J. Crabtree and B. Wailes (eds). Philadelphia, PA: University of Pennsylvania Archaeology and Anthropology Museum, 225–244.

Stahl, A. M. and Glynias, J. 2020. "The Transition From Byzantine to Islamic Coinage in Antioch and its Implication for the History of Settlement in the City," in *Dinars and Dirhams: Festschrift in Honor of Michael L. Bates*, Virginie Rey et al. (ed.). Irvine, CA: UCI Jordan Center for Persian Studies.

Stenger, J. R. 2018. "Healing Place or Abode of the Demons? Libanius' and Chrysostom's Rewriting of the Apoloo Sanctuary at Daphne," in *Antioch II. The Many Faces of Antioch: Intellectual Exchange and Religious Diversity,* CE *350–450*, S. P. Bergjan and S. Elm (eds). Tübingen: Mohr Siebeck, 193–220.

Stephen of Taron. 1907. *Des Stephanos von Taron armenische Geschichte.* H. Gelzer and A. Burckhardt (eds). Leipzig: B.G. Teubner.

Stillwell, R. J. 1961 "Houses of Antioch," *DOP* 15: 45–57.

———. 1942. *Antioch-on-the-Orontes. The Excavations, 1937–1939.* Princeton, NJ: Princeton University Press.

———. 1938. *Antioch-on-the-Orontes. The Excavations, 1933–1936.* Princeton, NJ: Princeton University Press.

Stinespring, W. F. 1932. "The Description of Antioch in Codex Vaticanus Arabicus 286," PhD diss., Yale University, New Haven, CT.

Stoneman, R. 1994. *Palmyra and Its Empire.* Ann Arbor, MI: University of Michigan Press.

Strootman, R. 2016. "The introduction of Hellenic Cults in Seleukid Syria: Colonial Appropriation and Transcultural Exchange in the Creation of an Imperial Landscape," in *Colonial Geopolitics and Local Cultures in the Hellenistic and Roman East (IIIrd Century B.C.–IIIrd century A.D.)*, H. Bru and A. Dumitru (eds). Conference paper.

———. 2011. "Kings and Cities in the Hellenistic Age," in *Political Culture in the Greek City after the Classical Age*, R Alson, O. van Njif, and C. Williamson. Leuven: Peeters, 141–153.

Sümer, F. 1963. "Çukur-Ova Tarihine Dair Arastirmalar," *Tarih Arastirmalari Dergisi* 1 (1): 1–112.

Ṭabarī. 1987. *Ta'rīh al-rusul wa al-mulū*. 3rd series, Part. 3. Leiden: Brill. 1987; republished 2010. As *The Ancient Kingdoms*. M. Perlmann (trans. and annot.), vol. 4. Albany, NY: SUNY Press.

———. 1992. *The Revolt of the Zanj*. D. Waines (trans.), vol. 36. Albany, NY: SUNY Press.

Tannous, J. 2014. "In Search of Monotheletism," *Dumbarton Oaks Papers* 68: 29–67.

Tate, G. 1997. "The Syrian Countryside During the Roman Era," in *The Early Roman Empire in the East*, S. Alcock (ed.). Oxford: Oxbow Books, 55–71.

———. 1992. *Les Campagnes de la Syrie du Nord du II au VII Siècle*. Paris: Presses de l'Ifpo.

Tchalenko, G. 1953. *Villages Antiques de la Syrie du Nord*. Paris: Geuthner.

Tekin, M. 1993. *Antakya'lı din şehidi Habib Neccar*. Antakya: [publisher not identified].

ten Hacken, C. 2006. "The Description of Antioch in Abu al-Makarim's History of the Churches and Monasteries of Egypt and Some Neighbouring Countries," in *East and West in the Medieval Mediterranean I: Antioch from the Byzantine Reconquest until the End of the Crusader Principality: Acta of the Congress Held at Hernen Castle in May 2003*. OLA 147, K. Ciggaar and M. Metcalf (eds). Leuven: Peeters, 185–216.

Theophanes. 1982. *The Chronicle of Theophanes*. H. Turtledove (trans.). Philadelphia, PA: University of Pennsylvania Press.

Theophilus. 2011. *Theophilus of Edessa's Chronicle and the Circulation of Historical Knowledge in Late Antiquity and Early Islam*. R. G. Hoyland (trans. and annot.). Liverpool: Liverpool University Press.

Thierry, M. 1993. *Répertoire des monastères arméniens*. Turnhout: Corpus Christianorum.

Thomas, D. 1997. *The Later Medieval City, 1300–1500*. New York: Longman.

Thomson, W. M. 1885. *The Land and the Book; or Biblical Illustrations Drawn from the Manners and Customs, the Scenes and Scenery of the Holy Land: Lebanon, Damascus and beyond Jordan*. New York: Harper & Bros.

Tiersch, C. 2018. "A Dispute -About Hellenism? Julian and the Citizens of Antioch," in *Antioch II. The Many Faces of Antioch: Intellectual Exchange and Religious Diversity, CE 350–450*, S. P. Bergjan and S. Elm (eds). Tübingen: Mohr Siebeck, 103–136.

Todt, K. P. 2004. "Antioch in the Middle Byzantine Period (969–1084): The Reconstruction of the City as an Administrative, Economic, Military and Ecclesiastical Center," in *Antioche de Syrie: Histoire, images et traces de la ville antique* (Colloque de Maison de l'Orient et de la Méditerranée, October 4–6, 2001). Topoi Orient-Occident Supplément 5, B. Cabouret, P.-L. Gatier, and C. Saliou (eds). Lyon: Maison de l'Orient Méditerranéen-Jean Pouilloux; Paris: De Boccard, 182–184.

———. 2000. "Antioch and Edessa in the so-called Treaty of Deabolis (September 1108)," *ARAM* 12: 455–501.

Treadgold, W. 1988. *The Byzantine Revival, 780–842*. Stanford, CA: Stanford University Press.

Treiger, A. 2020. "The Beginnings of the Greco-Syro-Arabic Melkite Translation Movement in Antioch," *Scrinium* 16: 1–27.

———. 2019. "Greek into Arabic in Byzantine Antioch: 'Abdallāh ibn al-Faḍl's 'Book of the Garden' (*Kitāb ar-rawḍa*)," in *Ambassadors, Artists, Theologians: Byzantine Relations with the Near East from the Ninth to the Thirteenth Centuries*, Z. Chitwood and J. Pahlitzsch (eds). Mainz: Verlag des Römisch-Germanischen Zentralmuseums, 227–238.

———. 2017 "Sinaitica (1): The Antiochian Menologian, Compiled by Hieromonk Yūḥannā 'Abd al-Masīḥ (First Half of the 13th Century)," *Christian Orient: Journal of Studies in the Christian Culture of Asia and Africa* 8 (14): 215–252 (St. Petersburg).

Triebel, L. 2005. "Die angebliche Synagoge der Makkabäischen Märtyrer in Antiochia am Orontes," *Zeitschrift fur Antikes Christentum* 3: 464–495.

Troadec, A. 2014–15. "Baybars and the Cultural Memory of Bilad al-Sham," *Mamluk Studies Review* 18: 113–147.

———. 2013. "Une lettre de Baybars au comte Bohémond VI de Tripoli (mai 1271): une arme dans l'arsenal idéologique des Mamelouks," in *La correspondance entre souverains, princes et cités-états. Approches croisées entre l'Orient musulman, l'Occident latin et Byzance (XIIIe-début XVI siècle),* D. Aigle and S. Péquignot (eds). Turnhout: Brepols, 107–125.

Troupeau, G. 2005. "Les églises et les monastères de Syrie dans l'oeuvre d'Abū al-Makārim," *Mélanges de l'Université Saint Joseph* 58: 573–586.

———. 2001. "Les églises d'Antioche chez les auteurs arabes," in *L'Orient au Coeur,* A. Miquel, B. Halff, and F. Sanagustin (eds). Paris: Maisonneuve Larose, 319–327.

Trovato, S. 2014. *Antieroe dai molti volti: Giuliano l'Apostata nel Medioevo bizantino.* Udine: Forum.

Tsetskhladze, G. (ed.). 1999. *Ancient Greeks West and East: Edited by Gocha R. Tsetskhladze.* Leiden: Brill.

Tyerman, C. 2011. *Chronicles of the First Crusade.* London: Penguin.

Uggeri, G. 2014. "Da Antiochia a Theoupolis: la Trasformazione Giustinianea di una Metropoli," in *La Teologia dal V all'VIII Secolo tra Sviluppo e Crisi.* Rome: Istitutum Parrtisticum Augustinianum, 867–877.

———. 2009. "Antiochia sull'Oronte. Profilo Storico e Urbanistico," in *Paolo di Tarso: Archeologia, Storia e Ricezione,* L. Padovese (ed.). Cantalupa: Effatà, 87–127.

2006. "Seleucia Pieria: il porto di Antiochia sull'Oronte," *Rivista di Topografia Antica* 16: 143–176.

———. 1998. "L'urbanistica di Antiochia sull'Oronte," *Journal of Ancient Topography* 8: 179–222.

Underhill, G. 1942. "A Tenth-Century Byzantine Silk from Antioch," *The Bulletin of the Cleveland Museum of Art* 29 (1) (January): 6–7.

Usama b. Munqidh. 2008. *Islam and the Crusades. The Writings of Usama ibn Munqidh.* New York: Penguin.

Van Berchem, D. 1985. "Le Port de Séleucie de Pièrie et l'Infrastructure Logistique des Guerres Parthiques," *Bonner Jahrbücher* 185: 47–87.

———. 1983. Une Inscription Flavienne du Musée d'Antioche," *Museum Helveticum* 40: 186–196.

Van Berchem, M. and Fatio, E. 1914–1915. *Voyage en Syrie.* Cairo: Imprimerie de l'Institut français d'archéologie orientale.

Van Egmond van der Nijenburg, J. A. 1759. *Travels through Part of Europe, Asia Minor, the Islands of the Archipelago; Syria, Palestine, Egypt, Mount Sinai…: Giving a Particular Account of the Most Remarkable Place, Structures, Ruins, Inscriptions… In These Countries; Together with the Customs, Manners, Religion, Trade, Commerce, Tempers, and Manner of Living of the Inhabitants.* London: L. Davis and C. Reymers.

Van Hoof, L. and Van Nuffelen, P. 2011. "Monarchy and Mass Communication: Antioch A.D. 362/363 Revisited," *Journal of Roman Studies* 1: 166–184.

Van Nuffelen, P. 2006. "Earthquakes in AD 363–368, and the Date of Libanius, Oratio 18," *Classical Quarterly* 56 (2): 657–661.

Verzone, P. 2011. *Palazzi e Domus dalla Tetrarchia al VII secolo.* Rome: "L'Erma" di Bretschneider.

Volney, C.-F. 1787. *Voyage en Syrie et en Égypte, pendant les années 1783, 1784 et 1785, avec deux Cartes géographiques et deux Planches gravées, représentant les Ruines du Temple du Soleil à Balbek, et celles de la ville de Palmyre, dans le Désert de Syrie.* Paris: Desenne, Libraire.

Vorderstrasse, T. 2015. "Re-Constructing a Medieval Painted Tomb from Antioch," in *Le patrimoine architectural de l'Église orthodoxe d'Antioche. Perspectives comparatives avec les autres groupes religieux du Moyen-Orient et des régions limitrophes*, M. Davie (ed.). Balamand: Publications de l'Université de Balamand, 79–92.

———. 2010. "Trade and Textiles from Medieval Antioch," *al-Masāq* 22 (2) (August): 151–171.

———. 2006. "Archaeology of the Antiochene Region in the Crusader Period," in *East and West in the Medieval Mediterranean I: Antioch from the Byzantine Reconquest until the End of the Crusader Principality: Acta of the Congress Held at Hernen Castle in May 2003*. OLA 147, K. Ciggaar and M. Metcalf (eds). Leuven: Peeters, 319–336.

———. 2005a. "Coin Circulation in Some Syrian Villages (5th–11th centuries)," in *Les Villages dans l'Empire Byzantin*, J. Lefort, C. Morrison, and J.-P. Sodini (eds). Paris: Réalités Byzantines, 11.

———. 2005b. *Al-Mina: A Port of Antioch from Late Antiquity to the End of the Ottomans*. Leiden: Nederlands Instituut Voor Het Nabije Oosten.

Waagé, F. O. 1948. *Antioch on the Orontes. Ceramics and Islamic Coins*. Princeton, NJ: Princeton University Press.

Waddington, W. H. 1870. *Inscriptions Grecques et Latines de la Syrie*. Paris: Firmin Didot.

Walbiner, C. M. 1999–2000. "The City of Antioch in the Writings of Macarius ibn al-Zaʿīm (17th Century)," *ARAM* 11–12: 509–521.

Walmsley, A. 2007. *Early Islamic Syria: An Archaeological Assessment*. London: Duckworth.

Weber, S. H. 1934. "The Coins," in *Antioch-on-the Orontes. The Excavations of 1932*, G. W. Elderkin (ed.). Princeton, NJ: Princeton University Press.

Welles, C. et al. 1959. *The Parchments and Papyri. The Excavations at Dura Europos*, Final Report, vol. 5.1. New Haven, CT: Yale University Press.

Weitenberg, J. 2006. "The Armenian Monasteries in the Black Mountain," in *East and West in the Medieval Mediterranean I: Antioch from the Byzantine Reconquest Until the End of the Crusader Principality: Acta of the Congress Held at Hernen Castle in May 2003*. OLA 147, K. Ciggaar and M. Metcalf (eds). Leuven: Peeters, 79–94.

Weltecke, D. 2006. "On the Syriac Orthodox in the Principality of Antioch During the Crusader Period," in *East and West in the Medieval Mediterranean I: Antioch from the Byzantine Reconquest Until the End of the Crusader Principality: Acta of the Congress Held at Hernen Castle in May 2003*, K. Ciggaar and M. Metcalf (eds). OLA 147. Leuven: Peeters, 95–124.

Weulersse, J. 1940. *L'Oronte: Étude de Fleuve*. Paris: Tours, Arrault, et cie Maîtres Imprimeurs.

———. 1934. "Antioche. Essai de géographie urbaine," *Bulletin d'Études Orientales* 4: 27–79.

Wheeler, E. L. 1996. "The Laxity of the Syrian Legions," in *The Roman Army in the East*, D. Kennedy (ed.). *JRA Suppl* 18: 229–276.

Whitby, L. M. 1989. "Procopius and Antioch," in *The Eastern Frontier of the Roman Empire*. Proceedings of a Colloquium held at Ankara in September 1988, D. H. French and C. S. Lightfoot (eds). Oxford: B.A.R., 537–553.

Whitcomb, D. 2011. "Qaysāriyah as an Early Islamic Settlement," in *Shaping the Middle East: Jews, Christians, and Muslims in an Age of Transition, 400–800 C.E.*, K. Holum and H. Lapin (eds). Bethesda, MD: CDL Press.

Whittaker, C. R. 1978. "Land and Labour in North Africa," *Klio* 60: 331–362.

Wickham, C. 2005. *Framing the Early Middle Ages: Europe and the Mediterranean 400–800*. New York: Oxford University Press.

Wiedeman, E. 1970. "Über die Stundenwage," in *Aufsätze zur Arabischen Wissenschafts-geschichte*. New York: Hildesheim, 57–68.

Wiemer, H. U. 2003. "Vergangenheit und Gegenwart im 'Antiochikos' des Libanios," *Klio* 85 (2): 442–468.

Wilber, D. N. 1938. "The Theatre at Daphne in 1938," in *Antioch-on-the-Orontes. The Excavations, 1933–1936*, R. Stillwell (ed.). Princeton, NJ: Princeton University Press.

Wilber Clarke, G. and Connor, P. J. (eds). 2002. *Jebel Khalid on the Euphrates: Report on Excavations 1986–1996. Vol. I. Mediterranean Archaeology 5*. Sydney: Meditarch, University of Sidney.

Wilbrand von Oldenburg. 2012. "Wilbrand of Oldenburg: Journey in the Holy Land (1211–12)," in *Pilgrimage to Jerusalem and the Holy Land*, D. Pringle. Burlington, VT: Ashgate, 61–94.

Wilkinson, T. J. 1997. "The History of the Lake of Antioch: A Preliminary Note," in *Crossing Boundaries and Linking Horizons: Studies in Honor of Michael C. Astour*, G. Young, M. Chavalas, and R. E. Averbeck (eds). Bethesda, MD: CDl, 557–576.

Wilkinson, T. J., Friedman, E. S., Alp, E. and Stampel, P. J. 2001. "The Geoarchaeology of a Lake Basin: Spatial and Chronological Patterning if Sedimentation in the Amuq Plain, Turkey," *Cahiers d' Archéologie du CELAT* 10: 211–226.

Will, E. 1997. "Antioche sur l'Oronte, Métropole de l'Asie," *Syria* 74: 99–113.

———. 1983. "La coupe de Césarée de Palestine au Musée du Louvre," *Monuments et Mémoires. Fondation Piot* 65: 1–25.

William of Tyre. 1943. *A History of Deeds Done Beyond the Sea*. E. A. Babcock and A. C. Krey (trans.), vol. 1. New York: Columbia University Press, 260–297.

Williams, W. 1974. "Caracalla and the Rhetoricians. A Note on the *cognitio de Gohariensis*," *Latomus* 33: 663–667.

Windham, A. L. 2005. "Coins," in *The Arts of Antioch: Art Historical and Scientific Approaches to Roman Mosaics and a Catalogue of the Worcester Art Museum Antioch Collection*, L. Becker and C. Kondoleon (eds). Worcester: Worcester Art Museum, 275–304.

Wintjes, J. 2018. "Die uberkannte Metropole–Antiochien und die römische Armee," in *Antioch II. The Many Faces of Antioch: Intellectual Exchange and Religious Diversity, CE 350–450*, S. P. Bergjan and S. Elm (eds). Tübingen: Mohr Siebeck, 75–102.

Woolley, C. L. 1955. *Alalakh: An Account of the Excavations at Tell Atchana in the Hatay, 1937–1949*. London: Society of Antiquaries.

Wortley, J. 2006. "Relics and the Great Church," *Byzantinische Zeitschrift* 99: 631–647.

———. 2004. "Relics of the 'Friends of Jesus' at Constantinople," in *Byzance et les reliques du Christ*, J. Durand and B. Flusin (eds). Paris: Association des amis du Centre d'histoire et civilisation de Byzance, 143–157.

Yakit, İ. 1992. *Türk-İslâm Kültürunde Ebced Hesabı ve Tarih Düşürme*. Istanbul: Ötüken.

Yāqūt. 1990. *Mu'jam al-Buldan*. Beirut: Dār al-Kutub al-'Ilmīyah.

———. 1955–57. *Mu'jam al-Buldān*, 5 vols. Beirut: Dār Sādir.

Yahya b. Sa'id al-Anṭakī. 1924, 1932, 1957. *Histoire de Yahya-Ibn Said d'Antioche*. I. Vasiliev Kratchkovsky (ed. and trans.), *Patrologia Orientalis* 18.5 (first part) and 23.3 (second part). Paris: Firmin Didot.

Yegül, F. 2000. "Baths and Bathing in Roman Antioch," in *Antioch, the Lost Ancient City*, C. Kondoleon (ed.). Princeton, NJ: Princeton University Press, 146–151.

Yener, A. et al. 2005. *The Amuq Valley Regional Projects. Vol. 1. Surveys in the plain of Antioch and Orontes Delta, Turkey 1995–2002*. Chicago, IL: The University of Chicago Press.

Yener, K., Edens, C., Harrison, T. P., Verstraete, J., and Wilkinson, T. J. 2000. "The Amuq Valley Regional Project, 1995–1998," *AJA* 104 (2): 163–220.

Yerasimos, S. 1988. "Le sandjak d'Alexandrette: formation et intégration d'un territoire," *Revue de l'Occident Musulman et de la Mediterranée* 48–49: 198–212.

Yücel, Y. 1989. *Timur'un Ortadogu-Anadolu Seferleri ve Sonuclari 1393–1402*. Ankara: Türk Tarih Kurumu Basimevi.

Zahir al-Din Nishapuri. 2001. *The History of the Seljuq Turks from the Jāmi'al-tawārīkh: An Ilkhanid Adaptation of the Saljuq-nama of Zahir al-Din Nishapuri*. K. A. Luther (trans.), C. E. Bosworth (ed.). Richmond: Curzon.

Zambon, M. Grazia, Bertogli, D., and Granella, O. 2000. *Antioch on the Orontes*. Parma: Edizionei Eteria.

Zayat, Habib. 1952. "Vie du patriarche melkite d'Antioche Christophore (1967) par le protospathaire Ibrahim b. Yuhanna. Document inédit du Xi siécle," *Proche Orient Chrétien* 2 (4): 11–38, 333–366.

Ziadeh, N. A. 1999–2000. "al-Antāqi and his Tadkhara," *ARAM* 11–12: 503–508.

INDEX OF PEOPLE

INDEX OF PLACES

VARIA INDEX

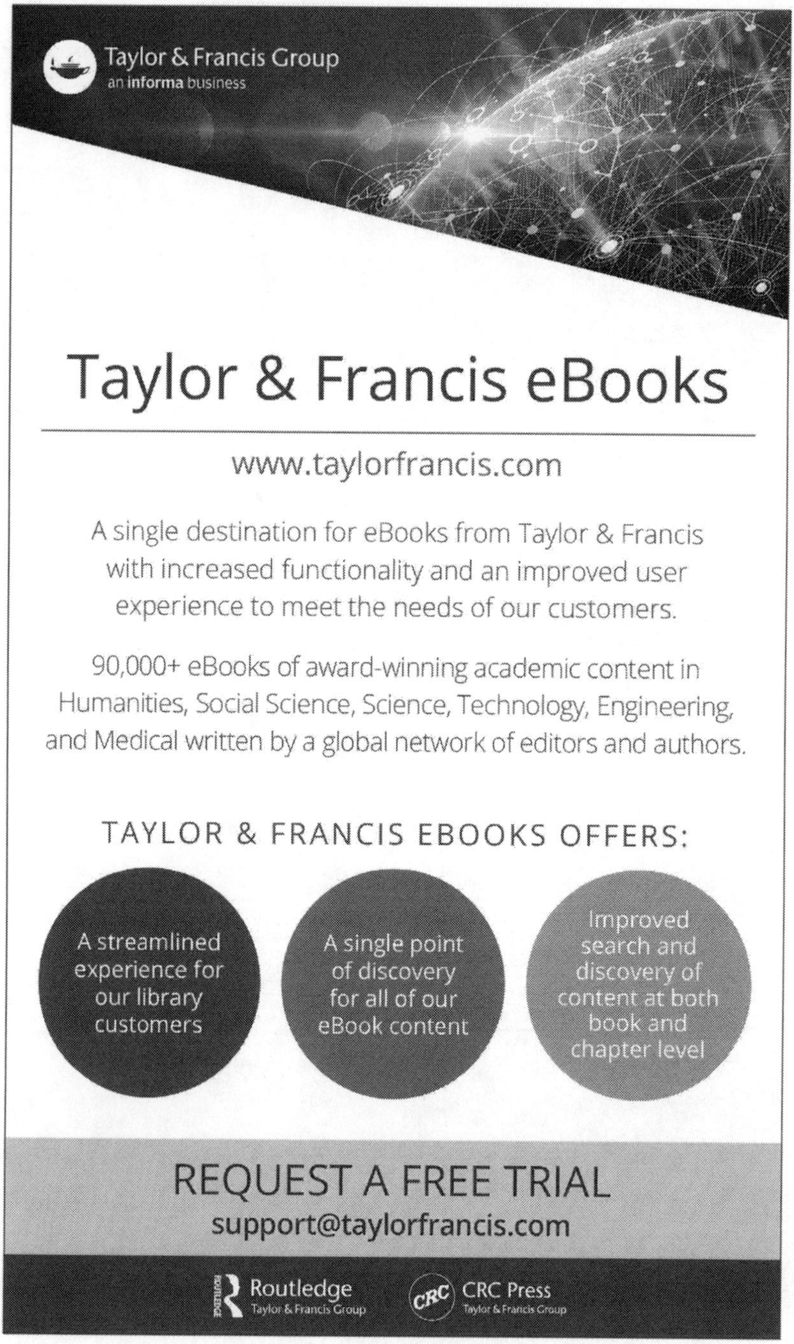
Taylor & Francis Group
an informa business
Taylor & Francis eBooks
www.taylorfrancis.com
A single destination for eBooks from Taylor & Francis with increased functionality and an improved user experience to meet the needs of our customers.
90,000+ eBooks of award-winning academic content in Humanities, Social Science, Science, Technology, Engineering, and Medical written by a global network of editors and authors.
TAYLOR & FRANCIS EBOOKS OFFERS:
A streamlined experience for our library customers
A single point of discovery for all of our eBook content
Improved search and discovery of content at both book and chapter level
REQUEST A FREE TRIAL
support@taylorfrancis.com
Routledge
Taylor & Francis Group
CRC Press
Taylor & Francis Group

Made in the USA
Middletown, DE
12 August 2024

58973454R00338